Jewish Nationality and Soviet Politics

Written under the Auspices of
The Research Institute on Communist Affairs
Columbia University

A list of other Institute publications
appears at the back of this book

Jewish Nationality and Soviet Politics

THE JEWISH SECTIONS OF THE CPSU, 1917–1930

By Zvi Y. Gitelman

PRINCETON, NEW JERSEY
PRINCETON UNIVERSITY PRESS
1972

LCC 77-154996
ISBN 0-691-07542-5

This book has been composed in Linotype Caledonia
Printed in the United States of America
by Princeton University Press, Princeton, N.J.

להורי היקרים

המחנכים לאהבת עם ישראל ותורת ישראל

Preface

THE MATERIALS on which this book is based are found in various libraries and archives located mainly in New York City. The Library and Archives of the Jewish Labor Bund in New York are rich in materials pertaining to the Jewish Labor movement, the dissolution of the Jewish socialist parties in Russia, and the origins of the *Evsektsiia*. The archivist of the Bund, Mr. Hillel Kempinsky, spared no effort in ferreting out sources, and shared his extensive knowledge of the socialist and Communist movements with me. The Library of the YIVO Institute for Jewish Research contains most of the *Evsektsiia* materials which were examined. Miss Dina Abramowicz, the librarian, graciously made these available to me. YIVO's archival collections, directed by Mr. Ezekiel Lifschutz, include the valuable Elias Tsherikover and Daniel Charney Archives. The Jewish and Slavonic collections of the New York Public Library were used extensively, and some materials in the library of the Jewish Theological Seminary proved useful. The late Alexander Pomerantz, a member of that library's staff, knew the *Evsektsiia* at first hand and, despite his serious illness, took the time to enlighten me on several points. Several interviews with Mr. Lazar Kling, who worked with the Belorussian *Evsektsiia* in 1926–27, were most helpful. The Smolensk Oblast Archive (on microfilm) and some important Soviet, *Evsektsiia*, and Jewish socialist periodicals were consulted in the Columbia University Library.

A grant from the Foreign Area Fellowship Program enabled me to explore the holdings of several libraries abroad during the spring and summer of 1966. The staffs of the Lenin State Library in Moscow and the Saltykov-Shchedrin Public Library in Leningrad made available much of their valuable collections to me. The staff of the Jewish Historical Institute in Warsaw was equally helpful. Several discussions with former *Evsektsiia* activists then residing in Eastern Europe were most enlightening. I was able to make use of the collection of the National and Hebrew University Library in Jerusalem. The library of the Historical Society of Israel was made available through the kindness of Professors Khone Szmeruk and Shmuel Ettinger of the Hebrew University. I owe a special debt to Dr. Mordechai Altshuler, of the Hebrew University and the Historical Society of Israel, for sharing freely his extensive knowledge and thorough research.

I am indebted to Professor Henry L. Roberts for his reading of an early draft of this book and for encouraging me to continue the project. I am profoundly grateful to Professor Alexander Dallin for having patiently given the manuscript a very close reading and for his helpful comments and suggestions. I benefited from Professor Alexander Erlich's knowledge of East European Jewish history and of Soviet modernization controversies. Professors Zbigniew Brzezinski, Leopold Haimson, Peter Juviler, William Zimmerman, Gregory Massell, and Alfred A. Greenbaum offered wise criticisms and comments which I acknowledge with thanks.

A modified version of the section in Chapter V on "The Attack on the Jewish Religion" appeared in *Aspects of Religion in the Soviet Union* (copyright © 1971 by the University of Chicago), and is incorporated here with the kind permission of the University of Chicago Press.

The heroic typing efforts of Christine Dodson and Michelle Elwyn of the Research Institute on Communist Affairs and of Colleen Glazer of the Center for Russian and East European Studies at the University of Michigan were truly beyond the call of duty. The financial assistance of the

Center for Russian and East European Studies helped accelerate the completion of the manuscript.

My wife Marlene prepared the index and helped in countless other ways for which thanks are inadequate.

All errors of fact and judgment remain, of course, my own.

Z. Y. G.

Ann Arbor, Michigan
June 1971

Contents

List of Tables

Illustrations

Introduction

THE CONCEPTUAL scheme or model with which historians and social scientists approach their subjects filters the facts available to them and often determines the weighting assigned to particular facts and predetermines which interrelationships between them will be discovered, and which ignored. Alex Inkeles has suggested that "there is no such thing as a right or wrong sociological model. There are richer and poorer ones. There are the more sensitive and the less sensitive. There are those which are more appropriate to one time or place than another. All have a piece of the truth, but it is rare that any *one* model is really adequate to the analysis of a richly complex concrete historical case." [1]

The study of Soviet politics and society has long been wedded to a totalitarian model, but serious doubts have been expressed about the continuing relevance of such models. Some have suggested that it might be more fruitful to study the Soviet Union as an early example of a modernizing society, while others have urged the relevance of bureaucratic models or of the analytical schemes recently developed by those engaged in the comparative study of politics.[2]

Without denying the usefulness of the totalitarian model in explaining much of Soviet history, we might find it more enlightening to view the first decade of Soviet power as a period in which an authoritarian regime attempted to

1 Alex Inkeles, "Models and Issues in the Analysis of Soviet Society," *Survey*, no. 60 (July 1966), p. 3.

2 See, for example, the symposium on the study of Communism in *Slavic Review*, XXVI, no. 1 (March 1967), particularly the contributions of John Armstrong, Alfred Meyer, and John Kautsky. See, more generally, Frederic J. Fleron, ed., *Communist Studies and the Social Sciences* (Chicago, 1969).

mobilize social and economic resources for the purpose of rapid modernization, political integration, and political development. Such is the approach of this book. For our purposes modernization can be defined as the "process by which historically evolved institutions are adapted to the rapidly changing functions that reflect the unprecedented increase in man's knowledge, permitting control over his environment, that accompanied the scientific revolution."[3] Modernization is a special case of development, which is, in turn, a particular form of social change.[4] Political integration is the development of loyalties to the defining values and aspirations of the political system. It is the achievement of a normative consensus governing political behavior.[5] Political development is a process that includes social and economic change, but whose focus is the development of a government's capacity to set new types of goals and demands and to direct the course and rate of social and economic change leading to those goals.[6]

Development results from the proliferation and integration of functional roles in a community and, in its broadest sense, is "the process by which secular norms of conduct are universalized."[7] Modernization involves a rapid increase in the complexity of human affairs within which the

[3] C. E. Black, *The Dynamics of Modernization* (New York, 1966), p. 7.

[4] David E. Apter, *The Politics of Modernization* (Chicago and London, 1965), p. x.

[5] For definitions of political integration, see Claude Ake, *A Theory of Political Integration* (Homewood, Ill., 1967), and Myron Weiner, "Political Integration and Political Development," *The Annals of the American Academy of Political and Social Science,* 358 (March 1965).

[6] See Karl Von Vorys, "Toward a Concept of Political Development," *Annals of the American Academy of Political and Social Science,* 358 (March 1965), and Alfred Diamant, "The Nature of Political Development," in Jason L. Finkle and Richard W. Gable, eds., *Political Development and Social Change* (New York, 1966), p. 92.

[7] Apter, pp. 67–68.

polity must act. Politics then becomes "the business of coping with role differentiation while integrating organizational structures." [8] The political system must develop a capacity for sponsoring and absorbing innovation, for encompassing flexible social structures and for providing the skills and knowledge needed by a technologically advanced society. The modernizing political system must be heavily involved in economic innovation and advance, which in almost all cases involves industrialization. The political system must find ways to integrate politically a society becoming ever more differentiated socially and economically.

But the social and economic change involved in modernization must be accompanied by the acceptance of new attitudes on the part of society and its culture, mainly attitudes of inquiry and questioning as to how men make moral, social, and personal choices and whether men can make such choices. In other words, the process of modernization has intellectual, social, and psychological dimensions as well as economic and political ones. The Russian Revolution was made possible by the intense questioning, the passionate search for ways and means to modernize Russia, which had characterized some segments of nineteenth-century Russian society. At the same time the Jewish minority in the Russian empire was wrestling with similar kinds of problems. Ever since the French Revolution and the emancipation from the ghetto, European Jewry had been burdened with the freedom of choice. For the first time in many centuries Jews could *choose* their religion and even their national identity. While many West European Jews embraced Christianity in the belief that this would guarantee total integration into the society surrounding them, East European Jews responded more conservatively to the attractions of emancipation, searching for ways to harmonize

[8] Apter, p. 3.

the acceptance of modernization which, to most, involved secularization, and the maintenance of ethnic identity. Modernity promised a new language, politics, culture, a new economy, and new forms of social life. Jewish identification offered the psychological security of tradition, of familiar behavior patterns, a sense of rootedness, and hallowed and cherished values. Between the two extreme solutions to the ethnic identity crisis—total assimilation or retreat into the ghetto—there developed a broad range of ideologies which tried to synthesize Jewish identity with modernizing political, social, economic, and cultural values. Zionists, socialists, Hebraists, Yiddishists, territorial autonomists, religious reformers, cultural reformers—all tried to reshape Jewry so that it would benefit from modernity while retaining a distinctive identity. The confrontation of particularistic Jewish values with universal modernizing ones generated a creative tension which made East European Jewry a bubbling cauldron of political, philosophical and ideological discussion and debate.[9] The need to reconcile these values animated individual Jews and Jewish movements in tsarist and Soviet Russia. As Russia was a modernizing country during the first quarter of this century and beyond, so too was the Jewish minority within her a modernizing society in microcosm, with unique modernization problems added to those experienced by Russian society as a whole.

The modernization strategy of the Bolsheviks in the 1920's

[9] For a discussion of a roughly analogous confrontation in contemporary Asia and Africa, see Clifford Geertz, "Primordial Sentiments and Civil Politics in the New States," in *Old Societies and New States,* ed. Clifford Geertz (New York, 1963), pp. 109 and 155. The extra-territoriality of the Jews, their status as a religious, as well as ethnic, minority, and the high cultural level they had attained even in the "pre-modern" stage make the problems of Jewish modernization different from those of African or Asian modernization—and perhaps makes them unique.

differed substantially from the Stalinist pattern of modernization and in many ways resembled the "nationalist revolutionary" pattern as seen, for example, in Mexico and Turkey. The Stalinist pattern involves a total transformation of the social, political, economic, and cultural orders, using a monolithic party, wide ranging coercion, and intense ideological appeals to achieve "close monolithic integration of all the various groups, movements and independent public opinion." Nationalist revolutionary regimes, on the other hand, "while aiming at long-range structural transformation in the society, did not envisage this transformation as a total revamping of the social structure and attempted also to take into account some of the major social strata and groups, or at least to permit them some autonomous expression, while at the same time they tried to regulate such demands." In short, they "laid the basis for a less coercive transformation bearing within itself some seeds of a new civil consensual order." [10] Naturally, different strategies for effecting change evolve different tactics and achieve results of different orders and magnitudes.[11] The Stalinist model, for example, calls for developing one sector, usually the industrial, very intensively, "while totalitarian instruments of control and repression are used to demobilize the other sectors, i.e., to inhibit popular demands for development in those sectors. The result is that if we compare a mature totalitarian mobilization system with a system undertaking balanced development (e.g., India), we find

[10] S. N. Eisenstadt, "The Development of Socio-Political Centers at the Second Stage of Modernization—A Comparative Analysis of Two Types," in K. Ishwaran, ed., International Studies in Sociology and Social Anthropology, IV: *Politics and Social Change* (Leiden, 1966), pp. 134–35.

[11] See Kenneth T. Jowitt, "A Comparative Analysis of Leninist and National Elite Ideologies and Nation-Building Strategies," paper prepared for the Summer Workshop on Comparative Communism, Stanford, California, 1968.

that the balanced system looks like a gray slab and the totalitarian system looks like a black-and-white checkerboard."[12]

Bolshevik modernization efforts before 1928 resembled the nationalist revolutionary pattern in that they did permit some carefully controlled but autonomous expression to groups, including ethnic ones, within Soviet society. If in the first phase of modernization one central problem is "the ways in which the broader groups and strata which have been undergoing more restricted processes of modernization can be drawn into the central institutions of society,"[13] then it is clear that the Bolsheviks approached this problem very differently in the 1920's from the way in which they were to handle it in the next decade. Our concern is to explore the consequences of the earlier Bolshevik strategy for the Jews of Soviet Russia, a group which had itself begun to undergo a variety of modernizing transformations, and to analyze the interaction between Bolshevik schemes of modernization and political development, on the one hand, with developments within the Jewish community, on the other.

European Jewish history has been written as the history of ideas, the history of religion, and social, political and economic history. It has been written as a threnody of unrelieved suffering imposed by a merciless Gentile environment and as sentimental reminiscences of a romanticized world of pure piety and purifying poverty. The historiography of Soviet Jewry might be better served by another kind of model. This study will attempt to view Jewish national life in the first decade of Soviet rule as a history of the modernization and secularization of an ethnic and religious minority resulting from attempts to integrate this

[12] Chalmers Johnson, "Comparing Communist Nations," in Johnson, ed., *Change in Communist Systems* (Stanford, 1970), p. 14.

[13] Eisenstadt, p. 120.

minority into a modernizing state. It will examine the nature of the challenge which modernization posed, the crisis it created, and the responses it evoked. Particular attention will be paid to one of these responses, the development of Jewish national programs in the socialist movement and, later, in the Soviet state. The programs were developed and discussed mainly by an agency that the Soviet government created to help in the social mobilization of the Jewish population. That is, it was to help integrate the Jews economically, socially, and politically into Soviet society. Its task, therefore, was to weaken primordial attachments and promote a sense of loyalty to the Soviet state, its goals and ideology.[14] But the Jewish Sections of the Communist Party of the Soviet Union went beyond this and gradually expanded their role and assumed the enormously heavy burden of planning and implementing the economic, social, and cultural modernization of Soviet Jewry. Their functions vis-à-vis the Jewish population paralleled the functions of the Party as a whole in regard to the general population. David Apter has described as "political religion" that which the modernizing state uses to replace primordial attachments. Political religion in new states comes to center on

[14] "By primordial attachment is meant one that stems from the 'givens'—or, more precisely, as culture is inevitably involved in such matters, the assumed 'givens'—of social existence: immediate contiguity and kin connection mainly, but beyond them the givenness that stems from being born into a particular religious community, speaking a particular language, or even a dialect of a language, and following particular social practices. . . . One is bound to one's kinsman, one's neighbor, one's fellow believer, *ipso facto;* as a result not merely of personal affection, practical necessity, common interest, or incurred obligation, but at least in great part by virtue of some inaccountable absolute import attributed to the very tie itself" (Geertz, p. 109). Others have described the same phenomenon as a "primitive belief." See, for example, Sidney Verba, "Comparative Political Culture," in *Political Culture and Political Development,* Lucian W. Pye and Sidney Verba, eds. (Princeton, 1965), p. 531.

four main tasks: breaking down primordial attachments, developing a simple system of central authority, developing the country materially, and institutionalizing "rationalistic values."[15] These were precisely the aims of the Bolsheviks and the functions of the Jewish Sections. The tasks of the Sections were made especially difficult by the strength of Jewish primordial attachments and competing Jewish authorities, by the poverty and economic marginality of the Jewish population, and by severe limitations placed on potential cultural development by Bolshevik ideology, on the one hand, and the attitudes of the Jewish population, on the other. The Jewish population seemed to be divided into two camps: those who were so strongly attached to traditional Jewish values and culture that they rejected almost any form of cultural modernization, and those who were convinced that they were imprisoned by a backward and parochial culture which had to be thrown off completely in order to become modernized.[16] The function of the Jewish Sections was similar to that of the leadership of new states: to try to synthesize traditional culture, transformed though it might have to be, with the imperatives of modernization, and to insure the integration of an ethnic minority into the polity as a whole. But since the Jewish Sections were not themselves the leaders of the Soviet state but rather their agents, the Sections were limited in the syntheses they could attempt. They were confined by ideological tenets and

[15] David E. Apter, "Political Religion in the New Nations," in Geertz, ed., *Old Societies and New States,* pp. 80–82.

[16] The sociologist Arthur Rupin pointed out that Jews in the Ottoman empire had not embraced Turkish culture because they saw it as a lower culture than their own, whereas they had accepted German and English culture because they perceived them as higher than Jewish culture. In 1913 he predicted that the "transformation of Russia and Turkey into constitutional states and their consequent provision for national education" would induce the Jews of those countries to assimilate linguistically and, eventually, in every other way. *The Jews of To-day* (New York, 1913), p. 117.

political principles which the Bolsheviks had evolved mainly in the pre-revolutionary period and which the leaders of the Sections tended to take more seriously, perhaps, than the Bolshevik leadership itself. They were dogged by a crippling insecurity arising from the awareness that most of them had come over to Communism from social democracy only after the Revolution.

The root of the problem confronting the Jewish Communists was that their perception of their own role and of the development of Soviet Jewry as a whole increasingly differed from the Communist Party's perception of these two related questions. While the Jewish Sections of the Party seemed to be increasingly committed to the simultaneous modernization of Soviet Jewry and the preservation of its distinctive identity, the Party as a whole judged that Soviet Jewry's economic, political, and cultural development could be accomplished as part of the total Soviet developmental effort, with no need for special measures vis-à-vis the Jews and with no compelling reasons for trying to insure the ethnic maintenance of the Soviet Jewish population. The Communist Party saw the Jewish Sections as a transient instrument through which the Jewish masses could be socialized, transformed, and integrated into the society as a whole, and if that integration meant the loss of a separate ethnic identity so be it, or even, some argued, so much the better.

In the end, all the programs the Jewish Sections had designed to combine modernization and ethnic maintenance failed for lack of support by the Party and state and by the Jewish people themselves. The regime found that substantial segments of the Jewish population were quite willing to abandon their ethnic identity for the emoluments of success as defined by general Soviet values; much of the Jewish population concluded that the radically transformed Jewish culture urged upon it by the Jewish Sections was an "impractical" one which could only impede the achievement of success in Soviet society while offering little in return.[17]

If the Sections failed, on the whole, in ethnic maintenance, they at least partially succeeded in modernization and political integration, though it is difficult to isolate their achievement in this regard from the success of the Soviet system as a whole. Whatever the outcome of the Sections' experience, the experience itself may be instructive in pointing to some characteristics and problems of the modernization of ethnic minorities in a multi-ethnic state. It also constitutes a crucial chapter in the turbulent history of European Jewry. Thus, this study is addressed both to those concerned with the general problems of modernization and political and national integration, particularly in Communist societies, as well as to those interested in a neglected area of Jewish history. It raises questions about the fundamental meaning of Leninist nationality policy, especially for a group whose nationhood is denied by an *a priori* definition, and it illustrates an early Communist attempt to achieve a synthesis of modernization, national integration, and political integration, syntheses with which the regimes in the USSR, Czechoslovakia, and Yugoslavia, among others, are still experimenting. All states, but especially multi-ethnic ones, are confronted by the task of a dual integration: a horizontal integration which will bind together individuals with different primordial and territorial allegiances in a sense of common nationhood, and a vertical integration

[17] Arthur Rupin remarked in 1913 that "As long as the new Jewish culture takes that of the old Ghetto for its foundation and becomes its organic continuation it will have a firm basis. But if, as has been occasionally attempted, a Jewish culture is built up without this foundation, the corner-stones of the new edifice being taken from the whole variety of possible sources, the result will be nothing but worthless talk. A civilization cannot be put together like a mosaic; it can only grow out of a living national life . . ." (Rupin, p. 234).

which will connect a political elite with the masses, whatever their primordial attachments. A great many combinations of different types of horizontal and vertical integration strategies have been observed, and even among Communist systems different integrative formulae have been tried.[18] The Jewish Sections were charged with major responsibility for achieving both kinds of integration among Soviet Jews: they were to resocialize the Jewish population so that it would become politically Bolshevized and sociologically Sovietized. Jews were to consider themselves, not part of a world-wide Jewish community, but a part of the Soviet family of nationalities.

Even though external political constraints make it impossible to generalize from the experience of the Jewish Sections to Jewish secularist experiments in different environments, some of the problems encountered by the Jewish Sections in their attempt to produce a new type of Jewish society and culture do raise serious questions about the viability of a secular form of Judaism which is not rooted in a particular territorial concentration. In fact, the religious component of Jewish identification may be so fundamental, especially in view of the fact that the only ethnic group practicing the Jewish religion are the Jews, that secular Judaism can only be a transient phenomenon, failing to maintain itself across more than two or three generations.

The reconstruction of Jewish national life on a secular, socialist basis was the ultimate goal which many activists of the Jewish Sections set for themselves, and it was in this aim that they seemed to have least Party encouragement. Two antecedent aims had to be accomplished before attention could be turned to the creation of a wholly new, historically unique Jewish community: the destruction of the

[18] See Zvi Gitelman, "Power and Authority in Eastern Europe," in Johnson, ed., *Change in Communist Systems.*

old order within the Jewish community, and the political resocialization of the Jewish population so that it would be politically integrated into the Soviet system. The Jewish Sections betook themselves to the task of destroying the old order with a zest that cannot be explained by enthusiasm for Bolshevism alone, but which probably drew just as much from pre-revolutionary cleavages and resentments within the Jewish community. In the destruction of the old order the Jewish Sections enjoyed a rather free hand, with the Party allowing Jewish Communists to do its destructive work within the Jewish community. The Jewish Sections had to share power and divide the labor when it came to Bolshevizing and reintegrating the Jews into the new order. The reconstruction of a Jewish national life was an aim articulated largely, though not exclusively, by members of the Jewish Sections' leadership. The Party did not support their particular vision of a Soviet Jewish society, but promoted schemes more in accord with its general political, economic, and military needs.

This study, then, follows the interplay of the Jewish Sections and the Soviet Communist Party through the three stages of revolutionizing the Jewish population, Bolshevizing it, and reconstructing the Jewish community so that it could become an integral part of the Soviet political and economic systems. It views this interplay in the perspective of modernization, a perspective infrequently adopted in systematic studies of politics and institutions in Soviet society, and even more rarely in the study of the Jewish minority in Eastern Europe. The somewhat unusual case of an extraterritorial minority with a distinctive religious identity may illuminate some aspects of the broader issues of modernization, social mobilization, and national and political integration that have not emerged from the many studies of territorially based ethnic groups in modernizing societies.

I

The Politics of the Jewish Question in Tsarist Russia

There are few intelligent people among us. We are, generally speaking, a gifted people, but intellectually lazy. An intelligent Russian is almost always a Jew or a man of Jewish blood.

Lenin to Maxim Gorkii

Absolutely untenable scientifically, the idea that the Jews form a separate nation is reactionary politically . . . that is precisely what the Jewish problem amounts to: assimilation or isolation? And the idea of a Jewish "nationality" is definitely reactionary. . . .

Lenin

"Judophilism" and "Judophobia" are closely related. A blind denial of a nationality engenders an equally blind affirmation of it. An absolute "Nay" naturally brings forth an absolute "Yea."

Dmitri Merezhkovskii

THE JEWS living in the western parts of the Tsarist Empire in the nineteenth century were a nationality, possessing their own language, religion, civil administration, judicial institutions, and educational system. For historical, cultural, and political reasons the Jews also developed a distinctive economic and social structure. The Jewish population was confined to a limited area, the Pale of Residence, which included the former Polish provinces incorporated into the Tsarist Empire in the 1770's and 1790's, Belorussia and Lithuania, the northeastern Ukraine, and areas near the Black Sea which had been colonized by the Russians in the early part of the nineteenth century. Only a privileged minority of highly skilled artisans, merchants of the first guild, certain veterans of the armed forces, and, for a time, university graduates, were permitted to live outside the Pale. The overwhelming majority of the Jewish population was forced to reside within the Pale (Table I). Of the people who lived in that area, more than four-fifths of the Jewish population lived in urban areas, and Jews constituted nearly forty percent of the urban population. One-third of the Jews lived in the *shtetls,* or market towns, which were small semi-urban communities in which the Jews had settled in the first decade of the nineteenth century after being driven out of the villages by imperial edicts.[1]

The urbanization of the Jewish population preceded the urbanization of the Slavic population of the Pale by nearly a century. Towns with a Jewish population of 10,000 to 15,000 increased in number by twenty-five percent in the second half of the nineteenth century. Those with Jewish populations of between 25,000 and 50,000 increased by 400 percent, and those with a Jewish population of over

[1] Schwarz, p. 11.

TABLE I
REGIONAL DISTRIBUTION OF THE JEWISH POPULATION IN THE RUSSIAN EMPIRE, 1897 [2]

Region	Jewish Population		Jewish Percentage of total Population
	Thousands	Percent	
In the Pale:			
Poland (10 provinces)	1,321.1	25.3	14.5
Northwest (3 Lithuanian and 3 Belorussian provinces)	1,422.4	27.3	14.1
Southwest (Ukraine west of the Dnieper-4 provinces and Bessarabia)	1,768.6	33.9	12.4
Southeast (Ukraine east of the Dnieper-3 provinces and the Crimea)	387.2	7.4	4.5
Total, 25 provinces	4,899.3	93.9	11.6
Outside the Pale	316.5	6.1	.4
Grand Total	5,215.8	100.0	4.1

50,000 increased by 500 percent. While the Jews in the various provinces of the Pale constituted between five and fifteen percent of the population, they formed between twenty-five and ninety percent of the urban population.[3] In 1897 over half the urban population of Belorussia and Lithuania was Jewish, and in the Ukraine Jews constituted nearly one-third of the urban population. Outside the Pale Jewish urbanization was even more pronounced: over eighty percent of the Jews living in St. Petersburg province

[2] Adapted from Solomon M. Schwarz, *The Jews in the Soviet Union* (Syracuse, 1951), p. 11. Slightly lower figures are cited in Salo W. Baron, *The Russian Jew under Tsars and Soviets* (New York, 1964), p. 76.

[3] Y. Yakhinson, *Sotsial-ekonomisher shtaiger ba yidn in Rusland in XIX y"h* (Kharkov, 1929), p. 15.

and ninety-seven percent of all Jews in the province of Moscow resided in the provincial capital.[4]

The governmental restrictions placed on Jewish residence were complemented by vocational and professional restrictions. Jews were excluded by law from public service. Jewish agricultural colonization, which had been growing slowly but steadily during the nineteenth century, was set back by the May Laws of 1882, issued by Tsar Alexander III, which forbade Jews to acquire rural property. The *numerus clausus* system prevented most Jews from obtaining secondary and higher education, effectively barring them from the professions, though there were some prominent Jewish attorneys. Enforced residence in the Pale prevented Jews from entering the heavy industries being built outside the Pale (Table II).

The overwhelming majority of Jews employed in industry

TABLE II

Occupational Distribution of Jews, 1897[5]

Occupation	Percentage of Economically Active Jews
Industry and handicrafts	36.3
Traders, storekeepers, peddlers, etc.	31.0
Manual laborers, domestics, private employees	11.5
Officials and professionals	4.7
Communication and transport	3.0
Agriculture	2.4
Profession unspecified	7.6
Military	3.5
	100.0

[4] Baron, pp. 82–83.

[5] Yaakov Lestschinsky, *Dos sovetishe idntum* (New York, 1941), p. 26. For a critique of the surveys on which these figures are based, see A. Menes, "Vegn der industrie-befelkerung ba idn in Rusland, 1897," in *Shriftn far ekonomik un statistik,* Yaakov Lestschinsky, ed. (Berlin, 1928), I, 255–56.

and handicrafts were actually artisans who were either self-employed or worked in small factories and workshops. At the end of the nineteenth century, of 300,000 Jewish industrial workers, 250,000 were employed in workshops and only 50,000 were in medium and large-scale factories.[6] Forty-three percent of the artisans were in the various branches of the garment industry.[7]

The artisans and the middlemen of all types, who constituted well over half the economically active Jewish population, led a precarious economic existence. Confinement within the Pale meant that economic competition was fierce. In the late nineteenth century in Kursk and Iaroslav provinces, where no Jews were allowed to reside, there was less than one artisan for every thousand inhabitants. In Kiev province, within the Pale, there were 2.6 artisans for the same number of inhabitants.[8] "As a rule Jewish artisans were deprived of capital, equipment, stocks of raw materials, and cheap credit facilities, and quite often worked for the account of middlemen supplying materials and accessories or acted as commission agents or subsidiary suppliers for manufacturers and wholesalers; or simply were exploited homeworkers as well as sweatshop sub-contractors for somewhat bigger jobbers."[9] Small wonder that many artisans joined impoverished traders and shopkeepers in the miserable crowd of *luftmenshn,* those without enough income to support themselves and their families, but with enough hope to loiter about the market square looking for the big break that only rarely came along. It was estimated that in

[6] Lestschinsky, *Dos sovetishe idntum,* p. 30.

[7] Yakhinson, p. 16.

[8] Louis Greenberg, *The Jews in Russia* (New Haven, 1944), I, 166. In the 1840's, 100 houses in the provinces of Kiev were occupied by 410 to 510 Christian inhabitants, while the same number of residences housed 1,299 Jewish tenants. Thus, the living space of Jews was one-third that of Christians (p. 162).

[9] Schwarz, p. 19.

many communities forty percent of the Jewish population consisted of *luftmenshn* and their families. In 1898 nearly twenty percent of the Jewish population in the Pale applied for Passover charities.[10] In 1900 an investigative commission in Odessa found that sixty-three percent of the Jewish dead were buried at the expense of the Jewish community. "He who understands what it means to a Jew to be buried in strange shrouds can appreciate the significance of this figure."[11] All in all, it was estimated that at the turn of the century between thirty and thirty-five percent of the Jewish population depended on relief provided by Jewish welfare institutions.[12] Some of this misery was relieved by emigration. Between 1897 and 1914 about 1,500,000 Jews emigrated from Russia, some seventy percent of them going to the United States. More than half of these emigrants were artisans.[13]

Many of those who remained sought economic relief in the rapidly developing industries of the Russian Empire. In the early part of the nineteenth century there were only a few hundred Jewish industrial workers, but by the turn of the century there were approximately 50,000. In cities such as Odessa, Vilna, Bialystok, Warsaw, and Lodz, the Jewish proletariat was a social and economic force to be reckoned with. Jews were concentrated in light industry, particularly in the related textile and garment industries. A microcosmic view of the Jewish labor structure is provided by the statistics for the city of Bialystok in 1887 (Table III).

The Jewish workers suffered all the disabilities of a laboring class in an industrializing, early capitalist social and economic order. Working hours were incredibly long, wages

[10] Baron, pp. 114–15.

[11] Lestschinsky, *Dos sovetishe idntum*, p. 39.

[12] Schwarz, p. 18.

[13] Yakhinson, p. 20.

TABLE III
Jewish Workers in Bialystok, 1887 [14]

Type of Factory	Number of Factories	Workers: Jews	Workers: Christians	Total	Percentage of Jews
Textile	60	774	449	1223	63
Weaving	4	101	117	218	48
Dyes	4	88	95	183	48
Shawls & scarves	9	276	123	399	69
Blankets	2	27	25	52	54
Gloves & stockings	2	12	—	12	100
Tobacco	4	527	—	527	100
Pigskin products	3	162	—	162	100
Breweries	1	10	—	10	100
Tanneries	1	20	4	24	84
Boxmaking	1	41	—	41	100
Lumber mills	1	10	1	11	91
Machine shops	4	20	1	21	95
Flour mills	3	27	10	37	73
Totals	99	2095	825	2920	72

abysmally low, conditions abominably oppressive. In Gomel in the late 1890's the working day was sixteen to seventeen hours; in Minsk sugar refining factories in the early 1900's Jewish girls worked a twenty-hour day; in Dubrovna weavers also worked a twenty-hour day. In 1900 the average worker's wage was twenty-four rubles a month.[15] Workers were frequently not paid on time and sanitary conditions in the factories and workshops were very bad.

Despite political and economic discrimination, a few individual Jews managed to attain economic affluence and social influence.[16] In 1904 Jews owned one-third of all sugar

[14] Leonty Soloweitschik, *Un Prolétariat Méconnu* (Brussels, 1898), p. 180.

[15] N. A. Bukhbinder, *Di geshikhte fun der yidisher arbeterbavegung in Rusland* (Vilna, 1931), pp. 14–15.

[16] Israel Brodskii and his sons were pioneers in the sugar refining industry, and by 1889 they owned some twenty-two major plants.

factories in the Ukraine. On the eve of World War I Jewish-owned factories were producing fifty-two percent of all the sugar produced in the Ukraine.[17] Jews were also prominent in the development of water transport, the oil industry and in banking.[18] In 1914 about forty percent of the directors of St. Petersburg banks were Jews.[19]

These men represented only a very thin layer of the privileged, while the great majority of Jews remained imprisoned within the Pale and its poverty, a self-contained and distinctive community. But there were signs that the cultural isolation of the Jews was being slowly eroded. The *Haskalah,* or Enlightenment movement, of the early and mid-nineteenth century had preached acculturation into the dominant Russian culture. Some had heeded this call and had gone so far as to convert to Russian Orthodoxy and assimilate completely. The pogroms of the 1880's had halted this trend, as Jews turned away from a culture which they perceived as not only alien but also hostile. In 1898 there were 375,000 children in Jewish religious schools, or *kheders,* six times as many as the number of Jews enrolled in Russian schools.[20] In 1897 ninety-seven percent of the Jewish population listed Yiddish as their mother tongue. At the same time, however, over thirty percent of Jewish men and sixteen percent of Jewish women could read the Russian language, while only twenty-one percent of the

---

Joseph (Evzel) Gunzburg and his son Horace were among the pioneer railroad builders in Russia, along with Samuel Poliakov (Baron, p. 107).

[17] Lestschinsky, *Dos sovetishe idntum,* p. 28.

[18] Baron, pp. 105–11.

[19] *Ibid.*

[20] Lestschinsky, p. 47. Lestschinsky estimates that this was roughly the situation obtaining in 1914 as well. On the *Haskalah* movement, see Jacob Raisin, *The Haskalah Movement in Russia* (Philadelphia, 1913) and Josef Meisl, *Haskalah: Geschichte der Aufklärungsbewegung unter der Juden in Russland* (Berlin, 1919). On the Haskalah in Germany and Galicia, see Maks Erik, *Etiudn tsu der geshikhte fun der haskole* (Minsk, 1934).

general population was literate.[21] Whereas in 1886 only 29,526 Jews had attended Russian schools, by 1911 126,976 Jewish students were enrolled in such schools.[22]

It was these people, having made contact with the world beyond the Pale, who first became aware of the possibilities of modernization, secularization, and assimilation. Nearly all of them felt a need to involve themselves in the economic, social, and cultural life around them, and many participated in political life as well. This made them painfully aware of the backwardness of Russia and her Jewish population. Most were convinced that both entities were in desperate need of modernization. As regards the Jewish people, some believed that modernization could be achieved only through secularization and assimilation; others agreed upon the need for secularization, but rejected assimilation; still others argued that modernization could be attained at the cost of only limited secularization of certain areas of life, and no assimilation at all. The assimilators would either convert to the Christian faith and thereby remove the legal and social impediments to their complete integration into Russian society, or they would simply adopt the Russian culture and try as best they could to integrate themselves into whatever segment of Russian society they chose. If they had a taste for politics, they were likely to join either liberal or revolutionary movements which pursued broad objectives and which only incidentally concerned themselves with "the Jewish question," if at all. Those who rejected assimilation but aimed at the modernization of the Jewish population devised various strategies for the attainment of their objectives.

[21] Schwarz, p. 13. The literacy of the general population is discussed in Michael T. Florinsky, *Russia: A History and an Interpretation* (New York, 1961), II, 1256–57.

[22] As late as 1840 only 48 Jews were enrolled in Russian primary and secondary schools, and only 15 attended universities (Baron, pp. 143–45).

These strategies were crystallized into programs formulated and enunciated by political parties.

The first political party to attempt a synthesis of general political goals, whose attainment would insure both the modernization of the Jewish and general populations and the preservation of Jewish identity, was the General League of Jewish Workingmen in Lithuania, Poland, and Russia, more frequently known as the "Bund."[23] The Bund was a Marxist party which, for a time, was an integral part of the Russian Social Democratic Labor Party (RSDLP), though it ran afoul of that party's—and particularly Lenin's—ideas on the organization of the party and of the future socialist state. The Bund's position and its historical evolution had profound implications for the nature and structure of the Russian Social Democratic Labor Party—and perhaps for the course of Russian history—as well as for Bolshevik policy toward the Jews in Russia. It was in the course of his struggles with the Bund that Lenin concretized his organizational theories. The conflict with the Bund molded and trained the highly disciplined, cohesive, monolithic party which came to be identified as a uniquely "Leninist" one. This same experience helped shape the future of Russian Jewry. Consciously rejecting the Bund's national program for the Jews, the Bolsheviks tried to formulate a policy which would preclude a recrudescence of Bundist notions and aspirations among the Jewish masses, while at the same time achieving the economic, political, and cultural modernization of Russian Jewry and their integration into the Soviet polity. In the pre-revolutionary period RSDLP policy was based on the naïve belief that the revolution would solve the Jewish problem automatically. Since the

[23] The name was originally "General League of Jewish Workingmen in Russia and Poland." It was lengthened in 1901. Ferdinand Lassalle's "Allgemeiner Deutscher Arbeiterbund" was the inspiration for the name.

Jewish problem was created by the injustices of the capitalist order and the idea of Jewish nationhood was but an exaggerated response to these injustices, both anti-Jewish discrimination and the "unscientific" notion of Jewish nationhood would be swept away by the majestic, impartial, liberating winds of revolution.

The revolution did indeed come, but both the Jewish people and the Jewish problem refused to go away. Confronted with these facts the Bolsheviks adjusted to them rather gracefully. A highly pragmatic Jewish policy was evolved, the specifics of which were to be dealt with by the Jewish Sections of the Soviet Communist Party. But this did not end the conflict between socialist and national aspirations; it merely shifted its locale.

The history of the Jewish Sections, and indeed the history of Soviet Jewry, is one of constant balancing, adjustment, and coordination of Jewish national motives and ideals with those of Communist ideology in its Soviet expression. Many of the Jewish Sections' activists were former Bundists, and within the Sections the old disputes and the old alignments on the national question continued. Furthermore, the Jewish Sections in effect implemented for the Party a national program which could easily be construed as the heretical national-cultural autonomy of the Bund. This irony was compounded by the fact that Lenin's writings on the Bund and on the claims of the Jews to nationhood were taken much more seriously by ex-Bundists in the Jewish Sections than they were taken by the Communist Party as a whole. Stained with original sin, the ex-Bundists felt obliged to be "plus catholique que le pâpe" and to pursue their national program with the greatest caution, even when urged to bolder actions by other Party leaders. For these reasons, in order to understand the history of the Jewish Sections—in Russian, the *Evsektsii* (or *Evsektsiia,* the singular form commonly used in Soviet Russia, even in reference to many sections)—it is necessary to examine the evolution of the national program of the Bund and Lenin's criticism of it. Because of its importance for the history of Soviet Jewry, the Bund must be examined in greater detail than the other Jewish parties of pre-revolutionary Russia.

Origins of the Bund's National Program

The founding of the Bund in September 1897 marked the consolidation of scattered Jewish labor and revolutionary groups into a highly organized socialist movement. Early in the nineteenth century the draconic laws of Nicholas I accelerated the development of class consciousness and class differentiation in the Jewish community, as the Jewish poor were forced by the leaders of the Jewish community to supply young boys to the army where they were to serve twenty-five year terms. Since one of the aims of this draft was to convert the recruits to Russian Orthodoxy, the recruit was seen by the Jews as a man lost to his family, his community, and his people. The *kahal,* the ruling body of the local Jewish community, was burdened with the responsibility of supplying a given quota of recruits, and it shifted this burden onto the poor.[24]

The growing number of Jewish artisans and laborers found that their interests were conflicting increasingly with those of the traditional leadership of the Jewish community. The rapid growth of the Jewish working class

[24] "The Grodno *kahal* reported that the draft quota of 1827 was 'successfully filled on the strength merely of the communal verdict.' Idlers who paid no taxes, and others not tolerated by the community, were summarily enrolled as recruits. The 'books of verdict' of Minsk for the same year reveal a similar procedure. Out of sixty-five recruits, not one was a taxpayer; none owned his home; twenty-five had no families; twenty, having families, lived apart from them; thirteen were vagrants, without passports; twenty-nine were unemployed; sixteen were servants, and seventeen were workers." Isaac Levitats, *The Jewish Community in Russia, 1772–1884* (New York, 1943), p. 63.

increased the dimensions and intensity of class conflict.[25] Jewish workers and artisans began to organize their own *khevrot*, or guilds, and, later, the more radical *kassy*. These organizations expanded their activities to include political, as well as economic, matters. Therefore, when thirteen delegates representing local underground labor organizations and two illegal newspapers founded the Bund, it was "already a mass party incorporating a wide network of workers' organizations, welded together over years of united struggle." [26] Led by intellectuals and worker-intellectuals, the Bund was enthusiastically received among the workers. The Jewish proletariat was susceptible to agitation because of its relatively high literacy and the fact that it was scattered among small workshops and factories where police supervision was more difficult than in the large-scale Russian factories and plants.[27] The Bund's recruitment efforts were well organized [28] and "Jargon Committees"—Yiddish

[25] For rich documentation attesting to increasing class conflict, see O. Margolis, *Geshikhte fun yidn in Rusland: Etiudn un dokumentn* (Moscow-Kharkov-Minsk, 1930) and the same author's *Yidishe folksmasn in kamf kegn zeiere unterdriker* (Moscow, 1940).

[26] Leonard Schapiro, *The Communist Party of the Soviet Union* (New York, 1959), p. 22.

[27] Jews remained in the small workshops because most of them refused to work on Saturday. Since the Christian worker took his day off on Sunday, employing both Jewish and Christian workers would mean that the factory would stand idle two days a week. Jews were also suspected of being more radical and more easily organized, and employers were leery of hiring them. Furthermore, Jews were barred by law from working in some branches of heavy industry. Finally, many of the large industrial centers of nineteenth-century Russia were outside the Pale of Residence. See Ezra Mendelsohn, *Class Struggle in the Pale* (Cambridge, Eng., 1970), pp. 18–23.

[28] "The Bund could . . . claim to have more working class support than any other Social Democratic organization in Russia at the time. . . . In two and a half years, 28,000 workers under its influence were said to have staged 312 strikes, of which more than 90 percent were successful. The very extent of these triumphs aroused some

was then known, somewhat deprecatingly, as "jargon"—were formed to translate, publish, and distribute socialist propaganda.

Finally, the Bund adopted a successful *modus operandi*, later adopted by the Russian Social Democratic Labor Party as a whole. The Russians had aimed at building small circles of select workers and indoctrinating them in history, political economy, and socialism. This was defined as "propaganda" by Georgii Plekhanov. These workers frequently used their newly-acquired knowledge to rise up out of the proletariat and become modest entrepreneurs themselves. Or, if they remained in the factories, they would frequently lord it over their "inferior colleagues."[29] The Bund engaged not in "propaganda" but in "agitation." In Plekhanov's terms, this meant the presentation of one or two ideas to a *mass* of people, concentrating on the enlistment of broad support for a general program. Arkady Kremer, a founder of the Bund, described the Bund's successes achieved by this method in his pamphlet *Ob agitatsii*, which was smuggled into Russia for use by RSDLP organizers. Much of the Bund's growth was undoubtedly due to the Jewish workers' thirst for knowledge and their hunger for economic justice.

> I see them now, crate makers . . . , soap workers, sugar workers—those among whom I led a circle. . . . Pale, thin, red-eyed, beaten, terribly tired. They would gather late in the evening. We would sit until one in the morning in a stuffy room, with only a little gas lamp burn-

---

distrust among Social Democrats in Russia proper; for the Bund's relatively high degree of organizational efficiency was due precisely to the presence within its ranks of that artisan element which in their eyes lacked proletarian virtues." J. L. H. Keep, *The Rise of Social Democracy in Russia* (Oxford, 1963), p. 44.

29 Oscar Janowsky, *The Jews and Minority Rights* (New York, 1933), p. 38.

ing. Often, little children would be sleeping in the same room and the woman of the house would walk around listening for the police. The girls would listen to the leader's talk and would ask questions, completely forgetting the dangers, forgetting that it would take three-quarters of an hour to get home, wrapped in the cold, torn remnant of a coat, in the mud and deep snow; that they would have to knock on the door and bear a flood of insults and curses from parents; that at home there might not be a piece of bread left and one would have to go to sleep hungry . . . and then in a few hours arise and run to work. With what rapt attention they listened to the talks on cultural history, on surplus value, commodity, wages, life in other lands. How many questions they would ask! What joy would light their eyes when the circle leader produced a new number of *Yidisher arbeter, Arbeter shtime,* or even a brochure! How proud a girl was when she would be given a black book to take home! She would hide it in her bosom, press it to her violently beating heart and fly home as if on wings in order to read it as soon as possible. At home, one would have to wait until father would have his fill of cursing and would fall asleep again, and then—very quietly—one would read by the covered light and swallow, swallow the holy burning little letters, and simultaneously keep an ear cocked lest someone should see. . . . How many tragedies young workers would suffer at home if it became known that they were running around with the "*Akhdusnikes*" ["Uniteds"], with the "brother and sisters," that they were reading forbidden books—how many insults, blows, tears! It did not help. "It attracts them like magnets," the mothers wailed to each other.[30]

[30] Esther [Frumkina], "Vi azoi mir hobn amol gelernt marksizm," *Liebknekhts dor,* I, no. 1 (January 1923).

But if the Bund was reaching out to the workers, its leadership was still dominated by intellectuals who came from families that had become acculturated into the mainstream of Russian life. Not surprisingly, therefore, the leaders of the Bund were unconcerned with giving the movement an especially Jewish content. "We were for assimilation; we did not even dream of a special Jewish mass movement. . . . Our task was developing cadres for the Russian revolutionary movement."[31] Imprisoned in the Pale, the early revolutionaries began to work among the Jewish laborers by necessity, and not by choice. Their aim was to prepare highly conscious socialist workers who would become thoroughly assimilated into the Russian culture and who could eventually go out to the centres of the Russian proletariat to preach the socialist doctrine.[32] Vladimir Medem, later the Bund's foremost theoretician on the national question, believed that the Bund leaders were not deliberately espousing a policy of assimilation, but were simply not conscious of the national question.[33]

Some early Jewish socialists did have a greater concern for national questions. In fact, as early as 1895, Julius Martov told a meeting in Vilna that "We have had to fit our propaganda and agitation to the masses, that is, to give it a more Jewish character."[34] In the establishment of the Bund, Martov wrote, "Our aim is to found a specifically

[31] T. M. Kopelson, "Evreiskoe rabochee dvizhenie kontsa 80-kh i nachala 90-kh godov," quoted in Henry J. Tobias, "The Bund and Lenin until 1903," *The Russian Review*, XXIX, no. 4 (October 1961), 344–45.

[32] See Moshe Mishkinsky, "Yesodot LeUmiyim Behitpatkhuta Shel T'nuat HaPoalim Hayehudim BeRusia," unpub. diss., Hebrew University (Jerusalem), 1965, pp. 37–39.

[33] Vladimir Medem, "Natsionale bavegung un natsionale sotsialistishe partaien in Rusland," in *Vladimir Medem tsum tsvantsikstn yortseit* (New York, 1943), p. 246.

[34] From Martov's address at the Vilna Conference, in *Di yidishe sotsialistishe bavegung biz der grindung fun Bund* (Vilna-Paris, 1939).

Jewish organization which will be the leader and educator of the Jewish proletariat in the struggle for economic, civil, and political liberation."[35] Ironically, Martov never joined the Bund and led the attack on it at the Second Congress of the RSDLP in 1903.[36] Nevertheless, when the Bund

[35] Quoted by Medem, *op. cit.*, p. 247.

[36] Martov was a grandson of Aleksander Tsederboim, editor of the first Hebrew and Yiddish periodicals in Russia, *HaMelitz* (1860) and *Kol Mevasser* (1863), respectively. Martov's father was a liberal, indifferent to Jewish affairs. Leopold Haimson notes that as a child Martov lived through a pogrom in Odessa, which obliged him to recognize his Jewish identity. "This recognition, which had come so traumatically . . . could not be rationalized . . . by an identification with the oppressed masses, for Yuri [*sic*] had been brought up as one of the privileged few; neither could it be balanced by a positive sense of the rich Jewish cultural tradition, for his parents had denied the value of this tradition in their efforts to assimilate. Jewishness was therefore to become in Martov's mind a weakness in his armor, a handicap with no compensatory rewards, and much of his subsequent hostility to the Bund may perhaps be attributed to this fact." Leopold H. Haimson, *The Russian Marxists and the Origins of Bolshevism* (Cambridge, Mass., 1955), p. 64. Haimson does not discuss Martov's 1895 Vilna speech. The Jewish historian Marc Yarblum reports that he met Martov several weeks before the latter's death and "he rained questions on me about the humanistic socialism of the Jewish workers in Palestine and listened with great curiosity and sympathy." M. Yarblum, "60 Shana LaBaaya Hayehudit Lehalakha UL'maase BeToldot HaBolshevizm," *HaPoel HaTsair,* November 26, 1963. Martov also wrote friendly greetings to the Bund on its twentieth anniversary, though he emphasized the role it had played in the *past.* See *Der veker* (Minsk), September 28, 1917. Bertram D. Wolfe states that Martov was "a member of the Jewish Bund," and "broke with it to become Lenin's chief collaborator in the Petersburg League." *Three Who Made A Revolution* (Boston, 1948), p. 184. Wolfe's statement is correct only if we accept the view that the Bund was an organized, identifiable movement before its official founding in 1897. Martov's biographer points out that even in 1895 "His advocacy of Yiddish was tactical and utilitarian, not surprisingly for Yiddish meant nothing to him. . . . It seems that Martov . . . by no means ever became . . . one for whom the preservation and cultivation of a national Jewish individuality in language, customs, and culture are worthwhile things in themselves. If he later made a volte-face, it

helped found the Russian Social Democratic Labor Party in March 1898, it entered the Party "as an autonomous organization, independent only in matters which specifically concern the Jewish proletariat." [37] The Bund explained that it required such autonomy so that it could propagate social-democratic ideas among the Jewish workers, most of whom understood only Yiddish, and so that the Jewish proletariat and its special problems could be effectively represented in party councils and publications.[38] The Bund was also admitted to the party as "the sole representative of the Jewish proletariat." Since there were no other Jewish proletarian parties at the time, the Bund's aim in gaining this status was to insure for itself a free hand among Jewish workers to the exclusion of other elements in the RSDLP. This claim was dropped in 1905 when other Jewish parties, which had since been organized, ridiculed it.[39] The formula

---

was not towards the Jewish nation; it was at most, in his own opinion of the correct relations between Jewish and proletarian disabilities, and between Jewish and Russian party structures." Israel Getzler, *Martov: A Political Biography of a Russian Social Democrat* (Cambridge, 1967), pp. 28–29. Getzler admits that "The importance of his contribution to *Iskra's* campaign against the Bund is difficult to overestimate" (p. 60), but speculates that "Martov was not so detached from his own people as to play his role against the Bund without pain or misgiving" (p. 62). "What did distinguish him from many a Jewish socialist was his personal involvement in the struggle against anti-semitism and anti-Jewish discrimination; he never abandoned that struggle and to that extent he remained true to his Vilno days and the family tradition of his grandfather Alexander Tsederbaum" (p. 60).

[37] *Pervyi s"ezd RSDRP, dokumenty i materialy* (Moscow, 1958), pp. 82–83.

[38] *Arbeter shtime,* nos. 9–10, 1898.

[39] The claim of being the sole representative of the Jewish proletariat was dropped because of pressure by the Zionists-Socialists, the "Sejmists," and the *Poalai Tsion.* The claim was revived at the Seventh Conference of the Bund (1906). See P. An-Man [Rozental], "Die fareinigungs frage af der VII konferents fun Bund," *Roiter pinkes,* no. 2, 1924.

of "sole representative" seems to have aroused little opposition at the time it was first made, but five years later *Iskra* was to repudiate even its historical accuracy.[40]

Dissatisfaction with the Bund's position on the national question began to grow as more unassimilated workers were drawn into the party. Jewish workers were attracted to the party not only because it promised to liberate them from economic misery but also because it offered them an opportunity to gain a general education. Furthermore, the Bund filled a psychological need by giving the Jewish worker, whose growing radicalism and low status increasingly isolated him from the Jewish community, a sense of his own dignity and a feeling of "belonging." George Theodorson, analyzing the social consequences of industrialization in non-Western societies, points to the emotional dependence of new proletarians on the traditional community, and adds that "a much more important and elusive point is that man gains most of his satisfactions and feelings of security from a well rounded and integrated pattern of interaction. This means that he needs an orderly life based on mutual patterns of expectations that cover all phases of his activities within and without the immediate factory situation. . . . A new social system is needed in the industrial community, a system which would integrate the new economic system with those aspects of the old culture which can be adjusted to industrialization."[41] The Bund increasingly became a kind of social system, rather than just a political movement, in that it provided cultural and social opportunities to the Jewish workers and evolved into an alternative style of life and social milieu which allowed Jewish workers to stand

[40] *Iskra,* no. 51, October 22, 1903.

[41] George A. Theodorson, "Acceptance of Industrialization and its Attendant Consequences for the Social Patterns of Non-Western Societies," *American Sociological Review,* 18, no. 5 (October 1953), 480.

apart from the traditional Jewish community but retain their Jewish identities and social ties.

Jewish workers saw themselves as a group apart from other Jews because of their class identity; they saw themselves as a group apart from other workers because of their national identity. They were "naturally" Jewish and needed no theories to justify the Jewishness of their movement. The Bund's strategy of agitation meant that the intelligentsia leadership was forced into constant, close contact with the rank-and-file Jewish workers, and the intelligentsia came to realize that it was dependent—and could rely—on them.

A tension began to be felt between those who desired complete assimilation and those who wanted only political and economic integration, but not cultural assimilation. This tension was not peculiar to the Bund, but was a reflection of moods within Russian Jewry as a whole. "If social exclusion from the dominant society hinders the minority from sharing the benefits of modernization, its members may seek assimilation individually and strive for equal civil and economic rights collectively. But if the cultural leavening of modernization poses a threat to cherished values and institutions, the minority may develop an impulse to preserve its own way of life in a changing world. Both of these tendencies were prompted among the Jews in pre-revolutionary Russia. In the Jewish parties formed to further the revolutionary cause, the conflict between politico-economic assimilation to Russian society and the preservation of cultural autonomy had to be resolved at every stage of organizational development and with every change in the political environment." [42] The only way this internal conflict could

[42] Charles E. Woodhouse and Henry J. Tobias, "Primordial Ties and Political Process in Pre-Revolutionary Russia: The Case of the Jewish Bund," *Comparative Studies in Society and History,* VIII, no. 3 (April 1966), 332.

be resolved was by changing the national program of the Bund.

External factors, too, helped change the character of the Bund. The Bund newspaper, *Arbeter shtime,* emphasized that tsarist policies directed against the Jews and other minorities "have created special interests which demand defense."[43] In March 1899, the former Populist, Khaim Zhitlovskii, wrote a series of articles in the Bundist *Yidisher arbeter* which attempted to define a tenable socialist position on the Jewish question. He preached a doctrine of secular Jewish "folk culture," rejecting Zionism as a purely bourgeois phenomenon and assimilation as national suicide. The editors of the newspaper were careful to note that Zhitlovskii was speaking only for himself.[44]

But by December, the same newspaper reported enthusiastically that the Brünn (Brno) Congress of the Austrian Social-Democrats had divided that party along federal lines and that this "is already almost an answer to the national question." The Bundist organ hailed "two great ideas" that were expressed at Brünn: that the proletariat should be concerned to allow national cultures to develop, and that even a people without land could demand national rights. The idea of cultural, non-territorial autonomy was very favorably received by the editors and they were moved to declare: "We must also give an answer to the national question. What that answer will be, we do not know yet. But an answer there must be and the sooner the better. The time has come."[45] Some elements in the Bund had moved from the cautious hesitations of March to this unequivocal call for a new position on the national question.

At the Third Congress of the Bund, held in Kovno in December 1899, the Bundist pioneer, John Mill, influenced

[43] *Arbeter shtime,* no. 11, July 1899.

[44] *Yidisher arbeter,* no. 6, March 1899.

[45] *Ibid.,* no. 8, December 1899, p. 27.

by Karl Kautsky's articles in *Die Neue Zeit* which defined "nation" on the basis of language rather than territory,[46] demanded that the Bund include "national rights as well as civil rights" in its program. But Mill's pleas fell on deaf ears, and a compromise resolution was adopted, declaring that the Bund fostered demands only for equal civil rights and not national rights. But the columns of the *Yidisher arbeter* were to be opened to full discussion of the national question.[47]

The internal pressures forcing the Bund to pay more attention to the national problem were complemented by external events. The Jewish historian Simon Dubnow was arguing that the *kahal,* the organ of communal government which had been abolished in the middle of the nineteenth century, could be revived and made to serve modern needs.[48] The Zubatov "police-socialism" movement, which was adapted for the Jewish workers with the creation of a Jewish Independent Workers' Party, was gaining popularity and this, too, pushed the Bund to appeal to the workers with a program more explicitly national than the demand for equal civil rights. Finally, the younger generation, and especially the students, had a "political outlook [which] differed radically from that of the 'praktiki' in Vilna's pioneer generation and approximated more to that of 'Der Judischer Arbeiter' under John Mill's editorship."[49] The students rejected Zionism as a quixotic fancy, yet wanted to express their national pride.

At the Fourth Congress, held in Bialystok in 1901, all agreed that the program of the RSDLP was unsatisfactory

[46] John Mill, *Pioneren un boier* (New York, 1946), II, 53–54.

[47] *Di geshikhte fun Bund* (New York, 1960), I, 156.

[48] Simon Dubnow, *Nationalism and History* (Philadelphia, 1961), pp. 73–233.

[49] Jonathan Frankel, "Socialism and Jewish Nationalism in Russia, 1892–1907," unpub. diss., Cambridge University, 1960, p. 178.

and that territorial solutions of the national question were irrelevant to the Jews. But while Mark Liber, a founder and leader of the Bund, urged that the Bund should favor "Jewish national autonomy," much as Mill had done at the previous Congress, Pavel Rozental and others regarded this as premature and a "foreign importation." A centrist group, led by Yekusiel Portnoi ("Noah") and Rakhmiel Veinshtain, argued that the issue was not a "foreign importation" and was a genuine concern of the Jewish masses; but national autonomy was an unrealizable aim and the Bund should content itself with demanding civil and political equality. Again, a compromise was reached. "A country such as Russia . . . which has so many nationalities has to become, in the future, a federation of nationalities with full national autonomy for each of them, independent of the territory upon which they reside. The Congress recognizes that the concept 'nationality' applies also to the Jewish people." The resolution went on to declare that "it is premature under present conditions to put forth the demand for national autonomy for the Jews," and so the Bund would content itself with fighting discriminatory laws, ever careful to avoid fanning the flames of national feeling "which can only dim the class consciousness of the proletariat and lead to chauvinism." [50] Mill added that this resolution was understood to be only a "principle" and not "an actual political slogan." [51] The *Arbeter shtime* took great pains to point out that "it is not to be concluded that the Bund wants to make itself independent. . . . On the contrary, separatism is a concept unknown to members of the Bund. . . ." [52]

Despite the cautious and elaborate hedging of the resolution, it quickly aroused opposition both within and with-

[50] *Yidisher arbeter,* no. 2 (1901), pp. 97–102.

[51] Mill, II, 311.

[52] *Arbeter shtime,* August 1901, p. 2.

out the Bund.[53] Many correctly judged that this was a turning point in Bundist thought and that the Bundist program would increasingly emphasize the national element, until it would become as vital a component of Bundism as the class struggle. The various attitudes towards the national question would remain represented within the Bund, but the general trend was to be unmistakably in the direction to which Mill and Liber had pointed.

The Social-Democrats grouped around the newspaper *Iskra,* including Lenin, were quick to recognize this. They had enjoyed good relations with Bund leaders and the first issue of *Iskra* had pointed to the Bund as an efficient organization which the Russians would do well to emulate. However, following the Fourth Congress of the Bund, *Iskra* commented, "From our side we can see this only as a political mistake, this attempt which artificially harnesses the Jewish workers' movement in the shafts of nationalism. The main trouble choking the Jewish masses in Russia is the government's policy." [54] This was the first volley fired at the Bund by *Iskra.* The attack was soon to become a barrage. The polemics between *Iskra* and the Bund grew sharper and Bund leaders had reason to believe that Lenin was carefully lining up support for an effort to discredit the Bund's national program.[55] But the Bund had grown more resolute on this point, in large part because of events beyond its control.

Zionism, officially consolidated as a movement in Basel, Switzerland, in 1897, had become a political force to be reckoned with in Russian Jewish society. The Bund had

[53] Medem "Natsionale bavegung," p. 250.

[54] *Iskra,* no. 7, August 1901.

[55] See Vl. Kossovskii, "Martov un di rusishe sotsial-demokratie," *Di tsukunft,* XXXII, no. 3 (March 1924), 176. See also A. Kirzhnitz, "Bund un RS-DAP erev dem tsvaitn tsuzamenfor," *Visenshaftlikhe yorbikher,* I (Moscow, 1929).

attacked Zionism as a bourgeois movement with close ties to anti-revolutionary "clericalists." In 1901 the first labor-Zionist groups were founded, but the Bund disposed of them easily by claiming that these groups had no interest in improving the lot of the Jewish worker or the Russian workers in general; the Zionists were offering the workers salvation in a future fairyland of Jewish independence and were thereby distracting them from the class struggle. Nevertheless, the fact that the Bund took the trouble to engage in public polemics with the Zionists seems to indicate that they were regarded as a potential threat.

On April 19, 1903, the pogroms in Kishinev broke out. These anti-Jewish riots had an enormous impact both in Russia and abroad and Medem observed that "in the Bund the impression was tremendous,"[56] arousing renewed dedication to revolution and leading to the founding of a Bund self-defense movement. The dark shadow of Kishinev could not but hang over the June Congress of the Bund.

The old divisions on the national question manifested themselves at the Bund's Fifth Congress: Kopelson and Franz Kurskii took the "assimilationist" position; Liber, Medem, and Kossovskii took the more positively national approach.[57] Veinshtain stated the issue bluntly: "Either the Bund is a national party, in which case it must have its national program, or the viewpoint of *Iskra* is correct."[58] The Bundists could not face the issue squarely. On the one hand, they did not want to give up their nationality policy; on the other, they did not want to break with the RSDLP. The Congress was deadlocked on the national issue, but a stand was implied when it was decided that the Bund would not insist on a federative party structure at the RSDLP Congress but that the Bund's status as the sole representa-

[56] V. Medem, *Fun mein lebn* (New York, 1923), II, 6.

[57] *Unzer tseit* (Warsaw), no. 2, November 1927, pp. 84ff.

[58] *Unzer tseit,* no. 4, December 1927.

tive of the Jewish proletariat, unlimited in its activity by geographical boundaries, was not to be given up, even at the risk of being forced out of the party. "The Bund's autonomy then [1898] was predicated on its representation of Jews in the Northwestern section of the Pale of Settlement and Poland, and on its ability to supply them with revolutionary literature written in Yiddish. But by 1901 the Bund's base of support had been extended to include Jewish workers in the South of Russia where many Russian Social-Democratic groups existed. To clarify its new position, the Bund, at the Second Congress of the RSDLP in 1903, asked to be recognized as the sole representative of the Jewish proletariat, with no territorial limitations on its activities."[59] The principle of federation, which would have meaning only in the future, was to be sacrificed in favor of a principle which justified the very existence of the Bund and its day-to-day activities. Essentially, then, the national program of the Bund remained unchanged.

Lenin launched an attack in February 1903, saying that the Bund had become an independent party and was splitting the proletariat.[60] "The Bund ought not to go beyond the demand for complete autonomy in matters concerning the Jewish proletariat."[61] Lenin devoted much time to the careful organization of the forthcoming Congress, cutting down Bund representation in favor of *Iskra*ists.[62]

At the Congress, Liber acted as the chief spokesman for the Bund. He argued that the RSDLP program was too vague, that regionalization of the party was unacceptable

[59] Woodhouse and Tobias, p. 343.

[60] *Iskra,* no. 34, February 15, 1903.

[61] *Iskra,* no. 33, February 1, 1903.

[62] "The most glaring disparity was that, whereas almost any of the Russian Committees, however small, could obtain permission to send a delegate . . ., the Jewish Bund, which could boast tens of thousands of members, had only five delegates from its central institutions" (Keep, *Rise of Social Democracy,* p. 110).

to the scattered Jewish proletariat—and besides, the Bund wanted a strong centralized party "as much as anyone"—that the Bund was not a technical translation committee, and, finally, that federation of the party would actually enhance centralization because the alternative of outright autonomy would cause each element in the party to concentrate exclusively on its narrow interests. In the end, the Second Congress rejected the Bund's demands for a federative party structure. This demand had been withdrawn, for tactical reasons, by the Bund spokesmen, but Martov claimed that the demand to be the sole representative of the Jewish proletariat amounted to the same thing and that the issue was one of principle and not of organization. The Bund's demands were overwhelmingly rejected, and Liber declared that the Bund was leaving the party.[63] John Mill commented that "our forced abdication from the party was seen by all of us, without exception, as a deep, painful tragedy. Some even took it as a colossal catastrophe, as a murderous stab in the heart of the organized Jewish proletariat."[64] The central committee of the Bund issued a statement which spoke bitterly about the Bund's constant struggle against Zionist nationalism—of which they were now accused! The statement explained that the Jewish proletariat had special national traditions and a national psychology evolved over hundreds of years. Therefore, only the Bund could carry on effective propaganda among the Jewish proletariat and could feel the "beat of its historical pulse." Some Bundists saw the issue not as "national disagreements but as organizational pettiness."[65] Pointing to the fact that those Social-Democrats who had led the attack on the Bund were themselves Jewish—Martov and Trotsky were the outstanding examples—Medem attributed their

[63] See *Vtoroi s"ezd RSDRP, protokoly* (Moscow, 1959), pp. 50–123.
[64] Mill, II, 119.
[65] Medem, "Natsionale bavegung," p. 270.

passion to the "self-hatred" which assimilated Jews often exhibit and he saw the Bund-RSDLP struggle as a civil war among Jews, not as an international dispute.[66] Perhaps all these elements entered into the struggle. For Lenin it was probably the organizational issue which was crucial. A federative party structure would have been detrimental to the type of party he was building—centralized, disciplined, and homogeneous. The fate of the Economists and the Mensheviks at the same Congress shows that Lenin had in mind uniformity and discipline, rather than diversity and discussion, for the party he now began to construct.

Lenin analyzed the break with the Bund in a series of articles in *Iskra*. "Once it had stepped on the inclined plane of nationalism, the Bund was naturally and inevitably bound to arrive at the formation of a particular Jewish party. And this is precisely the direct object of paragraph two of the by-laws, which grants the Bund the *monopoly* of representing the Jewish proletariat."[67] Lenin tried to show that the Bund was not, in fact, the sole representative of the Jewish workers and that neither logic nor history could justify the Bund's separate existence.[68] For the first time, Lenin explicitly denied that the Jews are a nation. He based himself on Karl Kautsky: "The Jews have ceased to be a nation, for a nation without a territory is unthinkable." He also quoted a French Jew, Albert Naquet,[69] who

[66] *Ibid.*, p. 271. It is also ironic that Knuniants, a Caucasian Social-Democrat, who sharply criticized the Bund at the Congress, demanded a separate regional organization for the Caucasus. He was reproved by one delegate who warned: "The Caucasian comrades are modest in their demands now, only because they are children compared with the Bund. Let them grow up and you will see, if not a Bund, then at least a Bundik." For an interesting discussion of the general phenomenon of "self-hatred," see Tamotsu Shibutani and Kian M. Kwan, *Ethnic Stratification* (New York, 1965) pp. 510ff.

[67] *Iskra*, no. 46, August 15, 1903.

[68] *Ibid.*, no. 51, October 22, 1903.

[69] Naquet was a leftist who later supported General Boulanger.

claimed that he was born a Jew, but was French by nationality. Lenin added that, "Not only national, but even racial peculiarities are denied to the Jews by modern scientific investigation." The Jews had been emancipated all over Europe and were being rapidly assimilated: therefore, it would have been "untenable scientifically" and "reactionary politically" if the future democratic Russia were to declare the Jews a nation and thus bar the way to progressive assimilation.

At the same time, Lenin was highly sympathetic to the Jews in Russia and later acknowledged that "No nationality in Russia is as oppressed and persecuted as the Jewish one."[70] Despite his clashes with the Bund he remarked that "it should be said to their credit that today the Jews provide a relatively high percentage of representatives of internationalism compared with other nations."[71] But he could not accept the idea that Jews were Jews because they were part of a Jewish nation. "The idea of a Jewish nationality runs counter to the interests of the Jewish proletariat, for it fosters among them, directly or indirectly, a spirit hostile to assimilation, the spirit of the 'ghetto'."[72]

He polemicized with Bernard Lazare, an early French Zionist, in *La Petite République*, September 24, 1903. It is interesting that Lenin made no reference at all to Karl Marx's writings on Jews and the Jewish question. Marx's writings on the Jews are almost never cited in Soviet discussions of Jewish nationality. The definitive treatment of Marx's ideas on the subject is found in Edmund Silberner, *HaSotsializm HaMaaravi Usheelat Hayehudim* (Jerusalem, 1955).

[70] Lenin, *Sochineniia* (2nd ed., Moscow-Leningrad, 1924), XVII, 291.

[71] Speech in Zurich (n.d.), in *Lenin on the Jewish Question* (New York, 1934). The speech is not included in the fifth Russian edition of Lenin's works.

[72] *Iskra*, no. 51, October 22, 1903. In *Critical Remarks on the National Question*, written in 1913, Lenin refers to the Jews as "the most oppressed and persecuted *nation*." But in the same work he defines the Jews of Russia and Galicia as a "caste" and the Jews of the rest of Europe as assimilated. These inconsistencies are probably

Lenin was confusing cause and effect in his analysis of the Bund's "nationalism." It seemed that it was not the Bund which was propagating Jewish nationalism among the Jewish workers, but the workers who were constantly pushing the Bund leaders to greater concern with national issues. "That which was previously seen as immature was now something which could not be postponed."[73] Pressed by the Zionists from one side and by the *Iskrovtsy* from the other—both claiming, for wholly different reasons, that Russian Jewry could not long survive—the Bund central

---

indicative of sloppy language rather than self-contradictory thought.

Stalin, of course, used the criteria of language and territory in his definition of a nation when he wrote *Marxism and the National Question* in 1912. This definition has been criticized, and in many cases abandoned, by Soviet and East European scholars. Thus, a prominent Polish sociologist writes: "Naturally, formulating one single definition of a nation is not only highly complicated; it is probably almost impossible. . . . If we do not want to arrive at a purely arbitrary, synthetic formula but an analytical one, we have to deal with highly varied social phenomena which cannot be comprehended within a unified and identical definition. If we depart—and on this we are almost unanimous—from the current Stalinist definition, it is mainly because it attempted to thrust the historical category of nation into the framework of unified characterizing features. . . . According to traditional Marxist thought we see a nation as a creation of historical development, a product of common history. This history is different for different nations which, in the concrete analysis of the history of these nations, thrusts various elements into the foreground." Jerzy Wiatr, in *Z Pola Walki,* IX, no. 3 (1967), 87. For Soviet debates on the Stalinist definition, see the series of "discussion" articles in *Voprosy istorii* for 1966 and 1967. See also Grey Hodnett, "The Debate Over Soviet Federalism," *Soviet Studies,* XVIII, no. 4 (1967). After defining nation as "a self-contained group of human beings who place loyalty to the group as a whole above competing loyalties," Dankwart Rustow suggests that "if a nation is conceived of as a group of people bound together by a common loyalty, it follows that nationhood, like loyalty itself, is a matter of degree. A given people at a given time may be more or less of a nation; and none fully approximates the ideal type." Rustow, *A World of Nations* (Washington, 1967), p. 24.

[73] Medem, "Natsionale bavegung," p. 250.

committee, which always prided itself on its responsiveness to the workers' sentiments, began to assert its national program with greater vigor. The Bund no longer had to restrain itself in its national demands for fear of RSDLP disapproval; and in 1904 "national autonomy" as a political demand began to appear in Bund propaganda. A Bundist commentator claimed that this was enthusiastically welcomed by the rank and file of the Bund. "A veritable wave of public opinion has come out for 'Bundist' national-cultural autonomy in one form or another, more or less explicit. Today it has become a topical question, a fashionable slogan."[74] In the revolutionary atmosphere of 1905 many Jewish groups—political, cultural, and economic—began to propose projects for Jewish self-government.

The New World of Politics and the Emergence of Jewish Parties

Until the 1905 Revolution the Bund had the field of Jewish politics pretty much to itself. While the Zionist movement had been founded in the same year as the Bund, many of its members were so intent upon establishing a Jewish state in Palestine that they consciously neglected the home front. Judging that the economic rehabilitation, political modernization, and cultural renovation of the Jewish people could come about only in a Jewish state, they considered wasted efforts to restructure Jewish economic life and to gain political rights. But under the pressure of a public opinion aroused by the stormy events of 1905, the Zionists, like the Bundists before them, were forced to concern themselves with domestic political questions. In November 1906, at their convention in Helsingfors, the Zionists adopted a platform which called for the democratization of the state,

[74] "Sovremennyi politicheskii moment i nashi natsional'nye trebovanii," *Posledniia izvestiia*, no. 250, September 1905.

autonomy for national regions, and guaranteed rights for national minorities, including the Jews. They demanded that the Jewish nation be given the right to administer its internal affairs and that an all-Russian Jewish national assembly be called to work out the mechanics and principles of internal national organization and administration. The Zionists demanded the right to use Yiddish and Hebrew in schools, courts and "public life," and the right of employed Jews to have Saturday, rather than Sunday, as their day of rest.[75] These remained the guidelines of Zionist domestic policy through World War I.

The Zionist movement appealed mainly to the middle class and the petite bourgeoisie, attracting some support from professionals and merchants as well. Some members of the intelligentsia and of the working class attempted to combine Zionist aspirations with socialist political and economic programs. The Zionist-Socialist Workers' Party, commonly known by the initials of its Russian name, S.S., held its first congress in 1906. The S.S. criticized the Bund for viewing the Jews of the Russian Empire as a separate nation with no ties to Jews elsewhere, and for overrating the importance of democratic freedoms to the welfare of the Jewish proletariat, thereby ignoring such important social phenomena as emigration and the failure to industrialize rapidly enough to rehabilitate Jewish economic life. The Zionist-Socialists urged that emigration be regulated in such a way as to concentrate large masses of Jews in one territory, not necessarily Palestine, where they could proceed to construct a viable socialist economy. To this end, the S.S. was willing to work with "bourgeois" Jewish organizations favoring territorialism as a panacea to Jewry's ills.[76]

[75] *Dos idishe folk*, no. 26, 1906, quoted in A. Kirzhnitz and M. Rafes, eds., *Der idisher arbeter* (Moscow, 1925), pp. 405–06.

[76] *Der neier veg*, April 28 and May 4, 1906, quoted in Kirzhnitz and Rafes, pp. 380–84.

The Jewish Socialist Workers' Party, popularly called SERP, after the abbreviation for its Russian name, or Y.S., after the abbreviation for its Yiddish name, was founded in April 1906 by a group of intellectuals who had been sympathetic to the S.S. and *Poalai Tsion.* The party "considered itself a division of the international socialist army" and its uniqueness lay in its platform calling for the formation of extra-territorial nationality parliaments, or *sejms,* which would have jurisdiction not only in cultural matters but also "in those political and economic questions connected with the historical conditions of the given nation." The Jewish *sejm* would have the power to regulate emigration so that it would concentrate itself in a free, uncolonized territory. The party disapproved of the willingness of the S.S. to cooperate with the bourgeoisie.[77]

The *Poalai Tsion* party, consolidated in 1906, was more truly Zionist and more strictly Marxian than either the S.S. or the Y.S. The *Poalai Tsion* based its platform on the ideas of Ber Borokhov, who had attempted to combine Marxism and Zionism.[78] His basic thesis was that normal social and economic development, and consequent class differentiation and class struggle in the Jewish nation, could occur only if the Jews were given one of the basic prerequisites for such development—land. Borokhov argued that "elemental [stychic] processes" are leading the Jews to Palestine, a primitive land remarkably well suited for experiencing the entire gamut of economic development as it had been classically described by Marx. "In free Russia we will successfully continue our work—the work of establishing normal conditions for the Jewish nation. . . . In the lands of

[77] From the report of the Central Committee of the party to the International Socialist Congress in Stuttgart, 1907, quoted in *Sotsialistisher teritorializm* (Paris, n.d.), pp. 54–56. The emphasis on a *sejm* gave this party yet another popular name, "Sejmists."

[78] See *Nationalism and the Class Struggle: A Marxian Approach to the Jewish Problem* (New York, 1937).

the diaspora conditions must be established under which the Jewish nation can breathe freely . . . , thereby making possible the achievement of the Zionist ideal—the establishment of a free Jewish society in Palestine. Only there can our national renaissance take place. . . . Through freedom in the diaspora to national renaissance in Palestine. Through renaissance . . . to socialism."[79] The *Poalai Tsion* demanded national political autonomy with broad economic, political, cultural, and financial jurisdiction for those nationalities whose needs could not be met by territorial (regional) autonomy. Jewish emigration was to be regulated so as to build up the Jewish settlement in Palestine. In July 1907 the *Poalai Tsion* claimed to have 18,000 members.[80]

In late March 1905 a group of Jewish lawyers, who had gained fame by their activities at trials following pogroms in Kishinev (1903) and Gomel (1904), proposed the formation of a non-party Jewish federation to fight for Jewish rights. While they neither had nor sought a mass following, these were prestigious and talented men. Maxim Vinaver, a leader of the new Russian Constitutional Democratic Party was "A man . . . with clear and masterful articulation and a rare gift not just for speaking but also for listening, for fathoming another's ideas. . . ."[81] Henryk Sliosberg was a lawyer whose specialty was Russian legislation about Jews,

[79] From a handbill of a *Poalai Tsion* group in Vitebsk, 1905. In the *Poalai Tsion* Archive, YIVO Institute for Jewish Research, New York City.

[80] Kirzhnitz and Rafes, pp. 387–90. On the various socialist-zionist or socialist-territorialist parties, see Jonathan Frankel, "Voluntarism and Determinism in Socialist Zionism (Russia, 1898–1923)," and Michael Astour, "Di problem fun tsvai flakhn in der sotsialistish-teritorialistisher bavegung in Rusland," both papers presented at the YIVO Research Conference on Jewish Participation in Movements Devoted to the Cause of Social Progress, New York, September 10–13, 1964.

[81] The description is by Simon Dubnow, *Dos bukh fun mein lebn* (New York-Buenos Aires, 1962–63), II, 28–73, quoted in Lucy S. Dawidowicz, ed., *The Golden Tradition* (New York, 1967), p. 462.

legislation which he frequently challenged in the courts and government ministries. "Compared to Vinaver the *political* leader, Sliosberg was more of a *communal* leader. He was a petitioner to the very government against which Vinaver had organized an opposition. Sliosberg belonged to the right wing of the Cadet party, whereas Vinaver belonged to the center." [82] Vinaver and Sliosberg were joined by Leon Bramson, later affiliated with the Trudovik party, and Mark Ratner, a member of the Socialist Revolutionary party.

This group of lawyers was joined by the historian Simon Dubnow who persuaded them that the non-party federation should demand national, as well as civil rights, and the Federation for Equal Rights for the Jewish People in Russia was born. Shortly thereafter the Zionist convention in Helsingfors "appropriated all the Federation's principles as part of their program, even the plank regarding national rights in the *galuth* [diaspora]. But they decided to support these policies only under their own party auspices." [83] This caused the anti-Zionists in the Federation, led by Vinaver, to create the own organization, the *Folksgrupe,* which adopted only minimal national demands and condemned the "principled emigrants" of the Zionist party. In turn, Dubnow began organizing a more nationalistic party, the *Folkspartai.* "Our political program was based on the principles of the Russian Constitutional Democratic Party (its left wing), whereas the Jewish National program was an extension of the Federation's, dwelling specifically on the institutionalization of autonomy through self-governing local and federated community councils," that is, through

[82] Dubnow quoted in Dawidowicz, p. 463. For the attitude of the Liberal movement and the Cadet Party on the Jewish question, see Yitzkhak Maor, *Shealat HaYehudim Batnua Haliberalit VeHa-Mehapkhanit Berusiya* (Jerusalem, 1964).

[83] Dawidowicz, p. 469.

kehillas which would be national rather than exclusively religious.[84]

The *Folksgrupe* called for equal civil and linguistic rights, recognition and subsidization of the *kehilla* by the government, and the guarantee of rights to national minorities. General education, as well as "the Jewish language," history and "ethical values" should be promoted among the Jews.[85]

The *Folkspartai* demanded democratization of the political order, strict parliamentarianism, rights for national minorities, autonomy for the various territories of the Russian Empire, and the right to use Yiddish in public life. A national Jewish assembly should be summoned to formulate the principles of internal national organization.[86]

The formation and activity of all these political groupings influenced the Bund to place greater emphasis on the national elements of its political program, in order to retain its appeal to the Jewish working masses. Bundist national consciousness had also been aroused by the pogroms of 1905.

The wave of pogroms which broke out in the early spring of 1905 caused the Bund to form armed self-defense groups (*boevye otriady*) in many cities. The Bund's national pride swelled, and it claimed that the pogroms would boomerang and aid the armed revolution.[87] "Jews are no longer weak cowards who flee from the Gentiles. We have healthy butchers, smiths, teamsters, stone-cutters, and porters. . . . Jews can form self-defense organizations, Jews are building barricades." [88]

Newly-acquired confidence was reflected in the decision

[84] *Ibid.*
[85] *Di idishe virklekhkeit,* quoted in Kirzhnits and Rafes, pp. 407–09.
[86] *Dos idishe folk,* no. 2, 1907, quoted in *ibid.,* p. 411.
[87] *Posledniia izvestiia,* no. 231, May 1905, pp. 2–3.
[88] *Arbeter shtime,* no. 40, September 1905.

of the Sixth Bund Congress of October 1905 to incorporate national-cultural autonomy into its "Program-Minimum." The resolution on this point declared that cultural matters, such as schooling, should be removed from the jurisdiction of the state and be transferred to special institutions—local and central—which would be selected by all members of a nationality on the basis of universal, free, direct, and secret balloting. This would not preclude the setting of general educational standards by central governmental organs. The Congress also demanded full civil and political rights for the Jews and the right to use Yiddish in all courts and organs of government.[89] This was to be the core of the Bund's national program until 1917.

Local Bund organizations had been cooperating closely with RSDLP units on an *ad hoc* basis during the Revolution of 1905. The RSDLP called for a unification congress and invited the Bund to rejoin the party officially. The RSDLP Congress met in Stockholm in the spring of 1906 and voted to readmit the Bund to the RSDLP.[90] The Congress resolved that the "question of the national program remains open in view of the fact that it was not reexamined."[91] Vladimir Medem asserted that the Bund's position had not changed and that "We enter the party to struggle. . . . The Bund was not, is not, and will never be the translator of Russian Social-Democracy into Yiddish. The Bund is the organized and conscious expression of the decisive, broad, and powerful currents in Jewish life. . . . The national program of the Bund cannot be changed by a directive

[89] *Der veker*, January 3, 14, 21, 1906.

[90] Neither the Bolsheviks nor the Mensheviks were united on the question of readmitting the Bund to the party, though the Mensheviks were the leading spokesmen against readmission. Lenin and Stalin voted for readmission.

[91] *VKP(B) v rezolutsiiakh i resheniiakh s"ezdov, konferentsii i plenumov TsK* (Moscow, 1936), I, 83.

from above."[92] A resolution approving reunification was passed by a large majority at the Seventh Congress of the Bund.

Having temporarily stabilized its "external" affairs, the Bund began to take a greater interest in all Jewish communal affairs. "We had to descend from the heavens to the grayness of daily life. . . . The feel for reality had been strengthened, the wish to enter all corners of Jewish life was deepened, [the desire] to be together with the Jewish masses in all the evolutions which they were undergoing."[93]

If the Bund was to make national-cultural autonomy an attainable goal, it had to involve itself with a Jewish culture which it could support. Therefore, the Bund entered a new field of operations—cultural activities. Besides, the political reaction which had set in after the abortive revolution prevented the Bund from carrying on much of its former political activity.

Since Jewish culture has always been essentially religious, the Bund had to promote a secular culture, consistent with the theories of social-democracy. Musical, literary, and dramatic societies were organized to develop such a culture. There was a political justification for the cultural work of the Bund. "In trade unions, educational societies and courses—everywhere we must build our islands . . . saturated with Social-Democratic ideas, with the Social-Democratic spirit."[94] The Bund also feared that the Zionists and bourgeois intelligentsia would gain influence among the workers if they were allowed to supply the proletariat's cultural needs. In fact, cultural activities helped keep the Bund intact during the post-1905 crisis in the

[92] V. Medem, "Ob"edinenie bunda s RSDRP," *Nashe slovo,* no. 4, July 1906.

[93] Medem, "Natsionale bavegung," p. 254.

[94] *Di shtime fun bund,* December 1908.

socialist movement. The Bund remained a viable organization at least partially "because what the members were doing was consistent with their traditional way of life, and because cultural aspirations were as valid as revolutionary political goals." [95]

Though, like the Bolsheviks, the Bund had boycotted the first Duma, it played an active role in the campaigns for the second and third Dumas in 1907. Here there was a confluence of political and national programs, as the Bund campaigned for candidates who would represent Social-Democracy and, at the same time, would fight for Jewish civil rights.

When non-Bundist Jewish deputies were elected, the Bund carried on a ceaseless campaign against their "timidity" in failing to press for Jewish national rights and equality for Yiddish. The Bund press charged that, while Caucasian and Polish representatives spoke up for better treatment of the nationalities, the Jewish deputies "sit as if they had a mouth full of water." [96] The Bund also pressed the non-Jewish Social-Democrats in the Duma to pay greater heed to the national, and particularly the Jewish, question. And, indeed, the Fifth (London) Congress of the RSDLP passed a resolution reproaching the Social-Democratic deputies for not having paid sufficient attention to the national question.[97]

The Bund began to concern itself with such matters as the secularization of the *kehilla,* Yiddish language schools, and Saturday as the day of rest for Jewish workers. The Bund now saw itself as the representative of the "broad masses in general" and not just the proletariat. The Bolshe-

[95] Woodhouse and Tobias, p. 348.

[96] *Folkstseitung,* July 3, 1906.

[97] *Piatyi (Londonskii) s"ezd RSDRP, protokoly* (Moscow, 1963), p. 614.

viks took this as confirmation of their fears regarding Bund nationalism and the decline of class consciousness.

> The maintenance of everything Jewish, the preservation of all the national peculiarities of the Jews, even those that are patently noxious to the proletariat, the isolation of the Jews from everything non-Jewish, even the establishment of special hospitals—that is the level to which the Bund has sunk.[98]

In the eyes of Lenin and Stalin, then, the Bundists had become nothing more than "Zionists afraid of sea-sickness" (Plekhanov's phrase).

Although the Bund continued to advocate national-cultural autonomy in its official program, there were really three schools of thought within the Bund. The national program had been molded by the hurly-burly of party politics and the exigencies of events. With the decline of political activity in the years after 1905, and the concomitant decline in Bund membership,[99] the Bund could afford to devote more time to the theoretical development of its program. A new generation of leaders, tempered in the fires of the revolution, was striking out in new directions. But the foremost exponent of the national program of the Bund was still Vladimir Medem.

Born into a Jewish family which had been baptized, as late as 1916 Medem still wrote his Yiddish articles in Latin script, and it was not until 1915–16, when he was active in Poland, that he became a fluent Yiddish public speaker.[100] Despite his background, Medem became the chief Bund

[98] Stalin, *Marxism and the National Question* (New York, n.d.), p. 42.

[99] The Bund claimed 40,000 members in 1906; 25,000 in 1907; "a few thousand" in 1908; and 30,000 in 1913.

[100] See V. Shulman, "Medem in Poiln," *Vladimir Medem tsum tsvantsikstn yortseit*, p. 144.

spokesman on the national question and devoted most of his writings to the formulation and definition of national-cultural autonomy. For Medem there were no national cultures *per se;* there were only national *forms* "into which general human content is poured."[101] But culture is so much a matter of form that each nationality was to be entitled to autonomy in cultural matters. Medem and the Bund did not oppose territorial autonomy for several regions of Russia, but Medem felt that such autonomy did not solve the national question, especially in view of the fact that capitalism had scattered members of the various nationalities over the length and breadth of Russia. "The concepts of 'nation' and 'population of a certain district' are not congruent."[102] Therefore, autonomy based on culture was necessary for all nationalities. What the Jews needed most were equal civil rights and the right to use Yiddish in the schools, courts, the press, and government institutions, since language is the basis of culture. This entire concept was rejected by Lenin who argued that national-cultural autonomy would weaken the class struggle by distracting the proletariat from its class obligations and attracting it to national struggles. Furthermore, the national struggle was a purely bourgeois phenomenon, and it would be anachronistic for the proletariat to participate in it. In the course of national struggle the proletariat would lose its class consciousness and join with the bourgeoisie in the struggle against the proletariat and bourgeoisie of another nationality. Schools and national culture in general "cannot be torn from economics and politics" and schools established on national lines would "perpetuate, intensify, strengthen 'pure' clericalism and 'pure' bourgeois chauvinism."[103] Thus Lenin opposed the Bund's national program, as well as its concept

[101] V. Medem, "Di sotsial demokratie un di natsionale frage," in *ibid.*, p. 188.

[102] *Ibid.*, p. 218.

[103] V. I. Lenin, *Critical Remarks on the National Question* (Moscow,

of a federative party. Medem, like all Bundists, was aware of the danger to which Lenin had pointed, and was torn between a "pure" social-democratic theory and the actual spirit and attitude of the Jewish workers. Medem tried to balance correct theory and pressing demands "from below," and was constantly forced to weigh one against the other. This balancing can be seen in his doctrine of "neutralism."

Medem opposed Zionism on the grounds that it neglected the real interests of the Jews and offered them an illusory panacea of a Jewish homeland. He also condemned activist assimilationism as being nothing more than a bourgeois lust for "an equal and fat share" with bourgeois citizens of the predominant nationality. But Medem was not satisfied with the RSDLP program.

> We ask the Program: What does Social-Democracy have to do in order to combat national persecution? And we hear an excellent answer: "We, the party of the proletariat, must always be unconditionally against national persecution." Hearty congratulations! We would very much like to know what the same comrades would say if in some Program . . . it would state in fine words, "We, the party of the proletariat, are always unconditionally against political despotism . . . against economic oppression." [104]

He felt that the program was meaningless because it offered no plan of action and was altogether too vague. Besides, equitable administration of national affairs would be too great a task for a central Russian government, even a democratic one. Furthermore, since this government would be dominated by the bourgeoisie, the old national enmities

---

1951), pp. 38–39. Lenin did not, however, deny the right of national minorities to be instructed in their native languages.

[104] Medem, "Di sotsial demokratie," p. 194.

and oppressions would not be effectively uprooted.[105] Once again the proletariat would be forced to march with the bourgeoisie of its own nation in order to protect itself from other nations.[106]

Because of the tension in Medem's thought between the elements of theory and reality, he adopted a "neutralist" position on the national question. In essence, his position was that only History could determine the fate of the Jewish people and that historical processes should not be interfered with in any way. Prognosis of the future is useless. "In actual work you cannot reckon with what might happen but only with what there *is* and with what is *needed*." Nationalists and assimilationists, seemingly diametrically opposed, have this in common: they confuse outcomes with goals. Instead of admitting that History might lead, either to assimilation or a national revival, they declare *a priori* that History is moving in a definite direction and make this direction their ideal. This does not mean that "neutralists" are indifferent to the fate of the nation. "For us, the most important thing is the actual interest of the working class . . .; for him [the nationalist] nationalism is an end in itself and its existence does not depend on any interests." If the masses have cultural interests, the Bund is bound to concern itself with them and try to establish schools. If no such interests exist, the Bund has no business undertaking cultural activities. Human efforts can influence the inexorable historical process only when these efforts "serve life-needs and life-interests."[107] Of course, any *forcible* assimilation is to be opposed since it interferes with the historical process.[108]

[105] *Ibid.*, pp. 200–01, 208.

[106] *Ibid.*, pp. 214–15.

[107] Vl. Medem, "Natsionalizm oder 'neitralizm,'" *Tseit fragn* (Vilna, 1910), pp. 15–24.

[108] Medem, "Di sotsial demokratie," p. 190. This is remarkably

The assimilationist tendency, the second school of thought, was never developed into a full-blown theory. Those who favored assimilation generally did so as much because of their personal background as because of intellectual conviction. There were some, however, who were influenced by the Russian Social-Democrats' charges against the Bund. Some of the older Bund leaders disapproved of the increasing national consciousness within the movement and were either pushed out of leadership positions, joined another wing of the RSDLP, or left political life altogether. But some members of the younger generation also favored assimilation. Thus, Moishe Rafes constantly emphasized the bourgeois nature of the nationalist viewpoint. "Not to take the side of one nationalism and help it against another, but to tear the working masses away from the influence of chauvinist ideology—this way and only this way can we

---

close to Lenin's language in *Critical Remarks,* pp. 36–37. For another expression of "neutralism," see articles by Bronislaw Grosser ("Aldor Shtein") in *Der sotsial demokrat,* nos. 48–49, Nov.-Dec. 1911. Lenin is reported to have said that until 1905 it was not certain that Russian Jews could and would assimilate as their West European co-religionists had. But when in the course of the 1905 revolution each stratum of Russian Jewry aligned itself with the corresponding stratum of the Russian population, Lenin said, "it became clear that it was the political order which was responsible for the isolation of the Jews." Lenin called Bundist neutralism "ignorance," and likened the Bundists to the Aesopian ass which could not decide which of two piles of feed to eat, and so died of hunger. "The same happens with the Bundists, for whatever measures are chosen to resolve the national question—every measure of this kind would aid either assimilation or differentiation of nations. Afraid of both these tendencies, the Bund is condemned to complete paralysis. But, in reality . . . the Bund, having condemned assimilation, stands for nationalism, for separation. Il'ich considered the worst evil of the Bund to be not its mistaken national program, consisting of cultural-national autonomy, but its organizational principle, dividing socialist workers of different nations into separate organizations." S. Dimanshtain, "Lenin i natsional'nyi vopros," *Molodaia gvardiia,* nos. 2–3, February-March 1924.

formulate our work. . . . Great care, consistency, fidelity to the basic principles of our old world-view, only this can guard us from the national tide which floods even the Jewish working mass." [109]

From the younger generation also came the outstanding exponent of the "nationalist" school of thought. Esther Frumkin was one of the most colorful figures of the movement. She was a passionate idealist, a gifted writer, and an incurable romantic. Esther, as she was known in the Bund, became prominent during 1906 and began her tortured and tortuous ideological and personal odyssey as a fiery orator, concentrating on two favorite topics, education and the Yiddish language.

Stalin had ridiculed the Bund for proposing autonomy "for a nation whose future is denied and whose existence has still to be proved." [110] Esther did not question the existence or the future of the nation; she was concerned for its national consciousness. The immediate task of the Jewish labor movement was to make the masses conscious of their national *needs* so that they could demand their national *rights*. In Esther's view this was entirely consistent with the class struggle because such an effort would oppose the *bourgeois* concept of national-cultural autonomy which "is a means of separating the Jews in order to preserve some sort of metaphysical 'Judaism' [while] for us it is a means of satisfying the needs of the masses." [111] National consciousness is, for Esther, "only a concrete form of political consciousness." [112]

Among the intelligentsia, and even among some of the masses, national consciousness is very weak and "too often

[109] *Tseit* (St. Petersburg), July 18, 1913, p. 2.

[110] Stalin, *Marxism*, p. 36.

[111] Esther, "Gleikhbarekhtigung fun shprakhn," *Tseit fragn*, v (Vilna, 1911), 21.

[112] *Ibid.*, p. 24.

serves as a holiday suit." "The task of the conscious proletariat is to . . . show the people the way to the fight for the rights of the Jewish language, of the Jewish school." The Bund must develop a proletarian Jewish culture for the masses who will then transmit it to the half-assimilated intelligentsia. The Yiddish language must be used in special Jewish schools because it is a link to the Jewish past and ties the child to the generations before him and to the nation around him. The Jewish child must receive a new intensive proletarian-national education. Esther said earnestly:

> When we speak of education in a proletarian spirit, we do not mean that children should recite part of the Erfurt Program instead of the "Shema" [Credo] or a chapter of the Communist Manifesto instead of the "Modeh Ani" [a morning prayer]. . . . But when we say "proletarian upbringing" we mean that Marxism is not only a political program but a *weltanschauung* . . . and in such a form it is never too early for a proletarian child. That which a child now feels he will later understand.[113]

The child must be told in Yiddish of his mother's suffering as a worker. Jewish holidays must be transformed into national-proletarian celebrations and solemn occasions. With unmistakable national pride, Esther confidently declared that "the proletarian children of that nation which from generation to generation handed down the Divine prophecies of Isaiah . . . swords shall be beaten into ploughshares and the lion shall lie down with the lamb—the proletarian children of that nation can understand our ideal."[114] Jewish kindergartens, libraries, courses in lan-

[113] Esther, "Vegn natsionaler ertsihung," *Tseit fragn*, I (Vilna, 1909), 24.

[114] *Ibid.*, p. 26. Lenin charged, falsely, that the Bund was supporting the establishment of "clerical schools" (*Critical Remarks*, p. 50).

guage and literature, plays, excursions—all these should be promoted in order to increase the national consciousness of the children of the proletariat.

Local organs of national-cultural autonomy [115] were to be established along the lines proposed by the South Slav delegation at the Brünn Congress of the Austrian Social-Democrats. A person whose language was locally recognized would have the right to use that language in any governmental and judicial institution and must be replied to in his language.

Esther disagreed with Medem and argued that the leaders of the Jewish proletariat should not stand passively aside watching the mysterious forces of history shape human events; they must play an active role in arousing the national consciousness of the proletariat and the intelligentsia.

Even the election of town officials should be conducted on the basis of proportional representation of nationalities. If a certain town has a total population of 100,000—40,000 Jews, 30,000 Poles, 20,000 Belorussians, and 10,000 Russians—and if ten judges are needed, there should be four Jews, three Poles, two Belorussians, and one Russian elected. This would prevent national hatreds from arising because it would fix national representation and the campaign would not be conducted with the slogans of "Elect a Jew" or "Elect a Pole."

Some Bundists were also taken aback by Esther's mixture of religious forms and socialism. "She became known for her brochure about 'our school,' about the education of the folk-child, of the working-child. She spoke about religion as a necessary element in the upbringing of the folk-child. She spoke with great warmth about the positive educational value of religious customs. She delighted in the custom of blessing the candles, for example. It did not occur to anyone that Esther Frumkin should be expelled from the party for her national-religious 'deviation'." H. Erlich, "Esther Frumkin," *Der veker* (New York), December 27, 1930.

[115] Others, such as nomads, would get "language help" from the central organs of the national autonomous groups.

Despite the various opinions on the Bund's national program, no significant changes were made in it between 1911 and 1913, although the question was in the forefront of discussion within the party.[116]

One of the last direct exchanges between Lenin and the Bund on the national question came in 1913. Peisakh Liebman ("Liebman Hersh") published an article in *Tseit* which once again charged that "self-determination" was too vague a term to have any real meaning. "When the Jewish working class . . . began to work out the concrete content which had to go into the program, the master theoreticians of Russian Social-Democracy raised the cry: Nationalism! . . . Every attempt at giving a clear and concrete content to this question was declared to be a petite-bourgeois heresy against Marxist teaching." [117] Liebman said that international culture is not "anational" culture and that only through his own national culture can the worker take part in international culture. Lenin admitted this to be true but asserted that every nation has a bourgeois culture which is the dominant one. "Therefore, 'national culture' in general is the culture of the landlords, the clergy, and the bourgeoisie." [118] Nevertheless, Lenin had modified somewhat his position on the national question. In November

[116] The Ninth Conference, held in Vienna in August 1912, protested against the Beilis trial and demanded that the Pale of Settlement be abolished. The Central Committee of the Bund proposed an agenda for the Eighth Congress (scheduled for August 1914, but not held because of the outbreak of war) which included the national question, Saturday and Sunday rest, schools, and the struggle for greater recognition of Yiddish. The conferences of the RSDLP Central Committee held in February and August 1913 condemned the Bund for obstructing unification of the branches of local party organizations and emphatically rejected national-cultural autonomy. See *VKP(B) v rezolutsiiakh,* pp. 205, 216.

[117] P. Liebman, "A neie oiflage fun an altn toès," *Tseit,* September 17, 1913.

[118] Lenin, *Critical Remarks,* p. 17.

1913 he specifically approved "broad self-rule and autonomy for regions which should be delimited, among other things also by national criteria. All these demands are compulsory for every consistent democrat and all the more so for a Socialist." [119] A year later he said, "only by means of autonomy for regions, large and varied in their national composition, can real democratic centralism be realized." [120] This did not mean the acceptance of national-cultural autonomy, nor did the Jews stand to gain from Lenin's new formulation, since they did not constitute a compact population, forming a majority in any one territorial area. Moreover, Lenin made no concessions on the organization of the Party, while the Bund continued to insist on its autonomy and the need to reconstruct the RSDLP on a federative basis.

The Mensheviks, on the other hand, "remained adamant in their hostility to the idea of federalism, but they slowly reconciled themselves to national-cultural autonomy." [121] The August 1912 conference of the right-wing Mensheviks, or "Liquidators," "took the first timid steps in the direction of a national program which the party had heretofore lacked. It asserted in its resolution that "national-cultural autonomy was not contrary to the party's program guaranteeing national self-determination." [122] By 1917 the entire Menshevik Party, which had many Jewish adherents and which had found the Bund sympathetic to its general political program, accepted national-cultural autonomy and that program was incorporated into the official party platform.

The Bund retained its platform through the first Revolution of 1917. The Tenth Conference of the Bund held in April 1917 demanded that the forthcoming Constituent

[119] V. I. Lenin, *Sochineniia*, XVII (3rd ed., Moscow, 1935), 65.

[120] *Ibid.*, p. 328.

[121] Richard Pipes, *The Formation of the Soviet Union* (rev. ed., Cambridge, Mass., 1964), p. 34.

[122] *Ibid.*

Assembly establish legal public institutions "for the organization and guidance of the cultural life of the Jewish nation in Russia." Any person declaring himself to be a Jew was to be a member of such an institution which would deal with schools, literature, art and the development of science and technology. All of these were to have a purely secular character. The language of this institution was to be Yiddish.[123] The Provisional Government should begin to implement this even before the convention of the Constituent Assembly.[124]

At the same time, Lenin was modifying his platform even further. He now saw some virtue in a federal state structure. "Even federation does not in the least contradict democratic centralism. Time and again, given a really democratic order, a federation . . . constitutes only a transitional step to a really democratic centralism." [125] But this in no way led Lenin to advocate any sort of autonomy for the Jews, despite the fact that they were concentrated very heavily in certain areas of Belorussia and the Ukraine, the area of the tsarist "Pale." Nevertheless, within a year of Lenin's death, attempts were made by the Soviet government to create autonomous Jewish areas and regions in Belorussia and the Ukraine.

The rejection of the Bund's proposal for a federated party was a crucial step in the formation of the Leninist party. It decisively established the party as a cohesive, tightly controlled unit which did not allow for ideological

[123] Browder and Kerensky, translating from Dimanshtain's Russian, incorrectly and incongruously render this as "Hebrew." Hebrew was considered by the Bund to be a language of religious ritual, artificially revived by the Zionists, whereas the true language of the masses was Yiddish. Robert P. Browder and Alexander F. Kerensky, eds., *The Russian Provisional Government* (Stanford, 1961), I, 428–29.

[124] *Ibid.*

[125] Lenin, *Sochineniia,* XXII, quoted in Julian Towster, *Political Power in the USSR* (New York, 1948), p. 63.

pluralism. Although "factions" were outlawed only by the Tenth Party Congress in 1921, the decisions of 1903 were the crucial ones and those of 1921 only their logical extension.

The Bund-Lenin debate and the internal debates in the Bund on the national question were to color all of Soviet policy toward the Jews and the reaction of the politically conscious Jews to the Soviets after 1917. It was against the background of the ideological formulations of *Iskra* that the Bolshevik leaders were to struggle with the Jewish problem they could not avoid. The creation and abolition of the Jewish Sections of the Communist Party, the *Evsektsiia,* the founding and withering away of the Jewish Autonomous Region in the Far East, and the policy toward Jewish culture all had to be enacted with "first principles" in mind. If the revolution forced a reassessment by the Bolsheviks of their nationality policy and of their Jewish policy, it also challenged the Bund and the other Jewish parties, excited by the revolution to heightened activity, to reexamine their own positions, the nature of the revolution, and the future of Jewish life and culture in the new Russia.

II

1917: Parties, Politics, and the Planning of Freedom

The autumn of Russian freedom has come. And after autumn comes the severe, long winter with all its different experiences, which can, it seems, dash all hopes and strike from memory the ray of light which flashed in March. But, no! True, our autumn is chilly and sad; severe and cruel is our coming winter. But spring will surely come again. Spring will surely come. . . .

B. Marshak in *Folkstseitung,* October 30, 1917

But when cities or provinces have been accustomed to live under a prince, and the family of that prince is extinguished, being on the one hand used to obey, and on the other not having their old prince, they cannot unite in choosing one from among themselves, and they do not know how to live in freedom, so that they are slower to take arms, and a prince can win them over with greater facility and establish himself securely. . . . It soon relapses under a yoke, oftentimes much heavier than the one which it had but just shaken off.

Machiavelli, *The Prince*

THE REVOLUTION of March 1917 was hailed by the overwhelming majority of the Jewish people in the crumbling Russian Empire. They had little cause to regret the downfall of a regime which had confined them to the Pale, had closed the professions, agriculture, and heavy industry to them and, during the war, had climaxed its treatment of the Jews by expelling thousands of them from their homes, particularly in the border areas of Poland and Lithuania, on the grounds that they were a disloyal element. This action was accompanied by seizures of hostages, rigged trials, and suppression of the press and other institutions of Jewish life. The collapse of the old regime aroused the Jews from their despondency, and a wave of expectation swept over the Jewish communities in Russian-held areas. "It is impossible," said a recent arrival from the United States, "to describe the exhilaration and the holiday atmosphere in the Jewish world immediately after the fall of tsarism. . . . Jews began to gather a huge sum of money in order to build a 'Temple of Jewish Freedom' in Petrograd. When the Provisional Government decided to float a 'freedom loan,' the Jews contributed tremendous sums; Moscow Jews alone contributed twenty-two million rubles. And when the imperialists began . . . further prosecution of the war, Jews supported the Provisional Government to the hilt, despite the fact that they suffered more than anyone from the war. There were no differences of opinion in the Jewish world. Class interests disappeared. The only desire of the Jewish bourgeoisie and the Jewish workers was to support the Provisional Government."[1]

[1] "Ben Khaim" [S. Agurskii], in "Di role fun di idishe arbeiter in der rusisher revolutsie," *Funken* (New York), I, no. 8, (March 25, 1920). The "Temple of Jewish Freedom" Agurskii refers to was

On April 2, 1917, the Provisional Government eliminated all restrictions imposed upon national and religious groups, but it chose not to take any further positive action in regard to the nationalities, deeming this to be the business of the forthcoming Constituent Assembly. This allowed the nationalities to formulate their national programs as they pleased and the unleashed energies of the Jewish community were soon directed toward planning the Jewish future in Russia. The revival of Jewish cultural and political life created psychological and institutional obstacles to the penetration of Bolshevik ideas and organizations. For this reason it is important to examine the cultural and political activity of Russian Jewry in 1917.

Jewish communal life emerged from its shadowy wartime existence, and local *kehillas* were reorganized. Adult education, primary and secondary schools, relief work, publication of Hebrew and Yiddish works, a daily press, and even musical and dramatic societies—all quickly blossomed in the spring of the Russian revolution.[2]

While cultural activity went on at a feverish pitch, the economic situation of the Jews hardly improved from the stagnation and backwardness of pre-revolutionary days. The entire Russian economy suffered severe dislocations, and that fragile periphery of it dominated by Jews—petty trade and small artisanry—was teetering on the edge of total collapse. "The situation of the working youth is now a very sad one. Unemployment is generally very high but it is especially rife among youth."[3] This situation was to affect

---

undoubtedly the "Temple of Equality" to which an "International Institute for the Study of National Problems" was to be attached. See *American Jewish Year Book 5678* (Philadelphia, 1917), p. 306.

[2] In 1917, 48 Jewish newspapers came into existence, whereas only one was carried over from 1916. See A. Kirzhnitz, *Di yidishe prese in ratnfarband* (Minsk, 1928), p. 68.

[3] *Der veker* (Minsk), November 10, 1917.

profoundly political developments in the Jewish community, especially within the Jewish working class.

Of the approximately 5,600,000 Jews in the Russian Empire in 1914, roughly one-quarter, or 1,400,000, were members of working class families. But the largest class was an impoverished petite bourgeoisie—mostly small shopkeepers, artisans, and a tiny group of peasants, who together constituted about half the Jewish population.[4] The working class was politically conscious compared to the relatively dormant petite bourgeoisie and the religious community. Generally, it joined Jewish socialist non-Zionist parties. There were also Zionist proletarian parties, such as the *Poalai Tsion,* although the Zionist movement attracted mainly the intelligentsia and some middle-class elements. The proletariat and socialist intelligentsia was concentrated in three parties in 1917: the Bund, the Jewish Socialist Labor Party (SERP) and the Zionist-Socialist (S.S.), the latter two merging in May 1917.

Political activity attained a hitherto unknown intensity among Russian Jews in 1917. There were six major Jewish political groups. The largest was the Zionist party which, previous to October 1917, claimed a "membership" of 300,000, with organizations in 1,200 localities.[5] Since the Zionists were concerned mainly with establishing a Jewish national homeland in Palestine, even after adoption of the

[4] This analysis is based on figures in Yaakov Lestschinsky, *Dos sovetishe idntum,* pp. 30, 41, 73.

[5] This is the figure cited in the Communist *Partai materialn,* no. 4, August 1921, p. 10. It is also cited by the Zionist Aryeh Tsentsifer in *Eser Sh'not Redifot* (Tel Aviv, 1930), p. 20. The rapid growth of the Zionist movement can be seen in the fact that in May 1917 there were 140,000 *shekel* holders in 700 communities, and in 1913 only 26,000. See J. B. Schechtman, "The U.S.S.R., Zionism, and Israel," in Lionel Kochan, ed., *The Jews in Soviet Russia Since 1917* (London, 1970), p. 101. It is curious that in his discussion of Jewish parties in Russia, Lestschinsky fails to mention the Zionists.

Helsingfors platform in 1906, their interest in Russian politics was relatively passive. Furthermore, many Zionists were politically inactive. They were "members" of the Zionist movement because they had bought the symbolic "shekel" which identified them as supporters of the idea of a Jewish national homeland in Palestine. For many, the purchase of the "shekel" was the extent of their politics.

The most powerful party intensely involved in Russian political life was the Bund, with a membership which reached 33,700 in December 1917.[6] It had 200 groups in the southwest of Russia and 102 organizations in the northwest. The Bund had generally followed a Menshevik line during the war years, though within the Bund, as within the Menshevik party, there were both "Internationalist" opponents of the war and "Defensists" who felt that Russia's participation in the war was justified. While the Zionists drew their adherents mostly from the middle and lower strata of the Jewish economic structure, the Bund's strength lay in the proletariat and in the artisan class. The Zionists also attracted many religious Jews and nationalistic members of the intelligentsia who favored the development of Hebrew as the Jewish national language. The Bund was hostile to the "clerical accomplices" of the bourgeoisie, and insisted upon recognition of Yiddish as the Jewish language. And, of course, the Bund was implacably opposed to any "romantic, utopian visions" of Palestine as a Jewish homeland.

The United Jewish Socialist Workers Party (UJSWP) stood somewhere between the Zionists and the Bund. It had been formed in May 1917 as a result of the merger of the Zionist-Socialists and the Jewish Socialist Labor Party (SERP). The Zionist-Socialists had been a basically Marxist

[6] V. Shulman, "Der bund in rusland far der tseit fun der revolutsie," *Unzer shtime (zamlbukh)*, August 1918, p. 84.

party whose "Zionism" consisted in their advocacy of the establishment of an autonomous Jewish territory, though not necessarily in Palestine. SERP, sometimes called the "Sejmists," had advocated national-cultural autonomy with a parliament, or *sejm*, for each nationality in the state. The UJSWP, in effect, dropped the territorialist program of the Zionist-Socialists by saying that "the question remains open and will be freely debated in party literature." [7] The UJSWP was particularly effective in the Ukraine and drew its strength mainly from secularized intellectuals who were staunch defenders of Yiddish. Formally associated with the Socialist-Revolutionary party (SR) by dint of the ties between the SERP party and the SR, in the trade unions the UJSWP was aligned with the Mensheviks. For the elections to the Constituent Assembly it linked itself to the SR.

The *Poalai Tsion* party, at once Marxist and Zionist, adopted Ber Borokhov's determinist Marxism which claimed that the Jews were being inexorably driven to Palestine, where they could develop a normal economic life. Within the *Poalai Tsion,* as within the Bund, there were "Internationalists" and "Defensists" on the war issue. Some of the *Poalai Tsion*'s members sympathized with the Bolsheviks after the "July Days" of 1917 but the Zionist component of their ideology kept them from throwing their full support to the Bolsheviks. In the Ukraine, however, the *Poalai Tsion* supported the Central Rada. The *Poalai Tsion* had a genuinely proletarian membership.

The *Folkspartai* was hardly the mass organization that its name implied. It remained a small coterie of intellectuals led by the historian Simon Dubnow. Dubnow's autonomist theories were the basis of the party's ideology.[8] The party attracted those who were sympathetic to national-cultural

[7] *Der idisher proletarier* (Kiev), no. 1–2, June 16 (29), 1917.

[8] Dubnow's theories are presented in Koppel Pinson, ed., Simon Dubnow, *Nationalism and History* (Philadelphia, 1958).

autonomy but who, for one reason or another, could not find a home in the Bund or the UJSWP. As one of its members remarked, the *Folkspartai* was "the party of all non-party people." [9]

All these parties were secular in outlook. Since the great majority of Russian Jewry was at least formally religious, it was natural that, despite the traditional reluctance of the religious leaders to engage in open political activity, religious parties should emerge out of the upheavals of 1917. In April 1917 the founding convention of *Masores V'kherus* (Tradition and Freedom) was held in Moscow. The convention demanded national autonomy with guarantees for Saturday as the day of rest and financial support by the government for the *kehillas.* Three months later representatives of fifty local religious political groups such as *Shomrai Yisroel* (Guardians of Israel) and *Kneses Yisroel* (Assembly of Israel) met and adopted a platform demanding an eight-hour working day, the right to strike, freedom of conscience, land distribution according to the SR program, and the promotion of religious education—hardly a "reactionary bourgeois" program. Finally, in the summer of 1918, 120 delegates from two religious parties, *Akhdus Yisroel* (Unity of Israel) and *Adas Yisroel* (Community of Israel) formed a united religious front in the Ukraine called *Akhdus.* In Belorussia the Orthodox *Agudas Yisroel* was active and even had a majority in the Minsk city duma.[10]

Aside from these parties, there was also the very small *Folksgrupe*—which certainly was only a group but hardly represented the "folk." This group, first formed in 1906, followed the general line of the Cadet party and was led by the prominent jurists Maxim Vinaver, Henryk Sliozberg, and Oskar Gruzenberg. Vinaver and Sliozberg were very

[9] Daniel Charney, *A yortsendlik aza* (New York, 1943), p. 205.

[10] Aryeh Refaeli (Tsentsifer), *Bamaavak Lageulah* (Tel Aviv, 1956), p. 79. On the Minsk *kehilla,* see Kirzhnitz and Rafes, eds., *Der idisher arbeter,* IV, 217–18.

active in Jewish life, serving as *shtadlonim*, or pleaders of the Jewish cause, and founding Jewish scholarly and civil rights organizations. Gruzenberg had received international publicity in consequence of his role in the defense of Mendel Beilis in 1911. The *Folksgrupe* demanded full civil rights for the Jews and an internal, independent, religious organization. The Jewish school was to teach both Yiddish and Hebrew and was to retain its religious character. Unlike the Bund, *Folkspartai*, UJSWP, and *Akhdus*, the *Folksgrupe* did not demand any sort of national autonomy.

The revolution had aroused these parties to an unprecedented flurry of activity, but it was the brief letter sent by Foreign Secretary Arthur James Balfour to Lord Rothschild on November 2, 1917, stating that "His Majesty's government views with favor the establishment in Palestine of a national home for the Jewish people," which affected their fortunes most profoundly. The impact of the Balfour Declaration on Russian Jews was tremendous:

> It is impossible to describe the joy which seized the Jewish masses all over the country. . . . On November 6 there was an unparalleled Jewish demonstration in Kiev which made a great impression on the population. . . . From early morning thousands of Jews, dressed in their holiday clothes and Zionist emblems, streamed to the university campus on Vladimir Street. All balconies of Jewish homes were decorated in blue and white. Three military bands marched at the head of the paraders and Zionist flags flew above. . . . The British consul . . . received a bouquet of flowers and expressed his gratitude in an emotional voice. . . . Professor Hrushevsky, president of the Rada, greeted us. Even many Bundists and sworn anti-Zionists were swept along in the general Jewish celebration.[11]

[11] L. Shapiro, *Bakalakhat HaRusit: Pirkai Zikhronot* (Jerusalem,

Already the largest political movement among Russian Jews, Zionism gained added strength from the British government's declaration. The Bund and other anti-Zionists tried to belittle the value of the Declaration and mocked the "naïve" Zionists for trusting the "British imperialists" to give the Jews a homeland. England had issued the Declaration, they said, in order that Russian Jews should urge their government to continue the war.[12] But the Jews were in no mood to denigrate the Balfour Declaration. A British officer in Siberia found it difficult to fathom the mood of the Jews.

> Many of those I talked with spoke with pathetic hope of the day when a Jewish state would be established in Palestine. Not that they all wished to go there—many of them felt that their *real* home was in Russia—but they harboured the strange hope that the future Ambassador or Consul from such a State would be able to

---

1952), pp. 44–45. Shapiro was a medical student at the University of Kiev and belonged to *Tseirai Tsion,* a socialist and Zionist party.

[12] *Folkstseitung* (Kiev), November 22, 1917. Actually, the British ambassador did tell the members of the Zionist Central Committee to use their "influence" with the Jewish Bolshevik leaders and persuade them not to withdraw from the World War. See Yitzkhak Grinboim, "Un dos is unzer goirl," *Letste neies* (Tel Aviv), November 15, 1963. Apparently, the British were persuaded that Trotsky, who did not even regard himself as a Jew, could be won over by nationalistic Jewish appeals. One writer, who says of the Balfour Declaration that "measured by British interests alone it was one of the greatest mistakes in our imperial history," sees the Declaration as a small part of Britain's *European* policy. "The British hope was that the influence of Russian Jewry would both keep Kerensky in the fighting line and prevent the Russian grain trade, which was largely in Jewish hands, from being diverted to the hungry Germans." Elizabeth Monroe, *Britain's Moment in the Middle East, 1914–1956* (Baltimore, 1963), p. 43. Of course, by the time the Declaration was issued, the Kerensky government had fallen. On the motives for the declaration, see also Leonard Stein, *The Balfour Declaration* (New York, 1961).

> secure them better treatment from the Russian Government. I used to point out to them that it was idle to expect that a representative of such a State would be listened to for a moment by any conceivable Russian government, but they remained unconvinced! "You are an Englishman," they said, "and if you are injured you go to your Consul and get redress; if we are injured, to whom can we appeal?" Apart from the large number who hope for such benefits, there are many, especially among the younger men, who are anxious to emigrate to Palestine, and a still more numerous class, who do not mind where they go, so long as they get out of Russia.[13]

These attitudes were reflected in the elections to the *kehillas*, the Jewish Congress, and the Constituent Assembly.

Almost all parties endorsed extraterritorial national-cultural autonomy for the Jews. The *kehillas* were now seen as capable of performing not only religious but also national-cultural functions, and elections to the *kehillas* were bitterly contested. All Jewish parties decided in March 1917 to convene an all-Russian, democratically elected Jewish Congress. The Bund, fearing rising Zionist sentiment among the Jewish population, declared that it would not be bound by the resolutions of the Congress which were to be understood as recommendations. The Zionists demanded that all resolutions bind all parties. Finally, a compromise solution was worked out on the sensitive issues of Palestine and the rights of Jews outside Russia. It was agreed that the question of Jewish rights would be included on the agenda, as the Zionists had demanded, and that the Palestine question be deleted, as the Bund had insisted. The Bund agreed to participate in the Congress,[14] and this was a triumph for

[13] Anonymous report, apparently by a British officer in Siberia, n.d., Joseph Rosen Archive, YIVO Archives.

[14] See M. Zipin, "Der yidisher kongress in rusland," *Die tsukunft*,

the Zionists, who were assured a victory at the Congress. The call to the Congress was full of hope and enthusiasm:

> Citizens, Jews! The Jewish people in Russia now faces an event which has no parallel in Jewish history for two thousand years. Not only has the Jew as an individual, as a citizen, acquired equality of rights . . . but the Jewish nation looks forward to the possibility of securing national rights. Never and nowhere have the Jews lived through such a serious, responsible moment as the present—responsible to the present and the future generations.[15]

The elections were held in the autumn of 1917 but, because of political developments in Russia, the Congress never met.

The results of elections to the *kehillas,* the Jewish Congress, and the All-Russian Constituent Assembly indicate clearly the relative strength of the Jewish political parties. The reports of 193 *kehillas* in nine provinces in the Ukraine showed that the Zionists had 36 percent of the delegates to the *kehillas,* the Bundists had 14.4 percent, *Akhdus* had 10 percent, the United Jewish Socialist Workers Party had 8.2 percent, the *Poalai Tsion* 6.3 percent, the *Folkspartai* 3 percent, the Cadet *Folksgrupe* one percent and various local groups 20 percent.[16] In most areas of the former Empire the *kehillas* were controlled by the Zionists, though the combined forces of the socialist parties did not lag far behind.[17]

XXVII, no. 1 (January 1919). See also Mordechai Altshuler, "Ha-Nisayon LeArgen Kinus Klal-Yehudi BeRusiya Akhar HaMahpekha," *HeAvar,* XII (1965).

[15] Quoted in Baron, p. 201.

[16] According to another source, in 161 *kehillas* the regular Zionists got 43.6 percent, the *Poalai Tsion* 8, and *Tseirai Tsion* 2.8; the Orthodox got 13.4, the Bund 19.6, the UJSWP 9, and the *Folkspartai* 3.6 percent. Abraham Heller, *Die lage der Juden in Russland von der Märzrevolution bis zur gegenwart* (Breslau, 1935), p. 19.

[17] The political configuration can perhaps be seen more clearly

The elections to the Jewish Congress held in January, 1918 showed a similar or even stronger Zionist predominance. The Zionists received approximately 60 percent of the vote, the socialist parties together amassed about 25 percent, and the Orthodox received 12 percent.[18] In the Ukraine, the Zionists received 33.6 percent of the vote and *Akhdus* received 15.2 percent, giving the "middle class" parties nearly half of the total vote. The Bund received 18.4 percent, the *Tseirai Tsion* 11.2 percent, the United Jewish Socialist Workers 9.6 percent, the *Poalai Tsion* 8.8 percent, and the *Folkspartai* 3.2 percent. Thus, in the Ukrainian Provisional Jewish National Congress (pro-parliament) the Zionists had forty-two delegates, the Bund twenty-three, *Akhdus* nineteen, *Tseirai Tsion* fourteen, USJWP twelve, *Poalai Tsion* eleven, and *Folkspartai* four.[19]

---

in individual *kehillas:* in the Odessa *kehilla* in the south there were 35 Zionist representatives, 26 Bundists, 11 Orthodox, 11 *Poalai-Tsion*ists, 9 members of the *Folkspartai* and 19 "others." In other areas of Russia similar patterns were established. In the Voronezh *kehilla* there were 14 Zionists and Orthodox, usually voting together, 4 Bundists, 3 members of the UJSWP and 3 *Poalai Tsion*ists; in Saratov there were 17 Zionists; 9 Orthodox (Akhdus), 6 Bundists, 6 *Poalai-Tsion*ists, one UJSWP member and 6 "Democrats" (probably aligned with the *Folksgrupe*). The Ukrainian figures are taken from *Novyi put'*, 1918, Nos. 3 and 4, and *Khronika evreiskoi zhizni,* 1918, no. 2, both quoted in Kirzhnitz and Rafes. See also *Di idishe avtonomie un der natsionaler sekretariat in Ukraine* (Kiev, 1920), pp. 16 and 210. Figures are also taken from *Evreiskii rabochii* (Petrograd), no. 10, July 31, 1918, pp. 13–15. It is interesting that while workers were only nine percent of the Jewish population in the ten central Russian areas cited, thirty-four percent of the elected delegates belonged to the labor parties, twenty-one percent representing the Bund. The explanation for this disparity may lie in the fact that the proletariat was the most politically conscious class in Jewish society and that it was joined in its socialist leanings by the secularized intelligentsia.

[18] Zipin, "Der yidisher kongress."

[19] See N. Gergel, *Di lage fun di yidn in russland* (Warsaw, 1929), pp. 152–53. See also Lestschinsky, p. 63, and Kirzhnitz and Rafes, p. 218.

If the *Tseirai Tsion* and *Poalai Tsion* are added to the general Zionist total, the Zionists emerge with 53.6 percent of the total vote. "A great deal of this success [of the Zionists] . . . must be ascribed to the abnormal condition of voting for the upper intellectual groups, to a very considerable absenteeism and chiefly to the great, ever increasing popularity of Zionism which has grown very considerably since Mr. Balfour's letter to Lord Rothschild was published."[20]

Finally, the election for the Constituent Assembly, held even before the *kehilla* elections, demonstrated Zionist predominance and socialist strength. These elections were very seriously contested by the Jewish parties. The Belorussian Bund alone held two hundred meetings reportedly attended by 127,000 people in its election campaign, and the Ukrainian Bund held two or three meetings a week. The atmosphere was tense, and "in Odessa there were even fist fights with the Zionists."[21] The final results proclaimed a tremendous Zionist victory. Out of 498,198 votes cast for Jewish parties, 417,215 went to Zionist and religious parties. The Bund received 31,123 votes, the other socialist parties 29,322, and the *Poalai Tsion* 20,538.[22] In Minsk *guberniia*

[20] "The New Jewish National Council—Extract from a report of the Committee's [committee of the British Board of Jewish deputies] Agent in Stockholm dated September 17, 1918," unpublished (Lucien Wolf Archive: Russia and the Ukraine 1918–28; YIVO Archives). Isaac Deutscher, whose scholarly objectivity seems to have failed him when he wrote of Jewish matters, claimed that "The great majority of East European Jews were, up to the outbreak of the second World War, opposed to Zionism. . . . The Zionists in our part of the world were a significant *minority,* but they never succeeded in attracting a majority of their co-religionists." "The Russian Revolution and the Jewish Problem," in *The Non-Jewish Jew and Other Essays* (London, 1968), p. 66.

[21] Shulman, p. 84.

[22] Oliver Henry Radkey, *The Election to the Russian Constituent Assembly of 1917* (Cambridge, Mass., 1950), p. 17. Radkey uses the category "nationalist" presumably to describe the Zionist and religious parties. N. V. Sviatitski, in *Kogo russkii narod izbral svoimi predsta-*

the Jewish Nationalistic Bloc got 65,046 votes to 11,064 for the Jewish Socialists; in Kiev *guberniia* the Nationalists garnered 24,790 votes, while the Bund and Mensheviks got 12,471.[23] Thus, the overwhelming majority of politically conscious Jews identifying with Jewish parties preferred the Zionist parties and programs to those of the socialists. Though it is difficult to ascertain how many Jews voted for the general Russian parties and for which parties they voted, it can be assumed that half-million Jews who voted for Jewish parties represented the great majority of Jews voting. It is also probable that the non-Jewish parties which received the most Jewish votes were the Mensheviks, drawing on the assimilated Jewish intelligentsia; the Cadets, attracting the tiny but influential minority of upper-class Jews and some Orthodox Jews; and perhaps the Socialist-Revolutionaries, in whose ranks there were some Jewish intellectuals. The Bolsheviks did get some Jewish votes, mainly because they were the only party opposing the ruinous war.[24]

Despite the fact that the Zionists were clearly the majority party among the Jews, they were destined to play a far less important role in the future of Russian Jewry than the socialists. Driven abroad, underground, or into exile by the Bolsheviks, active Zionists became a semi-legal or illegal opposition to the Soviet regime. Some of the more radical socialist Zionist parties were recognized by the Bolshevik government but these had little opportunity to pursue an independent course. On the other hand, the Jewish socialist parties seemed for a time to be capable of

viteliami (Moscow, n.d.), gives the "nationalist" bloc an even higher total of 550,075 (cited in Radkey).

[23] Radkey, p. 31 and appendix. Radkey's figures for Minsk are confirmed by those cited in Kirzhnitz, pp. 163–64. However, Kirzhnitz gives the Nationalist Bloc in Kiev a total of 90,704 and the socialists (Bund, UJSWP, and Mensheviks) 25,402.

[24] See Raphael Abramovich, *In tsvai revolutsies: di geshikhte fun a dor*, II (New York, 1944), 193.

coexisting or even competing with the Bolsheviks "on the Jewish street." Their view of the Russian Revolution and of the Bolshevik turn it took was crucial for the political future of Russian Jewry.

The Bund and the Revolutions of 1917

The Bund, of course, greeted the March revolution as enthusiastically as the other socialist parties did. Its view of the revolution was a traditional Marxist one: "Our revolution with its proletarian forms is not a proletarian one in content. This is a political revolution and not a social one. The counterrevolution has not been choked with the old regime." [25] Some Bundists urged the Jewish workers to fight for the revolution in the ranks of the Russian socialist parties and not to devote their energies to the fulfillment of national programs at the expense of general revolutionary goals. Thus, David Zaslavskii, at that time a Bundist publicist, declared that

> The Jewish proletariat will be a force in Jewish life only as long as it is a force in the ranks of revolutionary democracy of the land. . . . The Jewish proletariat must remember that all tasks, both of groups and of the nation, must be subordinated to the overall interest of the revolution.[26]

Other Bundists, however, warned the Jewish people to raise specific national demands and fight for them.

> In the new Russia, national disabilities will naturally be removed. . . . But does that mean that the Jews should demand no more? . . . The government is now in the hands of the Cadets and Octobrists. Both parties are supporters of "Great Russia." . . . Both have recently

[25] *Arbeter shtime* (Petrograd), March 8, 1917.
[26] D[avid] Z[aslavskii] in *ibid.*, May 12 (25), 1917.

tried to prove that in Russia there are no national cultures, but a single "Great Russian," all-encompassing culture. It is possible that under the pressure of the revolution their outlooks have changed. But it is also possible that later on, when things will quiet down, they will begin to implement the "Great Russian" principle and will not want to recognize Jewish schools as part of the educational system. This would be national oppression, and the Jewish parties will now arm themselves against this possibility.[27]

Preaching self-restraint of all parties, the Bund tended to lose sight of power realities because of a deeply ingrained Marxist concept of the nature of the revolution.

It was clear from the very beginning how the unity of the revolution could be preserved: the bourgeoisie must reject the desire for complete power, the proletariat must abjure the seizure of power. Each of the antagonistic classes limits itself by its good will until the revolution will be strengthened.[28]

[27] Moishe Olgin, "Tsu vos darfn de yidn fun rusland natsionale rekht," *Arbeter shtime,* July 16 (29), 1917. The article appeared originally in the New York *Jewish Daily Forward.* Olgin came to New York in 1914 from Vienna. He was extremely anti-Bolshevik until 1920 when he went to Soviet Russia. Then he became an important figure in the American Communist Party and was always "brimming with enthusiasm for each party line . . . always defending or attacking, he never permitted himself the luxury of silence . . . the perennial nightingale of the Soviet Union and of Communism." Melech Epstein, *The Jew and Communism 1917–1941* (New York, 1959), pp. 383–85. Olgin was a brilliant, if erratic, man. He received a doctorate in 1918 at Columbia University and published his dissertation as *The Soul of the Russian Revolution* (New York, 1918). Olgin knew Hebrew, German, French, Spanish, Yiddish, English, and Russian and was a sentimental romantic. According to Lazar Kling, who knew him in New York, Olgin returned from Russia and with tears of joy in his eyes described how "every day they give free milk to children over there."

[28] *Arbeter shtime,* no. 7, May 1917, quoted in *Tsum XV yortog*

Like Georgii Plekhanov and the Menshevik leadership, the Bund believed that a socialist-proletarian revolution must be preceded by a capitalist-bourgeois regime. The Bund was confident that its national program would ultimately be accepted by the new Russian government and believed that the Congress of Soviets would implement national-cultural autonomy. "Yes, we Bundists can be happy with the evolution of Russian democracy in the last few years. Then we were the only ones adhering to this position—today all are with us." [29] Indeed, national-cultural autonomy was endorsed by the Socialist-Revolutionary party in May, by the Cadets in July, and by the Mensheviks in August.[30] The Provisional Government, however, did not institute national-cultural autonomy.

Members of the Bund played an active role in local soviets, often serving on soviet executive committees. In the Berdichev soviet, for example, there were seventy-one Bundists, and its chairman was the Bundist David Lipets. Outside the former Pale, in cities like Irkutsk and Tashkent, a total of fifty-three Bundists were in soviets. Mark Liber and Raphael Abramovich were outstanding figures at the Congress of Soviets in July 1917, and the former's proposal for an administrative system which was in effect national-cultural autonomy, was passed over Bolshevik opposition. There was a seventeen-man Bund delegation to the Congress, of whom five were elected to the central executive committee. Bund delegates were active in trade union congresses, conventions of artisans, and teachers' congresses. Bundists were especially prominent in city dumas. In fifty-one cities 247 Bundists were elected to city dumas; 175 of these were in twenty-five cities within the former Pale. Over

---

fun der oktiabr revoliutsie—historisher zamlbukh (Minsk, 1932), p. 71. Henceforth cited as *Zamlbukh*.

[29] *Arbeter shtime,* June 29 (July 12), 1917.

[30] Schwarz, p. 92.

five hundred Bundists were in city dumas all over Russia. In Dvinsk, Odessa, Gomel, and Bobruisk Bundists served as deputy chairmen of the dumas, while in Minsk Rakhmiel Veinshtain chaired the municipal duma.[31] Bundists were so prominent in government posts even after the Bolshevik revolution that Jewish Communists in Belorussia complained, "at present, the most important commissariats dealing with the broad working masses . . . are in the hands of the Bundists. An impression is created among the masses that the Bund and not the [Communist] Party is in power." [32]

Among the socialist parties in Russia, the Bund had been noteworthy for its organization and discipline. In its twenty years of activity there had been important differences of opinion within the party, especially on the national and war questions, but unlike almost every other socialist party, the Bund had never split, surely a remarkable achievement in light of the history of the Russian Social Democratic Labor Party. The cohesiveness of the Bund was at least partially due to the fact that this was no ordinary political party or movement. In a sense, the Bund was a secularized Jewish community held together by class and national bonds. "Ideally," writes a contemporary sociologist, "the recruits for ideological groups should . . . stand outside normal social ramifications. They should be individuals who have lost the sense of personal identity and belonging; that is, they should be socially uprooted and alienated from the surrounding world." [33] Although Jewish workers were probably less "uprooted" than the Russian workers, since the Jews did not have to make the painful transition from rural to urban life, they had become increasingly

[31] See V. Shulman, pp. 77–78.

[32] Quoted in *Zamlbukh*, p. 31.

[33] Vladimir C. Nahirny, "Some Observations on Ideological Groups," *American Journal of Sociology*, LXVII (1962), 405.

estranged from the Jewish community and its bourgeois-dominated institutions. The very existence of the Bund was a product of this alienation, and one of its functions was to give its adherents a spiritual home in a kind of secular religion. As modernizing movement, the Bund had succeeded in developing a political religion. "The collective passion is sustained by frequent communion [and] inflamed by periodic rites such as meetings, processions and demonstrations."[34] By maintaining a remarkably close relationship between leadership and mass following and between intelligentsia and proletarians,[35] and by adjusting its programs and policies to changing times and shifting needs, the Bund managed to avoid the schisms and splits which so often occur in ideological movements.

In 1917, however, the Bund seemed to grow fretful about its ability to maintain organizational unity. "Even if we reconsider our position, we can do this proudly, not fearing that our party will split. Our ranks are firmly closed and we can entertain internal criticism often, for everyone to see."[36] This turned out to be whistling in the dark, and by August the seriousness of ideological differences was more frankly acknowledged. Viktor Alter wrote: "Let us say openly: the official policy of the Bund causes a deep dissatisfaction among part of the membership. And this dissatisfaction continues to grow. . . . The main question is the attitude toward the war."[37] The war-weary population was in no mood to support a "Defensist" position, but the Bund adopted a position of "revolutionary defensism."

Although the Bund had supported the anti-war position

[34] Jules Monnerot, *Sociology and Psychology of Communism* (Boston, 1953), p. 135.

[35] See Woodhouse and Tobias for statistical proof of this close relationship.

[36] *Arbeter shtime*, April 23 (May 6), 1917.

[37] V. Alter, "Diskusie: iz der bund in gefar?" *Arbeter shtime*, August 3 (16), 1917.

of the Kienthal and Zimmerwald conferences of 1915, by April 1917 many leading Bundists had moved to the "revolutionary defensist" position advocated by the Mensheviks Dan, Tsereteli, Chkheidze, and Skobelev, some of whom had earlier adhered to a grouping known as "Siberian Zimmerwaldists." The "revolutionary defensists" argued that the war had to be prosecuted, not for the "social-patriotic" reasons advanced by such "extremist" defensists as Potresov and Plekhanov, but in order to preserve the revolution from its destruction at the hands of imperialist Germany. Within the Bund this position was advocated by Henry Erlich and Mark Liber, who were also in the Menshevik leadership, and by Esther Frumkin, among others. In the spring of 1917 Raphael Abramovich was the only Internationalist in the central leadership of the Bund, but his position was supported by Bundist activists such as Vladimir Kossovskii, Benjamin Kheifetz, and Viktor Alter who were returning from abroad.[38] While the Menshevik "revolutionary defensists," particularly Dan and Tsereteli, favored the participation of socialists in the Provisional Government, the Bundist Defensists Liber and Erlich opposed it, though Rafes was in favor of participation. The April 1917 conference of the Bund voted against socialist participation in the government, though the majority of the Mensheviks at that time took the opposite position.[39] There was a movement afoot to split with the Mensheviks on this issue. But Raphael Abramovich acknowledged that the Bund could not really afford a split. "We always tried to be the left wing of the Mensheviks . . . the revolutionary

[38] Abramovich, *In tsvai revolutsies,* II, 47–53.

[39] *Geshikhte fun Bund,* III, 95. The divisions on the war issue within Menshevism are treated in B. I. Nikolaevskii, "RSDRP (Men'sheviki) v pervye gody revoliutsii (1917–1918)," Inter-University Project on the History of the Menshevik Movement, New York, typescript.

conscience of Menshevism. We knew that, were we to leave Menshevism, we would have to unite with the Bolsheviks. Are we ready to do that? No, because a great abyss separates us! Therefore, a split in the Menshevik party would mean only a weakening of the working class because we would have to build a *third* party."[40]

The stresses and strains in the Bund, cautiously alluded to by its leaders, were quite natural under the circumstances of 1917. Aside from the psychologically and economically devastating effects of the war and tsarist persecution, there were also the very immediate hardships imposed by the revolution. While there was no land hunger among the Jews, there certainly was a pressing need for bread and a burning desire for peace. In such a situation, the rank-and-file Bundist, especially the genuine worker, would have to place immediate needs above principled positions established by the leadership. Furthermore, much of the Jewish population had been uprooted by the war. Of ninety-seven organizations which had the right to send delegates to the

[40] Raphael Abramovich, in *Arbeter shtime*, August 20 (September 2), 1917. Soviet Jewish historians have tried to equate the Internationalist-Defensist split with a pro-Bolshevik and pro-Menshevik division within the Bund. The former Bundist Kirzhnitz (pp. 20–21) claims that the arrival of the Internationalists from Switzerland in 1917 temporarily postponed a split in the Bund because it gave the more radical members a chance to stay in the Bund, associating themselves with Bundist-Internationalists; only after the Internationalist-Defensist issue had become academic did the Bund split into pro-Bolsheviks and Mensheviks. That this is a false equation is most strikingly demonstrated by the fact that Abramovich, leader of the Internationalists, was one of the most prominent of the anti-Bolshevik Bundists from October-November on, when he walked out of the Second Congress of Soviets to protest the Bolshevik coup. Among the most prominent Defensists were Aaron Zolotariov and Moishe Rafes; Rafes later led the pro-Bolshevik wing of the Ukrainian Bund, and Zolotariov joined the Communist party. Viktor Alter, an Internationalist, remained a Social-Democrat, while the Defensist David Zaslavskii eventually joined the Communist Party.

Eighth Congress of the Bund in December 1917, forty were outside the old Pale.

Of the twenty-five *gubernii* of the former Pale, thirteen were under occupation, as were parts of two others. A total of fifty-eight cities and towns where Jews were not allowed to live before the war now had Bund organizations. The new organizations had little time to develop local prestige and firm allegiance among the membership. While some members of these young organizations had been in the Bund apparatus in the Pale, many were newcomers to the Bund. This was due to the fact that in the "years of reaction" following 1905 many of the smaller Bundist groups had disappeared. When, in 1917, there was a revival of Bundist activity, a large part of the membership was completely new to the Bund and did not have the almost fanatic loyalty to the party which "old-timers" displayed. A Bundist activist explained:

> The organizations which we now have arose mostly at the time of the revolution. . . . Who are the masses and leaders of these organizations? The workers themselves. The intelligentsia now follows the bourgeois parties or is entirely passive. . . . Everywhere you find old comrades who set the tone. But—for the most part—new, fresh forces. Often people of limited development, with little political experience, they nevertheless always find the correct line, the correct answer to all questions, [and] they work out a real proletarian class tactic.[41]

In the Ukraine, for example, there were only ten Bundist groups in February 1917. After the February revolution this figure rose astronomically, and in a matter of months, by the fall of 1917, there were 175 such groups, with the main

[41] Sara Fuks, in *Der veker*, August 1, 1917.

committee in Kiev.[42] Rafes points out that many Jewish workers in 1917 "had no tradition of petit bourgeois socialism"—that is, Bundism. For example, large garment workshops had been established to supply military needs; most of the tailors in these shops were impoverished Jews recruited from the war-torn cities and towns. The war had left them homeless and they sought security and work in the larger population centers.[43] This new composition of its membership is important to bear in mind when examining developments in the Bund.

The other major Jewish socialist party was the United Jewish Socialist Workers Party. The party was born in May-June 1917 as a result of the union of the Zionist-Socialists and SERP,[44] and was popularly known as the *Farainigte* (United). This party, dominated by intellectuals, evolved an interesting national program. The best form of government for Russia, the *Farainigte* argued, would be a federative republic similar to the United States of America. This would partially solve the national question. "If there were but one nation in the Ukraine, regional autonomy would solve the national question." Because this was obviously not the case in the Ukraine and in other regions, proportional representation of nationalities in regional *sejms* might be instituted. Since this would result in the tyranny of the national majority, as had happened in the Polish Ukraine, "national-*personal*" autonomy was necessary. A central organ would be created to deal with the affairs of Jews or Poles, or Letts or Tatars, wherever in Russia they happened to reside. Personal autonomy would be based "not on the

[42] M. G. Rafes, *Dva goda revoliutsii na ukraine* (Moscow, 1920), p. 13.

[43] Rafes in Kirzhnitz and Rafes, p. 19. "These workers," says Rafes, "must have been the first to come to the Bolsheviks," though he cites no evidence for this.

[44] See *supra*, p. 72.

objective fact that I live in the Ukraine, but on the subjective will to consider myself a member of this nation. We do not mean to say by this that personal autonomy excludes territorial autonomy. They complement each other." A central parliament would concern itself with matters of general interest—foreign relations, military affairs, post and telegraph, and the like. Education and social welfare would be left to the national *sejms*. Regional *sejms* would be the third level of government, dealing with sanitation, industrial development, trade, agriculture, and similar overall regional concerns.[45]

The Jewish national assembly, or *sejm*, elected on the basis of universal, equal, secret, proportional, and direct voting, would be the highest authority in Jewish life. Citizens would subordinate themselves to it voluntarily, that is, by declaring their affiliation with the Jewish people. Locally, *kehillas* would be formed where there were more than 300 Jews.[46] The *kehilla* would decide, for example, how many schools were needed in its locality and then set about establishing them and determining their curricula within the broad guidelines drawn by the Jewish *sejm*. Jewish institutions would receive a budget, proportionate to the population they served, from the central, provincial, and local governmental organs to which the Jews would pay taxes. If one million rubles were allocated by the central government to education, the Jews, being four percent of the population, would get 40,000 rubles for education, possibly supplemented by funds from the Jewish national organs. Religion would be separated from the national organs and would be dealt with by associations of

[45] This outline is based on Yaakov Lestschinsky, *Unzere natsionale foderungen*, published by the Central Committee of the *Farainigte idishe sotsialistishe arbeiter partai* S.S. *un* Y.S. (n.p., n.d. [1917?]).

[46] Where there were fewer Jews, the closest *kehilla* would have jurisdiction. *Ibid.*, p. 20.

the believers. The class struggle would express itself within the national organs, as each class would fight to have its curriculum adopted or its ideas on social welfare accepted.

This carefully elaborated scheme was perhaps broader in scope than Bundist notions of national-cultural autonomy; it was certainly more specific. Of course, neither the Bund nor the *Farainigte* was given the opportunity to test the practicability of its national program. With the Bolshevik seizure of power, schemes for national autonomy receded into the background, and the task of Jewish politicians became the evaluation of this latest crisis in the unhappy history of twentieth-century Russia.

The long-standing antagonism that had existed between the Bolsheviks and the Bund was exacerbated in the spring of 1917 when the Bund impatiently scoffed at Bolshevik claims that the time was ripe for a socialist revolution. Characterizing Leninism as an "ugly disease," V. Kantorovich demanded to know,

> If the proletariat calls now for dictatorship, who will follow it? No one! Who will be against it? Everyone! A leader from whom all have turned away is powerless. . . . Will the bourgeois American republic (as yet there is no socialism there!) lend money to the government of Lenin and Company? Of course not! . . . The Leninists are the enemies of the revolution. This must be firmly established once and for all.[47]

When Mark Liber and Lenin clashed at the Congress of Soviets over the timing of the socialist revolution, the Bund branded Lenin an "anarcho-syndicalist." Liber asserted that the proletariat must remain the leading class but should be careful not to run too far ahead of the masses and be prepared to halt at times, in order to avoid isolation. Lenin

[47] *Arbeter shtime,* May 25 (June 7), 1917.

took an opposite tack: push on and seize power, no matter what the consequences. Liber challenged Lenin: how could he maintain power and check the anarchic forces in the country? The *Arbeter shtime* reported sarcastically, "Lenin's answer will go down in history: 'We have to arrest fifty or one hundred capitalists.' Lenin wants to fight the capitalist order by putting capitalists in jail." Some Bundists, particularly of the rank-and-file, continued to make this ironic error, mocking the Bolsheviks as irresponsible, impractical dreamers. A day before the Bolsheviks took power in Petrograd, B. Marshak ridiculed Piatakov and the Ukrainian Bolsheviks for putting their trust in the ability of the Petrograd Bolsheviks to become the rulers of Russia.

> They fail to see that the Bolshevik war horse which looks so big and fierce is only papier-mâché and is absolutely incapable of galloping into the fray. . . . They don't know that the entire power of the Bolsheviks consists in frightening the audience from time to time: "Be careful, we're meeting on the twentieth. . . . Repent—we're quitting [the Petrograd Soviet] on the twenty-fifth" . . . to shout, to frighten, and nothing else. And suddenly the naïve Kiev Bolsheviks rush to the artillery which cannot shoot and to the horses who cannot run. . . . If the Great Bolshevik Trotsky had arms long enough to stretch from Petrograd to Kiev, he would grab the little Bolshevik Piatakov by the ear: "Don't be a little hoodlum [*sheigetz*], ask your elders." [48]

The Belorussian Bundists were not so cocky as their Ukrainian comrades. Their organ, the *Veker*, warned that the Bolsheviks were preparing to create a new government, by force if necessary.

> The great discontent of the masses, the bitterness, the

[48] *Folkstseitung*, October 24, 1917.

weariness—all is useful for the Bolshevik propaganda. . . . The result will be clear: once again the July days. . . . Our comrades everywhere must display an energetic resistance to the Bolshevik plans. . . . Work for the Constituent Assembly—all who still have some feeling of responsibility for the fate of the revolution must agree on that.[49]

The central leadership of the Bund unanimously condemned the Bolshevik uprising of October 1917. The great majority seemed to believe that this was simply a military *coup d'état* "made by a few adventurers, carried out with a small contingent of soldiers and armed workers. . . . We believe that the Bolshevik coup is insane." The coup was also a great crime against freedom and the revolution because it had been timed for three weeks before the elections to the Constituent Assembly. The Bolsheviks had opened the way for the counterrevolution and had to be overthrown on the condition that "the Bolshevik adventurers be liquidated by the forces of democracy themselves." A new socialist coalition would convene the Constituent Assembly, hand over the land to the land committees, and proceed with peace negotiations.[50]

The leaders of the Bund did, however, differ in their assessment of Lenin's maneuver. While Abramovich thought it essentially a military coup made possible by the sympathy of the broad masses of workers and soldiers, Zaslavskii recalled that Engels had warned against a premature seizure of power which could lead only to disaster. Zaslavskii called the Bolshevik coup a 'garrison revolt with no mass support," and so "Lenin's and Trotsky's socialist revolution is about to burst." The coup was nothing but a grotesque parody of the Paris Commune. Abramovich took a more charitable view of

[49] *Der veker,* October 18, 1917; quoted in Kirzhnitz and Rafes, pp. 134–36.

[50] *Arbeter shtime,* November 13 (26), 1917.

the Bolsheviks, though he by no means condoned their actions. "Every oppressed class, especially the working class, tends always to 'maximalism' . . . especially in times of revolution." The masses were ripe for Bolshevik demagoguery because they could not understand more sophisticated socialist doctrine. Military opposition to the Bolsheviks would only drive the masses into their hands, because the people see everything in black and white terms.[51] Henryk Erlich tried to locate the social base of Bolshevism. "Today Bolshevism has not even a tinge of socialism; today it is the lowest form of anarchism . . . the rejects of society, the chaff of the proletariat and peasantry." Since the cultural level of Russian workers was lower than that of their West European counterparts, Erlich argued, it was understandable that in the early stages of its development the Russian proletariat took on the uncultured forms of Bolshevism. Since Jewish workers belonged in the main to the more cultured segment of the proletariat, Bolshevism had only a small following among them. But, Erlich warned, many Jewish workers in Kiev voted for the Bolshevik ticket in the elections to the Constituent Assembly. Erlich predicted that "it would be surprising if a movement as powerful as Bolshevism would bypass the Jewish street" but he felt that this would be temporary because the Jewish workers could never support a party "which lives complacently with Black Hundreds in its own neighborhood." [52]

Some Bundists, along with some Mensheviks, expressed the fear that militant opposition to the Bolsheviks would allow the forces of reaction to split the revolutionary camp and move toward regaining power. Moishe Rafes, a prominent Bund leader in the Ukraine, warned that "all reactionary forces" might join with the Provisional Government

[51] *Ibid.*

[52] H. Erlich, "Bolshevizm un antisemitizm," *Folkstseitung*, December 8, 1917.

in suppressing the Bolsheviks and then demand "privileges" as their reward. "We should not forget that a part of the working class, misled by the Bolsheviks, is fighting in the streets of Petrograd; complacently to choke this uprising means to disrupt many soviets of workers' deputies, many trade unions where the Bolsheviks are strong and feel at home." While the Bolsheviks had perpetrated a crime against the revolution, the Bund could not possibly support the Provisional Government because this would throw the revolution into the arms of the bourgeoisie. The only way out of this dilemma would be a new government.[53]

Another Ukrainian Bundist also argued that Bolshevism was

> a mass movement, and a mass movement absolutely cannot be created artificially by the caprice of a few people such as Lenin, Trotsky, etc. That this is a mass movement is proved by the fact that the majority of the Petrograd proletariat and garrison supported it. . . . We have to remember that in this movement are heard the despairing voices of millions of workers and soldiers, the voice of hunger, need, and poverty . . . and if this is a mass movement, a justified human cry of pain, we socialists cannot remain indifferent to it. We cannot approach it with the old, tried and tested means—suppress, choke, and it will be quiet.[54]

Similar views were expressed in the Belorussian Bund. While viewing the Bolshevik coup as "the greatest danger to the revolution," the Belorussian Bund acknowledged that there was a mass underpinning to it, the result not of "the

[53] *Folkstseitung*, October 28, 1917, quoted in Kirzhnitz and Rafes, p. 154.

[54] *Folkstseitung*, October 28, 1917. I have dwelt at some length on these different reactions to the coup because they were soon transformed into definite attitudes toward it and ultimately hardened into political positions.

fury of agitators" but of hunger, need, and fatigue.[55] A conference of Bundist organizations in Belorussia pointed to the accumulated grievances of the working class and army as the impetus pushing them "on to the path of anarchy."

However differently Bundists assessed the Bolshevik coup, they all remained resolutely opposed to a Bolshevik monopoly of power. As far as is known, only one prominent Bundist abetted the Bolshevik takeover in any way. This was Benjamin Kheifetz, an Odessa Bundist who had declared the Bolshevik coup an "adventure" but who had joined the local military-revolutionary committee. The Bund immediately challenged him to clarify his position, which he justified by simultaneously attacking the Bolsheviks as "adventurers" and yet arguing that the mass nature of the coup allowed it to be turned into a struggle "for general democratic slogans" which would avert civil war.[56]

It appears that two Bund organizations—those of Odessa and Ekaterinoslav—entered the Bolshevik military-revolutionary committees, while continuing to proclaim their ideological opposition to Bolshevism.[57]

There was some disagreement on the practical steps to

[55] *Der veker,* November 10, 1917.

[56] *Folkstseitung,* November 10, 1917, quoted in Kirzhnitz and Rafes, p. 156. Kheifetz, one of the more radical Bundist Internationalists, turned on the Bolsheviks when the Constitutent Assembly was forcibly dissolved. At the end of 1918, however, he was one of the organizers of the Communist fraction in the Bund and later was a *Evsektsiia* official in the Ukraine. Raphael Abramovich describes him as "a person of strong temperament and the oratorical abilities of the mass agitator type. Dark as a Tatar, with burning black eyes and smooth long hair which was always falling over his forehead, he would speak unusually heatedly and quickly. He was not a great politician. He did not have any ideas of his own. But the masses were fond of him for his revolutionary fire and boiling temperament. . . . In 1923 he was in Berlin. . . . Together with Karl Radek he prepared the German 'October Revolution'." Abramovich, p. 127.

[57] M. G. Rafes, *Dva goda revoliutsii,* p. 49.

be taken toward ousting the Bolsheviks, or at least "controlling" them. These disagreements closely paralleled those among the Mensheviks. Zaslavskii and Esther Frumkin, adamant Defensists, agreed that the Bund should make no concessions to the Bolsheviks and should not participate in soviets where the Bolsheviks were strong. Esther attacked the Bolsheviks as a minority group creating a dictatorship. "Unity achieved by suppressing the majority is no unity at all. . . . We cannot limit ourselves to protests. We can and must show resistance by not helping them, by doing nothing for them."[58] Abramovich was less militant. "Our aim should not be to 'suppress' Bolshevism but to unite all forces of the working class and the revolution." If the Bolsheviks would make no concessions, "the naïve, honest, unconscious but genuinely revolutionary masses of workers and soldiers will force them to do so." Abramovich urged a socialist coalition *including* the Bolsheviks. This would effectively stifle them and would at the same time clearly distinguish the democratic foes of Bolshevism from the counter-revolutionary camp which had also taken up the cry, "Down with the Bolsheviks."

Abramovich's position had its origins in developments within Menshevism. As early as July, Martov had come out for a democratic government based largely on the parties represented in the soviets. He proposed a coalition ranging from Bolsheviks to *Trudoviki* as a prophylactic measure to prevent the Bolsheviks from "going it alone." The Mensheviks accepted this line at their Extraordinary Congress in December.[59] Only the extreme right wing, including Potresov and the Bundist Liber, continued to oppose this policy.[60]

[58] *Der veker,* November 5, 1917, quoted in Y. A., "Unzer partai prese in rusland," *Unzer shtime* (Warsaw), August, 1918.

[59] Getzler, *Martov,* pp. 155–59.

[60] B. I. Nikolaevskii, "RSDRP (Mensheviki) za vremiia s dekabriia 1917 po iiul' 1918," Inter-University Project on the History of the Menshevik Movement, New York, typescript, p. 1.

With the Internationalist wing now in control of the Mensheviks, the Defensist Henryk Erlich joined the Internationalist Raphael Abramovich, just as Fedor Dan had joined Martov, in favoring negotiations with the Bolsheviks in order to create a socialist coalition government.[61]

In late October and early November, Martov and Abramovich brought together members of various socialist parties who had expressed interest in a post-coup coalition of socialist parties. This attempt had the enthusiastic support of the All-Russian Executive Committee of the Railwaymen's Union, known as the *Vikzhel*. Despite the fact that private conversations with Kamenev, Zinoviev, Riazanov, Lunacharskii, and Tomskii had convinced Abramovich that some Bolsheviks were interested in the *Vikzhel* idea, the Bolsheviks rejected the plan.[62]

Since neither the Mensheviks nor the Bund would oppose the Bolsheviks militarily, the only thing to do was to go along with Abramovich's proposals and the *Vikzhel* program. The Ukrainian Bund demanded that city dumas create special revolutionary committees which would be coalitions of all "democratic forces" which would act as watchdogs over the military. All energies were to be directed toward gaining a non-Bolshevik, democratic majority in the Constituent Assembly. The *Veker* agreed with this policy and urged that the Bolsheviks be allowed to participate in a new coalition government.[63] Moishe Rafes

[61] B. I. Nikolaevskii, *Men'sheviki v dni Oktiabr'skogo perevorota,* Inter-University Project on the History of the Menshevik Movement, Paper No. 8 (New York, 1962), p. 7.

[62] See Getzler, pp. 168–70, and Abramovich, *In tsvai revolutsies,* pp. 179–80.

[63] *Folkstseitung,* November 3, 1917. Some Bundists opposed a coalition with the Bolsheviks because "the Bolshevik eye will be turned not to the Russian revolutionary democracy but to the 'power-reserves' of workers in Western Europe. . . . I am doubtful whether in a revolutionary-democratic united government the Bolsheviks will not be an alienated group pulling in another direction." "Shimoni" [Sh. Dobin], in *Folkstseitung,* November 7, 1917. The editors

went so far as to suggest that a new coalition government have only a minority of social-democrats—Bolshevik and Menshevik.[64] All Bundist newspapers now carried the slogan, "The Constituent Assembly is the only hope." The Ukrainian Bund evolved a four-point program: (1) a coalition government ranging from *Trudoviki* to Bolsheviks; (2) education of the public to the threat posed by the Bolsheviks to the revolution; (3) safeguarding the Constituent Assembly and relying on it to create a stable government; (4) strengthening local democratic government.[65] This program was also adopted, in effect, by the Belorussian Bund [66] and by local organizations of the *Farainigte*.[67] The Bund was very active in the election campaign for the Constituent Assembly, and the Assembly did, in fact, have a non-Bolshevik majority. The forcible dispersal of the Assembly by the Bolsheviks in January 1918 rendered meaningless both this majority and the Bund program.

The Bund's opposition to the Bolshevik coup was probably representative of the feelings of most Russian Jews. While the Bundists feared that the Bolshevik coup would provoke a counter-revolution which would nullify all the gains made since the collapse of tsarism, most Russian Jews were fearful of the economic and political policies the Bolsheviks were proclaiming. The Bolsheviks were well aware of Jewish opposition and apathy. "So you want to know what's doing on the Jewish street? It would be better not to ask. . . . Some kind of revolution took place, first in February, then in October . . . some business with socialism, decrees, dictatorship of the proletariat and the

---

hastened to point out that "Shimoni's" views did not represent their own.

[64] *Folkstseitung,* November 6, 1917.

[65] *Ibid.,* November 24, 1917.

[66] *Der veker,* November 10, 1917.

[67] *Ibid.,* November 9, 1917.

like. Oh, well. The Jews couldn't care less. Let 'them' tear each other to pieces. It doesn't matter to us. . . ."[68] To most Jews the difference between the revolutions was clear. "Who can ever forget what great enthusiasm, what deep spiritual wonder, what ecstatic joy and heavenly pleasure . . . the first Russian revolution aroused in the very depth of our hearts? The soul itself sang the Marseillaise. . . . The essence of the second, Bolshevik Revolution was not the same as the first. The essence of the February Revolution was freedom; the essence of the October Revolution was dictatorship . . . the premature dictatorship of the minority over the majority."[69]

Aware of these feelings, the Bolsheviks initiated efforts to enlist support among the Jewish masses and break the stranglehold on Jewish politics held by parties whose sympathies lay with the Mensheviks, SRs, or Cadets. They introduced a new actor on the stage of Jewish political life. The despised tyro, playing only a minor role, was destined to steal the scene.

[68] B. Friedland, "Partai politik un folks-interesn," *Di varheit*, May 1, 1918. *Varheit* was controlled by the Bolsheviks.

[69] Y. Blumshtain, in *Kavkazer vokhenblat* (Baku), April 14, 1919.

III

The Establishment of The Jewish Commissariats and Jewish Sections

The national and agrarian questions—these are the basic questions for the petit bourgeois masses of the Russian population at the present time.

Lenin

In my mental equipment, nationality never occupied an independent place, as it was felt but little in everyday life . . . it was lost among all other phases of social injustice. It never played a leading part—not even a recognized one—in my list of grievances.

Trotsky

THE BOLSHEVIKS had conducted practically no agitation or propaganda among the Jewish masses prior to 1917. Consequently, there were very few Jewish Bolsheviks, and almost no Bolsheviks who were familiar with the Yiddish language or with Jewish life. In 1922 there were only 958 Jewish members of the Communist Party who had joined before 1917,[1] while the total Party membership in January 1917 was 23,600. Less than five percent of Jewish Party members in 1922 had been Bolsheviks before 1917.

Within the Russian Social Democratic Labor Party the Jews were concentrated in the Bund and in the Menshevik faction. For example, there were almost one hundred Jewish delegates, one-third of the total, to the RSDLP congress in 1907; of these, fifty-seven were Bundists. One-fifth of the pro-Menshevik delegates were Jews. "This can hardly have been accidental. But when one further considers that over a considerable period the Bund and the Mensheviks shared the same outlook in many important respects on party policy, we are entitled to conclude that we are dealing in each case with an interpretation of Marxism which found a particularly responsive chord in Jewish tradition and temperament."[2] While there might be some doubt as to the connections between Jewish tradition and Menshevism, it may be more safely asserted that the as-

[1] This figure is given in the 1922 Party census and is cited in *Alfarbandishe baratung fun di idishe sektsies fun der Al.-K.P. (B)* (Moscow, 1927), p. 83. A figure of 964 is cited in Ia. Sh. Sharapov, *Natsional'nye sektsii RKP (b)* (Kazan, 1967), p. 239.

[2] Leonard Schapiro, "The Role of the Jews in the Russian Revolutionary Movement," *The Slavonic and East European Review*, XL (1961), 160. For an analysis of the ethnic composition of the Bolshevik and Menshevik delegations to the Fifth Congress, see David Lane, *The Roots of Russian Communism* (Assen, The Netherlands, 1964), p. 44.

similated Jews who joined the RSDLP were in the main "intellectuals," rather than workers at the bench, and that they gravitated toward the Menshevik faction which attracted an intellectual, European-oriented type, whereas the Bolsheviks attracted more ethnic Russians and more genuine proletarians.

By 1917, however, there were some prominent Bolshevik leaders who were of Jewish origin. Of the twenty-one Central Committee members in August 1917, six were of Jewish origin: Kamenev, Sokolnikov, Sverdlov, Trotsky, Uritskii, and Zinoviev.[3]

These Bolsheviks were Jewish by family background only. Trotsky, for example, explicitly declared his lack of interest

[3] Schapiro states that *five* members of the Central Committee were Jews, (*op. cit.*, p. 164). Perhaps he excludes Kamenev, who was a half-Jew. In "Evrei v russkoi revoliutsii," *Evreiskii mir*, II (New York, 1944), David Shub states that seven of twenty-four Central Committee members were Jewish. Shub includes A. A. Ioffe, who was only a candidate member and who was apparently of Karaite origin. Furthermore, if candidate members are to be included, the total membership would be not twenty-four but thirty-one. See *Bol'shaia sovetskaia entsiklopedia*, 1st ed., LX (Moscow, 1934), 555–56. Leonard Schapiro lists only four candidate members in August, 1917. *The Origin of the Communist Autocracy* (Cambridge, Mass., 1956), p. 367. At the Party congresses held between 1917 and 1922 between fifteen and twenty percent of the delegates were Jews. See Y. Kantor, "Yidn in kamf far dem nitzokhon fun der oktober revolutsie," *Folksshtime* (Warsaw), October 3, 1967. It is worth noting that Jewish representation in the Menshevik Central Committee was even higher than in the Bolshevik Central Committee. In June 1917 eight out of seventeen Central Committee members were Jews—and Martov and Deich were not on the Committee at the time ("The Political Situation in Russia," June 7, 1917: report in the Lucien Wolf Archive, item 14750, YIVO Archives). William McCagg, Jr. has found that "Some thirty of the forty-eight people's commissars in the Hungarian Soviet Republic of 1919 were Jewish, or of Jewish origin," and he interprets this as a reflection of the Jews' role in "Hungary's urban revolution in the nineteenth and early twentieth centuries." "Hungary's Jewish Ministers and Commissars, 1905–1924," unpublished paper, March 1969.

in Jewish life and recalled the rather tenuous ties his family had with Judaism. He was supposed to study the Old Testament in Hebrew but "the extent of the instruction . . . was left rather vague. . . . It is strange that my first school left very few impressions. . . . I had no intimate friends among my schoolmates, as I did not speak Yiddish." Trotsky's father was a farmer, an unusual occupation for a Jew. He "did not believe in God from his youth, and in later years spoke openly about it in front of mother and the children. Mother preferred to avoid the subject." Leon Trotsky felt no cultural kinship with Jews, nor did he feel especially persecuted as a Jew.

> In my mental equipment, nationality never occupied an independent place, as it was felt but little in everyday life. . . . National inequality probably was one of the underlying causes of my dissatisfaction with the existing order, but it was lost among all other phases of social injustice. It never played a leading part—not even a recognized one—in my list of grievances.[4]

Trotsky apparently rejected any trace of Jewish identity. He is reported to have said, "I am not a Jew but an Internationalist." [5]

Trotsky's attitude toward Judaism and Jews was fairly typical of that of other Bolshevik leaders of Jewish origin and of some other prominent figures in the world Marxist movement. One of Karl Radek's boyhood friends reports that Radek "was not in the least bit interested" in the Jewish people and Jewish problems and that his family made sure

[4] Leon Trotsky, *My Life* (New York, 1930), pp. 37–38, 86–87. For an exchange between Medem and Trotsky on the question of anti-Semitism, see Vladimir Medem, *Fun mein lebn,* (New York, 1923), II, 9.

[5] G. Ziv, *Trotsky: Kharakteristika* (New York, 1921), p. 46. Quoted in E. H. Carr, *A History of Soviet Russia: Socialism in One Country* (London, 1964), I, 143, n. 2.

that he would learn German rather than Yiddish.[6] According to J. P. Nettl, Rosa Luxemburg's grandparents had already assimilated into Polish culture and "Any self-consciously Jewish atmosphere grated on her at once." [7] In 1917 she wrote to a friend, "Why do you come with your special Jewish sorrows? I feel just as sorry for the wretched Indian victims in Putamayo, the negroes in Africa. . . . I cannot find a special corner in my heart for the ghetto. I feel at home in the entire world wherever there are clouds and birds and human tears." [8]

The leading Bolsheviks of Jewish origin seem to have had many of the characteristics of the "marginal man." As first described by the sociologists Robert Park and Everett Stonequist, the "marginal man" is "one whom fate has condemned to live in two societies and in two, not merely different, but antagonistic cultures," a man "poised in psychological uncertainty between two (or more) social worlds." Some of the consequences of marginal status are that the marginal individual develops, "relative to his cultural milieu, . . . wider horizon, the keener intelligence, the more detached and rational viewpoint." [9] But, as Simpson and Yinger point out, marginality is also associated with "an ambivalence, a strain

[6] Warren Lerner, *Karl Radek: The Last Internationalist* (Stanford, 1970), pp. 3–4.

[7] J. P. Nettl, *Rosa Luxemburg* (London, 1969, abridged ed.), pp. 32. Nettl argues that Rosa Luxemburg was not a true "internationalist" in the sense of uprooting all feelings of patriotism, but rather "succeeded in transposing her loyalties from *nation* to *class*—intact" (p. 518).

[8] *Ibid.*, p. 517.

[9] Everett V. Stonequist, *The Marginal Man* (New York, 1937), pp. xv, xvii. For some critiques and refinements of the concept, see Arnold Green, "A Re-examination of the Marginal Man Concept," *Social Forces*, 26, no. 2 (1947); David I. Golovensky, "The Marginal Man Concept: An Analysis and Critique," *Social Forces*, 30, no. 2 (1952); and Aaron Antonovsky, "Toward a Refinement of the 'Marginal Man' Concept," *Social Forces*, 35, no. 1 (1956).

of roles, that heightens self-consciousness and attention to oneself. This may take the form of self-hatred . . . and an inferiority complex, or it may express itself in egocentrism, withdrawal, and/or 'aggressiveness'. . . ."[10] Since many of the Jewish Bolsheviks were born outside the Pale, or if they were born in the Pale tended to shy away, consciously or unconsciously from Jewish culture and a Jewish social milieu, they were never well integrated into Jewish society. On the other hand, because of the official and social barriers erected by the tsarist system against the Jews they could never really be fully integrated into the mainstream of Russian society, though they clearly regarded Russian culture as "higher" than Jewish culture. These "doubly alienated" people, shunning Jewish society and shunned by the Gentile world, resolved the dilemma and their role strain by creating an alternative society, the revolutionary movement, which itself constituted a little world of social relations and which aimed to remake the entire world over in its own image. Undoubtedly, the social democratic movement's conscious downplaying of ethnicity appealed to these "non-Jewish Jews" and provided them with a theoretical and practical solution to a painful psychological experience. This does not mean, however, that ethnicity became a matter of no concern to the Bolshevik Jews, however much they refused to see themselves in ethnic terms. "The stable desegregating individual consciously seeks to avoid a particular racial, national, or religious identity which may be ascribed to him by others or which he himself may formerly have made. He is likely to be critical of all segregating persons, especially those of his 'own' ascribed ethnic identity, and he shares out-group prejudices towards them. This is what Lewin calls 'self-hatred' in Jews, and it is also en-

[10] George Eaton Simpson and J. Milton Yinger, *Racial and Cultural Minorities* (New York, 1965, third ed.), p. 143.

countered frequently in the Negro middle and upper classes and in American-born orientals not living in homogeneous ethnic communities."[11] "Self-hating" Jews see the group as nothing but a burden on them and seek to leave it as quickly and decisively as possible. According to Lewin, the Jew desiring dissociation from the Jewish group will be frustrated, highly tense, and therefore have aggressive tendencies. "The aggression should, logically, be directed against the majority, which is what hinders the minority members from leaving his group. However, the majority has, in the eyes of these persons, higher status. And besides, the majority is much too powerful to be attacked. Experiments have shown that under these conditions, aggression is likely to be turned against one's own group or against one's self." While the Bolshevik Jews may have exhibited "self-hatred," as in their virulent opposition to the Bund, to Zionism, and even to attempts by members of the Jewish Sections to promote a Sovietized Yiddish culture, they also dedicated their lives to attacking the "majority group" which they defined broadly as bourgeois society and its manifestation in Russia. Blocked by the majority from assimilation, refusing integration into the existent minority, they created another minority culture, not defined in ethnic terms, which they were able to transform into a majority culture by political means.

Among the nationally conscious Jews who did not become "marginal men" the Bolsheviks had almost no following. Semën Dimanshtain, the only fairly prominent Bolshevik who was familiar with Jewish life, admitted that "during the fifteen years of the existence of the party only the program of the All-Russian party, translated into horrible Yiddish, and a few Yiddish proclamations, appeared. . . .

[11] Daniel Glaser, "Dynamics of Ethnic Identification," *American Sociological Review*, 23, no. 1 (February 1958), 36.

[12] Kurt Lewin, *Resolving Social Conflicts* (New York, 1948), p. 176.

This is all the party did especially for the Jewish street."[13] Dimanshtain recalled that although he had sometimes debated with representatives of Jewish parties during the "years of reaction," "I never conducted any positive work in Jewish society."[14] Soviet historians later claimed that

[13] Introduction to Sh. (S) Agurskii, *Di yidishe komisariatn un di yidishe kommunistishe sektsies* (Minsk, 1928), p. 2. Such assertions were condemned as heretical in the 1930's. Soviet Jewish historians labored to "prove" that Bolshevism had been popular among Jewish workers even before 1917. Soviet Yiddish newspapers would sometimes appeal to readers to submit any documents which would substantiate this claim. As far as is known, no such documents were ever produced. The Historical Section of the Institute for Jewish Proletarian Culture in Kiev was reported to be preparing a study entitled "Studies and Materials on the History of Bolshevism among the Jews," *Visnshaft un revolutsie,* no. 1–2 (April-June 1934). As far as I have been able to determine, this study was never published. There was a "Section for Research on the Revolutionary Movement Among Jews" attached to the Society of Former Political Prisoners. Founded in 1926, it was disbanded in 1931, and its only publication was *Revoliutsionnoe dvizhenie sredi evreev* (Moscow, 1930).

The later revision of history by Soviet historians is seen, for example, in A. Osherovich, "Di oktiabr revoliutsie un der kamf far der bolshevizatsie fun di yidishe arbeter," *Zamlbukh.* Osherovich states: "The history of the revolutionary Jewish workers' movement unfolded not in the Bund, S.S., [or] P[oalai] Ts[ion], but in the Bolshevik groups, Bolshevik organizations where Jews were also members. . . . The fact that the Jewish Bolsheviks did not organize special Jewish organizations, leads many 'historians' into the error of thinking that the history of Bolshevism among the Jewish workers lies outside the compass of the 'history of the Jewish labor movement' when they [the Bolsheviks] alone decide the fate of the Jewish labor movement. From this it is obvious [*sic*] that the deciding factor in the history of the Jewish labor movement was Bolshevism."

[14] Introduction to Sh. (S) Agurskii, *Der idisher arbeter in der komunistisher bavegung* (Minsk, 1925), p. vi. A Soviet historian lists various "Iskrist" proclamations which were issued in Yiddish. Internal evidence suggests, however, that the author is unfamiliar with the Yiddish language and may have attributed proclamations issued in the name of "The Social-Democratic Committee"—almost always meaning the Bund—to *Iskra* groups. See T. Iu. Burmistrova, *Leninskaia politika proletarskogo internatsionalizma v period obrazovaniia RSDRP (1898–1903 gg.)* (Leningrad, 1962), pp. 175–76. The

after the 1903 RSDLP congress some Jewish workers left the Bund and joined the Bolsheviks. However, "there are, unfortunately, no figures on the number of Jewish workers who transferred to the [RSDLP] party after the Second Congress." Dimanshtain admitted that, while

> rather significant groups of Jewish workers left the Bund, [they] did not enter our party. They worked independently and made contact with new strata of Jewish workers. . . . These comrades opposed the nationalism and opportunism of the Bund, but they were inconsistent; being terrorized by . . . "assimilation," they believed that *Iskra* would do no work in Yiddish, that *Iskra* was setting up circles where Jewish workers would first be taught the Russian language and then all work would be conducted in Russian. When I told them that . . . such a method would never be used in the mass work of the Party, they regarded this with suspicion. . . . We felt the consequences of the fact that we conducted little work among the Jewish workers in their mother tongue. All the difficulties derived from the fact . . . that our *Iskra* activists, even the Jews among them, did not know Yiddish . . . and at this crucial moment we had no literature in Yiddish.[15]

Dimanshtain complained that Bundist activists enforced party discipline and prevented Bolshevik pamphlets from

---

first Yiddish brochure published by the Bolsheviks was the report on the Third RSDLP Congress. Lenin wrote the foreword to this 1905 publication. See Avrom Pribluda, "Di ershte bolshevistishe broshur in Yiddish," *Sovetish haimland,* x, no. 4 (April 1970), 108.

[15] Sh. Dimanshtain, *Di natsionale frage afn tsvaitn tsuzamenfor fun der partai* (Moscow, 1934), pp. 59–60. Apparently, the *Iskra* groups were generally regarded as hostile to any kind of national culture and activity and those who joined them were regarded as "traitors" and "assimilationists." See, for example, A. Bailin, "Zikhroines," *Roite bleter* (Minsk), I, 23.

reaching Jewish workers. Besides, "our job was to lead the non-Jewish masses in the Jewish areas, because there was no one aside from us who could organize and serve them." [16]

In January 1904 the RSDLP formed a committee in Polesie, a region with a large Jewish population, and in March the North-West Committee was formed in the city of Minsk, another Jewish center. In 1905 these two organizations had a total membership of 970, of whom 575 were Jews.[17] The Polesie Committee ceased operations in September 1905 and was reactivated in 1910, only to be shattered by the arrest and exile of its leaders in 1915.[18] During the brief period of its existence the Committee was ineffective. While the North-West Committee actively fought the Bund, the Polesie Committee agreed to abstain from any activity among the Jewish workers, thereby tacitly acquiescing to the Bund's monopoly in this area.[19] Furthermore, neither Committee was firm in its Bolshevik allegiance, and both tended to oscillate between Bolsheviks and Mensheviks, sometimes even cooperating with the Bund.[20]

[16] Sh. Dimanshtain, "Di ershte trit fun der yidisher bolshevistisher prese," *Oktiabr,* May 10, 1927. In another article Dimanshtain admitted that "until the eve of the 1905 events the Bund was the most powerful S.D. organization in Russia in terms of a firm apparatus, discipline, flexibility and conspiracy. . . . There was even a popular anecdote going around at the time: if you ask a Bundist 'what time is it?' he will not answer you immediately. He will tell you that he must first ask the party committee. . . ." "Di revolutsionere bavegung tsvishn di yidishe masn in der revolutsie fun 1905-tn yor," *Roite bleter,* p. 12.

[17] See A. Kirzhnitz, "Di partai arbet in der idisher svive nokhn tsvaitn tsuzamenfor," *Der emes,* August 4, 1928. Bund membership at the time was between 30,000 and 40,000, a total dwarfing the alleged number of defectors to the RSDLP.

[18] *Revoliutsionnoe dvizhenie v Belorussii 1905–1907 gg. dokumenty i materialy* (Minsk, 1955), pp. 661–62.

[19] Dimanshtain, "Di revolutsionere bavegung," pp. 18, 21.

[20] K. P. Buslova, ed., *Iz istorii bor'by za rasprostranenie marksizma v Belorussii (1893–1917 gg.)* (Minsk, 1958), p. 43. In the summer

Despite the overwhelming evidence that Bolshevism was in no sense a "Jewish movement," both the opponents and the supporters of Bolshevism saw it as such. Adherents of the old regime called the new Soviet government a "Jewish government" and professed to believe that Russia had "fallen into the hands of the Jews." The British consul in Kiev was convinced that the Bolshevik leadership could be influenced by the Zionists since, after all, they were of the same people. According to one report, converted Jews in Moscow "reconverted," believing the Bolsheviks to be very pro-Jewish, and "there were instances where Christians, genuine Christians, decided to convert to Judaism after the Revolution." [21]

The idea that the Bolshevik regime was a Jewish one gained popularity probably because of the relatively large numbers of Jews who in 1917 suddenly rushed into governmental posts from which they had been barred under the tsars. So striking was the presence of Jews in high places that when it was proposed that a Jewish ticket be put forth in the elections to the Constituent Assembly, Maxim Vinaver commented, "Why do we Jews need a separate ticket? Whichever party wins, we will still be the winners." [22] I. N.

---

of 1905 the Minsk Bolsheviks had 300 organized workers (p. 49). In 1904 the Bund had 1,200 members in the city of Minsk alone (see *Geshikhte fun Bund,* II, 144). For a city-by-city breakdown of the membership of the North-West Committee, see the report of the Committee in *Iskra,* no. 78, 1904, reprinted in Sh. (S) Agurskii, *1905 in Veisrusland* (Minsk, 1925), p. 197. See also I. Iurenev, "Rabota R.S.-D.R.P. v. severozapadnom krae (1903–1913 gg.)," *Proletarskaia revoliutsiia,* no. 8–9 (31–32), August-September 1924. For an interesting account of the Bund and *Iskra* group in Berdichev, see *1905 yor in Barditshev: Notitsn un zikhroines* (Berdichev, 1925). On the North-West Committee, see also T. Iu. Burmistrova, *Natsional'naia politika partii bol'shevikov v pervoi russkoi revoliutsii 1905–1907 gg.* (Leningrad, 1962), pp. 84–86.

[21] Charney, *A yortsendlik aza,* p. 205.

[22] Quoted in M. Zipin, "Di bolshevikes, di kadetn un di idn,"

Steinberg, Commissar for Justice in the short-lived Bolshevik-Left Socialist Revolutionary coalition of 1917–18, was an Orthodox Jew who seemed to feel completely at home with the atheistic socialists. "All knew that when he went to a Duma session on the Sabbath, a Gentile would carry his briefcase for him.[23] They told of a fiery leftist speech to the peasants on the Eve of Yom Kippur, and about tears and strict fasting in the House of Study on Yom Kippur." [24]

Jews were especially welcomed by the Bolshevik government because a large part of the old bureaucracy and intelligentsia refused to serve it. Lenin was aware of this. He told Dimanshtain that the wartime migration of the Jewish "middle intelligentsia" to the big cities had "great significance for the revolution." This Jewish intelligentsia had neutralized the boycott of the Bolshevik regime by the

---

Di tsukunft, XXVI, no. 9 (September 1918). Some Jewish leaders, particularly among the Zionists, did not look favorably upon the situation. "The fact that almost our entire Jewish intelligentsia has raced into the soviets and republic ministries evokes another feeling within us. They have made the Jewish democratic street even poorer than it was. . . . Talented people leave us, the politically impoverished nation, in order to work with the wealthier, where there is wider scope for all sorts of ambitions." "Baal Makhshoves," in *Togblat* (Petrograd), October 27, 1917. As a result of their engagement in government work Jews "are forced to neglect their own relief work, and, at the last conference of the Relief Committee, a striking decrease in the number of Jewish intellectuals on the Relief Committee was noted." "The Political Situation in Russia," item 14730, p. 11.

[23] Jewish law forbids carrying on the Sabbath.

[24] A. Mokdoni, "Di S.R. regirung, Kolchak un yidn," in A. Tsherikover, ed., *In der tkufe fun revolutsie* (Berlin, 1924), I, 104. Some of his party comrades charged Steinberg with inconsistency: "It seemed odd that even after the February Revolution so prominent a leftist should have been willing to run on the same ticket with the Moscow rabbi Maze as an exponent of the preservation of Jewish nationality through clerical schools." Oliver Henry Radkey, *The Sickle Under the Hammer: The Russian Socialist Revolutionaries in the Early Months of Soviet Rule* (New York, 1963), p. 134.

Russian intelligentsia. In Lenin's words, they had "sabotaged the saboteurs." At the same time, Lenin suggested that this should not be emphasized in the press because "in a peasant land one must sometimes also reckon with such hateful phenomena as anti-Semitism." [25]

The rush into government offices by Jewish bookkeepers, statisticians, artists, and teachers did not mean that Communism had suddenly seized the minds and hearts of all literate Jews. As a matter of fact, in 1922 there were only 1,175 Jews in the Party who had joined during the course of 1917.[26] This rush into official posts meant simply that government employment was one of the few sure ways to avoid starvation and to hold a decent, dignified job. Then, too, Jews were fascinated with the wholly new possibility of being rulers as well as ruled. There can be little doubt that the thirst for power had been exacerbated by centuries of drought and that Jews were determined to drink deeply of the sweet waters of power. Professor Minor, a neurologist whose father was the former chief rabbi of Moscow,[27] explained that "though in the old Russia I could get no promotion for twenty years by reason of being a Jew, today I am not only a professor but also dean of the medical school. I am not a radical but I must acknowledge the debt of the Jews to the new rulers." [28]

[25] From Dimanshtain's introduction to N. Lenin, *O evreiskom voprose v Rossii* (Moscow, 1924), p. 17.

[26] *Alfarbandishe baratung*, p. 83. Sharapov lists 2,182 Jews as having joined the Party in 1917 (p. 239).

[27] A post filled by a so-called *kazioner rabbiner*, or "official rabbi," appointed by the crown, in this case largely for ceremonial purposes but also to serve as a sort of "Court Jew."

[28] Boris D. Bogen, *Born a Jew* (New York, 1930), p. 339. Bogen was a Russian-born American Jew who was sent to Russia to direct the Joint Distribution Committee's relief work.

George Katkov traces the influx of Jews into government posts to the hatred of tsarism intensified by the expulsions of 1915. "For millions of Russian Jews, the revolution, with its proclaimed slogan

The high visibility of Jews in the Bolshevik regime was dramatized by the large numbers of Jews in the Cheka. The reasons for the popularity of Cheka service among Jews are not altogether clear but since Jews could hardly be suspected of devotion to the tsarist regime, they would be considered reliable opponents of the Whites. From the Jewish point of view it was no doubt the lure of immediate physical power which attracted many Jewish youths, desirous of avenging the crimes perpetrated against their people by anti-Soviet forces of all sorts. Whatever the reasons, Jews were heavily represented in the secret police. "Anyone who had the misfortune to fall into the hands of the Cheka stood a very good chance of finding himself confronted with, and very possibly shot by, a Jewish investigator." [29] Since the Cheka was the most hated and feared organ of the Bolshevik government, anti-Jewish feelings increased in direct proportion to Cheka terror.

Most Jews were ambivalent in their feelings toward the Bolsheviks. "The Jews in Russia were, on the one hand, proud that Trotsky stook at the head of the heroic struggle against the *pogromchikes,* but, on the other hand, they were afraid that if the Bolsheviks were to fail, Heaven forbid, they would have to pay heavily for Trotsky-Bronshtein." [30] The Jews had much to lose from the Bolshevik prohibition of free commerce and "the masses of traders and handicraft

---

of 'equality of all Russian citizens before the law' came as a liberation at the moment of the greatest danger for the physical and moral existence of the Jewish nation. . . . The fear that . . . next day they might wake to see the old order restored, was naturally an obsession of many of these ex-refugees. . . . This is why a large number of Jews offered their loyal services as 'Soviet employees' to the Soviet regime in the years of civil war and reconstruction." George Katkov, *Russia 1917: The February Revolution* (New York, 1967), p. 61.

[29] Schapiro, "The Role of the Jews," p. 165. Other national minorities, such as the Latvians, were also heavily represented in the Cheka.

[30] Charney, p. 243.

workers could look upon the Communist experiment only with fear." [31] At the same time, some Jews seemed to take genuine pride in the fact that Trotsky, "one of their own," had attained such a high position. With typical Jewish humor, they fancifully reinterpreted the initialed institutions which were being created daily by the Soviet Government. Thus, they quipped that VTsIK (Vserossiiskii tsentral'nyi ispolnitel'nyi komitet or All-Union Russian Central Executive Committee) really stood for *"vu tsen idn komandeven"* (where ten Jews give the orders). To the Jew, *trest* (trust, or industrial grouping of the NEP period) meant "Trotskii razreshil svobodnuiu torgovliu" (Trotsky has permitted [the Jews] to engage in free trade).[32] Many Jews were sympathetic to the Bolsheviks only because they feared and hated the Whites. " 'If only the Bolsheviks would retain power,' the Jews of Berezin prayed to the Almighty. 'Whatever they may be, the Bolsheviks don't bother the Jews.' " [33] This attitude became more prevalent as anti-Jewish excesses were committed by the Whites, Ukrainian nationalists, and bandits.

Lenin valued not only the contribution of the Jewish intelligentsia to Soviet administration but also the revolutionary activities of many Jews. While condemning Jewish nationalism, as he defined it, Lenin had pointed out that the "percentage of Jews in democratic and proletarian movements is everywhere higher than the percentage of Jews in the population as a whole." [34] Dimanshtain related how "in

[31] Avrahm Yarmolinsky, *The Jews and Other Minority Nationalities Under the Soviets* (New York, 1928), p. 50. Some Jews took a dim view of Trotsky: " 'Leibele Bronshtain,' they say, is killing their business and economy. He is much more radical than Lenin who would allow free trade but for Trotsky's pressure." Rachel Figenberg-Imri, *Megilot Yehudai Rusia* (Jerusalem, 1965), pp. 281–82.

[32] Charney, p. 283.

[33] *Ibid.*

[34] "Kriticheskie zametki po natsional'nomu voprosu," in N. Lenin,

conversations with me, Lenin quite often remarked on the great significance of the Jews for the revolution, not only in Russia but also in other lands. . . ."[35] Of course, Lenin would never generalize about "the Jews" without taking into account the class structure of the Jewish population, and he realized that the vast majority of Russian Jewry was not in the least committed to Bolshevik ideology. While he had refused to recognize a Jewish nation, Lenin could not very well deny the hard fact that the Russian Jews had a distinct language. For most, it was their only language. Furthermore, Lenin acknowledged that the disabilities imposed on the Jews under tsarism had produced effects which could not be done away with by Bolshevik decrees. There was obviously a need for some sort of special governmental agency to deal with Jewish needs and, at the same time, bring the Bolshevik message to the Jews in a language they would understand. In late 1917,

> after negotiations with certain Jewish Communists, it was decided to make me [Dimanshtain] Commissar for Jewish National Affairs. The question of Party sections did not exist at the time. I then had a long conversation with Lenin about the general line in the forthcoming work and I suggested that we also have some Party forms for work among the Jewish workers, mainly because we would have to struggle against the Jewish socialist parties and it would be very difficult to do so without giving Jewish Party work some organizational form. By chance, Sverdlov came in and Lenin asked him his opinion of my suggestion. Sverdlov strongly opposed any organizational forms for Jewish Party work. Moreover, he said, we would thereby create an internal Bund with all its faults,

Izbranniye stat'i po natsional'nomu voprosu (Moscow-Leningrad, 1925), p. 29.

[35] Dimanshtain's introduction to Lenin, *O evreiskom voprose.*

and we would end up with a federation of parties. . . . The only thing necessary for Jewish work is a daily newspaper—and no more. . . . Lenin said that he found no Bundist ideas in what I had said. . . . Lenin said that you could not go against national needs, but that we should be careful not to fall into Bundism. Sections were not mentioned.[36]

Lenin suggested that a conference be called of Jewish *intelligenty* of all parties for the purpose of explaining the nature of the Soviet government and informing them of the opportunities for developing the culture of the Jewish toiling masses. The meeting was held, but the Bolsheviks failed to convince the audience to cooperate with the Party.[37]

Dimanshtain received permission from Yakov Sverdlov, "the Party factotum," to publish a Yiddish newspaper, *Shturem glok* (Storm Bell). But there were more pressing needs and Dimanshtain was dispatched to the front as an agitator.[38] In early December 1917 two recent arrivals from America began to plan publication of Yiddish material which would be "friendly to the Soviets." Boris Reinstein, an American citizen of Russian origin, was in charge of the International Revolutionary Propaganda Section of the Commissariat for Foreign Affairs.[39] This section included

[36] Sh. Dimanshtain, "Lenin un di idishe komunistishe arbet," *Emes*, January 27, 1924.

[37] *Emes*, February 7, 1924.

[38] Sh. Agurskii, "Di antshaiung fun di ershte komunistishe tseitung in yidish," *Komunistishe fon* (Kiev), March 7, 1923.

[39] Reinstein had come to Russia as the representative of the American Socialist Labor Party. He attended an "international Socialist conference" in early 1918 and then the first congress of the Comintern, claiming to speak for the Socialist Labor Party. That party, however, disowned him. See E. H. Carr, *A History of Soviet Russia: The Bolshevik Revolution 1917–1923*, III (London, 1961), 116–17.

such luminaries as John Reed, Karl Radek, and Bela Kun. Among the lesser lights of the section was Samuil Agurskii, a tailor by trade. Agurskii had been a member of the Bund in the early years of the century but was forced to flee Russia after the 1905 revolution. He returned from the United States in May 1917 with the second group of political emigrants. Reinstein suggested to Agurskii that a Jewish department be organized within the International Propaganda Section. The department's function was to publish newspapers and brochures in Yiddish. These would not be strictly Bolshevik in outlook but "periodicals supporting the Soviet state." Agurskii eagerly accepted the suggestion but apparently could not himself edit and publish such material. Nor could he find a single Jewish editor willing to work for the new regime. Finally, two recently returned exiles from England were enlisted to publish a pro-Soviet Yiddish newspaper. These were A. Shapiro, a London anarchist, and A. Kantor, former secretary of the Jewish Workers Fund and the Board of Jewish Trade Unions in London. They had a newspaper already on the presses when Reinstein informed them that a Jewish Commissariat had just been formed and that they were to attach themselves to it.[40]

Reinstein informed Agurskii that Dimanshtain had been appointed Commissar for Jewish Affairs, but at a meeting in the Smolny Institute, Pestkovskii, Deputy Commissar in the Commissariat of Nationalities, told Agurskii that the meeting had been called to "elect" Dimanshtain. This done, the Left SR, Ilya G. Dobkovskii, was made Vice-Commissar for Jewish Affairs.[41]

By this time, Muslim, Polish, Latvian, and Belorussian Commissariats had been organized. A Jewish Commissariat

[40] Agurskii, *Der idisher arbeter,* pp. 5–6.
[41] *Ibid.*

had not been established "because there was simply no one to do it." [42] This was a problem common to all the nationality commissariats. "The lack of cadres of workers among the nationalities was the greatest difficulty in the organization of the apparatus of *Narkomnats* and its departments." [43] However, Dimanshtain had returned from service at the front, and there were the three emigrants in the International Revolutionary Propaganda Section. By January 1918 it was decided to create Jewish "organizational forms" within both the state and Party apparatuses. A Commissariat for Jewish National Affairs, abbreviated as *Evkom*, was formed as a section of the People's Commissariat for Nationality Affairs. Unlike the other nationality commissariats, the Jewish Commissariat was designated "temporary." [44]

[42] Sh. Dimanshtain, *Beim likht fun komunizm* (Moscow, 1919), p. 280.

[43] E. I. Pesikina, *Narodnyi komissariat po delam natsional'nostei i ego deiatel'nost v 1917–1918 gg.* (Moscow, 1950), p. 51. By the fall of 1918 there were seven national commissariats—Armenian, Belorussian, Jewish, Latvian, Lithuanian, Muslim, and Polish—and eleven national departments (*ibid.*, p. 61). The Armenian and Muslim Commissariats had great difficulty recruiting experienced cadres. See G. P. Makarova, *Osushchestvlenie leninskoi natsional'noi politiki v pervye gody sovetskoi vlasti* (Moscow, 1969), pp. 77–79.

[44] See *Dekrety sovetskoi vlasti* (Moscow, 1959–64), I, 370, quoted in M. Altshuler, "Reshit HaEvsektsiia," unpub. M.A. thesis, Hebrew University (Jerusalem), 1966. Altshuler reasons that the *Evkom* was labeled "temporary" because its officials knew very well that they would have to obtain the cooperation of non-Bolsheviks in "Jewish work." "They wanted to leave the door open to such groups and the Commissariat was designated temporary [to indicate] that this Commissariat was appointed from above, as in tsarist days, but the imposition from above was but a transitional phase until the Jewish population would itself set its organizational forms within the context of the Soviet reality and Bolshevik legality" (p. 6). This line of reasoning is supported by Dimanshtain's assertion in 1918 that "As a Marxist I know quite well that, disregarding all logic, the Jewish petit bourgeois element will not lose its essence and become Communist. But I have faith in the 'petit bourgeois by mistake' who has

Early Days in the Jewish Commissariats and Sections

In the fall of 1918 Jewish Sections (*Evreiskie Sektsii*, or *Evsektsii*, popularly referred to as "the *Evsektsiia*") were established within the Bolshevik Party. There was some controversy over the creation of such sections. Dimanshtain wanted to form not just sections but an organization "somewhat similar" to the independent Jewish labor parties, "and afterwards, in the course of the work, in time, the Jewish activists would become convinced that they must tie themselves closer to the party and reject their isolation." Sverdlov, who as secretary of the Central Committee had jurisdiction over such matters, strenuously opposed this. "He wanted only a Jewish party newspaper and no more. I remember how some respected comrades accused me of wanting to create a new Bund within the party. . . ."[45]

become greatly proletarianized [i.e., impoverished] thanks to our requisitions and nationalizations. The majority of the Jewish population in Russia consists now of such elements. . . . There is no salvation for Jews on any road other than Communism." Sh. Dimanshtain, "Veiter idishe pogromen," *Emes*, November 27, 1918. The Communist journal *Kamf un lebn* explicitly appealed to non-Communist Jewish *intelligenty*. See no. 1–2, April 1919.

[45] Sh. Dimanshtain, "10 yor komprese in yidish," *Emes*, February 29, 1928. It is interesting to speculate on who these "respected comrades" were. One might have been Stalin who, as Commissar of Nationalities, presumably had a say in the matter. Writing in 1928 when Stalin was consolidating power, Dimanshtain may have felt it impolitic to describe Stalin as having attacked him and ultimately being overruled by Lenin. There seems to be no information on Stalin's attitude toward the Jewish Sections or Commissariat. We do know that Stalin endorsed the creation of separate national battalions, presumably including a Jewish one, in the Ukraine. See S. M. Dimanshtain, ed., *Revolutsiia i natsional'nyi vopros* (Moscow, 1930), III, 34. In a long article on Stalin's role in the formulation of Soviet nationality policy, Dimanshtain failed to mention Stalin's attitude toward (or in connection with) the *Evsektsii* or *Evkomy*; see *Emes*, December 21, 1929. Agurskii, who worked in Narkomnats, wrote in 1920 that Stalin was "seldom in the Commissariat. . . . The work of the Commissariat is conducted by a collegium composed of the

Dimanshtain appealed to Lenin and "in the presence of Comrade Sverdlov and several others, Lenin approved my views, and the possibility of far-reaching Jewish work was created." [46] Thus, while the Jew Sverdlov opposed "separate forms for Jewish work," it was Lenin, the militant opponent of Bundist "separatism," who finally approved the creation of Jewish sections within the Bolshevik Party—a party upon whose indivisibility he had so adamantly insisted.

The Jewish Commissariat, organized at both the central and local levels, was seen as an administrative organ.

> The Jewish Commissariat sees its task as the reconstruction of Jewish national life on a proletarian-socialist basis. The Jewish masses have the complete right to control all existing Jewish social institutions, to give a socialist direction to our people's schools, to give Jews the opportunity to enter agricultural work on the socialized land, to concern themselves with the fate of the homeless, to see that the needy get government relief, to fight anti-Semitism, pogroms, etc.[47]

The plans of the Jewish Commissariat in 1918 spoke of

---

national commissars. And they . . . meet together every week with the assistant to the People's Commissar [Pestkovskii]. Each national Commissariat reports on its activity, and new plans for further activity are worked out together." "Ben Khaim," "Di role fun di idishe arbeiter in der rusisher revolutsie," *Funken*, April 15, 1920. "Stalin really had no definite duties. The Commissariat of Nationalities, especially at the beginning, took very little of his time. He, therefore, played the role of chief-of-staff or of clerk on responsible missions under Lenin." Leon Trotski, *Stalin: An Appraisal of the Man and his Influence* (London, 1947), p. 245.

[46] Dimanshtain, "10 Yor."

[47] *Di varheit*, June 2, 1918. On the structure and functions of the central and local nationality commissariats, see Alexander G. Park, *Bolshevism in Turkestan, 1917–1927* (New York, 1957), pp. 116–19. See also M. P. Iroshnikov, *Sozdanie sovetskogo tsentral'nogo gosudarstvennogo apparata* (Moscow-Leningrad, 1966), pp. 260–61, and Sharapov, *Natsional'nye sektsii.*

the creation of Jewish sections within the local soviets. The local Jewish sections of the soviets would be subordinated to regional Jewish soviets which would hold their own congresses. "At the All-Russian Congress of Jewish Soviets the general policy will be decided for all questions touching upon Jewish social life. The Jewish Commissar and Commissariat will also be chosen [there]."[48] The Jewish Commissariat also entertained a proposal, probably put forth by Dimanshtain, to create a non-party organization of proletarian elements which would merely "stand on the platform of the Soviet government." But the proposal for Jewish sections in the soviets won out. However, this scheme, seemingly very similar to the national program of the *Farainigte,* was quietly abandoned in the summer of 1918, and emphasis was shifted to the creation of Jewish sections in the party.[49] The party sections were probably

[48] *Di varheit,* June 2, 1918. A Jewish soviet was actually organized in Elets. It had 4 Bundist deputies, 4 Bolsheviks and 2 *Poalai Tsion*ists. The soviet dissolved the *kehilla* and took over its institutions. But inter-party differences and the refusal of the local soviet of workers and peasants to recognize the Jewish soviet led to the replacement of the latter by a *Evkom. Emes,* September 26, 1918.

[49] Schwarz (p. 95) erroneously states that "the notion that the soviets should be composed of various national sections, obviously a slip on the part of the writer, was never mentioned again," after having been put forth in the first issue of *Di varheit.* Schwarz himself then proceeds to quote from the June 2, 1918 issue of *Varheit* where the scheme is elaborated, as quoted above. Apparently the idea of Jewish sections in the soviets was not "obviously a slip on the part of the writer" but was seriously entertained for at least four months. The plan for Jewish sections in the soviets, or rather for "soviets for Jewish affairs," was discussed in *Di freie shtime,* no. 1–2, April 1918. This was the organ of the Petersburg Commissariat for Jewish Affairs. The plan was abandoned probably because of its striking similarity to the proposals set forth by the "petit bourgeois" *Farainigte* and because it did not guarantee a Bolshevik majority in such soviets. Altshuler (p. 11) argues that opposition by local soviets and *Narkomnats* combined with lack of cooperation by the Jewish population to defeat the idea of Jewish soviets. Sharapov writes of "groups of Jewish

less controversial than the extraterritorial organs to be created under the scheme for Jewish soviets, a scheme which came perilously close to the national-cultural autonomy demanded by the Bund and the *Farainigte.* After the Left SRs attempted an insurrection on July 5, 1918, the leaders of the Central Jewish Commissariat decided to abandon the scheme of non-party Jewish workers' soviets, and "Jewish sections of the Communist Party began to be established at once." [50]

While debating the relative merits of Jewish soviets and Jewish sections, the Jewish Commissariat tried to carry out the duties outlined by Dimanshtain. But the Commissariat, or *Evkom,* immediately ran into difficulties. The main problem was to recruit ideologically reliable personnel who had some knowledge of Yiddish and of the Russian Jewish community.

> Among the few Jewish Communists who had gathered round the Jewish Commissariat there was none who could have written a Yiddish pamphlet for publication. Consequently, translations had to be made from the Russian. But even translations were hard to make. Everybody had so much work to do that you did not know where to start. We had to look for Jewish writers willing to do the job for a substantial fee. But no money in the world could produce a Jewish writer willing merely to translate Bolshevik literature.[51]

When a young man named Kaplan turned up in Moscow, claiming to have published a Yiddish weekly in America,

---

Communists" attached to the Jewish Commissariat in five cities. "In some cities there were united soviet-party sections" (p. 76).

[50] Agurskii, *Der idisher arbeter,* p. 23n. Altshuler points out that nationality sections existed in the Bolshevik party as early as August 1917 (p. 32).

[51] Agurskii, *Der idisher arbeter,* p. 9.

he was snapped up by *Evkom* and was put to work translating into Yiddish Lenin's speech at the Third Congress of Soviets. *State and Revolution* was translated by a member of the *Folkspartai,* Kalmanovich, who insisted that his name be kept off the title page. This was no doubt due less to modesty than to fear of being identified with the Bolsheviks.[52] Finally, *Evkom* managed to obtain the dubious services of Moses and Sobelson, two Jews from Norway.[53] One of them knew no Russian and the other knew no Yiddish, so they worked with two dictionaries—a Yiddish-Russian and a Russian-Yiddish! [54]

In the hallowed tradition of small revolutionary groups, *Evkom's* first enterprise was the publication of a newspaper. The first issue of *Di varheit* appeared on March 8, 1918, and the newspaper appeared irregularly thereafter.[55] Of the three members of the original editorial board, Dimanshtain, Torchinskii, and Bukhbinder, the last two did not know Yiddish, and *Di varheit* was really a Dimanshtain *tour de force.* The newspaper was the official organ of *Evkom* and as such was a joint Bolshevik and Left SR organ. There were three Bolsheviks and one Left SR on the editorial board, but "we did not print a single major article which expressed a Left SR point of view." [56] Thus, the newspaper defended the Treaty of Brest-Litovsk though the Left SRs had attacked it. It was a rather amateurish sheet that the *Evkom* published. While Left SR ideology may very well have been excluded from *Di varheit,* the

[52] *Ibid.*

[53] *Ibid.,* p. 3.

[54] Charney, pp. 211–13. These two "Jewish experts" soon left for Poland.

[55] Agurskii, "Di antshaiung," incorrectly gives the date as March 7. A reproduction of the first issue in Agurskii, *Der idisher arbeter,* p. 12, shows the date as March 8.

[56] Dimanshtain, "10 yor."

newspaper did carry news of the *kehillas*;[57] and the ideological purity of *Evreiskaia tribuna,* published by *Evkom,* was sullied by a faithful report of the Petrograd religious *kehilla* which deplored the fact that Jewish youth were not receiving the proper Jewish religious-national upbringing. The orthography of *Di varheit* was a chaotic mixture of the old Yiddish style, which spelled words of German origin in their German form and spelled Hebrew words in the unvocalized Hebrew manner, and the newer phonetic style, which spelled all words according to their sound.[58] This was due to the fact that the articles were naturally written in the older style; the copy editor, Kantor, was a proponent of the new orthography but had no time to change all the articles since he also served as an official in another Soviet office. Kantor corrected what he could, and the rest was printed as it was written.[59]

The comic-opera flavor of the *Evkom* lingered on when the Commissariat moved from Petrograd to Moscow in the spring of 1918 and the name of *Di varheit* was changed to *Der emes* in August.[60] Some fresh personnel were re-

[57] See, for example, the issue of June 11, 1918.

[58] Thus, for example, in the more traditional spelling "to see" would be *zehen* and the Hebrew "summing up" would be *sakh hakol;* in the new spelling these would be *zen* and *sakhakel,* respectively. On the Communist attitude toward Hebrew and the Yiddishization of Hebrew words, see Chapter V.

[59] Agurskii, "Di antshaiung."

[60] Both *varheit* and *emes* mean "truth" and were intended to correspond to the Russian *Pravda. Varheit,* however, is an almost strictly Germanic form, the Hebrew *emes* being more frequently used. Schwarz speculates that *varheit* was chosen at first because "Either the editors knew German better than Yiddish, or they believed . . . that it was necessary to liberate Yiddish from the 'reactionary' influence of Hebrew." Dimanshtain, however, wrote that "I opposed the name *emes* because it reminded one of the old Hebrew journal *HaEmeth.* But when we had to change the name of the newspapers for political reasons we adopted the name *emes*" (see Dimanshtain, "10 yor"). The "political reasons" alluded to by Dimanshtain refer

cruited but these were hardly the most talented writers of their day.

> The first Jewish "Bolsheviks" who came to the Jewish Commissariat . . . were, for the most part, half and quarter writers. The October Revolution gave them a good opportunity to take revenge on the "bourgeois" and "petit bourgeois" editors who always obstructed their path to "immortality." With the power of the Jewish Commissariat you could expropriate Jewish presses and appoint yourself editor of the first Jewish Bolshevik newspapers and magazines. Who had ever heard . . . of these newly arrived editors, poets and publicists who suddenly betook themselves to the "cultural revolution" on the Jewish street? [61]

Despite the best efforts of these self-proclaimed writers, the circulation of *Emes* was infinitesimal. Five thousand copies were printed daily but most were smuggled into territories occupied by the German army, the Polish Legions, or Ukrainian nationalists. *Emes* printed Bolshevik placards in Yiddish, and they were pasted up all over Moscow. Unfortunately, *Emes* hired non-Jewish boys to do this and they pasted them upside down, making the posters the laughing stock of Moscow Jewry. "Even the employees of the editorial board itself failed to show proper respect for the first Jewish Communist newspaper. They knew that

---

to the provision of the Brest-Litovsk Treaty forbidding distribution of government newspapers in occupied territories while allowing distribution of party papers. *Emes* became an organ of the Communist Party. (The Jewish socialist Aaron Liberman published three issues of *HaEmeth* in 1876. This was the first Hebrew socialist publication.) The organ of the *Evkom* and *Evsektsiia* first appeared as *emeth* in the original Hebrew spelling (Aleph, Mem, Tav) but was soon "Yiddishized" into *Der emes* ('Ayin, Mem, 'Ayin, Samekh). *Evkom* decided on November 20, 1918 to Yiddishize the orthography of Hebrew words.

[61] Charney, p. 214.

the Jewish *Emes* of today was the Russian *Pravda* of yesterday." Each typesetter and most of the other employees took home one hundred copies every day to use as fuel.[62]

This unprofessional *modus operandi* of *Evkom* is understandable in view of the great dearth of personnel and the hostility of the Jewish intelligentsia and politically conscious Jews.[63] If one examines the background of *Evkom* personnel, the reasons for *Evkom's* blunders and failures become readily apparent. The only person who combined pre-revolutionary Bolshevik affiliation with good knowledge of Jewish life was Semën M. Dimanshtain. Born in 1888 [64] in Sebezh, a town in Vitebsk *guberniia,* Dimanshtain was the son of a poor tinsmith. Living in the same house as the local rabbi, young Dimanshtain grew up in an Orthodox religious atmosphere. At the age of twelve he started studying in Yeshivas. He showed his revolutionary mettle at a tender age when he was asked to leave the famed Telshe Yeshiva for having participated in a *hopke,* a strike of sorts against the faculty. Dimanshtain then studied in the

[62] *Ibid.,* pp. 224–26. As a result, Agurskii was said to be the only one to have a complete file of the first years of *Emes.* It seems that there are no complete files in the Soviet Union today.

[63] It was not necessary to be a Bolshevik in order to organize and work for a national Commissariat or department. A person or party had merely to "stand on the Soviet platform" (see Pesikina, p. 52). *Di varheit* wrote, "We turn to all Jewish comrades who support the platform of the Soviet government [Bolsheviks, Left SR's, *Poalai Tsion,* Left Bundists, etc.] to help us in our work . . ." (June 11, 1918).

[64] This date was given by Dimanshtain in an autobiography he wrote for Daniel Charney when the latter worked in *Evkom.* In Zalman Reisen's *Leksikon fun der yidisher literatur, prese un filologie* (3rd rev. ed., Vilna, 1928–29), I, 694, Dimanshtain is said to have been born "around 1885." *Sovetish heimland,* I, no. 2 (February 1965), writes that Dimanshtain was born "eighty years ago"—i.e., in 1885. This date is accepted in Hersh Smoliar, "Der ershter: tsum 80 geboirntog fun Shimon Dimanshtain," *Folksshtime* (Warsaw), February 24, 1965.

famous Yeshiva of Slobodka where he became a follower of the *musar* movement.[65] Later, Dimanshtain was attracted to Hasidism and left Slobodka for the bastion of Hasidic learning, the Lubavicher Yeshiva. Once again he underwent a spiritual transformation, rejected Hasidism in favor of "open wisdom" (*nigleh*) and led the life of a *masmid*, or Talmudic scholar, poring over the Talmud for fourteen and even sixteen hours a day. Like most yeshiva students, he ate at the homes of the wealthier residents of the town and earned a meager salary as a private tutor. Dimanshtain climaxed his religious-scholarly career when he received rabbinical ordination from several rabbis, including Khaim Ozer Grodzenskii of Vilna, one of the greatest authorities of the day. But the young rabbi was still not at peace with himself, and in 1903 or 1904 he decided to enter a *gymnazium*, at a time when he was so poor that he was sleeping in the streets. Preparing, as an extern, for the examinations, he was drawn into the illegal socialist circles in Vilna and was assigned to "literary" work, translating the program of the RSDLP into Yiddish and Hebrew.[66] Arrested in 1906, Dimanshtain made a dramatic escape to Riga where he was rearrested in March 1908, at a Bolshevik conference. He was sentenced to five years' exile in Siberia and served some time there before fleeing abroad.[67] In Paris, Dimanshtain

[65] The *musar* movement was founded in the second half of the nineteenth century by Rabbi Israel Lipkin Salanter. It emphasized the ethical life together with intensive Talmudic study and introduced such works as Bahya ibn Pakuda's *Khovot Halevavot* (Duties of the Heart) and Moses Hayim Luzzatto's *Mesillat Yesharim* (Path of the Righteous) into the yeshiva curriculum. The movement flourished in Belorussia and Lithuania.

[66] Dimanshtain later called the translation "horrible!" The Hebrew text was published in the Vilna *Hazman* in 1906. The Yiddish text is reproduced in *Tseitshrift* (Minsk, 1930), IV, 261–78.

[67] Again, the accounts in Charney and in the *Leksikon* differ slightly. Charney says Dimanshtain served his full sentence and went

was graduated from a school for "electro-technicians" and was active in the Bolshevik organization.[68] He worked in a factory and founded a Jewish workers' club in Montmartre. In May 1917 Dimanshtain returned to Russia, working first in the Petrograd Bolshevik organization and then on the Northern front where he helped edit *Okopnaia pravda.*[69] The paper was closed by the Provisional Government. Dimanshtain was arrested but was soon released and became chairman of the Bolshevik organization on the Northern front. In January 1918 the former yeshiva student, *musarnik,* Hasid, and rabbi became the Bolshevik Commissar for Jewish National Affairs.[70]

The rest of the *Evkom* staff did not quite measure up to Dimanshtain, either in Jewish learning or in Bolshevik pedigree. Ilya Dobkovskii, Dimanshtain's vice-commissar, was a Left SR who had been designated by that party as its representative in *Evkom.* Dobkovskii announced himself a

---

to Germany in 1913, going afterwards to Paris. The *Leksikon* says he escaped to Paris in 1910.

[68] According to Walter Z. Laqueur, *The Soviet Union and the Middle East* (London, 1959), p. 12, Dimanshtain was a locksmith. This is also reported in Smoliar, *op. cit.*

[69] See D. I. Grazkin, *Okopnaia pravda* (Moscow, 1933), p. 18.

[70] Pesikina, *op. cit.,* never once mentions Dimanshtain who, after all, was the secretary of *Narkomnats* and as such was close to Stalin. Neither is he mentioned by the former *Narkomnats* functionary, S. Pestkovskii, in his article, "Vospominaniia o rabote v narkomnatse," *Proletarskaia revoliutsiia,* no. 6 (101), June 1930. Dimanshtain was purged and disappeared in 1937, and by 1950 had apparently become a "nonperson." Pesikina also avoids any discussion whatsoever of *Evkom.* Writing two years after the Yiddish newspaper *Einigkeit* and the *Emes* publishing house had been closed down, Pesikina apparently thought it wise to refrain from any mention of *Evkom* and Yiddish work. Dimanshtain has been rehabilitated and was mentioned as a Soviet leader in Lithuania in 1918. See "Niezapomniany Rok, Dziejowe Wdarzenie 1918–1963," *Czerwony Sztandar,* reproduced in *Evrei i evreiskii narod* (London, 1964), no. 14, p. 18. See also *Sovetish haimland,* v, no. 2 (February 1965) where there is a brief summary of Dimanshtain's career.

writer and in his brief tenure wrote a book on Moses Hess, attacking the latter as a utopian socialist but acknowledging that for his "humanitarian" nationalism he deserved "the deepest respect." [71] It was soon discovered that Dobkovskii had worked for the tsarist secret police as an *agent-provocateur,* and some asserted that he had been converted to Christianity. Dobkovskii was immediately removed from his post.[72]

Aside from Dimanshtain, the only *Evkom* employee who was to play a significant role in the future of the *Evkom* and *Evsektsiia* was Samuil Agurskii. The man who was to become one of the most controversial figures in the Jewish sections came from humble origins. Born in 1884, he was the son of a worker in the huge Shereshevskii tobacco factory in Grodno. At the age of thirteen Agurskii became a manual laborer, then a tailor. He joined the Bund but never became more than a rank-and-file member. He fled to England in 1905 and joined an anarchist group in Leeds. A year later Agurskii emigrated to Omaha, Nebraska, hardly a hotbed of Jewish revolutionary activity. In 1913 he moved to Chicago, where he worked as a tailor, and, fancying himself a Yiddish writer, attempted without much success to contribute to the Yiddish press in that city. Agurskii seems to have had some connection with the IWW in Chicago.[73] In May 1917 he left the United States with the second group of political emigrants bound for Russia. After an exhausting trip through Japan and Siberia, Agurskii arrived in Petrograd, where he worked for the International

[71] I. Dobkovskii, *Moshe Hess—als sotsialist, id un denker* (Moscow, 1918), esp. p. 8.

[72] In 1926 Dobkovskii testified in the Paris trial of Schwartzbard, the assassin of Petliura. On Dobkovskii, see Agurskii, *Di yidishe komisariatn,* p. 55n, and *Unzer veg,* Warsaw, no. 39–40 (48–49), October 8, 1919.

[73] See his article "Di idishe arbeter un zeire ershte kamfn kegn religie," *Der veker,* September 19, 1923.

Propaganda Bureau and then the *Evkom.* "Sam," as he was known in Russia, was the butt of many jokes and was generally thought of as a buffoon with ridiculous pretensions to being a first-rate propagandist and writer. He was said to have "dreamed a great deal about being editor of his own journal so that his friends and enemies should see how great he had become among the Bolsheviks." [74] In 1918 he chanced to travel on the same train as Mikhail Kalinin and became friendly with him. In later years he would often cite this—along with his meetings with Lenin and his friendship with John Reed—as proof of his revolutionary antecedents. In 1919 Agurskii was supposed to make a short return trip to the United States. Traveling by way of Poland, Murmansk, and Norway he was somehow left stranded in Holland, where he mailed a revolutionary manifesto, addressed to American workers, to an American acquaintance. "Because of the poor communications we had with the American Communists in 1919," the manifesto fell into the hands of the New York *Jewish Daily Forward,* whose editors destroyed it.[75] From that point on, Agurskii confined his activities to Soviet Russia.

[74] Charney, p. 250.

[75] Agurskii, *Der idisher arbeter,* p. 96. See also the Reisen *Leksikon,* I, 39ff., and Moishe Litvakov, "Der 'ekspert' Agurskii," *Emes,* December 9, 1928. Lazar Kling, one of the founders of the American Communist Party, claims that Agurskii was sent by Bukharin to the United States in 1921 in order to heal a split in the Party. Disguised as a sailor, Agurskii entered the country and sold a diamond for a substantial amount which he was to deliver to the Party and, especially, its Jewish bureaus. According to Mr. Kling, Agurskii gave most of the money to the American Communist *Labor* Party and only under pressure did he agree to deliver it to its original destination. Mr. Kling, a former yeshiva student and then a Bundist, held the fifth membership card issued by the American Communist Party. He returned to Russia in 1926–27 and worked with the Jewish Sections in Belorussia. Shortly after his return, he quit the Party. He has recounted various anecdotes which demonstrate the low regard in which Agurskii was held by his co-workers. At a meeting of Jewish

Some better qualified Jewish *intelligenty* began to offer their services to the *Evkom* as the economic situation in the country deteriorated. *Evkom* was perhaps the only Jewish institution at the time able to pay writers and teachers. The rations which the Commissariat provided literally saved the lives of some starving intelligentsia. *Paiok* (rations) won out over principle. "For a herring more or a herring less you could reorient yourself from one group to another. . . ." [76] When herrings became more plentiful, most of these writers, such as Daniel Charney and his brother Shmuel Niger, severed their connections with *Evkom* and either found other employment or emigrated.

Despite its small and inexperienced staff, the Jewish Commissariat did manage to undertake a whole range of activities, in addition to publishing. The *Evkom* tried to act as an office which would deal with problems of all Jews, whatever their social class or political affiliation. This was especially true of Commissar Dimanshtain. "Dimanshtain was at that time still 'good to the Jews' . . . he did not rush to implement the October Revolution on the Jewish street," and some believed that Lenin had ordered him "to go slow on the Jews" because they had been so persecuted under the tsars.[77]

---

women in Minsk, Agurskii praised the women's sections of the Communist Party and concluded triumphantly, "You see how much we Communist men have done for you—we even have an organ designed specially for women!" The veracity of such anecdotes is not so important as the testimony they bear to the low regard in which Agurskii was held by the more cultured *Evsektsiia* personnel.

[76] Charney, p. 297.

[77] *Ibid.*, p. 221. One of the Zionist leaders of the time, Ben-Zion Katz, later expressed the belief that Dimanshtain would not have persecuted the Zionists, nor closed the Hebrew schools, had not the ex-Bundists in the Jewish Sections pushed for such measures. Of course, it is difficult to maintain that Dimanshtain had complete autonomy in deciding policy on Jewish questions and that his personal inclinations could be equated with *Evsektsiia* policy. Katz

Evkom even shared quarters "with the representatives of the Jewish *haute bourgeoisie.*"[78] The publisher of the Hebrew newspaper *Haam* (The Nation)[79] was the wealthy Jewish merchant Persitz, whose wife, Shoshana, was a Zionist leader. *Evkom* was lodged in his villa, where two Zionist journals and a Zionist legal society also had their editorial offices. Mrs. Persitz supervised the kosher kitchen which was used both by the Zionists and the *Evkom.* On Passover, the employees of *Evkom* ate the traditional matzoh and could not bring any non-kosher food to their offices. "The household harmony between the floors was extraordinarily good; while the Zionists upstairs eagerly studied every word of the Balfour Declaration, the Jewish Communists downstairs pored over Bukharin's *ABC of Communism.*"[80]

Evkom at first tried to gain support for the Bolsheviks by appealing directly to the public. Its first two public meetings in Petrograd were total failures because they were attended mainly by Bundists who shouted down the speakers and disrupted the meetings and because the *Evkom* novices had not the foggiest notion of organization and tactics. Dobkovskii spoke at the second meeting. "He did not speak of the tasks of the Jewish Commissariat because neither he nor the rest of us really knew what the tasks of the Jewish Commissariat were to be."[81] *Evkom* then tried to organize its activities along staff lines and created a number

---

also asserts that Dimanshtain "was dubious about the anti-religious war of the *Evsektsiia.* He himself came to *Kol Nidrai* on *Yom Kippur.*" See Ben-Zion Katz, "Al Shisha Harugai Malkhut," *Hadoar* (New York), May 25, 1956, p. 536ff. Katz came into daily contact with Dimanshtain since both worked in the same building, the Persitz villa.

[78] Agurskii, *Der idisher arbeter,* p. 19.

[79] Ben-Zion Katz was editor.

[80] Charney, p. 213.

[81] "Ben Khaim," Di role fun di idishe arbeiter," *Funken,* April 15, 1920.

of departments to deal with specific problems. There were departments for culture and education, press, provinces, war refugees, combatting anti-Semitism, and economic work.[82] Much attention was devoted to resettling refugees and the homeless. They were even directed to local *kehillas* which would provide them with a kosher meal and lodging. But *Evkom* did not miss this opportunity to spread Bolshevik propaganda, and sent both propaganda and activists—the latter disguised as refugees—into the occupied territories.[83] *Evkom* also served as a clearing house for letters from abroad to Jews who had become homeless during the war, and aided in the reunification of families and their emigration.

A local Jewish Commissariat, ostensibly responsible to the Central Jewish Commissariat, had been set up in Moscow by a group of Left *Poalai Tsion*ists, members of a party which advocated cooperation with the Bolsheviks. When the Petrograd *Evkom* moved to Moscow, the *Poalai Tsion Evkom* was closed but the new *Evkom* retained the services of the *Poalai Tsion*ist, Zvi Friedland. He headed the department charged with combatting anti-Semitism. Together with Maxim Gorkii, Friedland saw to it that the press carried many articles condemning anti-Semitism. *Evkom* also exposed some anti-Semitic incidents in the Red Army and the Cheka.

Evkom then tried to encourage the establishment of agricultural cooperatives as one way of relieving hunger and unemployment among Jews. As in every other area, its first attempt ended in failure. In the summer of 1918 it or-

[82] S. Agurskii, ed., *Di oktiabr revolutsie in veisrusland* (Minsk, 1927), p. 304. The departments varied in number and nature in the various national commissariats. Some departments were common to all. The Polish Commissariat had departments for military affairs, refugees, culture and education, and the press (Pesikina, p. 55).

[83] Agurskii, *Di yidishe komisariatn,* p. 13.

ganized a commune near Moscow, made up almost entirely of Jewish anarchist immigrants from England. The crop was to be divided equally among employees of *Evkom*, but frost ruined it before it could be harvested.[84]

The department for the "provinces" was in charge of setting up local *Evkomy* and was headed by Julius Shimiliovich. Thirteen such local offices were established in 1918, but only two of them were in localities which had large Jewish populations.[85] The instructions carried by the *Evkom* emissaries stated that all those "who accept the platform of the Soviet government" could serve in the *Evkomy* and join Jewish workers' clubs. This included Communists, Left SRs, *Poalai Tsion*ists, Left Bundists and non-affiliated workers. Indeed, the *Evkom* in Perm consisted of two "Left Bundists, two members of the *Poalai Tsion*, one Left SR, and not a single Bolshevik."[86]

As far as *Evkom* was concerned, the *Poalai Tsion* were the most cooperative party. Although they had opposed the Bolshevik coup on the grounds that Russia was too economically backward to sustain a socialist revolution, the *Poalai Tsion*

> were careful not to obstruct them [the Bolsheviks] in their work, but rather helped them in order that the experiment would succeed. True, there had been no need to seize power through an armed uprising. But since this

[84] Charney, p. 222.

[85] These two were Vitebsk and Dubrovna. The other cities were Moscow, Petrograd, Kursk, Oriol, Perm, Tambov, Elets, Voronezh, Saratov, Nizhni-Novgorod, and Tula. See *Zamlbukh*, p. 82. The late Yankl Kantor, in an article published posthumously, lists local *Evkomy* in Oriol, Nizhni-Novgorod, Bonoradsk[?], Smolensk, Vitebsk, Orsha, Kursk, and Kostroma. He cites no sources, nor does he indicate the precise period he is discussing. Y. Kantor, "Der yidisher komisariat—zeine oifgabn un oiftuen," *Folksshtime* (Warsaw), November 6, 1967.

[86] *Di varheit*, June 21, 1918.

had already occurred we believed that it would be very bitter for all of us, should the Bolsheviks suffer a total collapse. . . . In truth it must be said that the government's attitude toward us then and throughout 1918 was a very good one. More than once the government proposed to us that we contribute personnel to the commissariats in the cities.[87]

This cooperation did not last long. Zvi Friedland doubled in brass as a member of the collegium of the Moscow *Evkom* and as a *Poalai Tsion* delegate to the national *kehilla* Congress held in May 1918. When he was asked at the congress why the *Poalai Tsion* worked in the *Evkomy,* he is reported to have answered that "he sits in the Jewish Commissariat in order to enable the *kehillas* to exist." He and the other *Poalai Tsion*ists were summarily expelled from the *Evkom.* When the attempted SR coup ended the phase of coalition government the *Evkomy* fell in line by removing all *Poalai Tsion*ists.[88]

Instructions to *Evkom* emissaries emphasized relief work, the struggle against anti-Semitism, and educational activities, a program which was hardly controversial. It was urged that the *kehillas* be "reorganized on the basis of the dictatorship of the workers and the poorest strata of the population."[89]

The organization of the local *Evkomy* was no simple task. For example, the Smolensk *Evkom,* organized by local *Poalai Tsion*ists, had "turned into a nationalist office which

[87] Nahum Nir-Rafalkes, *Ershte yorn* (Tel-Aviv, 1960), pp. 296, 337.

[88] "Ben Khaim," "Di role," *Funken,* May 20, 1920. The *Evkom* went very far indeed in its attempts to enlist the cooperation of Jewish groups. It negotiated with Jewish military organizations and individual Zionist and *kehilla* leaders. See M. Altshuler, pp. 7, 20, 21.

[89] The instructions are found in Sh. (S) Agurskii, "Di ershte arbet fun yidishn komisariat in veisrusland," in Agurskii, *Di oktiabr revolutsie,* pp. 293–94. On the role of *Narkomnats* emissaries, see Park, *Bolshevism in Turkestan.*

the Smolensk soviet had to close," and Agurskii failed to revive it "because of the lack of a Jewish laboring mass." [90] Agurskii tried his luck in Orsha, where he lectured on "The October Revolution and the Jewish Workers."

> A few dozen people came, mostly intelligentsia. There was no chairman. The Jewish comrade assigned by the party to organize the meeting failed to show up and I had to chair the meeting and introduce myself. . . . After the meeting only one person asked a question and when I had answered it the audience left and I remained all alone in the hall. . . .[91]

The obvious isolation of the *Evkom* "temporarily depressed" Agurskii who began to believe that all "Jewish work" was a waste of time. But he refused to give up and finally scored a succeess in Vitebsk where he revived a *Evkom* originally founded by two Left SRs. The local soviet appointed Agurskii Jewish Commissar. His inaugural speech drew large crowds "most of whom came to fight the speaker or completely obstruct the meeting." [92]

By dint of hard work Agurskii managed to build up the Vitebsk *Evkom* until it employed thirty officials and had its own building, despite great hostility on the part of the local Jews. When it tried to open schools, no teacher would serve in them and no parent enrolled his child. A series of meetings was then organized by the *Evkom* in an attempt to allay the fears of the parents "that *Evkom* wants to turn the children into *goyim* [Gentiles]" and where the

[90] Agurskii, *Di oktiabr revolutsie,* p. 294.

[91] *Ibid.*

[92] Agurskii cannot resist an opportunity to reaffirm the longevity of his own Bolshevik affiliation in contrast to the "late-comers." He says: "It is interesting to note that the biggest troublemakers and insulters . . . were the late Comrades Khrapovskii, Eidelman, and a few others who a while later entered the Communist Party and became workers in the Jewish Commissariat" (*ibid.,* p. 299).

children were won over with gifts. Toys for the children and brochures for the parents was the strategy of the *Evkom,* and it was partially successful.

The *Evkom* did try to serve the needs of the local Jewish population. When in 1918 there was a general government reorganization and the Vitebsk Commissariat for Social Welfare assumed responsibility for Jewish welfare institutions, non-kosher food was introduced to the old-age home, and the residents refused to eat it. The local Commissar for Social Welfare, a Jew and a former Zionist, would not allow kosher food to be prepared for the home, and some residents actually died of starvation. *Evkom* protested to no avail until July 1919, when Kalinin came to Vitebsk and upheld the *Evkom.* The commissar was tried and convicted for "using medieval methods and thereby destroying the confidence of the masses in the Communist principle of social welfare." [93]

When the Vitebsk soviet demanded a "contribution" from the local Jewish "bourgeoisie" and was refused, the latter were arrested. The soviet wanted them to work on Saturday to pay off their "debt," but *Evkom* protested against this method of extracting the contribution.[94]

Beginning in August 1918, when the Left SRs had been removed from the *Evkomy,* Jewish Sections of the party came into being. In some cases they were formed by the *Evkomy.* In 1918 there was hardly any distinction between the Central *Evkom* and the Central Bureau of the Jewish Sections of the Communist Party. Dimanshtain was in charge of both. When he appointed Daniel Charney literary

[93] *Ibid.,* p. 307.

[94] The Vitebsk *Evkom* was later attacked at the first conference of *Evkomy* and *Evsektsii* for trying to act as the national organ of all Jews, regardless of class. See Agurskii, *Di yidishe komisariatn,* p. 50. The *Evkomy* themselves frequently imposed forced "contributions" on the local population. See *Di yidishe komisariatn,* pp. 108–111, and *Emes,* December 25, 1918.

editor of the journal *Komunistishe velt,* he was not sure whether to pay Charney from the *Evkom* or *Evsektsiia* budget. "Both 'budgets' were in his pocket and he would pay me at one time from one budget, another time from the other."[95] Because of this blurring of jurisdictional lines, *Evkom* officials sometimes tried to form Jewish Sections rather than Commissariats. When Agurskii and Mandelsberg went to Mogilev in December 1918, they attended Bundist meetings and participated in all discussions, trying to win over the Bund membership. A section was eventually founded and Mandelsberg became its chairman.[96] Agurskii founded and headed a section in Vitebsk in September 1918, and by the middle of October it claimed more than eighty members.[97]

In Kostroma, too, the *Evkom*—composed of nine Bolsheviks and six *Poalai Tsion*ists—initiated the establishment of a Jewish section, and the same was done in Tula.[98] To make this association of *Evkom* and *Evsektsiia* even closer, Shimiliovich, in charge of *Evkom* activity in the provinces, was made both deputy commissar to Dimanshtain and a member of the Central Bureau of the Sections. Shimiliovich, no desk-bound bureaucrat, made frequent tours of the provinces himself. He helped found the soviet in Vilna while the city was still under German occupation, and was elected its secretary. He published the first Jewish Communist newspaper in Vilna and made secret preparations for the entry of the Red Army. But when the Germans left Vilna, the Polish Legions entered, surrounded the soviet, and tried to arrest its leaders. After trading shots with the Poles for two days, the soviet members ran out of ammunition. On January 2, 1919, the twenty-eight year old

[95] Charney, p. 254.
[96] Agurskii, *Der idisher arbeter,* pp. 54–56.
[97] Agurskii, *Di yidishe komisariatn,* pp. 74–76.
[98] *Ibid.,* pp. 120, 130.

Shimiliovich committed suicide to avoid capture by the Poles.[99]

Another *Evkom* official assigned to work in the provinces was the former Socialist-Zionist Zalman Khaikin. He joined the Bolsheviks in 1917 and was on the staff of *Di varheit.* Khaikin worked in Smolensk and single-handedly published a newspaper, *Der shtern.* He brought type, machinery, and paper from Petrograd.

> Meanwhile, a dispute arose between me and a responsible Party member who stubbornly insisted that there was no need for a Yiddish newspaper in Smolensk. . . . Five or six weeks passed. . . . I ran around in the Central committee, in *Narkomnats,* from Comrade Sverdlov to Comrade Radek, from him to Commissars Stalin and Pestkovskii. Finally . . . Comrade Y. M. Sverdlov called me, wished me good luck with a warm smile and sent me to Smolensk. . . . I must say that from the very first day Comrade Sverdlov supported the proposal to publish a Yiddish workers' newspaper in Smolensk or Vitebsk.[100]

Upon arriving in Smolensk the editor found that there were no Yiddish typesetters. "So once again I ran pell-mell to Moscow and Petrograd. The Zionist *Togblatt* closed down in Petrograd and six typesetters were unemployed. I put them in a separate car, stole a machine [typewriter] . . . a stereotype, and a press, talked the Petrograd *Sov-*

[99] See Agurskii, *Der idisher arbeter,* pp. 173–76, and Sh. Dimanshtain, "Der 10-ter yortzeit nokhn toit funm kh'Yulius Shimilovich," *Emes,* January 3, 1929. Shimiliovich was born in Riga, the son of a sexton. He joined a Bund youth group in 1905 but by 1917 was part of a local Military Revolutionary Committee and in January 1918 helped persuade the Twelfth Army to support the Bolsheviks. Dimanshtain then recruited him for *Evkom* work.

[100] Khaikin in *Der shtern,* April 1, 1919.

narkhoz into giving me enough Yiddish type—and I arrived in Smolensk." [101]

When the Germans ended their occupation of Minsk, Khaikin moved *Der shtern* there and was able to recruit a staff. While he was on a short trip to Vilna, the Poles captured the disputed city, and after three days of fighting Khaikin was felled by a Polish bullet on April 19, 1919. He was thirty years old.[102]

The First Conference of the Jewish Commissariats and the Jewish Sections

In August 1918 Dimanshtain decided to pull together the strands of *Evkom-Evsektsiia* work. He proposed to the Bolshevik Central Committee that a central conference of *Evkomy* and *Evsektsii* be called in order to raise morale, to acquaint the leadership with the local activists, and to coordinate activities. Since the line between *Evkom* and *Evsektsiia* was still imaginary, the conference was to be a joint one. Sverdlov opposed Dimanshtain's proposal, claiming that "the party physiognomy of the *Evsektsiia* is not clear enough" and that this form of national section within the party would not last very long.[103] But Dimanshtain got his way, and finally, on October 20, 1918, the conference of the Jewish Commissariats and Sections met in Moscow. Sixty-four delegates attended—thirty-three of them non-Bolsheviks. The thirty-one Bolsheviks were almost all

[101] *Ibid.* One of the reporters on *Shtern* described its first day of operation. "We get telegrams to translate. 'Comrade Hurwich, what is *obstrel* in Yiddish?' 'I don't know. Comrade Tsorfas, how do you say *obstrel?*' 'Ask Comrade Reisin.' 'Hey, what do you say?' In the end, *obstrel* remained *obstrel*. . . . It was with such 'powerhouses' that *Shtern* began its work." A. Volobrinskii, "Der ershter tog in 'Shtern,' " *Der veker,* March 4, 1923.

[102] Agurskii, *Der idisher arbeter,* pp. 177–79, and Charney, pp. 215–16.

[103] Dimanshtain, "10 yor vuks."

representatives of provincial commissariats, while twenty-eight of the thirty-three non-Bolsheviks were teachers in Yiddish schools. Shimiliovich and Dimanshtain spoke on political problems, Agurskii on the national question, and the Left Bundists Torchinskii and Orshanskii on cultural matters. Shimiliovich was "the heart of the conference and Dimanshtain was its head," the latter acting as mediator and final authority.[104] The non-Bolshevik delegates created an uproar by demanding that the supervision of education be removed from *Evkom* jurisdiction and transferred to the *kehillas*. When a member of the presidium spoke in Russian they demanded that all speeches be made in Yiddish. They also protested against the decision to deprive them of voting rights on all except educational questions. The Left Bundists, Tomsinskii, Orshanskii, and Katznelson, also attacked as "nationalistic" Dimanshtain's proposal that Jewish Communists should actively promote Jewish agricultural settlement. Dimanshtain was elected central Jewish Commissar, and a collegium of the Commissariat was elected. Within this mixed bag of delegates, a separate "Communist fraction" caucused to agree on a Party line.[105] Dimanshtain explained that the Communist Party is "incapable of conducting its work in different languages," and so Jewish Communist Sections were necessary. The Sections had a two-fold responsibility: to agitate among the Jewish workers

[104] Y. Katznelson, "Di ershte konferents fun di idsektsies," *Emes*, October 20, 1928.

[105] The members of the *Evkom* collegium were Shimiliovich, Agurskii, Rappaport, and Mandelsberg. The central bureau of the Communist fraction consisted of Dimanshtain, Shimiliovich, Agurskii, M. Alskii, Dashkovskii, Torchinskii, and Krinitskii (Bampi). Agurskii, *Di yidishe komisariatn*, p. 62. Krinitskii-Bampi joined the Bolsheviks in February 1918 in Minsk and became secretary of its underground committee during the German and Polish occupations. He quickly disappeared from "Jewish work," as did many of the early *Evkom* personnel. Krinitskii served for a time as secretary of the Belorussian Communist Party.

and to "carry out the dictatorship of the proletariat on the Jewish street," that is, to become the supreme political force in Russian Jewry. This second task implied that the *Evsektsiia* would also devise the means by which the dictatorship was to be implemented, that is, it would exercise autonomous judgment and discretion in matters of Jewish social and political life. The Sections would consist of new members entering the party—the old Jewish Bolsheviks remaining in the general party—and, therefore, special care should be taken that no "petit bourgeois nationalist tendencies" be infiltrated into the Sections. "We are not a special party, but a part of the Communist Party consisting of Jewish workers. Being internationalists, we do not set ourselves any special national tasks but purely class proletarian ones." [106] Despite this assertion there is reason to believe that most of the members of the "Communist fraction" saw the Sections as something more than a mere division of the Party apparatus. Some of them spoke of a "Jewish party," a "large Jewish party" or a "Jewish Communist party," and Dimanshtain himself said that the position of the *Evsektsiia* within the Party "does not have to be federative, but autonomous." [107] Local Sections had indeed acted as independent political organizations. They held their own meetings, accepted members directly into the Section, published their own periodicals and often failed to coordinate their activities with the local Communist Party committee or

[106] *Ibid.*, p. 22.

[107] M. Altshuler (p. 50-52) argues convincingly that the members of the fraction were really talking about some sort of autonomous party. He shows (p. 58, n. 24) that Agurskii, in *Di yidishe komisariatn* (p. 61) changed Dimanshtain's statement to read, ". . . [The *Evsektsiia*] should be neither autonomous nor federative." Altshuler reasons that in the latter half of 1918 the Party was prepared to tolerate such talk of autonomy because it was believed that a revolution in Germany was imminent and that autonomous Communist parties in the German-occupied areas would be useful for agitation and propaganda purposes. Such ideas were especially popular within the *Narkomnats,* of which Dimanshtain was a leading functionary.

even with the higher organs of the *Evkom* and *Evsektsiia.* Mandelsberg reported that in Oriol the local soviet refused to recognize the *Evkom.* Furthermore, in disregard of the Central *Evkom's* instructions, the Oriol *Evkom* refused to sponsor education in Hebrew.[108] The autonomist tendencies of the local Sections were simultaneously a cause and effect of the attitude of the local *partkomy* (party committees). The latter often refused to recognize the legitimacy of the Sections, claiming that they represented a nationalist deviation which could not be tolerated. "Our first task was convincing our own comrades that the Jewish Commissariat is not a nationalistic institution."[109] Jewish Party members, especially, despised the Sections and refused to work with them. "Most of the Jewish workers who entered the party used Russian as their language; some had a knowledge of Yiddish, but they had a negative attitude towards work in Yiddish and considered it superfluous, a nationalistic invention."[110] The Party also had difficulty with the Latvian Sections which purportedly tried to include all Latvian nationals within the Sections and resisted control by local *Partkomy.*[111]

An attempt at solving the problem of Sections-Party relations was made two months after the first central conference of the *Evsektsii.* In December the Central Bureau decided that Sections should exist on the *raion* or "sub-*raion*" levels and that their members should attend all party meetings but retain the right to call special Section meetings. Income from membership dues should be turned over to the general party treasury, and the Sections would receive a budget proportionate to their memberships. The Sections were to be allowed to recruit members, but they had to be approved by the *partkom* as a whole and had to become

[108] Agurskii, *Di yidishe komisariatn,* p. 40.
[109] *Ibid.,* p. 39.
[110] M. Kiper, *Tsen yor oktiabr* (Kiev, 1927), p. 21.
[111] Sharapov, p. 74.

members of the *partkom.* The Sections were to recruit only people unfamiliar with the local language. This was a change from Dimanshtain's statement at the First Conference that new members of the Party would enter the Sections. *Guberniia* Sections were to hold periodic conferences and a general party congress of national Sections was to be held twice a year.[112] The new arrangement meant that Sections would have both vertical and horizontal responsibilities and affiliations. They were attached to local *partkomy* but also reported to higher levels in a distinct Section hierarchy. This arrangement was hardly likely to improve the relations of the Sections with the local *partkomy* and the conflicts built into this structure soon flared up.[113]

While the Jewish Sections were struggling to define themselves, to recruit new personnel and to establish their "dictatorship on the Jewish street," the Jewish socialist parties were battling to maintain their unity and independence in the face of internal and external difficulties. Their eventual failure to overcome these—admittedly, in the face of overwhelming odds—redounded to the benefit of the Jewish Sections, which were then able to establish a political monopoly among the Jewish people in Soviet Russia. The Sections were soon to gather in fresh talent, including some of the outstanding leaders of the Jewish socialist parties.

[112] Agurskii, *Di yidishe komisariatn,* pp. 134–35. The last two provisions were never fully implemented.

[113] Altshuler (pp. 54–55) suggests that this structure was evolved because the Party was liquidating the autonomous nationality sections in the areas liberated from German rule and was transforming them into territorial Communist parties (of Belorussia, Lithuania, and Latvia). Since there was no territory with a Jewish majority, no Jewish territorial party was formed. "But the Jewish Communist organization wanted to continue its existence and so tried to accommodate itself, as far as possible, to the territorial forms which were evolving at the time and which were becoming the only legitimate form of Communist organization."

IV

Disappearing Alternatives: The End of the Jewish Socialist Parties

But the Pole fired at me, kind sir, because he was the Counterrevolution. And now you're firing because you're the Revolution. But surely, Revolution means joy, and having orphans in the house does not contribute to joy. A good person does good deeds and the Revolution is a good deed of good people. But good people don't kill. Then Revolution is made by wicked people. But the Poles are wicked people too. Who, then, will explain to Gedali where Revolution is and where Counterrevolution is?

Isaac Babel, "Gedali"

If the victory of the Bolsheviks was facilitated by the fragmentation and disunity of the Whites and the anti-Bolshevik parties, the expansion and strengthening of the Jewish Sections was even more directly the result of the disintegration of its political rivals by internal and external forces. In a larger sense, the destruction of the traditional structures of political authority within the Jewish community, together with the retention of some of the familiar political leaders in positions of new authority, made easier the social and political mobilization of the Russian Jewish population. The unity of the Bund was severely tested by the difficult political questions it had to answer, by the dispersal of its membership, and by the arrival in the party of new masses of workers with no deep loyalties to it. The majority of those who made up the membership in 1917 had not experienced the trauma of 1903—the parting of the ways of the Bund and the RSDLP. Nor had they been in the Bund from 1906 to 1917 when it followed the Menshevik line, by and large, in general political questions. To many of the new proletarian elements, the conservatism of the intelligentsia leadership after November 1917 was a stubbornly dogmatic allegiance to abstract and outmoded principles. The proletariat had indeed seized power and there seemed to be no sense in giving it up just because things had not been envisioned in precisely this way. It is not at all surprising, therefore, that in a few localities there were subterranean pro-Bolshevik tendencies within Bund organizations. According to Soviet sources, in late November 1917 the Bobruisk Bund organization split into Menshevik and Bolshevik factions, the latter enrolling fifty members and calling itself "Bund-Bolsheviks."[1] In the Ekaterinburg

[1] *Sovetskaia pravda* (Minsk), December 12, 1917, quoted in Kirzh-

organization, formed only after the downfall of the tsarist government, there appeared a group of Bolshevik sympathizers, but they failed to split the organization because of the lack of intelligentsia leadership and the staunch opposition of old-time Bundists.[2] Apparently, no pro-Bolshevik group attempted to leave the Bund entirely. When a split took place in the Perm Bund, the pro-Bolshevik group declared that "We Perm Jewish workers unite under the banner of the Bund [left]. . . . We are sure that the Bund will lead us to our final goal—to socialism." [3] The Bobruisk, Ekaterinburg, and Perm factions were probably the only organized pro-Bolshevik groups within the Bund, though in many Bund organizations, pro-Bolshevik stirrings were felt. But by July 1918 the Bund confidently asserted that "the influence of Bolshevism on some elements of the Jewish working masses is disappearing lately" and, citing the Iaroslavl organization as typical, claimed that Bolshevism had lost its appeal to Jewish workers.[4]

Within the Menshevik party, as within the Bund, there were differences of opinion on the correct attitude toward Bolshevism. In 1918 there emerged a right wing, led by

---

nitz and Rafes, eds., *Der idisher arbeter,* p. 163. This organization disappeared during the German occupation in 1918, but a new group of Bundist-Communists was organized when the Red Army took Belorussia in 1919. Belorussian cities with large Jewish concentrations such as Minsk, Gomel, Slutsk, and Mogilev had either very weak Bolshevik organizations or none at all, even after the Bolshevik seizure of power. In the Mogilev city duma, for example, of 64 deputies only one was a Bolshevik—and this duma was elected two days after the Bolshevik coup. Where Bolshevik groups did exist, their strength lay with the soldiers, arsenal workers, and metal workers, among whom Jews were under-represented. See *V bor'be za obtiabr' v Belorussii i na zapadnom fronte* (Minsk, 1957).

[2] Agurskii, *Di yidishe komisariatn,* pp. 100–03. See also *Emes,* October 1 and 3, 1918.

[3] Agurskii, *Di yidishe komisariatn,* pp. 104–05.

[4] *Evreiiskii rabochii,* July 12, 1918, p. 13.

Mark Liber, which advocated Menshevik participation in a "national struggle" against the Bolsheviks, and a left wing which believed that a world revolution along Bolshevik lines was in the offing and which therefore sought a "bridge to the Bolsheviks." [5]

In the spring of 1918 the Central Committee of the Bund decided, in line with Abramovich's policy and against Liber's, that Bundists could hold posts in soviets on condition that they maintain their political independence.[6] Bund conferences held in Moscow and Minsk in December 1918 declared their opposition to the "Bolshevik dictatorship" and called for free local elections, freedom of speech and the press, the supremacy of the soviets, the cessation of terror, and the proclamation of a democratic constitution. The conferences did, however, acknowledge that if the Bolshevik regime were defeated by the Entente powers, "international reaction" would be the gainer.[7] The Minsk conference stated specifically that "the all-Russian worker-and-peasant Soviet regime is the only center capable of conducting the struggle for the socialism of the all-Russian proletariat in connection with the world [proletariat]." [8] Yankel Levin, a young carpenter who was one of the Bund's most effective organizers, warned that since the bourgeoisie had adopted "democracy" as its slogan, as a cover for a bourgeois dictatorship, the Bund must counter by moving closer to the idea of a proletarian dictatorship. The Bund still would be clearly distinguishable from the Bolsheviks because of its emphasis on the power of the workers' soviets and on genuine labor democracy.[9]

[5] Getzler, *Martov,* p. 184.

[6] *Geshikhte fun Bund,* III, 207.

[7] *Folkstseitung,* February 19, 1919. The Moscow conference also reaffirmed the principle of national-cultural autonomy, and called the Jewish Commissariats "incapable of creative work."

[8] *Emes,* December 31, 1918, quoted in *Zamlbukh,* pp. 117–18.

[9] *Der veker,* December 22, 1918.

The ambivalence of the Bund was increased by the outbreak of what appeared to be a proletarian revolution in Germany in November 1918. Germany had always been the crucial country for European socialists because it was considered most technologically advanced and it had the largest socialist party in Europe. A revolution in Germany would be the herald of world revolution. When, in November 1918, German sailors revolted in Kiel and uprisings took place in Munich and Berlin, it seemed that the fires of revolution were spreading and that it would only be a matter of time before the conflagration would engulf all of Europe. Of course, "The German revolution was . . . a 'collapse' rather than a revolution. . . . The old authority broke down and the Social Democratic leaders were the 'official liquidators.'"[10] But this "revolution" made an immediate and profound impression on the Bundist intelligentsia who were compelled to reexamine their orthodox belief that the bourgeois revolution had not yet been completed and that a Russian proletarian revolution was a premature freak of history. Raphael Abramovich noted that "the German revolution . . . created new tendencies in the ranks of the Bundists. The 'miracle' of the German revolution stimulated pronounced Communist tendencies among the Jewish masses."[11] The same tendencies were observed among the Mensheviks. Even Martov called revolutionary changes in Germany and Austria the "beginning of the socialist revolution in the West" which might "straighen out" the Bolshevik revolution.[12] In late 1918 Martov complained of Menshevik defections to the Bolsheviks and of "waverers" who were thinking of forming new

[10] Koppel S. Pinson, *Modern Germany: Its History and Civilization* (New York, 1954), pp. 350–51.

[11] Abramovich, *In tsvai revolutsies*, p. 310.

[12] Getzler, pp. 184–85.

groups.[13] A Menshevik conference in December 1918 resolved to support the German revolution "as the spearhead of the world socialist revolution." At this conference Dan called on the Mensheviks to abandon the idea of a constituent assembly and urged increased participation in the soviets which would be freely elected. This "struggle on the basis of Soviet legality" was to be the cornerstone of Menshevik policy in the next few years.[14]

It was in the Ukraine that the events in Germany made the strongest impression. The Ukrainian Bund was beset by countless excruciatingly difficult policy decisions, and it looked to the German revolution for the solution to some of its vexing problems. A new platform was adopted by the provisional bureau of the Main Committee of the Ukrainian Bund. It declared that the German revolution "places on the agenda of the entire world proletariat the question of the immediate liquidation of the foundation of the present social order and the immediate shift to socialist construction. . . . The struggle which has begun sets for the entire world proletariat the task of taking over government power." [15] But the Bund was not prepared to endorse the Bolshevik seizure of power since the revolution would "be victorious only when all its forces are united on an international scale." [16] The new platform attacked the "anarcho-Blanquist tendencies" in Russia and called for a military alliance with the Bolsheviks against the Whites while "resolutely opposing all attempts to fuse with the Communists who only yesterday were in the Bund." The new platform condemned the suppression of socialist parties, "The dicta-

[13] Letter to A. N. Shtein, quoted by David Dallin, "Men'shevizm v period sovetskoi vlasti," Inter-University Project on the History of the Menshevik Movement, pp. 95–97.

[14] *Ibid.*, pp. 144–46.

[15] *Neie tseit*, January 12 and 14, 1919.

[16] *Ibid.*

torship of the Communist Party over the Soviets," the Red Terror, ruination of the economy by "anarchic" factory committees, and the "cosmopolitan ignoring of the peculiarities of economic, cultural, and national development of different lands and areas." The platform called for national-cultural autonomy in the Ukraine, the convening of a provisional Jewish national assembly and a Jewish workers' congress.[17]

If the German revolution forced a reorientation of the Ukrainian Bund, albeit into a highly ambiguous new stance, it was by no means the sole or even crucial determinant of the Ukrainian Bund's behavior. The Bund was a key actor in the complex drama of Ukrainian politics and the course it chose in 1918 and 1919 can be understood only in the chaotic context of Ukrainian as well as Jewish politics.

The Ukrainian Central Rada, in which the Jewish socialist parties were represented, had granted the Jews broad national, political, and cultural autonomy in 1917.[18] The Rada appointed three-vice-secretaries for Russian, Jewish, and Polish affairs. The Jewish representatives voted for the Third Universal which proclaimed the Ukrainian People's Republic on November 20, 1917, but they did so reluctantly, for they feared that this would weaken the revolutionary front.[19] On January 9, 1918, the Rada guaranteed national-personal autonomy to all of the nationalities within the Ukrainian People's Republic and simultaneously elevated the vice-secretaries to ministers. But when the Fourth Universal, issued on January 22, declared complete Ukrainian independence from Russia, the Bund and the Menshe-

[17] *Ibid.*

[18] "This was the first time in the history of the Jews in any European state that such far-reaching national-political and cultural autonomy, based on a legal foundation, had been attained." Heller, *Di Lage der Juden*, pp. 17–18.

[19] See Jurij Borys, *The Russian Communist Party and the Sovietization of the Ukraine* (Stockholm, 1960), p. 115.

viks voted against it, while the *Poalai Tsion,* the *Farainigte,* and Jewish parties on the right abstained.[20]

The bulk of the Jewish population remained unenthusiastic about Ukrainian independence. There was a widespread suspicion that any Ukrainian government would soon be infiltrated and captured by anti-Semitic elements. Furthermore, an independent Ukraine would break up the Jewish community of the old Russian empire. The fifteen-thousand-member Ukrainian Bund [21] tried to use the Rada for its own purposes, especially as a bludgeon against Bolshevism. The Internationalist Bundists were not overly enthused about Ukrainian independence, and in November 1917 the Bund declared itself against "any separatism expressed in the striving toward an autonomous Ukrainian republic." [22] However, the Defensist Moishe Rafes served the Rada as assistant secretary of labor, and the Defensist Zolotariov was general comptroller of its General Secretariat.[23] The Bund straddled the issue of Ukrainian independence by advocating a federated Russia. This policy, when combined with vociferous hostility to the Bolsheviks, insured that the Bund would be distrusted by Ukrainian autonomists, on the one hand, and by the Bolsheviks, on the other. When Russia became Bolshevik, the Bund was forced to face the problem squarely, and it was only when the Bund split that its factions could take definitive stands. Despite the granting of national-personal autonomy by the Rada, the Bund feared that in an independent Ukraine the Jewish nation would be subject to severe disabilities, if not

[20] *Ibid.,* pp. 119–20. On the shifting policies of the Jewish parties see Elias Tsherikover, *Di ukrainer pogromen in yor 1919* (New York, 1965), pp. 39–47.

[21] This is the figure given in *Der veker,* September 29, 1917. A figure of sixteen thousand is cited in *Arbeter shtime,* August 20, 1917.

[22] *Folkstseitung,* November 29, 1917, quoted in *Zamlbukh,* p. 93.

[23] V. Shulman, "Der bund in rusland," pp. 84–85.

outright persecution.[24] The Bund demanded national-cultural autonomy and national minority rights, but was unwilling to support consistently the national aims of other nationalities. At the Eighth Congress of the Bund in December 1917 Abramovich castigated federalism as petit bourgeois and disruptive of the unity of the revolutionary forces. It is hardly surprising, therefore, that Ukrainian politicians suspected the Jewish socialists of being agents of Russification. Jewish hesitancy in embracing Ukrainian nationalism contributed to the outbreak of anti-Semitic pogroms among the Ukrainian populace. Jewish suspicion of the Ukrainians and Ukrainian distrust of the Jews thus reinforced each other in a vicious and tragic cycle.

The outbreak of pogroms dampened any enthusiasm some of the Jewish parties might have had for Ukrainian independence. In December 1917 the Rada's Vice-Secretary for Jewish Affairs, Moishe Zilberfarb, urged the members of the Central Rada to take effective measures against the pogroms,[25] and Bundist representatives tried to have resolutions passed by the Rada condemning pogroms. But the Rada was afraid of antagonizing its local organs, which it

[24] As early as June 1917 David Zaslavskii warned that the Ukrainian government would carry out a policy of Ukrainization which would affect the Jews adversely, both economically and socially. *Arbeter shtime,* June 25, 1917, quoted in *Zamlbukh,* p. 83.

[25] *Folkstseitung,* December 15, 1917, quoted in *Zamlbukh,* p. 96. In October 1917 Jewish soldiers in Kiev demanded the right to organize a Jewish self-defense against pogroms. The Ukrainian nationalist leader, Petliura, agreed to this in principle, but the Jewish socialist parties and the *Folkspartai* were unenthusiastic, fearing that this would arouse anti-Semitic feelings. Nevertheless, such groups were formed on the initiative of Jewish soldiers. The most powerful group was organized in Odessa where there were 400 to 600 regulars who were well armed. This organization remained intact for over two years and saved the Jews of Odessa from pogroms. See I. B. Shekhtman, "Evreiskaia obshchestvennost' na Ukraine (1917–1919 gg.)," in Ia. G. Frumkin, G. Ia. Aronson, and A. A. Goldenveizer, eds., *Kniga o Russkom evreistve* (New York, 1968), pp. 31–32.

could not effectively control anyway, and it did not want to risk losing mass support by condemning anti-Jewish outbreaks. Anti-Semitism manifested itself even in the central government. In January 1918 it was proposed to the Rada that all those who had settled in Kiev during the previous two years—in effect, Jewish war refugees—be expelled.[26]

The Bund remained in the Central Rada when German troops retook Kiev from the Bolsheviks at the end of February 1918. Anti-Semitism increased greatly during the months of German occupation and the Skoropadskii regime. "The peasant had to surrender his produce, and was given a low fixed price, while manufactured articles were practically unobtainable. The villagers were incensed by the fact that the Jews had an abundance of factory products which they were keeping for themselves. Nor did the presence of a common enemy in the shape of the foreigners succeed in uniting the Ukrainian radicals with the Jewish socialists."[27] The oppression of the Skoropadskii regime radicalized some elements of the Jewish proletariat and pro-Bolshevik tendencies appeared in Bund organizations in April and May 1918. But the Bund's leaders refused to acknowledge that the time had come for a socialist revolution. "Having turned to the left, the Bund still remained in the anti-Bolshevik camp."[28] The fall of the Skoropadskii regime and the withdrawal of German troops left the Ukraine in the hands of the Directory in Kiev, headed by Simon Petliura, and a Bolshevik government in Kharkov. As time went on, it became clear that Jews could not support the Petliura regime. Beginning in March of 1919, soldiers of the regime carried out the most violent anti-Jewish excesses in Eastern Europe since 1648. "The pogroms took on a mass character, the character of a great and

[26] Rafes, *Dva goda revoliutsii,* quoted in *Zamlbukh,* p. 97.

[27] Yarmolinsky, *The Jews,* p. 53.

[28] Rafes, *Dva goda revoliutsii,* p. 95.

lasting national misfortune."[29] It was the storm of pogroms more than anything else which forced the Jews to look to the Bolsheviks, and especially the Red Army, as their only saviors. "As a rule, the appearance of a Soviet detachment meant comparative safety for the Jewish population. . . . On one occasion the entire Jewish population of a town, some four thousand persons in all, trooped after a retiring Bolshevik regiment."[30] But Bolshevik rule also exacerbated anti-Semitism. "Many peasants who had their grain requisitioned by young Bolshevik commissars of Jewish descent hastily concluded that the movement was a Jewish phenomenon. This tragic notion was seemingly corroborated by the fact that many of the poorer Jewish workers and craftsmen . . . supported the Bolsheviks in the hope of obtaining some measure of economic justice."[31] Thirty major pogroms occurred in the Ukraine in 1918; by the end of 1919, after the White armies of Denikin had done their bloody work, 685 more "major attacks" on Jews had been carried out, in addition to 249 "minor attacks."[32]

The White armies of Denikin and Wrangel were supported by many Russian clergymen. They felt it their duty to fight a holy war against the godless Jews who had usurped power in Holy Mother Russia. "Anti-Semitic agitation was not a rarity among the clergy under White jurisdiction."[33] A message written by Dean Vostorgov for obligatory reading by the clergy to their parishioners provided

[29] E. Tsherikover, *Antisemitizm un pogromen in ukraine 1917–1918* (Berlin, 1923), p. 1.

[30] E. Heifetz, *The Slaughter of the Jews in the Ukraine in 1919* (New York, 1921), p. 112.

[31] John S. Reshetar, Jr., *The Ukrainian Revolution* (Princeton, 1952), p. 253.

[32] Baron, *The Russian Jew under Tsars and Soviets*, p. 220.

[33] John Shelton Curtiss, *The Russian Church and the Soviet State 1917–1950* (Boston, 1953), pp. 100–01.

this pithy formula for the salvation of Russia: "Bless yourselves, beat the Jews, overthrow the People's Commissars." [34]

Caught between the armies of Denikin,[35] the Bolsheviks, and the Directory, the Jews came to fear the latter most of all. Though there has been considerable debate as to whether Petliura was personally anti-Semitic or not, the fact remains that he was at least unable to control his armies and is reported to have said, "It is a pity that pogroms take place but they uphold discipline in the army." [36] The reputation of the Directory army can be seen from the reply given by a character in a Russian novel to the question as to who occupied the town on that day: "Let's wait a bit and see; if they start pillaging the Jews, we shall know it's Petliura's men." [37] Rafes reports that one member of the Directory told another: "Just wait. We have not yet used our trump card. Against anti-Semitism, no Bolshevism will be able to stand." [38]

It has been calculated that of the 1,236 pogroms in the Ukraine in 1918–19, 493 were committed by elements of the Ukrainian nationalist military.[39] Their methods were as brutal, if not quite as efficient, as those the Nazis were to employ on the same blood-soaked soil some twenty years later. Men were buried up to their necks and were then killed by the hooves of horses driven over them. Children

[34] *Ibid.*, p. 69.

[35] On the pogroms of Denikin's forces, see William Henry Chamberlin, *The Russian Revolution*, II (New York, 1935), 219.

[36] A. Revutski, *In di shvere teg oif ukraine* (Berlin, 1924), p. 290. For conflicting views of Petliura's attitude and behavior toward Jews, see Taras Hunczak, "A Reappraisal of Symon Petliura and Ukrainian-Jewish Relations, 1917–1921"; and Zosa Szajkowski, " 'A Reappraisal,' etc.: A Rebuttal," *Jewish Social Studies*, XXXI, no. 3 (July 1969).

[37] Nikolai Ostrovskii, *The Making of a Hero*, tr. Alec Brown (New York, 1937), p. 77, quoted in Baron, p. 219.

[38] Rafes, *Dva goda revoliutsii*, p. 132.

[39] N. Gergel, "Di pogromen in Ukraine in di yorn 1918–21," in Lestschinsky, ed., *Shriftn far ekonomik un statistik*, p. 110.

were smashed against walls and their parents butchered savagely. Thousands of women were raped and hundreds were left insane as a result of their experiences. Forced "tributes" and the burning of entire hamlets were the order of the day. The extent of the pogroms and the destruction wrought by them is difficult to determine, but it may be safely asserted that in the years 1917–1921 more than 2,000 pogroms took place, and half a million Jews were left homeless as a result of the burning of twenty-eight percent of all Jewish homes and the abandonment of others. The direct loss of Jewish life easily exceeded 30,000, and together with those who died from wounds or as a result of illnesses contracted during the pogroms the number of Jewish dead probably reached 150,000, or ten percent of the Jewish population.[40]

The effects of the pogroms were felt for many years. Jewish economic life did not recover until the 1930's and a general pall continued to hang over the Ukrainian Jewish community throughout the 1920's.[41] The terrible consequences of the pogroms for Jewish youth could be observed in the 1920's when thousands of homeless children wandered the streets, begging or stealing. "Children without a home.

[40] These figures are based on Baron, pp. 220–21, and Lestschinsky, *Dos sovetishe idntum,* p. 70. There is a substantial literature on the pogroms. Among the most important works are A. D. Rosental, *Megillat HaTebakh* (3 vols., Jerusalem, 1927–1931); Elias Heifetz, *The Slaughter of the Jews in the Ukraine in 1919;* and Elias Tsherikover, *Antisemitizm un pogromen in ukraine 1917–1918,* and *Di ukrainer pogromen in yor 1919.* An abbreviated Hebrew version of the earlier Tsherikover work is found in his *Yehudim BeIttot Mahpekha* (Tel Aviv, 1957), p. 421–558. A balanced overview is found in Reshetar, pp. 253–56.

[41] On the long-term effects of the pogroms in Odessa, a city which was relatively free of such occurrences and where a six-hundred-man Jewish self-defense organization existed, see B. Rubshtain, "Di oisshtarbung fun di rusishe idn," *Di tsukunft,* XXX, no. 3 (March 1922). On Jewish self-defense units, see several articles in *HeAvar,* vol. 17 (1970).

You see them all over in the cities and towns, in the villages, in the railroad stations, hungry, sick, naked, shoeless. . . . They wander about first with a bewildered, forlorn expression, then with a hand stretched forth for a donation, and finally in a camp of little criminals . . . embittered, degenerate. . . . In Kiev there are about five thousand such children and in Kharkov, three thousand." [42] Even those with homes were not much better off. An official of the American Relief Administration visited a town in the Ukraine in 1922 which had a population of about 15,000, "one-third destitute, among them 2,500 children; 25 to 30 deaths daily, almost half being children. . . . We entered another house where there were two orphans. The older, a boy about fourteen, had a bunch of grass neatly piled on the table with a few grains of salt alongside and was preparing to cook this, his only food. . . . Families were known as cat, dog, or horse families, the title indicating the character of their food." [43]

The pogroms were a major factor in the decline of the Jewish population of the Ukraine in the first quarter of the twentieth century. While the overall population of the area increased by 35.7 percent between 1897 and 1926, the Jewish population declined by 4.7 percent, and the Jewish share of the total population dropped from 8 to 5.6 percent.[44]

[42] *Emes,* February 2, 1922, quoted in Lestschinsky, *Dos sovetishe idntum,* pp. 320–21. Homeless, wandering children called *bezprizorniki,* were a general problem in Russia of the 1920's. Charney (p. 316) describes how they would grab passers-by in Moscow and beg or rob. The Cheka seemed to be powerless against them.

[43] Letter of William R. Grove to Col. William N. Haskell, May 1, 1922, in Archive of Dr. Joseph Rosen, Box 70, "Agro 18," in the YIVO Archives.

[44] Y. Kantor, *Di yidishe bafelkerung in ukraine* (Kharkov, 1929), pp. 16–20. In the 1897–1926 period the Ukrainian population increased by 43 percent, the Russian by 11.2 percent, and the Polish by 27 percent. In 1897 there were 1,644,488 Jews in the Ukraine, while in 1926 there were 1,565,194. Kantor's figures take territorial changes in the Ukraine into account.

Although Petliura's forces were most closely identified with the pogroms, numerous attacks were carried out by various bandit groups, the Polish military, the forces of Atamans Hryhoryiv and Bulak-Balakhovich, and even by the Red Army.[45] Serious Red Army pogroms took place in Glukhov and in Novgorod-Seversk in 1918, but the Red Army command failed to take any punitive action.[46] However, the Red Army pogroms were "mild" compared to the others. While the Red Army killed 725 Jews in 106 pogroms, Hryhoryiv's bands killed 3,471 in 52 pogroms. Petliura's forces were the most murderous, accounting for 16,706 deaths. The year 1920 saw a series of Red Army pogroms. They were carried out almost exclusively by Semën Budënny's First Cavalry, especially the Tarashchan division and the Bohun regiment. Most of the soldiers in these regiments had previously served under Denikin. In Kremenchug, for example, Jews recognized them as having pogromized the city a year before while fighting under Denikin's flag.[47] The Red Army command vigorously condemned these pogroms and sent a regiment composed only of Communist party members to disarm the Bohun regiment.[48] In October 1920 Kamenev, Kalinin, and Preo-

[45] According to Gergel, "bandits" conducted 207 pogroms, Hryhoryiv's troops 52, the Poles 32, and Balakhovich's bands 9.

[46] It appears that these pogroms were perpetrated by bandit elements which had entered the Red Army. See Tsherikover, *Antisemitizm,* pp. 146–47. Tsherikover gives the most comprehensive description of pogroms initiated by the Red Army in 1917–18; see pp. 140–49. See also his *Di ukrainer pogromen,* pp. 270–84.

[47] See Yaakov Lestschinsky, "Tsu der frage vegn di pogromen fun der roiter armai in Ukraine," *Di tsukunft,* XXIX, no. 10 (October 1921).

[48] For an eyewitness description of the sixteen-day Red Army pogrom in Liubar, see Menakhem Ribalow, "Der shreklikher emes fun ukraine," *Di tsukunft,* XXIX, no. 7 (July 1921). Agurskii reported hearing "horrible stories about wild anti-Semitism in the Red Army" on the southern front. "A reize oifn 'oktiabr revolutsie' tsug," *Di komunistishe velt,* no. 5 (August 1919).

brazhenskii attended a military parade in the Ukraine and Kalinin made a speech condemning anti-Jewish actions on the part of the Red Army and demanding that the Red Army fight a class war, not a national one.[49] In the same month three regiments of the Red Army were dismissed for "criminal acts" and pogroms.

The official attitude of the Red Army and the relative mildness of Red Army pogroms allowed the Jews to regard that army as their protector. Obviously, this had important political implications, although many Jews mentally divorced the Red Army from the Communist Party and government. Jewish youths volunteered for service in the Red Army out of a desire to avenge the crimes committed against their people. When the Bolsheviks drove Petliura's forces from a Ukrainian town, they began to execute the wounded left behind by the retreating Directory army.

> A Jewish soldier from Berdichev ran amok. He would wipe his bayonet in the grass to remove the blood and with every head he cut off he screamed, "This is my payment for my murdered sister, this is my retribution for my murdered mother!" The Jewish crowd . . . held its breath and kept silent.[50]

A special recruitment section of the Red Army, *Evreiskaia voennaia sektsiia* (*Evvoensek*), was set up to enlist Jewish youth.[51] The Red Army welcomed Jewish volunteers but

[49] *Krasnyi kavalerist,* October 19, 1920, quoted in E. Tsherikover, "Di ratnmakht un yidishe pogromen," *In der tkufe fun revolutsie,* ed. Tsherikover, pp. 377–80. On anti-Semitism in the Red Army and among Communists, see Chamberlin, p. 143. "In the Ukrainian town of Elizavetgrad, after the Petliurists had been driven out and a Soviet regime had been established, seventeen speakers in the local soviet debated for four and a half hours whether or not to 'beat the Jews,' finally deciding in the negative" (p. 364).

[50] L. Shapiro, *Bakalakhat,* p. 62.

[51] See *Di roite armai,* no. 1, supplement to *Komunistishe fon,* June, 1919. *Evvoensek* existed in at least thirteen cities and towns in the

also recognized that "many enter the Red Army partially out of hatred for the White pogromists" and called for intense agitation and propaganda among the Jewish volunteers.[52] In a letter written during the Civil War, Trotsky noted that Jews were highly urbanized and that "in this urban population the intelligentsia-petit-bourgeois elements in Jewry, as well as the Jewish workers (along with the Russian), were pushed to the road of revolution by the unbearable living conditions created by the tsarist regime. Among the *arrivé* Communists there are many whose Communism stems not from a social base, from a class source, but from a national one. It is clear that these are not the best Communists and the Soviet regime does not base itself upon them."[53] This analysis of Jewish motivations was correct; even those who opposed Bolshevism on ideological or political grounds supported the Red Army.

> In the Klinovka station I was surprised to see a Red Army company composed entirely of Jews and even including some wearing earlocks. These were yeshiva students from Proskurov who joined the Red Army after Petliura's riots in order to take revenge . . . and I, the Zionist opponent of Communism, I who saw it as a fatal danger to Judaism—I was filled with pride seeing those Jewish fellows. . . .[54]

Ukraine. In the small town of Smilè 200 Jews were enlisted in two days. Odessa and Cherkassy enlisted 1,000 each. *Komunistishe fon,* June 18, 1919.

[52] *Zhizn' natsional'nostei,* February 29, 1920. See also *Roite armai,* July 2, 1919.

[53] Quoted in *Der veker,* June 21, 1923.

[54] L. Shapiro, *Bakalakhat,* p. 160. About 1,500 Jews were murdered in Proskurov. This pogrom changed the attitude of many Jews and Jewish parties toward the Ukrainian national movement (Tsherikover, *Di ukrainer pogromen,* pp. 158–59). Hryhoryiv's pogroms also drove many Jews into the Red Army. Tsherikover quotes an eyewitness report: "Jewish youth leave the *shtetls* and run to Kiev for one

Among the Jewish proletariat, however, there was a closer identification of the Red Army with Bolshevism, and a greater willingness to accept both. When the Bolsheviks had taken Kiev in February 1918, the Jewish socialist leaders condemned them as "an occupation army which has driven out all of democracy . . . with their 'socialist' artillery the Bolsheviks carried out Shulgin's work—they bombed out all the national achievements of the revolution in the Ukraine." [55] The Kiev Bund voted 762–11, with seven abstentions, not to recognize the Bolshevik government.[56] Jewish socialists had even gone so far as to deny that the

purpose—to enter into the Red Army. They are not Bolsheviks at all . . . but they go to the Red Army because there one can die 'rifle in hand.' And when they pass by a Soviet military post the Red Army men call out after them, 'You accursed Jews, you're going to speculate'" (p. 327). There was considerable debate both within the Jewish parties and the Communist Party about the advisability of organizing separate Jewish units in the Red Army. The Jewish parties in Belorussia generally favored the creation of such units, while those in the Ukraine, with the exception of the *Poalai Tsion,* opposed it. Trotsky apparently favored the idea, and on May 14, 1919, the Bolshevik Politburo approved the creation of such units on condition that they be in nationally mixed regiments or brigades. Nevertheless, with only minor exceptions, such Jewish units were not formed, possibly because of the strong opposition of the *Evsektsiia* (Tsherikover, *Di ukrainer pogromen,* pp. 285–89). The reasons for *Evsektsiia* opposition are perhaps best reflected in the report of a Jewish Red Army man whose commanding officer had assigned all Jews to seize and hold one factory. "Our Gentile comrades began treating us as strangers. . . . We felt . . . an abyss suddenly separating us from those with whom we had lived in such comradely fashion." The fear was openly expressed that if Jews were placed in separate units and were thus made less visible, other Red Army men would accuse the Jews of shirking their military duty. *Komunistishe fon,* July 21, 1919.

55 M. Rafes, "Ikh vel pruvn fargleikhn," *Folkstseitung,* January 30, January 31, and February 1, 1918, quoted in Tsherikover, *Antisemitizm,* p. 108.

56 Rafes, *Dva goda revoliutsii,* p. 81.

pogroms were incited by Ukrainian nationalists.[57] But by the time the Bolsheviks returned to the Ukraine in 1919 few could entertain any illusions about the attitude of the Rada towards the Jews, or at least about its ability to halt anti-Jewish terror. For the Jewish worker, the pogroms had obscured the old theoretical differences between the Bund and the Bolsheviks. The most important thing was that the Red Army offered protection against the Petliura or Denikin forces. The fact that in 1903 Lenin had rejected national-cultural autonomy paled into insignificance before this question of life and death. As Rafes put it in Bolshevik rhetoric, "The national factor again began to take the highest place in the Bund, as it had in 1907–1910, at the expense of general proletarian considerations." [58] The intelligentsia leadership of the Bund, however, never lost sight of the important ideological differences it had with the Bolsheviks. But, as we have seen, the German Revolution of 1918 seemed to confirm both the Bolshevik analysis of the Russian Revolution and the ability of the world proletariat to seize power. In the fall of 1918 and winter of 1919 the Jewish socialist intelligentsia, like the Menshevik leadership, began to reassess its analysis of the nature of the Revolution, becoming increasingly receptive to the Bolshevik view.[59]

[57] M. Brenner, "Pogrom rekhilus," *Neie tseit,* February 19, 1918.

[58] Rafes, *Dva goda revoliutsii,* p. 59.

[59] When large parts of the Jewish socialist parties and their leadership went over to the Communists, great stress was laid on the fact that the "masses" had pushed the leadership toward Bolshevism. Moishe Litvakov wrote that "The working masses . . . were very reserved and cold in their attitude toward the Rada and the struggle for national autonomy. This was all the 'high politics' of the party great. . . . In Kiev, in opposition to the line of the [*Farainigte*] Central Committee, party members—workers—enlisted in the Red Guards; in Ekaterinoslav the party coordinated its policies with those of the Bolsheviks." From the brochure *Na povorote* (Moscow, 1920), quoted in Tsherikover, *Antisemitizm,* p. 113. Earlier in the very same year, Litvakov had expressed an opposite view: "The Jewish

The Split in the Ukrainian Bund

The Ukrainian Bund was cut off from the rest of the party and had to work out its own destiny. "No one . . . was aware that a central committee of the Bund existed, that it was necessary to coordinate one line with the other: on the one hand, there was the physical separation and, on the other, the complicated local political struggle. . . ."[60]

In the fall of 1918 three factions began to emerge in the Ukrainian Bund: Kheifetz headed a left wing, Rafes led the center, and Litvak was the chief spokesman of a right wing. According to Rafes, September 1918 was the crucial month for the political stance of the Bund,[61] since the combination of turmoil in the Ukraine and "the revolutionary struggle" in Germany forced a political reorientation. Nevertheless, "In December, the Bund (even the most left-oriented) still believed in a pact with the Directory. In

---

socialist parties—the Bund and the *Farainigte*—which are now building the United Bund in Russia, won the greatest victory—victory over themselves. Not under the pressure of the broad working masses which, unfortunately, remained inert and apolitical, but under the influence of world events and their own socialist understanding they came to their present Communist position. . . . Unfortunately—and we emphasize *unfortunately*—you cannot accuse the United Bund of coming to Communism because of pressure from the masses. These masses are apathetic and stand aside from the approaching struggle." Moishe Litvakov, "Der geist fun komunizm," *Der veker,* July 15, 1920.

[60] Rafes, *Dva goda revoliutsii,* quoted in V. Kossovskii, "Farvos un vi azoi der bund hot zikh geshpoltn," *Di tsukunft,* XXIX, no. 1 (January 1921).

[61] *Dva goda revoliutsii,* pp. 96–97. Elsewhere Rafes explained that the ineffectiveness of the non-Ukrainian left reduced the choice of the Bund to a dictatorship of the right or a dictatorship of the Bolsheviks. The latter was seen as the lesser of two evils. See M. G. Rafes, *Nakanunie padeniia getmanshchiny* (Kiev, 1919), pp. 49–50, cited in Altshuler, pp. 97–98. On the relations between Mensheviks, SR's, and the Bund, see S. Volin, *Mensheviki na Ukraine (1917–1921),* Inter-University Project on the History of the Menshevik Movement, Paper No. 11 (New York, 1962), pp. 18–35.

order to obtain this pact, Kheifetz demanded of the Directory that it conclude a military alliance with the Soviet republic, and of the Bolsheviks [he demanded] a so-called broadening of the base of Soviet power." [62] But by January 1919 the Bund saw control over its local organizations slipping away, and because of the differences among the leadership, it was difficult to lay down a definitive party line.

> The acuteness of the differences within the Bund has led to several sad developments in our party life. In some cities whole groups split off and joined the Communist party, thereby completely losing their political independence and forgetting the special national tasks which the Jewish working class has even today. . . . In other cities the party organizations almost disintegrated and lost their political influence because of the stand taken by local committees which are entirely alien to the revolutionary tasks of the present epoch.[63]

When Red Army troops attacked the forces of the Directory, the provisional bureau of the main committee of the Ukrainian Bund voted 3–2 to support "Soviet power," and a military alliance with the Bolsheviks was concluded. The minority promptly withdrew from the bureau. Similarly, a leftist group which found itself in the minority of the Bund delegation to a Workers' Congress refused to be bound by the decisions of the delegation.[64] The new platform adopted by the Main Committee bore the stamp of the left wing, though it expressed serious reservations about Bolshevik terror, and economic and nationality policies. It

[62] Rafes, *Dva goda revoliutsii,* p. 116.

[63] "Tsirkular numer 1," February 1, 1919, published in *Folkstseitung,* February 19, 1919.

[64] *Der veker,* February 25, 1919. See also M. Ravich-Cherkasskii, *Istoriia kommunisticheskoi partii (B-ov) Ukrainy* (n.p., 1923), p. 106.

became increasingly clear that the Bund could not continue to function effectively while it was being pulled in different directions by the three factions within it. A decision on a single policy for the Bund could not be avoided. The Bundists were aware that in January 1919 the Ukrainian Social Democratic Workers' Party had split, the left wing arguing that only a Soviet Ukraine could deprive the Russian Bolsheviks of a pretext to make war on and annex the Ukraine. The left wing also cited the German and Austrian revolutions as proof that the world revolution had begun. The Ukraine had to become part of it.[65]

The third All-Ukrainian Conference of the Bund was scheduled for February 25, but on the eighteenth the leftist provisional bureau announced that regardless of the outcome of such a conference a "Communist Bund" must be formed.

The statement of the bureau reflects both the soul-searching and the determination of the leftist elements in the Bund.

> The social revolution has come and we have to reorient ourselves, purge ourselves of all the ideas which have grown as responses to the needs of the day, to the demands of another epoch. . . . This is an enormous task, made more difficult by the fact that it has to be done in the very midst of struggle. . . . Within each party member there is a real battle between two ideologies . . . the old ideology is retreating bit by bit . . . the party tries to survive the crisis as a united political entity and must therefore take smaller steps in order to retain its weaker elements and not leave them to our opponents. The impatient, more activist elements refuse to adjust to this party task; they take longer strides and simply go over to the Communist Party. They cannot, by this means,

[65] Borys, *The Russian Communist Party*, p. 247.

> ease the crisis in any way. . . . It was not easy for us to take the steps [of a military alliance with the Bolsheviks against the Directory in January 1919]. . . . In the declaration, the most prominent place was given to everything which *differentiates us from the Russian Communist Party.* Two months of cooperative work greatly furthered the process. The rapprochement grows. . . .[66]

On February 20 the pivotal Kiev organization met to act upon the demands of the provisional bureau. Rafes, one of the most prestigious of the Ukrainian Bundists and leader of the centrist faction, chaired the meeting. The existence of the three factions was formally acknowledged by having them meet separately and formulate their positions.

> The difference between the "center" and the "left" as it manifested itself at the conference was, one might say, of a purely historical nature. . . . It seemed to the veteran Internationalist Kheifetz that his present position was simply the continuation of the Internationalist line, formulated long before the revolution, at Zimmerwald and Kienthal. . . . Therefore, Kheifetz's speech was little concerned with criticisms of the past and concentrated mainly on the present tasks of the revolution. The position of the representatives of the "center" was different; their task was to sum up the party development of the Bund, root out of the consciousness of the party those deep splits wihch had already entered the minds of the leadership and which had convinced them of the possibility of retrogression and the still inevitable defeat of the revolution. The "centrists," who best reflected the mood of the majority of the party, underlined in their speeches and platform that which differentiated the position of the Bund from that of the Communists.[67]

[66] "Der krizis in bund," *Folkstseitung,* February 19, 1919. Italics in the original.

[67] Rafes, *Dva goda revoliutsii,* pp. 138–39.

Rafes' position emerged as the one most acceptable to the three groups. He explained that the Kiev Bund had planned to go over to the Communist Party "organically," that is, as a whole organization, in order to isolate the opponents of Communism and leave them without an organization. This was the position of the left. But "it became evident that the other [non-Communist] faction is not a small but a significant group." Therefore, "we have to tear the thread binding both groups and make the revolution within the Bund, and not wait for the Conference." Rafes explained that both anti-Communist and pro-Communist factions would elect delegates to the All-Ukrainian Conference, thereby forcing a split there similar to the one taking place in the Kiev organization. This split would create a focus of loyalty for pro-Communist Jewish workers. "There would thus be no place for a Jewish Section in the Communist Party." Attempting to allay fears regarding the nationality policy of the Communists, Rafes assured the Kiev organization that "the Communist Bund as an independent party of the Jewish proletariat, will defend its national demands." He then outlined a plan whereby Jewish national autonomy would be guaranteed. A "revolutionary socialist" organ of government, which Rafes did not define, would be formed in the Ukraine and would be connected with the central organs of government. Furthermore, there would be established a provisional Jewish national council with representation mainly from the working class. Finally, a Jewish workers' congress would be called.[68]

Litvak, speaking for the minority Menshevik-oriented faction, brushed aside Rafes' argument that a revolution must take place within the Bund. Litvak charged: "You are not splitting the Bund; you are leaving it." He ridiculed Rafes' proposal to by-pass the Jewish Sections and "save

[68] These proposals were identical to those put forth in the January 14 platform of the provisional bureau.

the national program" by forming a separate Jewish Communist labor party. ". . . If you give up democracy you will also have to give up national autonomy, because the Bund national program is a democratic one." Finally, two resolutions, presented by Rafes and Litvak, were offered to the conference. Litvak's stated that "the Kiev organization of the Bund remains with its former position of international social-democracy together with the other parts of the Bund in Lithuania, Poland, and Russia." Rafes' resolution stated that "the Kiev organization of the Bund declares itself to be the Kiev organization of the Jewish Communist Workers' Bund." Rafes' resolution was carried by a vote of 135–79 with twenty-seven abstentions.[69] Two organizations were created by this vote and they adjourned to different rooms. Those who cast their lot with the new Communist Bund sang the "Internationale"; the others sang the traditional Bund hymn, *Di Shvua.* "Upon leaving, they meet as two separate parties. The crowd slowly drifts away. . . ."[70]

Almost simultaneously, a similar split occurred in the Ekaterinoslav Bund and there, too, a Communist Bund, or "Kombund," was formed. As Rafes had predicted, the All-Ukrainian Conference thus lost almost all significance, and so few delegates arrived that it was changed from a conference into a council. Rafes and Litvak again played the leading roles and the script was much the same. Once more the factions proved irreconcilable, and when the final curtain came down each walked off into opposite wings of the political stage.[71]

[69] This is the figure given in *Folkstseitung,* February 22, 1919, and in *Der veker,* March 10, 1919. Agurskii gives a figure of 139–79 with no mention of abstentions (*Der idisher arbeter,* p. 83).

[70] The account of the split in the Kiev organization is taken from *Folkstseitung,* February 22, 1919.

[71] Litvak refused to cease his attacks on the Bolsheviks and was later shadowed by the Cheka. Daniel Charney enabled him to escape Russia by sending him to Minsk to found a branch of the *Kultur-Lige,*

The split at the Third Conference was a signal for local Bund organizations in the Ukraine to divide into regular Bund organizations and Kombund groups. In Ekaterinoslav the Bund voted 130–108 to become a Kombund; in Poltava the Kombund was voted into existence unanimously. In some organizations, the situation changed from day to day. Thus, in Kharkov fifty-four voted to adhere to the Moscow Conference (1918) platform, while fifty-two voted for a Kombund; on the very next day, the Kombund proposal got sixty-eight votes, the Moscow Platform fifty-three, while eight abstained.[72]

It is important to note that the split in the Ukrainian Bund came about not so much on the national question but on the broader political question of the nature and future of the revolution. Furthermore, the left Bundists were very careful to assert both their organizational independence of the Communist Party and the right to formulate their own nationality policy. The split was an agonizing experience for the Bund, and even the Left Bundists felt uncomfortable with it. They attempted to explain that it was forced upon them by circumstances beyond their control and that it was inevitable. The split was seen as the only solution to a dilemma which had constantly plagued the Ukrainian Bund. It was the only way out of the isolation which slowly enveloped the Bund, cutting off all avenues of escape. One Bundist put it this way. "To whom can we turn? . . . To civilized Europe which signs treaties with the anti-Semitic Directory?" The Bolsheviks, "the armed carriers of socialism, are now the only force which can oppose the pogroms. . . . For us there is no other way. . . . This is the best and perhaps the only way to combat the

of which Charney was secretary-general. There Litvak used his real name, Khaim Yaakov Helfand, and escaped to Warsaw. See Charney, p. 269.

[72] *Folkstseitung*, February 15 (28), 1919.

horrible Jewish pogroms."[73] While the Bundists were forced into acceptance of the Bolsheviks by Jewish considerations, they, like the Mensheviks, also realized that "By the latter part of 1918 the civil war had become a simple struggle between Reds and Whites. In this, neutrality and the role of 'third force' were unthinkable. Mensheviks and Bolsheviks saw eye to eye on the matter of foreign intervention."[74] Thus, in light of the pogroms, the German revolution, and the absence of any effective democratic alternative to the Red Army and Bolshevik power, a Communist orientation seemed both inevitable and politically justifiable to the Ukrainian Bundists.

The acceptance, with important reservations, of the Communist platform did not gain the Kombund recognition by the Ukrainian Communists. At the Third Congress of the Ukrainian Communist Party in March 1919 it was resolved by 101–96 that the Kombund and the Left Ukrainian Socialist Revolutionaries (*Borot'bisty*)[75] would be refused "group-entry" into the Ukrainian Communist Party.[76] Indeed, there was much hostility between the local organizations of the Communist Party and the Kombund, with the latter often leading an independent political life.[77]

[73] *Ibid.* See also Israel Getzler, "The Mensheviks," *Problems of Communism,* XVI, no. 6 (November-December 1967), 28–29.

[74] Getzler, *Martov,* p. 185. The extreme right wing of the Mensheviks, led by Mark Liber, did not support the Bolsheviks against the Whites.

[75] The Bund had not supported the *Borot'bisty* on the grounds that the latter represented the peasantry, and their formation of a Council of Revolutionary Commissars created a government of peasants, divorced from the proletariat, and separating Ukrainians from Russians and Jews. See Iwan Majstrenko, *Borot'bism: A Chapter in the History of Ukrainian Communism* (New York, 1954), p. 10.

[76] Agurskii, *Der idisher arbeter,* p. 86. The vote figure is given in Rafes, *Dva goda revoliutsii,* p. 162.

[77] Kheifetz, however, soon left the Kombund and entered the Ukrainian Communist Party, creating a sensation in the Kombund (Rafes, *ibid.,* p. 155). The Kombund did have representation on

The sequence of events leading to the formation of a Kombund in the Ukraine was loosely paralleled by occurrences in Belorussia. In late 1918 *Evkom* and the Central Bureau of the *Evsektsiia* asked Left Bundists in Perm, Ekaterinburg, and other Ural cities to return to their original homes in Belorussia, most of which was conquered by the Red Army in December 1918, and to conduct pro-Bolshevik agitation in the Belorussian Bund. The Bundists responded favorably to this appeal and began to organize small groups of "Bundists-Communists" who had a pro-Bolshevik orientation in general political matters but who insisted on maintaining national-cultural autonomy as part of their program. The Belorussian Communist Party was prepared to cooperate with the Bund, especially with "Bundists-Communists." In fact, a contemporary Soviet historian asserts that after the February 1917 revolution "many Bolsheviks in Belorussia, having no confidence in their own powers, mistakenly proposed that it would be easier for them to carry on a struggle for the masses within the more powerful Bundist, Menshevik, and SR organizations." [78] Even after October, the Party was very weak in the cities—precisely where the Bund was strong—and it calculated that a temporary toleration of the Bund and limited cooperation with its more radical elements would be necessary to insure the maintenance of the Bolshevik power in Belorussia. This policy was opposed by the Belorussian *Evsektsiia* which entertained notions of exercising total authority in Jewish affairs in Belorussia.[79] The Belorussian *Evsektsiia*, based in Minsk and led by Zalman Khaikin and Mandelsberg, maintained outwardly cordial relations with these

---

the presidium of the Kiev *gubispolkom* (provincial executive committee).

[78] E. Bugaev, *Voznikovenie bol'shevistkikh organizatsii i obrazovanie kompartii Belorussii* (Moscow, 1959), p. 97.

[79] See Altshuler, pp. 62–64.

"Bundists-Communists" but violently opposed their insistence on a separate Jewish organization and the Bund's national program. Nevertheless, the Minsk *Evsektsiia* appears to have aided the "Bundists-Communists" financially and placed a "Bundist-Communist" on the editorial board of the *Evsektsiia* newspaper, *Shtern*. In this way the *Evsektsiia* hoped to induce the leaders of the "Bundists-Communists" to dissolve their organizations and enter the Communist Party. The leaders of the "Bundists-Communists" refused to give up national-cultural autonomy and even demanded that the Communist Party allow them to create a separate Jewish Communist organization along the lines of the Bund. On January 15, 1919, this demand was discussed by the Central Bureau of the Belorussian Communist Party. Some Russian members of the Central Bureau expressed willingness to accede to the demands of the "Bundists-Communists" but, as might have been expected, Khaikin vigorously opposed them and said that they should be content with a Jewish Section of the Belorussian Communist Party. After lengthy debate, it was decided by vote of six to two to organize a Jewish Communist party which would not include "Bund" in its name.[80] The "Sectionists," as they were called, and the Bundists negotiated the establishment of

[80] Altshuler (pp. 65–67) argues convincingly that the JCP was formed because the centrist faction in the Belorussian Communist Party opposed the Jewish Sections on the grounds that they were natural allies of the Belorussian Sections, then the backbone of a nationalist tendency which wanted to maintain a Belorussian apparatus—in the form of Sections—throughout what was to become the USSR. The center also feared that the third grouping within the Party, a Russifying faction, would point to the subordination of the *Evsektsiia* to the RCP as an example of what the Belorussian Party should become—a subordinate part of the RCP. When the center won out, it found it convenient to support the idea of a Jewish Communist party against the will of the *Evsektsiia* whose existence was being used to support the conflicting claims of the Russifiers and the Nationalists. On the Belorussian Sections see Bugaev, p. 186.

such a party and a provisional main committee was agreed upon. It included the Sectionists Mandelsberg and Kaplan and the Bundists Abram, Krol, and Sverdlov.[81] On the editorial board of *Shtern* the proportion of Bundists to Sectionists was reversed, with Khaikin and Kaplan representing the latter and Sverdlov the former. At the end of January the formation of the "Jewish Communist Party" was announced. This victory for the Bundist-Communists, who had achieved their aim of founding a separate Jewish Communist organization, illustrated both the weakness of the Belorussian Communist Party and its Jewish Sections, as well as the importance that pro-Bolshevik Bundists attached to having a separate organization.[82]

The Jewish Communist Party seems to have been nothing but a paper organization. It declared "dictatorship of the proletariat on the Jewish street" to be its slogan regarding national cultural life but did little to put this into practice. The Party called its first, and, as it turned out, its last, congress for February 28, 1919. The call to the conference gave eloquent expression to the deeply felt resentments and grievances of at least part of the Jewish proletariat.

[81] A contemporary Soviet historian lists the "leaders" of the Jewish Communist Party as "Krol, Tanin, and Abramov" and cites no source. B. K. Markiianov, *Bor'ba kommunisticheskoi partii Belorussii za ukreplenie edinstva svoikh riadov v 1921–1925 gg.* (Minsk, 1961), p. 36.

[82] The above account is based on Agurskii, *Der idisher arbeter,* pp. 63–67. Of the "Bundist-Communist" leaders, Krol and Abram were the only two to gain any prominence under the Soviets. Krol became chief of police in the Belorussian SSR and deputy in the Commissariat for Internal Affairs. He was awarded the Order of the Red Flag and the Order of the Red Labor Flag. Abram, a genuine worker, became an important *Evsektsiia* official in Belorussia and in Odessa. Abram became the leading political figure in Kalinindorf, a Jewish national district in the Ukraine, but was exiled to Siberia in 1938. He was still alive in 1948, but his subsequent fate is unknown. His brother, William Abrams, was a leader of the American Communist Party and was active in its Jewish Bureaus.

> At the time the tortured and disillusioned Jewish workers were gagging in the barren, stifling swamp of the Jewish Pale . . . the Jewish and Russian bourgeoisies knew nothing of a "diaspora." The Jewish bourgeoisie, factory-owners who refused to let a Jewish worker set foot in their plants, merchants of the first and second guilds, the well-educated whose capital enabled them to attend Russian middle and high schools—this Jewish bourgeoisie was "permitted" to live in all Russian cities where a Jewish worker was not allowed to set foot. And in the "Pale," where Jewish workers choked in the cellars and in the garrets—there the Jewish bourgeoisie sucked the last bit of blood from the Jewish workers, there the Jewish worker had to pay all sorts of taxes, and had no voice even in the management of the Talmud-Torahs where his children studied. And in the fearful days of pogroms the Jewish bourgeoisie always found aid at the *Nachal'stvo,* at the very moment when Jewish workers were being robbed and beaten. . . . It was not only the Jewish bourgeoisie which denied the existence of classes among Jews but also . . . the great majority of the Jewish intelligentsia. These latter, on the one hand coming out of the Jewish bourgeoisie and educated in the spirit of the middle and high schools of the time, and on the other hand coming out of the Jewish yeshivas, saturated with the spirit of antiquated, dead Jewish culture—they failed completely to understand the Jewish worker. They did not know his sufferings, his joys and his demands. . . . The bourgeois-intelligentsia called him to assimilation and Russification, and the yeshiva-intelligentsia called him to Hebraism, to the "science of Judaism," to the old, dead "cultural work" permeated with clericalism.[83]

Declaring that "the Jewish 'socialist' labor parties, be-

[83] *Ibid.*, pp. 158–60.

ginning with the Bund and ending with the *Poalai Tsion,* militantly opposed the revolutionary proletariat," the Jewish Communist Party saw itself as the Moses that could lead the proletarian children of Israel out of a hopeless wilderness inhabited by a grasping bourgeoisie, an irrelevant intelligentsia, and a traitorous labor movement. The party's program stated that it "entered the Belorussian Communist Party as an autonomously organized branch" and that its members were automatically members of the BCP. In general political questions the JCP would accept all policies of the BCP, but on Jewish questions it remained "entirely independent," with its own press, meetings and congresses, and party cells. Any Jewish worker "in agreement with the aims and tasks of the JCP" was eligible for membership, and no approval by the Belorussian Communist Party was necessary.[84]

The Congress of the Jewish Communist Party was crippled by the sharp division between the Sectionists, who saw it only as a temporary means to an end, and the Bundists who clung to national-cultural autonomy as a necessity of political life. Ironically, while the Sectionists demanded that the Party deal with the pressing problem of the economic ruination of the Jewish population, the Bundists insisted that this was a nationalist heresy and that the party ought to deal only with cultural matters. The Bundists accused the Sectionists of lapsing into a *Poalai Tsion*ist error, and the disputes grew so harsh that the congress threatened to break up, and with it, the party. Dimanshtain rushed to Minsk to prevent a rupture, and he rammed through a so-called "compromise" whereby no "question of principle" would be discussed. This saved the formal unity of the party but meant that no resolutions whatsoever were passed by the congress.

[84] The program of the JCP is reprinted in *ibid.*, pp. 163–65, and in *Folkstseitung,* March 11, 1919.

A second issue agitating the congress was the name and organizational form the party was to adopt. Some delegates favored the establishment of a "Jewish Communist Party of Soviet Russia," a centralized organization, while others argued for a "Communist Alliance of Soviet Russia" which would include, on a federated basis, Jewish Communist organizations of Lithuania, Belorussia, the Ukraine, and Great Russia. The Sectionist Zalman Khaikin, arguing that Jewish proletarian interests were the same everywhere, strongly supported a centralized all-Russian Jewish party. "We are not bashful, and we proclaim that just as the revolutionary nests of Moscow and Petrograd are dear to the Russian revolutionary proletariat, so are . . . Vilna and Minsk—our revolutionary nests—dear to us." [85] Nevertheless, it was decided to change the name of the Jewish Communist Party to the Communist Alliance of Belorussia and Lithuania (*Komunistisher farband fun Veisrusland un Lite*, or *Komfarband*). A new Main Committee was elected. It reflected a balance between the former "Bundist-Communists" Abram, Sverdlov, Gorelik, and Krol, and the Sectionists Dimanshtain, Mandelsberg, Khaikin, and Altshuler.[86] Two Sectionist candidate members, Kaplan and Agurskii, were also elected.

Thus was the Jewish Communist Party dissolved after six weeks of quiescent existence. It was replaced by an equally sterile *Komfarband*. "In the Jewish Communist

[85] Z. Khaikin, "A aigene, iber alts," *Der shtern*, February 28, 1919. See also Kh. Ber, "A partai oder a sektsie," *Emes*, January 31, 1919. Altshuler (p. 71) points out that Agurskii falsely presents the debate on the organizational form of the JCP as a debate between those who favored the establishment of an independent party and those who favored the Sections. *All* the delegates favored an independent party.

[86] Dimanshtain served as Commissar for Labor in the short-lived Lithuanian-Belorussian ("Litbel") republic in 1918–19, until the Poles took Vilna, whereupon he fled—on foot, at first—to Moscow.

world the death of the 'Jewish Communist Party' met with great indifference."[87] The Bund pointed to the dissolution of the JCP as further proof that Bolshevism had not changed the attitude it had taken in 1903 and that no attention would be paid by the Bolsheviks to Jewish national needs and aspirations.

The Split in the Belorussian Bund

While internal struggles were paralyzing the Jewish Communist Party and Komfarband, the Belorussian Bund, too, was experiencing a severe internal crisis.

> Everywhere you hear the same sad dirge: party life is near death. . . . We Bundists must also say: yes, with us, too, all is not in order. . . . Our Minsk organization is passing through a crisis. No spark of life is left . . . all shake their heads . . . and that's all. . . . The library! It hardly exists. Why? There's no one with sufficient energy to undertake to put it in order. The *Veker!* It's in a difficult situation. . . . Hunger is increasing and, with its bloody hands, it grabs the broad masses. . . . We dreamed of a radiant, free, happy life. And the reality . . .[88]

The Bund comforted itself with the thought that "all over there are Bundists, not from yesterday but from many years ago. The Communists have nothing in cities where there are Jewish workers. There are no oldtimers among them and those who have become Communists are only

[87] *Der idisher arbeter,* p. 70. Within the Komfarband there was sharp disagreement between former *Iskrovtsky* who opposed "separatism," former Bundists who wanted to limit Komfarband jurisdiction to cultural affairs, and former *Farainigte* who wanted to include economic work in the Komfarband's program. See *Neie tseit,* April 25, 1919.

[88] *Der veker,* February 5, 1919.

guests on the Jewish street."[89] The Belorussian Bund was also well aware of the fact that it had longer traditions and a firmer social base than the Ukrainian Bund. There had always been a greater proportion of Jewish artisans and factory workers in Belorussia than in the Ukraine and they had constituted a larger percentage of the total labor force. The greater concentration of the Jewish population of Belorussia gave it more political power and greater psychological security than Ukrainian Jewry. It also kept the Jewish workers less assimilated and more concentrated in the Bund than the Jewish proletarians of the south who frequently knew Russian and were to be found in the factions of the RSDLP as well as in the Bund.[90] However, the fact that the Communist Party seemed to evoke relatively little enthusiasm among the Jewish masses could in no way hide the critical situation of the Bund. Though Belorussian Jewry had not experienced the nightmare of pogroms that Ukrainian Jewry had seen, it had suffered much in the World War, under German occupation, and in the conflict between Russians and the Polish legions. Various White Armies had penetrated Belorussia, and hunger and disease were as great as in the Ukraine. The German revolution had impressed the Belorussian Bundist intelligentsia no less than it had their Ukrainian counterparts. Furthermore, the Bundists, like other socialists, feared an imminent Entente

[89] *Ibid.*, March 4, 1919. In 1921 the Belorussian Communist Party had only about 2,000 members, while the average Russian *guberniia* at the time included 12,000–15,000 Party members (Markiianov, p. 22).

[90] See Moshe Mishkinskii, "Regionele faktorn bei der oisforemung fun der yidisher arbeter-bavegung in tsarishn rusland," Paper for the YIVO Research Conference on Jewish Participation in Movements Devoted to the Cause of Social Progress (New York, September 10–13, 1964), mimeo. On Bolshevism among Jewish workers in the Ukraine see H. Spektor, "Masn shtreikn in Ukraine in 1905 yor un der kamf fun bolshevikes kegn bund," manuscript in Vilna Archive, YIVO.

attack. This attack could lead to a monarchist restoration or another kind of reactionary counter-revolution. When the Red Army took control of Belorussia in late 1918 and early 1919 the question of a Bolshevik orientation impinged itself more forcefully on the consciousness of the Bund's leaders. And from the membership were heard the first rumblings of discontent.

These internal and external developments were assessed at the Eleventh Conference of the Bund held in late March 1919 in Minsk. The differences of opinion in the Bund were clearly reflected in the vote of the Minsk organization, held to determine the delegation to the Eleventh Conference. The left got eighty-five votes, the center seventy-nine, and the right twenty-nine. So the delegation consisted of two leftists, two centrists, and one rightist.[91]

Because of the suspension of railway passenger service only thirty-nine delegates and thirty observers were able to attend the conference. Those who attended were fairly young people, the vast majority under forty, and about half of them were workers at the bench. After agitated debate, it was decided by a margin of two votes that Moishe Rafes, recently arrived from the Ukraine, be given the status of observer. Rakhmiel Veinshtain expressed the hope that while "with sadness we learned that our organization in the Ukraine did not pass the test and split . . . we will leave the conference strengthened in our unity and will have ended the process of fractionation."[92] Rafes lent support to Veinshtain's hope by explaining that the Ukrainian Bund had to split because of the extreme polar nature of the divisions within it, but that the Belorussian factions might be reconciled.[93] Indeed, the conference formally

[91] *Unzer shtime* (Vilna), March 18, 1919.
[92] *Ibid.*, March 21, 1919.
[93] *Der veker*, March 21, 1919.

acknowledged the existence of factions within the party by electing a presidium strictly along factional lines. Rakhmiel, Esther, and Svetitskii, veterans of the Bund, represented the center, with the first two really belonging to a "left-center"; the twenty-nine-year-old carpenter Yankel Levin and the forty-year-old economist Nakhimson represented a left wing; and the longtime Bundist Yudin-Eisenshtadt represented the uncompromising social-democratic right.

The programs and beliefs of these factions were clarified at the conference. The right, whose position corresponded to that of the extreme right of the Menshevik Party, condemned the Bolsheviks as "Blanquist-Utopians," opposed indiscriminate nationalization of industry and called for democratization of the regime and its bureaucracy. The right did not disassociate itself entirely from the Soviet regime because its members held government posts. But it would not accept responsibility for the overall situation and its policy was to "criticize from within."

Speaking for the left, Yankel Levin argued that a choice had to be made between dictatorship of the proletariat and dictatorship of the bourgeoisie. He called the center opportunist for its support of the Communists' economic policy and its simultaneous adherence "to the old traditions and forms appropriate to the pre-revolutionary era." "You don't have to be afraid of the word Communism," Levin taunted the center. " 'Bolshevik' used to be a dirty word but so was 'Bundist' once upon a time." [94]

Veinshtain attempted to define the position of the center. While socialism had definitely arrived, Veinshtain maintained, a dictatorship of the proletariat is possible only in Western Europe where the proletariat has a majority in the population. "Don't we feel in our entire Soviet work that power is lacking, that there is no order because the regime

[94] *Ibid.*

is weak? We need a broad and powerful social base. . . . The regime must build itself upon the spontaneous activity of the masses, on their organized will." On a more concrete level, the statement of the center was a plea for the cessation of the Red terror and, in Esther's words, "the dictatorship *over* the proletariat." [95] At the same time, Esther said that "We cannot give up power to the bourgeoisie. In this sense we are against democracy . . . we are together with the Communists. . . . The Red Army is our army—its faults, our faults. There is no way back." [96] Esther attempted to draw a fine line between her own position and that of Yankel Levin: "Dictatorship is genuine only when it bases itself on all workers and oppressed people, when it is the regime of the majority of the people." The immediate task is to implement the lofty principles of the Soviet constitution. Never one to be fazed by a paradox, Esther argued that this will lead to the achievement of "dictatorship *through* democracy. Democracy is dear to us as a *means* to dictatorship." [97]

Three resolutions, expressing the views of the three main factions, were presented to the conference. The resolution of the left, apparently tempered with some centrist ideas, was passed by a vote of 31–17.[98] It called for support of the socialist revolution in all countries and of the Soviet government in Russia. At the same time, it condemned "the Bolshevik policy of directionless, incessant nationalization" which was, of course, hurting the Jewish population, since

[95] Raphael Abramovich commented that "the question of Bolshevik terror was for him [Rakhmiel] as it was for Esther, one of the most difficult questions of conscience. . . . Were it not for the terror, not only they, but other socialists would have joined the Bolsheviks at that time [winter of 1918–19]." *In tsvai revolutsies,* II, 311.

[96] *Der veker,* No. 507; quoted in *Folkstseitung,* April 2, 1919.

[97] *Der veker,* February 17, 1919.

[98] *Ibid.,* March 23, 1919. *Der veker* of March 25, 1919 gives the results as 32–16.

most Jews made their livelihood as small shopkeepers, peddlers, and traders. The left resolution also approved of the dictatorship of the proletariat to be expressed in the rule of the soviets. But *within* the soviets, democratic rule must obtain. "The Bolshevik party has created its own dictatorship over the working masses. The soviets are turning into an ornament adorning the regime. . . . The Soviet constitution must be effected immediately: freedom of speech, press, assembly, etc., must be restored. . . . The policy of terror ought to be halted." [99] The left resolution also asked for more autonomy for local government and urged Bundists to take government posts while accepting no responsibility for government policy and reserving the right to criticize the regime. Since thirty-three of the sixty-two Bundists held "responsible posts in Soviet institutions," this ambiguous resolution was comforting and highly acceptable.

Because the majority resolution actually hedged in its attitude toward the Bolsheviks, the minority declared itself in agreement with the "practical program" of the resolution and declared itself able to "work on that basis." [100] Furthermore, Esther had asked the Bund to maintain ties with both the Second and Third Internationals, thereby emphasizing the "wait-and-see" nature of the majority position. The resolution on the national question, too, merely empowered the Central Committee of the Bund to "work out concrete plans for activity in this area." [101] By avoiding some potentially troublesome issues and by taking an ambiguous stand on others, the Belorussian Bund managed to avoid a split.[102]

[99] *Ibid.*

[100] *Ibid.*

[101] *Ibid.*, April 6, 1919.

[102] There are some interesting statistics on those who attended the conference. Of 62 people polled, 21 were between 30 and 40 years old and 30 were between 20 and 30. Only one person was over 50. There were 36 workers, 13 officials, 9 teachers, and 4 students at the conference. Only 15 of the delegates had a secondary

The new Central Committee chosen by the conference consisted of five veterans of the committee and five newcomers. The veterans were Yudin-Eisenshtadt, Rakhmiel, Litvak, Esther, and Abramovich. The new members were A. Svetitskii, a veteran Bundist who had been arrested six times and exiled once; Nakhimson, who had been a member of the Bund for twenty years; Henie Gorelik, a fifteen-year member who had spent six years in Siberia and had been a firebrand orator in Mozyr; a twenty-nine-year-old shoemaker from Minsk, Alter Rumanov; and Yankel Levin, who had joined a Bund organization at the tender age of thirteen and had been a Bund leader in the large cities of Poland, Lithuania, and the Ukraine.[103]

The new Central Committee was elected according to the factional composition of the Bund. Levin, Nakhimson, and Rumanov—two youthful workers and one older *intelligent*—represented the left; Rakhmiel, Esther, and Gorelik represented the left-center; Abramovich, Svetitskii, and Litvak were considered centrists; and Yudin-Eisenshtadt was the sole voice of the extreme right.[104]

The Left Bundists were by no means ready to leave their party and enter the Communist Party, and they were espe-

---

education and 14 had received higher education. Of the 62 attending 33 held soviet posts as managers of departments, members of collegia, instructors, etc. Interestingly, while 44 of those attending had been in the Bund for more than five years—32 had been members for 10–20 years—22 were participating in a Bund conference for the first time. This would indicate that a new leadership generation was playing an important role at this time. The unsettled political and military situation prevented some old-time leaders from traveling to the conference and others found themselves beyond the borders of the Soviet state—in Lithuania, Poland, etc. Finally, of the 62 delegates, 21 had been in prison twice or more, 11 had been imprisoned once, and 26 had not been educated in this highest of revolutionary schools. See *Der veker,* April 7, 1919.

103 *Ibid.*

104 *Unzer shtime* (Vilna), March 26, 1919.

cially hostile to the *Evkom* and *Evsektsiia*. They had not even gone as far as the Ukrainian Kombund which had split the organization. The leftist Nakhimson criticized the "freshly-baked" Jewish Communists who had attacked the Eleventh Conference because the split they had hoped for had not occurred.[105] The Jewish Sections and *Evkom* had always been favorite targets for the Bund.[106] The Bund called the Jewish Communists "national-Bolshevik comedians," and assimilationists who overnight "changed from Savlov [Saul?] into Pavlov [Paul?]." Simultaneously, the Bund attacked the *Evkom* for concerning itself with the Jewish homeless and Jewish economic difficulties. These, the Bund said, were general problems not to be solved by specifically Jewish institutions whose sole functions should be in the cultural field. Such a broad spectrum of activity by national organs "can lead to the isolation of individual nations and the strengthening of nationalist tendencies which can retard the development of class consciousness of the Jewish proletariat in its struggle with the bourgeoisie." [107] Oblivious to its own blithely paradoxical characterization of the members of the *Evsektsiia* as both "assimilationists" and "nationalists," the Bund gloated over the predicament of the former Socialists-turned-Communists. "Their heart aches—they know where the shoe pinches—but what can you do when you have to fight the Bund? Two souls, pulling in opposite directions, live within their breasts. And the result—sad, depressed creatures." [108] Even the Leftist Yankel Levin ridiculed both the Communist

[105] *Ibid.*, April 8, 1919.

[106] See, for example, Zaslavskii's article in *Evreiskii rabochii*, June 20, 1918, and the sarcastic article by D. Chertkov (N. Vladimirov) in no. 8, July 4, 1918.

[107] "Declaration of the Moscow city and *raion* committee of the Bund, 1918," quoted in Kirzhnitz and Rafes, eds., *Der idisher arbeter*, p. 248.

[108] *Der veker*, February 13, 1919.

Party and its Jewish Sections. He charged that the Communists were rigging local elections, that few real workers adhered to their organizations and "in many cities it is in fact the Bundists who carry on the work of the Commissariats, and they are so involved in their work that they have no time to come to our meetings."[109]

Esther was willing to concede that "on the Russian street you can speak of the Soviet regime as being representative of ninety percent of the population." But "on the Jewish street, the matter is clear: a proletarian minority has to rule over a non-proletarian, albeit poor and toiling, majority. And that is why the Jewish Commissariats and Jewish Sections have that certain flavor of working under the masses, over the masses but not with the masses. . . ."[110]

Another general attitude and policy uniting all factions of the Belorussian Bund was support for the Red Army. Immediately after the Eleventh Conference, the Bund, like the Mensheviks, declared a party mobilization affecting all members over twenty-five years of age. This was designed to meet the threat of the Polish Legions who by April 1919 had seized Vilna. The First Minsk Guards Battalion of the Red Army consisted of seventy percent *Poalai Tsion* members, twenty percent Bundists and ten percent Communists. After six weeks training they were sent to the front where, after an initial victory at Olekhnovich, the battalion was cut to ribbons.[111]

Support for the Red Army and derision of the *Evsektsiia* were perhaps the only issues upon which the various factions in the Bund could agree. Formal unity had been pre-

[109] *Ibid.*, March 4, 1919.

[110] *Ibid.*, February 6, 1919.

[111] See Agurskii, *Der idisher arbeter*, pp. 106–08; *Der veker*, March 11, 1919; M. Finkelstein, "Der bund un di idishe arbeter bavegung in sovet rusland," *Di tsukunft*, XXVIII, no. 2 (February 1920); and Yoiel Hurvich, "Veisruslander idishe arbeter un di roite armai," *Der veker*, February 23, 1923.

served at the Eleventh Conference but this was a hollow achievement. When the Polish Legions took large parts of Belorussia, including Minsk, in the spring of 1919, the Jews were once again forced to face the dilemma of the one alternative. The Poles, like the Russian Whites, identified the Jews with Bolshevism and fought both with equal fervor. In Pinsk, for example, thirty-three Jews were dragged out of a community relief meeting, lined up against the wall and shot—to suit the fancy of a Polish officer. Just as the Ukrainian excesses had driven the local Jewish population towards the left, so did the attitude and policies of the Polish Legions push the Jews nearer to the Bolsheviks who had, to borrow a Marxist term, become their "objective" defenders if not their "subjective" saviors.

But if the Red Army afforded protection to the Jewish population and included many Jewish soldiers, the Communist Party did not compromise with the Jewish parties and, by the same token, was only slowly gaining Jewish adherents. The Bolsheviks had pursued a policy of repressions against the Bund in 1917 and 1918,[112] and as Bolshevik power grew they were able to implement this policy more consistently. Military repressions of non-Bolshevik parties and rigged elections were frequently employed in the isolated small towns of Belorussia in 1919. Working their way from the periphery, Bolsheviks would gradually gain control of the larger cities, such as Vitebsk, Gomel, and Minsk, destroying all opposition by a methodical policy of attrition, using semi-democratic and half-legal means to legitimate their actions. In Baranovich, for example, Jewish Communists sponsored a Jewish workers' meeting. Seeing that no Bundists were present, the chairman announced that if there were no objections, he would declare all parties and

[112] See, for example, the dispatch by A. Korovkin from Vitebsk, in *Evreiskii rabochii,* July 31, 1918, and the reports from Smolensk in *Der veker,* December 18, 1917.

organizations dissolved. A member of the *Poalai Tsion* quickly protested and thus at least postponed the Bolshevik monopoly.[113] In Gomel the Bundist newspaper, *Golos rabochego,* was closed because it was deemed a "social compromiser" and "compromise is the weapon of capital." [114]

The Final Split

The fragile unity of the Bund was soon smashed by the twin hammers of Polish persecution and Communist coercion. The final blows were delivered at the Twelfth Conference of the Bund, held in Gomel in April 1920. Twenty-nine local organizations were represented by sixty-one delegates. Esther sounded the tone of the conference when she declared that "the Soviet system is gaining ever wider recognition in the ranks of the proletariat. . . . The Bund has a great responsibility—to carry these principles [of Communism] to the broad masses of the Jewish workers and the greater mass of former petit bourgeois elements who have to be led into productive work. . . . Soviet power is firmly taking the only road which can guarantee the revolution." [115] Esther said not a word about Bolshevik terror and the repression of democracy, the two main reasons for her opposition to complete acceptance of Communism in 1919. In her allusion to the need for introducing the Jewish masses to productive work, she implicitly repudiated her previous castigation of *Evkom* and *Evsektsiia* economic policy as "nationalistic." Perhaps somewhat embarrassed by her *volte-face,* Esther tried to prove that "already at the Eleventh Conference the Bund stood, in principle, on the platform of Communism." She asked that the Bund drop its officially oppositionist attitude toward the Communist

[113] *Der veker,* February 6, 1919.

[114] *Ibid.,* February 7, 1919.

[115] Gomelskii gubernskii komitet Bunda, *XII konferentsiia Bunda,* (Gomel, n.d.), pp. 10–11.

government and that it accept responsibility for its policies. But on one point Esther had not changed. She remained firm in her conviction that the Bund must lead an autonomous existence.[116] The Bund was the "distinct form" of the Jewish proletariat struggling with the "remnants of bourgeois ideology" among the Jews, in contrast to the unrepresentative Jewish Sections.

Again, on the question of national-cultural autonomy Esther retreated—but she held firm on the principle of Bundist organizational autonomy. Since the destruction of the bourgeois dictatorship "establishes for the first time in history the possibility of fraternal cooperation of nations on an overall governmental scale in all spheres, not excluding culture," the demand for national-cultural autonomy "put forth under the capitalist order, loses its meaning." However,

> The Bund holds to its previous position that cultural work should be the province of the working masses of the nationalities . . . that a system should be constructed whereby local, county, provincial, and central national organs elected by the toiling masses of the given nationality perform the tasks of cultural construction, decide all problems of an internal national character.[117]

How this differed from national-cultural autonomy, Esther did not make clear.

Esther's report and proposed resolution were countered by a report on the political situation by Abramovich, who expressed the views of the Menshevik faction. Veinshtain then tried to establish a center, thinking perhaps to avoid a split, by introducing amendments to the resolutions of the left. The amendments underscored the importance of spontaneity of the working masses and the fruitlessness of using

[117] *Ibid.*, p. 22.
[116] *Ibid.*, p. 20.

terror against the socialist parties, but they were unanimously rejected by the left and a split could no longer be avoided.[118]

The resolution of the left, accepted by the majority of the delegates demanded "recognition of the organizational principle of the Bund, recognition of the Bund as an autonomous organization of the Jewish proletariat which autonomously carries out the tasks of the socialist revolution among the Jews."[119] The Bund was to enter the Russian Communist Party on exactly the same basis as it had entered the Russian Social Democratic Labor Party in 1898. Coupled with the demand that the Jewish Sections be absorbed into a "General Jewish Workers Bund," this meant that the Bund was asking for *carte blanche* in Jewish politics and an eventual political monopoly "on the Jewish street."[120] "The Jewish Communist Sections, established for the specific purpose of fighting the Bund—this artificial institution which has continuously been a façade, giving the Jewish workers the impression of an independent organization, cannot in the least implement the dictatorship of the proletariat among the Jews. . . . The only Communist force around which the Jewish proletariat can unite is and will be the General Jewish Workers League, the 'Bund'."[121]

When the resolution of the left obtained a majority of the votes, the right faction walked out of the party and called its own conference. The majority declared itself a Kombund and the minority a Social Democratic Bund.[122]

[118] See *Di neie velt* (New York), VIII, no. 316 (February 4, 1921), 21.

[119] *XII konferentsii Bunda,* p. 24.

[120] See A. Kirzhnitz, "Der bund un di komunistishe partai in rusland," *Di tsukunft,* XXIX, no. 8 (August 1921).

[121] *XII konferentsii Bunda,* pp. 26, 28.

[122] See [Grigorii Aronson] *K raskolu Bunda,* (Vitebsk, 1920). The Social Democratic Bund's program called for the establishment of "cultural-national soviets chosen by the Jewish toiling masses on the basis of the Soviet constitution." These would appear to be akin to

Fourteen months after the Ukrainian Bund had split with a bang, the Belorussian Bund drifted apart with a whimper.

The reaction in the localities followed the pattern established in the Ukraine. The Gomel organization voted 127–44–13 to accept the resolutions of the Twelfth Conference. Within a few days, thirteen of those who had voted not to accept, or had abstained, came over to the majority. When, as in Orsha, the majority refused to accept the Conference resolutions, the left simply walked out, chose a provisional committee and began registering members. In some organizations, those who did not accept the resolutions of the Twelfth Conference were expelled from the organization.[123]

It is difficult to assess the nature and extent of Kombund activity in Belorussia. On the one hand, there were many complaints of the lack of activists and literature—and, in fact, Kombundist newspapers like *Der veker* appeared only irregularly; on the other hand, the Kombundists claimed that there was a revival of interest among the membership and that the Social Democratic Bund was completely dormant. Actually, it appears that most Bundists simply withdrew from political activity altogether. This is indicated by the size of the local Kombund organizations. In the Ukraine, for example, the Kiev Kombund seems to have had only sixty members in 1920—including "some former *Evsektsiia* personnel"—and the Kharkov group had twenty-

---

the Jewish soviets originally called for by the Jewish Commissariat in 1918 and then quietly dropped as nationalistic. In the name of the Social-Democrats, Abramovich had warned that the Kombundists would soon be swallowed up by the Communist Party. "Your fate as an organization of the Jewish proletariat is foreordained. The example of Rafes' group, rolling from step to step, from Communist Bund to Farband, from Farband to Sections, from Sections to a technical commission, shows us clearly what awaits you in the not too distant future." *XII konferentsii Bunda,* p. 38.

[123] See *Der veker,* May 29, 1920.

four members.[124] In May 1919 the Kiev Bund had claimed three hundred members, including one hundred and seven workers. Only fifteen members of the Kiev Kombund were over thirty-five years old.[125]

The Dissolution of the Farainigte

The *Farainigte* did not escape the fate which befell the Bund. In early 1918 the *Farainigte* leadership in the Ukraine unanimously condemned Bolshevik policy and tactics.[126] Reacting in the same way as other Socialists to the events in the Ukraine and Germany, the *Farainigte* began to divide into three factions. The left was led by the former "Sejmists" Levitan and Novakovskii, the center by Moishe Litvakov, and the right by Moishe Zilberfarb, who served for a while as Minister for Jewish Affairs in the Rada government. The smaller *Farainigte* groups in Central Russia and Belorussia were not subjected to the same pressures as their Ukrainian comrades, and a party conference of the *Farainigte* outside the Ukraine adopted a resolution in January 1919 calling for a united socialist front and Jewish soviets, but condemning the economic policies of the Soviet government.[127]

A similar conference was held by the Ukrainian *Farainigte* in the same month. All factions were represented, and the sessions were stormy. Litvakov emerged as the pivotal figure. The former Talmudist, Zionist, Sorbonne student, and Hebrew writer declared that "we are entering the socialist revolution but remain, meanwhile, in bourgeois society." He dismissed the question of the Constituent Assembly with the argument that "you cannot be meticulously observant in matters of democracy when the socialist revolu-

124 *Ibid.*, July 15, 1920.

125 *Folkstseitung*, May 3, 1919.

126 *Neie tseit*, February 16, 1918.

127 *Unzer veg* (Warsaw), April 14, 1919. See also *Neie tseit*, January 1 and 2, 1919.

tion is taking place." The resolution he presented, together with Novakovskii, followed the Menshevik line of the time and accepted the "rule of the soviets" but rejected the "rule of the Communists." The resolution carried by 25–2–2.[128]

As time went on, the "United" party became more divided. By March 1919 the Kiev organization declared its support for Communism, but demanded that the national question be solved by introducing national-personal autonomy. That is, Jewish soviets should be established with jurisdiction in cultural and even economic affairs.[129] The party did, however, declare itself the "United Jewish Workers Communist Party,"[130] though it is not clear what it hoped to accomplish thereby. At this juncture, Litvakov submitted his resignation from the *Neie tseit* staff, refusing "to take responsibility for the tactics of the Communist Party in the Ukraine which lead to the inevitable shrinking of the social base of the revolution . . . the hateful nationalizations and socialization . . . the policy of ignoring national autonomy. . . ."[131] As a further protest against the Communist tendency in the *Farainigte*, Litvakov resigned as its representative in the Kiev *ispolkom*.[132]

Litvakov was swimming against the current. In July 1919 the *Farainigte* in Belorussia held a conference in Gomel at which four factions were clearly identifiable: a Communist faction, a left—now headed by Litvakov—a center, and a right faction. Litvakov presented the resolution on the political situation. Curiously, the "Communists" declared their dissatisfaction with Bolshevik policy, especially

[128] *Ibid.*, January 31, 1919. Ravich-Cherkasskii comments that the leftward movement of the *Farainigte* came "not out of Marxist considerations, but owing to depression at the sight of Petliura's anti-Semitic pogroms."

[129] *Neie tseit*, March 5, 1919.

[130] *Folkstseitung*, March 30, 1919.

[131] *Ibid.*, April 14, 1919.

[132] *Ibid.*, April 2, 1919.

in the Ukraine, were opposed to a split of their own party into Communist and Social-Democratic wings, and refused even to be identified as a separate faction within the party. They also stated that they were "more nationally inclined" than the Jewish Communists. The conference resolved to accept the fact that the socialist revolution had come, but "the conference categorically states that we are not Communists, and our Communists would remain with our center and even with our right rather than enter the Communist Farband." [133] The party rejected Litvakov's proposal to initiate negotiations with the Bund for unification of the parties, and urged the formation of Jewish soviets. All factions declared their allegiance to the party, and a central committee was elected which included five centrists, four leftists, and three "Communists." [134]

As the Belorussian Bund had discovered, such unity could not last long. In April and May 1920, at the Second General Party Conference of the *Farainigte* in Gomel, came the predictable final split into Communist and Social-Democratic parties. As in the Ukraine a year earlier, two parties emerged, one calling itself the United Jewish Communist Workers Party and the other retaining the name United Jewish Socialist Workers Party.[135] The logical next step, uniting with the Kombund in a single Jewish Communist party, was taken quickly by the Belorussian Communist *Farainigte*, just as the Ukrainian *Farainigte* had done before them.

The Ukrainian *Farainigte* had entertained notions of a merger with other pro-Bolshevik groups in 1919 and had held talks with the *Poalai Tsion* regarding unification.[136]

[133] *Unzer veg* (Warsaw), August 29, 1919.

[134] *Ibid.*

[135] See the resolutions of the conference in Leon Khazanovich, ed., *Arkhiv fun'm idishn sotsialist* (Berlin, 1921), p. 47.

[136] *Kommunar*, March 16, 1919.

These apparently came to nought, and negotiations were begun with the Bund. The Bund and *Farainigte* had differed on the type of national autonomy Ukrainian Jewry ought to demand.[137] Basically, the Bund demanded only cultural autonomy, while the *Farainigte* demanded a broader autonomy, paying lip service even to the old territorial program of the Socialist-Zionists. In March 1919, at a meeting of representatives of the *Evsektsiia,* Kombund, and Communist *Farainigte,* the latter refused to accept any notion of a Jewish Section in the Ukrainian Communist Party, while the Bundists found the idea acceptable "in principle" if a stronger central executive and press would be established and if the Sections would become not merely *agitprop* organs but a "mass organization with its own congresses, conferences and central office." [138] The Bundists proposed the formation of a "Jewish Communist Alliance (*Farband*) Section of the All-Ukrainian Communist Party." The *Evsektsiia* representatives agreed in principle but declared that they needed the prior approval of the Central Committee of the Ukrainian Communist Party. Approval was never given by the Ukrainian Communist Party which was consistently hostile to any separate Jewish entity within the Party.

Rafes' proposal to skip the "stage" of Bund-*Farainigte* unification and form a Jewish Communist organization immediately was rejected.[139] Instead, in May 1919 the Kom-

[137] Mykola Skrypnik, leader of the "Centrist" faction in the Ukrainian Communist Party, characterized them as follows: "while the proposal of the *Farainigte* was written by people who think Jewishly, the proposal of the Bund was written by people who think in the Jewish language." For the substantive differences between the two parties, see *Neie tseit,* February 11, 1919.

[138] See *Der idisher komunist* (Kharkov), March 12, 1919 and March 17, 1919.

[139] See *Folkstseitung,* April 19 and May 9, 1919. See also the article by D. Shlossberg in *ibid.*, May 16, 1919.

bund and Communist *Farainigte* in the Ukraine established a commission of three representatives from each party to work out the merger. The commission adopted a Communist platform, declared national-personal and national-cultural autonomy appropriate only to a bourgeois regime, but demanded Jewish sections in various Commissariats such as those for education and social welfare. These sections would meet the special needs of the Jewish people and "in their work should rely on the Jewish Communist cultural and political organizations."[140] The commission also proposed that the Jewish Sections in the Ukraine fuse with the Jewish Communist Alliance, or Komfarband, and that the Komfarband "as a whole work as a Jewish section of the Communist Party of the Ukraine."[141] On May 22, 1919, the Kombund and Communist *Farainigte* parties accepted the proposals of the commission and the Ukrainian Komfarband was born. The infant organization was rejected, however, by its putative parent, the Ukrainian Communist Party. Although the Ukrainian Party was badly split during all of 1919, no group within the Party, apparently, favored accepting the Komfarband as an autonomous organization loosely associated in some manner with the Party. In 1925 Moishe Rafes claimed that "The creation of the Komfarband came, not against the will of the Communist Party, but in accordance with the demand of the Ukrainian Communist Party." But he did admit that "the Ukrainian Central Committee adopted an incorrect position, which was corrected by the direct intervention of the Central Committee of the Russian Communist Party."[142] In any case, the attitude of the Ukrainian Communist Party toward

[140] Report of the founding conference of the Jewish Communist Alliance (*Farband*) in the Ukraine, quoted in Agurskii, *Di yidishe komisariatn,* p. 172. See also *Komunistishe fon,* May 29, 1919.

[141] *Ibid.,* p. 173.

[142] M. Rafes, "A bletl geshikhte," *Emes,* August 9, 1925.

the Komfarband is not very clear. On the one hand, it argued that the creation of a Komfarband diverted the energies of Jewish Communists to purely national concerns at a time when the Communist cause in the Ukraine needed all the support it could muster; on the other hand, the Central Executive Committee of the Ukrainian Soviet Government did include three representatives of the Komfarband, apparently as full-fledged members.[143] According to Agurskii, the Ukrainian Party refused to accept the Komfarband as an associated but autonomous organization, and demanded that Komfarband members join the Communist Party on an individual basis.

Meanwhile, there were bitter debates within the Komfarband on the organizational and national questions. Some favored the establishment of Jewish sections within the Ukrainian Communist Party. A number of former Bundists demanded an autonomous Jewish organization within the Communist Party which would deal only with cultural matters, and some former *Farainigte* urged that the Komfarband become an autonomous organization within the Party with jurisdiction in cultural and economic affairs.[144] Moishe Rafes charged that the Ukrainian Communists opposed the admission of the Komfarband, not because they feared contamination by a nationalist heresy, but because they would lose their "organizational hegemony . . . because in many places former members of the Farband would form the majority in a united Communist organization."[145] Meanwhile, in Moscow, Dimanshtain succeeded in having the Central Committee of the Russian Communist

[143] *Komunistishe fon,* June 16, 1919.

[144] *Neie tseit,* April 25, 1919.

[145] *Komunistishe fon,* August 9, 1919. The Komfarbandists charged that, in the absence of Jewish socialist politicians, Zionists and bourgeois *intelligenty* had infiltrated the Ukrainian Communist Party. See Y. Solomonov, "Ukraine," *Di komunistishe velt,* no. 10–11, November, 1919.

Party pass a resolution urging the Ukrainian Communist Party to accept the Komfarband. The Russian Party had prevailed upon the Ukrainian Party in April 1919 to accept members of the *Borot'bist* party into the Ukrainian Soviet government, and it is likely that Dimanshtain cited this precedent, especially since the Russian Party was becoming increasingly persuaded of the ineffectiveness of the Ukrainian Communist Party. Furthermore, the Komfarband proved its revolutionary worth by actively participating in the struggle against Denikin's forces in August 1919.[146] In that same month the Ukrainian Communist Party finally agreed to accept the Komfarband into its ranks. A compromise was reached whereby the Komfarband would not be an autonomous organization but would transform itself into Jewish Sections of the Party, subject to more direct Party discipline and direction. Bureaus of the Sections were to be attached to *gubkomy* and the Central Committee. Any decisions of the bureaus "which are in the nature of principles" were to be approved by the *gubkom* or Central Committee. The bureaus and their chiefs were to be elected at All-Ukraine or *guberniia* meetings of the Sections. "For the time being" they were appointed by the Central Committee. They included the former Bundists Kheifetz, Orshanskii, Chemeriskii, Frenkel, and Rafes, and the former *Farainigte* leader, Levitan.[147] Apparently, many Ukrainian Komfarbandists either refused to enter the Communist Party or were denied admittance to it. In June 1919 the Ukrainian Komfarband claimed four thousand members.[148] However, according to a survey made in 1927 of surviving Jewish members of the Ukrainian Communist Party, only

[146] Agurskii, *Der idisher arbeter,* p. 86. On the divisions within the Ukrainian Communist Party and the attitude of the Russian Communist Party, see Pipes, pp. 137–50.

[147] *Komunistishe fon,* August 21, 1919.

[148] Agurskii, *Di yidishe komisariatn,* p. 187.

1,757 joined the Party in 1919 and 1,190 in 1920.[149] Thus, it appears that many Komfarbandists, while accepting Communist ideology, refused to acquiesce in the liquidation of an independent Jewish party.[150]

As usual, the political evolution of the Belorussian Jewish socialists lagged behind that of their Ukrainian comrades. The final split of the *Farainigte* and the unification of the Communist wing with the Communist Bundists came a year after these had been accomplished in the Ukraine. When unification came, the Jewish socialists in Belorussia proved to be more reluctant to enter the Communist Party than had the Ukrainian Komfarbandists. Rakhmiel Veinshtain claimed that only the Bund could bring the Jewish masses into the Communist fold, and disparaged the Jewish Sections: "We have adopted a Communist platform. We are not people who follow the latest fashions—we adopted the platform after much deliberation, after a bitter internal struggle, after having had a rich experience. We are not among those who only speak and take no action."[151] The Communist Bundists in Belorussia mocked the *Evsektsiia* and professed to see a longing among the Sections for a Bund-type organization. "The 'dry bones' of the individual sections long for the living flesh and blood of a united homogeneous organization. . . . [They are] wandering souls in a chaotic world where hidden hopes of entering

[149] Kiper, *Tsen yor oktiabr*, p. 97.

[150] It might be argued that many more Komfarbandists actually joined the Communist Party in 1919 but were then purged, only 1,757 remaining in the Party in 1927. However, the party purge of 1921 which resulted in the expulsion of so many ex-Bundists, was directed mainly against those Bundists who had fought to the bitter end and had entered the party only in 1921 (see *infra*). This supposition is borne out by Kiper's figure of only 656 Jewish members of the Ukrainian Communist Party in 1927 with a party *stazh* of 1921, a drastic decline from the 1,190 of 1920.

[151] *Der veker,* May 29, 1920.

a homogeneous Communist Bund have been aroused."[152] Esther was the most passionate defender of Bund autonomy. She tried to allay the fears of the Communist Party by declaring that the Jewish worker would be "separate only to the extent that life itself separates him." That is, the "Jewish environment" has certain distinct characteristics, "with a specifically Jewish clericalism and chauvinism, with an *Agudas Yisroel,* with plain Zionists and *Poalai Tsion*ists, with Hebraists, with *Tarbuth* schools, with a EKOPO, OZE, ORT, *Kultur-Lige,* with pogrom victims, with American relatives, with *kheders,* with *yeshivas*—in short, our Jewish microcosm." Because of the richly developed and variegated nature of Jewish life in Russia, only an organization such as the Bund, with its roots deep in Jewish history and the Jewish people, could hope effectively to propagate Communist ideology among that people.[153] While carefully emphasizing that the Communist Bund would not be a separate party, Esther took equally great pains to point out that the Communist Party needed a mass Jewish *organization,* and not merely a technical *apparat;* the Jewish Sections were merely "a bureaucratic *apparat.*"[154]

The Russian Communist Party was well aware of the stubborn resistance it would encounter should it attempt to force the Belorussian Bundists into a merger. The Bund had apparently appealed to the Communist International for a ruling on its organizational status and future, even though the Comintern had earlier refused to admit the *Borot'bisty* to its ranks, in a ruling issued in February 1920.[155] In November 1920 the Executive Committee of the Comintern asked the Central Committees of the Bund and Russian

[152] *Ibid.,* July 15, 1920.
[153] *Ibid.*
[154] *Ibid.*
[155] On the negotiations between the *Borot'bisty* and the Comintern, see Majstrenko, pp. 184–87, and Borys, pp. 258–60.

Communist Party to form a commission, chaired by a Comintern functionary, to work out the conditions whereby the Bund could unite with the Communist Party. N. N. Krestinskii, Y. A. Preobrazhenskii, and A. Chemeriskii represented the Central Committee of the RCP, while Esther, Rakhmiel, and Moishe Litvakov represented the Communist Bund and *Farainigte,* now united in a Belorussian Komfarband. The chairman of the commission was the Bulgarian Comintern official, Shablin.[156] The Komfarband delegates were in an unenviable position. The realities of power pointed to a clear Communist Party victory but, at the same time, local Komfarband organizations were pressuring their representatives to hold firm. Telegrams poured in urging Rakhmiel, Esther, and Litvakov to adhere to the resolutions of the Twelfth Conference and preserve organizational autonomy. Four hundred Jewish workers in Minsk sent a telegram urging the representatives "energetically to defend the organizational principles of the Bund."[157]

The Bundists fought valiantly. The proposals they offered declared that "the Bund enters the RCP as a Communist organization of the Jewish proletariat, unlimited in its activity by any geographical boundaries." This was nothing less than the demand of the Bund rejected by Lenin in 1903. The Communist Bundists also demanded autonomy in agitation, propaganda, and organization, meaning that the Jewish Communist organization would have its own local organizations, central organs, congresses, representation in the central committee of the RCP, and delegations to international congresses. The Bund also stood by the national program adopted at the Twelfth Conference and

[156] Agurskii, *Der idisher arbeter,* p. 119. Chemeriskii was, of course, a former Bundist. He was not a member of the RCP Central Committee but was included in the commission probably because it was felt he could exercise some influence over his former comrades.

[157] Kirzhnitz, "Der bund un di komunistishe partai in rusland."

demanded the right to have direct relations with "similar organizations abroad and under occupation." The Bund would absorb the Jewish Sections and the new organization would be called the "General Jewish Workers' Bund." [158]

Clearly, this was unacceptable to the RCP. The Bundist proposals were the *beau geste* of a proud party, determined to defend its revolutionary honor. But in view of Bolshevik nationality and organizational policy the Bund's demands could not possibly gain acceptance. The Bund's position was made even more difficult by the troubles plaguing the Bolsheviks in late 1920 and early 1921. Within the Party the "Workers' Opposition" and "Democratic Centralists" factions, together with divisions within the Central Committee on the issue of Party discipline, thrust the question of Party unity and Bolshevik dictatorship into renewed prominence. A wave of strikes in Petrograd in February 1921 and the Kronstadt rebellion of the following month made the Bolsheviks even less patient with small groups trying to avoid complete subordination to the Party. Nevertheless, the commission of the Comintern, Bund, and RCP held many meetings with both sides holding steadfastly to their positions. The Bund won a skirmish when a representative of its central committee was assigned to the Central Bureau of the Jewish Sections as an observer. In a letter to Krestinskii, Rafes warned that even some *Evsektsiia* personnel were "psychologically and politically half-Communists" because they could not bring themselves to subordinate the interests of Jewish work to those of the party. He suggested that the negative attitude of the RCP toward Jewish Communist work reinforced separatist tendencies among the Jewish workers. Rafes even claimed that some *Evsektsiia* people were ready to go over to the Bund.[159] Rafes pleaded

158 For the text of the Bund proposals, see Agurskii, *Di yidishe komisariatn*, pp. 390–92.

159 *Ibid.*, pp. 401–04. According to A. Osherovich, there were

that in view of these sentiments among the Sectionists, the RCP should not rush the process of fusion.

Of course, Krestinskii was neither intimidated nor persuaded. It was not the RCP but the Komfarband which began to retreat. The Komfarband tried to stall in every way possible but it had to yield. Rakhmiel was apparently ready to give up the fight in February 1921 and to agree that the Komfarband should unconditionally enter the RCP. But Esther Frumkin, with whom Rakhmiel had a symbiotic intellectual relationship and to whom he was intensely loyal, refused to yield, and Rakhmiel agreed to continue the struggle.[160] Finally the central committee of the Komfarband voted six to five to accept the decision of the mixed commission, whatever it might be, if the executive committee of the Comintern would approve it. The Komfarband desperately hoped that the Comintern would save it from extinction, but the latter duly approved the recommendation of the commission that the Komfarband unconditionally merge with the RCP.[161]

"The decision of the commission . . . obviously did not please even the most extreme Communists in the Bund. It was clear to all that the liquidation of the Bund was a powerful blow to the Jewish labor movement."[162] Many local Bund organizations balked at the decision, and the Gomel *Veker* mourned the action which "snapped the

---

indeed "cases where Sectionists went over to the Bund." *Zamlbukh,* p. 25.

[160] *Dos freie vort* (Vilna), February 5, 1921. "Veinshtain, a calm, self-controlled and stable person of strong character, was nevertheless the type who always needed someone to admire and to obey." Raphael Abramovich, *In tsvai revolutsies,* II, 311.

[161] As might be expected, Shablin, Krestinskii, Preobrazhenskii, and Chemeriskii voted for merger, while Rakhmiel, Esther, and Litvakov voted against it. *Der veker,* March 16, 1921.

[162] Kirzhnitz, "Der bund un di komunistishe partai in rusland," p. 709.

golden thread of the Jewish labor movement."[163] The Mogilev organization rejected the decision outright, calling it "a violent crime" and asking that the question be referred to the Third Congress of the Comintern.[164] But it was the Minsk organization which voiced the predominant sentiment. It expressed regret at the Comintern decision but "in this transition period the Communist forces cannot be diffused," and it held out the hope that "in the ranks of the RCP we will carry on a legal struggle for our organizational principles, and surely we will be guaranteed a victory."[165] As could be expected, Esther Frumkin made the most dramatic gesture of all. A few days before an Extraordinary Conference of the Bund was to meet to decide whether or not to accept merger with the RCP, Esther wrote in the *Veker,*

> Let it be said clearly and precisely at this, the last moment, that whatever happens to the name of the Bund, to the form of the Bund, whatever the conference should decide—Bundism will live as long as the Jewish proletariat lives, Bundism will live—and will be triumphant![166]

The last act of the drama was played in Minsk on March 5, 1921. By this time all political parties, save the Bolsheviks, had been liquidated or rendered totally ineffective. Within three days the Tenth Congress of the Bolsheviks would assemble to outlaw factions from the Party. In such an atmosphere, seventy-three Komfarband delegates, representing three thousand members, gathered to do away with the remnants of the Bund, a task which they knew would be accomplished by the Bolsheviks even if they refused to

[163] Quoted in Agurskii, *Di yidishe komisariatn,* p. 382.
[164] *Ibid.*
[165] *Ibid.*
[166] Quoted in *ibid.*, p. 382.

preside over their own dissolution. No one really doubted the outcome and the only question was whether the minority would accept the decision to liquidate. Even the majority resolution was unenthusiastic and insisted on reasserting the correctness of Bund autonomy. "If the name 'Bund' were retained within the Communist Party, the best foundation would be laid for the Communist education of the broad Jewish toiling masses of Soviet Russia." But unity of all Communist forces is essential in the transition period. Were the Bund to remain outside the ranks of the RCP it would be—"objectively, independent of its will"—compelled to conduct an open struggle against the RCP on behalf of the organizational principles of the Bund.

Some delegates bitterly attacked the Bundist representatives to the Comintern commission for having "betrayed" the party. Esther defended them and expressed poignantly the painful responsibility she felt.

> You can force us, you can break us, but you cannot make us over. We remain what we were. Comrades, can you possibly imagine that the Bund should reach such a point where its own leaders would betray it? . . . Let us prove that the form of the Bund has so molded the Jewish labor movement that it will be able to live without it and lead the Jewish working-nation. From this point of view we must guard the head, which will lead you further in your struggle. The head is bloodied most of all, because it *is* the head. . . .[167]

In a lengthy and emotional *apologia pro vita sua,* Esther attempted to explain her actions. She freely admitted that she had opposed the Bund's entry into the RCP. "My opposition was in large measure personal" and so she had kept silent on the issue. But "I begin to see that what I took

[167] Quoted in *ibid.,* pp. 382–83.

to be personal is actually typical for a certain group of Bundists. Let this then be not so much a discussion article as a human document which might help some comrades compose their inner souls." The choice for the Bund had been narrowed to entering the RCP on its terms or remaining a "sect." Esther chose the former even though it meant

> bearing all the responsibilities of a Communist, while not having his rights. . . . And why was I ready to take upon . . . ourselves this undoubted martyrdom? In order to save the idea of the Bund, in order to at least preserve the Bund as an *apparat* until the inevitable moment (I believe in it even now) when the RCP will recognize our organization principle, in order to preserve the great treasure smeared with the blood and tears of the Jewish proletariat, soaked with the hopes and sufferings of generations of fighters, with memories of superhuman achievements. I say superhuman achievements because the revolution the Bund made in the Jewish worker [who was] in the forefront of the Russian labor movement was perhaps greater than the transition to Communism made in the last few years. Now we have to climb from one peak to a much higher one, to a Mont Blanc. Thirty years ago we had to first crawl out of a thousand-year grave. . . . Tradition? Emotions? No! This is a living force! [168]

It would be difficult to "subjugate ourselves in our Communist and soviet work to such Communists who are less suited than we, and make more mistakes than we would make"—a clear reference to the *Evsektsiia*— ". . . but all will be comforted by the consciousness that in this manner we take responsibility for the Bund, and that in this way we preserve the Bund also for the Jewish masses of other

[168] Esther, "Tsu unzer diskusie," *Der veker,* February 18, 1921.

countries." Esther made very clear that she saw the merger as a holding operation, designed to preserve a maximum of Bund influence in the Party. The Bund had willingly remained a sect because it believed that "history is with us." And it was a mistake not to remain a sect even longer, not to stall for time.

Even while suffering her own pain, Esther tried to comfort her flock.

> Comrades, what this has cost each of us will perhaps one day inspire an artistic genius to create a great tragedy. But let us rather be silent about this, friends. Let us lock it into our hearts and let us not sully the tragic holiness of our suffering with petty discussions and cries of woe. The discussion must end. The Jewish proletariat must live and be faithful to the oath it has sworn—to carry on the holy struggle until the world is reborn. And we, comrades, we must remain with [the Jewish proletariat] and spin our thread anew.[169]

Thus did Esther struggle to maintain her cherished loyalties—to the Jewish workers, to the Bund, and to the vision of a new and better world. She, and no doubt others, entered the RCP in the firm belief that Bolshevik policy would change and that Bundist autonomist principles would ultimately be vindicated. That this belief proved groundless was as much the tragedy of the RCP as it was the tragedy of Esther.

Rakhmiel expressed similar sentiments in a calmer and more reasoned manner. While denying that the Bund was ever a sect, he agreed that "we face the dilemma of independent existence or Sections, with the hope that we will be able to remake the Sections and suit them to the needs

[169] *Ibid.* The text in *Der veker* has *traditsie* (tradition) at the end the first sentence, but it is clear that the context demands *tragedie* (tragedy).

of the Jewish proletariat."[170] He reaffirmed his belief in the self-activity (*zelbsttetikeit*) of the Jewish worker. "We remain loyal to this outlook. This is our Bundism, this is the Bund. Not a single one of us has ceased to be a Bundist, nor will any of us cease to be. Therefore I can close my speech with the cry 'Long live Bundism, long live the Bund!'"

After a series of mournful speeches, the majority resolution was presented:

> The conference is convinced that the Jewish labor movement, within the ranks of the Communist Party, will sooner or later assume the normal and correct forms which were given to it heretofore by the Bund; the further evolution of party construction in the RCP, together with the overall strengthening of Communism, will make the realization of these forms inevitable. Taking this into account, the conference resolves: The order of the Comintern commission, regarding fusion of the Bund and RCP, is accepted.

The final resolution, a short and swift death blow, was approved by forty-seven delegates to the accompaniment of "hysterical shouts and weeping by some of the delegates."[171]

[170] *Der veker,* March 7, 1921.

[171] Agurskii, *Der idisher arbeter,* p. 121. See also *Der veker,* March 16, 1921. One Bundist present at the conference wrote: "No one proposes any amendments. What purpose would that serve? . . . No one applauds. . . . The fate of the Bund has been sealed. . . . Does the Bund still live? Does it live even after the majority resolution? Of course. That which generations created with their blood and marrow cannot die off. . . . We are celebrating an extraordinary anniversary—twenty years since Comrade Veinshtain entered the Central Committee of the Bund . . . and the celebrant [*baal simkha*] sits unsmiling, deep in thought. . . . And I wanted so much to assuage the psychological pain this man is experiencing—this man whose whole life, creativity, and influence are so strongly tied to the history of the Jewish labor movement. What does he feel, what is he

The twenty-six delegates who abstained then declared that they would be bound by the majority decision. The conference continued to sit, in order to work out elaborate explanatory statements and appeals to its reluctant constituents. The Bund spoke to its members as a guilt-ridden, wayward father to his uncomprehending children. It paid tribute to the Bund "which was born among you, in the tiny houses, in the suffocating cellars, in the cold attics, in the crooked, filthy streets."

> Jewish workers! The Bund is not leaving you. It remains with you. It leads you under the banners of the All-Russian Communist Party. Jewish workers! Carry your love, your trust, your fidelity to the Jewish Labor Bund into that great alliance [bund] in which the organization of the Jewish proletariat will in time emerge. . . .[172]

Even after the death of the Bund, its ghost continued to haunt the old leadership who tried to salvage what they could of their honor, position, and influence. Rakhmiel fought successfully to have three Bund members rather than two in the Central Bureau of the Jewish Sections; he succeeded in having the Bundist names of Jewish workers' clubs retained; he succeeded in preserving the Bundist names of the party press, now the press of the *Evsektsiia.* All members of the Bund were to become members of the RCP upon approval of local commissions composed of one representative each from the local RCP, Bund, and *Evsektsiia.* Ex-Bundists needed no recommendations, nor did they have to serve a period of candidature, in order to become members of the RCP,[173] privileges which had been accorded to the *Borot'bisty* as well.

---

thinking when his anniversary falls out on a day when it is resolved to reject the name 'Bund'?" Y. Teumin, in *Der veker,* March 16, 1921.

[172] The entire text of this moving appeal is found in Agurskii, *Der idisher arbeter,* pp. 166–70.

[173] This arrangement has been attacked by the Soviet historian

The actual merger began in April 1921. The Bund organization in Minsk, the birthplace of the party and always one of its greatest centers, marked the merger with a dramatic ceremony. One hundred and seventy-five Bundists, a pitifully small number compared to the hundreds of pre-Bolshevik days, marched with their banners to a local theater and, in military fashion, surrendered them to representatives of the Belorussian Communist Party. Rakhmiel Veinshtain delivered a valedictory address in which he traced the history of the Bund. V. G. Knorin, secretary of the Central Bureau of the BCP, welcomed the Bundists into its ranks. After twenty-five years of struggle, the Bund had fought its last battle.[174]

The Splitting of the Poalai Tsion

While the Bund and *Farainigte* were hesitantly groping their way along the tortuous path to Communism, a third party, the *Poalai Tsion,* was moving in the same direction. This party had the misfortune to be regarded as a pariah both by the Zionists, who were suspicious of its radical

---

Markiianov on the grounds that it admitted to the Belorussian Communist Party ex-Bundists who "could not outlive their petit bourgeois nationalistic traditions" as expressed in "the idealization of the historical past of the Bund, in the support and propagation by several former leading Bundist activists (Veinshtain and others) of the 'theory' of the dual origins of the CP(b)B (from the Bund and the Bolsheviks), in identifying the activity of the Bund with the entire Jewish labor movement" (Markiianov, *Bor'ba,* p. 43). Markiianov notes that the first organization to merge with the Belorussian Communist Party was the Belorussian Communist Organization, a small, ethnically Belorussian group of rural intelligentsia which entered the BCP in August 1920 (pp. 34–35).

[174] The Social Democratic Bund continued to lead a shadowy existence, harassing the *Evsektsiia* at public labor meetings. As late as February 1923 it issued a *Biuleten' tsentral'nogo komiteta 'Bunda'* in Moscow which was labeled "Number 26" and which spoke of "Moscow and Vitebsk organizations of the Bund and RSDLP." The *Biuleten'* is in the Jewish Labor Bund Library and Archives, New York.

socialist program, and the Communists, who were repelled by its Zionism. Like other Jewish parties, the *Poalai Tsion* supported the Rada, but remained loyal to it even after all other Jewish parties had withdrawn their support.[175]

In early 1919 a Communist faction made its appearance in the *Poalai Tsion* and was recognized by the international *Poalai Tsion* movement. Like the Communist Bundists, the Communist *Poalai Tsion*ists attacked the *Evsektsiia*. Even two years later a conference of Communist *Poalai Tsion*ist youth declared, "One of the main tasks of conscious Jewish Communist youth is a merciless and implacable struggle with the *Evsektsiia*."[176] They formed their own Jewish Communist Party (*Evreiskaia Kommunisticheskaia Partiia*) in Gomel and were known popularly as "EKOP-ists." This party placed many of its members in Soviet posts, to the intense irritation of the *Evsektsiia*. The latter tried desperately to "unmask" the EKP as a catch-all for impostors and adventurers whose allegiance to Communism was purely opportunistic, though there is some evidence that in the summer of 1918 Dimanshtain had offered the EKP newspaper a subsidy if it would work with the Bolsheviks.[177]

The EKP proposed to the Comintern that the Bund and EKP unite into a Jewish Communist party and enter the Comintern on that basis. The Comintern insisted that the EKP drop its Palestine program and rejected the "scholastic-nationalistic dichotomy" made by the EKP in accepting Communist doctrine on general political matters and that of the World Union of the EKP-*Poalai Tsion* on Jewish

[175] Revutskii, the last Jewish minister of the Ukrainian Directory government, was a member of the *Poalai Tsion*.

[176] Evreiskii kommunisticheskii soiuz molodëzhi, *Protokoly i rezoliutsii i-ii vserossiiskoi konferentsii* (Moscow, 1921), p. 32.

[177] See *Letste naies*, no. 14, 1919, quoted in *Unzer shtime* (Vilna), January 21, 1919. Dimanshtain explained that the Bolsheviks had supported Left Socialist Revolutionaries and anarchists also. "But at the same time . . . we struggle against them."

affairs. The EKP replied that in each country it would be entirely subordinated to the national Communist party, but on international Jewish questions—those affecting Jews equally in different lands—the Comintern, with its Jewish Communist constituent, would be the final arbiter. When the Komfarband entered the RCP in March 1921, it cut the ground from under the EKP, and an "*anschluss*-faction," favoring merger with the RCP, formed within the EKP. At the Third All-Russian Conference of the EKP-*Poalai Tsion* in December 1922 the "*anschluss*-faction" declared that the EKP's national program had become an obstacle in the path toward full Communism. The faction split off and its members joined the Russian Communist party, while the rest of the EKP continued to exist legally until 1928.[178]

The Ex-Bundists and the Evsektsiia

The dissolution of the Jewish parties was significant both for the Communist Party as a whole and for its Jewish Sections. The liquidation of the Bund and the *Farainigte* meant that the *Evsektsiia* now had a political near-monopoly "on the Jewish street." Furthermore, the demise of the Bund ended in a formal way the possibilities for truly autonomous Communist-oriented parties or organizations within the RCP. Finally, as Kamenev remarked, "Menshevism has lost its last and best fortress—the Bund." [179]

[178] The 1922 split in the EKP is described in detail in *Emes,* November 23, 1922; and in nos. 264, 265, and 269 of the same year. For an account of the intra-party politics of the early 'twenties see Z. Abramovich, *BeSherut HaTnua* (Tel Aviv, 1965), and L. Tarnopoler, " 'Poalai Tsion' bamaavak im HaKomintern," *Baderekh,* no. 4 (August 1969). On the history of the various branches of the *Poalai Tsion* see Y. Peterzil, ed., *Yalkutai Poalai Tsion: HaMahpekha HaRishona VeHashniya BeRusiya* (Tel Aviv, 1947); *Yalkutai Poalai Tsion: HaMa'vak BaZira Haprolitarit HaBainLeUmit* (2 vols., Jerusalem, 1954, 1955). On the policies of the legal EKP in the USSR, see its organ *Der proletarisher gedank,* especially nos. 43–50, 1923 and 1924.

[179] Quoted in *Der veker,* July 15, 1920. Markiianov draws a

The Communization of the Bund has long been a sensitive issue for Jewish historians and politicians. There are those who claim that the activists of the *Evsektsiia* after 1921 were nothing but the old Jewish socialists, without whose participation the *Evsektsiia* would have died a quick natural death. Soviet Jewish historians, however—especially those writing in the late 1920's and early 1930's—have attempted to minimize the role played by former Bundists. In this attempt they have been joined by Social Democratic Bundists, who strive for the same conclusions from very different motives. Obviously, the question is a touchy one and has been beclouded by partisan claims and counterclaims. Perhaps some statistical analysis would help clarify the issue.

In 1917 the Bund had approximately 33,000 members. Many of these found themselves beyond the borders of the Soviet state at various times between 1918 and 1921, and it is probably impossible to determine how many of the 33,000 were living under Soviet rule in 1921. Nevertheless, the number must have been significantly larger than the 6,000 former Bundists and *Farainigte* who belonged to the Belorussian Komfarband in 1921 (2,000) and to the Ukrainian Komfarband in 1919 (4,000). Since the Social Democratic Bund had fewer members than the Komfarband, the total number of Bund-affiliated Jews in 1921 could not have been more than about 11,000. This indicates that by 1921 large number of Bundists had withdrawn from political activity altogether,[180] either because they disagreed with the prevailing tendencies within the Bund, or because they saw no

---

parallel between the splits and mergers of the non-Communist parties in Soviet Russia and those which occurred in Eastern Europe in the late 1940's (p. 32).

[180] Since not even Communists have claimed that many Bundists joined the RCP *individually* in 1918–1921, it seems safe to assume that those who dropped out of the Bund remained apolitical.

future in it, or because the struggle for sheer personal survival did not permit the luxury of political activity. There was a drop in Bund membership when the Bund adopted a Communist platform, and there was apparently a further decline in political affiliation, similar to the decline in the Ukraine, when, in 1921, the Komfarband dissolved itself into the RCP. It seems that precise figures as to the number of Komfarbandists entering the RCP in 1921 are either unavailable or have been suppressed. Agurskii, disparaging the notion that the Komfarband brought many people into the RCP, claims that only 2,000 Komfarbandists entered the RCP in 1921. The great Jewish labor center of Minsk contributed only 175 members and Moscow but 115, of whom only 20 were workers.[181] Agurskii fails to cite exact figures and seems to base himself on figures for 1925 which show that among 31,200 Jewish members of the Communist Party on January 1, 1925, only 2,799, or 0.4 percent of the total Party membership, were former members of the Bund.[182] But neither Agurskii nor his source points out the obvious fact that ex-Bundists made up nine percent of the *Jewish* Party members. If these figures are correct, it may be concluded that fully one-half of the Komfarbandists refused to enter the Communist Party or that they failed, for some reason, to be approved by the mixed commissions supervising the entry of Komfarbandists into the

[181] *Di yidishe komisariatn,* p. 415n.

[182] 2,409 were full members of the Communist Party and 390 were candidate members. The figures are given in A. Chemeriskii, *Di alfarbandishe komunistishe partai (bolshevikes) un di idishe masn* (Moscow, 1926), p. 25. The author was secretary of the *Evsektsiia* Central Bureau and a former Bundist who had entered the RCP before 1921 and had served on the Comintern Commission which decided the fate of the Bund. The number of ex-Bundists in the Party rose slightly in 1925–26. On January 1, 1926, there were 2,865 ex-Bundists in the Communist Party. *Bol'shaia sovetskaia entsiklopediia* (Moscow, 1927), VIII, 118, cited in Yarmolinsky, p. 112.

Communist Party. We have already seen that while the Ukrainian Komfarband had 4,000 members in June 1919, only 1,757 Jews joined the Ukrainian Communist Party in that year. In 1922 there were 715 former Bundists and 308 former members of other Jewish parties in the Ukrainian Party which had 54,818 members in all. At the same time, there were 6,981 Jews in the Party. Thus, most Ukrainian Jewish Communists had not been previously affiliated with a Jewish Party, and only 1,887 gave Yiddish as their language.[183] The number of ex-Bundists in the Ukrainian Party remained fairly constant. In January 1927 while there were 20,306 Jewish Party members and candidates in the Ukraine only 794 were former Bundists and 147 had belonged to the Komfarband. A total of 2,236 Jews had previously belonged to other parties. They came from nineteen different parties—six Jewish and thirteen general[184] In Belorussia the percentage of ex-Bundists was considerably higher, as was the percentage of all former members of other parties. Of 1,253 Jewish Communists in the Belorussian Party in 1924, 365 were former Bundists, and 60 were former *Poalai Tsionists*.[185]

It is evident that most of the Bundists who embraced Communism as an ideology nevertheless remained fiercely loyal to the Bundist idea of a separate Jewish organization. Their loyalty was due in part to organizational pride and jealously, but also to nationalistic motivations and a desire

[183] Ravich-Cherkasskii, pp. 241–42. "The Ukrainian data indicates [*sic*] that approximately half of the Ukrainians and two-thirds of the Jewish members [of the Ukrainian Communist Party in 1922] were Russian in the cultural sense of the word. A similar situation probably prevailed in neighboring Belorussia" (Pipes, p. 278n).

[184] Kiper, *10 yor oktiabr,* pp. 97 and 98.

[185] *Emes,* March 11, 1924. In late 1920 there were 30,000 members of the various territorial Communist parties who were former members of other parties. This represented only four percent of the total Party membership. But in the Belorussian Communist Party 17 percent were former members of other parties (Markiianov, p. 62).

to retain a distinctly Jewish political identity. It must be remembered, however, that wherever possible, ex-Bundists in the RCP tried to hide their previous affiliation, and so the figure of 2,799 may be somewhat too small. It seems entirely probable that *initially* perhaps the overwhelming majority of the Komfarband entered the RCP, but that in the Party purge of 1921 many former Bundists were expelled. Lenin wrote that "in my opinion only one out of every hundred Mensheviks who entered the party later than the beginning of 1918 should be allowed to remain in the Party; and those who are allowed to remain must be checked three and four times."[186] In 1922 there were only 1,975 Jews left in the Party who had joined it in 1921. When this figure is compared to the 5,672 left in the Party with a 1919 *stazh,* and the 5,809 with a 1920 *stazh,* it becomes clear that a large number of those entering in 1921 had been purged by 1922.[187] One observer described purge commission sessions which he had witnessed.

> Not infrequently, they would ask a "former" [Bundist]: what would he do were he now in Poland—in what party would he work? Frequently, they would get the following answer: In Poland he would work in the Bund. The reason—here in Soviet Russia the Bund no longer exists and therefore he finds himself in the Communist Party, but in Poland there is still a Bund.[188]

[186] Quoted in *Zamlbukh,* p. 44. About 6,000 former members of other parties were expelled in 1921–22. One-third of them were former Mensheviks, and this may include Bundists. Leonard Schapiro, *The Communist Party of the Soviet Union,* p. 232, n. 4. On the purges in Central Asia in 1922–23, see Park, p. 192. On the Party purge see also T. R. Rigby, *Communist Party Membership in the U.S.S.R., 1917–1967* (Princeton, 1968) pp. 96–100.

[187] Figures are from *Alfarbandishe baratung.*

[188] *Ibid.* The Party purge of 1929 also hit ex-Bundists especially hard and there were complaints in the *Evsektsiia* press about the severity of the purge (*ibid.,* pp. 59–60).

The purge wreaked havoc among the Jewish members of the Party: in 1920, 834 Jewish Party members in Odessa filled out Party questionnaires.[189] After the purge in 1921, it was reported that 400 Jews had been re-registered, that is, had survived the purge.[190] In other words, over half the Jewish members had left the Party. Undoubtedly, former Bundists were especially hard hit by the purge. "In places with a Jewish population, former members of the Bund, now members in good standing of the RCP, suffered greatly. . . . They are not in the party very long. . . . They may be very respected and responsible Communists, but their recommendations are not valid, nor are they taken into account, and very few Communists of 1917 know them."[191] The purge affected the *Evsektsiia* so severely that Moishe Litvakov felt compelled to warn against distortions and deviations in the process of cleansing the party.[192] The Central Bureau of the *Evsektsiia* received so many complaints from people being purged because of previous affiliation with Jewish parties that on three separate occasions it pleaded with the central purge commission to issue clear directives to the local purge commissions regarding the proper attitude toward former Bundists and Komfarbandists.[193] Merezhin admitted that "it is no secret that we have members who were won over to the Party solely because the Soviet government does not pogromize the Jews. The

[189] Y. Rabichev, "Ainike statistishe datn vegn di idishe mitglider fun R.K.P.," *Emes*, October 15, 1921.

[190] *Emes*, November 17, 1921.

[191] Kh. Shekt, "A nit gevinshter toës," *Emes*, December 2, 1921. Shekt claimed that it was much easier for Belorussians to survive the purge. See *Emes*, November 29, 1921, where it is noted that people who joined the Party in 1919 and 1920 were hardest hit in the purge. See also the report from Mozyr in *Emes*, March 15, 1923, which states that after the 1921 purge "many of the former Bundists remained outside the Party ranks."

[192] See *Emes*, November 17 and 18, 1921.

[193] *Emes*, December 9, 1921.

Jewish question was the door through which they came to us. . . . This is not the fault but the misfortune of the national minorities. All this must be taken into account and carefully weighed during the Party purge. Stress should be laid not on the question of *stazh* but on whether these members have truly freed themselves of petit bourgeois and religious beliefs. . . ."[194]

Similar patterns to these may be discerned among the *Borot'bisty*. In 1923 Mykola Skrypnik claimed that out of the 5,000 *Borot'bisty*, 4,000 had joined the Communist Party (Bolshevik) of the Ukraine.[195] By 1923 only 118 former *Borot'bisty* were left in the CP(B)U. "The others went to Russia, left the CP(B)U, or, and this applied to the majority of them, were excluded from the CP(B)U during the purge for the alleged reason that 'they preserved nationalist survivals'."[196]

In Belorussia, of 6,398 Party members, 1,495 were expelled in the purge of 1921. Nearly 60 percent of those purged had entered the Party in 1920–21, 148 of them (9.3 percent) having been members of other parties.[197]

The statistical evidence which exists is probably too fragmentary and unrepresentative to enable one to draw any definite conclusions regarding the role of former members of the Jewish socialist parties in the Communist Party and in the *Evsektsiia*. But it does seem fair to say that ex-Bundists were more prominent in the leadership echelons of the *Evsektsiia* than at the lower levels, though even at the lower levels they tended to be involved more in *Evsektsiia* work than in general Party work. Thus, at the Fourth All-Russian Conference of the *Evsektsiia* in 1921, of 144 dele-

[194] A. Merezhin, "Di rainikung fun der partai ba natsionale minderheitn," *Emes*, September 16, 1921.

[195] Majstrenko, pp. 206–08.

[196] Borys, p. 260.

[197] Markiianov, pp. 72–77.

gates, 116 had belonged to the Bund and the *Farainigte.*[198] Twenty-four delegates had entered the Ukrainian Communist Party when the Ukrainian Komfarband was dissolved in 1919, and 49 entered in 1920–21 with the Belorussian Kombund. Fifty-eight delegates entered on an individual basis in various years.[199] But this was before the purge of 1921 decimated the ex-Bundists in the RCP. Some statistics regarding the rank-and-file Jewish worker show a different trend. Of over 500 Jewish artisans in Gomel, for example, 90 had belonged to Jewish parties before 1917, but only 26 of the 500 became Communist Party members and even these "soon left the party," either in the purge of 1921, or voluntarily.[200] As Leonard Schapiro observes, "The contraction of the party during the years 1921–2 was not due solely to expulsions. Many people were leaving the party of their own free will."[201] People entering the Communist Party from the Bund with the same kinds of motivations as Esther and Rakhmiel became disillusioned when they saw that a holding operation was impossible, that the Communist Party had secured its political monopoly and that there was no chance for meaningful reform from within. Many *Borot'bisty* undoubtedly underwent the same process. Finally, tightened Party discipline as a result of the factional disputes of 1920–21 and the decisions of the Tenth Party Congress undoubtedly caused numerous departures from the Party.

Perhaps the most sensible conclusion that can be drawn is that while rank-and-file Bundists—Jewish workers—shied

[198] Eighty-six to the Bund and thirty to the *Farainigte.*

[199] Details on thirteen delegates were lacking. *Partai Materialn,* no. 6, September 1921.

[200] I. Pul'ner, "Iz zhizni goroda Gomelia," in B. G. Tan-Bogoraz, ed., *Evreiskoe mestechko v revoliutsii* (Moscow-Leningrad, 1926), pp. 175, 176, 193.

[201] *Communist Party of the Soviet Union,* p. 232.

away from the Communist Party,[202] it was ex-Bundists who assumed high- and middle-level leadership roles in the *Evsektsiia*. The high visibility of former Bundists in the *Evsektsiia* leadership, created the impression that the *Evsektsiia* was "heir" to the Bund. Thus, of the fifteen members of the Bund Central Committee elected at the Tenth Conference in April 1917, at least four were later identified with the *Evsektsiia* (Rakhmiel Veinshtain, Esther Frumkin, Moishe Rafes, and Aleksander Chemeriskii), and three others, including David Zaslavskii, entered the Communist Party, apparently taking little part in *Evsektsiia* work.[203] Also, of the eighteen Bundists nominated by their party as

[202] "We must remember that in the revolutionary years of 1905 [–1906] we had tens of thousands of Jewish workers . . . and others who were members of the petit bourgeois parties. They are now mostly non-party people but are quite often activists in all sorts of social organizations." Sh. Dimanshtain, "Afn ideologishn front," *Emes,* December 17, 1926.

[203] Zaslavskii had been one of the staunch opponents of Bolshevism in 1917. He had also emphasized that the revolution and its preservation were to be given priority over the national question. *Arbeter shtime,* May 12 (25), 1917. In *Evreiskii rabochii* he published violent attacks on the *Evsektsiia.* By 1920 he "retired" from all political activity, but he joined the Communist Party in 1923 and publicly confessed the errors of his Bundist past in *Pravda,* July 26, 1925. He wrote the uncomplimentary article on the Bund in the *Bol'shaia sovetskaia entsiklopedia* and became one of the most prominent Soviet journalists. Bukharin mentioned Zaslavskii as the man who attacked Gorkii when Stalin had become estranged from Gorkii. "Zaslavskii is usually employed for jobs of this kind. He writes well but has no moral principles" ("Letter of an Old Bolshevik," in Boris I. Nicolaevsky, *Power and the Soviet Elite,* New York, 1965, p. 58). In 1952 after the "Doctor's Plot" had been "exposed," Zaslavskii was excluded from the Party "allegedly because one of his editorial colleagues had declared that he was unable to work 'together with the son of a people of traitors and poisoners.'" Solomon Goldelman, "Zur Frage der Assimilierung und Denationalisierung der Juden in der Sowjetunion," *Sowjet-Studien* (1961), quoted in Baron, *The Russian Jew,* p. 324. Zaslavskii survived the 1952 purge, however, and died in 1965 in Moscow. A two-volume collection of his articles was recently published in the USSR.

delegates to the Constituent Assembly, four became *Evsektsiia* activists; again, they were Veinshtain, Frumkin, Rafes, and Chemeriskii. A. Zolotariov, another delegate, also joined the Communist Party. A sixth delegate was the colorful David Lipets, formerly a trade union organizer in the United States, where he was known as Max Goldfarb. Lipets-Goldfarb was elected mayor of Berdichev and chairman of the local *kehilla,* as well as a member of the Central Rada. He later became the head of the Red Army training schools and went by the name of General Petrovskii.[204] Finally, of twelve members of the Bund Central Committee elected in December 1917, five became leading *Evsektsiia* activists.

On lower levels, it might reasonably be assumed, the proportion of Bundists in the *Evsektsiia* was higher than their proportion in the Party's Jewish membership as a whole. The great majority of Jewish Party members lived outside the old Pale areas and here there were fewer Sections.[205] The ex-Bundists had originally come from

[204] Lipets also served as a Comintern agent in London in the 1920's in the guise of a trade official under the pseudonym A. J. Bennett. According to Raphael Abramovich, Lipets played an ambiguous role as far back as the summer of 1917. "As the careful statesman which he had now become, he decided to work for both sides. He remained officially in the Menshevik party but worked unofficially for the Bolsheviks, keeping this from us, his old comrades. When Bolshevism finally won out, he officially went over to them. . . ." Abramovich, *In tsvai revolutsies,* II, 124. Apparently, Lipets was not overly concerned with the national question. While in the Jewish language federation of the American Socialist Party in 1912–1915, he had consistently placed socialism ahead of "a positive concern for Jewish values." Melech Epstein, *The Jew and Communism* (New York, 1959), p. 60. In the 1920's he wrote a few articles in *Der emes,* usually on festive occasions such as the anniversary of the October Revolution, but was not consistently active in Jewish affairs.

[205] See M. Kiper, "Tsu der alfarbandisher baratung fun di idsektsies," *Emes,* March 6, 1924. Kiper shows that only 8,500 out of 19,500 Jewish Party members were living in the "Jewish areas,"

the Pale areas, and though war, revolution, and civil war had dispersed them beyond the boundaries of the Pale, many drifted back to their former homes and some were sought out by the Party and reassigned to work in areas with heavy concentrations of Jews.[206] Secondly, ex-Bundists were "naturals" for Jewish work in the eyes of the Party. Then, too, many ex-Bundists probably welcomed Jewish work as the nearest approximation to a continuation of the Bund. Thus, there was probably a high proportion of ex-Bundists in the *Evsektsiia* at least until the mid-1920's when new cadres with no previous party affiliations were recruited, but because the *Evsektsiia apparat* was always small—never more than 2,000—the absolute numbers of ex-Bundists in the *Evsektsiia* was not very great.[207]

It is always risky to analyze the motives of politicians, especially those who claim to be guided by an elaborate ideology. There can be little doubt, however, that different motives impelled different Jewish socialists to follow the same path to Communism. It would be incorrect to assume that the split between Communists and Social-Democrats in the Bund paralleled an assimilationist-nationalist divergence on the national question. The fact that the more nationally

---

that is, where 2.5 million Jews were residing. "These statistics show us clearly that the greatest part of Jewish Communists are even territorially separated from the Jewish masses. They neither live nor . . . work among them."

[206] See *Partai materialn* (Moscow), no. 3, March 1921, p. 7.

[207] Reading the Soviet Yiddish press, one gets the impression that ex-Bundists played leading roles in *kustar* (artisan) organizations and trade unions in the 1920's. That there was a new cadre of *Evsektsiia* activists recruited in 1924–25 can be seen from the Smolensk *oblast'* data: of 33 *Evsektsiia* activists, only 3 had been engaged in Jewish work for two years or longer. While there is no data on previous party affiliation, the youthfulness of the activists makes it doubtful that they had such affiliations. Smolensk Oblast Archive, Microfilm in Columbia University Library, WKP 303.

conscious Esther and the assimilationist Rafes led the Belorussian and Ukrainian Bunds, respectively, towards Communism indicates that initially the crucial questions were the general political situation, the historical nature of the revolution, its chances for survival, and the possibility of a proletarian dictatorship in a proto-capitalist country. The German "revolution" and the Entente threat answered these questions for the intelligentsia; the pogroms obscured these questions for the masses. After the commitment to a Communist orientation had been made, the Bundists pulled up short and demanded separate Jewish Communist organizations. The stubborn insistence on organizational autonomy was probably also an affirmation of distinct Jewish identity, at least for some Bundists. Rafes may well have been concerned only with organizational autonomy and his own position as leader of an independent political force;[208] Esther was undoubtedly concerned for the separate identity both of the Bund and of the Jewish "toiling nation" as a whole. Faced with the undeniable fact of Bolshevik power, both Esther and Rafes had to give up the independence of their organizations. The splitting of the Bund was probably less traumatic for both leaders and rank and file in the Ukraine than it was for the Belorussian Bundists. Rafes in the Ukraine was less of a party patriot than Rakhmiel and Esther in Belorussia.[209] Moreover, Rafes

[208] In 1925, when Rafes had drifted away from the *Evsektsiia* and Jewish affairs, a former-Bundist-turned-Communist commented that "it is already five years that Comrade Rafes has a monopoly on shaking off the national dust from himself. With great alacrity, often more than is necessary, he keeps insulting the Bund, keeps answering that he, Rafes, is not 'nationally disposed.' His national nihilism has reached the point where he completely denies the national environment and the need to accommodate it." M. Ravich-Cherkaskii, "Nokhamol vegn der kiever khrestomatie," *Emes*, August 12, 1925.

[209] Grigorii Aronson comments that "More than for other Bundist-Communists, the turning of the Bund to Communism was for them [Rakhmiel and Esther] not so much a political move as a tragic

was somewhat of an opportunist, while both Esther and Rakhmiel were obviously people of principle. In 1918 David Zaslavskii, no mean opportunist himself, wrote about his colleague Rafes that "he has made opportunism an easy profession for himself. He is not afraid of defeat because he always manages to save himself. He has a talent for accommodation, and when democracy triumphs—he is a democrat; in a time of autonomy—he is an autonomist; when the Bolsheviks arrive—he is a Bolshevik. . . . To him it is all the same with whom he goes, as long as he goes forward. All questions of program he turns into questions of tactics, and therefore he can so easily change his position."[210] To a more sympathetic observer who considered Rafes "undoubtedly the most brilliant personality of all politicians in Kiev," Rafes was, at the same time, "not one of those people who sacrifice success for the sake of ideas and principles." While "he had inexhaustible energy and strength," he was "in truth, 'of a doubting and negative spirit'; opposition and political intrigue were his real *métier* . . . of an active and practical nature, he changed fronts many times."[211] Rafes and Esther entered the Communist Party with very different intentions; judging by their own statements and their subsequent careers, Esther probably intended to maintain a unique Jewish position within the Communist Party, whereas Rafes took a more "cosmopolitan" view of the future of nationalities in Russia and, therefore, did not play a very active role in Jewish affairs.[212]

---

experience." "Di iluzies un der gorel fun di 'kombundistn' in sovetrusland," *Unser tseit* (February 1962), p. 23.

[210] F. Bogrov (David Zaslavskii), "Vyrozhdenie Bunda," *Iskra* (Kiev), December 31, 1918.

[211] A. A. Gol'denveizer, "Iz kievskikh vospominanii," in G. V. Gessen, ed., *Arkhiv russkoi revoliutsii*, VI (Berlin, 1922), 183.

[212] Curiously, in 1921 Rafes criticized the Soviet government's nationality policy for its "naïve cosmopolitanism" and neglect of the cultural needs of the national minorities. "There must be special

The liquidation of the Jewish socialist parties meant that the Communist Party, acting through the *Evsektsiia,* was now the sole effective political force within Soviet Jewry. The *Evsektsiia* and the RCP now bore full responsibility for the political, social, and cultural life of the Soviet Jewish millions. In 1918–19 the *Evsektsiia* was clearly incapable of bearing this responsibility. But the absorption of the Bund and *Farainigte* infused new blood into the *Evsektsiia* and the transfusion may well have saved its life. The first few years of the *Evsektsiia,* like the first few years of its parent party, were years of struggle on many fronts—against the bourgeoisie and the old culture, against the socialist parties, and even against some elements within the Communist Party and the *Evsektsiia* themselves.

---

organs in the Party and government apparatuses" to serve the cultural needs of the national minorities in their native languages. This criticism was published abroad. M. Rafes, "Di natsionale minderheiten," *Der veg tsum zieg* (*A proletarish zamlbukh*) (Vienna, 1921).

V

"Revolution on the Jewish Street"

I burned to ashes songs of old
Long chanted in serfdom's day,
Tore to pieces the ancient hold
Of a past, left far away.

"Kloinimus" (a Yiddish poet), 1919

I gaze through thirsty eyes
And further—further I stretch my neck:
There were little *shtetls* spread about here
Quietly resting . . .
But I myself helped to wreck them
And sent them all up in smoke
Now I hear the stars atrembling
I am drawn away and carried on high.

Izi Kharik (a Yiddish poet), 1924

THE JEWISH Commissariat, established in 1918 to direct the cultural, political, and economic reconstruction of the Jews of Soviet Russia, was largely ignored by the Jewish people and the Soviet state alike, and it led an insecure life in 1918–19. "In those days we would count the weeks that we would be able to hold out, and then we were convinced that we would be allowed to exist for only a few months."[1] As Soviet power consolidated and the Jewish community disintegrated, *Evkom* acquired new confidence, fresh reserves of personnel, and additional budgetary allocations. *Evkom* assumed broad responsibility for the social welfare of the Jewish people, and—despite later protestations that "the Jewish Commissariat was not created in order to be an all-Israel institution . . . its goal was not to concentrate around it the entire people of Israel"—*Evkom* tried to serve almost any Jew who was in need of a home, a job, or a visa.[2]

War and revolution had made a shambles of Jewish economic life. It has been estimated that between seventy and eighty percent of the Jewish population of Russia was without a regular income in the years 1918–1921, and, for many, "speculation" was the only way to avoid starvation.[3] Even the Jewish farming colonies had been ruined by the World War, the Civil War, the pogroms, and the famine

1 Dimanshtain in Agurskii, *Di yidishe komisariatn,* p. 5.

2 The quotation is from a speech by Agurskii on "Idishe kultur problemn in sovetn rusland," delivered in Berlin on November 28, 1922. The late Alexander Pomerantz was kind enough to show me the manuscript of the speech, which was in his possession.

3 Lestschinsky, *Dos sovetishe idntum,* pp. 92–93. There is a very interesting account in Lestschinsky (pp. 94–95) which describes how a Jewish storekeeper whose store was seized by the state was forced to turn to speculation after having sold all his belongings.

of 1921. Ekaterinoslav Province had embraced 10,622 Jewish farmers in 1919, but by 1922 only 4,263 were left.[4]

Evkom was well aware of the desperate need of the Jews. In December 1918 it established a department of economic statistics whose real function was to encourage Jewish agricultural activity, but, according to the chief of this department, it remained a stepchild in *Evkom,* and Dimanshtain ignored it completely, though the Central Committee of the RCP expressed its satisfaction with the department's work.[5]

In June 1919 the Second All-Russian Conference of the Jewish Sections and Jewish Commissariats resolved that the economic transformation and rehabilitation of the Jewish population was the most important task facing *Evkom* (the Jewish Commissariat) and the *Evsektsiia* (the Jewish Section of the Party). The Council of People's Commissars approved a five-hundred-million ruble allocation for this purpose, but gains made by the White General Denikin in the south and the Poles in the west put an abrupt end to these plans.[6] *Evkom* tried to solve both the immediate and the

[4] Baron, *The Russian Jew under Tsars and Soviets,* p. 260. In 1804 Alexander I barred Jews from the liquor trade but permitted agricultural colonization in the Kherson and Ekaterinoslav provinces. Nicholas I continued this policy and granted the colonists exemptions from military service. Under Alexander II much of the land was taken from the Jewish settlers, and in 1882 Jews were forbidden to rent, lease, or buy any more land.

[5] See B. Rubshtain, "Di idishe sektsie in moskve un di 'idishe teritorie' in krim," *Di tsukunft,* XXXII, no. 9 (April 1924). Rubshtain, head of the department of economic statistics, was a former Zionist and Bundist who worked in *Evkom* until 1920 or 1921. He then left for Poland, made his way to Palestine, and there actively promoted Jewish colonization in the Soviet Union. He was hounded out of Palestine for this activity and returned to Odessa in 1926, where he continued to work for Jewish agricultural settlement in the USSR. See Reizin's *Leksikon,* pp. 288–92.

[6] S. Agurskii, "Di ekonomishe lage fun di idn in sovetrusland," *Di tsukunft,* XXIX, no. 4 (April 1921), 215.

long-range economic problems of the Jews. The Central Jewish Commissariat aided in reuniting families separated by war and revolution. *Evkom*, and its successor, the Jewish Department (*Evotdel*) in *Narkomnats* (Commissariat of Nationalities) tried to help the thousands of Jews massed near the Latvian and Rumanian borders in the hope of emigrating.[7] It allowed some people to leave so as to join families in America; and it asked the Commissariat of Foreign Affairs to make certain revisions in the 1920 treaty with Poland so that Jewish rights in Poland would be safeguarded.[8] In regard to emigration, the Jewish Department of *Narkomnats* did adopt a class policy. Merezhin, administrator of the department, distinguished three classes of potential émigrés: (1) capitalists who refused to come to terms with the Soviet system—they were to be vigorously opposed; (2) the "panicked" victims of war and pogroms who believed they would find safety in capitalist countries—these victims of "petit-bourgeois nationalist ideas" were to be educated and informed that anti-Semitism is a counter-revolutionary capitalist phenomenon which they could not escape by fleeing to Poland, Rumania, or America; (3) those who had close relatives abroad. The families abroad were to be encouraged to return to Soviet Russia, said Merezhin, but he implied that if they refused to do so, their Soviet

[7] There were reports that Merezhin had sent a secret memorandum to the Cheka stating that all Jews approaching the Rumanian-Ukrainian border with intent to cross it were speculators and counter-revolutionaries. It was charged that "hundreds of Jews" were shot as a result. *Unzer gedank* (Vilna), March 31, 1923. In view of the fact that no hue and cry was raised about this, it seems safe to assume that the report was unreliable.

[8] Chicherin, Commissar for Foreign Affairs, answered that the *Evotdel's* recommendations had been forwarded to A. A. Ioffe and that the *Narkomindel* (Commissariat of Foreign Affairs) approved of them. See *Sovet politik tsvishn di yidishe masn: dekretn, dokumentn un materialn*, ed. [?] Meyersohn (Vienna, 1922), pp. 12–16. See also *Arbeter kalendar afn yor 1924* (Moscow, 1923), p. 135.

relatives would be permitted to join them.[9] Working through the Jewish Social Committee (*Idishe gezelshaftlikhe komitet*), or *Idgezkom,* which it had created in 1920, the Jewish Department of *Narkomnats* secured Latvian and Lithuanian visas through the good offices of the Jewish Emigration Directorate in Berlin. It arranged to have pogrom victims exempted from passport fees and provided temporary living quarters for those waiting for visas. This work was conducted by three men: Kheifetz of the Jewish Department, Mandelsberg of *Idgezkom,* and Zilpert of the Jewish Department's Emigration Bureau.[10] Despite the tightening of American immigration restrictions, a significant number of Russian Jews entered the United States in 1921–23. Most of them were traders, unemployed, or charity cases.[11]

Emigration was probably the most desirable form of relief from the point of view of the emigrants, but perhaps the least desirable from the standpoint of *Evkom.* The new Russia could not very well achieve its economic successes by exporting its economic problems. *Evkom* therefore devoted much attention to relief work within Soviet Russia. In July 1920 it set up *Idgezkom* in an attempt to cure a host of economic and social ills. *Idgezkom* was ostensibly a non-Party umbrella organization including such Jewish welfare organizations as EKOPO, OZE, SETMAS, and ORT.[12]

[9] *Zhizn' natsional'nostei,* July 16, 1921.

[10] *Komunistishe fon,* December 6, 1922.

[11] See B. Zilpert, "Ob evreiskoi emigratsii v ameriku," *Zhizn' natsional'nostei, kniga* 2 (1923), p. 75.

[12] EKOPO was the *Evreiskii komitet pomoshchi*—Committee for Jewish Relief—established in 1916 to aid war victims. OZE was the *Obshchestvo zdravookhranenia evreiskogo naseleniia*—Society for the Preservation of the Health of the Jewish Population. SETMAS was the *Soiuz evreiskikh trudiashchikhsia mass*—Union of Jewish Toiling Masses—led by the quixotic Rabbi Zhitnik (see *infra*). ORT, which exists to this day, though not in the Soviet Union, is the Organization for Rehabilitation and Training founded in St. Petersburg in 1880, as the *Obshchestvo remeslennogo i zemledel'cheskogo truda*

These organizations were forces to be reckoned with. At the end of 1916 EKOPO was supporting over 250,000 people; ORT had 70 employment agencies which served 80,000 homeless people and found employment for 25,000. Its own workshops employed 15,000, and it sponsored 40 vocational schools which had 6,000 students. OZE had 42 medical dispensaries and 105 ambulances, and was connected with 23 hospitals. It also administered 125 kindergartens and 115 playgrounds.[13] Because the Jewish Communists insisted on dictating *Idgezkom* policy and administering the dole on a class basis, the non-Communist organizations pulled out of *Idgezkom* in January 1921.[14] By 1922 *Idgezkom* claimed to be subsidizing 132,192 children, 1,440 institutions of all types, and 100 vocational schools. *Idgezkom* also processed almost 100,000 food and clothing parcels sent from America. Of 23,935 people registered by its emigration bureau in 1921–24, 12,576 managed to leave Soviet Russia.[15]

Communist claims concerning the activity of *Idgezkom* are misleading because much of the money, personnel, and other material assets used for relief work in Russia were supplied by American Jewish organizations. The Joint Distribution Committee had promised aid on condition that non-Communist organizations be included in *Idgezkom*.

---

sredi Evreev—The Society for Artisanal and Agricultural Work Among Jews.

[13] N. Gergel, *Di lage fun di yidn in rusland* (Warsaw, 1929), 161–62.

[14] The Communists dominated *Idgezkom* by virtue of the fact that its Central Bureau included representatives of the *Evsektsiia*, The Jewish Department of the *Narkomnats*, and of the Central Jewish Bureaus of *Narkompros*, *Narkomtrud*, *Rabkrin*, and the *Komsomol* (Commissariat of Education, Commissariat of Labor, Workers-Peasants Inspectorate, and Communist Youth League, respectively).

[15] *Arbeter kalendar*, pp. 141–43; *Komunistishe fon*, October 24, 1922.

Narkomindel welcomed this as the first breach in the capitalist wall which had been built up around Russia, and Chicherin apparently pressured the Jewish Sections and Jewish Department to accept the offer.[16] Over ten million pounds of food, clothing, and medicine were sent to Russia through *Idgezkom* and it received a direct grant of $500,000.[17] The Joint Distribution Committee spent $8,048,-711 for Russian relief, between August 1921 and January 1923, with $3,827,386 of that total allocated for non-sectarian purposes and administered by the American Relief Administration. An additional $10,000,000 was collected in individual food remittances. In 1924 the JDC spent nearly $10,000,000 for relief and reconstruction.[18]

Idgezkom began to fall into disfavor as the economic crisis eased somewhat in the early 1920's. Some attacked it for helping non-proletarian Jews, claiming to see in this a dangerous "community-of-Israel" heresy.[19] As both the Soviet state and the Communist Party grew more confident of their viability, a supposedly non-partisan organization—a fiction which *Idgezkom* continued to maintain—became anomalous. Besides, the ex-Bundists in the *Evsektsiia* had always regarded specifically Jewish welfare activities with

[16] See *Partai materialn,* no. 3, March 1921, p. 10.

[17] Charney, *A yortzendlik aza,* p. 285. According to Charney, a ten-dollar food package could feed a family of four or five for an entire month. One dollar could buy three *poods* of corn and thirty *poods* would purchase a "good pre-war house in town."

[18] See *The American Jewish Joint Distribution Committee in Russia,* January 1924, report in the YIVO Archives, New York. For the 1924 figures, see the *American Jewish Year Book* (Philadelphia, 1925), p. 353. The JDC also supplied tractors, seed stations, 3,000 horses, 1,000 cows, and 6,100 agricultural implements. On relations between the JDC and the *Evsektsiia,* see Bogen, *Born a Jew,* pp. 273–74. Bogen was succeeded as director of JDC activities by Dr. Joseph Rosen, an agronomist and economist who also proved to be an able diplomat, even winning the grudging respect of the *Evsektsiia.*

[19] M. Altshuler, "Af a falshn veg," *Emes,* September 7, 1922.

distaste and they no doubt hastened *Idgezkom's* end. *Idgezkom* was dissolved in 1924 with the explanation that Jewish Communists were not slaves of "organizational fetishism" and that some "bourgeois elements—and even some Communists—figured that we will transform the *Idgezkom* into a Jewish *kehilla.*" [20]

Idgezkom was preceded to the grave by a most curious organization, the *Soiuz evreiskikh trudiashchikhsia mass* (Union of Jewish Working Masses), or SETMAS. SETMAS was the creation of a small-town rabbi in the Ukraine named Zhitnik, who moved to Kiev during the war. He saw the Bolshevik Revolution as the triumph of the poorest, most oppressed elements of Russian society, and it seemed to him to open the way for setting aright the grave social injustices which had corrupted the Jewish community in Russia. Zhitnik was elected to the Board of the Kiev *kehilla,* but acted as an internal opponent of that body. When the Bolsheviks entered Kiev in February 1918 Zhitnik organized "Jewish People's Soviets" and seized the offices of the *kehilla*—for which he was promptly suspended from that body. Upon the Bolsheviks' return in 1919 he "returned to power," this time with the support of Moishe Rafes, hardly a sympathizer of the clerics. Zhitnik now organized SETMAS and received a government subsidy for it. The "Bolshevik rabbi," as he was known, went to Moscow, shaved his earlocks, donned the quasi-military uniform of the revolutionaries, and began to publish two newspapers, *Horevanie* (Toil) and *Horepashnik* (Menial Laborer). While Zhitnik was probably a naïve and quixotic character, if not a charlatan, his organization and its platform seemed to strike a responsive chord among some of the poorer elements of religious Jewry. Zhitnik preached a sermon of social justice and class struggle within the

[20] *Komunistishe fon,* April 24, 1924.

religious community, urging the lower strata of Jewish society to cut all ties with the hypocritical religious leaders, who bent to every whim of their wealthier congregants, and to take care of their own religious needs. Indeed, SETMAS did supply kosher meat, matzohs, and other religious items—all at the expense of the officially atheistic Soviet Government. SETMAS might have been attractive to the indigent religious Jews who were psychologically in sympathy with socialism—or, better, anti-capitalism—but who could not bring themselves to join Jewish socialist parties or the Bolsheviks, both of which were hostile to religion. SETMAS announced plans to organize artels and agricultural communes, and hired a large staff, consisting of unemployed Jews, to work on these projects.

In December 1919 a Vitebsk *raion* conference of the *Evsektsiia* warned SETMAS to organize only the "half-proletarian urban masses" and to accept only those who clearly have citizenship rights according to the criteria of the Soviet Constitution. The Conference forbade any Communist Party member to join SETMAS or work in its apparatus.[21] In late August 1920 when an All-Russian SETMAS Conference was held in Moscow, the Central Bureau of the *Evsektsiia* decided that it was time to end this romantic adventure before SETMAS acquired too much social power: "It became manifest that the leaders of the Union displayed in their activity a tendency to become an independent political party."[22] The *Evsektsiia* asked the Jewish Department of *Narkomnats* to halt all cooperation with SETMAS, but *Narkomnats* pleaded that it was unable to cope with the great and urgent needs of the Belorussian Jewish population, and so SETMAS was given a suspended sentence. By 1921, however, SETMAS had apparently degenerated into

[21] Agurskii, *Di yidishe komisariatn*, p. 245. See also *Horevanie*, March 26, 1920.

[22] *Partai materialn*, no. 3, March 1921, p. 10.

a small clique dominated by Zhitnik and his brother. At the same time, the Jewish Department had become better equipped to take over SETMAS' functions. SETMAS was dissolved, and some of its officials were arrested. Zhitnik and his brother eventually found their way to the United States.[23]

The Emigration Bureau, *Idgezkom*, and SETMAS were all stopgap measures to meet the immediate crisis. The Jewish Communists also had long-range programs for economic rehabilitation. For a variety of reasons, they concentrated on agricultural settlement. The Jew had always been a "superfluous man"—prohibited from engaging in the most basic forms of production and confined to those secondary functions in the economy which can be easily manipulated, altered, and sometimes dispensed with altogether. The Jewish Commmunists were probably unconsciously influenced by an idealized peasant mystique, the idea that agricultural work is one of the most basic, necessary, and ennobling ways of life, that a life close to the soil is somewhow pure and healthy, and that a communal life is best suited to ridding the Jew of his individualistic, petit-bourgeois competitive mentality.[24] What could be better for the pale Jew of the ghetto, emaciated in body and twisted in spirit, than to breathe the invigorating air of the steppes and to sink his hands into the rich

[23] On Zhitnik's activities, see A. Tsherikover, "Di yidishe komunistn un di gezelshaftn in Ukraine, 1919" and "Der 'rov der bolshevik' un di kiever kehilla," both in *In der tkufe fun revolutsie*, A. Tsherikover, ed. (Berlin, 1924). See also the SETMAS pamphlet, *Genug!*; *Partai materialn*, no. 3, March 1921; and *Emes*, June 5, 1923.

[24] Writing about pre-revolutionary attempts to settle Jews on the land, Lucy S. Dawidowicz comments that "the ideal of Jewish agricultural pursuits was a heritage of the haskala, reinforced by Populist notions about Jewish unproductivity. (That concept was a staple of anti-Semitic propaganda, deriving from an agrarian, anti-industrial, and anti-urban mentality.)" Dawidowicz, ed., *The Golden Tradition*, pp. 48–49.

black soil? His natural suspicion of the peasant and his feeling of cultural superiority had to be replaced by a healthy respect for village life and the spirit of cooperation rather than competition. Aside from the intangible aura surrounding agricultural work, it was attractive as the most direct way of avoiding starvation, a daily problem for many Russian Jews. The energetic head of the economic statistics department, Rubshtain, organized eight agricultural artels and twenty-five others of unspecified nature in Belorussia during 1919, but his efforts went for nought since the Polish Legions gained control of Belorussia and the communes fell apart.[25] Other efforts were made, but most communes disintegrated because of their small size, lack of experience, the hostility of Ukrainian peasants, "infiltration" of déclassé elements who saw the commune as a temporary means of surviving their economic misfortunes, and the indifference of the central government which ignored *Evkom*'s pleas for more financial support.[26] The communes failed in their avowed purpose and, especially in 1921–22, a great hunger ravaged them. In one colony, 117 people starved to death, in another, 37, in a third, 22 people perished in the course of two weeks.[27] Despite widespread failures, agricultural communes were still attractive to the famished masses. In Gomel *guberniia,* 128 Jewish agricultural collectives, encompassing 20,000 Jews, were organized during 1918–1920. Most of these were only consumer artels, and the "farming" that was done consisted

[25] Agurskii, *Der idisher arbeter,* p. 87. The same author, in his article "Di ekonomishe lage," cites a figure of forty-nine artels in Belorussia before the entry of the Poles.

[26] See Agurskii, *Der idisher arbeter,* p. 88. See also S. Rapaport, "Nazrevshie voprosy," *Zhizn' natsional'nostei,* May 11, 1919. On the harassment of Jewish settlers by the surrounding Ukrainian population, see Order No. 962 in *Visti* (Kiev), August 4, 1921, quoted in Meyersohn, *Sovet politik,* p. 11.

[27] *Zhizn' natsional'nostei,* April 26, 1922.

of little more than planting a small vegetable garden. Almost all these artels melted away when NEP was declared.[28] The influx of ex-Bundists into *Evkom* and the *Evsektsiia* did not add much impetus to the economic efforts of the Jewish Communists. When still in opposition, the Bundists had ridiculed the Jewish Communists for engaging in "Zionist work," and when they entered the RCP they did not completely abandon this attitude. Dimanshtain tried to explain the position of *Evkom* and the *Evsektsiia* by taking Lenin's NEP policy of conciliation of the middle peasant as a signal for the Jews to conciliate their own middle element, namely, the ruined traders and petite bourgeoisie.

> Our Bundists, whether of the right or the left, get very angry when we speak of a nationality's economy. . . . This attitude is the result of a long struggle with Zionism. The trouble is that they are bad Marxists. They do not see that times have changed and clearly, the means of struggle must change. . . .
>
> When we speak of a special Jewish economy we do not use this term in the Zionist sense, which means the creation of a separate Jewish economy. We only fit the Jewish masses into the Russian economic reality in order that these masses shall strike roots in the general productivity of the country, in all its branches.[29]

Just as SETMAS and *Idgezkom* had been destroyed by the increased politicization of all organizations, *Evkom* also fell victim to an emphasis on the Party at the expense of the state. As the Party organ, the *Evsektsiia,* increased in strength, the government organ, *Evkom,* declined. Then, too, local and regional soviets began to administer the

[28] Lestschinsky, p. 188. It is not clear what role the *Evkom* played in the organization and operation of these artels.

[29] *Zhizn' natsional'nostei,* May 18, 1919, quoted in *Neie tseit,* May 26, 1919.

hospitals and schools that had been *Evkom*'s responsibility.

The Ukrainian Communists, always suspicious of their Jewish comrades, whom they saw as agents of cultural and political Russification, were especially quick to reduce the effectiveness of the Jewish Commissariat. Two Commissars for Jewish Affairs had been appointed in January 1919, but did very little. In March 1919 most of the Ukrainian *Evkom* staff was fired as an economy measure.[30] By May, however, a "department for work among the Jewish toiling masses" was set up and Kheifetz was put in charge. The department was mainly concerned with *agitprop*.[31]

In 1920 the Central Jewish Commissariat was downgraded to a Jewish Department in *Narkomnats*. When the former Jewish socialists entered the *Evsektsiia* leadership, they began to drive a wedge between the Jewish Department and the *Evsektsiia*, attempting to reduce the influence of the Department, whose functions they saw as illegitimate. "Officially, the Jewish Commissariat still functioned, but its direction was entirely in the hands of the *Evsektsiia*. . . . The former Bundists and SSniks [*Farainigte*], especially Litvakov and Chemerinki [*sic*], wanted very much to take over the administrative functions, that is, to write decrees and orders in regard to matters other than those concerning the Party. Litvakov was greatly insulted when Dr. Rosen went to the *Evkom* rather than to the *Evsektsiia* for information."[32]

In April 1922 the Belorussian *Narkomnats* was closed, despite the protests of Merezhin, the head of the Jewish Department in Moscow. Merezhin complained that since the Jewish Department in Minsk had been opened only a year earlier—and its administrator, Kiper, had been reassigned within a month of his appointment—the Belo-

[30] *Nei lebn* and *Neie tseit*, March 1, 1919.

[31] See *Kommunist* (Kiev), May 25, 1919.

[32] Charney, *A yortsendlik aza*, pp. 288–89.

russian government could not possibly evaluate its worth with any degree of objectivity. Nevertheless, the Central Executive Committee of the Belorussian Republic assumed full jurisdiction over Jewish Affairs.[33]

A different pattern was followed in the Ukraine. In 1921 a Commission for National Minorities was placed in the Commissariat of Internal Affairs and nationality departments were set up in the various commissariats. In 1924 these were reorganized into a Central Commission for National Minorities which was attached to the All-Ukrainian Central Executive Committee, and into local commisisons attached to *ispolkomy*. There were Jewish representatives in the Central Commission, in thirty *kraiispolkomy* and fifty-five *raiispolkomy*. Their function was to advise on economic and cultural matters.[34] In 1924 *Narkomnats* was dissolved on the All-Union level as well and replaced by a nationality department of the Presidium of the Central Executive Committee. A special "instructor for Jewish affairs" was appointed to the new department. He was assigned to handle all cases of "national injustices" brought by Jewish complaints, to advise on the redistricting of *raiony* in line with national demographic shifts, and to initiate the establishment of Jewish courts or Jewish divisions of general courts.[35] The instructorship was merely a vestigial organ, attesting to the extinction of *Evkom* and the Jewish Department. As if to symbolize the end of the *Evkom* period, the

[33] *Zhizn' natsional'nostei,* June 1, 1922; *Emes,* February 5, 1922.

[34] See Y. Kantor, *Ratnboiung in der idisher svive* (Kiev, 1928), p. 29–50. See also Kiper, *Tsen yor oktiabr,* p. 71. Kantor, scion of a religious merchant family of Pinsk, was a former member of the *Poalai Tsion* and the S.S. In 1917–19, he worked for ORT in Petrograd. The leading proponent of Yiddish language soviets, he was a member of the VUTsIK's Central Commission for National Minorities. Kantor made significant scholarly contributions to Jewish demography and statistics. He died in 1964 in Moscow.

[35] *Emes,* March 10, 1925.

first Jewish Commissar, Dimanshtain, was sent to Central Asia, where he became a member of the first Kazakh military-revolutionary committee.[36]

The locus of power, prestige, and responsibility had definitely shifted to the *Evsektsiia.* In June 1919 the Second Conference of the *Evsektsiia* met in Moscow.[37] Twenty-five delegates from Soviet Russia claimed to represent eight hundred Jewish workers organized in Jewish Sections. The five Belorussian Komfarband delegates spoke for three thousand constituents and the Ukrainian Komfarbandists for four thousand. Thus, the Sectionists were but a small part of the Communist-oriented Jewish proletariat.[38] Some delegates demanded the immediate liquidation of the Komfarbands, which were uncomfortably close to Bundism, but representatives of the Belorussian and Ukrainian Komfarbands insisted that "the Jewish Communist movement still needs its independent forms." [39] On the other hand, Kheifetz, who always seemed to be a few steps ahead of his more conservative comrades, argued that even Sections

[36] Carr, *The Bolshevik Revolution,* I, 376. Dimanshtain returned to "Jewish work" and in 1927 became All-Union chairman of GEZERD, a society to promote Jewish agricultural colonization. He was the most prestigious Bolshevik identified with Jewish work. It is doubtful whether he was involved in day-to-day Jewish work in the 1920's when he edited books on the nationality question, served in Central Asia, and was connected with institutes of oriental studies. However, he did serve as head of the National Minority Department of the Central Committee and, presumably, the Central Bureau of the *Evsektsiia* reported directly to him. When GEZERD was abolished in 1937, Dimanshtain was sent to a labor camp and was never heard from again.

[37] The conference was originally scheduled as a congress, but because of the precarious military situation, only some thirty delegates managed to attend and the meeting was listed as a conference.

[38] Agurskii, *Di yidishe komisariatn,* p. 187.

[39] This claim was made by Gorelik, Abram, and Mandelsberg, of the Belorussian Komfarband, and Levitan, of the Ukrainian Komfarband. *Ibid.,* p. 186.

were only a transitional form and that as Communism was realized, national problems and peculiarities would disappear. "We must make clear once and for all that every implementation of Communism does away with any national problems."[40] At this stage of *Evsektsiia* history, Kheifetz was alone in his opinion, though Manevich and Alskii joined him in viewing the *Evsektsiia* as a purely technical apparatus.[41] Dimanshtain stepped into the debate and agreed that Kheifetz was correct but only in long-range terms and that he confused the ideal with the real. "Our dreams of an ironclad international alliance," he declared, "should not hinder us in our present practical work." Warning against taking an independent political line, Dimanshtain nevertheless asserted that, while the *Evsektsiia* was responsible to the RCP, "we are even more responsible to the Jewish street."[42] The *Evsektsiia* should not concern itself with the Jewish proletariat exclusively, but should reach out to the "*lumpen*-bourgeoisie, the middle element which has a proletarian pocket and a petit-bourgeois psychology."[43] Dimanshtain was repeating his favorite theme, the economic and social reconstruction of all of Russian Jewry. Kheifetz immediately reacted by insisting that the dictatorship of the proletariat demanded a small, united, and strong party, whereas Dimanshtain's program would dilute the party. Furthermore, the Jewish bourgeoisie was so intractable that it could never be won over; and agricultural colonization was impossible because of peasant anti-Semitism.[44]

The confusion of the *Evsektsiia* as to its proper role, reminiscent of the debates of 1903 in the RSDLP, was aggravated by the exhortations of Mikhail Kalinin. If the Sectionists were "more Communist than the Communists,"

[40] *Ibid.*, 223. [41] *Ibid.*, 206. [42] *Ibid.*, p. 209. [43] *Ibid.*, 210.
[44] *Ibid.*, pp. 215–19.

Kalinin was "more Jewish than the Jews." Agurskii had made Kalinin's acquaintance in 1918 and invited him to the Second Conference of the *Evsektsiia* to represent the VTsIK. Kalinin began to speak of the pogroms but broke down and cried so that he could not complete his address.[45] Kalinin asked his audience to "tell the Jewish bourgeoisie" that the pogroms and the counter-revolution went hand in hand and that with the defeat of the counter-revolution, the pogroms would come to an end. Alskii and others, hypersensitive to any intimations that they were in any way associated with a homogeneous Jewish society, excitedly told Kalinin that this was a conference not of "Jewish national-Communists but of Communist Jews who have no connection with the Jewish bourgeoisie." Kalinin was chagrined by this unlikely attack and he left the hall, stunning the delegates—who then proceeded to berate Agurskii for not having adequately briefed Kalinin.[46]

Perhaps because of the ideological differences at the conference, the elections to the Central Bureau were a lively contest. There were seventeen candidates for nine posts, and the results reflected an even balance of "nationalists" such as Mandelsberg, "assimilationists" such as Kheifetz, and men like Dimanshtain who accepted Kheifetz's more cosmopolitan views in theory but who wanted to strengthen the Sections "temporarily." Dimanshtain, with twenty-seven votes, led the field, as might have been expected. Mandelsberg received twenty-four votes, and Kheifetz twenty-two.[47]

While the obvious differences regarding the nature, func-

[45] *Ibid.*, pp. 218–19; Charney, p. 251.

[46] This does not appear in the official minutes edited by Agurskii, but is recorded by Charney, p. 252.

[47] Others elected to the Central Bureau were Einshtain, Orshanskii, Sverdlov, and Segal. Candidates were Alskii, Tomsinskii, and Mikhail Charney. Charney was killed a few months later by Denikin's forces. Rafes and Novakovskii, representing the Ukrainian Komfarband, were also made members of the Central Bureau.

tion, and future of the *Evsektsiia* were hurriedly patched over,[48] much attention was paid to the organizational structure of the Sections. The ground rules of the *Evsektsiia* were firmly laid down at its Second Conference in an attempt to bring administrative and functional order out of the chaos which prevailed in the local *partkomy*. Members of the *Evsektsiia* were to be members of the RCP; new members could be accepted by the Sections but had to be approved by the *partkomy* according to the general principles determining acceptance; members of the Sections were to participate in Party functions, meetings, and elections as individuals. However, the Sections were to have their own congresses and conferences, to be called by permission of the RCP Central Committee, and their own local, regional—later republic—and central bureaus. The Sections' task was to publish Communist literature in Yiddish, found Yiddish Communist clubs, Party schools and libraries, and to recruit Jewish members for the Party. They were also to control and direct the work of the Jewish Sections in various central, regional, and local organs of the Soviet government, "within the guidelines of RCP directives to its regional organizations and the relevant People's Commissariats." [49] Thus, the Sections were conceived of as propaganda agencies with no responsibility for independent policy formulation. It was only several years later that they were to take upon themselves additional tasks related to the modernization of Jewish economic life.

[48] See Dimanshtain's article in *Komunistishe velt,* no. 3–4, June 1919, where he admits the existence of a "right, left, and center" but calls them "nuances" and expressions of wholly unimportant prejudices. Quoted in *Di yidishe komisariatn,* pp. 237–38.

[49] *Ibid.,* pp. 227–32. Excercising its rights within the principles of democratic centralism, the Central Committee amended the decisions of the Conference in two respects: the Jewish Sections were to have conferences, not congresses; the Central Committee had to give prior approval to any new Yiddish publication.

The Conference also moved toward establishing the "dictatorship of the proletariat," in its terms, on the Jewish street. It resolved that the Central Bureau "approach the responsible institutions with a demand to decree that all activity of the Zionist party in the economic, political, and cultural fields be ended." The Komfarbands were to be permitted a legal existence since they actively supported the Soviet government and the Red Army.

The *Evsektsiia* resolved that the Jewish sections of the departments for national minorities within the Commissariat of Education must come under *Evsektsiia* control and must be approved by it.[50]

In the localities, too, the *Evsektsiia* was trying to assert itself. It was still faced with the task of overcoming the distrust both of local and regional Communist Party committees and of the Jewish population. When the Bolsheviks first took Minsk an attempt at organizing a *Evsektsiia* failed because the *partkom* considered it a nationalist deviation. After the Jewish Communist Party collapsed, the *partkom* again expressed its suspicion of the *Evsektsiia* but a local Section was finally organized in 1919. The Minsk Section had two hundred members, ninety percent of whom were former Bundists. The Section soon fell apart, however, when ninety-five percent of its membership was drafted into the Red Army to fight the Poles.[51] Many of the local Sections complained that the center was not providing enough direction, that it was, in fact, ignoring the local Sections, and that it was too lenient with the "bourgeois" Jewish community. The Sections suffered from a lack of capable personnel and from the intrusions of the Civil War and the Russo-Polish War.[52]

[50] *Ibid.*, pp. 228, 231.

[51] Mandelsberg's report, in *ibid.*, pp. 196–202.

[52] *Ibid.*, pp. 239–40.

Nationality Sections were to be formed upon declaration by twenty Party members that such Sections were needed. The *gubkom* or *obkom* would then decide whether to approve this initiative. Should a Section be established, it was to be part of the *gubkom agitprop* department's subdepartment for national minorities. Local Sections, however, were attached to the organizational-instructional department of the *partkom*.[53] The formal organization of a local Section often bore only a vague resemblance to its actual structure and method of operation. Each local Section was to elect a bureau, usually consisting of three men. One of these, the secretary, was to have "consultation rights" in the local *partkom*. Representatives of local bureaus were to attend *guberniia*-wide meetings and elect a *guberniia* bureau. The local bureaus were to submit monthly reports both to their *partkom* and to the Central Bureau of the Sections. Thus, the local Section was simultaneously part of a vertical *Evsektsiia* hierarchy and a horizontal Party organization. Especially in 1919–1922 the local Sections had to tread carefully in coordinating the sometimes conflicting demands of the two hierarchies. The situation became so unsatisfactory by September 1919 that the Central Bureau appealed to the Central Committee to make budgetary provisions for the *Evsektsiia* on all levels. The Central Committee refused to take the local frictions very seriously and ordered local Sections to continue receiving their budgets from the local *partkomy*.[54] The Central Bureau cautiously avoided any direct clashes with local *partkomy* and rarely went above their heads in a direct appeal to the Central Committee. This sometimes aroused the impatience, and even disgust, of local Sections which

[53] See Rossiiskaia kommunisticheskaia partiia (Bolshevikov), *Spravochnik partiinogo rabotnika* (Moscow, 1921), pp. 66–67; and *Partai materialn,* no. 7, October 1921, pp. 15–16.

[54] *Komunistishe velt,* no. 6–7, September 1919, p. 41.

felt that they were not being given sufficient support by the Central Bureau.

There was a middle level in the *Evsektsiia* structure. In the Ukraine, and later in Belorussia, a Main Bureau (*Hoipt biuro*) was in charge of regional—later republic—*Evsektsiia* activities and organizations. A provisional Ukrainian Main Bureau was chosen by the Central Committee of the Ukrainian Communist Party in August 1919.[55] The Bureau began systematic work in January 1920, and Rafes became its chairman. It demanded semi-monthly reports from the secretaries of the *guberniia* and *uezd* (district) Sections, in addition to copies of all minutes and publications. The Bureau debated such questions as the solution to the economic problems of Ukrainian Jewry, and, at least in the early 1920's, seemed to tolerate differences of opinion and to resolve them by majority vote.[56]

The *Evsektsiia* in the Ukraine found the early going very difficult indeed. In August 1919 the Ukrainian Communist Party actually dissolved the Sections and replaced them with Jewish divisions in the *agitprop* departments. Upon appeal by the Komfarband the Central Committee of the RCP intervened and ordered the Ukrainian Party to accept Komfarbandists into its ranks and to re-establish Sections.[57] The liquidation of the Komfarband actually took a number of months, and its members proved very re-

[55] Its members were B. Orshanskii, Aleksander Chemeriskii, A. Kheifetz, M. Levitan, P. Frenkel, Moishe Rafes, and Mikhail Charney. Frenkel was the Bureau's delegate to the Central Committee and was also in charge of *Evsektsiia* activity in the eastern Ukraine. Levitan, Orshanskii, and Rafes were the editors of *Komunistishe fon. Di yidishe komisariatn,* p. 250.

[56] See the account of a Bureau meeting of February 1920, in *ibid.,* pp. 271–75.

[57] *Zhizn' natsional'nostei,* August 3, 1919; and *Di yidishe komisariatn,* p. 242. On Ukrainian opposition to the nationality commissariats, see *Neie tseit,* March 28, 1919; and the debate between Feliks Kon and Piatakov, reported in *Folkstseitung,* May 5, 1919.

luctant to give up their separate organization. Some even claimed not to have heard of the dissolution of the Komfarband, and others tried to revive separatist ideas within the *Evsektsiia*.[58] This exacerbated the hostility of the Ukrainian Communists. The *partkomy* in Ekaterinoslav, Berdichev, Kremenchug, Poltava, and Vinnitsa refused to allow Jewish Sections to be formed in their bailiwicks. In turn, the attitude of the Ukrainians fed the fires of Jewish separatism, and some Sections undertook independent recruitment of members, creating a party within a party.[59] The Central Bureau, Ukrainian Main Bureau, and representatives of local Sections met in Kharkov in March 1920 and, curiously enough, did not decry the attitude of the Ukrainian Party toward the *Evsektsiia*. This is partially explained by the attitude of the Ukrainian *Evsektsiia* leadership—Moishe Rafes in particular. Rafes wrote that "work among the Jewish toiling masses is a barren field. In order to carry it on there is a need not for national organizations but for Soviet and Party organs. All Communist forces must be united and fused . . . at present . . . it is our duty not to expand but, on the contrary, to reduce the number and activities of mass national organizations."[60] The Ukrainian Communist Party had its own ideas on how to deal with the problem. On April 15 the Central Committee of the UCP suggested that the Sections be reduced to Departments of Agitation and Propaganda among the Jews. The Ukrainian Main Bureau did not protest this. Rafes and Frenkel voted to accept the change and only Levitan opposed it. Almost all *Evsektsiia* activists were assigned to general, rather than Jewish, work.[61] This completely demoralized

[58] Kiper, p. 27.

[59] Agurskii, *Di yidishe komisariatn,* p. 277.

[60] M. Rafes, "Kommunisticheskii bund i evreiskie sektsii," *Zhizn' natsional'nostei,* January 22, 1920, quoted in Altshuler, p. 141.

[61] *Di yidishe komisariatn,* p. 302. Rafes explained the Ukrainian

the Ukrainian *Evsektsiia*, and many Sectionists withdrew from the Party. Some concluded that Jewish Communist work could be conducted only by a separate Jewish organization and they joined the Kombund. Others cautiously expressed their sympathy with the Kombund which was then negotiating with the RCP.[62] The reorganization was a particularly sharp blow because a similar attempt by the RCP to reduce its Sections to Departments had been successfully resisted by those Sections in December 1919.[63] Actually, the Ukrainian Departments were not formed immediately, and their central organ was established only in June 1920, when instructors were borrowed from various Soviet offices and sent to five *gubernii* in the Ukraine.[64] The conversion from Sections to Departments was completed only in August-September.[65] Even then the Departments encountered the "impermissible, often harmful attitudes of some *partkomy* to the Jewish Departments. There were cases where they would not allow Jewish clubs, party publications, instructors, etc. This led to the complete withdrawal from the work on the part of many active Jewish Party workers." [66]

CP action as due partially to anti-Semitism but mainly to the fact that the Sections were dominated by the intelligentsia who were "divorced from the masses" and who did not help the Party during important campaigns. Besides, he argued, they were so weak and ineffectual that dissolution was only a formality.

[62] See Altshuler, pp. 145–46.

[63] *Di yidishe komisariatn*, p. 264. The Moslem and Latvian Sections supported a *Evsektsiia* memorandum to the Central Committee of the RCP which explained the need for the Sections. A defense of the Sections, as conducting "important and responsible work," was made by Dimanshtain and Mandelsberg in *Zhizn' natsional'nostei*, February 8, 1920. At the Third Conference of the *Evsektsiia* in July 1920 Mandelsberg vehemently denied that he favored Sections for nationalist reasons; he claimed that they were needed strictly on practical grounds.

[64] *Der komunist* (Kharkov), no. 2–3, July 1920.

[65] *Partai materialn*, no. 3, March 1921, p. 19.

[66] *Ibid.*

In July, the Third All-Russian Conference of the *Evsektsiia* resolved that Sections were a proper organizational form for contemporary conditions, implicitly criticizing the Ukrainian Communist Party. It also explicitly stated that the Ukrainian action was "contrary to Party spirit." In November the administrators of the local Jewish Departments met in Kharkov and expressed dissatisfaction with their new status. Altshuler, a member of the central organ of the Department, reported that the change from Sections to Departments had in no way changed the attitude of the Ukrainian Party toward Jewish work.[67] It was obvious that neither the Jewish Communists in the Ukraine nor the Central Bureau in Moscow were very happy with the Departments. In January 1921 the Ukrainian CP finally yielded and abandoned its attempt to get rid of the Sections. Sections were re-created, though they were subordinated to the *agitprop* departments of the *partkomy*, as were all nationality sections everywhere made part of the *agitprop* apparatus. The Sectionists began to return and there were soon 186 activists in eleven Ukrainian provinces.[68]

While the Ukrainian Sectionists were fighting to maintain their position, a storm was brewing at the center. The Third Conference of the Jewish Sections of the Communist Party was held in Moscow on July 4–10, 1920. This time the national-organizational question could not be hushed up. Trouble developed partially because many of the delegates were "freshly baked" Communists: of sixty-four voting

[67] *Komunistishe fon,* December 4, 1920.

[68] *Partai materialn,* no. 3, March 1921. The Minsk *Shtern's* comment on the change was that the Departments had begun to operate like Sections anyhow and that the creation of Departments had strengthened the connection between general Party and Jewish work (*Shtern,* March 8, 1921). There is an obvious error in the text where it is claimed that there were 1,661 *Evsektsiia* activists in January 1921. The accompanying figures for individual provinces add up to the far more realistic total of 186.

delegates, thirty-four were ex-Bundists, eleven had belonged to the *Farainigte,* seven to the *Poalai Tsion,* two to the Mensheviks, and one was a former anarchist. They claimed to represent 1,743 Party members.[69] The delegates were mostly young people, the oldest delegate being forty-nine.[70]

In what apparently was becoming an inviolable tradition for Jewish political groups, three factions appeared at the conference. A "nationalist" wing, which was labelled a "right" wing, was led by Novakovskii, late of the *Farainigte,* and argued that Communism and "*Iskra*-ism" were not the same, that "the existence of the Bund was very useful in earlier times." Another "rightist," Arsh, said that "the Sections must be a mass organization which must *alone* decide all questions of Jewish life."[71] In other words, the right wing was arguing for some sort of *Evsektsiia* autonomy, probably akin to that enjoyed by the territorial Communist parties.

Avrom Merezhin, an ex-Bundist, took the opposite tack and argued that economic work should not be a specifically Jewish concern—an old Bundist argument. Merezhin denied that he was in favor of assimilation but contended that *Iskra*-ism was the correct policy and that Arsh and others were inadvertently adopting the *Borot'b*ist program. He thought Sections were unnecessary and should be replaced by a purely technical—that is, translation—apparatus, perhaps in the form of Departments, with no need for a central organ.

Moishe Rafes, in a familiar role, led the center. His

[69] This probably meant that they represented Sections which had enrolled 1,743 Jews in the Communist Party. They could not have represented 1,743 *Evsektsiia* activists, for the number of such activists was closer to 200. Apparently, the notion of a *Evsektsiia* as an *organization* enrolling its own members had not yet been displaced by the definition of the *Evsektsiia* as a technical apparatus.

[70] Agurskii, *Di yidishe komisariatn,* p. 33.

[71] *Ibid.,* p. 307. Italics added.

centrism consisted in a somewhat scholastic differentiation of "political assimilation," which he favored, and "cultural assimilation," which he claimed to oppose, and in the view that Sections should ultimately be abolished but that they were temporarily useful in some areas, particularly Belorussia. He conceded that the Sections should be "multifaceted mass organizations," but he qualified his endorsement of Sections by saying that they were needed only because of practical, not national, considerations. Arguing dialectically, Rafes charged that by advocating abolition of the Sections, the left was objectively aiding the right, since abolition would arouse and highlight nationalistic tendencies. According to Rafes, the national problem could be solved by fighting the petit bourgeois elements which had infiltrated the Sections, but he argued that the Sections ought not to be dissolved because "for the Jewish workers, an autonomous revolutionary organization plays the same role as the idea of political autonomy does for the proletariat of other oppressed nations." [72] Dimanshtain reacted as he had at the Second *Evsektsiia* Conference. He tried to wave away these theoretical differences, pooh-poohing them as abstract arguments. "We should not squabble about philosophy but rather consider burning questions of civil war. . . . I am for Sections and against Departments, not on principle but for practical reasons—because the experience of Departments has been a sad one." [73]

A preliminary vote was taken on three resolutions which embodied the ideas of the three factions. Novakovskii's resolution got twice as many votes as Rafes', and only eight of the voters cast their ballot for Merezhin's resolution. A clear victory for the "right wing" was indicated, and a commission of five was appointed to work out a final

[72] M. Rafes, "Kommunisticheskii bund i evreiskie sektsii," *Zhizn' natsional'nostei,* June 29, 1920.

[73] Agurskii, *Di yidishe komisariatn,* p. 309.

resolution, using Novakovskii's as a starting point.[74] This disconcerted the left and center, who then tried to put through a resolution stating that a tendency toward forming an autonomous organization had manifested itself at the Conference. This would have placed the legitimacy of the Conference in doubt and would have served both to nullify the gains of the nationalist faction and to remove the stigma of heresy from the others. After a preliminary vote had approved the resolution 28–16, the right marshaled its forces for the final vote which saw twenty vote "yes" but thirty-two abstain.[75]

The resolution on the organizational question was finally passed by 36–21–3. The resolution affirmed the correctness of establishing Jewish Sections and their suitability for the tasks of the period. At the same time, it warned that the tendency towards organizational separatism must be checked, blaming this tendency partially on the *partkomy* which ignored the needs of the Jewish workers and paid little attention to the Sections. The Sections were eminently useful at a time when Jewish leftist groups were still splitting off from old parties, when Jewish workers in Poland and elsewhere were still wavering. But, the resolution continued, the Conference rejects proposals to make the Sections an autonomous Jewish organization. "In the questions posed by the specific conditions of Jewish life, the Jewish Section is also not an autonomous organization, but it has the task of preparing, working out, and presenting to the party . . . its projects and proposals."[76] Thus, the resolution did manage to assert *Evsektsiia* initiative, and for all practical purposes, responsibility and power in all Jewish

[74] Merezhin's group and Rafes' group refused to serve on the commission and the conference moved on to the next item on the agenda. Who actually wrote the resolution is unclear.

[75] The figures are in Agurskii, *Di yidishe komisariatn,* p. 323.

[76] *Ibid.,* p. 342.

questions—though it formulated this in a somewhat sophistic way. The Sections were urged to have fewer meetings and concentrate more on *agitprop,* thereby avoiding autonomist tendencies and inbreeding. Finally, with a flourish of what seemed to be sheer double-talk, the resolution defined the Section as a "multi-faceted technical mass apparatus of the Party." So the Section was multifaceted, but technical; a mass group, but only an apparatus! This kind of "compromise," wherein conflicting ideas were harmonized by a juxtaposition of antonymous words, resulted undoubtedly from the revision of the original Conference resolution by the RCP Central Committee, which made the Centrist resolution, rather than the "rightist," appear as the majority resolution.[77] "Democratic centralism" was apparently invoked to curb the Jewish Sections.

The disputes over the national-organizational question were the most serious of the conference but there were many squabbles concerning other matters. The delegates were unsparing in their criticism of Dimanshtain and the Central Bureau (C.B.), charging inactivity, ineffectiveness, inconsistency—"you cannot find a political line in the work of the C.B. even with a searchlight"—and insufficient initiative. Indeed, a resolution was passed stating that the "insufficient results achieved in Jewish Party and Soviet work are in large measure due to lack of initiative and energy of the C.B. . . . There is no general political and organizational system. The C.B. is weak in instructing the regional and *guberniia* bureaus of the Sections." [78]

There was no lack of personal bickering either. Cheskis accused Rafes of deliberately obstructing C.B. work, while Merezhin accused Cheskis of "provincialism" and a "*galuth*

[77] See Altshuler, pp. 172–73 and 187 for evidence that such a manipulation of the resolution took place.

[78] Agurskii, *Di yidishe komisariatn,* p. 338.

[diaspora] mentality."[79] Despite this highly charged atmosphere, the Conference took a long step forward in defining the organizational principles of the *Evsektsiia.* The membership of the Central Bureau, the highest organ of the *Evsektsiia,* was set at nine, with five members to be permanently stationed in Moscow. There were to be Main Bureaus in the Ukraine and "Lithuania,"[80] composed of three members together with a member of the Central Bureau.[81] *Guberniia* bureaus could be established when twenty or more Section members declared the need for them. Approval of both the *partkom* and the next highest *Evsektsiia* body was necessary. Such a bureau would consist of a secretary and two members. If there were less than twenty Yiddish-speaking Communist Party members who wished to form a Section, no bureau would be established, but a secretary would be elected, subject to approval by the *partkom* and *Evsektsiia.* Where no bureau or secretary was elected, the *guberniia* bureau of the Sections, in consultation with the local Party committee, appointed them. The *guberniia* bureau or Central Bureau could also appoint an *uezd* secretary; *uezd* bureaus in areas having more than five local bureaus could be created on approval of the *guberniia*

79 Merezhin's behavior is puzzling. Here he emerged as the most radical of the anti-nationalists whereas at a Conference of the Bund in Petrograd in 1917 he was a member of the "national opposition" and, according to a Bundist present at the Conference, expressed "Zionist belchings" about consolidating the Jewish population and curing its economic ills. See B. Z. Dinur, *BiYmai Milkhamah UMahpekha* (Jerusalem, 1960), p. 159. Merezhin was later the administrator of the Jewish Department of *Evkom,* a post which involved much "Jewish" economic activity. In the 1920's he was very active in Jewish agricultural colonization and devoted himself to the economic problems of Russian Jewry.

80 At that time the Bolsheviks held part of what was to become Lithuania. Later on, the Main Bureau was set up in Minsk, Belorussia.

81 The latter was not an *ex officio* member but actually worked with the Main Bureau in Kiev or Minsk.

bureau. The *uezd* secretary, like his *guberniia* and local counterparts, had consultation rights in the *partkom*. *Guberniia* bureaus were established in Vitebsk, Gomel, Smolensk, and Samara within the RSFSR and others were later added in the Ukraine and Belorussia. The bureaus were to organize lectures, meetings, discussions, party schools, workers' clubs, commissions for political work among women, newspapers and periodicals—all in the Yiddish language.[82] Persons sent by the Central Bureau to "do Jewish work" could not be diverted to other areas by Party organs without the express consent of the Central Bureau.

Because of the serious factional differences at the Third Conference, the election to the new Central Bureau was by lists. The Novakovskii group got thirty-two votes, Rafes' center, sixteen, and the Merezhin radicals, six.[83] The center and left then refused to enter the Central Bureau and take responsibility for its actions, but Mandelsberg and Rafes did eventually opt for power over principle. The new Central Bureau consisted of Novakovskii, Cheskis, Levitan, and Orshanskii—all identified with the "right wing"—together with Rafes, Mandelsberg, Dimanshtain, and Sudarskii of the center, and Shakhne Epshtain of the "left." Dimanshtain was soon reassigned by the Central Committee,[84] and he

[82] See *Yedies fun tsentral biuro fun di idishe sektsies beim tsentral komitet fun der ruslander komunistisher partai,* no. 1, October 1920. The *gubpartkom* was to pay for publication costs. This was changed when NEP and *khozraschet* were introduced.

[83] Agurskii, *Di yidishe komisariatn,* p. 331. According to a center group which later protested the nationalist tone of the Conference, Merezhin's group got only five votes. See p. 370.

[84] Possibly to assume his post as labor commissar in the short-lived "Litbel" republic. The Conference was held July 4–10, and "Litbel" collapsed later that same month. E. N. Shkliar, *Bor'ba trudiashchikhsia Litovsko-Belorusskoi SSR s innostrannymi interventami i vnutrennei kontrrevoliutsiei* (Minsk, 1962), pp. 164 and 168. Shkliar mentions a labor commissariat but does not say who was commissar (p. 34).

was replaced in the Central Bureau by Aleksander Chemeriskii. At the same time, the rightist Orshanskii was replaced, on orders from the Central Committee, by the leftist Merezhin. The Central Committee apparently also asked for the resignations of the rightists Novakovskii, Levitan, and Cheskis, but nothing was done about this and they remained in the Central Bureau.[85] As the Conference had established in the organizational rules, five of the Central Bureau members worked in Moscow. Chemeriskii was made secretary of the Bureau, Epshtain was appointed editor of *Emes,* Mandelsberg and Merezhin were assigned to work in *Evkom,* and Cheskis was placed in charge of a Jewish Bureau of the Comintern Executive Committee, where he was assisted by Chemeriskii. Rafes and Levitan were assigned to the Main Bureau in "Litbel," while Sudarskii was sent to the Ukraine along with Novakovskii.[86]

The Central Committee overruled the *Evsektsiia* on other matters, in an attempt to curb the latter's appetite for authority. The Committee initially refused to accept the *Evsektsiia*'s demand that the Ukrainian Jewish Departments be reconverted to Sections, though this step was soon taken. The Central Committee also rejected *Evsektsiia* claims to jurisdiction over Jewish departments in *Narkompros* or other commissariats. Furthermore, it placed the Sections under the jurisdiction of the *agitprop* departments of the

[85] Orshanskii was accused of publishing an article in the Vitebsk *Shtern* which defended nationalism and a federative party structure. This was communicated to Krestinskii and the Central Committee by the disaffected centrist group. There is no doubt that the Central Committee viewed the Third Conference with some apprehension and was eager to balance the Central Bureau with less "nationalistic" personnel. See *Partai materialn,* no. 5, August 1921.

[86] *Der komunist* (Kharkov), September 15, 1920, p. 8. There is no mention here of Novakovskii's assignment, but it is mentioned in *Partai materialn,* which also says that Cheskis "had no assigned task in the C.B." Either he had lost his job in the Comintern by 1921 or the Jewish Bureau had itself been abolished by that time.

gubkomy and Central Committee, thus partially altering the horizontal structure whereby the Sections worked as part of the local *partkomy*. In practice, however, the Central Bureau, at least, continued to work with the Central Committee directly, and not with its *agitprop* division.[87]

Despite the restrictions placed on the *Evsektsiia* by the Central Committee, relations between the two began to show definite signs of improvement. Whereas the Central Committee of the "Litbel" Party had opposed the formation of Jewish Sections, its successor, the Central Committee of the Belorussian Communist Party, cooperated fully with the Main Committee of the *Evsektsiia* in Belorussia.[88] Relations improved at the center, also. The Central Bureau submitted a list of 140 Party members it wanted reassigned to the *Evsektsiia*. The Central Committee agreed to send twelve to the Ukraine, eight to Belorussia, seven to Vitebsk, seven to Gomel, and ten to other parts of Russia. The status of thirty-five was undecided, and nineteen could not be spared by the Central Committee.[89] These new Jewish activists helped in the rapid expansion of *Evsektsiia* activity. By October 1920 there were about forty local Sections in Russia;[90] and this number had grown to sixty-six by August 1921. By that time fifty additional Sections existed in Belorussia and the Ukraine, though in the latter Party indifference and hostility to the *Evsektsiia* lingered on with the result that several large centers of Jewish population had no Sections at all.[91] The Central Bureau also managed to pry loose some more activists from the jealous hands of the Central Committee. One hundred and sixty-eight Jewish Communists were transferred to the *Evsektsiia* in 1921.[92]

[87] See *Partai materialn*, no. 3, March 1921, p. 2.

[88] *Ibid.*

[89] Forty-two were unaccounted for. *Ibid.*, p. 7.

[90] *Yedies*, p. 30.

[91] *Partai materialn*, no. 5, August 1921, p. 5.

[92] *Ibid.*

The staff of the Central Bureau itself increased, especially after the last Bundist holdouts entered the Party. The Central Bureau had between twelve and fourteen political functionaries, four instructors, a public relations officer ("administrator for information"), and a technical staff, including thirty-five printers.[93] Between February and August 1920 the Central Bureau had received 179 letters and memoranda and had sent out 586. But after the Third Conference the tempo increased. In the single month of August 1920, 172 letters and publications were received by the Bureau and 496 were sent out.[94] Between January and July 1921, 1,049 additional pieces of correspondence were received and 3,429 were sent out.[95] In the year following July 1920 the Central Bureau held 75 meetings at which 485 questions were taken up.[96] Thus, on the average, the Central Bureau met as a body nearly twice a week. All told, by August 1921, there were between 350 and 400 "active Jewish Party workers," meaning *Evsektsiia* functionaries, in Russia, Belorussia, and the Ukraine.[97]

This upsurge of activity and increase in personnel still left the *Evsektsiia* woefully inadequate resources with which to achieve the tasks it had set for itself—establishing the dictatorship of the proletariat on the Jewish street. In Vitebsk, for example, there were ten thousand Jewish

[93] *Ibid.*

[94] The Central Bureau received, between August 1920 and January 1921, 541 pieces of correspondence from 50 localities and sent out 1,596 to 94 places. *Partai materialn,* no. 3, March 1921, pp. 6 and 22.

[95] The calculation is based on figures in *Partai materialn,* no. 5, August 1921, p. 3. These figures are somewhat deceptive in regard to *Evsektsiia* activity "in the field." In the eleven-month period between August 1920 and July 1921 only 818 pieces of correspondence came in from outside Moscow. The 772 others must have been mainly intra-governmental memoranda.

[96] *Ibid.,* p. 1.

[97] *Ibid.,* p. 5. For some details on the increased activities of the *Evsektsiia,* see *Arbeter kalendar afn yor 1924,* p. 91.

workers alone, but only one hundred Jewish Communists and only ten *Evsektsiia* activists. The Mogilev Section had five or six activists; the Samara Section, which was a *guberniia* bureau, had only five. The relation between Jewish population, Jewish workers, and *Evsektsiia* activists in the fall of 1920 may be seen in Table IV.

TABLE IV

Evsektsiia ACTIVISTS IN 1920 [98]

City	Jewish Population	Number of Jewish Workers	Number of *Evsektsiia* Activists
Vitebsk	—	10,000	10
Mogilev	—	—	5–6
Smolensk	15,000	1,000	5
Samara	40,000	4,000	5
Saratov	20,000	3,000	4
Oriol	—	—	4
Kirsanov	—	—	3–4
Kazan	8,000	1,500	5
Irkutsk	18,000	—	4–5
Orenburg	5,000	500	—
Omsk	10,000	—	2–3
Cheliabinsk	8,000	2,500	—
Ekaterinburg	3,000	300	—
Rostov	45,000	2,000	5
Petrograd	12,000	3,000	2–3

These figures include almost exclusively Great Russian cities, where the Jewish population was relatively new. The figures for such cities as Minsk and Kiev would probably show a similar trend or one even less encouraging from a *Evsektsiia* point of view, because of the reluctance of former Komfarbandists in the Ukraine to enter the Party, and because of the continuing existence of an independent, albeit Communist, Bund in Belorussia.

[98] Based on *Partai materialn*, no. 3, March 1921, pp. 14–15.

Nevertheless, some localities did report progress. The Gomel Section, created in August 1919, had enlisted 175 members for the Communist Party by May 1920. Considering the fact that there were thousands of Jewish workers in Gomel, this seems like a modest achievement indeed, but the Gomel *Sektsiia* was apparently proud of its work. The *Sektsiia* sponsored a series of lectures aimed at drawing the Jewish workers away from the Bund. It helped form Party cells in factories with a high concentration of Jewish workers: in one factory the cell grew from three members to seventy. The Gomel *Evsektsiia* organized a Jewish workers' club, "open daily until midnight," which also included a two-month Party school. The Section boasted that there were "110 members and candidates *of the Section.*" [99] Interestingly, all of the Section members were former Socialists—fifty Bundists, forty *Farainigte,* and twenty *Poalai Tsion*ists. The Section held, on the average, weekly meetings. The Section Bureau and its presidium held forty-eight meetings during the year. The Section also reported that there were 337 "members of the *Evsektsiia*" in the Gomel *guberniia* as a whole—which, it admitted, was a pitifully small number. "Unfortunately, only one percent of the Jewish working masses in our province has joined the Communist Party." [100]

The Attack on the Old Order

The weakness of the *Evsektsiia* on the local level was not an insurmountable obstacle in revolutionizing and seizing control of Jewish communal life. The *Evsektsiia* could always play its trump card, its ace in the hole: it had the full force of Soviet power to fall back on, to use when all other expedients failed. When the *Evsektsiia* was un-

[99] Italics added.

[100] *Zhizn' natsional'nostei,* May 23, 1920.

successful in using pseudo-democratic means to gain absolute power in the Jewish community, it relied on force and coercion.

The old Jewish community began to distintegrate in 1917. "One of the chief consequences of the revolution is that the removal of the external pressure has brought, and is bringing about, a certain relaxation in the bonds which have . . . kept tightly together all the groups and classes of the Jewish community."[101] The Petrograd *Togblat* reported that "we have a constant flow of reports from cities and towns telling of the closing of Jewish institutions for lack of funds. . . . People have stopped giving private donations because the former contributors, having lost their say [*deah*], refused to give their pay [*meah*]. And this is the uniquely Jewish result of the struggle for democratization, of the 'class struggle' which has been conducted in Jewish institutions since the revolution. The struggle is won and the institutions close, because the winners cannot keep them up and the losers don't want to. We are all taken up with high politics, we destroy and build worlds, and we have no time for lesser work, for the usual daily tasks without which nothing can be built."[102] Dissatisfied with the pace at which the community was decaying, the Jewish Communists initiated their campaign against the old Jewish order in 1918, shifting it into high gear in 1919.

It is not surprising that the first large-scale and generally successful efforts of the *Evsektsiia* were in the direction of destroying the old Jewish order. For the *Evsektsiia* was beginning to assume some of the characteristics of a mobilization agency of a modernizing party-state, that is, it was entrusted with the task of the social mobilization of

[101] "On the Political Situation and the Jewish Aspects of the Revolution," report dated May 5, 1917, in the Lucien Wolf Archive, Box 16, Packet 110, item 14698, YIVO Archives.

[102] *Togblat,* August 24 (September 6), 1917.

Yiddish-speaking Jews—a "process in which major clusters of old social, economic, and psychological commitments are eroded and broken and people become available for new patterns of socialization and behavior."[103] In this process of social mobilization the *Evsektsiia* acted as a "political entrepreneur" on behalf of the Communist Party. The role of the entrepreneur is to organize

> individuals for particular purposes: party rallies, voluntary labor, mass literacy campaigns. . . . Particularly in societies where there are many institutions of a mixed traditional and modern nature that contain traditional, accommodationist, and innovative roles—such as churches, separatist movements, charitable and social organizations, clubs, and fiscal and burial societies—the political organizers are likely to embody roles that spread the value of modernity by focusing on particular instrumental ends. On the other hand, they are also potential centers of separatism, parochialism, and the perpetuation of nonmodern values. In order to attain modernization without parochialism, the society must infuse its intermediate groupings with a sense of corporate responsibility by means of an ideology of modernism. Typically, this is the work of the political entrepreneur.[104]

Amitai Etzioni has argued that Deutsch's conception of mobilization involves a sequence of nearly total disintegration of traditional authority and commitments followed by a process of reintegration. Whether or not this is a correct interpretation of Deutsch's thesis, we can agree with Etzioni that a totally disintegrated collectivity is difficult to organize and mobilize. "Traditional units can serve as

[103] Karl Deutsch, "Social Mobilization and Political Development," *American Political Science Review*, LV, no. 3 (September 1961), 494–95.

[104] Apter, *The Politics of Modernization*, p. 168.

effective foundations of mobilization for modernization if they are transformed rather than disintegrated." In the State of Israel the integration of immigrants was initially attempted through the dissolution of traditional groupings and "mixing" immigrants of different origins in the classroom, the army, and new settlements. "Actually, this approach seems to have generated a ritualistic adherence on the part of the immigrants to their old norms and groupings. It became increasingly evident that effective acculturation required gaining the support of the existing leadership of the immigrant groups and maintaining the groups or providing them with new 'Israeli' leadership, attempting to *transform* their cultures and structures rather than attempting to 'erode' or 'disintegrate' them." [105] A somewhat parallel process came about in the Bolshevization of Soviet Muslims. The mobilization of the Soviet Jewish population, as well as the Muslim population, had to be of a more radical kind, involving the near-disintegration of traditional structures and values, for several reasons. First, those structures and values were so alien to the spirit and content of Marxist-Leninist ideology as to render them unsuitable for transformation. Some attempts were made to remake the institutions of the Jewish religion and culture but all ended in complete failure. Secondly, Soviet Communism demanded an increasingly higher level of commitment to its own values and institutions which did not permit simultaneous adherence to alternative belief systems, even if those systems could be seen as merely different, but not competitive. Bolshevik ideology was too specific and demanding to allow

[105] Amitai Etzioni, *The Active Society* (New York, 1968), p. 420. Gregory Massell has described Bolshevik attempts to use Muslim women as a "surrogate proletariat" in an unsuccessful effort to "loosen and disintegrate traditional social relationships, then to rebuild society when its very dissolution compelled reconstruction." "Law as an Instrument of Revolutionary Change in a Traditional Milieu," *Law and Society Review*, II, no. 2 (February 1968).

for the existence of syncretic value structures. Finally, the *Evsektsiia* was extremely jealous of its prerogatives and would brook no political or social rivals in the Jewish community. Its acknowledged weakness both in the Jewish community and within the Party made it especially sensitive to any potential alternative source of authority. However, the *Evsektsiia* itself was in a way a "traditional unit" in that its very existence was a concession to the "traditional" idea of a distinct Jewish nationality. Furthermore, its leadership after 1921 was drawn in part from familiar Jewish political parties which some saw as having been "transformed" into the Jewish Sections. To the degree that it could be identified by Jews as a legitimate *Jewish* institution the *Evsektsiia's* mission of mobilization and transformation would be made easier.

The first step in the mobilization-transformation process was to clear away the traditional institutions and loyalties which stood as a barrier in the path of the Bolshevik drive for the economic modernization and political integration of Soviet Jewry. Chief among these were religion, Zionism, Jewish socialist parties, non-Communist social, cultural, or economic organizations, and even Hebrew language and culture.

The first act of a local *Evkom* was almost invariably to close all organizations, societies, and institutions or to place them under *Evkom* supervision. It would also take over all capital assets, including the buildings and offices of such institutions.[106] Most often, the *Evkom* did not abolish these

[106] See, for example, the decrees of the Vitebsk *Evkom* of September 5, 1918, in Agurskii, *Di yidishe komisariatn,* p. 78. The Vitebsk Society for Poor, Handicapped, and Orphaned Jews was taken over on the pretext that it was discriminating against the poor and keeping donations for itself. The *Evkom* seized the 43,155 rubles the Society had in the bank "in order to use them for the impoverished masses, to open a Jewish soup-kitchen and to build orphanages."

organizations' welfare services, so desperately needed by the stricken Jewish population, but dispensed them under its own aegis. The national organizations, such as EKOPO, ORT, and OZE, were first drawn into *Idgezkom* and then either Communized or abolished. ORT and *Idgezkom,* which survived the longest, had constitutions which provided that "applications for membership must be endorsed by the Jewish Section with the result that only communists and their sympathizers are admitted to membership."[107] The organizations had interlocking directorates, were not allowed to compete with each other, and were completely dominated by the *Evsektsiia.*

The *Evkom* and *Evsektsiia* were often inadvertently aided by members of the Bund, *Farainigte,* and *Poalai Tsion* who were also dissatisfied with the "bourgeois-clerical" domination of the Jewish *kehillas* and communal organizations. They tried to wrest control of these institutions, and sometimes succeeded, only to be usurped later by the *Evsektsiia.* It was SETMAS which made the first attack on the *kehilla* in Kiev, literally smashing and wrecking its offices,[108] and it was the Ukrainian Kombund which destroyed the Society to Aid Pogrom Victims in May 1919.[109]

In April 1919 a decree had been drafted abolishing the *kehillas.* The decree was not published until June-July "because the *kehillas* had a whole range of institutions which had to stay open and the Jewish Commissariats did not have the personnel needed to take over the work of the *kehilla.* It would have been senseless simply to close the

[107] H. S. Linfield, "The Communal Organization of the Jews in Soviet Russia," address delivered at the National Conference of Jewish Social Services, Toronto, June 25, 1924. Published in New York, 1925.

[108] Visual proof of the ferocity of SETMAS' attack is found in a picture on p. 346 of *In der tkufe fun revolutsie,* ed. E. Tsherikover.

[109] Rafes told V. Latskii, "We hate any social independence." *Ibid.,* p. 316.

kehilla because the Jewish poor, who came to the *kehilla* for aid, would have suffered."[110] In June, Stalin and Agurskii signed an order demanding that the monies and inventories of local *kehillas* be turned over to local *Evkomy*, formalizing a procedure which had been followed in practice for some time.[111] The religious functions of the *kehillas* were to be carried on by individual religious congregations and the welfare services were to be assumed by the appropriate offices, though temporary exceptions could be made for relief organizations. Frequently, the dissolution of the *kehilla* was followed by its reconstruction in another guise,[112] and *kehillas* continued to exist well into the 1920's. Cultural activities were to be taken up by the *Evkomy* or the Jewish departments of the Commissariat of Education.

The Second Conference of the *Evsektsiia*, held in June 1919, urged the forcible cessation of all Zionist activity. On the night of July 5–6, 1919, the offices of all Zionist organizations in the Ukraine, including even a sports club, were raided and closed. The Zionist leaders and officials were arrested, questioned, and released.[113] On July 12, 1919, the Ukrainian Commissariat for Internal Affairs decreed—"with the agreement of the Jewish Departments and Komfarband"—that "all bourgeois-Zionist and Jewish clerical, political, economic, educational, and cultural societies and organizations" were to cease operations.[114] Officials of these organizations were required to sign affidavits stating

[110] Agurskii, *Der idisher arbeter*, pp. 88–89.

[111] The text of the order is found in Agurskii, *Di yidishe komisariatn*, p. 237. In *Der idisher arbeter*, Agurskii states that "the order of the Central Commissariat was only a formal approval of what the local commissariats had done" (p. 89).

[112] See documents on the dissolution of the Berdichev *kehilla*, which reconstituted itself as a "committee dealing with all facets of religious life," in the Tsherikover Archive, YIVO Archives.

[113] *Komunistishe fon*, July 10, 1919.

[114] *Yedies*, no. 7, supplement to *Komunistishe fon*, July 12, 1919.

that all activities had been halted, that complete records would be turned over to the Liquidation Commission consisting of Rafes, Kulik, Frenkel, and Mikhail Charney, and that the activities would not be continued in another guise.[115] Moishe Rafes boasted that "the ban on Zionist activity in the Ukraine was put into effect on the initiative of *Jewish* Communists. This means that we are dealing with a manifestation of *Jewish civil war*. . . . This concretizes the dictatorship of the Jewish proletariat on the Jewish street." [116] The Odessa *Komunistishe shtim* exuberantly announced that "the time has come when the civil war in the Jewish world will be, not a paper revolution, but one of deeds, sweeping out Jewish Reaction." [117] Jewish socialist institutions were not suppressed at this time and even some "bourgeois" organizations managed to stay in existence by appealing to the Commissariat of Internal Affairs.[118]

A good case study in the Communization, rather than liquidation, of a Jewish organization is provided by the history of the *Kultur-Lige*. A secular cultural organization, the *Lige* had been founded in 1918 in Kiev. It had sections for literature, music, theater, painting and sculpture, people's schools, pre-school education, and adult education.

[115] Rabbi Oleshkovskii reminded Rafes that the affidavit followed very closely the form of a loyalty oath Jews had been required to take under tsarism. The rabbi refused to sign unless certain changes were made. Tsherikover, *In der tkufe*, p. 327. *Komunistishe fon*, July 26, 1919, reports that a telegram had been received from the Central Bureau of the *Evsektsiia* asking the Main Committee of the Ukrainian Komfarband to close all Zionist schools, in line with the resolutions of the Second Conference. The Komfarband seems to have acted even before getting word from Moscow.

[116] "Birger krig oif der idisher gass," *Komunistishe fon*, July 8, 1919.

[117] Quoted in Tsherikover, *In der tkufe*.

[118] Thus, OPE, the Society for Relief of War Victims, was allowed to continue operations—probably because it partially relieved the government of the burden of providing for Jewish war victims.

It planned a Jewish national theater, and its Jewish national university began giving summer courses in 1918.[119] By the summer of 1918 the *Lige* had twenty-seven branches in the Ukraine. It had a central committee which was officially non-political but whose members were affiliated with the *Farainigte* (9 members), Bund (7), *Poalai Tsion* (2), and *Folkspartai* (3). The *Lige* was very active in publishing and worked through existing cultural organizations so that its influence was felt in every sphere of Jewish secular culture. By the end of 1918 the *Lige* had 120 branches in the Ukraine, and similar groups had sprung up in Russia, Bessarabia, the Crimea, Lithuania, and even Siberia. Where the socialists had a majority in the *kehilla,* the latter would support the *Lige.* In January 1919 the obvious strength of the *Lige* had prompted A. Revutskii, a *Poalai Tsion*ist and the last Jewish minister of the Ukrainian Directory, to offer it complete control of Jewish education under the Directory.[120] The *Lige* officially turned him down, since its directors were members of anti-Directory parties, but many of its officials began to work for the Directory in the hope of getting a subsidy which would enable the *Lige* to expand its activities. This arrangement lasted only three weeks because the Directory left Kiev in February 1919. The leftist elements in the *Lige* now bitterly attacked the central committee for having looked the other way while *Lige* functionaries cooperated with the Petliura regime. When Soviet power was consolidated in the Ukraine, the differences of political opinion were resolved and "it may be said that the most brilliant period in the activity of the

[119] *Evreiskii rabochii,* July 12, 1918, p. 12; Moishe Katz, "Di kultur lige in ukraine," *Di tsukunft,* XXIX, no. 3 (March 1921).

[120] Some indication of the resources of the *Lige* can be gotten from the fact that in early 1919 one of its functionaries ordered half a million rubles worth of books from abroad and paid in advance. Katz, *ibid.,* p. 185.

Kultur-Lige began under the Soviet regime."[121] At the end of July 1919 the *Lige* had 250 students in its "people's university," four evening schools for workers, six adult schools on the elementary and secondary levels, a *gymnazium* and a teacher's seminary, a large publishing house and bookstore, fifty-six local libraries, and fourteen playgrounds and kindergartens.[122] Under a compromise worked out with the Bolsheviks, the *Lige* was not responsible to any commissar, but its educational institutions were placed under Soviet control. The Soviets subsidized the university at a cost of 250,000 rubles a month and theaters were also subsidized. The *Lige* managed to maintain almost complete control of Jewish culture even under the Soviets. When the Soviet government would establish any Jewish cultural office or institution, its officials would be recommended by the *Lige.* In fact, when Denikin's army temporarily pushed the Bolsheviks out of Kiev in August 1919, the latter left the *Lige* five million rubles to tide Jewish institutions over the crisis.[123] The romance of the Communists and the *Kultur-Lige* was a short one because the *Evsektsiia* acted the part of the jealous lover in the triangle. Rafes and Matz, a former S.S. member, opposed the *Lige* as nationalistic.[124] In December 1920 the *Lige* was officially reconsecrated to the Revolution when its presses were nationalized, its paper supply cut off by the *Evsektsiia,* and its central committee disbanded, after having had a two-thirds Communist majority imposed on it.[125] The *Lige* continued to operate as a

121 *Ibid.,* p. 187.

122 *Unzer veg* (Warsaw), November 21, 1919.

123 Katz, p. 188.

124 Esther and Litvakov, however, urged continued government support for it.

125 *Unzer gedank,* August 12, 1922; *Unzer tseit* (Vilna), January 28, 1922. "Baal Dimyon," "Der idisher komunist, di kulture-lige un dos idishe bukh," *Di tsukunft,* XXXI, no. 1 (January 1923). See also *Kultur lige: ershtes zamlheft* (Warsaw, 1921). *Lige* officials were al-

Communist organization, but still retained a Yiddishist tendency. There were complaints that its local branches were so anxious to publish anything in Yiddish that books "unfit for print" were published without previous consultation with "higher authorities." [126]

The main thrust of the *Evsektsiia* drive for total domination was directed at the "bourgeois-clerical-Zionist" camp. The destruction of the *kehillas* had been accomplished with relative ease, using administrative fiat with the ever-present threat of force to give it authority.[127] Communal organizations were taken over by the tactics of infiltration and "bogus coalition," leavened with proper doses of coercion. The Hebrew language, the Zionist movement, and the Jewish religion were the next targets. Because they were so antithetical to Communism and the *Evsektsiia* program, they could not be subverted and "transformed" but had to be confronted directly and assaulted frontally.

There had long been a conflict between the Yiddishists and Hebraists in Russian Jewry. Writers such as "Mendele Mokher Sforim" and I. L. Peretz had written in both languages, but around the turn of the century linguistic co-existence became increasingly difficult to maintain, as the language problem became a political one. Though practically no European (Ashkenazic) Jews used Hebrew as an everyday language—it was almost exclusively the language of prayer, study, and rabbinic correspondence—the Zionists among them aimed to revive Hebrew as a spoken language. This would be a part of the national renaissance which was to cast off the shackles of the diaspora, the *galuth.* As the *galuth* would disappear, so would its stultifying customs, backward economy, borrowed language, and even a per-

---

lowed to work as *spetsy* for the "new" *Lige* and in the harsh winter of 1920–21 many saved themselves from starvation by this means.

[126] "Alef," "Geferlikhe initsiativ," *Emes,* November 11, 1922.

[127] By 1923, however, many *kehillas* had reconstituted themselves.

nicious psychology which the Zionists referred to—and still do—as "*galuth* mentality." Most Jewish socialists, however, opposed the Zionist idea of a separate Jewish national homeland, and saw Jewish life in a socialist world as viable and productive, desirable and possible. Yiddish, the language of the masses, embodied within it the Ashkenazic Jewish culture which had been developing in Europe for hundreds of years. It would have been unhistorical and anti-Marxist to shunt aside the Yiddish language and artificially impose a Semitic language upon a people whose warp and woof was woven of the fabric of Europe. Moreover, since the early Zionists were mostly of the middle classes and intelligentsia, the linguistic debate could be identified with the political one, and the battle lines of language and politics were drawn congruently. The Hebrew-Yiddish struggle was taken very seriously by all combatants, but the most radical Yiddishists could not match the *Evsektsiia* in the fury with which it pursued the Hebrew language. Even more than the Jewish Socialists, *Evsektsiia* activists identified Hebrew with bourgeois culture and Zionist political persuasion. They exerted relentless pressure on the Soviet authorities to crush and obliterate both.

The Second *Evsektsiia* Conference had resolved to close all Hebrew schools, especially those of the Zionist-oriented *Tarbuth* (culture) network. The Jewish Communists explained that the struggle against Hebrew was not a struggle against a language, but one directed against an ideology—Zionism—of an enemy class—the bourgeoisie.[128] *Evkom*

[128] H. Freier, "Nit kain shprakh-kamf," *Komunistishe fon,* July 31, 1919. Earlier in July the Commissariat of Education had declared that Hebrew had the status of a foreign language and had decided that children in the second grade who had begun their studies in Hebrew could complete their education in that language. Forcible seizures of and requisitions from Hebrew schools were to be ended forthwith. This decision was sharply criticized by the Jewish Section of the All-Russian Education Conference of National Minorities. See *Kultur un bildung,* no. 1, February 1920, pp. 32–34.

had shared office space with Hebrew publications, but once the Jewish socialists entered the *Evsektsiia* coexistence was no longer possible. The Fourth *Evsektsiia* Conference, held in August 1921, dealt with concrete, rather than ideological, issues, and served to realign the *Evsektsiia* leadership and policy in light of the final liquidation of the Jewish socialist parties.[129] The new Central Bureau included Chemeriskii, Novakovskii, Sudarskii, Cheskis, Levitan, Merezhin, Mandelsberg, and Rafes as holdovers from the Central Bureau elected in July 1920, but added Moishe Litvakov, Esther Frumkin, and Rakhmiel Veinshtain, late of the Komfarband.[130] Whether the new members were directly responsible for the greatly stepped-up drive against Hebrew—

[129] There was a brief exchange between the former Hebrew teacher Kazakevich, on one side, and Esther and Abram, on the other, regarding the Jewish cultural heritage. Kazakevich argued that there need be no fear of talking about "national culture" and "if Yiddishism can serve the revolution we need not fear Yiddishism." Esther and Abram viewed this as nationalistic and said that a *new* culture is being created in Yiddish (*Komunistishe fon*, April 12, 1924). Yiddishism as a cultural ideology was always being denounced by the *Evsektsiia* which declared itself opposed to "linguistic fetishism and chauvinism" and saw Yiddish as a political instrument rather than an end in itself. In this light, Esther's hostility to Yiddishism is quite consistent with the "nationalist" position she had taken in her Bundist period. Her nationalism consisted in the desire to create a *new proletarian* Jewish culture. The Soviet regime, with its great power to destroy the old bourgeois culture, would be an admirable instrument for accomplishing this aim. Esther's view of the *Evsektsiia's* mobilization function emphasized "transformation" rather than total destruction.

[130] Litvakov replaced Shakhne Epshtain as editor of *Emes*. Epshtain was a former Bundist, "a Rightist of the Right." A. Litvak charged that in the spring of 1919 Epshtain was part of a delegation to the United States sent by the Petliura Directory. Epshtain went to Odessa to board a ship but the Red Army attacked and he was unable to leave. He joined the Red Army under an assumed name. See article by "A. Muk" (Litvak) in *Unzer gedank* (Vilna), October 20, 1923. Epshtain went to the United States, where he became a leader of the Jewish Bureaus of the Communist Party and later an agent of the OGPU. He returned to Russia briefly in

and against Zionism and religion, too—is difficult to ascertain. But the fact remains that Esther and Litvakov, especially, towered above their new colleagues intellectually and brought with them well-defined theories and programs relating to Jewish culture. Litvakov, who had a large personal Hebrew library including many works on Hasidism and the *Khabad* (Lubavicher) Hasidic movement, was especially hostile to Hebrew, perhaps because he had written in that language and now felt the need to prove his ultraorthodoxy, or because he already had a deep commitment to the radical transformation of Jewish culture.[131] In any case, it is certain that the campaign against Hebrew was initiated

---

1929–30. Litvakov became one of the outstanding figures in the *Evsektsiia* and was a sort of Jewish cultural commissar, though his abrasive personality and sarcastic pen assured him bitter opposition. When Litvakov heard that mice had eaten the manuscripts of Moscow Yiddish writers, he said gleefully: "Good. Now we will finally be rid of the mice. There is no better poison for them" (Charney, *A yortsendlik aza*, p. 311). Esther was put in charge of liaison with localities and in this capacity she made frequent trips outside Moscow. She was also the head of the Jewish desk in the Central Office of Political Education and later served as vice-rector of the Communist University of the National Minorities of the West and was also in charge of the Jewish Party School attached to the University. Esther wrote Yiddish books dealing with the life and work of Lenin and a short memoir of Hirsh Lekert (the Bundist cobbler who shot the governor of Vilna) for which she was later accused of nationalism and latent Bundism. She also edited children's magazines and wrote a number of political education pamphlets for the *Komsomol*. On the assignments of the Central Bureau in August 1921, see *Partai materialn*, no. 5, August 1921.

[131] On Litvakov's radical critique of Jewish culture, see Yosef Berger-Barzilai, "Moshe Litvakov—kavim lidyokno al-pi reshamim ishiyim," *Bekhinot*, no. 1 (1970). Esther did not particularly stand out in the campaign against Hebrew. Her specialty seems to have been the anti-religious campaign. One source reports that in a lecture at the Communist University for the National Minorities of the West in 1926, Esther declared that "the Jewish proletariat will not give away the talented, youthful, beautiful, rich Hebrew language." Letter of Sh. D. Niepomniashchi to Y. Opatoshu, dated November 4, 1928. In the Daniel Charney File, YIVO Archives, New York. Niepomniashchi adds, "Of course, this is *Zukunfts-musik*."

by the *Evsektsiia* and not by the Soviet government or Communist Party. Lunacharskii and other Soviet officials were caught in a crossfire as both the Hebraists and Sectionists attempted to gain a definitive ruling on the status of Hebrew. The *Evsektsiia* worked on Professor M. N. Pokrovskii, at that time one of Lunacharskii's chief advisers, while the Zionists pressured Kamenev and Lunacharskii himself. The success of the *Evsektsiia* was foreordained. As Lunacharskii pointed out to Rabbi Mazeh, a Zionist leader who served as Chief (Crown) Rabbi of Moscow and who had played an important part in the defense of Mendel Beilis,

> I do not know who would doubt the value of Hebrew, except for the Jewish Communists. And they, after all, are our allies and we can hardly disbelieve them when they say that Hebrew is the language of the bourgeoisie and not of the people. . . . It is not such a great tragedy if the Jewish people remain without a distinct language; but that Hebrew is the language of the poor—that is something new to me, though I remember that you have a poet, Bialik; is he of poor people? [132]

As a matter of fact, Khaim Nakhman Bialik, the foremost Hebrew poet of his time, and other leading Hebrew writers were constantly harassed by the *Evsektsiia.* Maxim Gorkii tried to secure permission for eighteen prominent Hebrew writers to leave Russia but the *Evsektsiia* effectively blocked this attempt. Finally, Felix Dzerzhinskii, the Cheka chief, was persuaded to intervene on their behalf, and Bialik, Saul Chernikhovskii, B. Z. Dinaburg, Moishe Kleinman, and other leading lights of the Hebrew literary world were

[132] Jacob Mazeh, *Zikhronot,* IV (Tel Aviv, 1936), 13. On Kamenev and Hebrew, see Bogen, *Born a Jew,* p. 322. See also B. Vest, ed., *Naftulai Dor* (Tel Aviv, 1945), pp. 304–11.

allowed to leave Soviet Russia in June 1921.[133] The famous Hebrew theatrical troupe, *Habimah,* also felt pressured not to return to Soviet Russia after a tour abroad, though Lenin is reported to have expressed his approval of it, Kamenev had seen several of its performances and was friendly with its director, Nakhum Tsemakh, and even Dimanshtain and his Russian wife attended one of its performances and were deeply moved.[134]

The *Evsektsiia* was eminently successful in its campaign against the Hebrew language, especially in European Russia. In 1925 a secret Moscow conference of the once-powerful *Tarbuth* society was attended by thirty-five people. In 1930 there were twelve students in an underground Moscow Hebrew Teachers' Seminary, but even this ceased to function after a year and a half.[135]

Nevertheless, there were quite a few Marrano (underground) Hebraists who continued to write Hebrew prose and poetry, some even teaching the language to their children.[136] The lonely hoplessness and bitterness of the

[133] M. Z. Frank, "Anshai S'arah," *Hadoar,* May 1, 1964. Ben-Zion Katz reports that Gorkii wanted to arrange a meeting of *literati* honoring Bialik but the meeting was cancelled and Gorkii told Bialik, "This is the work of those vile Evseks." Katz, *Zikhronot,* p. 281.

[134] Katz, p. 270. On the Habimah theater, see R. Ben-Ari, *Habimah* (Chicago, 1937). On Dimanshtain, see Yitzhak Rabinovich, *MiMoskva ad Yerushalayim* (Jerusalem, 1957), p. 48.

[135] Vest, p. 311.

[136] Yehoshua Gilboa has edited a volume of Hebrew prose and poetry written in the Soviet Union, *Gekhalim Lokhashot* (Tel Aviv, 1954). The outstanding Hebrew poets in the Soviet Union were Khaim Lenskii and Elisha Rodin. On Hebrew culture and writers, see Aryeh Refaeli (Tsentsifer), *BaMaavak LiGeulah* (Tel Aviv, 1956), pp. 177–80; Wolf Blattberg, "The Story of the Hebrew and Yiddish Writers in the Soviet Union" (New York, 1953), mimeo; Alfred A. Greenbaum, "Hebrew Literature in Soviet Russia," *Jewish Social Studies,* xxx, no. 3 (July 1968); and Y. A. Gilboa, "Hebrew Literature in the U.S.S.R.," in Kochan, ed., *The Jews in Soviet Russia since 1917.*

Marrano Hebraist were expressed by Barukh Shpilberg, a Hebrew writer in the Ukraine.

> Sometimes when I fall ill with a fever and I look around and see that I have no one to leave the few books to, that I am the last . . . I fall into a black melancholy. . . . You write something in Hebrew, you come up with a new idea—there is no one to whom you can show it, there is no 'learned man' [*Yodaia Sefer*] in Berdichev. . . .[137]

There was one Hebraist who was also a devoted Communist. Shlomoh Yaakov Niepomniashchi was one of those fascinating and enigmatic personalities who, like Esther Frumkin, tried to create unusual syntheses which must have strained even his muscular mind. Niepomniashchi studied in yeshivas in Russia and in Palestine. In 1917 he was secretary of the Poltava Zionist Committee, but two years later, swept up by the storm of pogroms raging in the Ukraine, he joined the Bolsheviks.

> We who have gone through so much terror are convinced that only the Soviet government saves us from a blood bath, and every weakening of the Soviet government is a danger to us. . . . The question is posed in a cardinal way: either with the Horthys and Mussolinis or with Lenin and Trotsky. . . . Of course I have reason to be displeased with the fact that they took away our house and possessions. But I tell you in all truth that I am heart and soul for the Soviet government and am strongly inclined to Communism. There is still a certain weak spot which does not allow me to become a Communist. After all, I am a factory owner's son, a yeshiva boy, far from the workers' life. . . .[138]

[137] Y. Opatoshu, "Drei Hebraier," *Zamlbikher*, no. 8 (New York, 1952).

[138] Letter to E. Tsherikover, June 12, 192[3?], in Tsherikover Archive, YIVO Archives.

Like Isaac Babel, Niepomniashchi served in the Cheka, in the anti-bandit department, and also in the Red Army during the Russo-Polish war. He worked on the staff of *Komunistishe fon* and later on the Russian-language Jewish newspaper *Tribuna*. Niepomniashchi could not forget his Zionist-Hebraist-Talmudist roots, and the twins of Jewish sentiment and Communist ideas struggled together within him.

> I will say, in Gordon's words, "I am a slave to Hebrew forever." No one will be able to uproot "Khumash-and-Rashi" from my soul. I gave my best years to these old writings. But here I stop and I go no further. I return the Torah to Mount Sinai, even though I know we remain naked without it. But that's all right! . . . We have to begin to write Genesis again. The old stuff—let it mold! And no matter how sorry I am to let the "Torai Zohov" rot away, no matter how insulting it is to tear off the "Khoshen Mishpot" and put on a campaign button, . . . I cruelly choke these sentiments in me so that they shall have no influence on our political line. . . . But how long can one be a tyrant over oneself? Ach, it is indeed bitter.[139]

Niepomniashchi explained that the Hebrew language and the Jewish religious heritage must, unfortunately, be abandoned because they did not conform to Communist ideology. "All the rich nuances of a Bialik poem must go for nought among us because it has no social-organizational worth. . . . For us ideology is the most important thing. We are rational thinkers, not emotional sob sisters!"[140]

[139] Letter to Daniel Charney, undated [1925], YIVO Archives.

[140] Letter to Y. Opatoshu, November 4, 1928, YIVO Archives. Of course, no one was more emotional in his attachment to "the old" than Niepomniashchi. He begged Charney to send him all Yiddish and Hebrew publications from abroad and he evidently read them very

Of course, Niepomniashchi was the exception among Jewish Communists.[141] But in Central Asia, Hebrew was the rule even among Jewish Communists. The sixty thousand "Bokharan" Jews, a loose designation for Jews of Central Asia, spoke mostly Tadzhik or Farsi in the nineteenth century, but by the time of the October Revolution Hebrew had become widespread among them. In 1919 a *Evsektsiia* was founded in Turkestan by European Jews. The Communist Party in Turkestan consisted in large part of Bokharan Jews. The European Jews demanded the replacement of Hebrew by Yiddish (!) or Tadzhik as the language of instruction in the Jewish schools.[142] The

---

thoroughly. He wrote Tsherikover: "To hell with politics, money be damned—I would give them up for a single poem, for a good literary piece. I can tell you that since I received the books I read the sonnets backwards and forwards several times and have memorized them. Colossal! . . . I have swum through so much water, have served so many strange gods, and yet the yeshiva boy who trembles over a point in biblical exegesis reasserts himself. . . . Intoxication with books, a 'librinizm,' like cocaine, if we can compare this to narcotics" (letter of December 17, 1923). Niepomniashchi was distrusted by some *Evsektsiia* activists for his Hebraism and was suspected by non-Communists of being a Cheka *provocateur*. See Blattberg, p. 11. He seems to have written a large number of Hebrew works which were never published. He died in 1930 at the age of thirty-three, after an operation. The obituary in *Emes* (January 15, 1930) called him a "capable journalist. . . . In the last few years Sh. Niepomniashchi worked in the scholarly field, having a special interest in bibliography and history. Some of his work was published in the Minsk *Tseitshrift*, in the Moscow *Visnshaftlikhe yorbikher*, etc. The deceased left behind some uncompleted works." See also the Reizin *Leksikon*, II.

141 A. Steinman published a pamphlet "HaKomunist HaIvri" (The Hebrew Communist) in 1919. This was reprinted in *Orlogin* (Israel), v, (1952), 311–16. Steinman left Russia shortly after his pamphlet appeared. On attempts to publish Hebrew Communist literature, see Yehudah Slutskii, "HaPirsumim HaIvriyim Bivrith Hamoetsoth Bashanim 1917–1960," in Kh. Szmeruk, ed., *Pirsumim Yehudiyim Bivrit Hamoetsot*, 1917–1960 (Jerusalem, 1961).

142 Some Jewish activists decried this as "a left-handed Zionism, a

Turkestan Communist Party ordered that Hebrew remain the language of instruction. "If not, not a single student will attend school. We find it necessary to warn that no coercive measures can stifle our desire to educate our children in the Hebrew language.[143] A great hullabaloo was raised when the Commissariat of Education agreed to print a Hebrew geography book, despite the protests of the *Evsektsiia* activist Bogod—himself a former Hebrew teacher. The book finally appeared.[144] This first Hebrew book published in Turkestan under Communist auspices was also the last. Despite the fact that in August 1920 the First Turkestan Congress of Cultural Workers among local Jews passed a resolution favoring Hebrew, the local *Evsektsiia* activists soon won out over their Bokharan brethren and Hebrew was suppressed in Turkestan as well, though it survived longer than in European Russia.[145]

---

sort of Pan-Yiddishism" (*Emes*, August 17, 1923). Niepomniashchi also attacked the "cosmopolitan-assimilationist" attitude of the European *"Evseks"* in an undated letter to Tsherikover.

143 Quoted in A. Tsherikover, "Komunistishe kemfer far hebreish in Turkestan," *In der tkufe fun revolutsie*, ed. A. Tsherikover, p. 358.

144 The book was Y. Z. Amitan-Shapiro's *Geografia K'lalith*, published by the Commissariat of People's Education of the Turkestan Republic, Tashkent, 1920. The title page and introduction are reproduced in Szmeruk, pp. 34–35. The author later repudiated Hebrew and the Hebraists. See Slutskii, p. 38.

145 As late as 1926, Chemeriskii found it necessary to state that "Hebrew is for us like any other dead language or previous cultures. Insofar as Hebrew is still tied to our Yiddish language and cultural creation, we introduce Hebrew in the Pedfak, Pedtekhnikum [pedagogical schools], INO [Jewish departments in the Odessa and Kiev Institutes of Social Sciences]. If adults wish to learn the language, we do not obstruct them. If students want to learn the language, in the higher schools, we allow it as an elective" (*Di alfarbandishe komunistishe partai*, p. 81). Of course, children under eighteen were not permitted to study Hebrew. Hebrew courses that were given in oriental institutes or *Evsektsiia* higher schools were carefully restricted to the language itself. Curriculum and materials were inspected before they could be introduced to the classrooms and "only

The suppression of Hebrew was but a reflex of the struggle against Zionism. Zionism was seen as a "response of the weak to the strong" in tsarist Russia, a "running away from the enemy." Since the Soviet regime had opened all doors to the Jews, Zionism was no longer relevant.[146] The ex-Bundists who entered the *Evsektsiia* brought with them a long tradition of anti-Zionism and the unshakeable conviction that Zionism diverted Jews from the realities of class struggle to the mirage of a mythical Jewish homeland. The Zionists, in turn, were unenthusiastic about the Bolshevik revolution. "The Russian revolution outdoes the French revolution in its negative features. We have one hope—that the government of the new inquisition will not last long."[147] A small faction of the *Tseirai Tsion* Party, calling themselves *Amailai Tsion* (Toilers of Zion), broke off and entered the Communist Party in Ekaterinoslav, Oriol, and Minsk. They saw themselves as "Zionist Communists."[148] In general, however, Zionists were hostile to the Bolsheviks. The Soviet government did not immediately reciprocate this hostility. On July 21, 1919, the VTsIK ordered that Zionist work not be interfered with.[149] The *Evsektsiia*, how-

---

persons loyal to the regime and to the new educational policy should be permitted to enroll" (M. Levitan, "Fun di lekher," *Emes*, June 4, 1922). Levitan indulged in a bit of dialectic when he said that if it is argued that such conditions in effect make Hebrew courses impossible to arrange, then "this is the best proof that there is something intrinsic in the idea of such courses which is in direct contradiction to Soviet educational policy." In 1926 Litvakov once again insisted on identifying Hebrew with Zionism while disclaiming any intention of barring study of Hebrew. "Hebrew is not persecuted . . . but Hebraism is persecuted" (M. Litvakov, "Tsu roidefn mir hebreish," *Emes*, January 15, 1926).

146 "Sionistki u sebia," *Zhizn' natsional'nostei*, December 7, 1919.

147 *HaAm*, December 7, 1917, quoted in Slutskii, p. 27.

148 Dan Pines, *Hekhalutz Bekur HaMahpekha* (Tel Aviv, 1938), p. 81.

149 Aaron Pechenik, *Tsionizm un idishkeit in sovet-rusland* (New York, 1943), p. 13; Pines, p. 84.

ever, constantly urged the government to take measures against its competitors.[150]

When in 1920 *Hekhalutz* (The Pioneer), a Zionist group which advocated the establishment of agricultural communes, appealed for official recognition, the VTsIK skirted the issue by declaring that "insofar as the activity of *Hekhalutz* does not violate Soviet laws, it is not prosecuted nor does it need special authorization."[151] This left *Hekhalutz* at the mercy of local officials, and the local *Evsektsiia* made sure that *Hekhalutz* would have rough sledding. When two *Hekhalutz* officials seeking some favors from the government were referred to Merezhin by an *agitprop* official, Kamenev is reported to have told the official: "Well, my friend, where are you sending them! After all, the specialty of the *Evsektsiia* is the destruction of all the other Jews."[152] In 1923 *Hekhalutz* and its seventy-five branches were finally explicitly legalized, but when the *Evsektsiia* started its own agricultural colonization campaign, *Hekhalutz*, which claimed a membership of three thousand, was liquidated.[153] Some *Hekhalutz* groups continued their

[150] One of the earliest *Evkom* publications was Zorakh Greenberg's *Di tsionistn oif der idisher gass* (Petrograd, 1918). This was a satirical, biting pamphlet which linked Zionism with illegal currency speculation. There was a great deal of variation in the attitudes of local *sektsii*, at least in 1918–19. See Pines, p. 82. In Oriol all Zionist organizations were abolished. When the Zionists argued that such organizations existed legally in Moscow, they were told: "Who cares about the center? We are more progerssive than they. We do not recognize any nationalities—and that's that."

[151] Pines, p. 85. For a *Evsektsiia* interpretation of this, see *Emes*, February 5, 1922.

[152] Pines, p. 152.

[153] The membership figure is given in *Jewish Daily Bulletin*, September 23, 1927, quoted in Yarmolinsky, p. 112. There is an undated letter to Dr. Joseph Rosen from *Hekhalutz*, which lists 12 colonies, most of them communes, with 333 working members. Total membership in the *Hekhalutz* movement, including its youth organization, was put at 8,140, with 1,250 in Odessa and 2,300 in Kiev. Joseph Rosen Archive, Agro 36, YIVO Archives.

activities under a variety of disguises. "In politics they give the impression of being children, but they lie like adults. They conceal their membership in and connection with the *Hekhalutz.*" [154]

The Zionist Central Office was closed in September 1919, and in April 1920 the participants in an All-Russian Zionist Conference were arrested. Communist persecution of Zionism in the Ukraine began in May 1922 when fifty *Tseirai Tsion* members were arrested at the conclusion of their conference.[155] In September the Cheka carried out simultaneous raids on Zionist groups in the Ukraine, Belorussia, and Central Russia. Exactly two years later 3,000 Zionists were arrested, most of them receiving sentences of three years' exile to Siberia, Kazakhstan, or the Solovetski Islands.[156] But the Zionists continued to be a thorn in the side of the Communists, especially the *Evsektsiia.* In some small towns they wielded considerable influence. In Skvir, for example, where there were almost no Jewish Communists in 1922, Zionists reportedly organized a Hebrew club, library, lectures, and dramatic performances.[157] Zionists circulated 100,000 brochures in the Ukraine in 1924, criticizing the economic and educational policies of the *Evsektsiia* and calling for a new regime of the "toilers themselves," a "toiler national-personal autonomy, freely elected Jewish soviets, free Jewish worker-cooperatives, the right to maintain ties with Palestine and take part in its socialist construction." [158]

[154] From a Communist Party report, quoted in Merle Fainsod, *Smolensk under Soviet Rule* (New York, 1963), p. 443.

[155] Shapiro, pp. 115–16. Ironically, the main speaker at the conference was Zinoviev's brother-in-law.

[156] Tsentsifer, pp. 97–113.

[157] *Emes,* no. 139, 1922, quoted in Joint Foreign Committee, Memorandum, p. 12.

[158] The text is quoted in I. N. Shteinberg, "Di neie heroishe idishe yugent," *Di tsukunft,* XXXVI, no. 5 (May 1928). See also Yehuda Erez, ed., *Sefer Ts'S* (Tel Aviv, 1963), pp. 102–22.

For this escapade 200 Zionists were arrested. By May 1925, 3,600 people had been arrested or investigated on suspicion of belonging to the *Tseirai Tsion.*[159]

In spite of repressions and arrests, the Zionists continued to harass the *Evsektsiia.* When Yiddish soviets and Jewish agricultural colonization were enthusiastically promoted by the *Evsektsiia* in 1924–1926, the Zionists tried to use the non-Party organizations created during these campaigns to criticize the *Evsektsiia.* The Zionists still exerted considerable influence among the youth, especially in the smaller towns and, for some reason, especially among the girls. The latter were often instructed to attend *Evsektsiia*-sponsored meetings and disrupt them, safe conduct for these "saboteurs" having been arranged by the underground Zionist organization. The Zionists hammered away at the dismal economic outlook as proof positive of the total inability of the Soviet regime to solve Jewish economic problems. When Yiddish soviets were established—by 1928 there were 131 such soviets in the Ukraine[160]—the Zionists tried to elect their followers to them. The *Evsektsiia,* seeing a Zionist lurking around every corner, reacted somewhat hysterically to this attempt. "These elections were conducted after a colossal revival and strengthening of the Zionist organizations which captured the minds and hearts of a significant segment of the youth, which exploit the truly difficult situation of the youth, especially in the first period of reconstruction. . . ."[161] At the same time, the *Evsektsiia* claimed that in the soviet elections of 1925–26, the Zionists had suffered a decline in strength and attributed this to

[159] Shteinberg, op. cit. In 1926 Moishe Litvakov characterized the *Tseirai Tsion* as "a catch-all for fragments of Menshevik and SR theories with a 'proletarian' phraseology" (*Alfarbandishe baratung,* pp. 152–53).

[160] Y. Kantor, *Ratnboiung in der idisher svive,* p. 60.

[161] *Alfarbandishe baratung,* p. 69.

enthusiasm for the *Evsektsiia* program of agricultural colonization, "the struggle for revolutionary justice," the more effective organization of the Jewish artisans and the increase in Communist propaganda.[162]

The other major arena where the *Evsektsiia* and the Zionists clashed was the OZET organization, set up to encourage Jewish rural settlement.[163] Since this was ostensibly a non-partisan organization, the Zionists exploited it as a forum in which to air their views.[164] Fearing that colonization in the Soviet Union might steal their own thunder, the Zionists warned that it was a temporary political expedient designed only to lure American Jewish capital which was expected to support the experiment. In a sense, then, the Zionists took the Communist assessment of the Balfour Declaration and turned it around as a weapon against the Communists. Sometimes, however, Zionists would join OZET colonies, either in the hope that they would gain valuable experience to be used later in Palestine or in the belief that they could effectively propagandize the settlers. But it was at the public meetings held by the OZET that the Zionists caused the most trouble. Often, fist fights would break out between *Komsomols* and Zionists. In Kiev, the Zionists staged a street demonstration which had to be broken up by mounted police. In 1925 in the town of Snobesk, after the Zionists had successfully disrupted two *Evsektsiia* rallies, a third rally was held and the police locked the audience in the hall in an attempt to weed out

[162] M. Kiper, *Tsen yor,* p. 125.

[163] OZET (Russian) or GEZERD (Yiddish) was the Association for the Rural Placement of Jewish Toilers.

[164] The executive board of OZET was dominated by members of KOMZET (KOMERD)—the Commission for the Rural Placement of Jewish Toilers, headed by the non-Jewish Communist Petr G. Smidovich, and attached to the Presidium of the Soviet of Nationalities. OZET itself was headed by Dimanshtain and, of course, was controlled by the *Evsektsiia,* or, at least, by the Communist Party.

and arrest the Zionists. It so happened that most of the firemen of the town were Zionists and they promptly unlocked the doors. Riots and street demonstrations followed and some policemen were disarmed by the rioters. An investigatory commission later blamed the *Evsektsiia.* "You do not know how to work tactfully. If they wanted to speak, you should have let them do so. But you should know what to reply." Even Moishe Litvakov was constantly interrupted during an address he delivered in Odessa.[165]

In 1928 the Zionists decided to abandon these flamboyant but costly tactics and to concentrate on educating the younger generation, lest Soviet education completely obliterate all traces of the Jewish nationalist idea. The Zionist movement went underground and even the EKP-*Poalai Tsion* was dissolved.[166]

The Attack on the Jewish Religion

The most tenacious, and perhaps most effective, resistance to the revolution on the Jewish street was offered by the Jewish religious community. "It should be noted that no Jewish socialist party—neither the Bund nor the *Farainigte*—fought for its principles with as much vigor and devotion as these Jews wrapped in their prayer shawls." [167] Again, there was an interplay of tradition and change in the formation of *Evsektsiia* policy toward the Jewish religion and

[165] Vest, pp. 153–59.

[166] Pechenik, p. 26. In 1937 about twenty representatives of fifteen tiny Zionist groups met secretly in Moscow and adopted a policy of limiting activities to studying and collecting information about Palestine. They decided that their organizational tactic would be to try to build very small circles of trusted friends. During World War II, Zionist activity revived somewhat as Nazi persecution aroused Jewish national consciousness and as Zionists from Poland, Rumania, and the Baltic areas came under Soviet Rule.

[167] Esther Frumkin, quoted in A. A. Gershuni, *Yahadut BeRusiya HaSovietit* (Jerusalem, 1961), p. 63.

its adherents. While the difference between the Bundist and *Evsektsiia* policies toward Zionism was one of degree and was conditioned by the power available to each, the Bundist and *Evsektsiia* policies toward religion differed in kind as well. While the Bund was basically areligious and anti-clerical, the *Evsektsiia* was both anti-religious and anti-clerical. As a socialist party, the Bund had a materialist philosophy and vigorously opposed what it saw as clerical subservience to the oppressors of the working class; as a part of a totalitarian organization, the *Evsektsiia* had a fiercely exclusivist outlook which could not brook the existence of any competing, dissenting, or merely different ideologies. It would be erroneous to assume, as many have, that *Evsektsiia* persecution of religion was merely the fulfillment of the old Bundist program, though there is no doubt that the leaders of the anti-religious campaign were the ex-Bundists and ex-*Farainigte* or *Poalai Tsion*ists in the *Evsektsiia.* The Bund had rarely attacked faith or religious customs and had concentrated its fire on the clergy. Believing, as Marx did, that religion was a phenomenon of the capitalist order, Bundists were confident that under socialism religion would die a natural death and it was useless to expend energy on combatting it in pre-socialist Russia. Furthermore, a campaign against religion would have served no purpose but to isolate the Bund from the Jewish community and alienate potentially sympathetic religious workers. Bundists were intellectually atheistic but many of them were psychically and emotionally tied to the religious symbolism and culture of the Jewish milieu.[168] Bundists generally were not inclined to the kinds of coercive methods the *Evsektsiia* employed, and even the militant atheists in the Bund would not consider forcible seizure of syna-

[168] On the role of religious customs and forms in the Jewish labor movement, see M. Mishkinskii, "Yesodot LeUmiyim," pp. 31–36, 262.

gogues or other religious institutions. Finally, the Bund may have refrained from attacking the Jewish religion because it was an oppressed religion not promoted by the tsarist order but barely tolerated by it.[169]

The cleavages created in the Jewish community by the tragic episode of the "Cantonists" in the early part of the nineteenth century were widened by the refusal of Jewish factory owners to hire Jewish labor and their vigorous opposition to the Jewish revolutionaries who wanted to undo the social and economic order. Since Jewish workers were often forced by economic necessity to work on Saturday and Jewish merchants and entrepreneurs kept the Sabbath, the rabbis regarded the former as sinners and desecrators of the Sabbath, and the latter as pillars of the community. In addition, it was the Jewish middle class which gave financial support to the *kehilla* and to the religious functionaries. Some rabbis were cognizant of the impossible situation of the workers, but others saw them only as dangerous sinners who could disrupt the religious life of Russian-Polish Jewry. Rabbi Khaim Zak, the rabbi of Mezrich, founded a *Makhzikai HaDat* Society (Upholders of the Faith) "to fight the Sabbath morning socialist meetings of boys and girls . . . who preach deviations from the ways of the Torah and Judaism and who oppose the government, thereby persecuting the entire Community of Israel and desecrating the name of God." [170] The rabbis, who certainly hated the Tsar and his government, the persecutors of the

[169] The reasons for the Bund's reluctance to attack the Jewish religion were outlined by Professor Erich Goldhagen in a talk on "The Fight Against the Jewish Religion in Russia in the 1920's and Its Implications Today," at the Thirty-Ninth Annual Conference of the YIVO Institute for Jewish Research, January 18, 1965. For the last point I am indebted to Mr. Hillel Kempinskii, archivist of the Jewish Labor Bund Library and Archives, New York.

[170] Quoted in Abba Lev, *Religie un klaikoidesh in kamf kegn der idisher arbeter-bavegung* (Moscow, 1923), pp. 25–26.

Jewish religion as well as of the Jewish people, not a whit less than the socialists, feared that Jewish revolutionary activity would only aggravate tsarist persecution and bring down the wrath of the authorities and the loyal population upon the heads of the entire Jewish community. Had the tsarist government adopted a more tolerant attitude to the Jewish religion and its institutions, it might have won some support among religious Jewry and might have driven an even greater wedge into Jewish society.

The opposition of many rabbis to the socialist movement did not, however, prevent religious workers from associating themselves with it. As has often been observed in developing countries, modernizing values are frequently expressed in traditional modes. Similarly, some of the more naïve Jewish workers saw the socialist movement as a quasi-religious one whose ideals of social justice were precisely those advocated by the Jewish religion. In fact, in the very town where Rabbi Zak was organizing against the socialists, there was a large number of religious workers affiliated with the socialist movement. Once, when a Bundist agitator had ended a speech, a religious worker asked him earnestly, "Tell me, Preacher, what will happen if the Messiah comes before we attain freedom and before socialism is introduced?" [171] The synagogue was often a rallying-point where meetings would be held and policies planned.[172] Religious brush-makers swore before an open Torah scroll not to become scabs. When a strike was prolonged by the refusal of the Jewish factory owner to negotiate, the workers would

[171] Lazar Kling, "Epizodn fun der amoliker bundisher tetikeit," *Buletin fun Bund arkhiv*, v, no. 3 (October 1964).

[172] Synagogues were often organized along occupational lines. Thus, there would be a butchers' synagogue, a tailors' synagogue, etc. The wealthier elements usually prayed in the "Great Synagogue," presided over by the town's rabbi. This structure was probably both a cause and effect of the growing class divisions within the Russian Jewry.

not permit the Torah to be read in the Great Synagogue and sabotaged the town's ritual baths.[173]

The Bund had sided with the religious community in its advocacy of Saturday as the day of rest, though its motivations were quite different.[174] As late as 1919 the Bund attacked the Bolsheviks for ordering certain Vilna factories with a large Jewish labor force to remain in operation on Saturday. "The government should also consider the religious feelings of its citizens if they do not conflict with the interests of the general community. But even the non-religious Jewish workers are part of an environment where the natural day of rest is Saturday." [175]

In 1917 religion became a live political issue because of the *kehilla* and Jewish autonomy questions. The Bund opposed an official state religion and demanded religious freedom for all citizens. There was to be complete separation of church and state so that even the *kehilla* would have no religious functions, and non-religious Jews would not have to provide financial support for religious institutions. The Bund carefully pointed out that "We do not at all wish to uproot the Jewish religion. Religion, in its pure form, is an intimate feeling . . . like love—and we do not

[173] Kling. See also Mishkinskii, *Yesodot LeUmiyim.*

[174] See *supra,* Chapter I.

[175] *Unzer shtime* (Vilna), quoted in *Der veker,* March 3, 1919. In 1917 a great uproar was caused when the Bund Central Committee approved a decision of the Mogilev soviet which called on Jewish workers to work on Saturday of the week of May Day holiday (which occurred on a Tuesday). The Bund explained its decision by arguing that "rest on Saturday makes it very difficult for the Jewish proletariat to participate in the economic life of the country, thereby weakening its class position." This was seized upon by all the Jewish opponents of the Bund and many local Bund organizations were discredited. They pleaded with the central committee to "clarify" its position, whereupon the committee, claiming it had been "misinterpreted," in effect annulled its previous decision. *Arbeter shtime,* nos. 6, 20, 29, 1919, quoted in Kirzhnitz and Rafes, eds., *Der idisher arbeter,* pp. 50, 71.

oppose it. We fight only against religion having the social power to force someone into doing something."[176]

A more hostile and emotional attitude was displayed by David Zaslavskii in a famous pamphlet, *Farshvekhte rainigkeitn.* Zaslavskii was prompted to write his "answer to the rabbis" by an incident which had occurred in Kiev at a Jewish convention. Following a report on White atrocities in Galicia, which had included the destruction of Torah scrolls, a delegate had asked all those "who honor the Holy Torah" to rise. A furor was created when the Bundists remained seated. Zaslavskii then wrote that he would honor the "bloodied and torn" scrolls which had been destroyed in the pogroms, but not those scrolls which had been presented by the Jews to the Tsar.

> Why don't you bury *those* scrolls? . . . Because they are witnesses to your shame. If only those scrolls could speak—"away from here!" they would say. You sold us into shame, you made slaves of us . . . you fine Jews and guardians of religion—you would bow to the earthly god, to the idol of autocracy, and you would bring a sacrifice of your holy Torah scrolls. . . . For pogroms—a Torah to the Tsar; for exiles—a Torah to the Tsar; for the Beilis trial—a Torah to the Tsar. . . . With hatred in your hearts and a hypocritical smile on your lips you presented your Torahs to the Tsar . . . you trembled like slaves, like beaten dogs, and thereby profaned your own holiness. . . . The people did not ask you to do this. The Jewish masses—they are no slaves. Simple Jewish workers and artisans did not go to prostrate themselves. . . . Slaves you were and slaves you have remained.[177]

[176] A. Zeldov (Nemanskii), *Di religie iz a privat zakh* (n.p., 1917), p. 13.

[177] Zaslavskii, *Farshvekhte rainigkeitn* (*An entfer di rabonim*) (n.p., 1917), p. 6. See also V. Z. Diskin, "Biymai HaMahpehkha BeRusiia," *Heavar,* vol. 16, 1969.

Even Zaslavskii's attack was a largely political one. He resented the efforts of the religious community to "preserve your rule over the nation with your Torah."

> But the Torah should be in the House of Study and only in the House of Study. . . . We respect sincere religious feelings . . . a private affair, a matter of conscience. With the greatest care we take the Torah out of your hands and carry it to its proper place—the House of Study. And now let us argue as good people do, and not involve God in our earthly affairs.[178]

The *Evsektsiia* inherited this righteous indignation but, like the Party as a whole, refused to draw any distinction between religion and politics, and insisted upon giving the Jewish religion a class character.

The abolition of the *kehillas* was only the first step in the campaign against religion. Though the lack of a *kehilla* structure atomized the religious community to some extent, it remained in a relatively strong position, partially because it was the chief recipient of American relief aid or at least was often the channel through which the Joint Distribution Committee and other organizations distributed their funds. Religion's moral force was even stronger and pervaded even the *sanctum sanctorum* of the *Evsektsiia*, its central daily newspaper, *Emes*. To the great chagrin of the editor-in-chief, Litvakov, the typesetters refused to work on the High Holidays. This was the unkindest cut of all. Immediately following the Holidays, however, they had to print Litvakov's sarcastic diatribe.

> Do they really fear the sound of the Great *Shofar* so much? Perhaps not. But the n'er-do-well inertia, lazy thinking, weakening of revolutionary resolve is so pronounced among them that they want to observe all the

[178] Zaslavskii, p. 6.

little Judaistic [*idishlakhe*] laws and customs. . . . Unfortunately, this is almost a mass phenomenon. The Jewish worker remains mired in the old Judaistic refuse: he sends his children to *kheder,* observes the Sabbath and holidays, and often trembles over the most minute religious detail.[179]

The anti-religious campaign was the main concern of the *Evsektsiia* in 1921–22. Basically, three methods were used: agitation and propaganda; feigned accession to the "demands of the toiling masses"; and naked force. This campaign was conducted almost exclusively by Jews against other Jews; the participation of non-Jews would have smacked of tsarist oppression of the Jewish religion and was therefore tactfully avoided.[180] In fact, the *Evsektsiia* jeal-

[179] M. Litvakov, "Habokhur hazetser," *Emes,* October 2, 1921. In Vitebsk in 1919 the presidium of the trade union council recognized Rosh Hashonoh as a non-working holiday. *Der shtern,* September 2, 1919.

[180] Jewish Communists failed to display a similar tact. Maxim Gorkii, a sincere and devoted friend of the Jewish people, pointed out that when the Russians, especially the peasants, saw young Jewish Communists wrecking the churches, anti-Semitic feelings were aroused. "Moreover: in the spread of Judophobia the Jewish speculators play a significant role. . . . They are helped by the orthodox Jewish Communists with their hostile attitude toward the teaching of Hebrew in the schools, to the magnificent products of Jewish talent such as the 'Habimah' theater and, in general, to the cultural activities of non-Communist Jews." Gorkii said that the activity of the "*Evseks*" is "devoid of all tact." He added, however, that "I know of cases where the Jewish Communists were purposely put in the ranks of those persecuting the Russian church and priests in order that the Russian peasants should see with their own eyes that the Jews are desecrating their holy places. . . . It seems to me that the Bolsheviks did this partly out of fear and a clear intent to compromise the Jews." Letter written on May 9, 1922, in the Levitas Archive II-1, YIVO Archives; printed in *Novoe russkoe slovo* (New York), December 2, 1954.

The "*Evseks*" were greatly embarrassed by Gorkii's letter, and Esther complained that "it is known that even Maxim Gorkii took part in the foreign hunt of the Jewish Communists for their self-

ously guarded its monopoly over the persecution of the Jewish religion. When the revolutionary tribunal in Smolensk decided to seize the choir-synagogue and give it to the *Evsektsiia*, the latter poutingly refused to accept it as a meeting place because the tribunal had "usurped" its prerogative. The *Evsektsiia* activists sulkingly halted the anti-religious campaign just to spite the tribunal.[181]

The *agitprop* and "mass participation" phases of the *Evsektsiia's* war on religion included meetings and lectures in places of work, floods of articles in the Jewish press, public debates reminiscent of medieval disputations, and elaborate show trials of religious functionaries and even of customs and institutions. At a workers' meeting a resolution to close the local *kheders* (religious elementary schools) would be presented by the *Evsektsiia*, and, of course, approved. A special commission would then be formed to aid in this project. Only then would the local government decree the closing of the *kheder*, but only feeble efforts were made to provide the children with another form of education.[182] The workers' meetings did not always go

---

sacrificing struggle against ignorance and fanaticism." Maria [Esther] Frumkina, *Doloi ravvinov* (Moscow, 1923), p. 40. Actually, had the Jewish Communists not played such an outstanding role in the anti-religious campaign, they probably would have been accused of sponsoring it anyway. The Russian church, some of whose leaders believed that Russian "had fallen under the power of godless men—Jews and Chinese" [!]—was prone to blame the Jews for its troubles. "The opposition to the confiscation of Church property is increasing and is causing anti-Jewish feeling, as the Jews are held responsible for the Decree." From a report of the U.S. Commissioner in Riga, April 21, 1922, in Boleslaw Szczesniak, ed., *The Russian Revolution and Religion* (South Bend, 1959), p. 70. The "theory" of "Chinese-Jewish" rule of Russia is expressed in an Epistle to Russian Refugees Abroad sent by the Metropolitan of Kiev, quoted in Szczesniak, p. 60.

[181] Merezhin scolded them in "Erger fun batlones," *Emes*, October 2, 1921.

[182] See M. Levitan, "Kul'turnye dostizheniia evreiskikh mass RSFSR," *Zhizn' natsional'nostei*, kniga I, 1923, p. 246.

smoothly for the *Evsektsiia.* In Gomel, Rabbi Barishanskii, one of the most courageous opponents of the *Evsektsiia,* defended the *kheder* vigorously and challenged the *Evsektsiia* to improve, rather than destroy it—the *Evsektsiia* having charged that it was unsanitary and injurious to the health of the students. A worker who was recognized as an "underground Bundist" protested against the resolution to close the *kheders* and argued that the struggle against religion should be conducted only on the ideological plane. But these protests were to no avail. A commission of twenty was formed to implement the *Evsektsiia* resolution.[183]

The press was mobilized for the fight against religion. Aside from a constant stream of articles, special newspapers and supplements were published, with eyecatching headlines and vicious cartoons which would have been branded anti-Semitic were it not for the fact that they were published by Jews themselves. The *Evsektsiia* was not above appealing to the prurient interests of the readers and sometimes printed lurid tales of rabbis who were sexual deviants, seducers of young girls, and the like. In the initial stages of its campaign, the *Evsektsiia* published more serious material, most of it in a mild, semi-scholarly tone.[184] Later on, the literature became more simplistic, more frankly polemical.[185]

The most bizarre aspect of the campaign was the show

[183] *Emes,* June 1 and 3, 1922.

[184] For example, the pamphlet *Yom Kippur,* by H. Lurie (Kharkov, 1923), used the writings of Edward Taylor, Herbert Spencer, Emile Durkheim, and George Simmel. Other pamphlets in this vein were Lurie's *Peisakh* (Kharkov, 1924), *Toire* (Kharkov, 1923), and *Shabes* (Odessa, 1922). Sometimes Yiddish translations of semi-scholarly Russian works were used. An example of this is Professor N. Nikol'skii's *Yidishe yomtoivim: zeier ufkum un antviklung* (Minsk, 1925).

[185] See, for example, I. Sudarskii, *Farvos kemfn mir kegn religie* (Kharkov, 1931), and Y. Novakovskii, *Gots strapshes* (Kiev, 1930).

trials. On *Rosh Hashonoh*, 1921, the *Evsektsiia* in Kiev "tried" the Jewish religion, ironically, in the same auditorium where the Beilis trial had been held. According to a non-Communist source, a weird cast of characters appeared before the "judges": a lady dressed in old-fashioned clothes explained that she sent her children to *kheder* because, she proclaimed haughtily, she was no "low-class tailor or cobbler" but of a "distinguished religious family." This was submitted as evidence that the Jewish religion was a creature of the bourgeoisie. A "rabbi" testified that he taught religion in order to keep the masses ignorant and servile. When someone in the audience accused him of being a "lying ignoramus," "stormy applause" broke out, according to the stenographic report. The interpellator in the audience was immediately arrested. After further testimony by a corpulent "bourgeois," bedecked with glittering gold and diamond rings, the *Evsektsiia* "prosecutor" summarized the "case against the Jewish religion" and asked for a "sentence of death for the Jewish religion." Moshe Rozenblatt, a Kiev Hebrew teacher, rose to defend Judaism and the sympathies of the crowd were clearly with him. He was arrested immediately after completing his speech. The "judges" retired to their chambers and returned with a verdict of death to the Jewish religion.[186] A similar trial—this time of the *kheder*—took place in Vitebsk.[187] The yeshiva was tried in Rostov, and circumcision was "put on trial" in Kharkov as late as 1928.

Pageantry was also used in another form. Realizing

[186] Y.D.K., "Der mishpet iber der yidisher religie," in Tsherikover, ed., *In der tkufe fun revolutsie*, p. 385ff. A partial Hebrew translation appears in A. A. Gershuni, pp. 21–25.

[187] For a detailed account of this, based on the stenographic notes of "Defense Attorney" Wolfson, see Gershuni, pp. 26–36. The *Evsektsiia* version of this trial is L. Abram, Y. Khinchin, and Y. Kaplan, *Der mishpet ibern kheder* (Vitebsk, 1922).

that "nature abhors a vacuum" and that there was a need felt by Jews for ritual and ceremony, the *Evsektsiia* designed an elaborate anti-religious ritual. It was suggested that greeting cards be sent on the anniversary of the October Revolution instead of on *Rosh Hashonoh,* that the traditional *khalah* be baked in shape of a hammer and sickle, and that the answer to the "Four Questions" on Passover be a recounting of the history of the October Revolution.[188] In Vitebsk in 1920 a *Evsektsiia* "Yom Kippurnik" consisted of a demonstration outside the main synagogue on the Day of Atonement. Using axes and saws, the holy vessels of the proletarian cult, the demonstrators created such a fearful racket that services were disrupted. This custom spread to other cities, with torchlight parades, clowns, and free lunches as added embellishments.[189] In 1924 a "*Red Haggadah*" was distributed which substituted the deliverance from tsarist rule for deliverance from Pharaonic oppression.[190] Following the example of the "Living Church," the *Evsektsiia* tried to set up a "Living Synagogue" in 1924. "Communism is the Mosaic Torah translated by Lenin into

[188] A. R. Tsveig, "Der neier shtaiger un der yontev," *Emes,* October 13, 1923.

[189] On events in Borisov, Odessa, and Minsk, see *Emes,* November 1, 1922, and Gershuni, pp. 82–85. These demonstrations sometimes got out of hand and led to miniature civil wars, especially in the smaller towns. M. Altshuler warned that demonstrations were fit for the larger cities, but that in the small towns they divided the community into "insistent believers and hesitant atheists," thus obscuring the class question. M. Altshuler, "Fragn fun taktik in kamf mitn klerikalizm," *Der komunist* (Kharkov), November 25, 1921.

[190] "Slaves we were to capital until the October Revolution came and rescued us with a mighty hand from the land of slavery. And were it not for October, then surely we and our children and our children's children would have remained slaves to capital. . . . Today the revolution is only here, next year—world revolution" (Gershuni, pp. 84–85). See also M. Libes, " 'Kamchatka' kievskoi gubernii," in Tan-Bogoraz, *Evreiskoe mestechko,* p. 81. For a complete description of a "Red Seder," see *Der veker,* April 3, 1923.

the Bolshevik tongue," declare one of its founders.[191] Apparently, the Jews preferred to study the Torah in their own tongue because the "Living Synagogue" died a quick death.

Propaganda and pageantry had almost no influence on the older generation, deeply rooted in the Jewish tradition and not seduced by "*Red Haggadahs*" or "Living Synagogues." In fact, the most reliable social class, the workers, disappointed the *Evsektsiia*. "The less conscious . . . Jewish worker at first did not understand why we so bitterly fight the whole clerical coterie. . . . He absolutely failed to understand what the Jewish Communists want of the rabbi and the *kehilla*, of the *minyan* and House of Study. . . . The rabbi, it seemed to him, is an innocent creature. Unlike the priest, he was never to be found in the tsarist regime."[192] To the annoyance of the anti-religious specialists, Jewish workers and, especially, their wives, observed Jewish customs and some rituals long after renouncing the Jewish faith. Osherovich complained that "the backward woman thinks that with the help of customs and traditions which her husband maintains (weddings, *seders*, *kiddish*) she will be able to strengthen the familial bond between herself, her husband, and her children."[193] The

[191] *Ibid.* Poltava had a "living Synagogue" derisively referred to as the *Evsov-Promoldom*—the Jewish Soviet Proletarian Prayer House. *Emes* satirized it in a hilarious article on June 5, 1924.

[192] Lev, *Religie un klaikoidesh in kamf*, p. 3. Abba Lev was one of the earliest figures in the Jewish labor movement. He was very active in antireligious work in the 1920's and 1930's, but in 1945, when he was archivist of the Jewish Anti-Fascist Committee, he was observed in a Moscow synagogue on Rosh Hashonoh where he came "in order to find some warmth," he said. Lev was completely crushed by the Nazi slaughter of the Jews. See Wolf-Hersh Ivan, "A bezbozhnik a ba'al t'shuve," *Dos yidishes vort* (Winnipeg), September 24, 1965.

[193] *Der veker*, April 8, 1923. The issue of April 19 cites the case of a Communist, a leader in the anti-religious campaign, who secretly observed Passover.

youth were more malleable and may have enjoyed the *Evsektsiia* celebrations and morality plays whose crude characterizations and simplistic black-and-white plots often resembled a children's puppet show. The younger generation was forced away from religion by the economic necessity of working on the Sabbath and holidays, and by social and political pressures which relegated the Jewish worker or employee to second-class citizenship if he sent his children to *kheder,* had them circumcised, or himself attended the synagogue.[194]

The propaganda campaign did not have much effect and sometimes boomeranged, as at the show trials. But there was a grimmer aspect to the *Evsektsiia's* anti-religious drive. If the Jewish Communists participated in the spoliation of Christian churches, they hurled themselves with such a frenzy into the battle against their own houses of worship that a non-Jewish Communist was moved to remark, "It would be nice to see the Russian Communists tear into the monasteries and holy days as the Jewish Communists do to *Yom Kippur.*"[195] The law was used to constrain religious

[194] For instance, a worker who donated money toward the purchase of a Torah was tried publicly (*Komunistishe fon,* February 12, 1924). Circumcision, the ceremony by which a male is initiated into the congregation of Israel, was one of the hardiest survivors among religious practices. Even sincere Jewish Communists would go to enormous lengths to have their children circumcised. Circumcision was discouraged as unhygienic, but Jews clung to it for nationalistic, as well as purely religious, reasons, circumcision being traditionally regarded as the rite of initiation into the Jewish people. The subterfuges used by secret policemen to have their children circumcised, and the tragi-comic results, are described in Gershuni, pp. 77–79.

[195] Quoted in Lestschinsky, *Dos sovetishe identum,* p. 313. Kalinin remarked that "As president of the Central Executive Committee, I have very often had to resist the demands of the Jewish youth who want to confiscate the synagogues and convert them into clubs" (M. I. Kalinin, "Evreiskii vopros i pereselenie evreev v Krym," *Izvestiia,* July 1926). Joshua Rothenberg, on the other hand, argues that "If the Yevsektsia had not existed, its acts would have been

activity. All religious associations were required to register with the authorities and submit membership lists. Premises for any sort of religious activity had to be leased from municipal housing departments. Rabbis and other religious functionaries were deprived of the vote and of all political rights. Religious instruction for persons under eighteen was made illegal. In 1922–23 over one thousand *kheders* were closed. In Vitebsk alone, thirty-nine *kheders* with 1,358 students and forty-nine teachers were shut down.[196] *Kheders* were closed despite the fact that even local *Evsektsiia* activists admitted that their students could not be provided with other schooling and protested against the forcible closing of the *kheders*.[197] "Comrade Fuks . . . comes to Dukor where he arranges a meeting in the House of Study. 'Sign the agreement,' he proposes, 'you have to accept the responsibility of maintaining a Yiddish Soviet school.' 'We don't need it, we don't want it,' the audience cries. 'Don't listen to them, the speculators!' shout the youth. . . . 'We'll sign on condition that the Bible and commentaries will be taught there.' 'That is unacceptable,' announces Comrade Fuks. The agreement is signed. (The audience wisecracks: by the time they ferret out a teacher, the *kheder* children will be adults.)" [198] Finally, gold and silver ornaments in the synagogues were seized and sold, purportedly to aid the poor.[199]

---

executed by some other agency of the regime" ("Jewish Religion in the Soviet Union," in Kochan, ed., *The Jews in Soviet Russia since 1917*).

196 *Doloi ravvinov*, p. 29.

197 *Emes*, June 23, 1922.

198 *Der veker*, February 14, 1923. This incident highlights (1) the bogus nature of the "mass meetings" which "demanded" the closing of *kheders;* (2) the fact that the older generation in the small towns was religious; (3) the wedge that was being driven between generations; (4) the difficulties of obtaining Yiddish teachers who would teach in Soviet schools.

199 The decision to seize the ornaments was taken on February 9, 1922. See *Emes*, February 12, 1922.

The velvet glove of the law was frequently dispensed with. When the *Evsektsiia* attempted to seize a synagogue in Vitebsk, the religious community staged a demonstration and when a detachment of fifteen men was sent to clear the synagogue they were beaten up and forced to retreat. Finally a cavalry detachment evicted the assembled Jews.[200] When a forcible seizure of the Minsk synagogue was attempted, two Jews were killed, and in a similar incident a rabbi in Odessa met the same fate. Most rabbis, however, abhorred the use of force and counseled restraint.[201]

In contrast to what was happening in the Russian Orthodox church, there were only isolated attempts by religious leaders to accommodate themselves to the new regime, perhaps because the Communist Party made no attempt to win over the Jewish religious establishment. The first rabbi to display a favorable attitude toward the Soviet regime was the rabbi of Slefianka who declared that "the present government tries to disseminate knowledge and work among the Jewish population, not the *luftmensh*ism and swindles which existed under the bourgeois order."[202] The *Evsektsiia* gleefully proclaimed a "split in the ranks of the Jewish functionaries," but this was hardly the case.[203] Actually, of the one thousand rabbis in the USSR only six are known to have had pro-Communist sympathies; only two rabbis attacked religion itself.[204]

[200] Gershuni, pp. 60–61.

[201] See Joint Foreign Committee, Memorandum, p. 4.

[202] *Emes,* July 6, 1923. This rabbi published an eight-page pamphlet, *Dos diment bletl,* which contended that "the diamond of Communism" had once hung on Abraham's neck.

[203] For other "pro-Communist" statements, such as "Moses was a Marxist," see Em. Iaroslavskii, trans. P. Shprakh, *Tsiln un metodn fun antireligiezer propaganda* (Moscow-Kharkov-Minsk, 1930), p. 46.

[204] Gershuni, pp. 109–10. An interesting, and apparently sincere, attempt to reconcile Judaism and Communism was made by Rabbi Samuel Alexandrov of Bobruisk. Alexandrov had corresponded with Rabbi A. I. Kook, Chief Rabbi of Palestine, Akhad HaAm, the

Some religious functionaries entered the Jewish colonies promoted by the *Evsektsiia*, and religious life was very

---

ideologist of "cultural Zionism," and M. J. Berdichevskii, a noted Hebrew writer. He emphasized "the justification of God's historical acts." The Communists were brought into being by God "who has wrapped himself in a cloak of materialism and in so doing has brought life to the world." Materialist Marxism is a prologue to the revelation of faith in one God. "Behold there are days which are coming in which the eyes of man will be opened to see the Divine, moral kernel which lies hidden in dialectical materialism." Quoted in A. Shauli, "Jewish Theology in Soviet Russia," *Reconstructionist*, October 4, 1957. Alexandrov apparently attempted a neo-Kabalistic metaphor in which God's Truth was seen as covered by the shell (*klipah*) of *diamat*. For a discussion of Alexandrov and his book, *Mikhtavai Mekhkar UBikoret* (Critical and Scholarly Letters), see Gershuni, pp. 126–28.

Although we are concerned only with the *Evsektsiia* campaign against religion, mention should be made of the resistance put up by the religious community, a chapter of Russian Jewish history which has not received the attention it deserves. Well into the late 1920's there existed in the Soviet Union a network of underground *kheders* and yeshivas. The leader of the religious resistance and the coordinator of much underground activity was Rabbi I. I. Schneerson, the "Lubavicher Rebbe." He was constantly hounded by the *Evsektsiia* and the secret police and was finally forced to leave the Soviet Union, but not before he had trained many teachers whose influence was felt in the USSR long after his departure. See *Di yisurim fun libavitshn rebn in sovet-rusland* (Riga, 1930); *Di rabonim in dinst fun finants kapital*—a *Evsektsiia* pamphlet attacking the *Rebbe* (Moscow, 1930), and Gershuni, pp. 156–208. The *Rebbe* failed in an attempt to raise large sums for the maintenance of illegal schools and an anti-*Evsektsiia* campaign ("Religious Instruction in Russia: Note by the Secretary," Joint Foreign Committee, June 21, 1928, Lucien Wolf Archive Box 17, Packet 114, YIVO Archives).

Cantors, too, played an important part in keeping the Jewish religion alive, by traveling around and giving popular concerts. In the smaller towns, especially, religion, and not Communism, was the dominating force in Jewish life until the 1930's. As late as 1926 a conference of Soviet rabbis was held and one publisher of religious books managed to print 100,000 books in 1927–29, while the presses of other religious publishing houses were also rolling. The extent of religious observance is impossible to measure, both because it was carried on clandestinely and because religious observance is inherently difficult to

strong in a number of colonies. The *Evsektsiia* was well aware of this and tried to force the colonists to break with tradition by raising pigs. But in 1929 only forty-five out of 235 Jewish collective farms were engaged in hog-breeding, and in some of these non-Jews were hired to tend the hogs. The *Evsektsiia* would frequently "unmask" rabbis and religious practices in these colonies and a great hue and cry would be raised in the press.[205]

In 1929 the *Evsektsiia,* to its horror, discovered that some Moscow workers and university students, among them members of the Communist Party, had joined a secret society, *Tiferes Bakhurim* (Glory of Youth). Founded by a Lubavicher *Hasid,* Rabbi Yaakov Landau, the society adopted as its slogan, "Be a complete Jew in your home, be a complete Jew when you go out into the world."[206]

---

quantify. For instance, in 1925 in Gomel of 560 Jewish artisans investigated, 431 rested on Saturday, 86 on Sunday, and 41 "undetermined"; 159 called themselves "religious," 104 "half-religious," and 275 "non-religious" (I. Pul'ner, "Iz zhizni goroda Gomelia" in Tan-Bogoraz, p. 196). The *Evsektsiia* invariably overemphasized the extent of religious commitment, while other Communists, such as Tan-Bogoraz, minimized it. See, for instance, A. Kirzhnitz, *Di "hailike" shediker un undzer kultur-revolutsie* (Moscow, 1929), pp. 10–26; and M. Kiper, *Dos yidishe shtetl in Ukraine* (Kiev, 1929). See also *Alfarbandishe baratung,* etc. for *Evsektsiia* fears of a religious revival in 1926. Foreign observers also differed radically in their assessments of the situation. Cf. Joint Foreign Committee, "Jewish Religious Education in Russia," May 28, 1928 (in the YIVO Archives), and N. Khanin, *Sovet rusland, vi ikh hob ihr gezehn* (New York, 1929), pp. 42, 44, 168.

[205] On religion in the colonies, see Kh. Szmeruk, "HaKibutz Hayehudi VeHahityashvut Hakhaklait Hayehudit BeByelorusia HaSovietit 1918–1932," Ph.D. diss., Hebrew University, Jerusalem, 1961, p. 126 (mimeo). For an eyewitness report, see an article by Louis Fischer which appeared in *The Forward* and *The Menorah Journal* [n.d.], in the Joseph Rosen Archive, Box 32, YIVO Archives.

[206] This was undoubtedly a parody of the dictum of Y. L. Gordon, a Hebrew poet of the *Haskalah,* or Enlightenment. Gordon had written in 1863, "Be a human being [Ben Adam] when you go out in the

The society demanded complete observance of Jewish law and daily study of Bible, Talmud, Laws, and Hasidism. The university students made no attempt to hide their religious beliefs and refused to take examinations on the Sabbath. The society had branches in Leningrad, Minsk, Smolensk, and Poltava. It ceased operations in 1930 but revived at a later date.[207]

The anti-religious campaign thrust Esther Frumkin into the limelight. If it is true that a Jew is like every other human being, only more so, then Esther was like every other Jew, only more so. She was a superb public agitator and this talent was put to good use in her capacity as Central Bureau member in charge of political education. It is difficult to fathom the inner workings of this complex personality. The granddaughter of a rabbi—a "dreamy, naïve Jew not of this world . . . poor, righteous, learned, who died over the Talmud"—Esther herself was married to a rabbi, her second husband, in 1917, and she bore him a child. Yet, by 1921 Esther was described as "a sort of frenzied Medusa, whose fury was on the head of the rabbis and who counted no day complete without assault on them." [208] The daughter of a rich lumber dealer and reader of the Torah in the synagogue, Esther passionately identified herself with the poor and abhorred the synagogue. This woman's paradoxical and pathological behavior might have had a peculiar logic of its own. Her constant theme was the need to create a new Jewish civilization, a proletarian Jewish culture. The first step in this process obviously would have

---

world, and a Jew in your own home." Many interpreted this, perhaps erroneously, as an exhortation to assimilate and to relegate Judaism to the privacy of one's home.

[207] Gershuni, pp. 131–33.

[208] Bogen, p. 328. The characterization of Esther's grandfather is by A. Liesin, *Geklibene verk: zikhroinos un bilder* (New York, 1954), pp. 278–80.

to be the radical transformation of the old culture. Thus, it might have been strangely twisted nationalist motives which impelled her to such ferocious attacks on the Jewish religion. As she explained to Boris Bogen,

> You do not understand the danger the Jews are facing. If the Russian people should once get it into their minds that we are partial to the Jews, it would go hard with the Jews. It is for the sake of the Jews that we are absolutely objective in our dealings with the clergy—Jewish and non-Jewish alike. The danger is that the masses may think that Judaism is exempt from anti-religious propaganda and, therefore, it rests with the Jewish Communists to be even more ruthless with rabbis than non-Jewish-Communists are with priests.[209]

Coming from anyone else, this dialectic might be thought a specious argument. However, Esther's sincerity is attested to by the fact that she repeated the same reasoning[210] along with a somwhat sympathetic discussion of the historical reasons for the power the Jewish religion had over its adherents. "Whoever has breathed the stifling air [in the synagogue on Yom Kippur] . . . has heard the wailings and sighings of hundreds of people, the trembling voice of the cantor—for the rest of his life he cannot free himself of the memory of this oppressive spirit."[211] Esther, like some others, had little difficulty in construing the anti-religious war as "good for the Jews." Some of her colleagues thought Esther prone to "simplicism and impressionism,"[212] while

[209] Bogen, p. 329. Esther's fears were supported by A. V. Lunacharskii's observation that "We are often reproached for fighing Orthodoxy but supposedly conducting no struggle against the Jewish religion, Muslim dogma, etc. . . ." From a lecture given in 1929, reprinted in A. V. Lunacharskii, *Pochemu nel'zia verit' v boga?* (Moscow, 1965), p. 315.

[210] *Doloi ravvinov*, p. 4. [211] *Ibid.*

[212] Grigori Aronson in *Undzer shtime* (Paris), November 5, 1938.

others thought her plainly "hysterical." Raphael Abramovich described her this way:

> You never saw Esther quiet. Her boiling temperament did not allow her to sit still for a moment. When she spoke it was with her eyes, with her hands, with her whole face, with her entire body . . . some considered her hysterical and she was perhaps hysterical in the broad sense of the word, if by "hysterical" you mean an extreme reaction, an exaggerated response . . . to external events. . . . She had masculine comprehension, good and clear logic, and the ability to grasp a new thought. Her hysteria was expressed in only one way: when she followed a certain line she was always too extreme, too exaggerated; she went too far.[213]

Curiously, Esther, the *bête noire* of the religious community, was the only one in the Central Bureau who voted to return the Houses of Study (*Batai Medrashim*) to the religious community of Vitebsk, after they had been seized by the local *Evsektsiia* in a particularly brutal manner.[214]

The anti-religious *jihad* was one of the wildest episodes in *Evsektsiia* history. It involved more people—on both sides of the fence—than any other Jewish Communist campaign heretofore. It ranged from clumsy buffoonery to riots and large-scale violence. And it is fair to say that it

[213] *In tsvai revolutsies*, II, 143–44. Abramovich's characterization well describes the pattern of Esther's anti-religious articles in *Komunistishe fon* of 1921. She started, on March 5, by attacking religion's ostensible *political* content but by July 16, 1921, she was directing an extremely vituperative attack against religion itself.

[214] Chemeriskii and Merezhin were in favor of unconditionally supporting the action of the local Section; Litvakov and Levitan wanted to reprimand the Section for insufficient *agitprop* preparation for the takeover but said that it was a *fait accompli.* Esther alone favored giving the Houses back. The Central Bureau adopted the position of Chemeriskii and Merezhin. *Partai materialn,* no. 5, August 1921, p. 12.

aroused both more support and more opposition than any other *Evsektsiia* activity. Local Sections, and especially their *Komsomol* adherents, often got so carried away that the center had to rein them in. Merezhin scolded, "It is not anti-clerical motives which should be the starting point but rather motives of economic utility" in the campaign to change the day off from Saturday. "This is the directive of the Central Bureau and the question has been formulated thus in the press and at mass meetings." [215] Criticizing the inactivity of the *Evsektsiia* in other fields, M. Altshuler pointed out that it came alive only at the time of anti-religious campaigns. "We are not a party of Sabbath desecrators—we are a revolutionary Marxist party. . . . A plan for work is necessary—not from holiday to holiday but from day to day; not from campaign to campaign, but on a regular basis." [216]

While in 1921 the anti-religious demonstrations were limited to the western provinces—Gomel, Minsk, and Vitebsk—by 1922 they had spread to the Ukraine. Esther claimed that between 25,000 and 30,000 Jewish workers were involved in the demonstrations of 1922.[217] Litvakov described the 1921 campaign as "a bitter military operation, . . . a grandiose attack on the camp of the ancient enemy. . . . It appeared to be a sort of national movement of the Jewish proletariat against *its* bourgeoisie." Litvakov applauded the fact that by 1922 non-Jews were taking part in the anti-religious campaigns, and that not only the *Evsektsiia* but the entire RCP was mobilized against religion. "This was not the cantankerous atheism of the small-town anarchists against small-town 'important Jews' . . . but a revolutionary demonstration of the entire Jewish working mass . . . against the tarnished Assembly of Israel.

[215] "A rikhtike taktik," *Emes*, December 25, 1921.

[216] *Komunistishe fon*, May 19, 1923.

[217] *Doloi ravvinov*, p. 20.

. . . Less *Evsektsiia,* more RCP—this must be the slogan of our work in all fields." [218]

The war on religion continued to smolder in 1923–24. There were campaigns directed against three major holidays in eighty-one different localities and thirty-nine campaigns to close *kheders,* abolish the day of rest on Saturday, and close Houses of Study. Of 303 *Evsektsiia* campaigns between January 1923 and March 1924 a total of 120 were anti-religious in nature.[219] Nevertheless, the campaign had been toned down. "This year we did not fire any heavy artillery in our anti-religious campaign [around the High Holidays]. . . . It is not for nothing that this year's anti-religious campaign was called 'new way of life' and not 'struggle against clericalism'—the struggle is really almost over." [220]

The Thirteenth Congress of the RCP held in 1924 resolved that the anti-religious campaign was to be conducted only with *agitprop* and educational methods.[221] In September 1925 the *Evsektsiia* Central Bureau ordered the cessation of "carnivals, demonstrations, etc." [222] From now

[218] M. Litvakov, "Di anti-religieze kampanie," *Emes,* October 18, 1922.

[219] The others were designed to increase the circulation of the *Evsektsiia* press, promote Jewish colonization, etc. *A yor arbet fun der RKP in der idisher svive* (Moscow, 1924), pp. 27–28.

[220] *Der veker,* September 21, 1923.

[221] *Izvestiia,* June 3, 1924, quoted in N. Gergel, *Di lage fun di yidn,* p. 215.

[222] *Emes,* September 15, 1925, quoted in Gergel, p. 206. Bogen commented, "Thereupon, Esther Frumkin who had been flaunting fiery banners lifted a white one of pity" (p. 329). Alfred A. Greenbaum suggests that "the militancy of this anti-religious work grew and waned in the same cycles as the general anti-religious campaigns" which were "curtailed or abandoned in response to considerations of foreign policy." In 1925 the Central Bureau was trying to get American funds for Jewish land settlement and it "informed the local branches not even to hold anti-religious lectures on Jewish *holidays,* let alone the usual demonstrations during the hours of worship." "Soviet Jewry During the Lenin-Stalin Period—I," *Soviet Studies,* XVI, no. 4 (April 1965), 410.

on the *Evsektsiia* campaign against religion was to be in the nature of sporadic skirmishes rather than a full-scale battle.

Despite the ferocity of the attack upon it, the Jewish religion continued to be an important factor in Soviet Jewish life. Even the *kehillas* showed remarkable resilience, though they had been officially stripped of all their social welfare functions and remained only congregations of worshipers. In 1925 there were 418 *kehillas* registered in the RSFSR, and in 1926 there were 1,003 *kehillas* registered in the Ukraine.[223] The children of religious functionaries could find no jobs and they sometimes changed their names and moved to other towns in order to do so.[224] Yet, there were small, isolated pockets of religious life. In the *shtetl* of Peresfe in 1929 there were eight Houses of Study, a yeshiva, a *kheder* and a branch of the *Tiferes Bakhurim* with twenty-four members, some of whom belonged to trade unions, among them a bookkeeper for the militia.[225] In many small towns the religious community was still the main welfare agency.[226] There were still about five hundred synagogues and Houses of Study in Belorussia.[227] In the Ukraine the number of synagogues had declined only from 1,034 in 1917 to 934 in 1929–30. The number of rabbis in the Ukraine had fallen from 1,049 in 1914 to 830 in 1929–30. All in all, 646 synagogues had been seized since the revolution.[228]

The "second revolution" of the 1930's, which transformed

[223] Each had a minimum membership of twenty and was registered with the local soviet. The Ukrainian *kehillas* included 137,000 members (Gergel, p. 206).

[224] Joint Foreign Committee, "Report of The Situation in Russia," March 5, 1930. Lucien Wolf Archive, Box 10, Packet 74, item 9747 (report of a Viennese traveler).

[225] *Oktiabr*, February 8, 1929.

[226] See the editorial in *Oktiabr*, November 1, 1929.

[227] *Oktiabr*, February 1, 1929.

[228] *American Jewish Year Book 5690*, pp. 68–69; *AJYB 5691*, p. 118.

Russia into a modern industrial society, produced the same effects upon religion as had been observed in America and Western Europe. As the Jew was drawn into the social and economic mainstream of society, he assimilated linguistically, culturally, and religiously. In an officially atheistic society the decline in religious affiliation was, of course, accelerated, and a synthesis of socioeconomic integration and religious identification was not possible. The Jewish religion in the Soviet Union fought a rear guard action against the forces which would destroy it; but fresh reserves were not forthcoming, and the army of the faithful dwindled into an aging and exhausted band of believers.

It is interesting that Islam was not consistently attacked by the same methods, though it resembled Judaism in regulating the entire life of its adherents and making great demands upon them. The Jewish *Halakha* and the Islamic *Shariat* are similar in their detailed prescriptions of daily conduct. Both the Muslims and the Jews were persecuted under the tsarist regime and both were economically backward, though the Jews were less so. But the anti-religious campaign among the Muslims was at first subtler and milder than the *Evsektsiia's* battle with the Jewish religion. Undoubtedly, this was due to the stronger hold of Islam on the Muslims, the lack of Communist Muslim cadres, and the fear of alienating such a large and powerful group. M. Sultan-Galiev, a prominent Bolshevik Muslim, acknowledged that "there are a number of reasons for adopting methods absolutely different from those used among other peoples" and cited the comparatively recent origin of Islam, and hence its vigor and strength, the "political, social, and economic enslavement of almost the entire Muslim world," and the Muslim identification of attacks on Islam with political oppression of Muslims. Therefore, Sultan-Galiev urged "a very careful and dexterous approach."[229]

[229] M. Sultan-Galiev, *Metody anti-religioznoi propagandy, sredi*

In contrast to the Muslims, the Jews had shown an eagerness to assimilate into European culture and had provided their own anti-religious cadres. Lacking their own territory and having proved adept at being absorbed into European society and making outstanding contributions to it, they were the natural vanguard of the movement toward a Luxemburgist cosmopolitanism or, at least, a Leninist internationalism. In 1948, of course, they were attacked for this cosmopolitanism, which was described as "rootless," implying non-allegiance to the Soviet state. Perhaps the conviction that the Jew is so assimilable contributes to the Soviet authorities' irritation with that part of Soviet Jewry which continues to insist on a distinct identity.[230]

The revolution had come to the Jewish street and, with

---

musul'man (Moscow, 1922); translated in Xenia J. Eudin and Harold H. Fisher, *Soviet Russia and the East 1920-1927* (Stanford, 1957), pp. 46–47. See also Park, pp. 204–48, and Massell, "Law as an Instrument of Revolutionary Change."

[230] Mention must be made of a misleading idea that "the persecution of Jews in Russia during the Revolution, in spite of the old anti-Semitism and anti-Jewish laws, was less severe than the persecution of other minorities and their national religions. In the well-documented works of the Jewish writers it is impossible to find statistics pertaining to the looting of synagogues, martyrdom of rabbis, burning of rabbinical schools, public court trials, and other things similar to the actions of suppression applied to other religions. The violent anti-Semitism of the Bolsheviks appeared after 1930, although it existed in mild form before that date" (Sczesniak, pp. 23–24).

If one speaks of the period "during the Revolution" it is difficult to call the murders of thousands and the pogroms in the Ukraine and Belorussia "less severe than the persecution of other minorities," though it is true that the makers of the Revolution did not persecute the Jews. If Sczesniak is really speaking of the Soviet campaigns against religion in the 1920's and 1930's, the evidence brought here suggests that he is ignorant of the facts. He is guilty of a logical error in identifying anti-Semitism and the drive against the Jewish religion, unless he considers the *Evsektsiia* and the Soviet regime of the 1920's anti-Semitic. Finally, if one speaks of "violent anti-Semitism of the *Bolsheviks*" it would probably be more nearly correct to place it in the 1940's and early 1950's than in the 1930's.

enormous logistical and political advantages, it had apparently succeeded in severely crippling the old order, if not quite destroying it altogether. The "revolution on the Jewish street" was an attack on the old order coordinated and, to a large extent, directed by the *Evsektsiia.* While the Communist Party set the overall goals and priorities in its efforts to break down the traditional sources of authority, among Jews, Muslims, and other ethnic and religious groups, it allowed Jewish and Muslim Communists an impressive amount of leeway in determining the tactics and pace of the battle against the old order.

When the smoke of battle had cleared and the Communists stood revealed as the victors, new problems presented themselves. Some Jewish Communists felt that their mission had been largely accomplished with the disintegration of the traditional community. Others believed that they had destroyed in order to build, and that the *Evsektsiia* program should be a positive one, with the annihilation of the old system only a prelude to the reintegration of the Jewish people around a new and unique Jewish sub-culture in a socialist society. This latter group saw the *Evsektsiia* not merely as an *agitprop* organ and instrument for mobilization, but as a planning and executive body which was to devise and implement a formula for the modernization of Soviet Jewry. Religion, the hallmark of Jewish civilization, was anathema to the builders of the new society. Jewish nationalism, preaching a return to Zion, was equally abhorrent. What, then, would be the content of the new Judaism? Indeed, was there to be a new Judaism at all, or should it be reduced to a few national "peculiarities" which time and a modernizing Soviet society would gradually eradicate? Within the seemingly monolithic Communist Party and its Jewish Sections there were proposed different answers to these questions. There were those who urged assimilation as rapidly as possible, judging that this was the quickest and least costly way of modernizing and integrating the Jews politically into the Soviet polity. Assimilation would also achieve *national* integration simply by merging the Jews into larger ethnic entities. Others rejected this cosmopolitan solution and sought to give content to their hopes for the new society, simultaneously defining their vision of the Jewish future. Their formula for national integration envisioned a pluralistic solution whereby distinct ethnic identities could be retained as long as the *political* integration of various nationalities could be achieved. This debate was no academic discussion of a theoretical problem; it profoundly affected the daily lives and the history of Soviet Jewry.

VI

The Constructive Years

The national cultures must be permitted to develop and expand and to reveal all their potential qualities, in order to create the conditions necessary for their fusion into a single, common language. The blossoming of cultures, national in form and socialist in content, under a proletarian dictatorship in one country, *with the object of* their fusion into a single, common, socialist (both in form and content) culture, with a single, common language, when the proletariat is victorious throughout the world and socialism becomes an everyday matter—such is the dialectical nature of the Leninist presentation of the question of national culture.

Stalin

To learn to use Belorussian so it will be easier to come to terms with the peasants, say while collecting taxes, this will not be a solution to the nationality problem. . . . This is a terribly harmful narrowing of the problem of national culture. It is the policy of the tradesmen from the market, who (I have observed this particularly) always address the peasants in their native tongue, in order to . . . fool them more easily. . . .

A Belorussian writer, quoted in
A. Adamovich, *Opposition to Sovietization in Belorussian Literature* (*1917–1957*) (Munich, 1958)

BY 1923 THE success of the "revolution on the Jewish street" seemed assured. The first stage in the social mobilization of Russian Jewry, "the stage of uprooting or breaking away from old settings, habits, and commitments," had been completed. But the *Evsektsiia* was also charged with the implementation of the second stage of social mobilization, "the induction of the mobilized persons into some relatively stable new patterns of group membership, organization, and commitment." [1] The *Evsektsiia* was well suited to the task. Since assimilation was the only realistic solution to the Jewish problem, according to Lenin, the *Evsektsiia* could not be anything more than a temporary apparatus designed to bring Communism to the Jews in their own language and to be dismantled once the linguistic barriers had been overcome, incidental "national pecularities" erased, and total integration of the Jewish population achieved. But the immediate need for *Evsektsiia* was indisputable in view of the fact that nine years after the revolution 71.9 percent of Russian Jews listed Yiddish as their mother tongue.[2] At the same time, the Jews were definitely in the proletarian vanguard: while, for the entire Soviet population, 8 percent of all trade union members in 1926 were members of the Party, 11 percent of Jewish trade unionists were Party members; Jews constituted 5.2 percent of the Party in 1922 and 4.3 percent in 1927, as against 1.8 percent in the total population, though the percentage of Jewish Communists was everywhere substantially lower than the percentage of Jewish city-dwellers.[3]

[1] Deutsch, "Social Mobilization," p. 494.

[2] According to the 1926 census. See Hans Kohn, *Nationalism in the Soviet Union* (New York, 1933), p. 156.

[3] Schwarz, *The Jews in the Soviet Union*, p. 261; Chemeriskii, *Di alfarbandishe komunistishe partai*, p. 23.

Thus, the potential of Russian Jewry for Bolshevization was manifest. Since the more Russianized Jews were less attached to the Jewish religion, to Jewish nationalism or to Jewish socialism, assimilation—which, for Soviet Jews, meant Russification—was desirable from a Bolshevik point of view. The *Evsektsiia* formally endorsed the Leninist position, though it rarely spoke of eventual assimilation. As we shall see, rather than pointing to its own built-in obsolescence, the *Evsektsiia* eventually defined for itself a role as a modernizing agency whose specific function was to serve the special needs of a nationality being revolutionized and modernized. At first, *Evsektsiia* leaders conceived of their role as a very limited one. Dimanshtain argued in 1918 that Bundist fears that a post-revolutionary government would pursue a policy of forced Russification had been rendered obsolete by the compression of the bourgeois and proletarian revolutions, it being assumed that no proletarian government could ever pursue such a bourgeois policy. Furthermore, many national questions were of a sufficiently general nature so that "a good translator is enough."[4] The *Evsektiia,* then, was to be a "good translator" and little else. Dimanshtain did admit that "in a certain sense there are *psychological differences* between Jewish and Russian workers" and that "the Jewish Communists Sections will no doubt pay attention to this." In the most authoritative definition of the *Evsektsiia,* Dimanshtain said that

> as internationalists, we do not set any special national tasks for ourselves . . . insofar as we speak a different language, we are obligated to make an effort to have the Jewish masses know their own language, satisfy their needs in their language. . . . We are not, however,

[4] S. Dimanshtain, "Prosveshchenie natsional'nykh menshinstv," *Zhizn' natsional'nostei,* December 29, 1918.

> fanatics of the Yiddish language. There is no "Holy Yiddish" [*yidish hakoidesh*] for us. . . . It is entirely possible that in the near future the richer languages of the stronger and more highly developed peoples will push aside the Yiddish language in every country. We Communists will shed no tears over this, nor will we do anything to obstruct this development.[5]

In 1922 Samuil Agurskii underscored the transient nature of the *Evsektsiia*'s mission.

> We must note that the future of the Yiddish language in Soviet Russia is not very bright. The new conditions created by the October Revolution make the basis for the future development of the Yiddish language very shaky. . . . These facts may not be pleasing to the lovers of the Yiddish language and Yiddish culture, but you cannot hide your head in the sand and refuse to see reality.[6]

Agurskii discerned a very direct and exclusive relationship between the Jewish proletariat and Yiddish culture. Since the Jewish proletariat was using the Russian language more and the Yiddish language less, the latter was bound to wither on the vine. Agurskii could not resist aiming a shaft in the direction of "many Jewish revolutionaries" who chose to devote themselves to general work, rather than Jewish work, "not only because of altruism . . . but out of egoism—because in general Russian work they have a wider field for their activity and can play a more prominent role

[5] *Emes,* September 12, 1918. Interestingly, in a book published in 1930, Dimanshtain spoke only of the inevitability of *bi*-lingualism among the Jews who were becoming increasingly urbanized. He did not mention total assimilation or the possibility of the Yiddish language being "pushed aside." See his *Di problemn fun natsionaler kultur* (Moscow-Kharkov-Minsk, 1930), pp. 18–19.

[6] "Idishe kultur problemn."

in political life." In an obvious reference to Lipets-Petrovskii, Agurskii gibed, "The test comes when one has to decide what to do: to be a leader of the Bund with a few thousand members and promote Yiddish culture, or a leader of all higher military schools in Russia." In view of Dimanshtain's and Agurskii's prediction that Yiddish could not last long, one can hardly blame a Lipets-Petrovskii for hitching his star to a going concern rather than to a doomed institution whose chief *raison d'être* was the Yiddish language. Agurskii was probably ordered by the Party to work in the Jewish field and thus had no choice. Otherwise it is difficult to understand why he should choose to link his career with an institution which, by his own analysis, was only temporary. However, he—and others—might have calculated that "temporary" could be a very long time, and that both Yiddish and the *Evsektsiia* might well exist beyond his lifetime.

Almost from the very beginning it was apparent that the *Evsektsiia* would be more than a translation service or even a Yiddish *agitprop* department, and that it had undergone a considerable role expansion, a phenomenon frequently observed in the behavior of organizations. By the mid-1920's it was acknowledged that the *Evsektsiia* had broader responsibilities. "As is known, Jewish work differs from other national minority work in that it embraces the most diverse branches of work, often those which have nothing to do with the *agitprop* functions of the Sections, such as court chambers, land settlement, etc."[7] Though the executives of the revolution were civil and general Party authorities, by 1925–26 it was the *Evsektsiia* which defined the scope and intensity of the revolutionary struggle for the modernization of Soviet Jewry and, in many cases, instigated and led it. This latitude was allowed it partially because

[7] Y. Rives, "Der 'emes' un di idishe arbet," *Emes,* January 20, 1926.

neither the Politburo as a body, nor any one of its members, seemed to have a constant concern with Jewish affairs, and partially for broader systemic reasons, especially the tolerance of autonomous authority structures within Soviet society.

The Party itself began to take a more positive attitude toward national aspirations. Almost imperceptibly, "national pecularities" became "national cultures." In contrast with Lenin's formula of 1913—"The proletariat not only does not undertake to fight for the national development of every nation, but . . . warns the masses against such illusions"—the Tenth Party Congress in 1921 affirmed "the right of national minorities to free national development." [8] The exigencies of the struggle for power, especially in Central Asia, had forced the Party to modify its attitude towards national cultures. "Whatever its motives, the Communist Party encouraged and developed cultural activities and was successful in raising the cultural level of backward national groups." [9] Stalin gave theoretical sanction to the new policy in his famous definition of proletarian culture as "socialist in content and national in form." True, the benefits of the new policy accrued more to the less developed peoples of Asia than they did to the Jews—hardly a culturally underdeveloped group, though the less assimilated Jews were sometimes so considered. Nevertheless, Soviet Jews also benefited from the new policy. For the *Evsektsiia* it meant a new status. No longer a temporary translation service, nor even another cog in the machinery mounted against the old order, the *Evsektsiia* had to assume the burden of a host of cultural and economic programs whose life span was calculated in years and even decades. In effect, it was assigned a major role in determining the

[8] Quoted in Schwarz, p. 37.
[9] *Ibid.*, p. 68.

future of Soviet Jewry—perhaps consciously, more likely by default. It is not clear whether the Party consciously entrusted the *Evsektsiia* with the formulation of cultural and economic programs for Soviet Jews (an unlikely possibility in view of the dubious antecedents of many *Evsektsiia* leaders), or whether the *Evsektsiia* filled a vacuum created by lack of Politburo interest in "Jewish questions" (if, indeed, the members of the Politburo believed that there existed special "Jewish questions" which could not be subsumed under general Soviet Russian problems). Whatever the case, the *Evsektsiia* did assume the responsibility of proposing alternative programs designed to achieve the economic and cultural reconstruction of Soviet Jewry.

This responsibility brought the *Evsektsiia* face to face with the problem that confronts the modernizing leadership of any nation or national minority: how to achieve the economic and social transformation of the nation or nationality while retaining at least some elements of its specific, ethnic culture and identity (or "transforming" these to fit new conditions). Some modernizing countries, such as Communist China, have placed economic, social, and political transformation far ahead of cultural continuity and preservation, while countries such as India have tried to strike a more equal balance between the new and the traditional. Within the *Evsektsiia* different leaders struck different balances between the imperatives of economic, social, and political modernization, on one hand, and the pull of primordial loyalties and purely ethnic cultural values, on the other. As we shall see, some Jewish activists were prepared to sacrifice the past on the altar of modernization. Others tried, in different ways, to revive and express in modern forms the cultural traditions of the Jewish people. This, of course, was the problem faced on an individual basis by every Jew challenged by a confrontation with a modernizing world. But in trying to develop its own balance between

Soviet socialism and Jewish identification, the *Evsektsiia* faced enormous difficulties.

The *Evsektsiia*, and especially that part of its leadership which had matured in the Jewish socialist movement, hastened to fill the vacuum created by the crippling of the old Jewish culture, in the full realization that the destruction of the old order does not automatically result in a new one. The *Evsektsiia* tried to construct a socialist culture encased in national forms. It found, however, that the national forms it could employ were severely circumscribed by the Party, for which national forms meant language almost exclusively, and by Jewish forms themselves, overwhelmingly religious in origin and otherwise ill-suited to the Soviet way of life. Almost the only national form left to the *Evsektsiia* was language, and although the *Evsektsiia* leaders periodically reaffirmed that they were not Yiddishists, they began to pour all their energies into the development and diffusion of Yiddish in and through all the channels of the Soviet structure. They tried to create a culture whose medium was Yiddish and whose content was, in the main, the depiction of the Soviet Jewish milieu, whether in the *shtetl,* in the cities, or in the agricultural colonies. Hence, when speaking of "nationalist" and "assimilationist" tendencies and viewpoints within the *Evsektsiia,* one is basically measuring attitudes towards linguistic independence and linguistic assimilation, though linguistic distinctiveness or assimilation is not the same as national identity or assimilation.

In a country such as the United States, Jews may be linguistically assimilated, but may retain a distinct identity, ultimately based on religion and its customary forms, on a subjective assertion of identification with other Jews and an allegiance to "Jewish culture," however defined, or an active sympathy for the Jewish state. The same holds true, *mutatis mutandis,* for other ethnic groups. In the Soviet

Union, allegiance to religion and support for a Jewish state were illegitimate or highly suspect; what remained, aside from official identification as a Jew, required by Soviet law, was linguistic-cultural identification and/or the essentially subjective sense of identity, without an elaborate cultural content, which is a function of external factors such as societal anti-Semitism. The American Jew could be linguistically assimilated but socially-subjectively distinct, and yet could legitimately identify himself as an American citizen. The Soviet Jew could be linguistically distinct but wholly identified with Soviet society, because that society sanctioned and even encouraged the use of different national languages. In theory, the Soviet Jew could be integrated into Soviet society—indeed, he could be a leader of that society, a Communist—while remaining committed to the Yiddish language and culture, though the latter was redefined and considerably narrowed for him. "Nationalist," in the Soviet context, thus indicates a positively affirmed Jewish consciousness and a desire to retain ethnic culture and identification for an indeterminate future. "Assimilationist" connotes the conviction either that Jewish culture and identification should, or—as was more frequently the case among the *Evsektsiia* activists—would disappear in the not too distant future. Since the discussion between "nationalists" and "assimilationists" was conducted in "objective" terms but undoubtedly reflected "subjective" attitudes, it would seem that those who unregretfully predicted the loss of Jewish identity were probably urging it, or, at least, were prepared to accept it.

"Nationalist" and "assimilationist," then, indicate attitudes more precisely than programs. Programs did, however, exist. The assimilationist program was simple: limit the use of Yiddish to the absolutely necessary, embark on no programs which might isolate the Jew and increase his national consciousness, promote industrialization and the use of Russian, combat anti-Semitism. This was a program which postulated modernization and integration as the sole objectives, with no value attached to ethnic maintenance and cultural continuity.

There was no single "nationalist" program. Some were content to promote the widespread use of Yiddish in schools, soviets, party cells, trade unions, the press, and the courts. Others, who had a broader conception of the *Evsektsiia* function, favored agricultural settlement in compact masses, the creation of Jewish districts, and even a Jewish republic. Still others emphasized the creation of a new proletarian Yiddish culture, truly socialist in content and national in form. Naturally, in the conditions of Soviet society, rapidly moving from extreme authoritarianism toward totalitarianism, different programs had to be put forth with extreme caution by the very vulnerable ex-socialists who felt a need to demonstrate their ultra-orthodoxy, to show that they were "more Communist than Lenin." There is therefore a danger of wrongly ascribing positions and beliefs to *Evsektsiia* activists and incorrectly classifying them as proponents of one or another viewpoint. Nevertheless, as Robert Conquest notes, "the careful consideration of all facets of an event in the field and of the relevant information about the people concerned at least reduces the possibilities to a limited number, till only some small move may be needed to reduce these to one. . . . The odd tooth or even jawbone may be susceptible to various explanations, but careful study of it is all that is open to the scientist. . . . In these sciences of defective information, indeed, no one can be sure of not being hoaxed by a Piltdown skull."[10]

The *Evsektsiia* was able to move from primarily destructive to constructive tasks, from the disintegrative to the integrative stage of the mobilization process, as a result of

[10] Robert Conquest, *Power and Policy in the USSR* (London, 1961), p. 4.

decisions taken by the Party in 1923, 1924, and 1925. At the Twelfth Party Congress in April 1923, a "resolute struggle with the survivals of Great Russian chauvinism" was called "the primary task of our party." One of the "survivals" explicitly condemned was the attitude of many Soviet bureaucrats at the center and in the localities who were charged with regarding the Soviet state structure, not as a permanent union of equal governmental units, but as a temporary arrangement soon to evolve into a centralized country with no republics.[11] This decision clearly implied more support and leeway for the national republics and, at least indirectly, for the national minorities as well. The *Evsektsiia* was certainly in need of such support since many Communists, within and without the *Evsektsiia,* were arguing either that Party work among the Jews was impossible because of Party indifference or, on the other hand, that there was no need for such work, and hence, no need for Jewish Sections, to begin with.[12]

The Thirteenth Party Congress, held in May 1924, went further in buttressing the legitimacy of the *Evsektsiia.* Dealing specifically with the rights of the national minorities, it resolved that too little attention had been paid to Party work among them. This encouraged *Evsektsiia* leaders to ask their local activists to assert their rights within the local Party committees and to base themselves on the resolutions of the Twelfth and Thirteenth Party Congresses.[13] Apparently, this was successfully done, and Dimanshtain observed that "after the Thirteenth Party Con-

[11] *Kommunisticheskaia partiia sovetskogo soiuza v rezoliutsiiakh i resheniiakh s"ezdov, konferentsii i plenumov TsK, Chast' I* (Moscow, 1953), pp. 713 and 715. On the Twelfth Congress and its decisions regarding the nationalities, see Pipes, pp. 285–93.

[12] See, for example, the report from Mozyr, in "Partai lebn," *Emes,* March 15, 1923.

[13] "A—skii" [Agurskii?] "Di natsionale frage afn 13-tn tsuzamenfor," *Der veker,* July 6, 1924.

gress national minority work grew significantly and became differentiated [multi-faceted]." [14]

The Communist Party began to display a more active interest in Jewish affairs during 1924–25. The formation of the USSR had aroused greater attention to the nationalities in general, and the Party began a campaign of "nativization" (*korenizatsiia*), which meant that cultural and political institutions, such as soviets and Party cells, in the national republics would conduct their work in the local language. This shift in policy affected the Jews, though they did not have their own republic. From April 1924 to October 1925 the Central Committee adopted 408 resolutions on Jewish matters.[15] The new emphasis on "Jewish work" included both acceleration of standing programs and initiation of new ones. The *Evsektsiia* implemented general Party policy, but did not yet assume the initiative in suggesting alternative paths to the modernization of Soviet Jewry. The Yiddish press and publishing, Yiddish schools, courts, and soviets were promoted with new vigor. A new policy was adopted toward the *shtetl,* or small Jewish hamlet, and toward the *kustar,* the self-employed artisan who occupied such an important place in the Jewish economic structure. These policies paralleled and complemented new Party attitudes toward the rural population and toward cooperative forms of economic organization. There was also a new emphasis on Yiddish in the trade union and in the Party

[14] S. Dimanshtain, "K postanovke partraboty sredi natsmen'shinstv," *Partiinoe stroitel'stvo,* no. 6, March 1930, p. 24.

[15] Smolensk Oblast Archives, WKP 303; and Chemeriskii, p. 28. Chemeriskii comments, "This shows that the *Sektsiia* cannot be considered the sole representative of the Jewish masses, as the Bundist Bible demands. It is understood that the *Sektsiia* is the most sensitive apparatus in relation to Jewish work and therefore almost all the work is conducted *through* the *Sektsiia,* though this is not an *obligation* upon the Central Committee."

cell.[16] Later on, these new policies and attitudes led to a large-scale effort to revamp completely the economy of the Jewish population and intensively involve the Jews in wholly new forms of political, cultural, and even social life. This was not an easy task. "Functional change depends on the few, and may often be rapid and easy. Structural change depends on the many, and is slow and painful. It is the task of leaders to mediate between function and structure—between the new knowledge and the old customs—and this is never easy."[17] It was the task of the *Evsektsiia* leadership to replace the "old customs" with the "new knowledge."

One set of instruments for the accomplishment of this task was obviously the mass media. The number of Yiddish books and brochures published annually in the Soviet Union, steadily declining in 1921–24, rose from 76 in 1924 to 168 in 1925; by 1930 it had reached 531.[18] In the Civil War period there had been a plethora of Communist newspapers in Yiddish, owing to the fact that they were totally subsidized by the regime. The military situation made it impossible to circulate central newspapers very widely, and local papers appeared in almost every city and town with a significant Jewish population. Paper and ink were very scarce, and many newspapers were printed on brown wrapping paper or the coarse blue cardboard used to wrap sugar. When cost-accounting was introduced as a part of NEP, the newspapers had to operate on a profit basis—and

[16] For some of the basic decisions concerning the new line of positive work and some discussion of these, see A. Bailin, "Tsum frabraitertn plenum fun der yidburo bam TsKKPV," *Oktiabr,* November 10, 1926, and the resolutions on Jewish work adopted by the Orgburo of the Ukrainian CP Central Committee, in *Der shtern,* July 15, 1925. See also M. L[itvakov], "Mitn 'neiem kurs'," *Emes,* January 9, 1924.

[17] Black, *Dynamics of Modernization,* p. 48.

[18] Szmeruk, *Pirsumim,* p. lxv.

most of them collapsed. The regime continued to subsidize three dailies which appeared in Moscow, Minsk, and Kharkov, along with some other newspapers in major Jewish centers. By the mid-twenties more newspapers were being published on a regular basis. There were twenty-one Yiddish newspapers published in 1923–25, twenty-six in 1926, and forty in 1927.[19]

The *Evsektsiia* press did not attract a wide readership. According to the 1926 census, there were 1,888,000 Jews whose mother tongue was Yiddish. Yet, in that same year the circulation of the three main Yiddish dailies was only 27,000, and this represented a significant increase from 1924.[20] In 1926–28 there was another gain, and the total circulation of the three newspapers reached 32,000. It has been estimated that each copy of the newspaper was read by three people. This would make the total readership of the Yiddish newspapers about 110,000, if one adds the circulation of 14,000 which the provincial and local weeklies enjoyed.[21] Some local figures will illustrate the relatively very low readership of the Yiddish newspapers. In Gomel, out of 353 *kustars* (artisans) who read newspapers, 271 read the Russian newspaper *Poleskaia pravda,* only 54 read *Emes,* and 28 read other Russian newspapers. This was among a group in which ninety-seven percent had given Yiddish as their mother tongue.[22] In Berdichev, out of 2,800 Jewish trade union members only 100 read Yiddish newspapers; after a "vigorous campaign" to increase readership 265 more readers were added.[23] In Kharkov, where

[19] *Ibid.,* p. lxviii.

[20] *Emes,* in 1926, had a circulation of 11,000; the Kharkov *Shtern* (previously *Komunistishe fon*) had 9,400; and the Minsk *Oktiabr* (previously *Veker*) had 6,800 (*Alfarbandishe baratung,* pp. 256–57).

[21] D. Charney, "Freint Khanin, ir zeint farfirt gevorn," *Bikher velt* (Warsaw), April 1929.

[22] I. Pul'ner, "Iz zhizni goroda Gomelia," p. 174.

[23] *Komunistishe fon,* February 12, 1924. In 1923 only forty sub-

there were 15,000 Jewish trade union members and 3,500 organized *kustars*, *Shtern* had a circulation of only 500, *Emes* only 120, and *Yunge gvardie* only 100.[24] Even the *Evsektsiia* functionaries themselves did not read the Yiddish press to the extent that one might have expected. Of thirty-three *Evsektsiia* workers in Smolensk *oblast*, only eleven read Yiddish newspapers and only four read Yiddish newspapers exclusively.[25]

The abysmally low circulation of the Yiddish press may be explained by the poverty of the Jewish masses and their inability to afford the luxury of a newspaper, the unattractive format of the papers, and the new orthography to which many older people were unaccustomed. In any case, it is fair to assert that the Soviet Yiddish press failed to strike a responsive chord among its potential readers, and this indicates perhaps the masses' indifference to the *Evsektsiia* and its conception of Soviet Jewish society.[26]

The literary tastes of the Jewish population support this

---

scribed to *Emes* and only seventy-five to *Komfon*. This circulation campaign, like most others, focused on the central organ, *Emes*, rather than the local or provincial one. *Evsektsiia* activists outside the center resented this and Litvakov had to assure them that the Central Bureau was not trying to increase the circulation of *Emes* at the expense of the other newspapers. Judging by the campaigns on behalf of *Oktiabr* and *Shtern*, this was probably true. Nevertheless, the Jewish reader may have preferred *Emes* as more authoritative and cosmopolitan.

[24] *Shtern*, May 11, 1927. For the demographic characteristics of *Shtern's* readers see F. Sh., "Der 'shtern' un zeine lainer," *Shtern*, January 5, 1928.

[25] Based on Party questionnaires in Smolensk Oblast Archive, WKP 303.

[26] For instance, many *Shtern* readers wrote to the editors that they should stop printing anti-religious articles since this was pitting one Jew against another. Fifty-two of 1,153 questionnaires filled out by the readers contained complaints of that nature. *Shtern's* reaction was to consider itself complimented since the complaints "proved" that it was following a "class," rather than "Jewish nationalist," policy. See "Der 'shtern' un zeine lainer," *Shtern*, January 7, 1928. The *Evsektsiia* itself was very critical of its own press, perhaps too much so. In 1924

conclusion. A survey conducted by the newspaper *Oktiabr* in 1928 found that Yiddish readers read mostly the Yiddish classics. Their second preference was for Yiddish translations of European classics. Soviet Yiddish literature ran a poor third. The survey cited complaints that contemporary literature was "artificial," as well as the demands of some older people for religious literature and more of the classics.[27] Nevertheless, there were some truly outstanding talents among the Soviet Yiddish writers, who were very productive in the middle and late 1920's. It was not only the central government which encouraged the Yiddish writers but also some of the Belorussian and Ukrainian authorities. One Jewish writer, perhaps oversimplifying, noted that "the Ukrainians and Belorussians drive us very hard to publish in Yiddish—of course, not as much from 'love of Mordecai' as from 'hatred of Haman,' hatred of the Russians."[28] The failure of the new writers to gain extensive popularity is understandable in light of the fact that the majority of Yiddish readers were of the older generation and felt more comfortable with Sholem Aleikhem's traditional wit and pathos than with the younger writers' experimental styles and contemporary subject matter.

The Evsektsiia *and the Soviet Yiddish School*

If Jewish culture was to continue in the Soviet Union, there had to be Jewish education. Traditional Jewish education, with its religious or Hebraist emphases, was being

---

Litvakov criticized his own newspaper, *Emes,* as "too Jewish." He excused himself by saying that "they do not give us" articles on general Soviet and Party problems, indicating that such articles appearing in *Emes* were merely translations from *Pravda* or *Izvestiia. Veker* was criticized for amateurishness and localism, while Litvakov said of *Komfon* that "it does not yet have a steady course" (*Komunistishe fon,* April 22, 1924). More detailed criticisms were made in 1926 at the All-Union *Evsektsiia* Conference. See *Alfarbandishe baratung,* p. 259.

27 Charney, "Freint Khanin."

28 Niepomniashchi to Charney, August 7, 1924, YIVO Archives.

destroyed in a war of attrition, and a wholly new Jewish school had to be constructed. The Jewish socialists had long dreamed of a Jewish secular school but until 1917 had been largely unsuccessful in their efforts to establish it.[29] The *Evsektsiia* had a better opportunity to implement its program for the new Jewish school, and it hastened to the task. Jewish bureaus were formed in the Central, Belorussian, and Ukrainian People's Commissariats of Education. Jewish bureaus also existed in all *guberniia* and *krai* educational departments of soviets located in areas with large Jewish populations.[30] Familiar problems, and some new ones, were encountered in the endeavor to create the Jewish school network: lack of teachers, lack of enthusiasm on the part of the Jewish masses, lack of a well-defined program and goals.

The new school could not be constructed as rapidly as the old was being destroyed. When a *kheder* was closed, its students were not transferred to other schools, but either enrolled in Russian schools, or, in most cases, remained without any schooling whatever. While the Communists could and did take over the buildings and equipment of Jewish schools and other institutions, they could not fill them. The buildings became hollow shells, mute testimony to the death of the past and the bankruptcy of the present. The silence in the Jewish school was broken only in 1923, and from then on the four- and seven-year Jewish schools grew at a steady and sometimes spectacular rate. From 366 Yiddish schools in 1923–24, the number rose to 775 in

[29] Within the borders of the tsarist empire in 1898 there were 375,000 Jewish children in religious schools, six times as many as were in secular schools (*Dos sovetishe identum,* p. 47). A figure of 363,000 is cited in Aryeh V. Yodfat, "The Soviet Struggle to Destroy Jewish Religious Education in the Early Years of the Regime, 1917–1927," *Jewish Education,* 40, no. 3 (Winter 1970), 33.

[30] There were also Jewish sections of the political education and the trade union educational apparatuses.

1926–27 and then to 1,100 in 1929–30.[31] Student enrollment jumped from 54,173 in 1923–24 to 130,000 in 1930.[32] Most significant was the fact that almost half of all Jewish children attending schools in the Belorussian and Ukrainian republics were attending Yiddish schools, though in the RSFSR only 16.8 percent of Jewish students were enrolled in Jewish schools.[33] Many Jewish children of school age were beyond the reach of any Soviet education. Forty percent in the Ukraine and twenty-five to fifty percent in Belorussia did not attend any school, though a good number may have been attending underground religious schools.[34]

The teacher was an important figure in the *Evsektsiia* scheme of things. He was often the only Communist sympathizer in the *shtetl* who had the political knowledge

[31] N. Gergel, p. 230. The 1930 figure is from Sh. Klitenik, *Kultur arbet tsvishn di yidishe arbetndike inem ratnfarband* (Moscow-Kharkov-Minsk, 1931), p. 9. Klitenik gives lower figures than Gergel for the previous years. For example, he lists 642 schools for 1926–27 while Gergel lists 775. Yankel Kantor cites still a third figure: 686 schools in 1926–27 (*Ratnboiung*, p. 212). According to figures cited at the All-Union *Evsektsiia* Conference of 1926, there were 692 schools in 1926 (*Alfarbandishe baratung*, p. 73). There is further confusion in figures for Belorussia. The All-Union Conference reported 141 schools in Belorussia in 1924–25 and 176 in the following year (p. 116), while the Main Bureau in Belorussia reported 134 in 1924–25 and 175 the following year (*Barikht fun der hoipt biuro fun di yidsektsies bam TsKKPV: far di tseit fun obtiabr, 1925 yor*, Minsk, 1925, p. 28). These discrepancies are not very significant and perhaps arise because the surveys were made at different periods during the years cited and because some schools were multilingual and difficult to classify.

[32] Gergel and Klitenik, *op. cit.*

[33] Gergel, p. 221.

[34] Kantor (p. 212) cites a 25 percent figure for Belorussia in 1927, while *Barikht, loc. cit.*, cites 50 percent in 1924–25. Chemeriskii, writing in 1926, states that 50 percent of all Jewish schoolage children attend school and 21 percent of all children are in Yiddish schools (p. 11). Yodfat (p. 39) cites reports indicating that in 1926 about 15,000 pupils studied in illegal *kheders*, and the same number attended illegal Zionist Hebrew schools.

and sophistication to lead political activities. The teacher was expected to "Sovietize" the *kustars* and work among the *shtetl* youth and its poor.[35] Russianized Jewish teachers vigorously opposed the conversion of Russian schools into Yiddish schools, since this would mean loss of their jobs.[36] The old secular teachers were suspected of "Yiddishism," and the Jewish Communists had little pedagogical training. To meet the constantly growing demand for teachers the *Evsektsiia* established a network of Yiddish pedagogical institutes, whose graduates were rushed into the breach.[37] Nevertheless, a constant crisis existed. Of 347 teachers in Belorussian Yiddish schools in 1924–25, only fourteen percent had any pedagogical training and thirteen percent did not even have secondary education.[38]

The lack of teachers and the failure to provide schooling for almost half the Jewish children of school age were essentially technical problems which might have been solved in due time. The *Evsektsiia* came up against a more serious difficulty, a manifestation of the problem inherent in the very idea of a *Evsektsiia* in particular and in the Stalinist nationality formula in general. The Jewish schools could be Jewish in language only. Jewish culture was largely inappropriate because of its religious and Hebraic roots. The Soviet government claimed that it was promoting national cultures, but with regard to the Jews, an extra-territorial minority, it was actually reducing culture and nationality to language alone. The Leninist definition of Jewry and the Jewish future was in fact being fulfilled, though that defini-

[35] A. Bailin, "Tsum aroisloz fun 125 neie yidishe lerer," *Oktiabr,* June 3, 1926. Often, teachers did not receive their salaries on time, and the salaries they did receive were quite modest. "Teachers see vacations as times of unemployment," *Shtern,* July 24, 1925.

[36] M. Kiper, "Di kampanie far idishizirn di arbet-shuln," *Shtern,* July 17, 1925.

[37] There were seven institutes with a thousand students, according to Kantor, *Ratnboiung,* p. 214.

[38] *Barikht,* p. 31.

tion preceded reality and shaped it, rather than vice versa. The Leninist-Stalinist formulation left the *Evsektsiia* with language and language alone; from an epiphenomenon of national culture it had become the sum and substance of national culture.

The Yiddish schools reflected this narrow concept of a Sovietized Jewry, which, in turn, was only an expression of the Soviet regime's vulgar Marxist approach to the history and literature of all nationalities, wherein most non-radical elements were ignored. They differed from the general schools in form and not in substance, though a course in Yiddish literature was required. "Even in the selection of Yiddish literary creations, communist rather than Jewish criteria were employed. If among the great literary figures Sholem Aleikhem and Mendele were paid particular attention, this preference was in part owing to their satirical descriptions of the ghetto community which could be used as a foil for contrast with the achievements of Soviet society." [39] The Jewish content of the curriculum was heavily propagandistic. "The very concept of 'Jewish history' is excluded from the school. Any general course in the history of the class struggles may include elements describing the struggle of Jewish artisans against their employers and of Jewish workers against the Jewish or any other bourgeoisie." [40] Of course, it was not only *Jewish*

[39] Baron, p. 271. One analysis of the Yiddish literature curriculum concludes that (1) Hebrew writers who also contributed to Yiddish literature were excluded; (2) few non-Communist writers living outside the USSR were studied; (3) a "large number of important writers were totally excluded from the texts." Harry Lipset, "Jewish Schools in the Soviet Union, 1917–1941: An Aspect of Soviet Minorities Policy," unpub. Ed.D. project, Teachers College, Columbia University, 1965, pp. 305–06.

[40] Y. Dardak, "Undzere dergraikhungen far 15 yor oktiabr afn gebit fun folk-bildung," *Tsum XV yortog fun der oktiabr revoliutsie—sotsial ekonomisher zamlbukh* (Minsk, 1932), p. 173. Lipset points out that only the history of the Jews in *Russia* was touched upon (p. 295).

history which was distorted almost beyond recognition. The violence done to history by the system which speaks in its name and claims a monopoly on its proper understanding is too well known to require elaboration.

In a second-grade curriculum the only "Jewish" content consisted of warnings against "non-hygienic customs such as kissing the Torah." The fourth grade learned about Jewish agriculture in the USSR and Palestine in order to show the "utopianism and harmfulness" of Zionism. The Jewish teacher was advised to highlight the pogroms as a natural bourgeois manifestation and a counter-revolutionary instrument, rather than as a national tragedy. He was urged to emphasize "how the Soviet government and the Party care for the Jewish workers." [41] In the fifth grade history was given a more prominent place in the course of study. The history of the Jews in Lithuania and Belorussia was given twelve out of 109 pages in the history book, but only economic history and class struggles were dealt with.[42]

Even the linguistic aspect of Yiddish education presented serious difficulties. When the graduate of a Yiddish school wished to continue his education, he had to relearn all his subjects in Russian because the entrance examinations to secondary schools were given in Russian. For this reason parents preferred to send their children to Russian schools. Others "found new jobs in the RSFSR or sent their children to school there. For the same reason Jewish middle schools, especially in the upper grades, were not full, having three to five students in a class." [43] The *Evsektsiia* constantly berated Jewish parents who argued that the Yiddish school was impractical because it closed off any opportunities for

[41] Y. Reznik, ed., *Programen fun der einheitlikher arbet shul* (Moscow, 1928), pp. 41, 64, 86.

[42] Rubin, et al., *Gezelshaftkentenish* (Minsk, 1928), p. 96ff.

[43] S. Krushinsky, *Belorussian Communism and Nationalism: Personal Recollections* (New York, 1953), p. 5.

advancement in education and in most careers. It was pointed out that Russian was always taught as a second or third language, but even the *Evsektsiia* admitted that graduates of Yiddish schools had only a nodding acquaintance with the rudiments of Russian grammar.[44] Furthermore, most religious Jews preferred to send their children to Russian, Ukrainian, or Belorussian language schools because the anti-religious propaganda in these schools was not aimed specifically at the Jewish religion, whereas in the Yiddish schools it was.[45] There were no Yiddish secondary schools, and Yiddish higher education was specialized education exclusively, training teachers and workers for the "Jewish street." Thus, there were Jewish teachers' institutes in some universities, Yiddish agricultural schools, and some Yiddish Party schools.[46] Often, the *Evsektsiia* forced Jewish parents to send their children to Yiddish schools.

> It was *not* clear to all cultural activists that Yiddish is not an end in itself but a means to ease the cultural development of the Yiddish-speaking masses. This led to the tendency to drag all Jewish children into Yiddish schools

[44] See, for example, "Di idishe shuln in veisrusland," *Der veker*, October 22, 1925.

[45] See the comments of delegate Shatzkii at the conference of Yiddish teachers attending the All-Belorussian Teachers' Congress. *Oktiabr*, May 14, 1926.

[46] There was a Jewish sector in the Communist University of the National Minorities of the West (itself an adjunct of the Sverdlov University), which was mainly a Party school; there were Jewish departments in the Belorussian State University, the Pedagogical Faculty of the Second Moscow State University, the workers' faculty of Leningrad State University, and the Institute of Belorussian Culture. There was also a chair of Jewish culture in the Ukrainian Academy of Sciences, Jewish departments of the Kiev and Odessa Institutes of Social Sciences, an agricultural *tekhnikum* and tractor courses, three Jewish state theaters which were also drama schools, and a music school in Kiev (Chemeriskii, p. 87). Sharapov (p. 202) mentions eleven local Yiddish Party schools in 1922–23.

> by force, taking no account of the language they use or the wishes of their parents. It turned out that we were building Yiddish schools not for Yiddish speakers who really need them, but for all citizens of Jewish origin. . . . This is how militant Yiddishism, though dyed in Soviet ideology, blatantly manifested itself. As a result gross distortions occurred in some cities where people who do not need Yiddish schools were forced—by use of terror—to attend them. This strengthened [the resolve] of some anti-Semitic elements not to admit too many Jewish children to the general schools.[47]

Many Jewish activists argued, however, that "We cannot take the desires of the parents into account. We must teach the child in the language he speaks at home."[48]

Yuri Larin, a prominent economist interested in national minority and specifically Jewish affairs, wrote an article in *Pravda* asking that parents be given complete freedom of choice in determining which school their children were to attend. This brought down the wrath of the Jewish educators on his head. "The will of the parents is not always an obligation on the child. In many, many respects we raise the children in a manner explicitly opposed to the desire of the parents. . . . A child should be educated in the language spoken at home."[49] The question had to be resolved at the highest levels of the *Evsektsiia*. Kiper suggested that children who speak mainly Yiddish should be assigned to Yiddish schools; children speaking mainly Russian or Ukrainian should attend Russian or Ukrainian schools; in the case of children speaking two or three languages well,

[47] M. Kiper, "Oifgabn in der kultur-oifkler arbet," *Shtern*, June 28, 1927.

[48] *Oktiabr*, May 11, 1926.

[49] A. B., "Di shprakhn frage in sovetn-farband," *Der veker*, March 24, 1925. See the attacks on Larin by David Matz and others in *Der veker*, March 24 and 28, 1925.

the choice of school would be left up to the parents. Propaganda should be conducted on behalf of the Yiddish school since it "revolutionizes the Jewish way of life more easily," but "in no case should freedom of choice be impeded."[50] Chemeriskii, secretary of the *Evsektsiia* Central Bureau, agreed that, if the child could demonstrate knowledge of two languages, his parents could choose the type of school they wished him to attend. Admitting that such a policy would mean that many more children would attend Russian schools, Chemeriskii asked, "What is more harmful? When children study in a Russian school or when you stir up the masses against you?"[51] Clearly, the educators and the politicians had different stakes to protect. The educators urged the forcible enrollment of children in Yiddish schools because this would beef up the Yiddish school system and, hopefully, its budget. The politicians knew this to be a very unpopular policy and their positions was dictated by a fear of alienating the Jewish masses from the *Evsektsiia.* Even children already enrolled in Yiddish schools were strongly attracted to Russian. A visitor to a Yiddish school in Kiev observed that

> some of the pupils were carrying Russian text-books; and to the enquiry as to whether no Yiddish books existed for these subjects, several pupils replied: "Oh, yes; but we like to read the Russian texts better than the Yiddish." . . . If they had been able to decide for themselves, it is possible that many of these children would have chosen to attend Russian or even Ukrainian schools. Russian is the language of a culture stronger than the secular non-Hebrew culture conveyed by the Yiddish language in the Soviet Union; Russian is also the language

[50] M. Kiper, *loc. cit.*

[51] Chemeriskii's speech at the Second All-Union Yiddish Culture Congress, in *Shtern,* April 24, 1928.

> spoken in Moscow and generally throughout the USSR; and all those pupils, and parents, too, who ever expect to move freely about the Union must have complete mastery of the Russian language.[52]

This problem was acknowledged by the *Evsektsiia,* and it was obvious that teaching Russian as a second language was inadequate to solve it. The situation was very complicated. Yiddish schools in the RSFSR taught Yiddish, Russian, and, in the higher grades, German. In the Ukraine and Belorussia the languages of those areas were also made a part of the curriculum. If the student did not learn Russian, he had no chance of continuing his education; if he did not learn German, he was at a disadvantage in competing for a place in a higher school. Chemeriskii tried to wish the problem away. "Disregarding the difficulty of learning four languages, which turns the school into a vocabulary-factory, one must learn all four. This is the new form of the language problem in our schools and we will solve it."[53] Belorussian or Ukrainian was introduced in the second grade, Russian in the fourth, and German was taught in the higher grades of the seven-year schools.[54] As if this were not enough of a burden for the child, "in the schools they teach Yiddish, the Pioneer groups in the school speak a

[52] Harold R. Weinstein, "Language and Education in the Soviet Ukraine," *The Slavonic Year Book,* vol. xx of *The Slavonic and East European Review* (1941), p. 138.

[53] Chemeriskii, pp. 79–80. David Matz suggested a more realistic solution. He proposed that German be made an elective since those who planned to go on to higher education could take quick preparatory courses enabling them to pass the German examinations. He also proposed that the four-year school teach two languages rather than three and that the third language be added either in new schools to be set up for working youth (aged twelve and up) or in a fifth grade to be added to the four-year school. D. Matz, "Tsu der frage vegn der filshprakhikeit in der yidisher shul," *Oktiabr,* May 27, 1927.

[54] *Rezolutsies funem tsvaitn alfarbandishen tsuzamenfor fun di yidishe kultur tuer* (Kharkov, 1928), p. 18.

broken 'Reisish'. . . . The parents demand that their children learn Ukrainian and not Russian."[55] This crazy-quilt curriculum and the linguistic facts of life were bound to make most children not polyglot prodigies but multilingual schizophrenics.

Granting that some coercion was used to enroll Jewish students in the Yiddish schools, the proportion attending such schools was an impressive achievement when compared to the enrollment figures of other countries, though it was qualified by the fact that in small towns the Yiddish school was often the only one and Jewish parents had no alternative; the proportion of Jewish students in urban Yiddish schools was much smaller than the overall proportion.[56] Other nationalities supported their national schools and languages better than Jews did, though Jews almost invariably had a higher percentage of children attending school than did most other nationalities. Table V, based on figures for the Ukrainian town of Vinnitsa in 1925, illustrates these points.

The percentage of Jewish pupils attending Yiddish schools did rise constantly—and sometimes dramatically—in the late 1920's. In Kamenets *krai* in the Ukraine, for example, only forty-eight percent of Jewish children attended Yiddish schools in 1923–24, but by 1925–26 the percentage had risen to sixty-four. In the same area only fourteen percent of Jewish first graders were in non-Yiddish schools whereas eighty-six percent of Jewish seventh graders were in such schools.[57] While the trend was encouraging from the *Evsektsiia*'s point of view, Jews did not compare favorably in proportion of children studying in the nationality language even with other national minorities in the Ukraine,

[55] Niepomniashchi to Charney, August 7, 1924, YIVO Archives.

[56] See Baron, pp. 272–73, and Schwarz, p. 135.

[57] M. Levitan, "Di vegn tsu idishizatsie fun der arbetshul," *Shtern*, April 27, 1926.

TABLE V

SCHOOLS IN VINNITSA, 1925

Nationality	Number of Children	Percentage of total child population	Number of schools (by language)	Percentage of children attending all schools
Jewish	3,055	44.82	3(24 classes)	70
Russian	1,335	19.59	5(39 ")	36
Ukrainian	1,882	27.62	7(50 ")	67
Polish	320	4.70	1(7 ")	81
Others	225	3.27		

LANGUAGE IN WHICH CHILD STUDIES [58]

	Yiddish	Russian	Ukrainian	Polish	Percentage of school children studying in nationality language	Percentage of all children of the nationality studying in nationality language
Jews	927	840	397		42	30
Russians		449	42		91	33.6
Ukrainians		234	1037		81	55.0
Poles		34	47	100	55	31.0

though the Jews were more highly urbanized and more widely dispersed—and therefore better able and more prone to send their children to Russian or Ukrainian schools—than these other national minorities (Table VI).

By 1927–28, 55.5 percent of Jewish pupils in Belorussia, 49.6 percent in the Ukraine but only 8 percent in the RSFSR were enrolled in Yiddish schools.[59] Nevertheless, the fact remains that more Soviet Jewish parents sent their children

[58] Based on statistics cited in A. Be., "Interesante tsifern," *Shtern,* July 23, 1925.

[59] *Natsional'naia politika VKP(b) v tsifrakh,* p. 278. An additional 3.4 percent in the Ukraine, 1.6 percent in Belorussia, and 3.1 percent in the RSFSR were attending schools where Yiddish was taught as a second language.

TABLE VI

NATIONAL MINORITY SCHOOLS IN THE UKRAINE, 1926 [60]

Nationality	Number of Schools	Number of Students	Approximate population of nationality in the Ukraine
Jews	432	70,887	1,700,000
Germans	621	38,736	375,000
Poles	337	20,550	400,000
Bulgarians	74	7,184	100,000
Tatars	31	1,500	10,000
Czechs	17	926	12,000
Armenians	5	—	9,000
Assyrians	3	250	—
Latvians	1	75	—

to Jewish schools than did American, British, and perhaps even Polish Jewish parents.[61]

It seems, too, that almost all social classes were represented in the Yiddish school. Of 15,293 children surveyed in Belorussia, 25.5 percent were children of workers, 8.0 percent of peasants, 27 percent of *kustars*, 28 percent "children of poverty," and 10.5 percent children of small shopkeepers

[60] Based on figures from *Shtern*, July 6, 1926, and January 11, 1927.

[61] In inter-war Poland, about 22 percent of Jewish children attended Jewish all-day schools and 50 percent received some sort of Jewish education. See Meyer, Weinryb, Duschinsky, and Sylvain, *The Jews in the Soviet Satellites* (Syracuse, 1953), p. 223. One author cites three different studies which showed that in the late 1930's either 77.6 percent, 66 percent, or 50 percent of Jewish children in Poland were attending non-Jewish schools. Many of these were also receiving some form of Jewish education. See Miriam Eisenstein, *Jewish Schools in Poland, 1919–39* (New York, 1950), p. 96. For comparative statistics on Jewish schools in Poland and the USSR, see Y. Mintsin, "Shul bildung ba idn in Rusland un Poiln," in Lestschinsky, ed., *Shriftn far ekonomik un statistik*, pp. 237–45. For a discussion of the attitudes of Polish Jews toward Jewish and Polish schools see Herbert Parzen, "When Secularism Came to Russian Jewry," *Commentary*, XIII, no. 4 (April 1952), 316ff. Lipset, "Jewish Schools in the Soviet Union," p. 246, points out that in the Baltic republics most Jewish children attended Hebrew or Yiddish schools.

who had managed to survive under the NEP.[62] The doctrines taught in Soviet schools fed the growth of generational conflict, which was also exacerbated by the very structure of the educational system. In 1928 fifty-one "toilers" wrote to the Jewish educational bureau in Berdichev complaining that, while Saturday was their day off, "and we dress a bit better and eat a bit better than usual," their children, students at the Yiddish school, were off on Sunday and so the family would never enjoy leisure time together.[63]

Among the specialized Yiddish schools were five two-year party schools, about thirty shorter Party courses, and, at the center, the "Mairevnik," or Jewish Party school in the Communist University of National Minorities of the West. The "Mairevnik," which was opened in June 1921, was designed to provide a six-month course in Yiddish Party work to one hundred "workers who know Yiddish and Russian well, who have proved themselves active workers in the labor movement, Party and trade union work, workers' clubs, etc." [64] Only a few students showed up, however, and they were not exactly the flower of Soviet Jewish youth. "They sent comrades who had tuberculosis, all sorts of nervous diseases, sick ones. . . . They sent whoever happened to be around, primarily people who had no place to go. . . . Some declared at the outset that they wished to enter the workers' faculty or Sverdlov University and they saw the Party school as a temporary stepping stone." [65] Further-

[62] *Barikht*, pp. 31–32.

[63] *Emes*, January 31, 1928. The *Evsektsiia* said that this complaint "obviously" had been written by Zionists with "religious motives."

[64] *Der komunist* (Ekaterinoslav), June 7, 1921. The Communist University of the Peoples of the East in Moscow and the Central Institute of Living Eastern Languages in Leningrad were designed to serve analogous purposes. See Park, pp. 134–35.

[65] *Emes*, April 27, 1922.

more, 58 percent of the students in 1923–24 were former members of other parties.[66] There were national frictions, too, but when Julian Marchlewski and Esther Frumkin were appointed to the administration, things took a turn for the better and a three-year curriculum was developed.[67] Admission requirements were tightened: the Central Bureau assigned a number of places to various Party and state organs (the Jewish Sections of the *Komsomol*, for instance, were allotted twenty places); students had to be Party or *Komsomol* members or candidates and had to be approved by their *gubkomy* and the Central Bureau. In an attempt to eliminate the tubercular types, the national sectors required a strict medical examination for admission.[68] The first graduating class included sixty-four diplomates of the

[66] *Mairevnik*, no. 2, December 1927. By 1927–28 the percentage of members of former parties had dropped to 18.

[67] Courses were given in national language and literature, history, "political physiognomy" of nationality, and history of the labor movement. Each national sector had an administrator, secretary, and pedagogical council which included a representative of the Central Bureau. "The sectors are naturally not national but language sectors. In the Polish sector there are Jews learning in the Polish language" (*Emes*, April 27, 1922). There was a lack of suitable books and lecturers.

Marchlewski's widow remembers Esther as a "talented woman . . . flaming orator, an activist with uncommon energy." Her reformist and experimental approach to education conflicted with Marchlewski's belief "that study requires concentration and quiet. By temperament and in their methods they stood at opposite poles. In the friction of these two currents Marchlewski 'lost out.' He was unsuited 'for war with women' as he jokingly said of himself, especially with such a good fighter as Esther. At meetings and commemorative events . . . where both were present Marchlewski usually remained in the shadows, Frumkina occupying the presidium herself. . . . She greeted guests, made a speech, organized entertainments of the most excellent sort, with youthful verve. . . . She was very sympathetic to her students and knew no rest in her work." Jadwiga Sierkerska, *Kartki z Przeszlosci* (Warsaw, 1960), p. 59.

[68] *Emes*, June 24, 1923.

Jewish sector[69] who were immediately rushed into Party work, not necessarily in the Soviet Union.[70]

Imprisoned by its own ideology and preconceptions, the Communist Party and its Jewish Sections had an extremely limited area in which to experiment with the creation of a Soviet Jewish culture and a Soviet Yiddish educational system. It is to the credit of the *Evsektsiia* that it conducted this experiment with great energy, even in the knowledge that the results could not have lasting significance. Jewish national feeling operated in a peculiarly ambivalent way with regard to the Yiddish school. Some parents saw Soviet-Jewish teachings as far more dangerous than general Soviet education where the propagandistic shafts were not so directly aimed at their beliefs. Thus, an adherence to traditional national forms and religious beliefs precluded support for the Yiddish school. On the other hand, a great number of people must have felt that the Yiddish school was, after all, a Jewish institution and as such deserved their support and loyalty. Why send a child to a school with an inferior physical plant and faculty and with a built-in brake on higher education, unless there was some powerful allegiance to things Jewish which impelled one to support the Yiddish school, no matter how truncated its national content? It is interesting that of the 1,358 children attending *kheders* in Vitebsk in 1922, about 400 were also enrolled in Soviet Yiddish schools.[71] Some Jewish parents apparently tried to combine traditional religious learning with Soviet Jewish education.

[69] Fifty workers, two peasants, and twelve officials.

[70] These sixty-four were the survivors of a class of 137: 37 were academic failures, 12 were discharged for reasons of health, and 13 others were discharged for "various reasons" (*Emes*, June 27, 1925). According to Alexander Pomerantz, Esther, who had become rector of the University following Marchlewski's death, cried bitterly when she learned that some of her students were being assigned to Poland rather than to the Soviet Union.

[71] Dardak, p. 166.

The Yiddishization of Political and Cultural Institutions

In 1923–24 the Party pursued a policy of "nativization" of cultural and political institutions in the national republics. "Ukrainization" and "Belorussianization," for example, meant that soviets, courts, and Party cells conducted their business in Ukrainian or Belorussian. The same policy was applied to the national minorities and a policy of "Yiddishization" was inaugurated. This began simply as an implementation of a general Party directive. The Yiddishization drive was the hallmark of the period of the *Evsektsiia*'s transition from the role of making the "revolution on the Jewish street" and serving as the Party's propaganda organ to its self-assumed role as the planner and executor of a thoroughgoing modernization of the Soviet Jewish population. Naturally, these role changes were not abrupt and the *Evsektsiia*'s perception of its roles changed only gradually. Nevertheless, it is possible to characterize the period between 1923 and 1926 as one of constructive activity and transition from disintegrative activity to a stage where the *Evsektsiia* would try to formulate and initiate programs designed to achieve political integration in an ethnically pluralist context.

The local soviet bore the most traffic of daily life, and the *Evsektsiia*'s Central Bureau and the VTsIK decided in 1925 to Yiddishize the soviets in areas of "compact Jewish settlement." In 1918 *Evkom* had been forced to retract its proposal for Jewish soviets; but by the mid-1920's the soviets were completely Bolshevized and could no longer serve as bases for political opposition. Similarly, the new soviets were not to be Jewish soviets, but Yiddish ones. In other words, they would be, not representative bodies reflecting diversity but Communist organs enforcing conformity. They were to be purely Communist in content, though Yiddish in form.

The establishment of a national soviet arouses, among

> certain strata of the workers, erroneous conceptions: "It is our soviet, a Jewish soviet"—and from this it is concluded that the Jewish soviet should be an internal [*haimish*], purely Jewish matter; the Jewish soviet should be concerned with the interests of the Community of Israel and it should protect the Jewish shopkeepers and NEP men from the financial inspector, if possible. . . . It is therefore necessary to make clear from the outset that a Jewish soviet differs only in the language in which it serves the population, but its role as an organ of the dictatorship of the proletariat is not thereby lessened by a hair. . . . It should, of course, energetically combat every manifestation of the anti-Semitism, every special attitude displayed toward the Jewish shopkeeper. . . . But it must be careful not to give cause for the slightest suspicion that a Jew receives any sort of "break" because he is a Jew.[72]

The Yiddish soviet faced the same practical difficulties the Yiddish school had faced. Which language to use in correspondence with higher soviet organs and with soviets of other nationalities and how to coordinate the work of "mixed soviets" which used several languages were some of the problems encountered. There were also instances where "the petite bourgeoisie and the clerical influence tore in through the too-widely opened doors of the soviets. . . . There was a case where a rabbi was invited to attend a meeting of the soviet in order to settle a question."[73]

The soviet was to concern itself with cultural and administrative matters, public health and sanitation, public improvements, and social organizations. Three sections were obligatory: communal, financial, and cultural-social. By 1927, 146 Jewish soviets had been set up, about 130 of them in the Ukraine where they embraced 11.6 percent of the

[72] Y. Kantor, *Ratnboiung,* pp. 61–62.

[73] *Ibid.,* p. 65.

Jewish population, and one Jewish *raion* had been created in the Ukraine which encompassed 16,000 Jewish farmers living on 27,000 *dessiatin* of land.[74] In 1929 a second Jewish *raion* was created in Zaporozh'e *krai* in the Ukraine. It was to embrace nine Yiddish village soviets. Seventy-three percent of the *raion*'s population was Jewish.[75] In 1927 the government gave the Jewish soviets a larger budgetary allocation and by 1930 there were 169 Jewish soviets.[76] Yiddish soviets could not possibly operate among all of the Jewish population because they could be established only in towns and villages with a majority of Jews. Since nearly seventy-five percent of Ukrainian Jews lived in large cities, they were almost automatically precluded from being served by a Yiddish-language soviet, unless a borough or district was so heavily Jewish that a Yiddish soviet could be justified. The *Evsektsiia*'s Main Bureau in the Ukraine considered the possibility of establishing Jewish sections within the city soviets but it was felt that this might lead to a loss of interest in Jewish affairs on the part of the soviet as a whole and, conversely, exclusive concentration on Jewish matters by the Jewish section. It was decided to establish a small number of such soviets on an experimental basis.[77] Yankel Kantor, the chief proponent of Yiddish soviets, nevertheless foresaw that "in six to eight years the entire state apparatus will be nationalized,[78] mostly in autonomous districts." [79]

[74] The *raion* was in Kherson *krai*. Eighty-six percent of its 18,000 inhabitants were Jews (*Shtern,* March 6, 1927). There were twenty-two nationality *raiony* all told (Gergel, p. 189; Yarmolinsky, pp. 105–06). Gergel cites a figure of 125 soviets in the Ukraine, and *Emes* (July 3, 1927) cites a figure of 130.

[75] *Shtern,* February 6, 1929.

[76] Heller, p. 118. According to Schwarz (p. 151) there were only 160 soviets in 1930.

[77] *Shtern,* April 9 and 18, 1926.

[78] That is, will use the nationality languages.

[79] *Emes,* February 1, 1925.

In a typical Jewish soviet in Baranovka, thirty-one plenary sessions were held between February 1927 and May 1928. Over half the questions taken up were "administrative," with social-cultural matters second. The various commissions—cultural, sanitary, financial, etc.—met rarely, and the presidium met only twenty-four times.[80] Even this sluggish activity soon petered out, and the number of Yiddish soviets declined very rapidly in the 1930's. This was a direct result of the urbanization of the Jews and the flight of the youth to the cities, which left the soviets in the hands of the older generation. "The flight of what might have been the *shtetl*'s Communist elite defeated the purpose of the establishment of Jewish local soviets."[81] Old-time Jewish leaders were excluded from the soviets on class grounds. "Hence, many Jewish soviets . . . had to get along with untrained, second-rate personnel enjoying little prestige among their own people."[82] Furthermore, a relatively high percentage of Jews was ineligible to vote in soviet elections. The number ineligible both in village and *shtetl* soviets was much higher than among other nationalities. Over forty percent of *shtetl* dwellers and fourteen percent of village dwellers were barred from soviet elections in 1927 in the Ukraine, on the grounds that they were—or had been—traders, clergy, or "NEP-men." In 1925–26 Jews constituted nearly forty-five percent of those ineligible to vote in the Ukraine, and in 1926–27 they made up nearly thirty percent of the ineligibles. Among the Germans, who had the next highest percentage of ineligibles, the overall figure was only about ten percent.[83] The government began to curtail Yiddish

[80] M. Kiper, *Dos yidishe shtetl in ukraine* (Kiev, 1929), pp. 10–11.

[81] Schwarz, p. 151.

[82] Baron, p. 225.

[83] Kantor, *Ratnboiung*, p. 56, and *Shtern*, March 24, 1927. For the social composition of the ineligibles, see Y. Levin, "Di valn in di ratn in 1925–6tn yor in ukraine," *Di roite velt*, no. 1 (28), January 1927. See also M. Kiper, *Sakhaklen fun di valn in di ratn un di arbet in*

language soviets in market towns "lest the Jewish soviets seem an instrument of 'Jewish domination' in the eyes of a restive and sometimes openly hostile peasantry." [84] Thus, the Yiddish soviet could play only a limited role in the political socialization and integration of the Jewish population.

"Face to the Shtetl"

Closely connected with the short-lived growth of the local Jewish soviet was the changed attitude toward the *shtetl,* the Jewish hamlet where, for example, more than one-third of the Jewish population in the Ukraine resided. This was the stronghold of the old way of life, where rabbis wielded more authority than Communists. In many ways it resembled the rural hinterlands of modernizing countries, as described by Daniel Lerner and others.

The Jews had been late-comers to the revolution and their "civil war" period began in earnest only in 1921. After the "Jewish civil war" had ended in 1923, a "Jewish NEP" was introduced. A policy of reconciliation with the "petit bourgeois elements" was announced by the Central Bureau. The *Evsektsiia* turned its "face to the *shtetl,*" hitherto regarded as a leper colony, outside the camp of Soviet society. Jewish Sections were formed at the *uezd* level in order to be closer to the *shtetl* where there were almost no Jewish Communists, and special *Evsektsiia* detachments were sent to work in picked *shtetls.* Many "plenipotentiaries" were appointed to do Jewish work in the *shtetls.* They were not fulltime *Evsektsiia* activists but part-time *agitprop* workers who were assigned to Jewish work.[85] In March 1924 there

shtetl (Kiev, 1929). For the legal definition of those deprived of voting rights, see Y. Kantor, *Vos darf visn yeder birger tsu di valn in di ratn* (Kharkov, 1926), pp. 17–18.

[84] Baron, p. 152.

[85] See *A yor arbet,* p. 13.

were 115 people doing Jewish work in the *shtetls* and by November 1925 there were 340, still a pitifully small number but an improvement.[86] Many of them did not know Yiddish, had little authority in the eyes of the *shtetl* population, and were overburdened with work. Almost all of them were members or candidates of the Party or the *Komsomol.*[87] In 1925 the secretary of the Central Bureau announced that "we can justifiably assert that politically—in principle—the problem of the *shtetl* exists no longer: the problem is solved." [88] He did not deny the lingering influence of religion or of Zionism. But he believed that once the basic strategic decision to invade the *shtetl* had been taken by the *Evsektsiia,* its enemies could be eliminated in a mop-up operation.

The *Evsektsiia* may have felt that the political problems of the *shtetl* were on the way to solution, but no one imagined that the ruined economy of the *shtetl* could be easily rehabilitated. The pogroms and the civil war, together with sporadic banditry that lingered into the early 1920's, had devastated many of the *shtetls,* particularly in the Ukraine. As a result, many of the most productive people emigrated to other countries or to the larger towns and cities. There was in the *shtetls* a disproportionate number of widows and others dependent on charity. The *kustars* who remained found it very difficult to obtain raw materials. The traditional role of the *shtetl* as the buyer from the farms and seller to the cities was undermined by the new economic system. Small wonder that a survey of six *shtetls* in 1923 concluded that the *shtetl* was in a worse economic situation than it had been before 1914 or even during the World War. The same was concluded by a survey of

[86] *Emes,* December 12, 1925.

[87] Y. Rabichev, "Unzere partai-bafulmekhtikte," *Shtern,* September 13, 1925. See also *Shtern,* October 13, 1925.

[88] Chemeriskii, p. 7.

shtetls in Belorussia. Many were unemployed; artisans and workers had declined in number while tradesmen had increased. There was almost no cultural life to speak of and no Soviet schools of any kind. Relations between Jews and non-Jewish peasants had deteriorated.[89] A statistical survey of forty-three *shtetls* in Belorussia with a total population of 91,130 showed that only one-quarter of the Jewish population had an identifiable profession or business.[90] The *shtetl* youth was in a particularly despondent state. "Only a small part escapes the *shtetl* to study; a second part flings itself into the arms of trade and speculation. The rest are in a depressed, hopeless situation."[91] When in 1925 the Central Bureau decided to establish soviets in the *shtetls* and to consider the possibility of according the working population there the same rights and obligations accruing to the working population of the villages,[92] it discovered that it had descended into a morass of economic devastation and disorganization, abysmal poverty and profound despair. A study of the *shtetl* Monastyrshchina, in the Ukraine, which was said to be typical of the majority of *shtetls*, revealed that while the number of craftsmen, workers, and officials—classified as productive elements—had increased by fifty-eight from 1914 to 1925, the number of those living on welfare or on money sent from America had increased by forty-eight. Forty percent of the 356 loans made by the savings and loan bank could not be paid back. Fully one-third of the *shtetl* population was classified as "half beggars"—some shopkeepers, religious teachers, widows (of whom there were 115), and those "without any profes-

[89] *Emes,* February 2, 1924.

[90] *Pravda,* August 1, 1924, quoted in Yaakov Lestschinsky, *Der emes vegn idn in rusland* (Berlin, 1925), p. 62. According to Chemeriskii, in 1926 "only" half the *shtetl* population was without an identifiable profession (p. 14).

[91] M. Kiper in *Emes,* February 2, 1924.

[92] *Der veker,* April 11, 1925.

sion."[93] The political situation in the *shtetls* was not much more encouraging. Of the 5,880 Jews in Nezhin only twenty-four were Party members; there were eighty-six *Komsomol* members whose political education, however, was quite elementary. A *Evsektsiia* was established in 1924, and during the next six months it organized ten meetings of the Jewish Communists and trade union members, assumed the management and direction of the *kustar* society and was active in Yiddish education.[94] Despite these kinds of effort the overall economic situation in the *shtetls* worsened in the late 1920's. The shopkeeper and middleman suffered most, but the *kustars* also found themselves in increasingly dire straits, and the youth was still unable to find work.[95] As late as 1929, 72.2 percent of the youth in three Belorussian *shtetls* were unemployed, and the number leaving the *shtetl* for the big cities was increasing every year.[96] In that year it was estimated that the *shtetl* population still accounted for one-third of the total Jewish population in the Ukraine, so that the problem remained of crucial importance.[97]

One way of improving the situation was to change the previously negative attitude toward the *kustars*[98]—who

[93] M., "Dos shtetl vi es iz," *Shtern,* March 14, 16, 17, 1926. For an analysis of another *shtetl,* see Y. Hershnboim, *Shchedrin: a shtetl in rekonstruktivn period* (Minsk, 1931).

[94] *Shtern,* August 5, 1925.

[95] See the reports by Yankel Levin and M. Kiper in *Shtern,* on June 17, 1927, and March 1, 1928, respectively.

[96] Shneider, "Vegn der ekonomisher einordnung fun der yidisher shtetldiker yugnt," *Oktiabr,* March 29, 1929. On the plight of *shtetl* youth in 1929, see also A. M. Kichaev and Y. R. Rubinov, *Sovremennoe sostoianie evreiskikh mestechek i perspektivy ikh ekonomicheskogo ozdorovleniia* (Kamenets-Podolsk, 1929), p. 15.

[97] Y. Kantor, *Di yidishe bafelkerung in Ukraine* (Kharkov, 1929), p. 79. For a survey of the economic, social, and political situation in thirteen Belorussian *shtetls* in 1931, see Y. Osherovich, ed., *Di shtetlekh fun USSR in rekonstruktivn period* (Minsk, 1932).

[98] The *kustar* was defined as "an artisan who works alone at his

formed nearly ten percent of the Jewish population of the Ukraine, Belorussia, Moscow, and Leningrad—and to aid them economically. The Bolsheviks had regarded the *kustars* with suspicion since they did not fit precisely into the Marxian model of class structure and class conflict. But since the *kustars* were the sole suppliers of processed foods and consumer goods in many areas of the country, and they could not be nationalized because they were so widely dispersed, the Bolsheviks made their peace with the *kustar* cooperatives as a legitimate part of the socialist system until such time as the *kustars* would become full-fledged proletarians.[99] In March 1924 Rakhmiel Veinshtain explained that the position of the Central Bureau of the *Evsektsiia* was not to alienate the "petit bourgeois" elements of the Jewish population but to "neutralize" them. "It is clear that in this way we can create a friendly attitude toward the Soviet regime among a significant part of the Jewish petite bourgeoisie. We can breed a friendly attitude on the part of the *kustars* toward the proletariat. Of course, the *kustar* question is not one of neutralization alone." Rather, it was the job of the *Evsektsiia* to "think about methods whereby the Party and Soviet government can approach the *kustars*." [100]

The Central Bureau's favorable attitude toward the

---

trade in his own home, using his own or his customer's raw material, and sells his product on the market either to retailer or to a customer. There are individual *kustars* who do not employ hired labor, and entrepreneur *kustars* who employ apprentices as well as other hired workers. The *kustar* differs from the entrepreneur capitalist in that the former not only organizes production but also participates in the work itself." B. Slutskii, Y. Liberberg, and H. Kozakevich, *Leksikon fun politishe un fremd-verter* (Kiev, 1929), p. 886.

[99] On Soviet *kustar* policy see Park, pp. 282–87, and especially A. F. Chumak, "K voprosu o vovlechenii kustarei i remeslennikov v sotsialisticheskoe stroitel'stvo," *Voprosy istorii KPSS*, XI, no. 7 (July 1967).

[100] *Der veker*, March 6, 1924.

kustars was undoubtedly an expression of the general Party line on socialist construction which between 1924 and 1928 reflected the ideas of Nikolai Bukharin. Bukharin's program of a gradual transition to socialism included the toleration and even encouragement of petty producers and "NEP-men," in addition to the peasantry. These groups would not be alienated from society and would provide the capital needed for investment in the expanding state sector of the economy. "Lest the proletariat alienate its political allies or precipitate class war, it must use only persuasion, incentives, economic competition, and other peaceful means to draw the peasantry and other small producers into co-operative enterprises, which in time may be gradually transformed into socialist, and ultimately communist, forms." [101]

The Central Bureau attempted to initiate this line in April 1924, at the All-Union Conference of the *Evsektsiia*. However, the leaders of the Main Bureau in the Ukraine engaged the Central Bureau in heated debate. Speaking for the Central Bureau, Merezhin drew analogies between the peasant and the *kustar,* both of whom were members of the "middle strata." The peasantry supported the proletariat, and the kustar could be won over to such support. The Party took advantage of the "positive features" of the peasantry and neutralized "negative features" by concessions. The same could be done with the *kustars.* Stalin had written that the greatest achievement of the Party was its correct attitude, a positive one, toward the middle strata. Furthermore, the Twelfth Party Congress had urged that there be greater reliance on local resources and initiative. Merezhin interpreted Stalin's statement and the Congress's resolutions to mean that the Jewish Communists must cultivate the middle strata. He seemed to equate the *kustars*

[101] Sidney Heitman, "Nikolai Ivanovich Bukharin," *Problems of Communism,* XVI, no. 6 (November-December 1967), 46.

with the middle and lower peasantry, and to support a favorable attitude toward them, similar to what Bukharin was urging vis-à-vis the peasantry. "Our Party, a ruling Party, has to conduct itself so that it has a majority behind it, even in the *shtetl* and the smaller cities. . . . Ukrainization and Belorussianization, absolutely necessary from an all-Union point of view, mean the strengthening of the influence of the village. Must we add to its strength by ignoring the middle strata of the *shtetl*? No, no! This could lead to a *de facto* bloc of peasants and *shtetl* bourgeoisie." [102] Merezhin admitted that the Central Bureau had not persuaded its subordinates of the correctness of this line. The Gomel *gubkom* activists had apparently argued that the best way to deal with the *kustars* would be to have them emigrate. The Belorussian Main Bureau had chosen to ignore the *kustars*, and so the latter set up their own organization and declared themselves "non-class" and equal to the proletariat.[103] The most serious opposition came from the Ukrainian Main Bureau. Altshuler, its spokesman and a congenital "leftist," argued that the *Evsektsiia* should concentrate its attention on genuine workers, rather than *kustars*. Savings and loan associations and separate production cooperatives should be organized for the *kustars*, but they were not to have general organizations which would include these two since this would be the *political* organization of an element which was not entirely reliable. The peasants might then emulate the *kustars* and try to achieve autonomous political power. The *kustars* should have "political rights but no political power. They should be organized only in cooperatives, savings and loan associations and no more." [104] Thus, Altshuler's distrust of the peasantry, and, by analogy, of the *kustars*, echoed Trotsky's and

[102] *Der veker*, April 13, 1924.
[103] *Emes*, April 9, 1924.
[104] *Der veker*, April 15, 1924.

Preobrazhenskii's view of the peasantry as a potentially hostile social class which ought to be exploited in the interests of the proletariat.

Yankel Levin, speaking for the Belorussian Main Bureau, agreed with Altshuler that the *kustars* were an unreliable element and that in Belorussia they ignored Party directives and went their own way. Levin charged that the Central Bureau had lost sight of the general Party line and was out of touch with the reality of the Jewish environment. He warned that the *Evsektsiia* "should not become a section of *kustars*" and he agreed with Altshuler that the proletariat should be the focus of *Evsektsiia* programs and activities. The Central Bureau defended its position on the grounds that in the *shtetl* the *kustars* were a larger and more important element than the workers and that "The Party is attracting the sympathies of the majority of poor toilers. We cannot allow a hostile void to exist only on the sector of the front where we '*Evseks*' hold the line. No—we have the opportunity to master the *shtetl*, the poor . . . should we not seize it?" [105] In the end the conference approved the line of the Central Bureau—and hence of the Party's Central Committee—and agreed to involve the *Evsektsiia* in *kustar* affairs, noting in passing that the Central Bureau was the leading organ of the *Evsektsiia* and that Main Bureau policies must be coordinated with it.[106]

Despite the formal adoption of the Central Bureau's policy, the Main Bureaus and local Sections continued to

[105] *Ibid.* The speaker was Moishe Litvakov. His sister Zlate, a delegate from the Ukraine, promptly attacked her brother, charging that "you have become *kustar*ified at the center."

[106] *Der veker*, May 20, 1924. If the analogy between attitudes toward the peasantry and attitudes toward the *kustars* is correct, then the Central Bureau seems to have been following a Bukharinist line, at that time the more or less general line of the Party, while the Belorussian and Ukrainian Main Bureaus adopted a "leftist" (Trotsky-Preobrazhenskii) line.

sabotage the *kustar* policy. The Central Bureau urged the creation of *kustar* organizations on the *krai* and *guberniia* levels. Cooperatives of all sorts were to be established, beginning with credit cooperatives and progressing to production cooperatives.[107] But Chemeriskii admitted that most activists still had a negative attitude toward the *kustars* and were actively sabotaging *Evsektsiia* policy.[108] Krinitskii, secretary of the Belorussian Party, noted in 1925 that "there is an opinion which holds that the work of the *Evsektsiia* is 'petit bourgeois' work which is not proletarian in spirit or in character. This is incorrect in principle."[109] Many *Evsektsiia* activists felt that they were becoming second-class Communists working with second-class citizens, members of a group of doubtful pedigree. Mikhail Levitan argued that just because there were more Jewish *kustars* than Jewish workers the *Evsektsiia* should not devote itself entirely to the former because "social groups are not only to be *counted,* but also *weighed.*"[110] Despite these widespread sentiments many *kustar* cooperatives of all kinds were organized and the *Evsektsiia* did involve itself very heavily in this kind of activity.[111] The Central Bureau adopted the slogan, "Don't act the boss, don't act the commissar" in regard to the *kustars.* When the Central Bureau was satisfied that individual *kustars* had come under Party influence, it turned to those who employed less than three people, the "middle *kustars.*" But, again, the local Sections simply ignored the new policy. Chemeriskii pointed to the fact that peasants who employed others but whose families

[107] *Der veker,* June 7, 1925.

[108] *Ibid.,* October 21, 1925.

[109] *Ibid.,* October 28, 1925.

[110] M[ikhal] L[evitan], "Merer oifmerkzamkeit der arbetershaft," *Shtern,* July 18, 1925.

[111] See *Prakticheskoe rasreshenie natsional'nogo voprosa v Belorusskoi sotsialisticheskoi sovetskoi respublike: Chast' II-ia: rabota sredi natsional'nykh men'shinstv* (Minsk, 1928), pp. 40–41.

worked were allowed to vote, and Stalin had emphasized the need to broaden the category of voting citizens. The Belorussian Main Bureau resisted the new policy, justifying itself by the claim that the new policy would open the floodgates to a powerful stream of petit bourgeois influence. The Central Bureau persisted and tried to organize *guberniia* and *uezd* organizations for the middle *kustar*. Ninety-seven such organizations, eighty-six percent of whose membership was Jewish, existed in 1926. They sponsored credit cooperatives, artels, and savings-and-loan associations.[112] The *Evsektsiia* policy worked fairly well and the situation of the *kustars* improved to the point where some considered them "the aristocracy of the townlet." [113] Foreign observers made a study in 1926 which "established the fact that the artisans, constituting about thirty percent of the population, were economically the strongest elements. . . . The improvement of the condition of the small producers was partly due to the fact that the Communist Party took them under its wing. . . . At present they are in a class with the peasants, and the theory prevails that, like the rural masses, the artisans will reach socialism by way of cooperation." [114]

Yiddishization of the Courts

The policy of Yiddishization was extended to the judicial system. Under the tsars the Jews had avoided the regular courts and had settled their cases in rabbinic tribunals. The rabbi continued to render judicial decisions in civil cases even under the new regime, and the *Evsektsiia* tried to undermine his authority by establishing Jewish courts of its own. By 1926 there were twenty-five Yiddish courts in the Ukrainian Republic and twenty-one more were to be added in 1927–28, along with twenty-two Ukrainian-

[112] Chemeriskii, p. 108.
[113] Yarmolinsky, p. 68.
[114] *Ibid.*, p. 68–70.

Yiddish courts.[115] Actually, a total of only forty-six courts had been established in the Ukraine by 1931, with Belorussia having ten and the RSFSR eleven.[116] The obstacles to the successful functioning of the courts were similar to those faced by the schools and soviets. Legal terminology had a distinctly rabbinical flavor and so a new language had to be invented; Yiddish-speaking lawyers were scarce; in a case involving Jewish and non-Jewish litigants obvious difficulties presented themselves; the procurators and militia rarely referred cases to the Yiddish courts and almost all cases were brought directly by citizens; Yiddish courts were territorially based and could not serve isolated and scattered Jewish communities; there were no appeals courts operating in Yiddish and litigants were reluctant to begin a case in Yiddish and then have to transfer it to a Russian-language court system; older litigants resorted to Yiddish courts, while younger, better educated ones preferred the Russian courts. The docket of the Yiddish court was not so full as that of the regular courts but was heavier than that of other national minority courts.[117] After 1931

[115] Kantor, *Ratnboiung*, p. 91. It may be noticed that Yiddish courts and soviets were concentrated in the Ukraine. This is due to the fact that the Jewish population in the Russian Republic was far more urbanized and scattered and so was ineligible for Yiddish courts, soviets, etc. In the other great Jewish center, Belorussia, the republic government made Yiddish an official language of the republic, and it was used on all governmental levels. Nevertheless, the structure of the Belorussian Republic was such that Jewish soviets were not easily accommodated. Yiddish courts in Belorussia operated on an extra-territorial basis, in contrast to the Ukraine, and this had the effect of reducing their numbers. See Baron, p. 224, and Binyamin Pinkus, "Batai HaMishpat beYidish Bivrit HaMoetzot," *Heavar*, XVIII (1971).

[116] Baron, p. 225.

[117] According to Kantor (p. 92), there was an average of 511 cases in the nationality courts in 1926–27 while the Yiddish courts handled 611 cases that same year. Yiddish courts also dealt with more civil than criminal cases. For a detailed breakdown on the number and kinds of cases handled in the Zhitomir, Kremenchug, and Berdichev Yiddish courts, see *Shtern*, July 11, July 30, and August 21, 1925, respectively; see also Pinkus, p. 145.

the Yiddish courts steadily declined in number and none were left by the eve of World War II.

Yiddishization in the Party

Until 1924 not a single Party cell had conducted its business in Yiddish; by November 1925 there were fifty-seven.[118] By 1926, Belorussia alone boasted twenty-five such cells comprising 654 members, with some Yiddish sub-cells formed as the situation required. A year later, fifty-five Yiddish cells were said to exist in the Ukraine. It was claimed that the Yiddishization of the cells improved the morale of the membership.[119] These cells existed almost exclusively in the larger cities and the Jewish agricultural colonies; the *shtetl,* the bastion of Yiddish, simply had no Party cells to speak of.[120] The Yiddish cells included only about 2,000 of the 45,000 Jewish Party members, of whom 18,000 considered Yiddish their mother tongue.[121] In other words, while 36.5 percent of all Jewish Communists considered Yiddish their mother tongue, only 4.4 percent conducted their work in Yiddish. This was due not only to the fact that most Jewish Communists lived outside the centers of Jewish settlement but also to a feeling on the part of Jewish Communists that Russian enjoyed a higher status than Yiddish and its use was a mark of education

[118] Fifteen of these worked only partially in Yiddish. *Emes,* December 12, 1925.

[119] *Alfarbandishe baratung,* p. 92; Kiper, p. 101. There were also 80 *Komsomol* cells, with 2,230 members, operating in Yiddish.

[120] Thus, of the 55 Yiddish cells in the Ukraine, 33 were in cities, 16 in the colonies, and only 6 in the small towns or *shtetls.* See also M. Kiper, "Der tsushtand fun der idarbet in ukraine," *Emes,* March 21, 1926.

[121] The 18,000 Yiddish speakers constituted 36.5 percent of all Jewish Communists in 1927; 73.7 percent of the Belorussian Jewish Communist were Yiddish speakers and 39.4 percent of the Ukrainian Jewish Communists spoke Yiddish. A. Brakhman and Y. Zhiv, eds., *Yidn in FSSR* (Moscow-Kharkov-Minsk, 1930), p. 107.

and sophistication. In Gomel, for example, only 197 out of 1,018 Party members were included in the four cells operating in Yiddish. "Some believe that in the street and workshop you are *allowed* to speak Yiddish, but party work *must* be conducted in Russian."[122] Even some *Evsektsiia* activists spoke Russian among themselves and sent their children to Russian language schools.[123] Of course, the selection of languages appropriate to different settings is a common phenomenon in polyethnic societies, as among Laplanders who invariably speak Norwegian in public interaction.[124] The choice of a non-native language for public usage betrays the user's sense of the relative worth and prestige of his own and other cultures.

Yiddishization and the Trade Unions

The weakest link in the chain of Yiddishized institutions was the trade union. Chemeriskii wrote, "We must admit that this is our weakest point, that we are tenuously tied to the Jewish workers; the greatest obstacle we faced in this area was the conservatism and immobility of the trade unions with regard to Jewish work."[125] Merezhin complained that the non-*Evsektsiia* Jewish *aktiv* of the Party and the trade unions had always opposed Jewish work. Fully eighty-four percent of the union *aktiv* did not consider Yiddish its language of daily use.[126] The *Evsektsiia*

[122] *Oktiabr*, January 28, 1928.

[123] "In very many Jewish institutions Russian is spoken. . . . The Jewish leaders almost always speak Russian amongst themselves." Y.Y. Zinger, *Neirusland* (Vilna, 1928), p. 226. See also A. Osherovich, "A noitike deklerung," *Oktiabr*, August 18, 1929.

[124] See Harald Eidheim, "When Ethnic Identity is a Social Stigma," in Fredrik Barth, *Ethnic Groups and Boundaries* (London, 1969).

[125] Chemeriskii, p. 10. See also Esther's complaint at the 1926 conference in *Alfarbandishe baratung*, p. 203.

[126] *Emes*, April 30, 1926. On the basis of a survey conducted among Jewish workers in the Ukraine in 1926, Lestschinsky calculated that 58 percent of the Jewish workers in the Ukraine considered Yiddish their language of daily use. *Dos sovetishe identum*, pp. 264–66.

did not mean for whole factories to be run in Yiddish but it urged the use of that language in the *agitprop* work in the factories. Its pleas went unheeded. In a Kiev candy factory, for instance, where sixty-five percent of the workers were Jewish, no Yiddish activity was conducted and there was not a single Yiddish book in the factory library; in a shoe factory with 500 Jewish workers there were two subscribers to the Kharkov daily, *Shtern*.[127] Kiper showed that of 1,696 trade union cells with Jewish majorities, adding up to 35,523 workers, only 57 cells conducted their business in Yiddish. This did not prove that *Evsektsiia* work had become "*kustarified*," as "some comrades" had argued. The fact was that Yiddish work "cannot be conducted from the outside by the *Evsektsiia*" but must be done by the trade unions themselves. Unfortunately, the unions "display great conservatism in implementing nationality policy in general and with regard to the Yiddish language in particular." [128] *Evsektsiia* leaders constantly criticized the hostility of the trade unions to "Jewish work," but this seemed to have no effect on union officials. The indifference and hostility of the unions may have been due to several considerations: they may have reasoned that the use of several languages in the factory, even if only for *agitprop* work, would be costly, cumbersome, and inefficient. Secondly, the unions may have felt very little real pressure for Yiddishization because, while some *Evsektsiia* leaders were highly placed in the All-Union, Belorussian, and Ukrainian Parties, they had no representatives in the trade union leadership and so no pressure was exerted from within the union hierarchy.

Furthermore, while the Party included many nationalities and was forced to conduct its activities in many languages,

[127] Smolensk Oblast Archives, WKP 449.

[128] M. Kiper, "Di arbet tsvishn idishn proletariat," *Emes*, October 31, 1926.

workers at the bench were a much more ethnically homogeneous group: in the Ukraine they were almost exclusively Russians, Ukrainians, and Jews, while the Poles, Germans, Greeks, Bulgarians, Tatars, and others were almost exclusively peasant elements. The Jewish workers themselves, displaying the "psychic mobility" that Daniel Lerner attributes to "transitional" types in developing societies, gave every indication of preferring Russian to Yiddish. "The Jewish worker does not want to read a [Yiddish] newspaper. He will break his teeth, he will not understand a word, but give him Russian. A Jewish comrade begins to speak in Yiddish at a workers' meeting—they don't want to listen. And when she finishes, they translate her [speech], even though you can't find a non-Jew here for love or money."[129] In a factory where 98 percent of the workers were Jews, "it often happens that comrades not only cripple the Russian language, breaking their tongues in order to speak 'po-russkomu,' but when someone makes a speech in his mother tongue there is a hullabaloo and derisive laughter."[130]

Jewish workers were hostile to Yiddish not only because they thought of it as only a "jargon," but also because they saw knowledge and use of Russian as a prerequisite to advancement. "A meeting of the transport workers. One comrade, a porter, takes the floor and comes out categorically against any work in Yiddish. When challenged, he answered: The matter is quite simple. . . . For many years I have carried hundreds of poods on my back day in and day out. Now I want to learn some Russian and become a 'kontorshchik' [office worker]."[131]

The *Evsektsiia* did not overcome the hostility of the workers nor of the trade unions to Yiddish. Painfully aware

[129] *Der veker,* February 16, 1923.

[130] *Der odeser arbeter,* January 6, 1930.

[131] *Emes,* April 6, 1924.

of the increasingly important role of the factory worker in Soviet planning and reality, the *Evsektsiia* desperately cast about for a way of exercising its influence over the proletariat. The Ukrainian Main Bureau abandoned the old argument about adherence to Leninist nationality policies and the need to serve the cultural needs of the workers as the rationale for work in Yiddish. Instead it justified trade union work in political and practical terms: since many Jewish workers were fresh from the *shtetl* they were still rooted in the miasma of chauvinism, religion, and individualism. They had no regard for collective property or labor discipline. The trade unions had failed to influence them, and if they were not reached by the *Evsektsiia* they could exercise a harmful influence on veteran workers.[132] The Main Bureau went so far as to resolve that since many Russian-speaking workers retained the "petit bourgeois narrowly national" outlooks and characteristics of their old environment, it was necessary for the *Evsektsiia,* which was well acquainted with that environment, to "reeducate" them in Russian.[133]

But the *Evsektsiia* never really succeeded in establishing itself in the factories and trade unions. Even after repeated campaigns and exhortations by the *Evsektsiia* and the Republic governments the situation did not change.[134] This failure was a critical one, for in the 1930's the factories emerged as the smithies wherein the Soviet society would be forged. They became the key sector not only of economic life but of the necessarily integrated Soviet milieu. The failure to implant Yiddish firmly in the trade unions, and hence in the factories, precluded the possibility of

[132] Lead editorial in *Shtern,* March 22, 1929.

[133] *Shtern,* January 19, 1929. See also N. Maidat, "Redt farshtendlekher far di masn," *Shtern,* January 25, 1929.

[134] See *Emes,* January 9, 1924, and L. Goldbert, "An alte frage," *Emes,* June 28, 1929.

identifying Yiddish with the new society and legitimizing it even in a predominantly industrial setting. The *Evsektsiia* failed to associate Yiddish with progress, prestige, and modernization. In the mind of the Jewish citizen it was linked to the abandoned *shtetl* and a backward, anti-modern culture. Since the Yiddish language had become almost the only legitimate expression of Jewish identity, this failure had profound consequences for the future of Jewish nationality in the Soviet Union. It meant that in the 1930's, when the city and the factory throbbed with the excitement of construction and development, Jewish identity was seen as superfluous and stultifying, as sometimes to be cast off as quickly as possible.

1. First Conference of the Jewish Sections, Moscow, October 1918. Samuil Agurskii is in the second row, the seventh person in from the right.

2. Former synagogue converted into Communist workers' club. The hammer and sickle has replaced the Ten Commandments on the wall.

3. Yiddish school newspaper staff meeting. Both Russian and Yiddish newspapers appear on the wall.

4. Mikhail Kalinin speaking at the first All-Union Congress of GEZERD, Moscow, November 1926. Rakhmiel Veinshtain is third from left in the first row on the dais, and Abraham Merezhin is sixth from left.

5. Speech at the GEZERD Congress, November 1926. Esther Frumkin and Semën Dimanshtain are on the speaker's left, and Rakhmiel Veinshtain is immediately to his right. The young man in the second row directly behind Dimanshtain is Sh. D. Niepomniashchi.

6. Temporary barracks for Jewish agricultural settlers, Kherson province, 1925.

7. Voting on a Jewish collective farm.

VII

The *Evsektsiia* and the Modernization of Soviet Jewry

These times of modernization are also times of experimentation. Exciting and even epic, they have a certain refreshing cheerfulness despite tragic undertones. When cherished institutions are swept away and beliefs come to be regarded as outmoded, a sense of foreboding for some has its counterpart in a sense of adventure for others. . . .

David Apter, *The Politics of Modernization*

THE POLICIES and programs adopted during the transition from disintegrative to integrative activity in 1924–26 did not cure the economic-political ills of Soviet Jewry. The *shtetl* remained a festering sore in Soviet society; the Party still could not make a lasting peace with the *kustar;* the Jewish social-economic structure continued to produce "unhealthy" manifestations. Just as Stalin and others in the Party began to turn away from Bukharin's gradualism, so too did the *Evsektsiia* begin to search for more potent medicines than the palliatives of Yiddishization, *kustar* cooperatives, and work in the *shtetl,* which had failed to stem the growth of unemployment, to supply the *kustars* with raw materials, or to bring new industries to the *shtetls.*

The Jewish population was relatively more urbanized and more literate than the general population; nevertheless, it suffered from a higher rate of unemployment and from underrepresentation in the favored classes—the peasantry and the proletariat. In 1926 in the former Pale, over sixty percent of the Jews lived in cities, nearly thirty percent in *shtetls,* and nearly ten percent in villages.[1] Jews constituted forty percent of the urban population in Belorussia and over twenty percent of the urban population in the Ukraine.[2] While in the Ukraine only 44.9 percent of the total population was literate, 70 percent of Ukrainian Jews was literate; in Belorussia 35.5 percent of the total population was literate, while the percentage among Jews was 68.8. Even in Moscow and Leningrad there was a substantially higher

[1] L. Zinger, *Evreiskoe naselenie v sovetskom soiuze* (Moscow-Leningrad, 1932), p. 14.

[2] *Ibid.,* p. 11. For a comparison with the urbanization of Jews in Poland, see Yaakov Lestschinsky, *Yidn in der shtotisher bafelkerung fun umophengikn Poiln* (New York, 1943).

TABLE VII

PERCENTAGE OF GAINFULLY EMPLOYED, 1926 [3]

	Jews	Total Population
Ukraine	38.9	61.8
Belorussia	37.1	63.0
Moscow	53.7	53.6
Leningrad	51.4	53.9
Smolensk *guberniia*	37.8	58.3
Briansk *guberniia*	38.5	60.5

proportion of literates among Jews than among the total population.[4] At the same time, however, the percentage of those gainfully employed—including those temporarily employed—was, with the exception of Moscow, everywhere lower among Jews than among the total population (Table VII). Whereas only a little over one percent of the total population was unemployed and 2.9 percent had no determinate vocation, 9.3 percent of Jews was unemployed and 7.8 percent had no definite vocation.[5]

The overall class structure of the gainfully employed Jewish population in Belorussia, the Ukraine, Moscow, and Leningrad can be seen in Table VIII.

The distinctive nature of the Jewish social structure may be appreciated by comparing it to the social structure of other nationalities (Table IX).

Finally, the geographical distribution of the various social classes is illustrated in Table X.

By the mid-1930's nearly half the Jewish workers had been drawn into larger industries, but a quarter of the Jewish proletariat remained in artisanal industries, concentrated in such fields as printing, needle trades, tobacco manufactur-

[3] Zinger, p. 32.

[4] Zinger, p. 30.

[5] Zinger, pp. 33–35.

TABLE VIII

CLASS STRUCTURE OF THE SOVIET JEWISH POPULATION, 1926 [6]

Social group	Percentage of gainfully employed Jews	Those supported by the income of the respective groups
Workers	14.8	14.6
Salaried employees	23.4	23.0
Kustars	19.0	23.7
Peasants	9.1	5.9
Traders	11.8	14.3
Free professions	1.6	1.5
Undetermined vocation	7.8	5.9
Unemployed	9.3	6.1
Others	3.2	5.0
Total	100.0	100.0

ing, woodworking, and tanning.[7] All told, Jews constituted over seven percent of all Soviet workers. In the Ukraine, where Jews constituted 5.4 percent of the population, Jewish workers formed 8.7 percent of the proletariat; in Belorussia, where Jews made up 8.2 percent of the population, Jews

TABLE IX

SOCIAL-ECONOMIC STRUCTURE OF THREE NATIONALITIES IN THE UKRAINE, 1926 [8]

Social-Economic Group	Ukrainians	Russians	Jews
Peasants	90.7%	51.8%	8.9%
Workers (including kustars)	3.8	20.0	40.0
Traders	0.8	3.3	14.9
Salaried employees	2.1	12.7	15.5
Total	100.0	100.0	100.0

[6] Zinger, p. 35.
[7] *Ibid.*, pp. 39, 40, and 43.
[8] Adapted from Borys, *The Russian Communist Party and the Sovietization of the Ukraine,* p. 63.

TABLE X

GEOGRAPHICAL DISTRIBUTION OF JEWS GAINFULLY EMPLOYED, 1926 [9]

	Percentage of total Soviet-Jewish population	Percentage Distribution Among Gainfully Employed Jews					
		Workers	Employees	Kustars	Peasants	Traders	Percentage unemployed
Ukraine	69.3	15.2	20.7	19.8	9.8	13.2	8.9
Belorussia	17.9	16.7	16.9	22.3	13.2	10.2	6.9
Moscow	5.8	8.3	50.1	9.1	0.04	4.9	14.5
Leningrad	3.7	13.3	40.1	9.2	0.11	4.5	15.5
Smolensk *guberniia*	1.6	8.9	17.5	26.2	11.5	17.4	7.2
Briansk *guberniia*	1.7	11.7	20.0	22.0	9.4	19.0	5.9
Total	100	14.8	23.4	19.1	9.2	11.8	9.3

constituted 20.7 percent of the proletariat. Nearly seventy percent of the Jewish workers were classified as skilled [*kvalifitsirovannye*], while seventeen percent were semi-skilled and about fifteen percent were unskilled.[10] This was a new and very young labor force—nearly forty-five percent of the Jewish workers were under thirty-four years of age.[11] This picture of a young, skilled labor force might have given the *Evsektsiia* cause for satisfaction, were it not for the fact that the Jews were an overwhelmingly urban population which could be expected to have a large proletariat. The economist Iurii Larin claimed that when the general non-agricultural population gainfully employed in the USSR was compared with the Jewish non-agricultural population, workers, employees and their dependents were found to constitute about thirty percent of the former, while

[9] Based on Zinger, pp. 37, 52, 57, 64, 68, and 70.

[10] *Ibid.*, pp. 42 and 45.

[11] *Ibid.*, p. 47.

constituting only about twelve percent of the Jewish population.[12]

While some progress in revamping the economic life of the Jewish population, and hence its social structure, had been made, it was painfully obvious that, given the values attached by the Soviet economic and political system to various occupations and social classes, much remained to be done in order to integrate the Jewish population into Soviet society. As the Party itself began to consider drastic measures designed to speed up the growth of the socialist-industrial sector of the economy, the *Evsektsiia*, too, began to explore various policies which could lead to the rapid modernization and concomitant political integration of the Jewish population. Many of the *Evsektsiia* activists were also anxious to combine this modernization and integration with the preservation of Jewish ethnic identity and the development of a new Jewish culture suited to a secular, modernized Soviet society. The *Evsektsiia*'s explorations led it to discuss various programs of industrialization and agricultural settlement which it considered not only in terms of their economic worth but also in terms of their effect on Jewish identity and culture.

Modernization through Agricultural Colonization

As was pointed out in the previous chapter, it was becoming apparent that industrialization would adversely affect the maintenance of ethnic identity and culture. But the *Evsektsiia* had an alternative means of simultaneously

[12] Iurii Larin, *Evrei i antisemitizm v SSSR* (Moscow-Leningrad, 1929), p. 85. For comparative data on the occupational and social structure of Jews in the various countries of Eastern and Central Europe, see Yaakov Lestschinsky, "Profesionaler bashtand fun di idn in mizrakh un tsentral eirope," in Lestschinsky, ed., *Shriftn far ekonomik un statistik*.

"productivizing the Jewish masses" and keeping them Jewish. One program would serve both the purpose of economic rehabilitation and of national preservation. This was the plan for mass agricultural settlement. In July 1924 the Belorussian and Ukrainian Central Committees created special commissions for Jewish agricultural resettlement and in August the All-Union Central Committee created the Commission for the Rural Placement of the Jewish Toilers, KOMZET (KOMERD). In 1926 the Presidium of the VTsIK approved a KOMZET plan to settle 100,000 Jewish families on the land in the course of a few years. Together with the Jews already on the land, they would constitute one-quarter of the Soviet Jewish population. OZET (GEZERD) was formed as a non-Party organization to recruit potential colonists and rally support—mainly financial—abroad. The American Joint Distribution Committee supported agricultural colonies in the Ukraine, ORT supported colonies in Odessa *krai* and Belorussia, while ICOR and PROKOR were leftist American organizations contributing money and tractors to OZET. Settlers received free land, machines and livestock could be purchased on credit, and the land was tax exempt for three years. Artels and collectives were the preferred, but not obligatory, forms of organization.[13] By 1928 the Jewish peasant population reached almost 220,000,[14] and a total of 29.5 million rubles had been spent on Jewish colonization since 1924.[15] Jewish colonization was progressively moving into higher stages—from the tsarist colonies revived under War Communism to the suburban agriculture which flourished in the Ukraine

[13] Y. Kantor, *Tsu hilf dem ibervanderer* (Kiev, 1927), pp. 8–43.

[14] Schwarz, p. 164.

[15] The state had supplied 6.5 million rubles, "social organizations" (including foreign ones) had supplied 20.5 million, and 2.5 million had been received as credit from agricultural banks. Brakhman and Zhiv, *Yidn in FSSR*, p. 67.

though unsupported by the state, and now to a massive effort which was widely publicized at home and abroad.

The colonization project had several aims: to rehabilitate the déclassé elements which were such a substantial portion of the Jewish population; to reduce Zionism's appeal by providing an alternative to the Palestinian communal settlements; to populate and secure certain border regions in the Crimea, the Far East, and Belorussia; and, at least in the minds of some, to brake the rush to assimilation. The project was fraught with difficulties, but they were not so basic as those inherent in the Yiddishization schemes. Colonization failed to attract those elements for whom it was designed. Of a sample of 260 families, 78.5 percent had been engaged in factory work, artisanry, or agriculture and only 11.9 percent were former petty traders or unemployed.[16] Of 15,000 families in the Ukaine who registered for settlement in 1925, seventy-one percent could be classified as "productive" (workers, officials, *kustars,* agricultural workers); of 7,000 families registered in Belorussia over sixty percent could be so classified. But only half of all the families were able to bring any capital at all to the colonies.[17] Within the colonies there was almost no political or cultural life and schools were rare. One Jewish peasant complained, "I am already an old man but I still want to know how to write Yiddish and Russian. This is all we want. Give us schools." [18]

There were some manifestations of religion and Zionism in the colonies.[19] *Evsektsiia* leaders complained that the Jewish peasants were too proud of their *national* identity and of the fact that there were high Party officials who were

[16] *Emes,* May 5, 1924.

[17] *Shtern,* August 29, 1925.

[18] *I-ter alveisruslendisher tsuzamenfor fun idishe poierim* (Minsk, December 4, 1924), p. 8.

[19] Of 99 delegates at the First All-Belorussian Congress of Jewish Peasants, 62 declared Saturday as their day of rest. *Ibid.,* p. 43.

Jewish. "Don't think that the Yankel Levins, the Osheroviches, the Orshanskiis, the Chemeriskiis and the Nodels are interested in you because you are Jews."[20] Party influence among the peasants was very weak, especially since Yiddish instructors were lacking and the struggle for existence left little time for political work.[21] In some areas, particularly in the Ukraine, local peasants were openly hostile to the recently arrived Jewish settlers. They felt that the settlers were receiving financial aid and tools while no one looked out for the interests of the long-time dwellers on the land.[22] At the Tenth All-Ukrainian Congress of Soviets, Vlas Chubar, Chairman of the Ukrainian Council of People's Commissars, found it necessary to warn the peasants not to be taken in by the rumors concerning Jewish settlement and to rest assured that the Jews were not being granted special privileges.[23] A Ukrainian journalist reported that " 'the yids will take over all power on the steppes,' hooligans whispered. And in some places priests even prayed to God to 'save us from the Jewish nemesis'."[24] There were technical problems, too. It was difficult to turn former traders into efficient farmers overnight. Farm implements were woefully scarce and livestock were rare.[25] Many of the settlers gave up and returned home. In Krivorog in 1928 thirty-three percent

[20] *Ibid.*, pp. 32–33.

[21] Of the 99 delegates at the Belorussian Congress, only six belonged to the Party and ten to the *Komsomol.*

[22] Report by Agronomist Zaichik from Kherson, June 26, 1926. Archive of Dr. Joseph Rosen, Box 70, Agro 13, p. 6, YIVO Archives. See also the report by Louis Fischer, manuscript in the Rosen Archive.

[23] *Shtern,* April 9, 1927.

[24] Semën Sumny, "Tsvishn a natsmindisher natsmerheit," *Shtern,* May 26, 1927.

[25] In seven collectives located in one area of the Ukraine, 369 Jewish colonists had only 59 horses, 49 cows, 3 iron hoes, 2 sowing machines, 5 harvesters, and 16 ploughs. A. Revutskii, "Idishe kolonizatsie in rusland in ihr emes'n geshtalt," *Di tsukunft,* XXXIII, no. 9 (September 1925).

went home; from Evpatoria *raion* twenty-five percent; from Birobidzhan thirty-five percent.[26] The situation improved when Agro-Joint set up cooperatives, loan associations, and trade and agricultural schools; [27] it supplied tractors, farm implements, seeds, and livestock.[28]

By 1925–26 almost all the Jewish colonies were collectivized but by the following year they were all de-collectivized.[29] Gradually, some of the settlements were re-collectivized and the collectivized percentage of Jewish land was usually higher than the collectivized percentage of Ukrainian or Belorussian land.[30] During 1928 the question of collectivization was constantly debated, with Kantor, who took great interest in the colonies, urging that collectivization be done gradually and cautiously. But the following year August 28 was proclaimed "collectivization day" and all Jewish colonies were called up to collectivize completely.[31] At about the same time a movement was begun to "internationalize" the Jewish colonies. Belorussians and Ukrainians were to be settled in Jewish colonies, and Jews were to be settled in non-Jewish collectives. Jewish and non-Jewish collectives were to be merged. This policy

[26] *Shtern,* December 18, 1928.

[27] Rosen Archive, Box 70, Agro 38.

[28] "Statement of Reconstructive Activities in Russia," April 12, 1934, typescript in Rosen Archive.

[29] Y. Kantor, "Kolektivizirung fun der yidisher landvirtshaftlekher bafelkerung in ukraine," *Di roite velt,* no. 4, April 1930. For an explanation of the disintegration of the collectives see A. Chemeriskii, A. Merezhin, and Y. Kantor, *Dos ferte yor yidishe erdeinordenung* (Kharkov, 1929), p. 37.

[30] Chemeriskii, Merezhin, and Kantor, p. 76. See also *Shtern,* June 23, 1929. Collectivization of Jewish land compared favorably with other national minorities as well. In 1928 in the Ukraine there were 24 Jewish collectives, 10 German, 7 Russian, 8 Greek, and no Polish. A. Glinskii, *Dergraikhungen un felern in der arbet tsvishn di natsionale minderheiten* (Kharkov-Kiev, 1931), p. 49.

[31] *Oktiabr,* August 24, 1929. The JDC opposed collectivization and soon liquidated its agricultural activities in the USSR.

was justified on the grounds that larger *kolkhozy* would be more efficient.[32] The policy was implemented despite vigorous opposition by the Jewish *kolkhozniki*.[33] Collectivization and "internationalization" led to a further exodus of the Jewish colonists. In February 1930 the Jewish Telegraphic Agency reported that seventy percent of the Jewish settlers in the Crimea had left.[34]

The new role and enormously expanded activities of the *Evsektsiia* posed new problems of organization, administration, and recruitment of personnel. Kiper noted that "many comrades who did rather well in 1923–24 when the Sections were concerned mainly with agitation and propaganda work now cannot cope with the expanded soviet, social, and cultural work." [35] Chemeriskii observed that Jewish work was growing "with such impetus that it is difficult to keep up with it." [36] While in 1925 Jews constituted 24.3 percent of the Belorussian Party, 11.8 percent of the Ukrainian Party, and 5.2 percent of the All-Union Party, in 1922 only 8,500 out of 19,500 Jewish Party members resided in the areas where the bulk of the Jewish population—2.5 million people—lived. In 1925 slightly less than half the Jewish Party members lived in Belorussia and the Ukraine.[37] "These figures explain not only why the Jewish Communists are often opposed to work in Yiddish but also why it is necessary to have a campaign among the Jewish masses—even when you have 19,500 Jewish Communists—in order to enlist them in the Red Army." [38] The *Evsektsiia* was

[32] *Oktiabr*, November 28 and December 10, 1929.

[33] *Oktiabr*, December 21, 1929. See also the anonymous report dated November 21 and 22, 1929, in the Rosen Archive.

[34] JTA Report, February 16, 1930, Rosen Archive.

[35] M. Kiper, "Fragn fun der idarbet," *Emes*, November 24, 1926.

[36] Chemeriskii, p. 12.

[37] *Ibid.*, pp. 23–24.

[38] M. Kiper, "Tsu der alfarbandisher baratung fun di idsektsie," *Emes*, November 24, 1926.

constantly plagued by a shortage of qualified personnel and found it extremely difficult to recruit activists. Often, activists assigned by the Central Committee to Jewish work were shanghaied by local Party committees for other, unrelated tasks. Jewish work had a very low status—Altshuler called it a "limited kind of work which does not satisfy the activists" [39]—and the more highly qualified Party members sought to avoid it. In discussing ways and means of recruiting more activists Kiper admitted ruefully that "We will come up against difficulties both from comrades themselves, who for the time being have no great desire to transfer to Jewish work, and from the general [Party] organs which do not want to give up useful activists." [40] Even the graduates of the "Mairevnik," which was supposed to be the main training center for Jewish activists, seemed to avoid *Evsektsiia* activity. Of twenty graduates working in Moscow in 1927 only two were engaged in Jewish work.[41] Those who did enter the Sections could expect to be enormously overburdened with work. Thus, the secretary of the Vitebsk Section was also a school administrator, a substitute lecturer, a student in the workers faculty, secretary of the local GEZERD organization and a member of a commission to investigate artels.[42] In Chernigov the Section secretary

[39] *Der veker,* April 11, 1924.

[40] M. Kiper, "Di raionirung un di frage vegn tuer far idarbet," *Shtern,* June 2, 1925. Describing a visit to the *Evsektsiia's* Central office located in the Party Central Committee building, the former chief of the Comintern's Middle Eastern section recalls his "great disappointment at the sight of a small and forlorn office . . . a tiny room within the office dealing with national minority questions. . . . Chemerinskii [*sic*] was a secretary without a staff—he had only one official [assisting] him and meetings and appointments were also held in his small office." Y. Berger-Barzilai, *Hatragedia shel HaMahpekha HaSovietit* (Tel Aviv, 1968), p. 33.

[41] A. Bukovich, "Vu zeinen unzere praktishe tuer," *Mairevnik,* no. 2, December 1927.

[42] *Oktiabr,* November 18, 1929.

served also as secretary of the tailors' Party cell, member of the tailors' union administration, chairman of the cultural section of the union, representative of the national minorities in the *ispolkom*, vice-chairman of GEZERD, head of the political school, and administrator of the savings and loan association of the *kustar* union.[43] It is therefore no surprise that most of the activists recruited in 1925 and thereafter were young, inexperienced, and often totally unprepared for Jewish work—to the extent that some spoke only a broken Yiddish.[44] Of thirty-three *Evsektsiia* activists in the Smolensk *guberniia* in 1926—there were 732 Jewish Party members and candidates in the *guberniia*—none had a higher education, though most had elementary and some had secondary schooling. They ranged in age from nineteen to fifty, with the average being twenty-nine. Only eleven read a Yiddish newspaper and the same number read Yiddish books, though only two said they bought any. One activist had been in the *Evsektsiia* for four years and two others had served for two years. The thirty others had either just begun *Evsektsiia* work or had been involved in it for less than two years. The Section complained of a lack of personnel, pointing out that the *gubsektsiia* had only one full-time worker and that contacts between the *gubsektsiia* and local *sektsii* were absolutely minimal and totally inadequate. One Sectionist remarked that "Among Party and *Komsomol* members there exists to this very day the question of whether Jewish work is necessary." [45]

The *Evsektsiia* claimed that there were between 1,700 and 2,000 activists in Jewish work. However, only 120 were fulltime *Evsektsiia* officials. They were aided by about 1,000 Komsomol members who did not confine themselves to

[43] *Shtern*, August 4, 1926.

[44] See *Oktiabr*, March 24 and September 8, 1926.

[45] Smolensk Oblast Archive, WKP 303.

youth work.[46] In addition five hundred "plenipotentiaries" were working in the *shtetls*, and teachers were also involved in essentially political *agitprop* work. In 1924 there were seventy Jewish Sections, and their number continued to grow, though at a rather sluggish pace.[47] The *Evsektsiia* made the perhaps exaggerated claim that Section work was being done on a regular basis in five hundred localities.[48] Sections existed in almost all *krais* of Belorussia and the Ukraine—though the Ukraine had only sixty-two full-time *Evsektsiia* workers—as well as in three *gubernii* in the RSFSR. Sections also existed in the Crimea, Orenburg, Astrakhan, Kazan, Baku, and Tashkent.[49]

A look at a locality where Jewish work was relatively well developed and successful will serve to portray more vividly the nature and extent of *Evsektsiia* activities. The Berdichev *krai* encompassed 64,298 Jews in 1926. Of this total, 5,700 were trade union members and 3,500 were *kustars*. There were 351 Jewish Party members or candidates in the *krai*. Forty-two of them, or twelve percent, worked in the *Evsektsiia*. There were twelve Sections in the *krai* and four Party cells—all in the city of Berdichev—conducting their work in Yiddish. There were three Jewish workers' clubs, four *kustar* clubs, four reading rooms and —atypically—thirteen trade union locals working completely in Yiddish. Two Yiddish soviets existed, and five more were being planned, along with a Yiddish court. In 1923–24 there were ten Yiddish schools, serving 5,149 students and employing 103 teachers.[50] In 1927 there was some

[46] Chemeriskii, p. 26, 30. For a breakdown by function of 1,763 Communists in Jewish work, see Kiper, *Tsen yor oktiabr*, p. 100.

[47] *Emes*, December 12, 1925.

[48] *Alfarbandishe baratung*, p. 85.

[49] The Baku Section was dissolved in 1926 and a Moscow Section was created. Leningrad had not a single Section. *Ibid.*, p. 88.

[50] *Tsu der 1-er kreiz-baratung fun di idpartsektsies* (Berdichev, January 10, 1926).

growth on all fronts but the picture remained essentially the same. There were now sixty-six *Evsektsiia* functionaries in the *krai,* an increase of almost fifty percent, and some interesting data, illustrating the composition of the *Evsektsiia* and its growth in the mid-1920's, was obtained from them. Of fifty-six respondents to a questionnaire only twelve had previously belonged to another party and four "had taken part in the revolutionary movement before 1917." Only one was a Party member in 1917 and none had joined in 1921—the year the remnants of the Bund entered the Party. This seems to confirm the impression that those who entered in 1921 did not last long in the Party, having probably been purged in that very year. The greatest single group was that of 1925 when ten of the activists had been recruited into the Party. Among the activists there were thirty-five workers, eighteen officials, two *kustars,* and one peasant.[51]

It seemed as though basic organizational problems could never be permanently solved. Having gotten the explicit blessing of the Party at the Twelfth and Thirteen Congresses, the *Evsektsiia* could conduct its work with greater self-assurance and more confidence. The Ukrainian *Evsektsiia,* conscious of the change of role that had come about, proudly observed that "from agitation, propaganda, and political education work *the Evsektsiia passed to broader, multifaceted activity in the economic, soviet, and social spheres.* Implementing the general Party and Soviet policy in the Jewish environment, *the Evsektsiia accepted the task of reconstructing the economic life of the Jewish masses on a productive basis, of enlisting the broad strata of Jewish working people into active state construction.*"[52] Exhilarated by a new sense of their own legitimacy and worth, some

[51] *Emes,* April 28, 1927.

[52] *Shtern,* October 15, 1925. Italics added.

Jewish activists began to hint that the *Evsektsiia* should increase its autonomy vis-à-vis the Party.[53]

> The growth and development which Yiddish work is undergoing creates . . . a danger of separatism . . . local Sections often overstep their boundaries and set themselves tasks which are in no way the business of the *Evsektsiia.* This is especially noticeable in Party and *Komsomol* cells which have transferred to Yiddish. Only the language of the work changes, but not the content.[54]

Several Sections demanded that they be part only of the vertical *Evsektsiia* hierarchy and that their agenda be set only by the Main Bureau and not the *Partkom.* Many Sections "not having outgrown the era when the Party was indifferent or hostile to them," referred all questions, even those of purely local interest, to higher *Evsektsiia* organs, bypassing the *partkomy.*[55] A prominent activist in the Ukraine even proposed that the Section no longer be subordinate to the *agitprop* department of the Party committee and Central Committee but should itself become a department which would have connections with *all* the departments of the Party. In Podolia, he pointed out, this was already the fact. "We put all questions, minutes, instructions, circulars, and reports directly to the meeting of the Party committee bureau." This forced all bureau members to concern themselves with Jewish work, whereas previously only a few had read the reports of the *agitprop* department.[56]

Undoubtedly, *Evsektsiia* work was better organized and

[53] See M. Kiper, "Fragn fun der idisher partai-arbet," *Emes,* March 2, 1924.

[54] M. Kiper, "Vegn einglidern di idishe arbet in der algemainer," *Emes,* June 18, 1926.

[55] *Ibid.*

[56] Alek, "Di organizir formen fun unzer arbet," *Shtern,* October 11, 1925. This proposal was not acted upon.

less episodic and fitful than in the 1918–1923 period. Section meetings and conferences were held on the city, *raion*, *krai*, *guberniia*, and republic levels. Sections also held several non-Party conferences during the year in an attempt to reach beyond the Party *aktiv*. In 1925, 246 such conferences were held.[57] Still, many Jewish and non-Jewish Party members took a dim view of the *Evsektsiia* and even within the Sections themselves "liquidationist tendencies" persisted. It was therefore necessary for the assistant for *agitprop* of the All-Union Central Committee to reaffirm the worth of national minority Sections and to declare the need for their continued existence. "We must achieve a reorganization of the nationality Sections into real cells of ideological leadership among the national minorities, into authoritative organs of leadership in ideological-educational work." He called on the Sections to investigate thoroughly the cultural and economic situation of their people—"Perhaps only the Jewish Sections can point to significant achievements in this regard"—and on the Party as a whole to pay more heed to "specific national conditions and characteristics when implementing Party policies." [58]

The Evsektsiia in the Belorussian and Ukrainian Communist Parties

The power and effectiveness of the *Evsektsiia* were determined in large part by its relationship with the Party on the local, regional, and republic levels. There were important differences in the structures and attitudes of the Belorussian and Ukrainian Parties which greatly affected the fortunes of the Jewish Sections within them. While Yiddish was one of the four official languages in the Belorussian Republic from the Republic's very inception, it was

[57] Chemeriskii, p. 53.

[58] A. Abalin, "Di natsionale sektsies als shlakhttsentrn fun ideologisher arbet," *Emes*, October 10, 1926.

not accorded this privileged status in the Ukraine, though in 1927 the Ukrainian government declared the equality of all languages—that is, they could be used in official transactions.[59] Attached to the Central Executive Committee of the Ukrainian Republic Government was a Central Commission for National Minorities which had no operational functions but was to help the government coordinate its general policies with the special characteristics and needs of each national minority.[60] While the Jews were considered a national minority in Belorussia as well, they enjoyed a special status. There were three categories of national minorities in the Belorussian Republic: (1) those who belong to a nation the majority of whose members lived abroad under bourgeois governments (Poles, Latvians, Lithuanians, Germans); (2) Jews—"the most cultured national minority in Belorussia, constituting twenty-five percent of the entire proletariat of Belorussia and having large Jewish national masses outside Belorussia in territories inhabited mainly by them but without their own governments"; (3) miscellaneous nationalities (Tatars, Gypsies), each of whom have special characteristics and must therefore be treated differently. Jews were only about nine percent of the Belorussian population but they constituted forty percent of the urban population and forty-two percent of workers who belonged to trade unions.

Therefore, [argued V. Knorin, the leader of the Belo-

[59] *Shtern*, July 12, 1927. A former Belorussian Communist notes that the insistence on the equality of four languages sometimes reached "absurd proportions." At a teachers' conference in Rechitsa in 1928 the director of a Yiddish school spoke in Yiddish and a translation was requested. A Belorussian teacher, known for his liberal attitudes, suggested that the speakers speak in the commonly understood language—Russian. For this he was accused of "Great Russian chauvinism," dismissed from his job, expelled from the trade union, and deprived of his pension. Krushinsky, *Belorussian Communism*, p. 13.

[60] Slutskii, et al., *Leksikon*, p. 7.

> russian Communist Party] if you can call the Jews a national minority at all, they are a *special kind of national minority.* Moreover, *Jews are a special kind of nation.* Therefore, special attention must be paid to Jewish work. . . . The Jewish population of the Belorussian SSR will become increasingly tri-lingual. The Jewish nation will become a tri-lingual one in the near future. . . . [But] even if the Jewish masses will master the language of the majority at a more rapid rate than heretofore, even then the needs of the Jewish population for all forms of cultural facilities in the Yiddish language will grow very strongly.[61]

Therefore, the most backward elements of the Jewish population, now under clerical influence, must be drawn into Soviet Yiddish schools; the leading Party cadres of Jewish origin must learn Yiddish so as to influence less developed elements; increased support must be given to Yiddish literature and to the Yiddish press and theater; finally, new Jewish cadres must be trained and sufficient numbers of them must be placed in all state offices.[62]

Evsektsiia leaders in Belorussia tried to reciprocate this support of Yiddish culture and Jewish national rights by urging Jews, especially those in the Party, to show their approval of the policy of Belorussianization by learning Belorussian. It was no secret that most Jewish Party and

[61] V. Knorin, "Vegn bashlisndike 'kleinikeitn' in a groiser frage: fragn fun kultureler boiung fun di natsionale minderheitn," *Oktiabr,* October 16, 1928. Italics in original. Knorin was then Secretary of the Central Bureau of the Belorussian Communist Party. His references to the Jews as a "nation" and other aspects of the discussion were completely out of line with Stalin's 1913 definition of a nation and remarks on the Jews. Another Belorussian leader, Cherviakov, dismissed the question of whether or not Jews are a nation as having no practical consequences. *Tsvaiter alveisrusisher tsuzamenfor fun yidishe poierim* (Minsk, 1928), pp. 34-35.

[62] Knorin, *op. cit.*

soviet officials looked down their noses at the Ukrainian, and especially, Belorussian languages and cultures. Just as many of them were sure that Yiddish was losing ground to Russian, so were they convinced that the Belorussian language and culture were artificial, evanescent inventions.[63] A leading member of the Belorussian *Evsektsiia's* Main Bureau, Osherovich, acknowledged that the Jewish worker in Belorussia

> feels himself a citizen of Moscow, of the USSR in general, and not of Belorussia where he actually lives. . . . Therefore, our first task is to make the Jewish worker a citizen of Belorussia so that he should feel that Belorussia is his own. . . . From this it follows that our culture should become "territorialized," so to speak. [It must gain] a local coloration, it must mesh with Belorussian culture which has shown signs of growth and development in the last few years. This is possible and necessary because Belorussian culture is manifesting tendencies toward becoming not a national-personal culture, but a national-territorial one, that is, not a culture of Belorussians as a people isolated in themselves but a culture of Belorussians as citizens living in the given territory. . . . Each and every worker in the Soviet Union has a dual citizenship. *First,* he is a citizen of his national state. *Second,* he is a citizen of the entire Soviet Union. These two can absolutely not conflict with each other.[64]

This remarkable endorsement of a kind of Belorussian autonomism and separate national identity to be supported by all the nationalities living in Belorussia was perhaps so overstated precisely because the realities were so radically

[63] Yankel Levin, "Ufgabn fun partai-arbet," *Der veker,* February 26, 1924.

[64] A. Osherovich, in *Der veker,* March 4, 1924. Italics added.

different. There were "national contradictions" in Belorussia which were to a large extent congruent with class differences. Thus, Krinitskii, the secretary of the Belorussian Central Bureau in 1925, pointed to the "main contradiction, that between the Belorussian peasant and the Jewish worker." There were further "contradictions" between the Polish peasants and Belorussian peasants, and between all of these nationalities and the Russians, who were often not accorded the same rights as other national minorities. For example, in the mid-1920's Russian was offered in schools as a foreign language, "on an equal footing with German and French. . . . Unlike the Jewish and Polish communities, the Russians had no courts of justice, no high schools, and no teachers' college of their own."[65]

There was a tendency in the Party, especially pronounced among Polish and Jewish members, toward a kind of national clannishness, perhaps in reaction to "incorrect attitudes toward the national minorities" sometimes displayed by Belorussians and Russians.[66] There was a very practical reason for the hostility of many Jewish Party members to the policy of Belorussianization. One aspect of this policy involved increasing the number of Belorussians or those who knew the Belorussian language—which meant the same thing for all intents and purposes—in the Party and state apparatuses. When this policy was announced, great care was taken to emphasize that there would be a parallel increase in the number of Poles, Lithuanians, and Jews in these apparatuses so that the respective concentrations of these nationalities could be better served. "Increase the number of Belorussians without decreasing the number of Jews"

[65] Nicholas Vakar, *Belorussia: The Making of a Nation* (Cambridge, Mass., 1956), p. 142.

[66] Krinitskii's speech to the Minsk Party Organization, in *Der veker*, September 27, 29, 30, 1925.

was to be the policy.[67] Krinitskii promised explicitly that the Party would not adopt nationality as a criterion for eligibility for leadership or cadre membership in the Party. While there was to be no *numerus clausus* in the Party, members would be expected to be familiar with the language and milieu of the people among whom they worked.[68] These assurances were welcomed by the *Evsektsiia* which stood only to gain from insistence that Party workers in the *shtetl* and among *kustars* speak the language of the latter,[69] but other Jewish Communists, working mainly in Russian, openly expressed the fear that they would lose their jobs.

Jews occupied a strategic place in the Belorussian Party and many people feared that they stood to lose from Belorussianization. On July 1, 1925, Jews constituted 25.5 percent of the Belorussian Communist Party.[70] Jews constituted 23.3 percent of the personnel in *kraikom* bureaus and 12.6 percent of all *raikom* secretaries.[71] In the state apparatus Jews occupied an equally prominent place, constituting 20.2 percent of the Central Executive Committee, 16.7 percent of the *kraiispolkomy*, 6.7 percent of the *raiispolkomy*, and 30.1 percent of the city soviets.[72] Somewhat panicked by the Belorussianization policy—which increased Belo-

[67] Resolution of the Belorussian Central Committee, *Oktiabr,* August 31, 1926.

[68] A. Krinitskii, "Ordentlekhe ufgabn in der natspolitik fun KP(B)V," *Oktiabr,* December 8, 1926.

[69] These are the points stressed in "A vikhtike bashtimung," *Oktiabr,* September 1, 1926, and "Klorkeit in di frage fun veisrusizatsie," *Oktiabr,* September 9, 1926.

[70] This is the figure cited in *Der veker,* supplement (Report of the Main Bureau for October 1924–October 1925) to the issue of October 18, 1925. Chemeriskii (p. 23) cites a figure of 23.4 percent. The differences are no doubt due to the inclusion of candidate members in the former figure.

[71] Krinitskii's speech to the Minsk Party *aktiv,* in *Oktiabr,* October 19, 1926.

[72] *Der veker* supplement, October 18, 1925.

russian representation in the BCP from about twenty percent in 1922 to nearly fifty percent in 1927—Jewish functionaries began to murmur about "anti-Semitism" in high places and in Party policy. "The fact is that there are among us those who see the Belorussianization of the state apparatus as an anti-Semitic act. When they see a Belorussian placed in the *apparat* they scream that the Jews are being fired. . . . Or when the Party says that Jewish workers ought to learn Belorussian again there are cries that this is a 'decree against the Jews.'"[73]

The *Evsektsiia* itself actually gained from the Belorussianization policy since obviously no Belorussian would replace someone doing Jewish work. Furthermore, some of the dispossessed Jewish officials found a new home in Jewish work. Finally, Belorussianization was accompanied by Yiddishization.

In general the Belorussian *Evsektsiia* enjoyed good relations with the Party as a whole, perhaps because the *Evsektsiia* leadership was well represented in the higher echelons of the Party. In 1924 Yankel Levin remarked that "almost the entire Belorussian Main Bureau [of the *Evsektsiia*] had entered the Central Bureau [of the BCP]. Thanks to this we could coordinate Jewish and general Party work . . . and the Party was sensitive to Jewish work. . . . A similar situation existed in the *uezdy*. . . . There were no conflicts in the Party regarding Jewish work."[74] In 1926 of the seven members of the *Evsektsiia* Main Bureau (sometimes called the *Yidburo*), three were members of the Belorussian Central Committee (formerly Central Bureau).[75] Of ten *Evsektsiia* secretaries on the *krai* level, two were members of the *kraikom* bureau and four were candidate

[73] *Oktiabr,* February 5, 1927.

[74] *Der veker,* March 5, 1924.

[75] One was a candidate member, one was a full member, and the third was a member of the bureau—or politburo.

members of the *kraikomy*.[76] B. Orshanskii, editor of *Oktiabr*, was assistant administrator of the *agitprop* department of the Central Committee, the office which had charge of nationality Sections.[77] As late as 1929 two members of the Main Bureau were on the Central Committee, and one was also a member of the politburo.[78] Thus, through elite representation the *Evsektsiia* was able to make its influence felt in the Belorussian Communist Party.

Jews did not enjoy a similar position in the Ukrainian Communist Party, nor did they occupy so strategic a location within the Ukrainian population. While in 1926 Jews were 8.2 percent of the population of Belorussia, they constituted 5.4 percent of the population of the Ukraine. Whereas they made up 40.2 percent of the urban population of Belorussia, they were only 22.7 percent of the Ukrainian urban population.[79] Whereas 20.7 percent of all workers in Belorussia were Jews, in the Ukraine only 8.7 percent were.[80] In the Belorussian Communist Party 26.6 percent were Jews, while in the Ukrainian Party the figure was 13.1 percent.[81] By 1927, 4.3 percent of the Ukrainian Central Executive Committee (VUTsIK) members were Jews, as were ten percent of the *kraiispolkomy* members and 19.3 percent of the city soviets' members.[82] There were no *Evsektsiia* leaders in the Party Central Committee.[83]

[76] *Oktiabr*, June 17, 1926.

[77] *Oktiabr*, September 18, 1926.

[78] *Oktiabr*, February 16 and 17, 1929. Osherovich was a member of the TsK and Bailin was a member of the politburo as well. At this time Yan Gamarnik, a Jew, was first secretary of the Belorussian Communist Party.

[79] Schwarz, pp. 15 and 261.

[80] Y. Kantor, "Di idishe bafelkerung in ukraine loit der folkstsailung fun 1926-tn yor," *Di roite velt*, no. 4, 1928, p. 133, and *Prakticheskoe rasreshenie*, pp. 22-24.

[81] Schwarz, p. 261.

[82] *Shtern*, November 29, 1927.

[83] For a list of the Committee members see *Shtern*, November 30,

The Ukrainian Party had never been overly enthusiastic about "Jewish work" or the *Evsektsiia*. As will be recalled, the Russian Communist Party had forced the Ukrainians to accept Sections as a legitimate organizational form within the Party. Nevertheless, by 1925 the Party seemed to be adopting a more positive attitude, and *Evsektsiia* spokesmen noted that "The Central Committee of the CPU is now entirely in agreement with the [Party] line in Jewish work, whereas heretofore it had not entirely agreed with it." This new attitude was said to be reflected on the local level as well.[84] Potential improvement in CPU-*Evsektsiia* relations was set back to some degree by strong Jewish opposition to Ukrainization.[85] Ukrainian nationalism was much more highly developed than Belorussian nationalism, both in the Party and the population. Therefore, Jewish opposition to Ukrainization had a much greater impact than did opposition to Belorussianization. The Ukrainian Party was divided into two main groups, one consisting of former members of other Ukrainian parties, particularly the *Borot'bisty,* and some younger nationally conscious Ukrainians, and the other made up mostly of Russians and Russified Ukrainians. In the late 1920's the Party was polarized between these two camps,[86] with the Jews tending to associate themselves with the Russifying camp. Since not even the more nationalistic wing espoused the Belorussian Party line of strengthening *all* national cultures and supporting Party work among the nationalities across the board, the *Evsektsiia* had no natural allies in the Ukrainian Party. Neither the Russifiers nor

1927. Lazar Kaganovich, a Jew, was general secretary of the Ukrainian Party at this time.

[84] Speeches by Kiper at the All-Ukraine *Evsektsiia* conference, reported in *Shtern,* October 18, 1927, and by Merezhin at the same conference, reported in *Shtern,* October 22, 1925.

[85] See, for example, *Shtern,* March 2, 1927.

[86] Hryhory Kostiuk, *Stalinist Rule in the Ukraine* (New York, 1960), p. 142.

the Ukrainifiers were interested in promoting Yiddishization, certainly not to a greater extent than Germanization, Polonization, Magyarization, etc. Moreover, the *Evsektsiia* and "Jewish work" were adversely affected by the existence of a native tradition of anti-Semitism in the Ukraine which even pervaded the Party. The lower apparatus was most hostile to the *Evsektsiia*, and there is scattered evidence that it was not immune to outright anti-Semitism.[87]

Iurii Larin, speaking at the Third Congress of Soviets of the USSR in 1925, pointed out that the creation of national republics and the "nativization" policy had only partially solved the nationality problem. He charged that the policy of Ukrainization was being used to force Russian, Jewish, and Polish nationals to learn Ukrainian. "As a result the Soviet policy of localization [nativization]—correct as a general policy—was being transformed into a device for repressing the separate minorities in the republics just as the majority groups in the border areas had been repressed earlier under tsarist rule. It was necessary, he concluded, for the majority nationality in each republic to recognize the same rights and guarantees for the minorities of the republic that the majority had demanded for itself from the USSR . . . it was plain that most of the delegates to the Congress of Soviets sympathized with Larin."[88] Larin's criticism of the national republics underscores the problems the *Evsektsiia* faced in the very nationally conscious Ukrainian SSR.

The various levels of the *Evsektsiia* hierarchy were con-

[87] See the calls for a "radical improvement in the lower *apparat*" and "firm revolutionary legality" coupled with talk of "counter-revolutionary elements who infiltrated us in order to destroy us from within" in *Shtern,* August 2, 1925. See also the story of a blood libel incident and Central Committee member Petrovskii's comment in *Shtern,* April 17, 1926.

[88] Robert S. Sullivant, *Soviet Politics and the Ukraine, 1917–1957* (New York, 1962), p. 125.

stantly plagued by the necessity of serving two masters whose wishes seemed to conflict more often than not. Relations with local, regional, or republic Party organs were always delicate and sometimes troubled; relations with higher organs of the *Evsektsiia* itself were not always very harmonious either. A particularly sensitive spot seemed to be the relationships between the Main Bureaus in Belorussia and the Ukraine, on one hand, and the Central Bureau in Moscow, on the other. At the 1924 All-Union *Evsektsiia* conference, for example, Abram pointed out that the Central Bureau had ridden roughshod over Main Bureau opposition on the *kustar* question and had bypassed the Main Bureaus completely, giving orders directly to the local Sections. Yankel Levin warned the Central Bureau to pay more attention to local conditions,[89] and Chemeriskii found it necessary to remind the delegates that the Central Bureau's directives were to be obeyed even when the Main Bureau did not approve them. Toward the end of the decade frictions between the Bureaus and the Central Bureau played an increasingly important and disruptive role in the work of the *Evsektsiia*. In December 1929 Abram complained that the *Evsektsiia* was relying too much on "the old forms and the old traditions in Jewish work," and that it was worrying too much about *kustars* and Jewish nationalism when it should be concerning itself with the current problems of the five-year plan, collectivization, and socialist competition. Kiper, too, lent his authoritative voice to this complaint and claimed that the *Evsektsiia*'s "forms and methods of work" were outmoded and should be made more suitable for work in the factories.[90] "All Jewish Sections, especially those in the larger [urban] centers, should take account of the most important phenomena and trends

89 *Emes,* April 6, 1924.
90 *Shtern,* December 21, 1929.

being created in the process of socialist construction . . . in order that they should themselves reconstruct the forms, methods, and substance of their work. . . . We must adjust Jewish work to the tempo, form and methods of general Party work and socialist construction." [91]

The Evsektsiia Debates The National Question

While organizational questions could be debated as essentially technical problems, they were often linked to the national program of the *Evsektsiia,* which, in turn, involved debates over alternative modernization programs. At the Third Conference the question of Sections versus Departments was really fought on national grounds, despite pious protestations that the issue was organizational functionalism. At the next All-Union Conference, held in 1924, the issues were debated openly. Altshuler claimed that Jewish workers often did not want any Yiddish work, and he vigorously opposed Esther's suggestion that separate meetings, conducted in Yiddish, should be held for the Jewish workers entering the Party in the "Lenin Levy," the mass recruitment into the Party following Lenin's death. Altshuler also attacked the Central Bureau's policy of working with the *kustars* and in the *shtetl.* While Merezhin called the *shtetl* "our Donbas," Altshuler insisted that "Donbas is our Donbas too—we have one Donbas for all workers of all nations." Moishe Litvakov attacked Altshuler's proposal that new Jewish Party members be asked if they knew Russian and if they did they should be assigned to general, rather than Jewish, Party work. Litvakov admitted that the "internationalizing" policy followed by the *Evsektsiia* in 1922 had been mistaken. He opposed the notion that the *Evsektsiia* should be a sort of "emigra-

[91] *Ibid.* Kiper's phraseology is strikingly similar to that used some two months later in explaining the dissolution of the *Evsektsiia.*

tion bureau for sending Jewish workers to another culture. Certainly we should think of ourselves as the Communist Party itself which serves the Jewish environment."

Altshuler's anti-*kustar* and "assimilationist" positions were logically related. The *kustar* predominated in the *shtetl,* and the *shtetl* was the stronghold of Jewish identity and traditional Jewish culture. To encourage the *kustar* would be to strengthen the *shtetl.* Altshuler's "leftist" economic position thus implied a concomitant "leftist" position on the national question. Indeed, logic would seem to dictate that the Trotsky-Preobrazhenskii economic program would have been welcomed by the anti-national elements in the Belorussian and Ukrainian Communist parties, since this program would have placed the greatest burden on the peasantry, heavily Belorussian or Ukrainian, and probably more nationalistic than the urban population.[92] Conversely, elements in these Parties more favorably inclined toward the preservation and promotion of their respective national cultures and identities might have been expected to favor Bukharin's economic proposals, though in the mid-1920's Stalin too was identified with Bukharin's economic line. If the analogy could be made between the peasant and the *kustar,* the same logic might apply to the disputing parties in the *Evsektsiia.* Unfortunately, the implications of the intra-party debate on economic modernization for ethnic maintenance or assimilation have not been investigated.

At least within the *Evsektsiia* two general approaches to the broad range of political and national issues could be discerned in the 1920's. One approach may be termed a "minimalist" or "gradualist" one. Its adherents, who logically belonged in the Bukharin camp, saw the modernization of Soviet Jewry as a gradual process. Economic rehabilitation could be accomplished by starting with agricultural coloni-

[92] Sullivant (p. 134) asserts that this was, indeed, the case.

zation, rather than by plunging into large-scale industrialization and urbanization. Similarly, national integration of the peoples of the USSR, including the Jews, could be accomplished, as Stalin said, by first promoting the national consolidation and cultural development of the individual ethnic entities. National integration would be achieved *through* political integration; the Uzbek, the Tatar, the Ukrainian, the Armenian, and the Jew would be united not by a common ethnic identity but by a shared political allegiance. Ethnic identity could co-exist with "Soviet patriotism." [93]

The second school of thought urged, in the manner of the Left Opposition, the most rapid possible attainment of maximum goals. Industrialization of the Jewish population, like industrialization of the population as a whole, was to proceed forthwith and with the greatest possible rapidity. National disintegration, a process initiated by the "revolution on the Jewish street," would be completed by the assimilatory consequences of industrialization-urbanization, and it would be wrong to slow the processes of history by "artificially" strengthening ethnic identity and promoting parochial cultures. National integration would be achieved simply by assimilation. The weakening of primordial loyalties would remove one of the barriers to political integration. Political integration without national integration via assimi-

[93] "In each national republic of the USSR Soviet patriotism has its *national distinctiveness* . . . has its unique characteristics . . . *but their patriotism has one socialist content.*" I. E. Kravtsev, *Proletarskii internatsionalizm, Otechestvo i Patriotizm* (Kiev, 1965), p. 45. Although the two concepts are often used interchangeably, we use national integration to mean the development of primary loyalties to and identification with the nation, whereas political integration is the development of loyalty to and identification with the defining values and aspirations of the political system. See Claude Ake, *A Theory of Political Integration* (Homewood, Ill., 1967), and Myron Weiner, "Political Integration and Political Development," *The Annals of the American Academy of Political Science*, 358 (March 1965).

lation was an impossibility. Thus, the gradualist or minimalist school emerged as spokesman for the "nationalist" viewpoint, while the maximalists defended rapid and conscious assimilation. The leadership of the *Evsektsiia* tried to steer clear of both positions by developing a "neutralist" theory.

While at the 1924 All-Union *Evsektsiia* Conference, Altshuler represented the "liquidationist" or "assimilatory" school of thought, Kazakevich emerged as the leader of the "nationalist" camp. "We are afraid of words like 'national culture' and the like. This fear is groundless. . . . We are creating a new national culture and we must see to it that it does not become crippled. If Yiddishism can serve the revolution we must not be frightened off by it." Esther attacked Kazakevich for his "nationalistic tendencies" and admitted that "our Party *uses* the nationalist strivings of the downtrodden masses." But then she went on to agree that "a new culture is being created" and that "The Sections absolutely must not limit themselves to specifically Jewish questions. The sections must grow into the whole range of local work."

Altshuler and Kazakevich were not speaking only for themselves. Speaking for the Central Bureau, Rakhmiel Veinshtain warned that two deviations from the Party and Central Bureau line were noticeable, especially in the Ukraine: "One is assimilationist (to put it crudely) and the other is nationalistic. The first was connected with liquidationist tendencies—we must liquidate Jewish work in many cities because the Jewish workers understand Russian. . . . The nationalist deviations led in the opposite direction. Were we to pursue them to their logical conclusion we would end up with independent Jewish work, the autonomization of Jewish life. . . . The Central Bureau fought both deviations most energetically."[94] Was the policy of the Party and the

[94] This account of the discussion at the conference is based on

Central Bureau one of "neutralism"? Was it nothing more than the Bundist program formulated by Vladimir Medem? The *Evsektsiia* took pains to point out the differences between Bundist "neutralism" and the main line of the Central Bureau. Bundist neutralism was said to be negative and passive—"To put it bluntly, we don't give a hoot [*moia khata s kraiiu*]. Neither here, *nor* there. Let nature take its course." The *Evsektsiia*, on the other hand, was neutral in a positive, active way: it actively attracted Jewish workers to heavy industry, a policy which "will probably lead to assimilation." But it also actively promoted Jewish agricultural colonization "though it is possible that this will lead to a consolidation of a part of the Jewish population into a nation." *Objectively*, two contradictory processes—assimilation and consolidation—were taking place among the Jewish population and the *Evsektsiia* supported both because, in the final analysis, both served the same end. "Neutralism pertains to the end, but not to the means, when two means can lead objectively to the same end—the strengthening of the dictatorship of the proletariat." [95]

Emes, October 14 and 16, 1924, and *Der veker*, April 11, 12, 13, 1924; Veinshtain's statement is in *Der veker*, May 6, 1924.

[95] A. Volobrinskii, "Notitsn iber der natsionaler frage," *Shtern* (Minsk), III, no. 2 (February 1927). Interestingly, within the Ukrainian Communist Party there were also three factions disputing Party policy on the nationality question. A small group led by Oleksander Shums'kyi wanted to accelerate Ukrainization and orient Ukrainian culture away from Russian culture. As was the case in the *Evsektsiia*, this nationalist group was a small minority. The majority group, including such leaders as Skrypnik, Chubar, and Kaganovich, supported continued Ukrainization but thought Shums'kyi's program too radically nationalist. A third faction, consisting mainly of non-Ukrainians, urged an "assimilationist" program. Its leader was Iurii Larin, who insisted that the culture of the proletariat and of the urban areas in general was almost exclusively Russian and that efforts to Ukrainize the urban proletariat would alienate them from the Party. See Sullivant, pp. 138–140. Larin's anti-Ukrainization position was

The movement to settle Jews on the land was seen as the chief instrument through which both large-scale economic modernization and simultaneous national consolidation could be achieved. There is some evidence to indicate that Jewish colonization was first proposed by the *Evsektsiia* and that it used the argument that such a project would steal the thunder of the Zionists.[96] The *Evsektsiia* could not call the Jews a nation because Lenin, basing himself on Kautsky, had "proved" the Jews were not a nation, as they had no territory. Now that the Jews were going to be settled on the land, there was a possibility of "creating the objective conditions" which would force a redefinition of the Jewish people, as the super-structure would have to accommodate itself to the all-determining base. In 1924 Chemeriskii said that the *Evsektsiia* was not opposed in principle to the idea of "an autonomous area" but that since the creation of such an area was not objectively possible at the time it would be foolish and unrealistic to "proclaim the slogan" of an autonomous area. "But we are categorically in favor of compact colonization in contiguous land areas."[97] In other words, if Jewish settlement were compact enough and on a sufficiently large scale, a Jewish territory might be established, removing all obstacles to the creation of a Jewish nation. While to the outside observer the mechanics of denying or creating a Jewish nation might seem artificial and absurd, the *Evsektsiia* was forced

---

consistent with his vigorous defense of the rights of national minorities living in the national republics.

[96] "The Jewish Communists, not those who hold responsible positions among us—they are already Jews only by descent—but those Jewish Communists who live among the Jewish masses, they turned to the government and asked that it make it possible for those emigrants wishing to go to Palestine to settle in the Soviet Union." M. I. Kalinin, "Evreiskii vopros i pereselenie evreev v krym," *Izvestiia,* July 11, 1926.

[97] *Emes,* October 12, 1924.

to work within this system which had been set in motion by an *a priori* definition.

The national question exploded into unforeseen and unwelcome prominence at the first All-Union Congress of GEZERD in November 1926. On September 4, 1926, the Central Bureau had adopted a resolution endorsing the idea of "Jewish territorial autonomy" but hedging it with a warning against "nationalistic overestimation" of this autonomy.[98] This cautious formulation was designed to protect the Central Bureau against charges of nationalism, to which it was hypersensitive in view of the "nationalist" past of some of the leadership. Some Jews and Jewish Communists not affiliated with the *Evsektsiia* felt no such inhibitions and eagerly seized upon the resolution to press for a Jewish autonomous territory, at the same time expressing impatience with the Central Bureau's timid and hesitant approach. The spokesman of the non-*Evsektsiia* "nationalists" was Abram Bragin, a former member of the *Tseirai Tsion* and the organizer of an agricultural exhibition in Moscow in 1923–24.[99] In 1924 Bragin had written that there were only two possible ways out for the impoverished Jews and youth of the *shtetl*—industrialization and settlement on land. Bragin argued that the first was impractical, presumably because of the USSR's general economic situation, and so for "ninety percent of the Jewish population there remains one way out—to agriculture." He suggested that Jews be settled on lands near Odessa and around the Black Sea.[100] Now Bragin minced no words in his interpretation

[98] *Alfarbandishe baratung*, p. 97.

[99] Born in 1893, Bragin was a law graduate of Kiev University and later became an agricultural expert. See *Bol'shaia sovetskaia entsiklopediia* (Moscow, 1927), VII, 283. Bragin was not mentioned in the 1951 edition of the *Entsiklopediia*.

[100] A. Bragin and Mikhail Kol'tsov, *Sud'ba evreiskikh mass v Sovetskom Soiuze* (Moscow, 1924), p. 12.

of the colonization plan and in his condemnation of the *Evsektsiia*.

> The significance of our work is that we are laying the foundation for national self-determination of the Jewish nation, as set forth in the policy of the Communist Party and the Leninist conception of the problem. Approaching the question in this way, we must say that all is not in order, that our little cigarette lighter pales in the great flame of socialist construction. We are guilty of being hypnotized by a breathing space. Because the situation of the *kustars* and small traders lately has improved somewhat, we have become complacent and think that we have enough time to work on the reconstruction of the Jewish economy. . . . We must fight the hypnosis of the hiatus. . . . We have to understand that building individual settlements which are not connected to one national union that has no representation of its own, nor its own state budget—*this is building on sand.* [Movement in the hall.] We demand that not only Petrovskii and Chicherin should make declarations, but our own leaders should demand in the name of the Jewish masses that we build our life on the basis of national self-determination, lest we be unworthy of the great movement which demands those rights to which we are entitled.[101]

Bragin was attacking the *Evsektsiia* policy of openly proclaiming territorial autonomy in the propaganda aimed at enlisting foreign support, while simultaneously quashing any "premature notions" of this sort within the USSR. In the course of the debates, this fearless "wild man in a starched white shirt"[102] charged that "the colossal move-

[101] *Ershter alfarbandisher tsuzamenfor fun 'GEZERD': stenografisher barikht* (Moscow, 1927), pp. 28-29.

[102] Niepomniashchi's description. Letter of November 22, 1926, to Daniel Charney, YIVO Archives.

ment has outgrown a large number of its leaders [disturbance in the hall]. . . . I was connected with the slogan of a republic and I am proud of it. There will come a time when Merezhin, too, will be married to this slogan, just as he is now to the slogan of 100,000 families [to be settled on the land]." Bragin deplored the fact that non-Jewish Communists were supporting the idea of a Jewish republic while the *Evsektsiia*, the "guards on the Jewish front," kept a timid silence. "You remain silent at a time when history demands a clear and detailed definition of the question." He demanded that the slogan of a Jewish republic be proclaimed forthwith, even though the republic could not be immediately established. Bragin shocked the audience by charging that the revolution "had passed the Jewish question by. Therefore, the question of a republic, just like the question of the 100,000 families, is a question only of the state's formulation of our affairs in the same manner in which they are formulated for all other areas and peoples." [103]

Kantor, the advocate of Yiddishized governmental organs, defended *Evsektsiia* policy: there was no need to set up a Jewish republic hurriedly in order to save the stricken *shtetl* population. Jewish work in the *shtetl* had done a great deal to ease the emergency and the situation would undoubtedly continue to improve. But it remained for Chemeriskii to spell out the definitive *Evsektsiia* position.

Chemeriskii had been the first prominent Jewish activist to raise publicly the possibility of a Jewish claim to nationhood in the form of an autonomous Jewish republic in the USSR and to speak about it favorably. However, Chemeriskii favored a multiple solution to the economic problems of the Jews. In 1925–26 he wrote that the Jews could come to socialism through cooperatives, agriculture, and

[103] *Ershter . . . tsuzamenfor*, pp. 84–85.

industry. But "the most comprehensive means of making the Jewish masses productive is *by transforming as many as possible into peasants.*" [104] Concomitantly, it was

> not only politically but also practically possible to create a Jewish autonomy. Is it worth creating such autonomy? Yes, *it is worthwhile.* . . . Yes, Jewish autonomy in the Soviet Union is worthwhile and useful and we may therefore have it as a perspective, as a practically feasible goal of our work, as a goal which we try to realize.[105]

Chemeriskii was careful to distinguish between this program and Zionist ideology. The Communist program was optimistic, limited to one country and but one of several possible solutions to the Jewish problem; the Zionist program was grounded in pessimism, sought to solve the Jewish problem in the same way in different countries wherein different socio-economic conditions obtained, and was an exclusivist, monistic approach. Finally, "For them it is an adventure which misleads the masses and which will never be realized, whereas with us it is a part of the practical policy of our Soviet state." [106]

The emphasis on colonization and autonomy was a new one for Chemeriskii who had usually emphasized the need for drawing the Jewish masses into industry.[107] Apparently, Chemeriskii soon had reason to abandon his new emphasis, perhaps out of fear that he had opened a Pandora's box of nationalistic forces, or in the conviction that it would be best not to alarm the Party with too much talk about the national aspect of the program. It would be better to pro-

[104] Chemeriskii, *Di alfarbandishe komunistishe partai,* p. 17. Emphasis Chemeriskii's.

[105] *Ibid.,* p. 74.

[106] *Ibid.,* pp. 76–77.

[107] See, for example, his article "Vegn areintsien idishe arbeter in der industrie," *Emes,* August 4, 1925.

ceed quietly in doing the *practical* work necessary to legitimize *theoretical* autonomist claims. Whatever the case, at the GEZERD conference Chemeriskii eschewed any talk of autonomy and pleaded for discussion of all questions in practical terms. The national question is, he said, only a function of the more fundamental economic one.

> When you declare that building individual colonies or groups of colonies had value for us only when this is connected with a national ideology, this is simply phraseology. When we build a textile factory in a distant Central Asian *raion*, it does not mean that we are specifically trying to solve the national question. But thereby we are carrying out a policy of bringing new productive forces to life and this perforce solves the national problem.[108]

Engineer Shmuel Weitzman was not satisfied with Chemeriskii's explanations.

> Let Comrade Chemeriskii say as much as he wants to that he acts strictly from the proletarian viewpoint—for us it's the results that count. Jewish schools, courts, and *raiony*—and in general the entire work of the *Evsektsiia*—show that the "*Evseks*" are on the right path to the solution of the Jewish question. The Russian comrades—official and responsible comrades—speak explicitly and categorically about a Jewish state unit in the Soviet Union. This fills us with enthusiasm. Comrade Ter-Gabrielian conducts agricultural settlement work among the Armenians and he does not minimize the significance of the national work he does. I don't think Comrade Veinshtain will be a worse Communist for calling his work "national work."[109]

[108] *Ershter . . . tsuzamenfor*, p. 31.

[109] *Emes*, November 23, 1926. Weitzman was a former member of

Chemeriskii tried to answer the attacks on the *Evsektsiia* leadership.

> Bragin said . . . that neither Comrade Petrovskii nor Chicherin should speak about Jewish agricultural settlement, but "we" should. Who are "we"? [Bragin, from the audience: "You, Comrade Chemeriskii, you as representative of the Jewish working class!"] I am not a "representative" of the Jewish working class. I am an ordinary soldier of the All-Union Communist Party [stormy applause]. . . . To say that Jewish agricultural colonization is our business, the business of Jewish "society," and not the business of the state—means to *lose everything*, means to veer off the proletarian tracks. . . . To say that only Chemeriskii and neither Petrovskii nor Chicherin can speak in the name of Jewish workers about agricultural settlement—this is nationalism in the highest degree. Bragin ended his talk by saying: "You act correctly but speak poorly." This is untrue. We also speak correctly.[110]

Chemeriskii undoubtedly thought that this pious and self-effacing, yet self-satisfied, answer to Bragin would settle the issue. His composure, and that of all his comrades, was rudely shattered as a bombshell was exploded by the "*starosta* of the USSR," the philo-Semitic Russian, the former peasant and worker, Mikhail Kalinin. Electrifying some of the audience and stunning others, Kalinin stated flatly that

> it is completely natural that the Jewish population, too—a lively [people], its masses quite cultured, politically and socially tempered in the constant struggle for its existence—also discovers itself, also strives to find its national place in the Soviet Union.[111]

the Socialist-Zionist party. His brother Khaim was a Zionist leader who later became first president of the State of Israel.

[110] *Ibid.*

[111] *Ershter . . . tzusamenfor,* p. 38.

In a gentle rebuttal to Chemeriskii, Kalinin agreed that the Soviet government had sound economic motives for promoting Jewish colonization, but "I must say that if we will approach this question ideologically, from the national point of view, I allow that beneath this desire lies buried a powerful, mass, unconscious phenomenon—the desire to preserve one's nationality. It seems to me that this phenomenon represents one of the forms of national self-preservation."[112] Kalinin charged the Jewish people to take advantage of the opportunity:

> *The Jewish people faces the great task of preserving its own nationality, and to this end a large part of the Jewish population must be transformed into an economically stable, agriculturally compact group which should number at least hundreds of thousands. Only under such conditions can the Jewish masses hope for the future existence of their nationality.*[113]

Kalinin insisted that it was in the government's interest to maintain the "national feeling of each small people living in the USSR. Only under such conditions, I repeat, will each nationality consider the Soviet Union its fatherland. . . . Comrades, I believe that the Soviet Union must become the

[112] *Ibid.*, p. 39.

[113] *Ibid.*, p. 41. Italics added. Alfred A. Greenbaum suggests that "It seems clear enough that he [Kalinin] expected land settlement to draw off some of the Jews streaming into the large cities and competing for employment and higher education." This would presumably dampen some of the causes of anti-Semitism. "Thus, in spite of Kalinin's undoubtedly sincere feeling that the time had come for the Jewish people to build a state of their own in Russia, there may have been something of an ulterior motive in the 'Jewish nationalist' sentiments which this Russian statesman expressed at the first OZET Congress and on many subsequent occasions." "Soviet Jewry During the Lenin-Stalin Period," *Soviet Studies,* xvi, no. 4 (April 1965), 413–14. While this may have been the calculation of some other Soviet leaders, I find no evidence to support this contention.

fatherland of the Jewish masses, ten times a more genuine fatherland than any bourgeois Palestine."[114]

Kalinin's speech further aroused the emotions of the "nationalists," and some were moved to tears by the sight of a Russian *muzhik* pleading with the Jewish people to preserve its national identity. The talk had quite a different effect on the *Evsektsiia* leaders. Kalinin's ideas on the preservation of the nation

> were so un-*Evsek*ish, so "new"—that the audience was trembling. The *Evsek*-haters, including Bragin, rubbed their hands with glee. . . . We constantly claim that we are not worried about the preservation of the nation; along he comes and tells us we must worry about this, that Moscow Jews are no Jews, they assimilate and intermarry—did you ever! This was very bewildering to our *Evseks* and right afterward they began to "twirl their thumbs" scholastically in *Emes,* saying that Kalinin's nation is not the "Hebraist-Orthodox" nation but the "Soviet" nation. I once wrote some articles on . . . the national question but this concept of a "Soviet" nation I hear for the first time—and "I know not what it means" ["*V'lo yadati pairusho*"]. Of course, Bragin had found himself a "supporting authority" ["*tana d'mesaio*"] and he began to wave his gilt-edged "white-blue-red" flag.[115]

Greatly vexed by this nationalist outburst from an unexpected source, the *Evsektsiia* leaders could only repeat that "the tendentious proclamation of the slogan 'republic' smacks of adventurism and irresponsibility."[116] Bragin pressed his advantage. "It is no accident that Comrade Kalinin used the words 'nation,' 'people,' 'nationality,' while Comrade Veinshtain . . . spoke only once, and then in-

[114] *Ershter . . . tzusamenfor,* p. 43.
[115] Niepomniashchi to Charney, November 22, 1926.
[116] Merezhin's phrase. *Ershter . . . tsuzamenfor,* p. 75.

cidentally, about the national fate. . . . I maintain that you fail to grasp the significance of the national element in our undertaking, even within the limitations imposed upon it by the Party."[117] Litvakov then rose on behalf of the *Evsektsiia* and the veteran polemicist lashed out at Bragin:

> Bragin says he accepts the leadership of the Communist Party and *Evsektsiia*—as if he had a choice [laughter]. But if he does accept the leadership of the Party, how does he permit himself to deny the history of the Party which, immediately after the October Revolution, placed the question of the Jewish masses on the agenda? . . . They say that a ruined Spanish hidalgo, whose dignity does not permit him to beg for a loan, appeals with "Give me a few thousand ducats!" In just this way Bragin throws around a thousand families and a Jewish republic. What does it cost him? . . . One must know when, how, and where to raise such matters; having a long tongue does not mean having profound ideas [laughter, stormy applause]. . . . They complain about us: "you conceal your national work." Really! A highly "conspiratorial" people we "*Evseks*" are. We built schools where 100,000 Jewish children study, soviets, village soviets, Yiddish courts, and more and more—and all of this in a "conspiratorial" way![118]

Litvakov's witty thrusts could not deflect the attention of the conference from Kalinin's challenge. Iurii Larin, one of the prime movers of the Crimean colonization project, accused Litvakov of attacking official Soviet policy by attacking Bragin. Finally, the Central Bureau was ready to make an official statement and its spokesman, Chemeriskii, was greeted by "stormy, prolonged applause turning into an

[117] *Ibid.*, p. 85.
[118] *Ibid.*, pp. 88–89.

ovation." Chemeriskii charged that Bragin and the intelligentsia were trying to push the *Evsektsiia* in the direction of "national Bolshevism" and attempting to drive a wedge between the *Evsektsiia* and the Party as a whole. In a flash of dialectic inspiration, Chemeriskii triumphantly explained away Kalinin's position: as a member of the former ruling nation, Kalinin must encourage oppressed-nation nationalism; as members of the formerly oppressed nation, the *Evsektsiia* leaders must encourage proletarian internationalism. Chemeriskii fell back on his favorite formula of the incidental national element acting as a superstructural reflex to the economic base. "*If* we are able to concentrate significant numbers of Jewish toilers in one place, then there will be neither political nor practical obstacles to the creation of a republic. Preparing these conditions, eliminating this 'if' was one of the aims of Comrade Kalinin's speech . . . and even Comrade Kalinin's speech contained no slogan directly calling for the establishment of a [Jewish] state. Why do we have to agree with his view of the preservation of the nation?" [119] Chemeriskii repeated his support for the multiple approach to the Jewish problem. The issue remained unsettled, with no resolutions passed on the national question. In fact, according to one non-Communist observer, the conference came to an end at a banquet where "we sang Hasidic melodies and folk tunes. . . . At this time there were no Communists or non-Party people—only Jews, plain Jews, united in Jewish song, in Jewish joy. Each table sang its own song. In the next room they were dancing. 'A Hasidic synagogue?' I asked myself." [120]

The national question was very much in the air. The highly charged atmosphere threatened to explode at the

[119] *Ibid.*, pp. 100, 105.

[120] Dr. M. Vishnitser, "Di GEZERD konferents in Moskve," *Di tsukunft*, xxxv, no. 2 (February 1927).

touch of the smallest spark.[121] The *Evsektsiia* was determined to avoid such an explosion at its Sixth All-Union Conference held in December 1926, only a month after the stormy GEZERD conference. Whereas at the GEZERD conference there had been a conflict between non-*Evsektsiia* "nationalists" and *Evsektsiia* "neutralists," the *Evsektsiia* conference was the scene of a clash between *Evsektsiia* "neutralists," "nationalists," and "assimilationists."[122] Chemeriskii led the "neutralist" forces, though perhaps he might more aptly be termed a "left-neutralist," and his passive determinism was remarkably akin to Vladimir Medem's. He had hurriedly abandoned the tentative, and probably only tactical, emphasis on agricultural settlement which he had put forth in 1925. He explicitly stated that experience, or "life itself," had corrected some of the points he had made in 1925. Specifically, agricultural colonization was *not* the "most comprehensive way of drawing the Jewish population into productive work." In fact, "the main road

121 See Niepomniashchi's letter to Charney, January 13, 1927.

122 Unfortunately, only an expurgated account of the proceedings was published and the floor discussion is omitted entirely. Schwarz reasons that the Central Bureau was "sharply attacked by less 'Bolshevized' former Bundists (Rafes and Kiper) and territorialists (Novakovskii). Both oppositions pointed out that if it was sincere in anticipating a rapid advance of assimilation, the special Jewish program made no sense and ought to be abandoned forthwith; but if it was really looking forward to the establishment of an autonomous Jewish national division, then the Jewish people would and indeed must be preserved outside of the autonomous territory as well, and this in turn required a firm stand *against* assimilation" (p. 122). As usual, Schwarz's observation is acute and perceptive. However, one can quibble with his apparent lumping together of Rafes and Kiper in the "assimilationist" camp. Rafes was certainly the assimilationist *par excellence* and had withdrawn from active *Evsektsiia* work. Kiper is more difficult to categorize. He stood at the helm of the Ukrainian Main Bureau when Jewish work was flourishing and on many occasions he pleaded for more Yiddish work among the proletariat.

to socialism is industrialization of the Jewish population" and only "insofar as the slackened tempo of economic development does not permit the more rapid absorption of all the masses into productive activity, the agricultural colonization, the creation of a peasantry, comes to our aid." [123] Industrialization was clearly linked with assimilation. Chemeriskii proclaimed nationalism a greater danger than assimilationism and "industrialism, not agricultural settlement (which can be used by nationalists for their own purposes) is the answer to this danger." Chemeriskii, the guardian of *Evsektsiia* orthodoxy, was leaning toward an industrialization-assimilationist position, toward the "maximalist" position, probably to counter the effect of the nationalist tendencies so much in evidence a month earlier and because he sensed that the Party was moving toward a policy of extremely rapid industrialization. At the same time, he disagreed with Rafes, apparently joined by Agurskii,[124] who said that nationalism is reappearing in the form of Bundism. Chemeriskii thought that "in the present conditions of industrialization . . . it is impossible to have this original combination of Menshevism and nationalism repeat itself. . . . Now in our day nationalism will take on new forms—forms of neo-nationalism and national Bolshevism." [125]

Surprisingly, it was Esther who was the chief spokesman on the national question. This time she was in the majority "neutralist" camp, but her emphases were different from Chemeriskii's, and a close reading of her report reveals a carefully hedged sympathy with the "nationalist" school of thought. Turning first to the "assimilationists," she attacked

[123] *Alfarbandishe baratung,* pp. 103, 105.

[124] Esther referred to "Belorussian comrades." Agurskii was in the Belorussian Main Bureau and, having an anarchist pedigree himself, was a voracious "Bundist-eater."

[125] *Alfarbandishe baratung,* pp. 108–09.

them for "mechanically" applying the Leninist-Stalinist definition of the Jewish problem, a definition formulated in the context of a bourgeois-democratic revolution. In this attack she was reportedly supported by no less an authority than Dimanshtain who explicitly rejected Stalin's definition of a nation. Referring to the absence of a territory, Dimanshtain quipped, "So what if we are missing a piece?" as his audience burst into peals of laughter.[126] Esther argued that "national nihilism" prematurely concludes that the Jews are not a nation and the sooner assimilation takes place the better. Admitting that the Jews are not a nation in the strict "scientific" (i.e., Leninist) sense of the word, Esther pointed out that the *practical* policy of the Party had always been to allow national development. "Under the dictatorship of the proletariat there is a possibility for the *Jewish people to consolidate itself into a nation.*" [127] Hitherto oppressed nations could now skip the capitalist stage and "undergo the process of national consolidation . . . in socialist forms." Esther's theory seemed to preclude a conscious policy of assimilation: if Lenin had proposed assimilation only for the bourgeois-capitalist order, and if this order was now to be skipped, there was obviously no need for adopting assimilation as a policy. Esther therefore opposed Rafes' proposal to junk the Jewish schools in order to speed

[126] This does not appear in the official report, for obvious reasons, but it is reported by Hirsh Smoliar who attended the conference. See Smoliar, "Der ershter: tsum 80 geboirntog fun Shimon Dimanshtain," *Folksshtime* (Warsaw), February 24, 1965. It seems hardly necessary to explain that the laughter was occasioned by Dimanshtain's unintended *double-entendre* which the audience related to the Jewish practice of circumcision.

[127] *Alfarbandishe baratung,* p. 126. Emphasis Esther's. Even the term "Jewish people"—*yidishe folk*—had disappeared from the Communist vocabulary by 1930 but it reappeared in 1938. See Alfred Abraham Greenbaum, "Nationalism as a Problem in Soviet Jewish Scholarship," *Proceedings of the American Academy for Jewish Research,* xxx (1962).

assimilation.[128] She did, however, admit that industrialization—a path to socialism which she explicitly endorsed—would lead to assimilation. When asked what use there was in Jewish work if such were to be the case, she brushed off the question: "To pose the question in this way means leaving the class viewpoint for the nationalist." Later on, however, Esther pointed out that just as the state and Red Army would eventually wither away, but must be supported and built with enthusiasm, so too all other *means* in the construction of socialism—including work among the Jewish people and the use of national sentiment—must be supported to the hilt.[129] Apparently, Esther saw assimilation as an event very far off in the future and of no great practical significance for the tasks of the moment. She thereby placed herself in the "minimalist" or "gradualist" camp. The practical national program was the crucial concern for Esther, and the hedging statements on assimilation and against nationalism were basically bows in the direction of theory, the ritualistic obeisances which were becoming increasingly necessary in Soviet Russia.[130]

That Esther leaned toward the "nationalist" group is evidenced by the Central Bureau's rejection of her theory that "in socialist society there might be some possibilities even for extraterritorial minorities to preserve their national existence." [131] She provided a revealing insight into the *Evsektsiia* psychology when she related how "one comrade said privately: you are right in theory [regarding the strong possibility of assimilation] but for tactical reasons we should

[128] *Alfarbandishe baratung*, p. 135.

[129] *Ibid.*, pp. 138–39.

[130] Esther put the matter this way: "Can you not build a Yiddish school for Saratov Jewish children whose mother tongue is Yiddish when you are given no guarantee that their grandchildren will be educated to Communism as Jewish grandchildren—and if not?" *Ibid.*, p. 142.

[131] *Ibid.*, p. 136.

keep quiet about this. . . . We cannot speak about the probability of assimilation since it vitiates our revolutionary pathos . . . when you build you must know that you will finish the job—we will repel the nationally-inclined intelligentsia." [132] Esther was not prepared to accept this argument and harked back to her old theme of cultural renovation.

> Comrades, we will certainly not repel but, on the contrary, attract the nationally-inclined intelligentsia . . . because it sees that we enthusiastically and properly create a new Jewish culture, that we lift up the Jewish masses. . . . Let the source of their pathos be the nation; let us pull them behind us in this channel. . . . But the source of *our* pathos and of our enthusiasm should not be the preservation of the nation but the victory of the proletarian revolution, the construction of socialism.[133]

Clearly, Esther was urging the kind of minimalist course very similar to that outlined in Lenin's writings of 1920 on the trade unions where the idea of attracting adherents to Bolshevism through ideologically dubious appeals was approved as a way of inducting them into the movement where they would then be politically resocialized.

Esther had tried to steer a safe course between the Scylla of nationalism and the Charybdis of assimilationism, but her previous momentum pushed her toward the former. Despite the valiant efforts of Chemeriskii, Soviet Jews—and the *Evsektsiia* with them—were drifting toward a more confident assertion of some sort of positive national future and "Bragin's ideas at the GEZERD conference no longer appear[ed] so crazy." [134]

[132] *Ibid.*, p. 137.

[133] *Ibid.*

[134] Niepomniashchi to Charney, July 3, 1927. The Sixth Conference elected a new Central Bureau consisting of Bailin, a member

Following the conference, Chemeriskii embarked on a campaign to convince the *Evsektsiia* and the Jewish masses that socialist construction and economic modernization were primary and national consolidation only their possible by-product. He stressed the many paths to socialism, sometimes pointing to industrialization as "a shorter and healthier path" which should be followed by as many Jews as possible, and on other occasions admitting that industry could not absorb very many Jewish workers and so agricultural work had great significance for the Jewish déclassé.[135] By late 1927 Chemeriskii was speaking of only two paths to socialism, judging that the co-operative movement was too sluggish to solve the economic problems of Soviet Jewry and that *kustar* work was a technically backward and outmoded sector of the economy which could serve only as a training area for future factory workers. At the same time, he pointed out that the Biro-Bidzhan project had given concrete content to the hitherto abstract talk of a Jewish republic: "We have achieved our goal: the question now

---

of the Belorussian Main Bureau who had been transferred from general Party work, Dimanshtain, Chemeriskii (secretary), Litvakov, Yankel Levin, G. Moroz (a former OGPU official), Merezhin, Esther, and Kiper. Candidates were Altshuler, Osherovich, Brakhman (a young graduate of the Jewish Sector of the Communist University of the National Minorities of the West), and Lezman (*Emes*, March 1, 1927). Bailin, Levin, Moroz, and Kiper were new members, replacing Levitan, Mandelsberg, Rafes, Novakovskii, Veinshtain, and Cheskis. Levitan and Novakovskii, both formerly in the Farainigte Party, had led the "nationalist" wing at the conference. Veinshtain had earlier been appointed first president of the TsIK of the Bashkir Autonomous SSR. "Desire to remove from Moscow a leader of a former Menshevik organization, whose loyalty to Bolshevism was not above suspicion, may have played its part in this appointment" (Carr, *The Bolshevik Revolution*, I, 376). Rakhmiel returned to Moscow in 1923 to take a post in Narkomfin and was active in GEZERD.

135 Chemeriskii, "Tsil un veg fun der idarbet," *Emes*, March 1, 1927, and "Di natsionale frage af der alfarbandisher baratung fun di yidsektsies bam TsKAl.KP(B)," *Oktiabr*, May 14, 1927.

concerns a concrete *raion*, a concrete territory where it is *possible* to create a territorial unit—and it is no longer a nationalistic slogan which mobilizes national feelings, but a practical task using the national dimension for its purposes." [136]

Chemeriskii warned that there was a general upsurge in nationalism among Soviet Jewry. The partial revival of NEP-type commerce, the increase in anti-Semitism, and the cutback in the number of government employees had contributed to a rise in clericalist and nationalist influence and activity. Furthermore, according to Chemeriskii, there was much Jewish support, especially among the intelligentsia, for the Kamenev-Zinoviev-Trotsky Opposition. "For example, at a speech I delivered, someone handed me a note which said that the whole struggle against the Opposition is nothing but an anti-Semitic trick . . . though this certainly does not mean that all Jewish cadres aligned with the Opposition are pervaded by nationalism." [137] Zionism had been replaced by clericalism as the focus of Jewish nationalism. The Left Opposition and, especially, "national Bolshevism and neo-territorialism," were the other breeding grounds of nationalism. The only way to overcome these tendencies was to reconstruct and modernize the social and economic physiognomy of the Jewish population. But Chemeriskii warned against following a policy of assimilationism, that is, actively accelerating the process of assimilation. Ukrainization and Belorussianization were still being implemented, and pushing Jews toward assimilation meant,

[136] Speech to a Belorussian conference of the *Evsektsiia* in *Emes*, January 31, 1928. Curiously, the Fifteenth Party Congress, held in December 1927, took a positive view of the role of producers' cooperatives. The Congress reflected the views of Bukharin. See Alexander Erlich, *The Soviet Industrialization Debate, 1924–1928* (Cambridge, Mass., 1960), p. 84.

[137] On Trotskyite sympathies among Jewish Party members see Chapter VIII, *infra*.

in reality, adding to the camp of the Russified. More importantly, assimilationist policies would open up an ever-greater gap between the progressive vanguard and the masses. "The greatest danger for our revolutionary socialist work would be to tear ourselves away from the masses, and this is what assimilationism must lead to. We must not confuse natural processes of assimilation with assimilationism." [138]

Suddenly, Chemeriskii was attacked by a nominal subordinate in Belorussia. Agurskii was quoting Chemeriskii's articles to "prove" that they were full of ideas of autonomy, territorialism, and nationalism. But instead of condemning these, Agurskii declared himself in agreement with them: the *Evsektsiia* is conducting a territorialist program and should not deny this objective fact. Chemeriskii was being hypocritical in condemning neo-territorialism. To these charges Chemeriskii retorted that Agurskii's was a "purely psychological" approach, that territorialism was an ideological-political movement which aimed to solve the problem of a "united Jewish nation" outside the confines of the general class struggle in a never-never land, and this had nothing to do with the concrete project based in the USSR and riveted to the socialist revolution.[139] Agurskii's mild attack was only a portent of what was to come.

Meanwhile, the persistent Chemeriskii doggedly pursued the "neutralist" line in the face of a growing nationalistic heresy. While praising industrialization as the highest form

[138] Speech to the Seventh All-Union Conference of the Komsomol *Evsektsiia, Emes,* November 4, 1927.

[139] *Emes,* February 1, 1928. In the same article Chemeriskii vigorously condemned "a certain comrade" who had said that the charge that the struggle against the Opposition is pure anti-Semitism was "exaggerated," but who had agreed that there was an element of truth in it. According to Lazar Kling, Agurskii was a supporter of the Opposition. Given the fact that the article was mainly an attack on Agurskii, he may well have been that "certain comrade."

of socialist salvation, Chemeriskii did not ignore colonization, and he became involved in the growing dispute as to *which* region was most suitable for massive Jewish colonization. He called Larin a "national nihilist" for disparaging Biro-Bidzhan and glorifying the Crimea as a Jewish center. Chemeriskii urged that colonization take place in Belorussia, the Ukraine, the Crimea, and Biro-Bidzhan. The Central Bureau approved his program. It supported both Crimean settlement and colonization of Biro-Bidzhan, while urging the Jewish youth of the *shtetls* to enter industry.[140]

At the very end of his tenure as Central Bureau secretary, Chemeriskii returned to a national emphasis and partially reversed himself once more. Answering the accusation that the slogan "to a Jewish land" had been proclaimed before a single Jewish foot had trod on Biro-Bidzhan's rich virgin soil, Chemeriskii maintained that the will to settle there and the resolve to have an autonomous area had manifested themselves long before Biro-Bidzhan was selected as a site for Jewish colonization. The *Evsektsiia* had to give a reason for choosing Biro-Bidzhan; it had to show that Biro-Bidzhan could become a Jewish autonomous area. Otherwise, the natural question would have been, "Why go to such a distant place? The Zionist slander that 'Jews are being exiled to Siberia' would have appeared to be true."[141] Merezhin's slogan, "to a Jewish land," might be somewhat unfortunate in that it reminded one of the arch-Zionist Theodore Herzl, but the idea behind it was good and was in accord with the Party line. Industrialization remained the main road to socialism and was to be welcomed even though it might lead to assimilation, but land settlement too was a legitimate path to socialism and, indeed, the only possible path for some strata of the Jewish

140 *Emes*, June 18, and June 20, 1929.

141 *Emes*, November 16, 1929.

masses.[142] The captain of the *Evsektsiia* ship was indeed steering a tortuous course in ever more troubled waters.

The agricultural settlement project provoked a new debate, again involving both *Evsektsiia* leaders and various other Party activists. The central issue of the debate was the location of the main center of colonization, and, hence, of the autonomous Jewish area or even republic. Apparently, one of the earliest proposals was to make the Crimea the center of Jewish settlement. Iurii Larin was the chief proponent of Crimean colonization, and he was supported by Kalinin. Larin believed that former traders and other "unproductive elements" should migrate to the Crimea, while *kustars* could move to centers of industrial development; and he calculated that by 1929 about 66,000 Jewish families could be settled in the Crimea.[143] Kalinin pointed out that while both the Crimea and Siberia held huge expanses of available land, Jews were better suited to the climate of the Crimea. Kalinin admitted that the government had been unable to finance the huge irrigation projects which the Crimea had to have if it was to become productive, and he reasoned that Jewish colonization there would attract foreign Jewish capital.[144] Thus, the Crimean project seemed to offer a happy coincidence of interests: the Soviet government would receive financial aid from Wall Street and some land would be settled and made productive; Jewish déclassé elements would be economically and socially rehabilitated; and Jewish national aspirations would be satisfied, with the Zionists upstaged.[145] KOMZET began to look elsewhere

142 Chemeriskii, " 'Fun links,' " *Emes,* November 15, 1929.

143 Larin, *Evrei i antisemitizm v SSSR,* pp. 180–81.

144 M. I. Kalinin, "Evreiskii vopros."

145 Louis Fischer was enthusiastic about Crimean colonization and pointed out that, while there were great stretches of empty land, there were also plenty of empty but intact buildings and houses abandoned by their landlord owners during the Revolution and civil war but not destroyed by local peasants. Manuscript report, 1925, in Rosen Archive, YIVO Archives.

for territories suitable for colonization, investigating areas in Kazakhstan, Tomsk *oblast,* near the Black Sea, near the Dnieper, around the Sea of Azov, in the marshlands of Belorussian Polesie and elsewhere.[146] The Biro-Bidzhan area was not listed among those investigated by KOMZET and it seems that this program was *not* born of Jewish initiative.[147] According to Dimanshtain the Biro-Bidzhan project was proposed by representatives of the People's Commissariat for Agriculture of the RSFSR, supported by experts from the People's Commissariat of Defense, the Agricultural Academy, and the Russian scientist Vladimir Komarov.[148] Kalinin also claimed to have been the first to propose the project.[149]

Whatever the case, it is clear that "not the settlement of the Jews, but the development of the region and strengthening it militarily and politically were the decisive reasons for proposing and approving the Biro-Bidzhan program." [150] The decision on Biro-Bidzhan was taken in December 1927, and by March 1928 the Presidium of the Central Executive Committee of the USSR publicly agreed to assign the area to Jewish colonization. Whereas an investigative mission sent out to the area in 1927 had recommended that settle-

[146] See Yaakov Lvavi (Babitzky), *HaHityashvut HaYehudit BeBirobijan* (Jerusalem, 1965), pp. 41–42.

[147] *Ibid.*

[148] *Forpost,* no. 1, 1936, p. 124. Quoted in Lvavi, p. 43.

[149] Lvavi, p. 46. A former *Evsektsiia* activist who served in its highest bodies told me in 1966 that the Biro-Bidzhan program originated with the "highest Party organs, not with the *Evsektsiia.*" Chicherin and Stalin supported the plan, though there was much opposition to it. Trotsky is said to have opposed the earlier plan to colonize the Crimea on the grounds that, should anti-Semitism manifest itself there, it would be exploited for purposes of anti-Soviet propaganda by the neighboring—and hostile—countries in the Black Sea area. But Stalin supposedly formulated his position in 1925 as follows: "The Tsar gave the Jews no land. Kerensky gave the Jews no land. But we will give it."

[150] Lvavi, p. 45.

ment begin not before 1929,[151] the first colonists were rushed to the Far East in 1928, probably because the Soviet authorities wanted to settle the area as quickly as possible for defense and diplomatic reasons which had to do with an expanding Chinese population and an expansionist Chinese government.[152] At the Second Ukrainian GEZERD Conference in December 1928, Rashkes, reporting on the Biro-Bidzhan project, said that the first colonists began to arrive there very soon after the decision to colonize the area was announced. Rashkes' assertion that "the comrades have agreed that this was a correct policy" indicates that this was debated and opposed within the *Evsektsiia* but "were we not to begin colonization . . . the area assigned to Jewish colonization would have been smaller because many non-Jewish settlers from the Ukraine and Belorussia are rushing there." [153] The threat of being pre-empted by other nationalities undoubtedly forced the *Evsektsiia* to push Biro-Bidzhan settlement much harder than it would have liked. Because there was no time to prepare the area for settlement, the first colonists faced an impossible situation. There was little machinery and horses had to be brought from near Baikal. The *gnus* insect, heavy rains, and a disease which killed two hundred horses added to the misery of the pioneers. Small wonder that of 654 settlers who arrived in the spring only about 325 were left by October 1.[154] Whatever their true feelings about the project, the politicians of the Central Bureau apparently felt that they had no choice but to support the project whole-

[151] Schwarz, p. 176.

[152] See, for example, A. Merezhin, *Vegn Biro-Bidzhan* (Kiev, 1929), pp. 8–14.

[153] *Shtern*, December 20, 1928.

[154] *Ibid.* One-third of the settlers made the long and arduous journey back to their original homes while the rest moved to cities in the Far East. By the spring of 1929 sixty percent of the settlers in the spring of 1928 had left. Lvavi, p. 79.

heartedly in public. Chemeriskii and Merezhin proclaimed the slogan, "To a Jewish land," and declared that while colonization in other areas would continue, Biro-Bidzhan presented "the broadest and sunniest horizons" for the "creation of a Jewish land." [155] Merezhin consciously used Herzl's famous dictum—"if you will it, it shall be no legend"—and argued that while Zionists might will to have a Jewish land they could never obtain one because they were trying to work within a capitalist order; but within a Soviet context the will of the people would be translated into policy and so only in the Soviet Union could the desire to have a Jewish land be fulfilled.[156] Chemeriskii enthusiastically commended a Jewish woman who spoke at a Belorussian Peasant Congress about " 'Eretz Yisroel' [The land of Israel] right here in our land. This shows that the new principle has been perceived by the people. Our new principles have been understood by the masses, and understood much better than by other so-called leaders and cultural activists." Chemeriskii implied that the focus of Jewish work had shifted from cultural to social and economic activities and that this meant that the *entire* Jewish population of the Soviet Union was properly the subject of "Jewish work," which now involved nothing less than the complete social-economic transformation of that population.[157]

James Marshall, an American attorney who went to the USSR in 1929 as a representative of the Agro-Joint, reports the enthusiasm of Pëtr Smidovich, chairman of KOMZET, and of Kalinin for the Biro-Bidzhan scheme. Kalinin met Marshall in Moscow, and

[155] *Oktiabr* and *Shtern,* January 22, 1928.

[156] Speech at the All-Belorussian Jewish Peasant Congress, *Shtern,* January 24, 1928.

[157] Speech to the Second All-Union Jewish Culture Congress, *Shtern,* April 13, 1928.

For some fifty minutes he talked about Birobijan, leaning across the desk . . . or standing beside a map and touching my arm sometimes to emphasize a point, offering us cigarettes. He was a very informal little man, as you know, a peasant by birth, who spent his vacations in the village he came from, which too he talked about. It was obvious that he hoped to have me interest the Agro-Joint and JDC group in Birobijan. I found that Birobijan had a small population, one person per square kilometer of Russian origin. There could therefore be no difficulty, Kalinin said, in obtaining ample land for Jewish colonization and the chance for a majority of population. In the Crimea it would be difficult to obtain free lands, and also there could be no majority of Jews because of local German, Russian, and Tartar populations. The government favored a Tartar state there because they had been much persecuted under the czars. The government wanted to increase population on the eastern borders. The Pacific coast, he said, is filling up rapidly. Kalinin believed that the Jews were content with too little. They should have their own territory to develop their own culture. Russia believed in encouraging each people to develop itself. He did not believe in the melting pot. . . . It would be easy, he thought, to get a majority at Birobijan and in ten years time [1939] a Jewish republic—Yiddish speaking—could be established. . . . I believe . . . that he also had in mind the fact that Jews were less likely to merge with the Manchurian population than other peoples. Jews, therefore, would be especially desirable as a border population. He said that the government would not move all Jews there but 500,000 to 800,000. Speed was desirable in order to give the Jews a quick majority. Speed depended on cash. He would like to see Americans investigate the project.[158]

[158] Letter from James Marshall to the author, December 2, 1970.

Despite the effusiveness with which the Biro-Bidzhan project was greeted, it is clear that there was strong overt and covert opposition to it. In fact, even Merezhin, who castigated the "hesitators and doubters in our ranks" and who constantly defended the slogan, "To a Jewish land" [159] —even he seems to have been covertly opposed to the entire scheme.[160] Active, open opposition came largely from two quarters: Larin and the advocates of Crimean colonization, and the Belorussian *Evsektsiia* backed by the Belorussian Communist Party. Larin charged that Biro-Bidzhan was basically ill-suited to agriculture and that climatic conditions, disease, permafrost, and the distance from the centers of Jewish population made any kind of settlement there extremely difficult, if not impossible. He pointed out that to achieve the five-year plan of settling 9,000 families in Biro-Bidzhan, the government would have to allocate at least twenty million rubles. In 1928–29 a total of only 3.3 million rubles had been assigned to Biro-Bidzhan. "This alone makes the program unrealistic, in contrast to the programs for the Crimea and the Ukraine which are financially underwritten by foreign organizations." He argued that the "unhealthy ballyhoo which was raised around Biro-Bidzhan is in inverse proportion to the real significance of the area for the Jewish poor," and that Biro-Bidzhan was attracting workers and *kustars* who emigrated for nationalistic reasons, not the poor and déclassé elements for whom

[159] See *Dos ferte yor,* p. 23.

[160] Dimanshtain listed Merezhin, together with Bragin and Larin, as an opponent of the Biro-Bidzhan project. "Di bashtimung vegn der idisher oitonomer gegnt," *Der hammer* (New York), IX, no. 11 (November 1936), 42. See also "Prezidium TsIK SSSR o evreiskoi avtonomnoi oblasti," *Revoliutsiia i natsional'nosti,* no. 10 (1936), p. 51. William Zukerman reported that Merezhin was dismissed from his posts because "it was suspected that he was not wholeheartedly in favor of the Far Eastern [Biro-Bidzhan] scheme." *Jewish Chronicle Supplement,* November 1932. Clipping in the Mowshowitz-Wolf Archive, YIVO Archives.

the program was designed.[161] Larin advocated instead large-scale colonization in Northern Crimea, with the addition of the neighboring lands bordering on the Sea of Azov. The capital of this territory would be the city of Kerch. Larin's position seems to have been based on his hard-headed appraisal of the economic situation and development potentials rather than on any romantic visions of Jewish autonomy or nationhood. He charged that "the choice of Biro-Bidzhan was dictated by the enthusiasm of Jewish workers [*Evsektsiia?*] striving for a 'large territory,' and not by the serious investigation of the area. . . ." He acknowledged that colonization was a brake on assimilation but "we personally see nothing especially positive in this for the poor who are embarking on agricultural labor." [162] Larin warned that even if a Jewish republic or *oblast* would eventually be created in the Crimea this would not guarantee the preservation of Jewish culture since a majority of Soviet Jews would continue to reside outside this area.[163] Declaring that assimilation was an inevitable process, Larin asserted that national differences would disappear with the world socialist revolution, especially since airplanes would facilitate international travel, and he spoke seriously of developing Esperanto as an international language.[164]

[161] *Evrei i antisemitizm v SSSR,* pp. 183–84. See also Larin's "Territorial'naia peregruppirovka evreiskogo naseleniia," *Revoliutsiia i kultura,* No. 15, August 15, 1928, and "Sostoianie i perspektivy evreiskogo selskogo khoziastva v SSSR," *Na agrarnom fronte,* no. 3, March 1929.

[162] *Evrei i antisemitizm,* p. 303.

[163] *Ibid.,* p. 308.

[164] *Ibid.,* p. 311. Larin's real name was Lurie and he was the son of a rabbi in Kiev who was one of the first Zionists there. Yitzkhak Rabinovich reports seeing a Christmas tree in Larin's Moscow home in 1924—a "Red Christmas tree," to be sure. Yet, "he was practically the only one of the 'greats' from among those of Jewish origin to whom [Jews] would turn privately in order to complain against the actions of the government in the provinces and in the capital." *MiMoskva ad Yerushalayim,* pp. 55, 98.

The motives of the Belorussian opposition to Biro-Bidzhan were more complex. The Jewish population in the Belorussian Republic was steadily declining both in absolute numbers and relative to other nationalities in the Republic. Between 1923 and 1926 the Jewish population had declined by 3.8 percent, while in the same period the Jewish population of the Ukraine had increased by 6.1 percent, that of the RSFSR and other parts of the USSR by 18 percent, and in the USSR as a whole, by 7 percent.[165] The officials of the Belorussian *Evsektsiia* sought to reverse this trend, probably because it meant that their own work would become less important and their budgets smaller and possibly because they saw this as a portent of assimilation. Therefore, despite the fact that only small, scattered plots of land were available in Belorussia for Jewish colonization, the leaders of the Belorussian *Evsektsiia* stressed the difficulties involved in migration to the Crimea, let alone Biro-Bidzhan, and urged the Jews of Belorussia to settle on lands within their own republic.

> We have stated several times . . . that migration to the Crimea is a difficult undertaking. It is in many ways much more difficult than settling on the land here in Belorussia. But it seems that there are some people who do not believe our warnings and must see for themselves. . . . But we consider it our duty to indicate once more the difficulties awaiting the migrant to the Crimea and to say that as long as one can still settle on the land here [Belorussia], one should not go to the Crimea. . . .[166]

Happily for the Belorussian Main Bureau, the Belorussian Communist Party also had an interest in opposing the Biro-Bidzhan program and promoting colonization in Belorussia.

165 Szmeruk, *HaKibutz HaYehudi,* p. 22. Over 80,000 Jews migrated from Belorussia in the period from 1926 to 1939.

166 M. Beinfest, "Vegn ibervandern in krim," *Der veker,* February 15, 1925.

The budget of the Belorussian republic could never support the gigantic task of draining the huge and potentially productive marshlands in the republic. Certainly, the central government was not going to allocate huge sums for this purpose since beyond the Urals lay enormous expanses of fertile, untilled soil. But foreign capital for swamp drainage could be obtained if it could be linked to a program of Jewish colonization. Secondly, the movement of some Jews to the land would reduce the large urban proportion of Jews giving the cities a more balanced ethnic make-up, with Belorussians filling the vacuum left by the Jews. Thirdly, such colonization would not arouse the hostility or jealousy of the Belorussian peasant, as had happened in other areas assigned to Jewish colonization. Finally, since the marshlands were a huge continuous expanse, it would be easy to establish an autonomous Jewish administration there.[167]

This convergence of interests allowed Bailin and his comrades to argue tirelessly that the marshlands must be settled, that "Moscow" did not properly appreciate the possibilities for colonization in Belorussia, that the central government should provide funds for this colonization and, finally, that Biro-Bidzhan should serve only as an ancillary to Belorussia, absorbing those for whom there was no room in the latter.[168] In December 1928 a plenary session of the Central Bureau passed a resolution strongly supporting Biro-Bidzhan as "the most important area for emigration" and "the only area which has a chance to develop into a large

[167] Szmeruk, *HaKibutz HaYehudi,* pp. 99–100.

[168] Some of the more important statements are: the report of the conference of Belorussian Jewish activists in *Oktiabr,* February 2, 1928; A. Bailin, "Elf yor oktiabr-revolutsie un di yidishe erd-einordnung in VSSR," *Oktiabr,* November 7, 1928; M. Baron, "Einike sakhaklen fun letstn plenum fun alfarbandishen 'gezerd'," *Oktiabr,* January 4, 1929; Bunin's report in *Oktiabr,* January 10, 1929, and the discussion that followed. Merezhin's veiled criticisms of the Belorussian Republic's government are especially interesting.

autonomous Jewish national-territorial unit." But the plenum also tabled the question of allocating funds for the drainage of the Belorussian marshlands.[169] Clearly, the Central Bureau had failed to beat down the opposition in Minsk completely. Undoubtedly it was the Belorussian Party, in whose Central Committee the *Evsektsiia* leaders were so well represented, that protected the Belorussian *Evsektsiia*. That protection soon melted under the intense fire directed at the Belorussian Party from Party organs in Moscow. The leaders of the Belorussian Party were charged with having countenanced and, indeed, supported "National Democratism," that is, Belorussian nationalism. The Commissar for Agriculture in Belorussia, Prishchepov, was accused of opposition to collectivization and sympathy for Bukharin's peasant program. Since the Belorussian Jewish activists had worked closely with the now discredited commissar—he was chairman of the Belorussian KOMZET—they were obliged to dissociate themselves from agricultural colonization programs which they had formulated together. Adding to their troubles, they were also the target of a direct attack from the *Evsektsiia* Central Bureau which was hurling charges of nationalism and "right deviationism" at the beleaguered comrades in Minsk. The latter chose to defend themselves by aiming the very same shafts at Moscow. But one of the costs of proving their internationalism and *partiinost'* by striking an ultra-leftist pose was the virtual abandonment of the Belorussian colonization program. Without energetic support from the Party the program was doomed to extinction, especially since "internationalization" of the colonies and collectivization were breaking up the colonies and discouraging potential settlers from leaving their homes and occupations.

The Belorussian colonization program had collapsed; the

[169] *Oktiabr,* January 25, 1929.

Crimean scheme never really got off the ground; the Biro-Bidzhan project never fulfilled its promise.[170] But at least the attempt had been made to remedy the economic ills of the Jewish people and to preserve and nourish the culture and nationhood of that people. The Jewish Communists had thrown themselves wholeheartedly into a search for an elusive synthesis of social-economic modernization and cultural renovation and renaissance. They tried to remake radically the economic base, while conserving at least some components of the cultural superstructure and transforming others to meet the demands of ideology. Whatever its ultimate results, this was a positive effort. But it was drowned in the wave of criticism, accusations, self-denunciations, and witch-hunting that engulfed the entire Party in 1928 and 1929 and which the *Evsektsiia,* with but a few exceptions, tried to avoid but to which it finally succumbed. The efforts and achievements of the constructive years were swept away on the tide of hysteria that lapped at the very foundations of the Communist Party.

[170] For a while, KOMZET continued to sponsor agricultural settlement in areas outside Biro-Bidzhan. These were funded largely by foreign capital: Agro-Joint provided aid for colonies in the Crimea, Kalinindorf (*Sde Menukhe*), Shterndorf (formerly "little *Sde Menukhe*") and Krivoi Rog; the Jewish Colonization Association aided colonies in Zaporozh'e and Mariupol in the Ukraine; and ORT was active in the Odessa area. See Yaakov Lvavi (Babitskii), "Tsiyunai Derekh BaHityashvut Hakhaklait Bivrit Hamoetzot," *Bekhinot,* no. 1 (1970).

VIII

Deviations, Dissension, Dissolution

Wherever there is a Right deviation there must be a Left deviation. The Left deviation is the shadow of the Right deviation. . . . Those who incline toward Trotskyism are in fact Rights turned inside out, they are Rights concealing themselves behind Left phrases.

Stalin

THE EXUBERANCE of the period from 1924 to 1928 was blunted somewhat in 1927 when the *Evsektsiia* tried to rein in the national enthusiasm which had burst forth uncontrolled.

> By 1927 there was no question that the initial enthusiasm which had launched the localization [nativization] program in the USSR was gone. . . . Emphasis was placed on the necessity of subordinating national rights to socialist demands. Local nationalism was described as a growing danger which had become more troublesome than Russian chauvinism and could no longer be explained away as a simple reaction to tsarist oppression. Even within the All-Union Central Committee it was urged that, in view of the new socialist centralization in the USSR, the national question was no longer of importance and that, consequently, the Party should place emphasis on the building of a single socialist culture rather than numerous local cultures.[1]

The Party was passing through a difficult period as Stalin was methodically eliminating the various oppositions and gradually gaining ascendancy over the rest of the leadership. Within the *Evsektsiia,* too, discontent and division began to emerge. This was linked to the specific issues in the general nationality policy, but the polemics and power struggles also provided a fertile breeding ground for the growth of personal and ideological frictions and rivalries specific to the *Evsektsiia.* Personal enmities were linked with theoretical positions, as in an ideology-oriented system personality and policy are inseparable. Nevertheless, it was clear that some of the debates were highly subjective and

[1] Sullivant, *Soviet Politics and the Ukraine,* pp. 165–66.

often centered around abstract and quite irrelevant issues which were used only to veil the personal antagonisms which were the real issues. When in 1928–29 the Party adopted a policy of intensive *samokritika,* a spate of self-criticism allowed these rivalries to emerge full-blown while simultaneously forcing the *Evsektsiia* into an orgy of self-castigation. Nationalism, "national nihilism," chauvinism, latent Bundism, disorganization, passivity, right and left deviations of all sorts, "pessimism" in literature, falsification of history, autonomism, territorialism, "organizational fetishism"—this was the *Evsektsiia's* catalogue of errors.

A campaign against "survivals of Bundism," initiated by the Belorussian *Evsektsiia* in 1925, was only a portent of things to come. The motivations behind this campaign and its precise aims were rather obscure, and both the Central Bureau in Moscow and the Ukrainian Main Bureau criticized the entire undertaking as unnecessary and harmful. In fact, even within the Belorussian Main Bureau itself there were those who opposed the campaign. At a *Evsektsiia* conference in October 1925, Krinitskii noted that "forty-five percent of the central *aktiv* of the BCP are former members of other parties" and might still be influenced by the traditions of those parties. But Krinitskii was careful to point out that the campaign was not directed at individual members, though he acknowledged that "some comrades" had misunderstood it in that way.

> Some comrades, mostly those who were in the Bund, believe that posing this problem 'sows distrust" among Party members. . . . A comrade comes to me and says, "Why, Comrade Krinitskii, must we now raise the question of the Bund. . . . Was not the Bund a forerunner of Bolshevism?" But this comrade is wrong. The Party must not cover up any dangers. . . . Each of us must examine himself: is not a retrogression to the old ideology

possible? . . . But clearly it is absolutely impermissible to act towards a Communist who was in another party as if he were a second class Communist. Such an attitude deserves punishment. There can be no talk of distrust of those comrades who were in other parties.[2]

It was, indeed, true that the Belorussian Party had very few members whose Bolshevik pedigree reached back to pre-revolutionary days. In fact, in 1928 when 10,758 members of the CPSU who had worked in the Bolshevik underground were surveyed, only 118 of them were then in the Belorussian Party, and of this number only ten were Jews.[3] But the Belorussian leaders insisted that the anti-Bundist campaign was not directed at individuals. Bailin emphasized that "The Party has not the slightest suspicion of members who came from other parties and have long since been remolded. . . . The Party makes no distinction among its members. The task of the Party is not to reject those comrades who came out of other parties if they have preserved certain ideological survivals of the petit bourgeois parties. . . . On the contrary, the task of the Party is to help them re-educate themselves, to outgrow the survivals."[4]

If the campaign was not designed to purge the former Bundists from the Party, what did its initiators hope to accomplish? To put the campaign in a positive light it was

[2] *Der veker,* October 28, 1925. Bailin made the same points at a plenary session of the Main Bureau (*Yidburo*) in 1926. See *Oktiabr,* November 13, 1926.

[3] *Oktiabr,* January 13, 1928.

[4] A. Bailin, "Di politik fun der partai in der yidisher arbetndiker svive," *Oktiabr,* May 30, 1926. The former *Borot'bisty* in the Ukrainian Communist Party constituted a group analogous to the ex-Bundists in the Belorussian Party. Ethnically distinct, they had entered the Communist Party only in 1920. The collective influence of the *Borot'bisty* on the policies of the Ukrainian Party was probably greater than the influence of ex-Bundists on the Belorussian Party's policy. See Sullivant, pp. 56–57, and Borys, pp. 155–56 and 261.

labelled "Bolshevization of the Jewish masses" and it was designed as an exercise in political education. The specific "survivals of Bundism" which were to be uprooted included: tailism (*ekizm*)—overemphasizing the initiative of the masses; guild (*tsekhn*) mentality—underestimating the role of the proletariat and ignoring the village; the idealization of the Bund's role in history and the mistaken notion that it was the progenitor of the "Jewish Communist movement" [*sic*]; and "national isolation"—interesting oneself only in Jewish work.[5]

Since it was difficult to point to concrete manifestations of such errors, except in historical and ideological literature, the campaign never really made much of an impact on Party members and their working methods. Despite the protestations of Bailin and Krinitskii, most members interpreted the campaign against Bundism as a campaign against ex-Bundists. One Party cell resolved, "Having read the letter of the TsK, the cell states that we have no Bundists among us, and should we find any we will turn them over to the OGPU [!]".[6] One of the few concrete results of the campaign was the replacement of Bundist names with Communist ones, as when *Der veker* became *Oktiabr*. Interestingly, the newspaper's circulation fell drastically when the name was changed.[7]

The Central Bureau looked askance at the doings of the Belorussian *Evsektsiia*. The latter had persuaded the Central Committee of the Belorussian Party to circulate a letter calling for an anti-Bundist campaign all over the USSR, and not just in Belorussia. In March 1926, Che-

[5] B. Z., "Vegn der bolshevizirung fun der yidisher svive," *Oktiabr*, January 24, 1926. The last point is made by Sh. Agurskii, "Der kamf kegn opnoign afn historishn front," *Shtern* (Minsk), v, no. 12 (December 1929).

[6] Cited by Bailin in *Oktiabr*, January 9, 1927.

[7] *Oktiabr*, January 24, 1926. Agurskii was credited with having initiated the change.

meriskii hastened to Minsk where he conferred with the Main Bureau. He completely rejected the premises of the campaign:

> The unhealthy manifestations in the Party . . . must be [explained] on the basis of the difficulties being experienced at present, and [we need not burrow] into the past. This is simply metaphysics, opposed to our dialectical method. I am convinced that all the deviations you have enumerated are caused by present difficulties and not by the past. If Zinoviev and Kamenev could exaggerate differentiation in the villages. . . . if Sokol'nikov—an old, unswerving Bolshevik, a member of the TsK since the October Revolution—if he could make mistakes, how can you ascribe deviations and unhealthy tendencies in the Jewish labor milieu to the Bundism of the past? By aggravating the question of Bundism you are deflecting the attention of the Party from the real dangers and causes of the deviations—this is a distortion, this is "political prostitution." [s]

The Central Bureau offered to compromise with the Belorussian Main Bureau by agreeing to adopt a resolution generally condemning *all* the "old ideologies" but refraining from singling out Bundism for special criticism. After all, a large-scale anti-Bundist campaign could be used to depose the vulnerable Central Bureau officials from their positions of power. It would not be very difficult to make a case against them. Litvakov, for example, had written in 1924 that the October Revolution was "the second breakthrough of proletarian internationalism in the Jewish milieu. The first was the rise of the labor movement and the appearance of the Bund . . . a penetration of the proletarian world

[s] Quoted in Agurskii, "Der kamf kegn opnoign."

force into the environment of the *Jewish nation. . . .*"[9] Sensing their advantage, the Minsk leaders rejected the compromise, and after "a bitter struggle" the matter had to be referred to a higher authority, the *Agitprop* Department of the All-Union Central Committee. This department—in actual fact the matter was probably adjudicated by Dimanshtain—delicately suggested that, while there were really no grounds for criticizing the Central Bureau, it would do well to "improve" its resolution so that there would be "no possibility for misunderstanding."[10] Despite the fact that the Central Bureau's position was supported by Kiper and the Main Bureau in the Ukraine,[11] and perhaps even by Osherovich in Belorussia,[12] the Bureau chose not to

[9] M. Litvakov, *Finf yor mlukhishe idisher kamer-teater* (Moscow, 1924), p. 20. Italics in the original.

[10] Report from Dimanshtain in *Oktiabr,* January 18, 1927.

[11] See M. Kiper, "Di oifgabn fun bolshevizirung un sovetizirung in der id-arbet," *Di roite velt,* no. 12 (27), December 1926.

[12] "Zionism is the only organized and active anti-Soviet and anti-Communist [ideology] in the Jewish milieu. There is no Bundism, no Menshevism. . . . The Jewish workers have uprooted Bundism, they swept out all Bundist remnants with an iron broom." A. Osherovich, "Kamf mit antikomunistishe gruppirungen," *Der veker,* October 17, 1925. Osherovich was a former Bundist and might have felt threatened by the campaign, especially since another former Bundist, Yankel Levin, was being transferred out of Belorussia, and Bailin, who replaced Levin as Secretary of the *Yidburo,* found it necessary to deny "false rumors spread by petit bourgeois elements" regarding the transfer. "The Party has the greatest respect for the Bundists who have honestly and completely severed all ties with their former party and who have become good Bolsheviks." Levin, too, commented that when he was in the Bund he had been a "Bundist patriot"—but now he was a "convinced Bolshevik" (*Oktiabr,* January 14, 1926). A recent Soviet publication wrote of Osherovich that in 1905 "Though he consider[ed] himself a Bolshevik, his organizational work was conducted within the Bund until the October Revolution." In 1930, after the dissolution of the *Evsektsiia,* Osherovich was sent to Lithuania where he was a member of the underground Central Committee of the illegal Lithuanian Communist Party. He returned to the editorship of *Oktiabr* in 1933. Osherovich died in 1938, apparently a victim of the Great Purge. See "Chelovek

wage an all-out struggle. It seems that a tacit agreement was reached whereby the All-Union Conference of the *Evsektsiia* (December 1926) would condemn Bundism and then the issue would be quietly dropped. At any rate this is what finally did happen, with Dimanshtain commenting that the question had been resolved to the satisfaction of all concerned.[13]

While the Belorussian *Evsektsiia* was trying to launch its anti-Bundism drive, the Party as a whole was involved in a much more important struggle, the campaign against Trotsky and "Trotskyism." While this did not directly affect the *Evsektsiia* in any special way, in the 1930's charges of Trotskyism were frequently brought against former *Evsektsiia* activists. There might have been some truth to them since fragmentary evidence indicates that there were strong Trotskyite sympathies among Jewish Party members. In the predominantly Jewish Gomel organization, for example, 92 voted for the line of the Central Committee at a 1924 meeting, but those who were unreservedly in favor of the "Sapronov-Preobrazhenskii Opposition" together with those who basically agreed with the Central Committee but felt that it was too militant and had exaggerated the danger of factions, managed to marshal 61 votes. "It is interesting to note that it was mainly older workers who voted for the first [Central Committee] resolution while students, *Komsomol* members, and former members of other parties voted for the second."[14] In another predominantly Jewish Party organization, that in Vitebsk, the Opposition gained a clear,

udivitel'noi sud'by," *Kommunist* (Vilnius), no. 12, December 1966, pp. 61–63.

13 It was only the fractious Agurskii who kept up a hail of criticism against Rafes, Kirzhnitz, Esther, Litvakov, Chemeriskii, Merezhin, and others, for their alleged "idealization of the Bund." His was a lone voice crying out in the wilderness—until 1928–29, when conditions were ripe for full-scale denunciations.

14 M. Kiper, "Di diskusie in der Homler organizatsie," *Emes*, January 5, 1924.

if temporary, victory.[15] In the "Mairevnik," the chief training center of the *Evsektsiia,* the sympathies of the students were overwhelmingly with Trotsky.[16] Finally, the Jews were said to constitute 67.6 percent of the Opposition in Odessa *krai,* though they were only 29.1 percent of the total Party membership in that area.[17] Admitting that "Trotskyism was quite widespread among Jews," Mikhal Levitan pointed to the fact that the proportion of Jews expelled from the Party for Trotskyite leanings was much higher than the proportion of Jews in the Party. Levitan tried to explain the popularity of Trotskyite ideas among Jews, though his logic was short of impeccable: (1) Former *kustars* and others who were now workers were receptive to the idea that state industries exploit their workers. (2) Jewish workers, recently arrived in heavy industry, were skeptical of the possibility of building socialism in one country. (3) Being an overwhelmingly urban group, Jews were naturally sympathetic to Trotsky's idea of exploiting the peasants for the benefit of the workers. (4) Jewish NEPmen and Kulaks tended toward Trotskyism because they hoped it would split the Party and allow for a capitalist restoration [*sic*].[18] Levitan failed to mention one

[15] Z. B. M-N, "Di diskusie in Vitebsk," *Emes,* January 6, 1924.

[16] Based on a conversation with a former student leader in the "Mairevnik."

[17] L. Abram, "Di idishe arbet in Odes vi zi iz," *Shtern,* March 17, 1928.

[18] M. Levitan, "Bakemfen di rekhte gefar in der idishe svive," *Shtern,* December 8, 1928. Levitan went so far as to claim that the fact that Jewish socialists supported Bolshevism only after the German revolution of 1918 "proved" that they were Trotskyites even then, having little faith in the viability of a Russian revolution unaccompanied by revolutions elsewhere. Isaac Deutscher notes the preponderance of Jews in the Trotskyite faction's leadership and says that though they were thoroughly assimilated, "they were still marked by that 'Jewishness' which is the quintessence of the urban way of life in all its modernity, progressiveness, rootlessness, and onesidedness. . . . The Bolsheviks of Jewish origin were least of all inclined to idealize rural Russia. . . . As a rule the progressive or revolutionary

of the plausible explanations for the strength of Trotskyism among Jewish Communists, especially in the Ukraine. Jewish Party members were generally hostile to the policy of Ukrainization, as we have seen. The Trotskyites, as well, were generally opposed to this policy [19] and thus gained the support of many Jews. This supposition is lent credence by the fact that *Shtern*, the *Evsektsiia* newspaper in the Ukraine, carried many more articles on Trotskyism than did *Oktiabr*, its counterpart in Belorussia where Jewish opposition to Belorussianization was not nearly so great.[20] In the intra-Party struggle "Stalin had been able with little difficulty to win the personal allegiance of anti-Centralist, anti-Russification Ukrainian Bolsheviks," largely because Trotsky and Zinoviev were perceived as centralizers and Russifiers.[21] Moreover, Trotsky "did not [even try to] take charge of the anti-Stalinist opposition among the minorities; and thus he failed to take advantage of an excellent opportunity to embarrass his principal rival at a critical phase in their struggle for power." [22]

Paradoxically, the campaign against Trotskyism had far less impact on the Jewish Sections than the drive against "right deviations," generally associated with Great Russians and the peasantry. In April 1928, the signal was given to begin a self-criticism campaign whose main purpose would be to uncover "right deviations" in Jewish work.[23]

Jew, brought up on the border lines of various religions, whether Spinoza or Marx, Heine or Freud, Rosa Luxemburg or Trotsky, was particularly apt to transcend in his mind religious and national limitations and to identify himself with a universal view of mankind. . . ." *The Prophet Unarmed* (New York, 1965, Vintage edition), p. 259.

19 See Levitan, in *Shtern*, December 20, 1928.

20 I am indebted to Dr. Mordechai Altshuler for this point.

21 Sullivant, p. 134.

22 Pipes, p. 289.

23 M. Levitan, "Zelbstkritik un di idishe masn," *Shtern*, April 21,

The Jewish activists were very reluctant to undertake such a campaign, both because they sincerely believed that there could be no right deviations among a people with a tiny peasantry and because they feared that such a campaign would do irreparable damage to *Evsektsiia* work. Since nationalism had traditionally been identified as a right deviation, an attack on such deviations might lead to an attack not only on nationalism but on work among the nationalities *per se.* Two months after the campaign was supposed to begin, the editors of *Shtern* remarked that there had been many articles about the need for self-criticism within the *Evsektsiia* but the criticism itself had not been forthcoming.[24] Levitan, apparently charged with the difficult task of leading the campaign, tried to convince the Sectionists that right deviations stemmed not only from the peasantry but also from traders, "*kustars,* kulaks, and NEPmen, all of whom were heavily represented among Jews."[25] Even some Main Bureau members disparaged the idea that right deviations existed in *Evsektsiia* work but they were forced to accept Levitan's somewhat ingenious theories.[26] Levitan explained that the abnormal social-economic structure of the Jews was an excellent base for right deviations; while forty-one percent of the proletariat in the Ukraine was white-collar, among Jews the percentage was fifty-seven. Furthermore, since one-quarter of all Jewish wage earners were in *kustar* industries and small workshops, they were "not only *surrounded* by the petit bourgeois atmosphere but actually *fused* into it." Traders

1928. Since it was not until the fall of 1928 that a serious campaign against "right deviations" was launched in the Party as a whole, it is unclear from where the signal for the *Evsetksiia* campaign originated, especially since the Central Bureau seemed hesitant about the campaign.

[24] *Shtern,* June 29, 1928.

[25] *Ibid.,* December 12, 1928.

[26] *Ibid.,* December 18, 1928.

formed only 0.6 percent of the general self-sufficient population, but they made up 13.3 percent of this population among Jews. Moreover, the traditions of the Jewish labor movement contributed to receptivity of Jews to right deviations.[27]

What were the concrete deviations of which the Jewish Sectionists were to purge themselves? According to Levitan these were mainly "an attempt to add an autonomist flavor to the activities of the Jewish Sections" and viewing the *Evsektsiia* as a defender of Jewish interests against the Party and state, a failure to understand anti-Semitism as a *class* phenomenon, and a failure to appreciate fully the harmfulness of Jewish chauvinism and considering it a justifiable response to anti-Semitism.[28] The Central Bureau went further and described nine "expressions of the right deviation in the Jewish environment," adding such errors as ignoring class differentiation in the *shtetl,* denigrating the roles of the Party and state in agricultural colonization, resistance to collectivization, tolerance of "petit bourgeois moods" and motifs in literature, attempts to form a "united front" with foreign Yiddishists, etc., etc.[29] Not to be outdone in revolutionary zeal, the Ukrainian Main Bureau, inspired by Levitan's report, adopted a resolution condemning over

[27] M. Levitan, "Bakemfn di rekhte gefar in der idishe svive," *Shtern,* December 5 and 6, 1928.

[28] M. Levitan, "Untern druk funm id. natsionalizm," *Shtern,* January 4 and 6, 1929. Sullivant (p. 169) points out that in 1928 "the left deviation in Soviet political life had been replaced by the right deviation as the principal threat to Soviet authority. In regard to the national question, this meant that local nationalism—which, it was argued, was identified with the right deviation—had now become a greater menace than great-state nationalism or Russian chauvinism. Hence [Ukrainian] Party emphasis should be shifted toward a more resolute battle with nationalists and a greater acceptance of Russian elements."

[29] Resolutions passed by a plenary session, *Oktiabr,* January 25, 1929.

twenty manifestations of right deviationism in the *shtetl, kustar* policy, agricultural colonization, cultural work, and nationality policy. It also offered an eight-point program for fighting these deviations, which amounted to nothing more than pious prescriptions for stepped-up *agitprop* work.

The right deviation was found to exist in Belorussia as well, and a special conference of Belorussian Jewish activists was called to deal with the problem. The right deviationists were charged with regarding socialist reconstruction as detrimental to the future of a consolidated Jewish people, failing to make proper class differentiations in *kustar* and colonization work, neglecting to condemn Jewish chauvinism while overemphasizing anti-Semitism, and incorrectly stressing that the *toiling* masses be drawn into productive work when Chemeriskii had asked that the déclassé elements be attracted to colonization, industry, and cooperation.[30] In September, the BCP Central Committee announced a campaign against the right deviation in Jewish work, opening the way to "a flood of self-criticism."[31] "Dangerous" terms, such as "déclassé" (dangerous presumably because it allowed enemy classes to remain unidentified as such), were to be avoided, as was the idea of "social reconstruction of the Jewish population" which might be wrongly interpreted to mean that the Soviet Union was seeking to modernize the economic-political structure of the *entire* Jewish population. Clearly, the minimalist-gradualist strategy of modernization and political-national integration was being rejected. Consolidation of the Jewish population was no longer a legitimate goal. Even the watered-down euphemism, "Jewish environment," was placed on the index of forbidden terms. · "At present a nationalist-kulak content

[30] A. Osherovich, "Di baratung fun di yidpart-tuer bam TsKKP(B)V," *Shtern* (Minsk), VI, no. 1 (January 1930), 45–56.

[31] *Vitebsker arbeter,* December 18, 1929. In the Smolensk Oblast Archive, WKP 449.

can certainly worm its way into this concept. . . . All those aiding the exploiting, speculating, criminal-déclassé, contrabandist elements of the Jewish population in their invasion of our economy and *kustar* cooperatives will now base themselves on it."[32] The effect of this hysterical self-flagellation was to paralyze *Evsektsiia* work in many localities. "There are many Jewish activists who were afraid of making right-opportunist mistakes and so they did nothing at all."[33] Osherovich criticized "some comrades . . . frightened by the heavy blows received by the right deviationists . . . [who] threw themselves 'to the left.' If so, they argued, we must liquidate Jewish work altogether."[34] Even Levitan was forced to reprove those comrades who were calling all errors "right deviations."[35]

Anti-Semitism and its obverse, "Jewish chauvinism," were both considered right deviations. The Soviet press devoted much space to the problem of anti-Semitism and several incidents in Belorussian factories became *causes célèbres*.[36] By participating in the campaign against anti-Semitism and "national chauvinism" the *Evsektsiia* was falling in line with the shift from "right" to "left" which was occurring in the Party as a whole. But there was a unique feature of the *Evsektsiia*'s attack on these "right deviations": the *Evsektsiia* press took great pains to emphasize the dangers of "Jewish chauvinism" much more than anti-Semitism. While Yan Gamarnik, speaking out at the Twelfth Congress of the Belorussian Party, did not mention Jewish chauvinism and attacked only anti-Semitism and Russian and Belorussian chauvinism,[37] the *Evsektsiia* went so far in its campaign

[32] *Ibid.* In his near-hysteria, the writer let slip the now-forbidden word "déclassé."

[33] *Oktiabr*, December 21, 1929.

[34] *Ibid.*, December 26, 1929.

[35] *Shtern*, February 22, 1929.

[36] See Schwarz, p. 243.

[37] *Oktiabr*, February 9, 1929.

against Jewish nationalism that it berated the highly placed Smidovich for having told some Jewish activists that since the "harvest day" fell on *Yom Kippur*, Jewish colonies might want to begin gathering their harvest a day or so later.[38] The Central Bureau resolved that it was the task of the Jewish Sections to "show initiative in organizing the struggle against Jewish chauvinism and nationalism . . . In this struggle Jewish Communists working in the Jewish environment must be foremost." [39] This formulation seems to reflect a dual-purpose *Evsektsiia* strategy. By demanding that Jewish activists combat chauvinism even more tenaciously than anti-Semitism the *Evsektsiia* was demonstrating its super-orthodoxy; simultaneously, it was serving notice that it would keep its own house in order and would need no outside help in attacking Jewish chauvinism in its ranks. Both of these were aimed at giving the *Evsektsiia* as an institution and Jewish activists as individuals a measure of security in a period of great uncertainty. This policy required the *Evsektsiia* to strike fine balances in its discussions of the two related deviations. It attacked Jews who blamed all their ills on the alleged anti-Semitism of government and Party officials [40] as well as those who wanted to hush up manifestations of anti-Semitism.[41] This second attitude led to a system of "double entry bookkeeping": when among non-Jews, Jewish workers would say nothing

[38] Dimanshtain, "A rekht-oportunistisher trit," *Oktiabr*, October 22, 1929.

[39] *Oktiabr*, January 25, 1929.

[40] See, for example, Kh[aim] D[unets], "Geferlekhe simptomen," *Oktiabr*, February 15, 1929; and Y. Hershnboim, "Faktn un maises vegn shovinizm un shovinistn," *ibid.*, February 1, 1929. Hershnboim comments that "Jewish NEPmen and kulaks take advantage of our fight against anti-Semitism. . . . We have many instances of NEPmen and kulaks trying to protect their little shops behind the shield of 'They are beating the Jews.' "

[41] M. Kiper, "Farshtarkn dem ongrif," *Shtern*, June 28, 1928.

about anti-Semitism, but among themselves they would speak bitterly and militantly. According to one's temperament one either became subservient or tried to take "national revenge," and both of these were deemed incorrect reactions based on the false premises of the "Jewish nationalist" approach to anti-Semitism.[42]

There seemed to be a general consensus within the *Evsektsiia* on how best to deal with anti-Semitism-chauvinism, and, like the Trotskyite deviation, this issue did not seriously affect the fortunes of the *Evsektsiia* itself. A more particularistic struggle, almost a family quarrel, had more important political ramifications. It revolved ostensibly around a historiographical issue.

There were such obvious personal stakes involved that the substantive issue was probably secondary to the struggle for personal ascendancy. The substantive issue was the "latecomer theory" propounded by Merezhin and supported by many other Jewish activists, including Esther. This theory held—quite correctly, in view of the facts—that the Jewish workers were two years "late" in coming to the Bolshevik Revolution. Not in 1917, but in 1919, when the Ukrainian Komfarband merged with the Communist Party, did the Jewish proletariat take its first firm steps toward Bolshevism. It embraced Bolshevism fully only in 1921, when the last remnants of the Bund entered the Party. The Jewish proletariat continued to lag behind, and its period of "War Communism" lasted until 1923 when a "Jewish NEP" was belatedly initiated, as the attitude toward the *shtetl* and the *kustars* softened appreciably. Even then the Central Bureau had to fight the energetic resistance of the local Sections which were reluctant to accept a truce on the Jewish street.[43] Esther explained that the tardiness

[42] M. Levitan, "Untern druk funm id. natsionalizm," *Shtern*, January 6, 1929.

[43] This theory is outlined in A. Merezhin, "Tsu di baratung fun di

of the Jewish toiling masses stemmed from their economic backwardness, the predominance of the petite bourgeoisie in the Jewish class structure, the artisanal character of the Jewish working strata, the extreme alienation of the Jewish from the non-Jewish workers—a result of "national persecution and religious fanaticism"—and, finally, the seduction of the masses by a petit bourgeois nationalist leadership which failed to realize that "what was correct in the epoch of industrial capitalism becomes incorrect in the epoch of imperialism." [44]

Agurskii violently attacked the "latecomer" theory as early as 1926 and he tried to present the issue as a battleground between two camps within the *Evsektsiia*.[45] He had been one of the founders of the *Evsektsiia* but had suffered an unjust fate at the hands of its later leadership. When the intellectuals of the Bund and *Farainigte* entered the *Evsektsiia,* they seized the commanding heights of the Central Bureau and shipped Agurskii off to provincial Minsk where he was a member of the Main Bureau. He never was re-elected to the Central Bureau and was generally regarded as a boor and despised by the intellectual "aristoc-

---

idsektsies," *Emes,* October 2, 1925. It is also summarized in Sh. Agurskii, *Afn historishn front (Kegn der idealizirung fun bund),* (Moscow-Kharkov-Minsk, 1930), pp. 128–29.

[44] Esther, *Oktiabr revolutsie* (Moscow, 1928), pp. 316, 328. Esther went so far as to say that only "tiny, isolated groups" of Jewish workers had taken part in the October Revolution and that "the conscious, organized sector of the Jewish working class remained with the Jewish parties," clearly a manifestation of "Bundist pride."

[45] Sh. Agurskii, "Historishe faktn anshtot verter," *Emes,* October 13, 1926; "Tsum 10-yorikn yubilai fun der oktiabr-revolutsie," *Oktiabr,* August 31, 1926. Dimanshtain intervened and tried to settle the dispute. He denied that there were two camps within the *Evsektsiia* and concluded that while Merezhin had given too much weight to the role of ex-socialists in leading the Jewish workers to Communism, Agurskii had given it too little. Sh. Dimanshtain, "Di idishe komunistishe arbet," *Emes,* October 24, 1926, and *Oktiabr,* October 26, 1926.

racy" in Moscow. Agurskii's smoldering resentments burst to the surface during the intensive criticism and self-criticism campaign of 1928–29. He judged correctly that the time was right for a thorough revision of history which could serve his own purposes. That Agurskii was motivated by calculations of personal advantage rather than establishment of historical truth is indicated by the fact that he himself had written that the Jewish working masses had not participated in the February Revolution and "did not want to play any part in the second revolution. Only a few conscious Jewish workers left their leaders and joined the ranks of the revolutionary camp. But the great Jewish masses . . . did not participate in the struggle. . . . There was no Jewish Bolshevist movement before the revolution." [46]

Now Agurskii's main point was to deny any Jewish revolutionary lag. He pointed out that *Evkom* and the infant *Evsektsiia* had existed in 1918, along with artels of workers and peasants, and that even SETMAS "did not have suitable leaders but had good intentions." He shifted the entire responsibility to the leadership of the Jewish socialist parties. "Yes, there was tardiness among the Jews, but absolutely not among the Jewish workers—the leaders of the Jewish petit bourgeois 'socialist' parties were the latecomers." [47] Agurskii stoutly maintained that the more revolutionary elements of the Jewish proletariat had joined the Bolshevik North-West and Polesie Committees in 1905 and that by no means had the Bund enjoyed a political monopoly among Russian Jews. Agurskii explicitly attacked Litvakov, Esther, Rakhmiel Veinshtain, Rafes, and Yankel Levin for continuing to overpraise and overestimate the Bund.[48] He berated

[46] "Ben Khaim," "Di role fun di idishe arbeter in der rusisher revolutsie," *Funken* (New York), no. 10, April 10, 1920.

[47] *Afn historishn front,* pp. 130–31.

[48] Sh. Agurskii, "Der kamf kegn opnoign afn historishn front," *Shtern* (Minsk), v, no. 11 (November 1929).

Chemeriskii for stating that "the unhealthy manifestations in the Party . . . must be investigated on the basis of present difficulties and [it is] unnecessary to dig into the past." This, Agurskii charged, was "political prostitution" and an attempt to cover up the latent Bundism which sullied the ideological purity of the *Evsektsiia*.[49] Agurskii placed the blame for revolutionary latecoming squarely on the shoulders of the "traitorous 'leaders' of the Bund and other Jewish 'socialist' parties" who were "morally guilty because they joined hands with the bourgeois[ie] right at the beginning of the proletarian revolution." [50]

The direction of Agurskii's thrusts was obvious. He aimed to discredit the "petit bourgeois Jewish 'socialist' leaders" now in the *Evsektsiia* leadership and thereby advance his own fortunes. After all, his revolutionary strain was purer than theirs, and yet it was the Litvakovs and the Esthers who were the rulers in Moscow while he languished in Minsk. The personal motivations in Agurskii's scheme were all too apparent to the apprehensive members of the Central Bureau, and they called upon their best polemicist, Moishe Litvakov, to take up the cudgels in their behalf.

Litvakov was eminently well qualified for the task. His

[49] *Ibid.*

[50] *Der idisher arbeter,* p. xvii. The vagaries of Soviet scholarship and politics being what they are, Agurskii was later mildly reprimanded for excessively minimizing the influence of the Jewish socialist parties on the Jewish proletariat. This, it was reasoned, might "demoralize" the Party activists from the just and necessary struggle against latent Bundism. "If we were to say that the Bund did not unite workers around it, then why is the struggle against the Bundist ideology necessary when it has left no traces amongst the Jewish workers?" (*Zamlbukh,* p. 21). Interestingly, the "latecomer" theory has recently been attacked by Jewish Communists in Poland and the USSR. See the editors' introduction to Y. Kantor, "Yidn in kamf far dem nitzokhon fun der oktober revolutsie," *Folksshtime* (Warsaw), October 3, 1967. See also, Hersh Remenik, "Di oktiabr-revoliutsie un di yidishe literatur," *Sovetish haimland,* VII, no. 11 (November 1967), 140.

prestige was enormous and he had the respect and admiration, if not affection, of Jews and non-Jews, Communists and non-Communists. Niepomniashchi called him "our Communist flag" [*Komunistishe fon*] while complaining that "we can and must put an end to the legend that the Marxist-Leninist Divinity speaks through the mouth and pen of Litvakov. . . ."[51] Another young writer described how

> From all cities and towns Jewish youth and their elders came to the Jewish Department of the Second State University in Moscow to hear Moishe Litvakov's course in Jewish literature. I cannot say that Moishe Litvakov was an excellent speaker. On the contrary, he stammered like an old Jew. But in his simple speech there was so much wisdom, so much good-natured humor and biting satire, that it attracted us and forced us to . . . listen, laugh, and marvel. . . . His articles in *Emes* were an event, a bombshell. We used to read the article until the paper had been worn through. . . . Litvakov was a surly individual and had almost no friends. Almost all of those whom he had helped in the literary world repaid his "bread" with "stones." This embittered him even more, and he could not abide criticism or disagreement. . . .[52]

Litvakov opened fire on December 1, 1928. He accused Agurskii of having campaigned against the editors of *Emes* and the Central Bureau, "against both the institutions and their personnel," since 1921, though until 1928 it had been a whispering campaign. At the 1926 *Evsektsiia* conference Agurskii had tried to introduce a resolution condemning the Central Bureau but his plans had been foiled. When, "through an error," *Emes* had failed to mark the August 7 anniversary of the transformation of *Varheit* into *Emes*, Agurskii had written such a "*khutzpedik* [presumptuous]

[51] Letter to Daniel Charney, April 29, 1929, YIVO Archives.
[52] Herschel Weinrauch, *Blut oif der zun* (New York, 1950), p. 52.

letter full of insinuations" to *Emes* that he knew beforehand they would not print it and he published it in *Bol'shevik belorusii,* where it was charged that only "the fifth anniversary of Comrade Litvakov's editorship of *Emes* had been celebrated."[53] Litvakov denied this and many other charges regarding the proper periodization of *Evsektsiia* history. He ridiculed Agurskii—"who derives so much satisfaction [*nakhes*] from every printed word of his"—for first writing a series of articles in *Emes* in 1927 about the *Evkom's* early agricultural efforts, and then, in 1928, accusing *Emes* of failing to mention this activity, finding it convenient to forget his own articles. "Now there's a self-sacrificing fellow for you."[54]

Having tried to answer Agurskii's accusations, Litvakov betook himself with evident zest to the offensive. "In order to immortalize Comrade Agurskii's name in Marxist literature even beyond the borders of Belorussia," Litvakov paraphrased some theses Agurskii had published in *Oktiabr*: (1) Tsarist oppression led to Jewish nationalism, especially among the intelligentsia, and to the formation of separate Jewish parties. (2) The Bolsheviks fought against this and urged that the Jewish problem be solved by the general revolution. ("Here every word is gold and the historian Agurskii attains such theoretical heights that every little Octobrist will certainly get dizzy.") Litvakov ridiculed this "theory" because it failed to differentiate any historical periods under tsarism, though Professor Pokrovskii had demonstrated that tsarism encompassed commercial capitalism, industrial capitalism, and even finance capitalism. Agurskii had also neglected to point to the classes and interests represented by the Jewish parties. In a word, Agurskii's theory was so superficial as to be totally useless.

[53] M. Litvakov, "Der 'ekspert' Agurskii," *Emes,* December 1, 1928.
[54] *Ibid.*

With unsuppressed relish, Litvakov mockingly applied Agurskii's theory to ancient Egypt. Pharaoh was a dictator, the Jewish nationality was oppressed, and a faction arose which wanted to "solve the Jewish problem" with separate Jewish organizations which urged "emigration." "Moses, for example, can thus be made out to be the first *Poalai-Tsion*ist."[55] Litvakov, the former Talmudist, adduced proof upon proof of Agurskii's most egregious error, the failure to differentiate properly classes within Jewry, even dredging up a 1918 brochure written by Agurskii showing excessive "idealization" of the Bund. In the tone of an impatient teacher who cannot abide the blatant stupidities of a dull student, Litvakov scolded, "Comrade Agurskii occupies himself with Marxist 'philosophy of history' without having the slightest notion of the ABC of Marxist methodology in history."[56]

On a more serious level, Litvakov defended the latecomer theory, acknowledging that the leadership had lagged behind the masses in coming to Communism and claiming that this had not been denied by the present *Evsektsiia* leadership. The latecomer theory, said Litvakov, was expounded by Dimanshtain in a foreword to Agurskii's own book, *Der idisher arbeter.* Litvakov argued that the theory was a Leninist one. Lenin had spoken of a vanguard leading the masses; the Jewish workers were necessarily excluded from the vanguard because the Bolsheviks had conducted very little work among them prior to 1918, and Lenin had "proved" that workers would not achieve full social-democratic consciousness without guidance from a group such as the Bolsheviks. Agurskii's contention that the majority of the Jewish workers had always been inclined toward Bolshevism was an "anarchist-spiritual retrogression"

[55] *Ibid.*, December 4, 1928.
[56] *Ibid.*

because it implied that a revolutionary spirit could arise among a people only if they were "critical thinkers"—a well-known anarchist heresy which placed spontaneity above consciousness. Furthermore, this contention was ideologically dangerous because it could lead to national pride, creating a basis for "right deviations and nationalist retrogressions." [57]

The embattled Agurskii replied by turning Litvakov's argument around: if Agurskii had been stained with the blot of nationalism and Bundism for all these years, why had not Litvakov condemned him until now? Why had he printed Agurskii's articles with nary a dissenting note? True, Litvakov had defended the *Evsektsiia*'s early work, but only because Agurskii had privately forced him to do so. Agurskii complained that his writings had been quoted selectively, tendentiously and unfairly, that he had sided with Larin and not Bragin at the 1926 GEZERD conference and, finally, that Litvakov's motivations were personal, rather than principled. "What were the basic motives behind Litvakov's attacks? I believe that it becomes clear to everyone in his last article where he explicitly states that he wrote the articles in order to remove the crown from Agurskii's head. How far Comrade Litvakov will succeed in this effort remains, for the time being, a large question mark." [58]

This was not a petty quarrel between two pugnacious individuals. The acrimonious debates were the public manifestations of a struggle for power. When Agurskii cast doubt on the legitimacy and propriety of the Central Bureau's leaders, he was clearly insinuating that they were no longer fit to lead and that leadership should devolve on more reliable persons—and he left little doubt as to who such persons might be.

[57] *Ibid.*, December 6, 1928.

[58] Sh. Agurskii, "An entfer dem kh'Litvakov," *Emes*, April 19, 1929. See also *Emes*, April 18, 1929.

It seems that the polemic had gotten out of hand and the Central Bureau judged that Litvakov had gone too far. The Bureau tried to pour oil on the troubled waters by admitting that Litvakov had been "too sharp," and by contending that all were agreed on the question of the Bolshevization of the Jewish proletariat, but there remained some differences "in clarifying certain periods of the Jewish labor movement."[59] The Bureau called for an end to the open polemic and asked that "serious study of the Jewish labor movement" be undertaken.[60] Agurskii had apparently rallied some influential support, probably the leadership of the Belorussian Party, to his cause. Though stung by Litvakov's barbs, he could not be destroyed by them.

A commission of the Central Committee of the BCP was charged with the task of settling the dispute. It decided that Agurskii might have used "too sharp a tone," but that this was justified in the light of the opposition and indifference he had encountered. Moreover, Agurskii had played an active role in Bolshevizing the Jewish masses, while his critics had played a more passive role.[61] In a private letter written in 1931, Agurskii remarked that "during the last seven years I have—by order of our Party—conducted a stubborn struggle against the attempts of a group of people to idealize the Bund and other petit bourgeois parties. This aroused a campaign against me by the former Bundists and others. The matter reached the highest Party organs, and they took my side."[62] Agurskii had been identified with the Left Opposition, but his extremely tendentious historiography, his violent anti-Bundism, and his zealous

[59] *Emes*, February 9, 1929.

[60] *Ibid.*

[61] *Oktiabr*, September 14, 1929. The Lenin Institute also supported Agurskii. See Adoratskii's letter to Gamarnik in *Shtern*, August 23, 1929.

[62] Letter to Kalman Marmor, August 20, 1931. In the Kalman Marmor Archive (Box 29–57, A-L), YIVO Archives.

guarding of orthodoxy were very much in the spirit of the time. As Stalin began to concentrate his fire on "right deviations" in late 1928 and 1929, Agurskii's "leftist" stance became politically legitimate and expedient. Furthermore, Agurskii's denigration of any sort of Jewish separatism and his assertion that the Bolsheviks had carried on Jewish work even before a Jewish Section was created (implying that such work could be effective even without a Section)—these were precisely what the Party welcomed as it became aware that its encouragement of a flowering of national cultures had "gone too far" and as it became more vigilant in guarding against nationalist deviations. Most importantly, Agurskii's attack on "Moscow" was welcomed and supported by his colleagues in the Belorussian Main Bureau who were carrying on their own feud with the Central Bureau.

As has been seen, there was a running argument for several years between the Main Bureau, which wanted to continue and accelerate Jewish agricultural settlement in Belorussia, and the Central Bureau, which tried to allocate maximum resources to Biro-Bidzhan. In 1929 this argument became part of a less substantive but more acrimonious debate over nationalist deviations and their practitioners. Already in 1926 Stalin had attacked nationalism within the Ukrainian Communist Party,[63] and in 1929 many Ukrainian intellectuals were arrested on charges of national deviationism. At the same time, Party members and non-Party intellectuals were being purged in Armenia, the Crimea, and Turkestan. In Belorussia a violent purge of Party leaders accused of "National Democratism" (Belorussian nationalism) threatened to strike at the *Evsektsiia* leadership which had worked so closely with the Belorussians. "By the fall

[63] See the letter to Kaganovich in *Marxism and the National Question*. On the Party's campaign against Ukrainian nationalism, beginning in 1926, see Sullivant, pp. 144–78, and Majstrenko, pp. 217–18.

of 1929, the whole Belorussian nationalist leadership found itself behind prison walls."[64] The *Evsektsiia's* Central Bureau, always insecure because of its doubtful revolutionary pedigree, also seemed to feel itself threatened by the purge of nationalists within the Party. In order to display their ultra-orthodoxy both the Main Bureau and Central Bureau tried to assume anti-nationalist postures. One of the ways of doing this was to accuse each other of nationalist deviations. Osherovich, editor of *Oktiabr* and apparently second in command to Bailin, posed as a defense attorney for Agurskii and struck out at Litvakov, accusing him of defending the poet Shmuel Halkin as a fellow traveler, when he was actually an unreconstructed petit bourgeois nationalist. Litvakov was accused of inventing a Minsk-Moscow split. "For several years now Comrade Litvakov has suffered from such a mania: Minsk is preparing a coup against Moscow. Kharkov is preparing a coup against Moscow. . . . Instead of thinking seriously about a matter and examining the substance of this or that literary or social phenomenon they look at the stamp: 'made in Minsk?' Good for nothing! [*toig oif kaporès*] Some city—Minsk! [*oikh mir a shtot!*] Real merchandise is to be found only in Moscow."[65] Litvakov replied that "The comrades of *Oktiabr* have found a new technique for themselves: first they sin and then they beat the breast—someone else's."[66]

The severity of Litvakov's criticisms forced the flustered editors of *Oktiabr* to appeal to their Ukrainian comrades for help, and Levitan responded by chiding Litvakov: "It is well known that in an ideological struggle he often attacks

[64] Vakar, p. 146. According to Krushinsky, "the leadership of the national movement in Belorussia was decimated" in the course of 1930–31 (p. 29).

[65] A. Osherovich, " 'S'iz gedekt' . . . vi azoi der kh'Litvakov gevint ois a zeks un zekhtsik," *Oktiabr*, December 6, 1929. See also Osherovich, "An entfer dem kh'Litvakov," *ibid.*, January 5, 1929.

[66] "Af tsvai frontn," *Emes*, December 12, 1929.

people too sharply. We would always forgive him, of course, for these weaknesses, the inability to control himself in polemics . . . byproducts of the difficult struggle against the petit bourgeois ideologies in literature."[67] Litvakov responded immediately and returned Osherovich's compliment by saying that the Belorussian comrades had dreamed up a Minsk-Moscow split and had interpreted Litvakov's criticism as based not on principle but on geography.[68] He demanded that Levitan choose one side or the other and, with a courage that was to become increasingly rare in the years ahead, stoutly maintained that "intermediate ideological forms [i.e., slight variations from the Party line] are not as numerous as they were in 1925 and the base for such positions has shrunk very much—*but to have shrunk is not to have disappeared.*"[69]

The Central Bureau had a better hand to play against the Belorussian Main Bureau. The Moscow group now revealed that at a plenary session of GEZERD in 1928 Bailin had supported his plea for funds for Belorussian swamp drainage with the argument that this was necessary "to preserve the specific weight [*spetsifishe gevikht*] of the Jewish population in the BSSR," clearly an expression of Jewish nationalism, perhaps combined with a kind of Belorussian localism.[70] Despite the fact that the first GEZERD congress in 1926 had decided not to consider the idea of "guaranteeing the existence of the Jewish nationality" as its fundamental *raison d'être,* Bailin had insisted that this was GEZERD's justification, saying this openly at a GEZERD plenum in 1928.[71]

[67] M. Levitan, "A feler vos muz farikht vern," *Shtern,* (clipping, n.d.), Smolensk Oblast Archive, WKP 449.

[68] "Af tsvai frontn," *Emes,* December 12, 1929.

[69] "Kegn 'linkn' trask un rekhte meisim," *Emes,* December 25, 1929.

[70] A. S., "Di rekhte opnoign in der natsionaler politik in Veisrusland," *Emes,* September 20, 1929.

[71] See Szmeruk, pp. 109–10.

Though the dispute between Bailin and the Central Bureau had begun long before 1929, it was only now that the Central Bureau mounted an attack on him, probably because Yan Gamarnik, secretary of the BCP and influential outside Belorussia as well, had acted as Bailin's protector. Furthermore, Bailin's policies could easily be construed as "rightist deviations" at a time when Stalin had swung the Party to the "left." When Gamarnik was transferred to the political administration of the Red Army in October 1929, the way was cleared for an all-out condemnation of Bailin.[72] Chemeriskii broadened the attack to include the entire Belorussian Main Bureau which he correctly called a united front supporting the policies enunciated by Bailin. The secretary of the Central Bureau summarized the case against the Belorussian *Evsektsiia* and its Main Bureau: they had included class enemies in the cooperatives and yet failed to discriminate between former class enemies, lumping together those who could be rehabilitated with the incorrigibles; they failed to condemn the "Larin-Alski-Pavlovich-Bragin" nationalist bloc at the All-Union GEZERD conference; they demanded the maintenance of the "specific weight" of the Jewish population, "an original, popularized edition of the old slogan 'unite the Jewish nation' "; they concealed their "objective" opposition to Central Bureau policy; they overemphasized anti-Semitism and incited to chauvinism; they attacked Chemeriskii for his support of the Biro-Bidzhan project, his opposition to "neo-territorialism," while refusing to brook any criticism of their own policies; finally, they had begun to adopt all sorts of resolutions without the consent of the BCP Central Committee, masking this autonomist deviation by changing their formal structure and becoming a Jewish Bureau [*Yidburo*] instead of a Jewish Section [*Yidsektsie*]. The Belorussian Jewish

[72] This thesis is advanced by Szmeruk, p. 120.

activists had then tried to recover their orthodoxy and legitimacy by shifting radically to a "leftist" position and accusing their accusers of rightist deviations. In a dialectical phrase, the Belorussian *Evsektsiia* manifested "pseudo-leftist distortions on an overall banner of right opportunism." [73]

Left without their protector, Gamarnik, and frightened by the severity of the Central Bureau's criticisms, the Belorussian activists tried to defend themselves by pointing to Merezhin and Chemeriskii as the real nationalists. Had not these Central Bureau members proclaimed the slogan "To a Jewish land"? Had they not spoken of Biro-Bidzhan as the white hope of Jewish nationality? While these charges may have been as justified as Chemeriskii's, they could not beat back the Central Bureau's attack. On December 17, 1929, *Oktiabr* announced the surrender of the Belorussian *Evsektsiia* by publishing a letter from Bailin to the Central Committee of the Belorussian Communist Party. He confessed that he had mistakenly directed that Jewish work focus on the *entire* Jewish population and that he had "not recognized the great possibilities of our socialist growth which also solves the problem of taking care of the Jewish working masses." He also confessed to opposing the policy

[73] A. Chemeriskii, "Di hoidelke," *Emes,* December 26 and 28, 1929. This formulation was frequently used to describe the Left Opposition. Right deviations attributed to Belorussian nationalists were strikingly similar, *mutatis mutandi.* See "Vegn rekhten opnoig in der KP(B)V iber der natsionaler frage," *Oktiabr,* July 28, 1929. Though there were deviations in the Ukraine, too, the Central Bureau was satisfied that they had been "quickly overcome," except in Berdichev where the *Evsektsiia,* it was claimed, was seen as the "defender of the Jewish people" against the Party and where Yiddish was "idealized" and made an end in itself. See Alek, "Shedlekher natsionalizm," *Emes,* August 8, 1929. Activists in the Ukraine generally supported the Central Bureau against the Belorussian Main Bureau. See, for example, L. Abram, "Kegn rekhte opnoign un 'linke' knaitshn in der idarbet," *Der odeser arbeter,* January 6, 1930.

of the All-Union KOMERD (KOMZET) which did not want to allocate funds to the Belorussian Republic and in this connection using the "inept phrase 'de-Yiddishization [reducing the number of Jews] of the Belorussian SSR.'"[74] Bailin repeated his "confession" at a conference of the Belorussian *Evsektsiia* and accepted all the blame for its errors.

> Some comrades tried in their speeches to ease Bailin's situation. No, comrades, the leaders are guiltier than the local activists. . . . I made many great political errors when I stood at the helm of Jewish work. Now it is my duty to acknowledge these errors so that others should learn from them. . . . This is how my letter to the TsK should be understood.[75]

Bailin apparently still had enough revolutionary credit and political protection to allow him to make his confession with dignity and without the abject self-denunciation which was later to characterize the trials of the 1930's. He was removed from his post but was not punished as a criminal. Bailin lost his position as secretary of the Main Bureau (now the *Yidburo*) to his colleague Osherovich. Osherovich, in turn, was replaced as editor of *Oktiabr* by Khaim Dunets, who had risen to prominence with his fire-breathing articles against right deviationism and every other imaginable sin.[76]

The intramural debates, the accusations and counter-accusations, and the personal vendettas had created a malaise which affected all those involved in *Evsektsiia* work. The Yiddish writer Peretz Markish described the situation as "very strained and aggravated. . . . In general we don't know what world we're in. In this atmosphere of trying to be terribly proletarian and one hundred percent kosher, much falseness, cowardice, and vacillation have

[74] *Oktiabr*, December 17, 1929.
[75] *Ibid.*, December 22, 1929.
[76] *Ibid.*

manifested themselves and it is becoming somewhat impossible [*sic*] to work."[77] There was no slackening of Jewish work and none of the protagonists in the family quarrel seemed demoralized or pessimistic, though they spoke of such moods seizing activists on the lower levels. It seemed that the minimalist strategy of development was inadmissible at a time when the Party as a whole had decided on the maximalist policies of collectivization and rapid industrialization. But there was much talk of the need to reorganize and reconstruct Jewish work. It was with a seeming confidence that the Central Bureau asked for reports from all *krai* Sections on Party education among the Jews, "in connection with the preparations for the [forthcoming] All-Union [*Evsektsiia*] Conference."[78] It seems that the conference was originally scheduled for December 1929,[79] and it was again alluded to in *Emes* on December 18, 1929, and January 1, 1930. On January 3, 1930, there was a meeting of the editorial board of *Emes* which discussed questions listed on the agenda of the still "forthcoming conference" of the *Evsektsiia*.[80]

The conference was never held. On January 8, 1930, a notice appeared in *Emes* calling all members of the *Evsektsiia*'s Central Bureau to what may have been an emergency meeting in Moscow. Five days later, a conference of representatives from the Central Committees of the republic Communist Parties, probably attended also by representatives of the Central Bureau, decided to reorganize the *apparat* of the national (republic) central committees.[81]

[77] Letter to Joseph Opatoshu, November 25, 1929, in Shlomo Bikel, ed., *Pinkes far der forshung fun der yidisher literatur un prese* (New York, 1965), pp. 328–29.

[78] *Emes*, September 28, 1929.

[79] See I. Veitzblit, "A por kritishe gedanken vegn undzer idkomprese," *Shtern*, November 29, 1929.

[80] *Emes*, January 7, 1930.

[81] *Ibid.*, January 17, 1930.

The reorganization was announced by the All-Union Central Committee on January 17, 1930. Apparently, the *Evsektsiia* was to be dissolved as part of this reorganization. But the first announcements of the decisions taken by the Central Committee made no explicit mention of the dissolution of the national minority sections, though all other changes in the structure of the Committee were described in detail.[82] Indeed, meetings of the Ukrainian Main Bureau were called for January 19 and January 23 as well.[83] On January 19 the First Conference of Toiling Jewish Youth in Biro-Bidzhan sent "warm greetings to the guardian of Party ideology in the struggle for socialist construction among Jews—the Central Bureau of the Jewish Sections of the Central Committee All-Union Communist Party."[84] There is no doubt that most *Evsektsiia* activists, even so prominent a figure as Kiper, were not expecting the dissolution of the *Evsektsiia*.[85] The delay in announcing this step may have been

[82] "Vegn reorganizirn dem aparat fun TsKAlKP(B)," *Oktiabr,* January 18, 1930. This is a faithful translation of "O reorganizatsii apparata TsK VKP(b)," *Pravda,* January 17, 1930. "Reorganizatsiia partiinogo apparata" in the same issue makes no mention of nationality sections. See also "Vi azoi darf reorganizirt vern der partai-aparat," *Shtern,* February 19, 1930.

[83] *Shtern,* January 22, 1930.

[84] *Emes,* January 19, 1930.

[85] Based on an interview with a former Jewish activist in the Ukraine. Kiper wrote that in December 1929 "the question of liquidating the *Evsektsiia* was not yet on the agenda." "A vort tsu der ordenung," *Di roite velt,* no. 6 (June 1930). Yitzkhak Rabinovich reports that in late April 1929, Dr. Joseph Rosen, the head of Agro-Joint in the USSR, informed him that "it has been decided in high places to liquidate the *Evsektsiia* because it had not justified the hopes put in it." *MiMoskva ad Yerushalayim,* p. 172. Boris Smoliar, then Moscow correspondent of the Jewish Telegraphic Agency, claims to have been told of the dissolution of the *Evsektsiia* by Party secretary Enukidze before any of the *Evsektsiia* personnel were informed. He also claims to have published the news in a Warsaw newspaper which was the source from which the Belorussian *Evsektsiia* learned of the dissolution. "Vi azoi di 'Evsektsie' iz likvidirt gevoren," *Forverts* (Forward), May 23, 1970.

dictated, therefore, by a need to prepare the activists for this change which would profoundly affect their personal fortunes as well as the cultural and political life of Soviet Jewry. It is also probable that the *Evsektsiia* leadership in Moscow was lobbying in an attempt to prevent the dissolution, and that when all other details of the reorganization had been worked out the *Evsektsiia*'s fate hung in the balance for a few days. But signs that the *Evsektsiia* had lost began to appear in the press. Without explicitly stating that it had been abolished—indeed, *Emes* still appeared as the organ of the Central Bureau of the Jewish Sections—the *Evsektsiia* discussed the newly stepped-up pace of industrialization and collectivization and explained that,

> Because of these phenomena, some forms of Party leadership are, of course, obsolete, and it became necessary to reconstruct the backbone of the Party in accordance with this. . . . Bolsheviks have never made a fetish of *given* forms. . . . The so-called Jewish work must also find its new forms, in accordance with the new developments whereby new masses of Jewish workers enter industry and, in Jewish villages, new mass collectives are being organized.[86]

Emes called for more and better Communist work among the Jews, as if to show that this was not a specious excuse for abandoning Jewish work—now downgraded to "so-called" Jewish work—but a sincere effort to adjust it to new conditions and make it more efficacious. The weaknesses in Jewish work, and the exploitation of these weaknesses by "bourgeois elements"

> is not the fault mainly of the Jewish activist but, most of all, of the local Party bureaus and committees. But to a certain extent, the weakness of Jewish work, and of

[86] *Emes,* January 26, 1930.

national minority work in general, stems from the fact that the proper *forms* of such work have not yet been found.[87]

Emes called for volunteers in the Party *aktiv* to replace the professional Jewish activists. It pointed approvingly to the Odessa *kraipartkom* where "Jewish culture brigades" had been formed and were led by volunteer Jewish Communists.[88] Evidence that the *Evsektsiia* had already been abolished began to appear in the form of announcements of personnel changes.[89]

By March 1930 the *Evsektsiia* had disappeared even from the masthead of its central organ, *Emes.* It remained only to write the obituary. Appropriately, Semën Dimanshtain, the most prestigious Jewish activist and the oldest in point of service, performed that melancholy duty. In contrast to the fulminations of Agurskii or Dunets which were to become the order of the day in later years, Dimanshtain spoke gently of the *Evsektsiia* and explained its dissolution purely in terms of the need to make more efficient the nationality work and the organization of state and Party. The existence of nationality departments such as the Jewish Sections in the Central Committee had bred "waste and duplication" since other sectors of the Committee were working with all nationalities and national minorities. The nationality departments could not hope to encompass all of nationality work which had become so multifaceted. Furthermore, as Sovietization and Communization progressed, the difference between nationality and general work had narrowed. Dimanshtain was arguing, no doubt correctly, that many "na-

87 "Iberboien di idarbet af neie formen," *Emes,* February 5, 1930.

88 *Ibid.*

89 See, for example, the announcement that Gulko, former administrator of the Kiev *Evsektsiia,* had been appointed senior inspector of the Central Jewish Education Bureau. *Shtern,* February 20, 1930.

tional peculiarities" had been outgrown and that the difference between the needs of the nationalities and those of the Russians had been reduced essentially to linguistic ones. Dimanshtain asserted that the national sections had done valuable work and had effectively brought Communism to their peoples. But the nationalities had drawn closer to "general life" and "internationalism" had grown apace. Instructors from the various national minorities would be assigned to nationality work within the Party and would serve as the link between the Party and the national masses. These instructors and other activists among the national minorities would meet in periodic conferences. The national commissions of the central executive committees and the *krai* executive committees would be strengthened, and the work of the Soviet of Nationalities broadened. Dimanshtain wrote the epitaph for the national sections: "The Sections are leaving after having fulfilled their task, but their accomplishments, which are the goals of the entire Party, will remain for a long time." [90]

This polite and respectful farewell contrasted sharply with the judgment pronounced on the *Evsektsiia* by another founder and erstwhile activist. Writing in 1932, Samuil Agurskii explained that "in order to get rid of all nationalistic tendencies still observable in the work of the *Evsektsiia,* it was reorganized into a Jewish bureau by decision of the Central Committee of the All-Union Communist Party (Bolsheviks). In January 1930 the Jewish Sections were liquidated both locally and at the center." [91]

[90] Sh. Dimanshtain, "Di natsmindarbet af a hekherer shtufe," *Oktiabr,* March 11, 1930, and *Shtern,* March 12, 1930. The article appeared originally in *Emes,* No. 57. The Russian version is "Natsmenovskaia rabota na vysshuiu stupen'," *Tribuna evreiskoi sovetskoi obshchestvennosti,* no. 9 (March 20, 1930).

[91] *Bol'shaia sovetskaia entsiklopedia* (1st ed., 1932), XXIV, 338. The article on *Evsektsiia* was signed by Agurskii. Not surprisingly, no article on the Jewish Sections appeared in the 1952 edition.

Agurskii was not alone in his judgment. In an article published in June 1930, Kiper explained that he had written it in December 1929, but had been dissuaded from publishing it by his colleagues in the Ukrainian Main Bureau who feared that it might be interpreted as "forming a bloc with 'Belorussia' (as is known, we have great specialists in the field of exegesis)."[92] But already in December, Kiper claimed,

> on the basis of the discussion of the Kvitko affair[93] which was conducted in impermissible forms and in general because of the constant internal discussions in the Jewish environment, about which the leading Party organs were not informed for the most part, I emphasized most sharply and clearly the negative sides . . . of Jewish work. . . . I posed the question of reorganizing the work of the *Evsektsiia,* refreshing the cadres, in order to liquidate every manifestation of separatism, of a private internal discipline and even of certain family relations which began to emerge among some groups. The liquidation of the *Evsektsiia* . . . therefore came at the right time.[94]

A lead editorial in a December 1929 issue of *Oktiabr* emphasized that "The remnants of sectionism and separatism must be liquidated. Jewish work must be an organic part of Party work as a whole and responsibility for it devolves on the Party committees."[95] Dunets pointed out, however, that "when we speak of survivals of sectionism . . . we do not mean that Jewish work be weakened in any way . . . but we must remember that the Jewish bureaus [Sections]

92 "A vort tsu der ordenung."

93 The prominent Yiddish writer Laib Kvitko had been accused of mocking Litvakov and attacking him as a "stink bird" and the dictator of Yiddish culture.

94 "A vort tsu der ordenung."

95 *Oktiabr,* December 17, 1929.

are no more than helping hands of the party committees."[96] He later argued that while "Sectionist separatism" should be condemned, it must be acknowledged that in its time the *Evsektsiia* was a necessary and useful aid to the Party. He criticized Agurskii for charging that the *Evsektsiia* was shot through with "national opportunism and survivals of Bundism."[97]

Senkevich, an official of the Belorussian Central Committee, combined the arguments of increased rationality and efficiency with that of a struggle against nationalism.[98] It is likely that both considerations were involved in the dissolution of the *Evsektsiia* and that the two were interrelated: a growing national assertiveness, observable not only in the *Evsektsiia* but among some other nationalities and national minorities within the USSR,[99] led to an administrative reorganization designed to initiate a gradual dampening of nationalist ardor and to further narrow the avenues of legitimate national expression. Stalinist totalitarianism was taking shape, and it could not abide pluralistic allegiances and competing loyalties. Certainly, by this time the Soviet government felt sufficiently confident of its own viability and internal strength not to make the kinds of concessions to the nationalities which had been proferred during the troublesome years of the civil war. The Stalinist policy of "socialism in one country" had reduced the importance to the regime of revolutionary and nationalist movements abroad, and it no longer needed to worry much about the

[96] "Di linie fun der yidarbet bam shain fun zelbstkritik," *ibid.*

[97] "Af ainen fun di sektorn fun der natsarbet," *Shtern* (Minsk), VI, no. 10–11 (October-November 1930).

[98] "Di reorganizatsie fun partaparat un di yidarbet," *Oktiabr,* February 28, 1930.

[99] On nationalist deviations among national minority Party workers in the Ukraine, see A. Glinskii, *Dergraikhungen un felern,* pp. 19–20, 33.

effects of Soviet nationality policy on these movements. After 1927, when industrialization, collectivization, and central planning required an increase in central prerogatives and activity, the nationalities and national movements were seen "not as neutral forces to be drawn to the Bolshevik cause, but as centers of opposition to be reconstructed or suppressed."[100] The attempt to minimize the abolition of the *Evsektsiia* could not hide the fact that a turning point had been reached in Soviet policy toward the Jewish minority.

The Communist Party strove to play down the importance and effect of its reorganization of the national minorities apparatus. The dissolution of the *Evsektsiia* was openly acknowledged only about a month or two after it had actually taken place and it was glossed over as a routine administrative reorganization. Superficially, at least, there was little real change at the center. The same personnel continued to lead Jewish work. The Yiddishization campaign, like Ukrainization, continued unabated, at least through 1930–31, and there were no other sudden major shifts in the Jewish policy of the Soviet government or the Communist Party. On the local level, the abolition of the *Evsektsiia* had more immediate and dramatic consequences.

> Jewish work has weakened in many cities and towns and we are in danger of having it liquidated entirely in certain places. Novozybkov can serve as an example. Until the Party *apparat* was reorganized, Party Jewish work was carried on systematically. What is happening now? No one takes an interest in Jewish work. . . . Jewish work in the Western Province is in terrible shape. There are no Jewish activists. The Party secretaries do not implement the directives of the Central Committee re-

[100] Sullivant, p. 129.

garding national minority work. Jewish work is a step-child to whom no one pays any attention.[101]

Viewed in historical perspective, the dissolution of the *Evsektsiia* in itself did not profoundly affect the course of Soviet Jewish history, nor did it mark a sudden change in Soviet policy. Far more important for the Jewish nation were the general economic policies and their social consequences which were to be pursued with single-minded persistence in the 1930's. The abrupt liquidation of the *Evsektsiia* did, however, clearly signal the refusal of the Party leadership to tolerate even the mildest forms of Jewish separatism or political autonomism. It was an effective means of further weakening a separate Jewish political and cultural consciousness and of amalgamating Jewish political and economic life with Soviet life as a whole. "The abolition of the *Evsektsiia,* unfavorably received by nationalist elements, made 'Jewish work' even more a general concern of the Party and soviet organs . . . Yiddish pages in newspapers, . . . Yiddish books in libraries, a whole range of new forms of mass work. At the same time the participation of Jewish masses in socialist construction has grown colossally."[102] There could be no room for particularistic interests and concerns in one of the greatest campaigns of social mobilization in history. All factions and leaders in the Communist Party favored planned economic growth

[101] *Emes,* October 22, 1930, quoted in *Dos sovetishe idntum,* p. 270. For a series of such statements collated from the Soviet Yiddish press, see Y. Khmurner, "Di likvidatsie fun di likvidatorn," *Neie folkstseitung* (Warsaw), March 30, 1930. The following statement is representative: "The dissolution of the Jewish Sections, which had as its aim to step up Jewish work, has not been used for this purpose in most localities. People contented themselves with liquidating the Sections. . . ." F. Rozenfeld, "Di idarbet in mairev-gegnt," *Emes,* September 13, 1930.

[102] Kh. Dunets, *Kegn sotsial-fashistishn 'bund'; kegn idealizatsie fun bundizm!* (Minsk, 1932), p. 58.

requiring central direction and authority. But while Bukharin's more moderately paced plan might have been compatible with local decision-making autonomy in economic and cultural affairs, the extremely rapid pace of development and its concomitantly high degree of centralization adopted and implemented by Stalin beginning in 1928 could not be reconciled with ethnic cultural autonomy. The Stalinist formula for modernization precluded ethnic maintenance. It was a strategy of rapid political integration, the immediate creation of high levels of commitment to defining and even secondary political values. This strategy of political integration precluded a minimalist or pluralist strategy of national integration wherein distinct ethnic identities could be maintained within a politically integrated society. Ethnic parochialism had to be replaced by universal commitment to extremely rapid economic development based on a rigid central master plan. This was maximal political integration, with the transformation or liquidation of any cultural or social values which might impede progress toward the stated development goals. Concentrated in the strategic urban center, potentially able to contribute heavily to development with their high level of motivation and culture, the Jews were too important—and too potentially disruptive—to be allowed to pursue even a distinct road to development: The dissolution of the Jewish Sections symbolized the total commitment to a meta-ethnic development goal which would be pursued relentlessly even if it involved costly attempts at homogenizing the wide range of cultures in the USSR and destroying the primordial ties of Soviet citizens.

IX

Conclusion

. . . It is impossible to compel the Jews to attend Jewish schools. Also, their interests are too divergent and often too much at odds to make it possible to satisfy them in any region where they would find themselves all together, face to face. This does not depend on the non-Jews. A true Jewish cultural community is no more possible of attainment than a political community: the Jews are interested in everything, want to get to the bottom of everything, discuss all topics and end up by having very diverse and deep cultural concepts.

In the USSR there are nationalities which are less numerous than the Jews, or who are less gifted. But these non-Jews are better at organizing a common existence. That is why it is possible for them to build durable national institutions.

Nikita S. Khrushchev

THE HISTORY of the *Evsektsiia* can be seen as a microcosmic manifestation of processes endemic to many modernizing societies. According to S. N. Eisenstadt, the first task of modernizing elites is to undermine traditional forces and create "free-floating" and mobile resources unfettered by particularistic and traditional loyalties. The new groups and activities created by this action are not always easily controlled or channeled by the ruling elites themselves and the elites are often forced to try to break up new centers of political and social allegiance or, if possible, preclude their development altogether.

> All these developments may create a situation in which it very often seems as if political leadership and organization is faced . . . with a choice between the development of one, very strong, unified, firmly centralized ruling party which aims at total control of all the social forces or the converse development of several weak, loosely integrated groups and associations which have almost no ability to implement efficiently executive decisions and policies. And yet it would seem as though such a picture is exaggerated. There may exist . . . ways of overcoming this dilemma. Among these the most important are: growing cooperation between "traditional" and modern leaders in common political frameworks; growing administrative experience in various fields . . .; common participation . . . in responsible local and national legislatures and executives; development by the parties in power of concrete constructive economic plans which draw into the orbit of modern political and administrative frameworks different new groups which may

become, to some extent, independent centers of power; and last, the spread of education at all levels.[1]

The Evsektsiia *and the Changing Soviet Political System*

In 1902–03 the Bolsheviks had decisively rejected the idea that the Party should merely preside over or coordinate "loosely integrated groups and associations." From the outset the Party was designed as a centralized, unitary, powerful director of all social and political life. In David Apter's terms, the Party was designed for mobilization—seeking to rebuild society "in such a way that both the instrumentalities of government and the values associated with change are remarkably altered"—rather than for reconciliation—compromising between "groups which express prevailing political objectives and views." [2]

But the realities of a huge, multi-ethnic, and unevenly developed state and society forced the Bolsheviks to make concessions to traditional economic, cultural, and national forces. The *Evsektsiia* was designed to straddle the worlds of the past and the future and to transform the present reality into the future ideal as rapidly as possible. It was indeed the meeting place for those who were both committed to a specific formula for modernization, because of their belief in Communist economic and cultural goals, and to ethnic maintenance, because of their connection with the pre-revolutionary labor movement and their devotion to Jewish culture, however transformed. The *Evsektsiia* also provided many Soviet Jews with their first administrative experience and actively promoted Jewish political participation. Finally, it was deeply committed to the economic

[1] S. N. Eisenstadt, *Essays on Sociological Aspects of Political and Economic Development* (The Hague, 1961), p. 38.

[2] David E. Apter, "System, Process and the Politics of Economic Development," in Jason L. Finkle and Richard W. Gable, eds., *Political Development and Social Change* (New York, 1966), pp. 444–45.

rehabilitation and reconstruction of the Soviet Jewish population.

In 1930 it had not yet completed these tasks, but it was dissolved anyway because the Party, or Stalin, deemed the time ripe for an unambiguous decision in favor of a monolithic Party and state, a highly centralized economy which would pay little attention to local conditions and peculiarities, and an essentially homogeneous culture whose universal content and purpose would be to serve the aims of the regime. The 1920's had been a period of slow revival and recovery rather than a period in which the major objectives of Bolshevik policy could be attained. But by 1930 the time for accommodation with even semi-autonomous groups and spontaneous social forces was over. The choice was made for a maximalist strategy of development, demanding intense and unambiguous commitments.

A profound systemic change was occurring whereby an "autocratic mobilization system" was being replaced by a "totalitarian mobilization system," to use Apter's terms.[3] This means that whereas in the 1920's the Soviet system could tolerate multiple and divided ethnic, institutional, and even, to a lesser extent, ideological loyalties, in the 1930's all competing or autonomist tendencies were viewed as unacceptable expressions of dissent from the system.

In the first decade of its rule, the Soviet regime could be described as authoritarian in the sense that it had limited, not responsible, political pluralism. Though the regime had an elaborate ideology, non-ideological groups were permitted to exist and many fields of endeavor, such as literature or science, were allowed to remain ideologically uncommitted or pluralistic. Relatively general, vague, and minimal commitments were all that were necessary to insure

[3] For an elaboration of these concepts in terms of the "process variables" of goals, costs, coercion, and information, see *ibid.*, pp. 449–50.

social and political acceptability. The leadership, or leader, exercised power within formally ill-defined but nevertheless real limits. In brief, the distinction between state and society had not been obliterated.[4] In the 1930's all institutions and fields of endeavor were politicized and state and society were no longer as distinct as they had been. In 1930 the republic commissariats of internal affairs were abolished and their functions were assumed by a single All-Union commissariat. Similar measures were taken in public health and in education. Culture could not be value-free or even vaguely "proletarian," but had to be transformed into an instrument for the mobilization of the population. "The areas of unregulated activity in the republics were reduced so far that little opportunity for original work remained. . . . Matters which had been considered 'form' in an earlier period and only of local concern were now examined for the most subtle political implications and brought under central direction."[5]

In 1925 the Central Committee had resolved that "The Party as a whole must not bind itself to any one tendency in the field of literary form. . . . The Party cannot support any one faction in literature. . . . The Party should declare itself in favor of the free competition of various groups. . . . Any other solution of this problem would be an official, bureaucratic pseudo-solution."[6] But by 1932 a single Union of Soviet Writers had replaced the many literary societies and groupings which had flourished in the previous decade and "A new slogan and a new method became com-

[4] For a definition of an authoritarian regime in these terms, and a comparison with totalitarian regimes, see Juan J. Linz, "An Authoritarian Regime: Spain," in Erik Allard and Yrjo Littunen, eds., *Cleavages, Ideologies and Party Systems:* Transactions of the Westermarck Society, X (Helsinki, 1961), pp. 297–301.

[5] Sullivant, *Soviet Politics and the Ukraine,* p. 186.

[6] Quoted in Edward J. Brown, *The Proletarian Episode in Russian Literature, 1928–1932* (New York, 1953), pp. 237–40.

pulsory for all Russian literary men. That slogan was Socialist Realism. From 1932 . . . 'socialist realism' has been the required style for Soviet literature." [7]

"On 'the scientific front of the cultural revolution' the great break took about two and a half years, from the middle of 1929 to the first part of 1932." [8] "Bourgeois" specialists gave way to "red" specialists, and ideology and politics intruded on the purest of sciences. Riazanov was removed as head of the Marx-Engels Institute and expelled from the Party in 1931 for refusing "to renounce his view that Lenin's genius was restricted to political science. A tolerable foible in the 'twenties, well known to those who honored him in 1930, this view of the Party's founder was inadmissible now that the separation of politics and philosophy was ended." [9]

The Russian Orthodox Church, too, faced a mounting anti-religious campaign in 1928–29, and all sorts of new laws and taxes were imposed on this semi-autonomous authority structure.[10] Thus, extra-political loyalties—whether they were cultural, academic, institutional, ethnic, or religious—and unpoliticized institutions were deemed intolerable and were subverted. This was a necessary step in the construction of a political system different from that which had existed between 1917 and 1928.

In the 1920's Jewish national allegiances could be expressed as long as it was made explicit that these allegiances not only did not weaken loyalty to the Soviet state and Communist ideology but, indeed, could be made to serve them. Political integration was compatible with—indeed could be served by—ethnic pluralism. Chemeriskii and

[7] Edward J. Brown, *Russian Literature Since the Revolution* (New York, 1963), p. 211.

[8] David Joravsky, *Soviet Marxism and Natural Science, 1917–1932* (London, 1961), p. 233.

[9] *Ibid.*, pp. 263–64.

[10] See Curtiss, *The Russian Church and the Soviet State*, pp. 228–39.

Kalinin were willing to accept the fact that some Soviet Jews might respond to agricultural colonization projects out of national Jewish motivations rather than on political-ideological grounds. The totalitarian system of the 1930's was more demanding and more confining. It was no longer sufficient to make the appropriate response to a political demand, but it was now necessary to make it from an appropriate and highly specified motivation. Just as in the arts and in literature the socialist message had to be encased in a particular esthetic form ("socialist realism"), so did "socialist content" predominate over and condition "national form" in the various national cultures in the USSR. The decline of Jewish culture as a national culture with unique characteristics was a reflex of broader systemic change affecting all areas of Soviet life.

The debates in the *Evsektsiia* and the nature of the decisions and actions it took demonstrate that it operated within a limited autonomy possible in an "autocratic mobilization system" or "authoritarian regime" but intolerable in a "totalitarian mobilization system." The *Evsektsiia*'s limited autonomy can be explained by specific institutional arrangements which were themselves reflections of broader systemic characteristics. Basically, the *Evsektsiia* gained a measure of autonomy by default. There seems to be no evidence from published sources which would indicate a continuous concern with "Jewish affairs" on the part of any Politburo leader or group of leaders. Even Kalinin's interest in Jewish matters does not seem to have expressed itself in close supervision of *Evsektsiia* activities or policies, nor did he seem able to impose consistently his own policy preferences, which might have been those of other Soviet leaders as well, on the *Evsektsiia* leadership. It would appear that the Central Bureau of the *Evsektsiia* reported to Dimanshtain in his capacity as head of the National Minorities Department of the Central Committee. But even Dimanshtain's concern with *Evsektsiia* affairs seems to have been spasmodic, limited mainly to settling serious intra-Section disputes and indicating broad policy guidelines for the *Evsektsiia.* It is not clear to whom, how frequently, and in what manner Dimanshtain reported, though, of course, he was generally responsible to the Central Committee.

If the *Evsektsiia* did, indeed, enjoy a significant degree of decision-making and executive autonomy in the authoritarian, rather than totalitarian, system of the 1920's, it is reasonable to ask whether the *Evsektsiia* was successful or not in achieving its stated goals. This question has to be considered from different points of view—that of the *Evsektsiia* itself, the overall Soviet perspective, and a Jewish one.

There were three basic tasks the *Evkom* and *Evsektsiia* had set for themselves: the destruction of the old order, the Bolshevization of the Jewish proletariat, and the reconstruction of Jewish national life. In the early days these were sometimes reduced to the formula of "establishing the dictatorship of the proletariat on the Jewish street." Later on, responsibility was assumed for the modernization of the Soviet Jewish population.

It was understood from the outset that the *Evsektsiia* would not bear the burden of these tasks alone, but would coordinate its activities with those of other Party and state organs. However, in the destruction of the old order the *Evsektsiia* dominated completely, though the ever-present threat of legal and police sanctions was crucial to its ability to undermine the old order. That way of life was seriously challenged by long-range modernizing trends, such as urbanization and industrialization. But direct governmental action and *Evsektsiia* activities, such as the campaign against religion, combined with the genuine appeals of the Revolution—especially to the Jewish youth who could, for the first time, enjoy the perquisites of power—to hasten the end of the traditional Jewish way of life in Russia. The *Evsektsiia,* going further than Party leaders such as Kamenev and Lunacharskii, was especially successful in destroying Zionism and Hebrew culture, which were relatively new and tender growths on Russian soil. It was less successful in its attempts to eradicate religion, so firmly rooted in Jewish life. But even in this area its attainments were considerable—though the Party would have accomplished as much even without a *Evsektsiia.* By depriving the majority of Soviet Jewish youth of the opportunity for traditional Jewish education, and by substituting its own brand of anti-religious Jewish education, the *Evsektsiia* probably insured that a religious renaissance in Russia would be impossible.

In its avowed purpose of destroying Jewish political life, the *Evsektsiia* ultimately succeeded, but it could hardly claim credit for the victory which properly belonged to the Party as a whole. The *Evsektsiia* itself failed to attract the politically conscious Jews until the pressure of events, at home and abroad, drove many of them into the Communist camp and some of them into the *Evsektsiia.* Just as Russian workers were pushed to the left by war weariness and military defeat rather than by intellectual-political considerations, so did the German Revolution, more than *Evsektsiia* newspapers, drive the Jewish intelligentsia to the left; the pogroms and the Red terror, not *Evkom* communes and welfare services, combined to force the Jewish masses passively or actively to accept Bolshevism. Even in the 1920's, the *Evsektsiia* itself failed to attract a great number of Jews, as is indicated by the fact that its new cadres were for the most part reassigned to it from other Party work. The relatively large number of Jews who entered the Party in the 1920's shunned the *Evsektsiia* for the more prestigious and promising areas of Communist activity.

> It is a fact that a large—not the largest—part of the Jewish Communists who not only have a lively interest in Jewish life but have explicit national leanings have alienated themselves from the *Evsektsiia* for a variety of reasons, mostly personal. Those who have remained in Jewish life consider themselves martyrs, in a certain sense, because this is work with no reward and without prestige.[11]

In the *shtetl* and even in the agricultural settlements it had so enthusiastically promoted, the *Evsektsiia* was frustrated in its attempts to convert the masses to the new faith. Its influence among the Jewish proletariat was minimal, as seen in the futility of its campaign to promote Yiddish in the trade unions. Thus, in those areas which the *Evsektsiia* had arrogated to itself for Bolshevization, it accomplished very little.

The *Evsektsiia*'s greatest failure was in the province of national reconstruction, the area of greatest need. The Jewish people desperately required economic, social, and sheer physical rehabilitation.[12] Admittedly, this was the area where the *Evsektsiia* had the least autonomy and minimal flexibility. Its program for the Jews was carefully watched and regulated by the Party as a whole. It is therefore especially difficult to differentiate between Party and *Evsektsiia* policy in this area. The nationality sections of the party had a dual task: to reach and teach the masses,

[11] H. D. Nomberg, "Mein reize iber rusland," *Gezamelte verk*, v (Warsaw, 1928), 257.

[12] Surveys taken in 1927 showed that Jews were shorter, weighed less, and had smaller physiques than Russians, Belorussians and Ukrainians. *Natsional'naia politika VKP(b) v tsifrakh*, p. 319. An examination of 1,500 Jewish schoolchildren in Gomel showed that a far larger proportion suffered from anemia and respiratory and circulatory illnesses than their Polish and Russian schoolmates. Sh. Palatnik, "An ernste frage," *Emes*, January 13, 1926.

and to report back to the Party on the needs of the masses and try to satisfy some of them. In trying to reach the masses the *Evsektsiia* became involved with the *shtetl*, the *kustars*, the poor and déclassé—and these may have had a "feedback" effect on the *Evsektsiia*. In the period of its most intensive and widespread activity the *Evsektsiia* found itself concentrating on these groups and, as many activists charged, it became "*kustar*ified," involved in the rehabilitation of the most "backward" elements of Soviet society. At the same time, it seemed unable to make its influence felt among the prestigious proletariat. The gigantic industrialization drive of the 1930's focussed the Party's attention on the workers, not on the Jewish colonists and certainly not on the *kustars*. Thus, the *Evsektsiia*, whether by choice or, more likely, by necessity, was riding the wrong horse. The decline of Jewish culture, while it was certainly most strongly affected by larger secular trends, was hastened by the fact that in the 1920's the supposedly most advanced class, or at least the favored one, was hardly touched by *Evsektsiia* work.

Secondly, the policy of the *Evsektsiia* and the Party was varied and changing, and therein lay its weakness. The effort toward national cultural and economic reconstruction was too sporadic and diffuse to be effective in the little time the *Evsektsiia* had. Rehabilitation of the *shtetl* and the encouragement of artisanry quickly gave way to industrialization; Yiddishization yielded to colonization. None of the policies was pursued long enough or intensely enough to have an appreciable impact on the decrepit Jewish economic structure. Neither the Party nor the *Evsektsiia* had a consistent, long-range plan which could evoke a general consensus. Indeed, throughout most of the 1920's the Party was engaged in an intense intramural debate on how best to modernize the Soviet Union. Shifts from "left" to "right" and back again in overall Party economic and political policy reflected themselves in corresponding shifts in *Evsektsiia* economic and political programs. The *Evsektsiia* had to be flexible enough to shift in whatever direction the Party pointed. Programs were adopted to meet the economic and political needs of the moment, and when immediate needs changed, programs were hastily abandoned. When all programs were in action simultaneously, a shotgun effect was produced: plenty of noise and shot, but isolated hits incapable of bringing down the target. In the end it was the Stalinist forced-draft industrialization and collectivization efforts of the five-year plans which leveled what remained of the old Jewish economy and absorbed Jewry into the mainstream of Soviet life.

From the overall Party viewpoint the *Evsektsiia* was a useful mobilization agency which succeeded fairly well in its assigned duties. In its early days it helped ease the transition from a lively and proudly independent Jewish labor movement to no movement at all; it recruited some of the best soldiers of Jewish labor and made them serve the Bolsheviks' purposes; and it was sufficiently cowed by the specter of its own suddenly disreputable past to prevent it from posing a serious threat of autonomism and of Bundist revival.

The *Evsektsiia* also carried out the Party's work on the Jewish street. The Party was able to draw on and exploit the genuine resentments and antagonisms of the Jewish socialist leaders toward the non-socialist Jewish community. By having Jews do its own destructive work, the Party "objectively proved" the existence of a pro-Bolshevik stratum in Jewish society and simultaneously avoided any suspicion of anti-Semitism, a suspicion which would have been held of any Russian government whose policies were directed against even a well-defined segment of Jewish society. Having destroyed the traditional Jewish community, the *Evsektsiia* absorbed, diluted, and channeled the still existent sentiments of part of the Jewish population and deflected at least some from irreconcilable opposition to the new regime.

If the *Evsektsiia* was partially successful by its own lights, and eminently successful from the overall Soviet point of view, it was a disastrous failure from a national Jewish perspective. It would be incorrect to separate the *Evsektsiia* from the Party. The *Evsektsiia's* national failure was the Party's failure. Still, one cannot escape the feeling that the *Evsektsiia* might have compiled a better record from a Jewish national point of view even within the constraints imposed upon it. Had the *Evsektsiia* been internally united and had it devoted all its efforts to one of its national programs, perhaps that program would have taken such strong hold that, were the Party or the state desirous of uprooting it, they would have been faced with an extremely difficult task.

For instance, if the Bailin plan for Belorussian colonization had been pursued with all the energies poured into the bottomless pits of industrialization, Yiddishization, Crimean colonization, Ukrainian colonization, and Biro-Bidzhan, it might have very well created such a compact Jewish population that Yiddishization and Jewish autonomy could have come about. Had the Central Bureau of the *Evsektsiia* joined forces with the Belorussian Party and the Belorussian *Evsektsiia's* Main Bureau, Bailin's plan might have been approved by the All-Union Central Committee. In contrast to Biro-Bidzhan, Belorussia was a traditional center of Jewish settlement and was close to other major centers, such as the Ukraine. Of course, urbanization would have taken its toll in any case, but there would still have been a viable alternative to journeying thousands of miles to a wild and unknown part of Asiatic Russia. Stained with the original sin of Social Democratism and hence terrorized by the error of nationalist deviation, and internally divided by personal and ideological differences, the *Evsektsiia* could not engage in a purposeful construction even of a Soviet-Jewish nation, whatever concrete content might have been given that elusive concept. But even when engaging in activities which could not but aid national consolidation and development, the *Evsektsiia* was impelled to constantly disavow any national motivations, rationalizing these activities mainly in terms of "socialist construction," that is, in terms of modernization, without ethnic maintenance.

The *Evsektsiia* was further confined by limitations for which it could hardly bear responsibility. One inherent restraint on the *Evsektsiia*'s ability to influence the Jewish masses was that it was forced by the Party's definition of the *Evsektsiia* function to ignore the Russian-speaking Jews —a group whose numbers were growing at a steadily increasing rate. The original *raison d'être* of the *Evsektsiia* had been the need to translate Communism into Yiddish for the benefit of those who could not receive its message in Russian. This rationale was never changed even when the *Evsektsiia* began to function as much more than a "translation service," though there was a half-hearted acknowledgement that "we do not say that no Jewish work should be conducted among Jews whose mother tongue is not Yiddish"—quickly qualified by the assertion that "the weight of Jewish work lies where there are compact Yiddish-speaking toiling masses." [13]

One of the basic problems dogging the *Evsektsiia* throughout its history was that its definition of itself was different from the definition that the Party gave it. The Party, *from the very beginning*, saw the *Evsektsiia* as a temporary organ,

[13] Brakhman and Zhiv, *Yidn in FSSR*, p. 6. In the 1930's OZET published a Russian-language newspaper, *Tribuna*. OZET explained that the publication was in Russian, rather than in Yiddish, because some non-Jews were members of the organization. Among its editors were Bragin, Dimanshtain, Zaslavskii, and Rashkes.

designed to destroy the old Jewish life and make the Jewish people economically productive and self-sufficient ("healthy"), to integrate the Jewish people into Soviet society. The *Evsektsiia,* or a significant part of its *apparat,* carried out precisely this program in the mistaken belief that the more successful it was in achieving this program, the stronger its position, the greater its indispensibility to the Party, the more effective an instrument of policy it would be adjudged. But the Party reasoned otherwise: the closer the *Evsektsiia* came to achieving its goal, the less it was needed, the closer it came to the completion of its historic task, the nearer it edged toward turning its activities to undesirable channels. The *Evsektsiia* began to look for new channels into which its energies could be directed, and it looked in dangerous places.

The "nationalists" within the *Evsektsiia* tried to insure that it would have a reason to exist far into the future through its school policy and its Yiddishization drive. But powerful and seemingly inexorable trends were working against them. In 1926, 82.4 percent of the Jewish population was considered urban.[14] This population was more apt to be assimilated—linguistically and in other ways—than a compact, rural Jewish population. Marriages of Jews to non-Jews in the Ukraine increased from 8.5 per hundred marriages involving Jews in 1924 to 11.1 per hundred in 1927.[15] In the RSFSR well over twenty percent of Jews intermarried.[16] Yankel Kantor pointed out that among urban Jews in the Ukraine the smallest percentage of Yiddish speakers was to be found in the five-to-nine year old group. This implied that parents were trying to bring up their children in Russian, and Kantor called this a "proc-

[14] The *shtetl* population was classified as rural. Baron, p. 246.
[15] I. I. Veitsbilt, *Di dinamik fun der yidisher bafelkerung in ukraine far di yorn 1897–1926* (Kharkov, 1930), p. 50.
[16] *Natsional'naia politika VKP(b)*, p. 41.

ess of denationalization": "This is proved by the fact that the percentage of Yiddish speakers among children below the age of four is greater than among those of nursery age. That is, the child's mother speaks Yiddish, but when he is of nursery age she breaks her teeth and speaks Russian to him so as to [make him] equal to the others."[17] Kantor noted that "the large city creates certain conditions for assimilatory processes and certain segments of the Jewish population become assimilated."[18] Although urbanization *per se* does not automatically lead to the dissolution of traditional cultures and to assimilation of ethnic minorities, Soviet urbanization did have these consequences for Jews because Soviet cities were the focal points of revolutionary, anti-traditional efforts, and because most of them did not develop ethnic neighborhoods.[19] For these reasons, a Soviet Jewish demographer was able to describe assimilation in these terms: "We are dealing not with a gradual fading away but with a massive development of the post-war period. . . ." He pointed out that the Jewish birth rate, "one of the basic elements of the concept of 'national growth,'" was declining.[20]

Ironically, Jewish values themselves contributed to Jewish assimilation and the decline of Jewish culture. Since Russian Jews generally considered Russian culture of greater practical value than Jewish culture—a large part of which had been actively and vociferously discredited by the Soviet regime—many Jews applied their traditional love of learning, respect for culture, and high achievement motivation to Russian culture. Furthermore, the Bolshevik hero image

[17] Kantor, *Di yidishe bafelkerung in ukraine*, p. 34.

[18] *Ibid.*, p. 33.

[19] On urbanization and assimilation, see Robert LeVine, "Political Socialization and Culture Change," in Geertz, ed., *Old Societies and New States*, pp. 284–85.

[20] Veitsblit, *Di dinamik*, p. 53.

probably contributed to Jewish self-contempt and self-hatred. The glorified picture of the militant rough-and-ready industrial worker overcoming great difficulties through sheer determination, physical strength, and singular dedication, stood in direct contrast to the gentle *luftmensh* of the *shtetl*, living by his wits and spending much of his time in abstract discussion and Talmudic learning. Soviet citizens were taught to despise the *shtetl* type, and the younger elements in the Jewish population sought to flee the stigma of the *shtetl* and to adopt modern roles, often trying to hide or deny their Jewish identity and desperately seeking acceptance by their peers of other nationalities.

The synthesis of modern Soviet values and Jewish ethnic identity offered by Soviet Yiddish culture appealed only to a minority of Soviet Jews. Both tradition-oriented or nationalistic Jews, on the one hand, and modernizing Jews, on the other, regarded the Soviet Yiddish culture being created by a handful of *intelligenty* as an ersatz product. Many Soviet Jews seemed to believe that "real" Jewish values and Soviet values were incompatible and that a choice had to be made between them. Soviet Yiddish culture thus remained a synthetic subculture created and supported largely by an intelligentsia-dominated minority and with a limited following among the Soviet Jewish population as a whole.

Jewish assimilation, in the sense of loss of ethnic distinctiveness, is a common phenomenon in many countries of the modern world. Whereas some other Jewish communities have tried to stem its tide by "modernizing" the Jewish religion, appealing to Jewish national sentiment, or increasing the scope and intensity of Jewish education, Soviet Jews were not permitted these options, except for intensifying a Soviet-style Jewish education, and even this option was closed off in the late 1930's. To the Soviet Jew it seemed that the price of integration into Soviet society was total assimilation, and that preservation of ethnicity was possible only at the cost of alienation from society and rejection of its modernizing values. The synthesis of integration and ethnicity offered by Soviet Yiddish culture was rejected as artificial, barren, and impractical. Moreover, the kinds of syntheses between modern and Jewish values made in other countries were not available to Soviet Jews. Jews have assimilated into every society which gave them the opportunity to do so. They have assimilated especially rapidly into industrializing-urbanizing societies—the kind of society the USSR was becoming. In such a society Jewish language and folkways usually fade away even among those who desire integration or acculturation without total assimilation.[21] Religion, however, can be accommodated, though not without difficulties and modifications. But in the USSR —unlike France, England, or the United States—religion was attacked and driven underground. Language might have been preserved if the Jews had their own territory. But economic necessity dispersed them and drove many into the large cities which, unlike American cities, did not have and did not develop ethnically homogeneous neighborhoods. Most Jewish folkways also could not be preserved because they were intimately bound up with religion. The Western Jew resolves the tension between his primordial sentiments and his desire to participate fully in the advances of his society by focussing those sentiments on a religious affiliation which hardly impedes his participation in secular life. His religion is relegated to the synagogue or

[21] The late sociologist Arnold Rose defines *acculturation* as "the adoption by a person or group of the culture of another social group. Or, the process leading to this adoption." *Assimilation* is defined as "the adoption by a person or group of the culture of another social group to such a complete extent that the person or group no longer has any particular loyalties to his former culture. Or, the process leading to this adoption." Arnold M. Rose, *Sociology: The Study of Human Relations* (New York, 1956), pp. 557–58.

temple, and even there it is often translated into the general vernacular. Outside the synagogue the Jew participates in civil life in exactly the same way as all other citizens. This solution to the tensions between ethnic identity and societal integration was not available to the Soviet Jews. Taking into account all the special limitations and restrictions imposed on the *Evsektsiia,* its experience still calls into question the viability of a radically secular Jewishness, the possibility of creating a Jewish culture, totally divorced from the religious tradition and its forms, which can be successfully transferred from one generation to another, surviving the disappearance of the specific circumstances which brought it into being.

The attempt to develop a secular Jewish culture was, of course, a response to a perceived necessity of choosing between modernization or preservation of Jewishness. This attempt had been made by Zionists and Jewish socialists before the *Evsektsiia.* Zionists and socialists in pre-revolutionary Russia agreed that the Jews were not only a religious group, but a nation as well.[22] This meant that one could completely reject the Mosaic faith and yet remain a Jew. But the Jewish nation could not—or should not—continue to exist in the tsarist empire. The Zionists argued that Jewish cultural, economic, and physical survival were threatened by the diaspora, regardless of the social or political order under which Jews lived. Most Jewish socialists believed that Jewish survival depended on the nature of the political system to which Jews were subject, not on their geographic location. Zionist-socialists and socialist-territorialists

[22] Walker Connor makes the sensible observation that in trying to define what constitutes a nation, "The coincidence of the customary tangible attributes of nationality, such as common language or religion, is not determinative. The prime requisite is subjective and consists of the self-identification of the people with a group—its past, its present, and most important, its destiny." Connor, "Self-Determination: The New Phase," *World Politics,* xx, no. 1 (October 1967), 30.

accepted the necessity of a Jewish national homeland, but demanded that it be constructed on a socialist foundation. All these arguments presupposed the fullest participation of the Jewish people in modern economic, political, and cultural life, whether as a nation-state, or as a national minority enjoying cultural autonomy within a socialist state.

Concomitantly, it was admitted that Jews were not yet fully suited for such participation, not only because of externally imposed constraints, but also because of internal Jewish backwardness. This backwardness might well have come about owing to external constraints on development, but it would have to be overcome by the Jews themselves—though not at the cost of abandoning Jewish identity. Thus, Zionists and socialists saw two related tasks at hand: internal modernization of Jewry, and the preservation of Jewish national identity in a secular sense. Both needs could be met simultaneously by a secular Jewish culture which would somehow integrate modern and Jewish values.

It is impossible to judge whether such a culture could have survived over several generations, or whether it would have been an effective vehicle of both modernization and national preservation. As we have seen, external forces cut short the experiment in Soviet Yiddish culture. Similar Jewish socialist experiments in Eastern Europe were ended by the advent of the Second World War. Thus, European experiments in creating a secular Jewish culture never enjoyed optimal conditions, and the European Jewish experience cannot serve as an adequate test of the viability of secular Jewishness.

It can be said, however, that the attempt to create a secular Yiddish-language culture in the United States has definitely failed, though some may argue that an English-language secular Jewish culture exists. Never an indigenous product, but an importation from Eastern Europe, the secular Yiddishist or Hebraist movements have not survived the immigrant generation. The native-born sons of this generation have, by and large, maintained some affiliation with the Jewish community, but rarely is this expressed in active participation in secular Yiddish culture, as distinguished from participation in Jewish organizational activities with broad secular aims. The network of secular Yiddish schools has shriveled to almost nothing. At the same time, religious Jewish schools have continued to grow in number and size.

It is also difficult to make a definitive judgment on the character and viability of whatever secular Jewish culture is evolving in Israel because the Israeli experiment is still in its early stages. But it must be noted that there has been widespread dissatisfaction in Israel with the Jewish component of its developing secular culture. About a decade after the founding of the State, the secularly-oriented population began to express fears that there was nothing particularly Jewish about the Israeli school curriculum and that the younger generation was assimilating modernizing values, but not Jewish ones. There seemed to be such a broad consensus on this judgment that the government instituted a program of "Jewish consciousness" *[toda'a yehudit]* in the curriculum. This is an attempt to instill traditional Jewish values, to preserve Jewish national customs—such as holiday observances—in a secular form, and to propagate the idea that the Jewish nation-state is characterized by a culture whose uniqueness extends beyond language and history to values, mores, and style of life.

The fact that such dissatisfactions can arise in a state where one's ethnic identity is automatically given and where there are no impediments to ethnic cultural expression suggests that the substance or content of a modernized Jewish ethnicity may not have yet evolved to the satisfaction of the majority of secular Jews. This kind of dissatisfaction with the ethnic components of a synthesis of modernization and ethnicity has also manifested itself in other countries. Several Communist states have attempted reconciliations of modernization and ethnicity in ways roughly similar to those described above, that is, by a combination of secularization, modification of some cultural values and forms, and the preservation of territorial and linguistic distinctiveness. This is particularly true for national or ethnic minorities in multi-national Communist states, but it also holds true for ethnically more homogeneous Communist countries.

Broadly speaking, the Soviet, Yugoslav, and Czechoslovak Communist regimes have pursued such policies in regard to their constituent nationalities. In more ethnically homogeneous countries, such as Rumania and Hungary, serious and intensive discussions have been conducted on the problem of maintaining a distinctive national culture and identity within a Communist context.[23] It is striking that in all these countries primordial sentiments seem not to have been substantially eroded even among those who completely accept modernizing values. On the contrary, even among modernizing Croats, Slovenes, Slovaks, Rumanians, Uzbeks, Armenians, et al., there seems to be a widespread sentiment that in the syncretic development of modernization and

[23] On the Hungarian discussions, see William F. Robinson, "Nationalism: Hungarian Problem Child," Radio Free Europe Situation Report, July 5, 1967. See also the same author's "Teaching the Party Cadres about Nationalism and Internationalism," Radio Free Europe Situation Report, September 25, 1967. Some representative Rumanian writings are M. Bulgaru, "Responsibility of the Present Generations for the Future of the Rumanian People," *Scinteia*, November 26, 1966. English translation in Radio Free Europe, Rumanian Press Survey No. 676, December 19, 1966; and D. Berci, "History: A Lesson in Patriotism and Humanism," *Scinteia*, March 14, 1967. English translation in Radio Free Europe, Rumanian Press Survey No. 694, April 27, 1967.

national culture there has been an imbalance in favor of modernization and that the ethnic component has not been adequately developed and expressed.

Walker Connor has argued that ethnic consciousness is increasing among the peoples of Asia, Africa, and Europe. Furthermore, "the inability of authoritarian governments to cope successfully with multi-nationalism must therefore be considered still another testament to the increasing power of ethnic aspirations, for it indicates that the immunity believed to be enjoyed by authoritarian governments four decades ago is no longer effective."[24] It might be added that ethnic consciousness has increased not only in multinational authoritarian states, but in ethnically homogeneous ones as well.[25]

In the Communist states, growing ethnic consciousness often implies heightened ethnic dissatisfaction, though it is difficult to determine which is cause and which is effect. In any case, the experience of Communist East Europe suggests that the *Evsektsiia* was not alone in failing to evolve a fully satisfactory synthesis of modernization and national culture, at least from the perspective of the members of the nation involved. The *Evsektsiia* was handicapped by the necessity of trying to preserve national identity and culture under a *Stalinist* type of modernization, which demanded total mobilization of the population and would not brook multiple loyalties. Perhaps some of the alternative strategies of modernization proposed in the USSR in the 1920's might have proved more conducive to ethnic

[24] Connor, "Self-Determination," p. 44.

[25] Ethnic persistence has also manifested itself in democratic states. The United States has usually been held up as the model of modernization accompanied by progressive ethnic integration. Michael Parenti has adduced much evidence to show that the extent of ethnic assimilation in the United States has been greatly exaggerated. See his "Ethnic Politics and the Persistence of Ethnic Identification," *American Political Science Review*, LXI, no. 3 (September 1967).

maintenance. But it might well be that all Communist regimes labor under an ideological handicap when dealing with the problems of nationalities, national cultures, and nationalism. The history of the *Evsektsiia* illustrates this most vividly.

The Evsektsiia *and Soviet Nationality Policy*

Assimilation and national identification were the two poles around which Soviet nationality policy revolved. It moved purposefully, and oscillated rather than vacillated. At a time when it was in the interest of a weak Soviet state to curry the favor of the nationalities, national identification was encouraged; when this was deemed to have gone so far as to have dangerous political consequences, and when Soviet power had increased vis-à-vis the nationalities, rapid, forced integration, often leading to assimilation, was promoted. This is not to say that Soviet nationality policy was an unmitigated success. Regarding it from the national point of view, it can be seen as at least a partial failure. The artificiality of the doctrine of self-determination quickly became apparent to all, and its successor, federalism, also gave way before the immediate military and economic needs of the Soviet state.

> The minorities were thus left without any effective guarantees against the encroachments of the central authorities; and yet they needed these more than ever in view of the unlimited authority enjoyed by the Communist Party over the citizenry. In the end, Lenin's national program reduced itself to a matter of personal behavior; it depended for the solution of the complex problems of a multi-national empire upon the tact and goodwill of Communist officials. . . . Lenin was unable to perceive that the failures of the Soviet national policy were due to a fundamental misinterpretation of the national prob-

lem and followed naturally from the dictatorial system of government which he had established.[26]

The Leninist nationality policy can be criticized also on more fundamental grounds. While the policy of reducing nationality to linguistic autonomy and, in most cases, a territorial base, was a highly effective compromise between Bolshevik doctrine and national reality, there was an irremediable failure in Bolshevik nationality policy, a failure to truly understand nationalism.

> Nationalism belongs to those political concepts which are at once impractical and indispensable. All discussions of nationalism in general are marked by the proliferous and glittering sterility characteristic of discussions of undefined and undefinable subjects. . . . We . . . are dealing with the shadowy realm of collective psychology, which eludes rational consciousness. Every attempted definition of "the nation," the "nationalist idea" or "national feeling" ends in mysticism or mystifications; it can only be expressed in images and symbols.[27]

Because Bolshevik ideology reduces every social and political phenomenon to class terms, because it is a materialist system, it cannot comprehend the true nature of nationalism, which is, after all, an idealist, intangible, subjective phenomenon. This leads to a kind of frustration with the persistence of national loyalties which is often relieved by castigating such feelings as deviationist. Of course, whether nationality policy is adjudged a success or failure depends on the point of view from which it is being examined.

Soviet nationality policy was especially successful, from a Soviet point of view, and especially sterile, from a Jewish

[26] Pipes, pp. 276–77, 287.

[27] Herbert Lüthy, "A Rehabilitation of Nationalism?" in K. A. Jelenski, ed., *History and Hope* (London, 1962), p. 85.

national point of view, in regard to the Jewish nationality. It began with a scholastic *a priori* denial of the existence of the Jewish nation based on the fact that the Jews did not meet the criteria established by one Marxist theorist and adopted by another. That many Jews themselves claimed they were a nation, not just a religious group or an ethnic minority, was of no consequence; indeed, the Jews had to be educated away from this false notion. When the reality of the existence of such a nation forced itself on the Bolsheviks, they were reluctant to deny their theoretical assumptions.[28] Those who held no brief for Jewish nationhood devised a series of temporary expedients which would quickly erase the embarrassing evidence for its existence; those who recognized its existence and wanted to maintain it, pleaded with the Jews to "legitimize" themselves by forming a compact territorial group and thereby meet even the Leninist criteria for national identity. However, the majority of Jewish and non-Jewish Communists judged this to be a regressive step. The Jews had excelled in their ability to assimilate, not only in Russia but in the rest of Europe and in the Western Hemisphere. Indeed, Lenin and Lunacharskii[29] explicitly stated that only assimilation would finally do away with anti-Semitism. The only way to make the Jewish problem disappear would be to make the Jews disappear. While some have been moved by hatred to advocate the extermination of the Jews, others have been impelled by a concern

[28] "Nationalism, like physical movement, proves its reality by marching on, and even when there had previously been nothing in existence resembling a national consciousness, agitation and struggle can in no time create a tradition and a consciousness and a legitimate claim based on them—for there is no other criterion" (Lüthy, *op. cit.*, p. 90). Or, as Hugh Seton-Watson puts it, "A nation exists when an active and fairly numerous section of its members are convinced that it exists. Not external objective characteristics, but subjective conviction is the decisive factor." *Nationalism New and Old* (Sydney, 1965), p. 3.

[29] A. Lunacharskii, "Der antisemitizm," *Emes,* October 7, 1926.

for their welfare to urge the Jews to disappear as a distinct group. To try to brake the assimilatory trend within Jewry would have been anti-historical, anti-Marxist. By reducing Jewish nationality to a denationalized Yiddish language and by suppressing more than a thousand years of Jewish culture, the Bolsheviks insured that the march of History would not be interrupted.

Epilogue
The Tragedy of the *Evsektsiia* Activists

SOME, PARTICULARLY Zionists, Bundists, and religious Jews, have seen the *Evsektsiia* episode as a Jewish national tragedy and consider the *Evsektsiia* activists traitors who deserted the Jewish labor movement and then destroyed Jewish life in Russia. Others view them as heroes who chose the excruciatingly difficult course of trying to salvage some sort of national life from the ruins of revolution. Whatever the objective results of their actions, it may well be that all the Jewish activists, even the "assimilationists," were sincerely concerned for the welfare of Soviet Jewry.

As time went on, it seemed ever clearer that a choice had to be made between the economic rehabilitation of the Jews—that is, drawing them into industry and, hence, into the cities—and the preservation of ethnic identity and culture which appeared to presuppose maintenance of compact Jewish settlements with Yiddishized institutions. This latter is what the *shtetl* could offer. But the *shtetl* was economically backward. In an attempt to combine economic rehabilitation with cultural preservation, the *Evsektsiia* hit upon the scheme of agricultural settlement which could combine both desiderata. But this really implied giving priority to Jewish national preservation, because by 1926 all were aware of the fact that the main road to economic progress was industrialization, and Chemeriskii explicitly said so while continuing to support agricultural colonization for the Jews. Even the Rafeses and the Altshulers who favored industrialization and the concomitant assimilation probably did so out of a desire to do "good for the Jews," deciding that since a choice was ineluctable, it had to be made in favor of modernization and economic viability rather than national consciousness.

Whatever the motivations of the *Evsektsiia* leaders, it cannot be denied that their own political careers had elements of a human tragedy. They were fraught with so many dangers and difficulties that these careers became a daily struggle for life itself. The Jewish activists were members of the Communist family but they were illegitimate children, having been born in Social Democracy. They were embarrassing to the older and more important members of the family who barely tolerated them. Their own sense of illegitimacy paralyzed their will and made them timid creatures whose natural spontaneity and spirit had to be tamed lest they incur the displeasure of their elders and superiors. Chemeriskii's fundamentalist Marxism and inflexible determinism, reflected in his essentially "neutralist" position on the national question, were perfectly appropriate to the *Evsektsiia*. The "neutralist" stance of most of the Central Bureau members allowed them to shirk responsibility, to avoid heresy—or so they thought. It also froze them into an immobility which eventually became *rigor mortis*.

The personal fate of the *Evsektsiia* activists was even more tragic than their political failure. Almost all of them were victims of the purges, though Chemeriskii apparently preceded his colleagues. According to some reports, he was arrested in 1930 and was sentenced to death some time later on the grounds that he had once belonged to the police-socialist movement founded by Zubatov. His sentence was commuted to life imprisonment out of deference to his service in the Communist cause.[1] Another source reports that after the dissolution of the *Evsektsiia* Chemeriskii worked as an archivist. In 1933 Emelian Yaroslavskii dis-

[1] *Leksikon fun der neier yidisher literatur,* IV, 154. He was also accused of having opposed the anti-Bundist campaign of the Belorussian Main Bureau and thereby having "idealized the Bund" and erroneously minimized the dangers of clericalism and Zionism. Dunets, *Kegn sotsialfashistishn 'bund',* pp. 28–29.

covered that Chemeriskii had been a *Zubatovets* and, despite Chemeriskii's protestations that he had repented and Lenin himself had approved his application for Party membership, Yaroslavskii insisted that "in the year 1933, he, Yaroslavskii, was unwilling to be in the same party with a former *Zubatovets*." Chemeriskii was allegedly expelled from the Party, arrested by the secret police, and sentenced to three years in a prison camp—from which he did not return.[2]

The fall of Chemeriskii and several of his colleagues was paralleled by the rise of those who had been most zealous in the prosecution of heresy, most notably Samuil Agurskii and Khaim Dunets. Agurskii was cast in the image of the new generation of Soviet leaders, just beginning to arrive in positions of power. The crude, opportunistic, power-seeking former tailor was more a man of the 1930's than were the flashy intellectuals, the brilliant polemicists, or the men of integrity who could be found in the old Central Bureau. At the end of the 1920's the Stalins were rising rapidly and confidently, while the Trotskys and Bukharins thrashed about in theoretical futility. Agurskii's career might well have been a prototype for Stalinist Man: from an undistinguished, despised Party hack he rose to a position of power achieved by terrorizing those who had looked down their intellectual noses at him. Then, in the 1930's he was in an uneasy and precarious position of leadership.

> Comrade Agurskii is not well liked in Moscow. They think he is not competent for editorial work. And he himself is aware of this. He is afraid of erring—especially politically. . . . For him, it is of supreme importance that

[2] This information was given to Y. Barzilai by Alexsander Khashin, a former *Poalai Tsion* leader who joined the Communist Party and became a Comintern agent. He was arrested and executed in 1937. Y. Barzilai, "Akhrito shel Aleksander Khashin," *Molad* (Jerusalem), July-August 1965, p. 219.

> they should not say *he* has not outgrown anarchist tendencies.[3]

In the end, he was destroyed by the very means which had made his career, by the monster he had helped to create. In 1937 it was alleged that

> Agurskii idealizes the counter-revolutionary past of the Bund and allows the Bundists to stealthily continue their destructive work. . . . Though he always poses as "an active fighter" against the Bund, his actions and his work as a hard-boiled Bundist betray him, working in the Party and smuggling in Trotskyite-Bundist contraband. . . . Comrade Agurskii slanders the Jewish people, falsifies history. . . . In his hostile work Agurskii has gone so far as to idealize the super-bandit Trotsky.[4]

Agurskii apparently survived this attack but disappeared at the end of 1948. Details regarding his fate are not known.[5] Dunets' turn came in 1935 when he was expelled from the Party for not having outgrown his Socialist-Zionist party past and for popularizing literature whose content was discovered to be Trotskyite.[6]

Though there were constant internecine battles among the former *Evsektsiia* activists, few were arrested until 1936. In that year Mikhal Levitan was imprisoned. In May of that year the "Mairevnik" was disbanded, and Esther Frumkin was appointed director of the Foreign Languages

[3] Letter of Kalman Marmor, who was trying to publish a book under Agurskii's supervision, to Alexander Pomerantz, April 30, 1935. In Alexander Pomerantz, *Di sovetishe harugai malkhus* (Buenos Aires, 1962), p. 364.

[4] V. Rokhkind, "Ufdekn bizn sof di trotskistish-bundishe kontrabande," *Oktiabr*, July 26, 1937. Agurskii's "idealization of the super-bandit Trotsky" consisted in his praise of the latter (during the 1920's) as the chief organizer of the Red Army.

[5] *Leksikon fun der neier yidisher literatur*, I, 19.

[6] *Neie folkstseitung* (Warsaw), March 14, 1935.

Institute in Moscow, an important post. But at the end of 1937 Esther lost her job and in January 1938 she was arrested. Suffering from various ailments, including diabetes, she was nevertheless sentenced to eight years in a camp in Karaganda. She served as camp bookkeeper and constantly wrote appeals for a review of her case. Finally, because she was an invalid, she received permission to leave the camp. But it was too late. Her diabetes worsened as a result of lack of insulin and on June 8, 1943, she died.[7] When Rakhmiel Veinshtain learned that Esther had been removed from her post, he decided to protest. Esther's old comrade in arms, the veteran organizer who had always admired the fiery ideologue, rose to defend her honor at a GEZERD conference in 1937. *Emes* described this startling event in its cryptic way.

> At the general plenum of the central board of GEZERD, Veinshtain openly idealized the Bund. With unmistakeable pride, he frankly declared that he had educated a former member of the Bund Central Committee, an unmasked enemy of the people, with whom he had always had a close relationship. He also candidly said that the unmasking of several enemies of the people had been a great blow to him. . . . This anti-Party, Bundist, hostile belching is not unexpected from such a disreputable character as Veinshtain.[8]

[7] E. Falkovich, "Ester—der lebnsveg fun der groiser revolutsionern," *Folksshtime* (Warsaw), May 22, 1965. Falkovich, a prominent contemporary Yiddish linguist in the USSR, was a student at the "Mairevnik." He writes with deep affection and respect for Esther: "Esther lives and will live long in the deeds of thousands of her students and those who respected her, in the hearts of those who knew her and had the good fortune to encounter her fine and rich soul—a soul who lived for one purpose: to make man better, nobler, happier." Esther's daughter and son-in-law, a graduate of the Institute of Red Professors, were arrested even before 1938.

[8] *Emes*, November 27, 1937. Quoted in Grigori Aronson, *Di yidishe*

Veinshtain was immediately imprisoned and ended nearly half a century of revolutionary activity by committing suicide.[9] Yankel Levin was denounced at the same 1937 GEZERD conference and was liquidated on charges of being a Bundist and "bourgeois nationalist." Moishe Litvakov, perpetually under fire in the 1930's, was removed from his post in 1937, just before *Emes* ceased publication, and died in prison.[10]

The most prominent purge victim formerly associated with the *Evsektsiia* was the Old Bolshevik, Semën Dimanshtain. It was his former superior in *Narkomnats* who had created the terror and Dimanshtain did not escape it. Perhaps because of his unsullied Bolshevik record and his pacific nature, Dimanshtain never engaged in the recrimina-

---

problem in sovet rusland (New York, 1944), pp. 153–55. Veinshtain was also Esther's brother-in-law, having married her sister Gite. After Gite's death in 1917 Esther took care of Veinshtain's children as well as her own. See Falkovich, *op. cit.*

[9] Aronson, *op. cit.* There is a second-hand report, no doubt apocryphal, that Rakhmiel was alive in the labor camps as late as 1949. He is supposed to have spoken to a group of arrested Jews who were passing through the camp in which he was held. "Old, emaciated, and sick, he was afraid that he would soon die. To the Jews gathered in that way-station—all of whom acted with great respect toward him—Veinshtain turned with a last will and testament: 'Tell all the Jews who will come here: Thus saieth Rakhmiel Veinshtain—'Next Year in Jerusalem'. . ." Y. Barzilai, *Zohar Bekhatsot* (Tel Aviv, 1963), p. 226. Of course, to an Israeli writer there is a great appeal in the picture of the veteran anti-Zionist-Bundist-turned-Communist coming to the realization that Zionism is the only solution to the Jewish problem. Unfortunately, the facts do not support this image. According to Soviet sources, Rakhmiel Veinshtain died in 1938. See *Piatyi (londonskii) s"ezd RSDRP, protokoly* (Moscow, 1963), p. 839.

[10] Melekh Epshtain, a prominent figure in the American Communist Party in the 1920's and 1930's, reports that Litvakov was expelled from the Party *twice*, though Epshtain does not specify when. He also claims that Litvakov was reinstated through the intervention of Bukharin. Epshtain, "50 yor yidisher bolshevizm in rusland," *Di tsukunft*, LXXII, no. 11 (November 1967), 433.

tions and accusations in which the *Evsektsiia* wallowed after 1929.[11] He also displayed unusual forthrightness in expressing his opinions, even when they seemed to run counter to official policy. In 1929 Dimanshtain argued that a national culture need not be expressed in its own national language, citing the Russian-language newspapers of Azerbaijan and Uzbekistan which wrote mainly about the life and culture of Azerbaijanis and Central Asians. He expressed the belief that nationalities and their distinguishing characteristics would persist for a very long time. When asked whether Stalin's definition of a nation was still operative, Dimanshtain had the courage to answer that "this question is irrelevant [*ne iavliaetsia aktual'nym*]. The declaration of rights of the peoples of Russia . . . speaks not only of equality of nations but also of the free development of national minorities and even ethnic groups. This development can also lead in the direction of the consolidation of different tribal groups into a nation." Dimanshtain maintained that the main task of the Soviet regime in the present epoch was to win the broad masses to Communism. This precluded the establishment of a single Turkic or Slavic language for several nationalities. In order to reach the masses it was necessary to speak to them in their own language, and therefore the present period would be characterized by a differentiation rather than amalgamation of languages.[12]

[11] Y. Berger-Barzilai, who had frequent contact with Dimanshtain in the 1920's and 1930's, comments that "his gentle and kindly spirit amazed me. He was not a fanatic by nature, and in his approach to various problems he was deliberate and calm. . . . I saw in him no hatred for the Jewish people and traditions. On the contrary, he was happy to learn that I knew Hebrew and he would sprinkle his Yiddish conversations with Hebrew quotations and would sometimes mention some passage learned in his youth." Y. Berger-Barzilai, *Hatragedia*, p. 31.

[12] S. Dimanshtain, "Problemy natsional'noi kultury i kulturnogo

In 1930, at the height of the collectivization campaign, Dimanshtain wrote an article in *Revoliutsiia i natsional'nosti* opposing full collectivization in the national *raiony*. For this he was immediately removed from the editorial board of that journal, but after making a public recantation he was restored to grace. He also maintained that "great-power [Russian] chauvinism" remained the chief danger to Soviet nationality policy and that it had become particularly blatant in work among the national minorities.[13] Again, in 1931, Dimanshtain was criticized, this time for a left deviation on the nationality question: he was accused of writing that Party policy was itself an outmoded right deviation, "national-opportunist and national-reformist." This was attacked as "profoundly revisionist and hateful to Leninism"; but in the same breath Dimanshtain's insistence that nationality differences would persist was also condemned.[14]

The resilient Dimanshtain survived this attack, but a few years later he came under fire once again for right deviation. With typical forthrightness, the former Jewish Commissar had written an article in *Emes* asking that "the national factor be taken into consideration" during the elections of 1937. Dimanshtain urged that candidates "should be people close to the national masses in their activities, in their language, in their knowledge of national life, etc." He also asked that candidates for the Soviet of Nationalities have a good knowledge of the language of the nationality they were to represent, an apparent allusion to the fact that some candidates from the Jewish *raiony* did not know Yiddish and that he, Dimanshtain, had not been nominated to a

---

stroitel'stva v natsional'nykh respublikakh," *Vestnik komunisticheskoi akademii*, kniga 31 (1), 1929.

[13] S. Dimanshtain, "Rekonstruktivnyi period i rabota sredi natsional'nostei SSSR," *Revoliutsiia i natsional'nosti*, I, no. 1 (May 1930).

[14] Ye. F. Hirtshak, *Di natsional frage un der rekhter opnoig* (Kharkov-Kiev, 1931), pp. 62–68 and 70–76.

Jewish candidacy.[15] This blatant nationalist deviation could not go unpunished and *Emes* dutifully turned on its organizer and first editor. On January 16, 1938, *Emes* announced the Central Committee's decision to remove Dimanshtain as editor of *Tribuna* and to liquidate the GEZERD house organ. It was twenty years, almost to the day, since Dimanshtain had been appointed Jewish Commisar in Petrograd.[16]

The mills of Soviet justice ground slowly, but they ground exceeding fine. One by one the former *Evsektsiia* leaders were ground under by the machinery which was tearing the old revolutionary leadership to shreds.

> The Russian Jewish revolutionary [writes Leonard Schapiro] was as much the victim of the Russian revolution as its instigator. The revolution which he wanted to create was not the kind of revolution which in the end he helped to create. He was not of course alone—many of the best and bravest of the Russian revolutionaries suffered the same fate. . . . In the main the Jewish revolutionary found himself in the Russian revolutionary movement fully convinced that in the brotherhood of international social democracy he could not possibly be anything other than an equal of the Russian, as indeed he was—outside the ranks of bolshevism. Once inside the bolshevik fold he readily jettisoned any claim to his

[15] *Emes,* September 11, 1937, quoted in Aronson, *Di Yidishe problem,* pp. 162–63. See also Dimanshtain's "Vybory v sovet natsional'nostei i natsional'nye men'shinstva," *Revoliutsiia i natsional-'nosti,* VIII, no. 9–10 (September-October 1937), esp. p. 31.

[16] Dimanshtain was shot later in 1938. He has been "rehabilitated." See *Sovetish haimland,* V, no. 2 (February 1965), 159. As far as I have been able to determine, Soviet sources and authorities have not had very much to say about the *Evsektsiia* since its dissolution. The Yiddish-language journal, *Sovetish haimland,* and several Soviet monographs have mentioned the *Evsektsiia* in passing, but I have not seen any extended discussion of its nature and functions.

> national rights, for the most part only to perish in the end as the victim of a new kind of nationalism which he had not been able to foresee. Perhaps in the end the *Bund* was right in trying to allow for some national apartness even if it ran counter to strict social-democratic theory. Of course the *Bund* failed—but it is perhaps better to fail with integrity, than to succeed—only to discover that one has succeeded in the wrong cause.[17]

The tragedy of the *Evsektsiia* was that it had succeeded in making the "revolution on the Jewish street" only to be betrayed by its mentor in the arts of revolution. Those whom it had revolutionized were ultimately rehabilitated economically, as the *Evsektsiia* had hoped, but the *Evsektsiia's* failure to devise a means whereby they could maintain and develop an acceptable national culture doomed them to a constant identity crisis, the psychological anguish of rootlessness.

There was a brief hope in the 1930's that the Jew could strike new roots by assimilating himself completely into Russian culture. This hope was dashed by growing societal and governmental anti-Semitism and was completely crushed by the Nazi invasion when the Jew discovered that he could not escape his Jewish identity. The reappearance of mass social anti-Semitism and the governmental anti-Jewish policies of the late Stalinist period combined to aggravate the pain of rootlessness. When many Soviet Jews reached out to the newly created State of Israel as a source of psychological security and spiritual identity the Soviet regime moved quickly to stifle the development of dual psychological and political loyalties. Soviet cultural and nationality policies in the post-Stalinist era have condemned the Jew to a psychological limbo: denied an opportunity to pursue and develop his own national culture, he must be

[17] Schapiro, "The Role of the Jews," p. 166.

acculturated into the Russian culture; at the same time, Soviet policies and social mores prevent the Jew from completely assimilating, that is, from becoming objectively and psychologically Russian.[18]

There can be no doubt that, at least in the 1920's, Soviet Jews were interested in some kind of ethnic maintenance and identity, though many of them were perfectly content to assimilate completely.

> The desire to live according to one's own rights and customs and to be ruled by one's fellow-countrymen is the natural desire of every population group that has developed its own customs and standards of behaviour; the rest is a matter of circumstances, of historical luck, of greater or less originality and stubbornness.[19]

Resistance and originality were impossible in a totalitarian society. Circumstances and historical luck worked against the national aspirations of Soviet Jews. The *Evsektsiia* and Soviet Jewry were quickly overtaken and enveloped by the long, dark Stalinist night which descended over all the Russias.

[18] For an elaboration of this argument, see my "The Jews," *Problems of Communism,* XVI, no. 5 (September-October 1967).

[19] Lüthy, "A Rehabilitation of Nationalism?", p. 91.

Bibliography

1. Bibliographies and Biographical Dictionaries
2. Manuscripts, Letters, and Archival Material
3. Documents and Collections of Documents
4. Non-Communist Newspapers
5. Bolshevik and Communist Newspapers
6. Non-Communist Periodicals
7. Bolshevik and Communist Periodicals
8. Non-Communist Source Material
9. Communist Source Material
10. Memoirs
11. Secondary Works
12. General Works

Note

Some special problems necessitated a somewhat arbitrary arrangement of the bibliography. Because of the changing political affiliations of many of the leading personages in the *Evsektsiia,* I have listed their works separately, depending on their affiliation at the time the work was written. For example, works by Esther Frumkin will be found under both "non-Communist sources" and "Communist sources." I have included under "secondary sources" articles or books written by *Evsektsiia* activists, Bundists, or other political figures, if those works were published when these people were no longer politically active but were observers and analysts. Thus, Grigori Aronson's writings while he was a Bundist in Russia are considered a primary source, while his analyses of Soviet politics written while he was living outside the USSR are listed as secondary sources. Memoirs have been listed separately. "General" works include those works of political science or history not dealing specifically with Communism, the Soviet Union, or East European Jewry.

The orthography of the Yiddish language is highly varied and unpredictable. Soviet Yiddish employs a unique orthography, while the Yiddish written outside the USSR also varies greatly in its spelling, syntax, and grammar. (Even the name of the language itself is variously spelled "idish" or "yidish.") Each Yiddish word has been transliterated phonetically from its original spelling, with no attempt at standardization. The modified Library of Congress system has been used for the transliteration of Russian words. Only the Hebrew titles have been translated in the Bibliography.

1. *Bibliographies and Biographical Dictionaries*

Altshuler, Mordechai, ed. *Russian Publications on Jews and Judaism in the Soviet Union, 1917–1967.* Jerusalem: Society for Research on Jewish Communities and the Historical Society of Israel, 1970.

Deiateli soiuza sovetskikh sotsialisticheskikh respublik oktiabr'skoi revoliutsii. Moscow: n.p., 1927.

Kirzhnitz, A. *Di yidishe prese in ratnfarband 1917–1927.* Minsk: n.p., 1928.

Niger, Sh., and Y. Shatskii, eds. *Leksikon fun der neier yidisher literatur.* 4 vols. New York: Congress for Jewish Culture, 1956–1962.

Nadel, Kh., and Y. Eliovich. *Literatur vegn der natsionaler frage, antisemitizm un yidisher erdeinordnung in ratnfarband.* Kharkov: Ukrgezerd, 1930.

Reizin, Zalman, ed. *Leksikon fun der yidisher literatur, prese un filologie.* 4 vols. Warsaw: Klatskin, 1927.

Shmeruk, Khone, ed. *Pirsumim Yehudiyim Bivrit Hamoetzot 1917–1960* (Jewish Publications in the Soviet Union, 1917–1960). Jerusalem: Historical Society of Israel, 1961.

2. *Manuscripts, Letters, and Archival Material*

Agurskii, Sh. "Idishe kultur problemn in sovetn rusland," speech made at the Kultur Ligè, Berlin, November 28, 1922. Manuscript in the possession of the late Alexander Pomerantz.

———. Letters to Kalman Marmor, 1931. In the archives of the YIVO Institute for Jewish Research.

Dallin, David. Untitled typescript on the Menshevik Movement, 1918–1921. Inter-University Project on the History of the Menshevik Movement, New York.

Frankel, Jonathan. "Socialism and Jewish Nationalism in

Russia 1897–1907," doctoral dissertation, Cambridge University, 1960. Typescript in the Library of the Jewish Labor Bund.

Gorkii, Maxim (pseud.). Letter to a Berlin newspaper, May 9, 1922. Copy in the YIVO Archives.

Lipset, Harry. "Jewish Schools in the Soviet Union, 1917–1941: An Aspect of Soviet Minorities Policy," Ed.D. project, Teachers College, Columbia University, 1965.

Kalman Marmor Archive. In the YIVO Archives.

Mendelsohn, Ezra. "The Jewish Labor Movement in Czarist Russia: From its Origins to 1905," Ph.D. dissertation, Columbia University, 1966.

Mishkinsky, M. "Yesodot leUmiyim BeHitpatkhutah shel T'nuat HaPoalim HaYehudim BeRusiya" (National Factors in the Development of the Jewish Labor Movement in Russia), doctoral dissertation, Hebrew University (Jerusalem), 1965.

Niepomniashchi, Sh. Y. Letters to Daniel Charney, 1924–1929. In the YIVO Archives.

———. Letters to Y. Opatoshu, 1928. In the YIVO Archives.

Nikolaevskii, B. I. "RSDRP (Men'sheviki) v pervye gody revoliutsii (1917–1918)," New York: Inter-University Project on the History of the Menshevik Movement, typescript.

———. "RSDRP (Men'sheviki) za vremiia s dekabriia 1917 po iiul' 1918 g.," New York: Inter-University Project on the History of the Menshevik Movement, typescript.

Joseph Rosen Archive. In the YIVO Archives.

Schulman, Elias. "Jewish Education in the Soviet Union 1918–1948," Doctoral dissertation, Dropsie College (Philadelphia), 1965.

Szmeruk, Kh. *HaKibutz HaYehudi VeHaHityashvut Ha-Khaklait BeByelorusia HaSovietit 1918–1932* (The Jewish Community and Agricultural Settlement in Soviet Belorussia 1918–1932), doctoral dissertation, Hebrew

University (Jerusalem), 1961. Mimeo in the YIVO Library.

Shukman, H. "The Relations Between the Jewish Bund and the RSDRP, 1897–1908," doctoral dissertation, Oxford University, 1960, typescript in the Bund Library.

Smolensk Oblast Archive. Microfilm in Columbia University Library.

Tobias, Henry Jack. "The Origins and Evolution of the Bund until 1901," Ph.D. dissertation, Stanford University, 1957, typescript in the Bund Library.

Elias Tsherikover Archive. In the YIVO Archives.

Vilna Archive. In the YIVO Archives.

Lucien Wolf Archive: Russian and the Ukraine, 1918–1928. In the YIVO Archives.

3. *Documents and Collections of Documents*

Akademia nauk Belorusskoi SSR. *Revoliutsionnoe dvizhenie v Belorussii 1905–1907 gg: dokumenty i materialy.* Minsk: 1955.

Alfarbandishe baratung fun di idishe sektsies fun der Al.K.P.(B). Moscow: Shul un Bukh, 1927.

Agurskii, Sh. (S). *Di yidishe komisariatn un di yidishe komunistishe sektsies (protokoln, rezolutsies un dokumentn 1918–1921).* Minsk: Histpart TsKKP(B)V, 1928.

The American Jewish Joint Distribution Committee in Russia. New York: (report in the YIVO Library), January 1924.

Barikht fun der hoipt biuro fun di yidsektsies bam TsKKPV: Far di tseit fun oktiabr 1925 yahr. Minsk: Shul un Bukh, 1925.

Browder, Robert P. and Alexander F. Kerensky. *The Russian Provisional Government.* 2 vols. Stanford, Cal.: Stanford University Press, 1961.

Chazanovich, Leon, ed. *Arkhiv fun'm idishn sotsialist.* Berlin: Farlag "Poalai Zion," 1921.

Deviatyi s"ezd RKP(b) mart-aprel' 1920 goda, protokoly. Moscow: Gospolitizdat, 1960.

Di ershte alukrainishe baratung fun idishe arbdorfkustkorn. Kharkov: Tsentrfarlag, 1927.

Dimanshtain, S. M., ed. *Revoliutsiia i natsional'nyi vopros*, 3 vols. Moscow: Komakademi, 1930.

Ershter alfarbandisher tsuzamenfor fun 'gezerd', moskve, 15–20 Nov., 1926—stenografisher barikht. Moscow: GEZERD, 1927.

l-ter alukrainisher tsuzamenfor fun gezerd. Kiev: Kultur-Ligè, 1926.

Evreiskii kommunisticheskii soiuz molodezhi. *Protokoly i rezoliutsii l-i vserossiiskoi konferentsii.* Moscow: n.p., 1921.

Farn proletarishn gerikht: protsess ibern fargvaltiker-farbrekher dem shoikhet Rapaport. Minsk: Melukhe-farlag, 1934.

Gomelskii gubernskii komitet "Bunda." *XII konferentsiia Bunda.* Gomel: n.p., n.d.

Grossman, M. et al. *Di idishe avtonomie un der natsionaler sekretariat in ukraine.* Kiev: n.p., 1920.

Lazovskii, I. and I. Bibin, eds. *Sovetskaia politika za 10 let po natsional'nomu voprosu v RSFSR.* Moscow-Leningrad: Gosizdat, 1928.

K raskolu Bunda. Vitebsk: TsK-Bund SD, 1920.

Kommunisticheskaia partiia sovetskogo soiuza v rezoliutsiiakh i resheniiakh s"ezdov, konferentsii i plenumov TsK;chast'I. Moscow: Gospolitizdat, 1953.

Kirzhnitz, A. and M. Rafes, eds. *Der idisher arbeter*, 4 vols. Moscow: Shul un bukh, 1927–1928.

Joint Foreign Committee of the Board of Deputies of the British Jews and the Anglo-Jewish Association. *Memorandum on the Correspondence with the Soviet Government Respecting the Persecution of Judaism in Russia.* London: n.p., 1923.

Materialy ob antievreiskikh pogromakh: seria l-aia, pogromy v Belorussi. Moscow: n.p., 1922.

Meyersohn [?], ed. *Soviet politik tsvishn di yidishe masn (Dekretn, dokumentn un materialn).* Vienna: Promachos, 1922.

Otchet VIII konferentsii bunda. N.p.: n.d.

Partai materialn, nos. 3–7 (November 1920; March, April, August, September, October 1921), (Moscow).

Pervyi s"ezd RSDRP, dokumenty i materialy. Moscow: Gosizdat, 1959.

Piatyi (Londonskii) s"ezd RSDRP, protokoly. Moscow: Gosizdat, 1963.

Protokoly s"ezdov i konferentsii. Moscow: Gosizdat, 1932.

Rezolutsies fun dem ershtn alukrainishn tsuzamenfor fun yidishe kultur un bildungs tuer. Kiev: n.p., 1922.

Rezolutzies funem tsvaitn alfarbandishn tsuzamenfor fun di yidishe kultur tuer. Moscow: Tsentrfarlag, 1928.

Rezolutsies ongenumene af der alukrainisher baratung fun di idsektsies fun KP(B)V. Kiev: Kultur-Ligè, 1926.

Sakhaklen fun der arbet iber der erdeinordnung fun der yidisher arbetndiker bafelkerung in der Veisruslendisher sovetisher sotsialistisher republik. Minsk: n.p., 1927.

Szczesniak, Boleslaw. *The Russian Revolution and Religion: A Collection of Documents Concerning the Suppression of Religion by the Communists, 1917–1925.* South Bend: University of Notre Dame Press, 1959.

Tsu der l-er kreiz baratung fun di idpartsektsies. Berdichev: January 10, 1926.

Tsvaiter alveisrusisher tsuzamenfor fun yidishe poierim. Minsk: Natskomisie beim Ts.I.K., 1928.

Vos'moi s"ezd RKP(B) mart 1919 goda, protokoly. Moscow: Gospolitizdat, 1959.

VKP(B) v rezoliutsiiakh i resheniiakh s"ezdov, konferentsii i plenumov TsK, vols. I and II. Moscow: Gosizdat, 1936.

Yedies fun tsentral-biuro fun di idishe sektsies beim tsentral komitet fun der ruslender komunistisher partai. No. 1 (October 1920), (Moscow).

4. *Non-Communist Newspapers*

Arbeter shtime (n.p., 1898–1899).
Der idisher proletarier (Kiev, May-July 1917).
Der glok (n.p., March 1918).
Der veker (n.p., 1906).
Der veker (Minsk-Gomel-Moscow-Vitebsk, 1917–1920).
Di neie velt (New York, 1921).
Dos freie vort (Vilna, 1920–1921).
Evreiskii rabochii (Petrograd, 1918).
Folkstseitung (n.p., 1906).
Folkstseitung (Kiev, 1917–1919).
Kavkazer vokhenblat (Baku, 1919).
Nakhrikhten (Kharkov, April 1917).
Nash golos (Odessa, June 1917).
Posledniia izvestiia (n.p., 1905).
Togblat (Petrograd, 1917).
Tseit (St. Petersburg, 1913–1914).
Unzer gedank (Vilna, 1922–1924).
Unzer shtime (Vilna, 1918–1920).
Unzer tseit (Vilna, 1922).
Unzer veg (Warsaw, 1918–1920).
Yidisher arbeter (n.p., 1899–1901).
Clippings in the Tsherikover Archive from: *Bor'ba; Kievskaia zhizn'; Nei lebn; Nei Tseit.*

5. *Bolshevik and Communist Newspapers*

Der arbeter (Berdichev, 1929–1930).
Der emes (Moscow, 1918–1930).
Der komunist (Ekaterinoslav, 1920–1921).
Der shtern (Minsk-Vilna-Vitebsk-Minsk, 1919–1921).
Der shtern (Kharkov, 1925–1930).

Der veker (Minsk, 1921–1925).
Di freie shtime (Petrograd, 1918).
Di komune (Petrograd, 1918).
Iskra (n.p., 1901–1903).
Komunistishe fon (Kiev, 1919–1924).
Oktiabr (Minsk, 1925–1930).
Clippings in the Tsherikover Archive from: *Der idisher komunist* (Kharkov); *Izvestiia TsIK; Izvestiia* (Moscow); *Kommunar; Kommunist* (Kiev).

6. *Non-Communist Periodicals*

Baderekh (Israel)
Bulleten' tsentral'nogo komiteta "Bunda" (Moscow, 1923).
Der proletarisher gedank (YKP-PZ), (Moscow, 1922, 1926–1927).
Di tsukunft (New York, 1917–1931).
Evrei i evreiskii narod (London, 1962–1968).
Jews in Eastern Europe (London, 1959–1970).
Evreiskaia proletarskaia mysl' (Kiev-Kharkov-Moscow, 1922–1926).
Horovanie (n.p., 1920).
Otkliki bunda (n.p., 1910).
Razsvet (Paris, 1930).
Tseit fragn (Vilna, 1909–1911).
Unzer gedank (Berlin, 1931).
Unzer tseit (Warsaw, 1927).
Yagdil torah (Bobruisk, 1927).

7. *Bolshevik and Communist Periodicals*

Der komunist (Kharkov, 1920–1921).
Di freie shtime (Petrograd, 1918).
Di komunistishe velt (Moscow, 1919–1920).
Di roite velt (Kharkov-Kiev, 1924–1930).
Kamf un lebn (Petrograd, 1919).
Kultur un bildung (Moscow-Petrograd, 1918–1920).

Liebknekhts-dor (Kharkov, 1923).
Mairevnik (Moscow, 1927–1930).
Shtern (Minsk, 1925–1930).
Sovetish haimland (Moscow, 1961–1970).
Tribuna evresikoi sovetskoi obshchestvennosti (Moscow, 1927–1930).
Visnshaft un revolutsie (Kiev, 1934–1935).
Zhizn' natsional'nostei (Moscow, 1918–1924).

8. *Non-Communist Source Material*

Biuletn fun tsk ykp (p.z.). Moscow: September 1922.

Di shtime fun bund, December 1908.

Esther [Frumkin]. "Gleikhbarekhtigung fun shprakhn," *Tseit fragn,* III-IV, Vilna: 1910.

———. "Gleikhbarekhtigung fun shprakhn," *Tseit fragn,* V, Vilna: 1911.

———. *Tsu der frage vegn der idisher folksshul,* 3rd ed. Petrograd: Di velt, 1917.

———. "Vegn natsionaler ertsihung," *Tseit fragn,* I, Vilna: 1909.

Genug! n.p. SETMAS, 1918[?].

Kultur lige; ershtes zamlheft. Warsaw: n.p., 1921.

Lestschinsky, Yaakov. *Unzere natsionale foderungen.* n.p.: TsK-Farainigter idisher sotsialistisher arbeiter partai S.S. un Y.S. [1917].

"Levi," "Vegn di frage fun shabes un zuntog ru," *Tseit fragn,* I, Vilna: 1909.

Liebman, P[eisakh]. "A neie oiflage fun an altn toès," *Tseit,* September 17, 1917.

Litvak, A. (Kh. Y. Ḥelfand). "Fragn fun der yidisher kehile," *Tseit fragn,* III-IV, Vilna: 1910.

Medem, Vladimir. "Natsionalizm oder 'neitralizm', *Tseit fragn,* III-IV, Vilna: 1910.

———. "Obedinenie Bunda s RSDRP," *Nashe slovo,* no. 4, July 1906.

Rafes, Moishe. *Oif'n shvel fund der kontr-revolutsie.* Ekaterinoslav: Di velt, 1918.

Ribalow, Menakhem. "Der shreklikher emes fun ukraine," *Di tsukunft,* XXIX, no. 7 (July 1921). (An eyewitness report on Red Army pogroms.)

"Shtein, Aldor" (Bronislaw Grosser). Articles in *Der sotsial demokrat,* nos. 48–49, November-December 1911.

Subbotin, A. P. *V chert' evreiskoi osedlosti.* St. Petersburg: n.p., 1888.

Vladimir medem tsum tsvantsikstn yortseit. New York: American Representation of the General Jewish Workers' Union of Poland, 1943.

Zaslavskii, David. *Farshvekhte rainigkeitn (an entfer di rabonim).* n.p.: Di velt, 1917.

9. *Communist Source Material*

Agurskii, Sh. "A reize oifn 'oktiabr revolutsie' tsug," *Komunistishe velt,* no. 5. Moscow: August 1919.

———. *Afn historishn front (kegn der idealizirung fun "Bund").* Moscow-Kharkov-Minsk: Tsentraler-farlag far di felker fun FSRR, 1930.

———. *Der idisher arbeter in der komunistisher bavegung (1917–1921).* Minsk: Melukhe-farlag fun veisrusland, 1925.

———. "Der kamf kegn opnoign afn historishn front," *Shtern* (Minsk), V, no. 11 (November 1929).

———. "Di ekonomishe lage fun di idn in sovet rusland," *Di tsukunft,* XXIX, no. 4 (April 1921).

———. "Di role fun di idishe arbeiter in der rusisher revolutsie," *Funken* (New York), I, 7–13, 16, 19, 22, 23 (March 18-July 29, 1920).

———. "Idishe ertsiung unter di sovetn," *Di tsukunft,* XXIX, no. 2 (February 1921).

———. "Tsen yor 'emes'," *Oktiabr,* August 8, 1928.

Bol'shaia sovetskaia entsiklopedia, 1st ed. Moscow: Ogiz, 1932.

Arbeter kalendar afn yor 1924. Moscow: n.p., 1923.

Barikht fun der amerikaner IKOR ekspertn komisie. New York: n.p., 1930.

Ber, A. "Kegn bundistisher farkriplung fun der partaigeshikhte," *Shtern* (Minsk, VIII, no. 1–2 (1932).

Brakhman, A., and Y. Zhiv, eds. *Yidn in FSSR*. Moscow-Kharkov-Minsk: Tsentraler felker farlag fun FSSR, 1930.

———, A. Merezhin, and Y. Kantor, *Dos ferte yor yidishe erdeinordenung*. Kharkov: Tsentrfarlag, 1929.

Bragin, A., and M. Kol'tsov. *Sud'ba evresikikh mass v sovetskom soiuze*. Moscow: n.p., 1924.

Bukhbinder, Nokhum. *Di oktiabr-revolutsie un di idishe arbeitsmasn*. Petrograd: Evkom, 1918.

Chemeriskii, A. *Di alfarbandishe komunistishe partai (bolshevikes) un di idishe masn*. Moscow: Shul un bukh, 1926.

Der veg tsum zieg (a proletarish zamlbukh). Vienna: January 1921.

Di rabonim in dinst fun finants-kapital. Moscow: n.p., 1930.

Dimanshtain, Sh. *Beim likht fun komunizm*. Moscow: Evkom, 1919.

———. *Der kamf fun leninizm kegn liuksemburgizm*. Moscow: Emes, 1933.

———. "Di bashtimung vegn der idisher oitonomer gegnt," *Der hammer*, x, no. 11 (November 1936).

———. *Di natsionale frage afn tsvaitn tsuzamenfor fun der partai*. Moscow: Emes, 1934.

———. *Di problem fun natsionaler kultur*. Moscow-Kharkov-Minsk: Tsentrfarlag, 1930.

———. "Evreiskaia avtonomnaia oblast' na novom etape," *Revoliutsiia i natsional'nosti*, VIII, no. 6–7 (June-July 1937).

———. "Ideologicheskaia bor'ba v natsional'nom voprose," *Revolutsiia i natsional'nosti,* I, no. 3 (July 1930).

———. "K postanovke partraboty sredi natsmen'shinstv," *Partiinoe stroitel'stvo,* II, no. 6 (March 1930).

———. "Lenin i natsional'nyi vopros," *Molodaia gvardiia,* III, no. 2-3 (February-March 1924).

———, ed. *Natsional'naia politika VKP(b) v tsifrakh.* Moscow: n.p., 1930.

———. "Problemy natsional'noi kultury i kulturnogo stroitel'stva v natsional'nykh respublikakh," *Vestnik kommunisticheskoi akademii, kniga* 31 (1), 1929.

———. "Rekonstruktivnyi period i rabota sredi natsional'nostei SSSR," *Revoliutsiia i natsional'nosti,* I, no. 1 (May 1930).

———. "Vybory v sovet natsional'nostei i natsional'nye men'shinstva," *Revolutsiia i natsional'nosti,* VIII, no. 9-10 (September-October 1937).

———. "Za klassovuiu chetkost' i prosveshchenii natsional'nostei!", *Prosveshchenie natsional'nostei,* no. 1, 1929.

Dobkovskii, I. *Moshe hess—als sotsialist, id un denker.* Moscow: Lebn, 1918.

Dunets, Kh. *Di dergraikhungen fun der natsionaler politik in VSSR.* Moscow-Kharkov-Minsk: Tsentrfarlag, 1930.

———. *Kegn sotsial-fashistishn "Bund"; kegn idealizatsie fun bundizm!* Minsk: Melukhefarlag, 1932.

Eisenshtadt, Maks. *Der arbeter klub.* Moscow: Shul un Bukh, 1926.

Epshtain, Shakhne, ed. *Di yidishe kinstlerishe literatur un di partai onfirung.* Kharkov: Melukhefarlag, 1929.

Esther [Frumkin]. *Oktiabr revolutsie.* Moscow: Tsentrfarlag, 1928.

Frumkina, Maria Ya. [Esther]. *Doloi ravvinov.* Moscow: n.p., 1923.

Glinskii, A. *Dergraikhungen un felern in der arbet tsvishn di natsionale minderheiten.* Kharkov-Kiev: Tsentrfarlag, 1931.

Hadad. *Der tsionizm vi er iz.* Moscow: Shul un Bukh, 1925.

Hershnboim, Y. *Shchedrin: a shtetl in rekonstruktivn period.* Minsk: Veisrusishe visnshaft akademie, 1931.

Hirtshak, Ye. F. *Di natsionale frage un der rekhter opnoig.* Kharkov-Kiev: Tsentrfarlag, 1931.

Kalinin, M. I. "Evreiskii vopros i pereselenie evreev v Krym," *Izvestiia,* July 11, 1926.

Kamenshtain, M. *Sovetskaia vlast', evresikoe zemleustroenie i OZET.* Moscow: GEZERD, 1928.

Kantor, Y. *Di yidishe bafelkerung in Ukraine.* Kharkov: Melukhe farlag, 1929.

———. *Ratnboiung in der idisher svivè.* Kiev: Kultur-Ligè, 1928.

———. *Ratnboiung tsvishn di yidishe masn.* Moscow: Emes, 1932.

———. *Tsu hilf dem ibervanderer.* Kiev: Kulture-Ligè, 1927.

———. *Vos darf visn yeder birger tsu di valn in di ratn.* Kharkov: Melukhe farlag, 1926.

Kichaev, A. M. and Rubinov, Y. R. *Sovremennoe sostoianie evreiskikh mestechek i perspektivy ikh ekonomicheskogo ozdorovleniia.* Kamenets-Podolsk: n.p., 1929.

Kiper, M. *Antisemitizm un yidisher natsionalizm.* Kiev: Kultur-Ligè, 1929.

———. *Der itstiker tsienizm un zein yeridè.* Kharkov: Tsentrfarlag, 1929.

———. *Di politik fun der KP(B)U in der natsionaler fragè.* Kharkov: Literatur un kunst, 1931.

———. *Dos yidishe shtetl in Ukraine.* Kiev: Melukhe farlag fun Ukraine, 1929.

———. *Tsen yor oktiabr.* Kiev: Kultur-Ligè, 1927.

Kirzhnitz, A. *Di "hailike" shediker un undzer kultur-revolutsie.* Moscow: Bezbozhnik, 1929.

———. *Di profbavegung tsvishn di idishe arbeter in di yorn fun der ershter revolutsie.* Moscow: Shul un Bukh, 1926.

Klitenik, Sh. *Kultur-arbet tsvishn di yidishe arbetndike inem ratnfarband.* Moscow-Kharkov-Minsk: Tsentrfarlag, 1931.

Larin, Iu. *Evrei i antisemitizm v SSSR.* Moscow-Leningrad: Gosizdat, 1929.

———. "Puti i metody preodolenia antisemitizma," *Molodaia gvardiia,* VIII, no. 13 (July 1929).

———. "Sostoianie i perspektivy evreiskogo sel'skogo khoziastva v SSSR," *Na agrarnom fronte,* XXIX, no. 3 (March 1929).

———. "Sotsial'naia struktura evreiskogo naseleniia SSSR," *Bol'shevik,* V, no. 12 (June 30, 1928).

———. "Territorial'naia peregruppirovka evreiskogo naseleniia," *Revoliutsiia i kultura,* no. 15 (August 15, 1928).

Lenin, V. I. *Collected Works,* 4th ed. Moscow: Foreign Languages Publishing House, 1960.

———. *Critical Remarks on the National Question.* Moscow: Foreign Languages Publishing House, 1951.

———. *Izbrannye stat'i po natsional'nomu voprosu,* 2nd ed. Moscow-Leningrad: Gosizdat, 1925.

———. *Lenin on the Jewish Question.* New York: International Publishers, 1936.

———. *O evreiskom voprose v rossii* (introduction by S. Dimanshtain). Moscow: Proletarii, 1924.

Lev, Abba. *Religie un klakoidesh in kamf kegn der idisher arbeter-bavegung.* Moscow: Tsentraler mairev farlag, 1923.

——— and Vin, R. *Klaikoidesh in kamf mit der arbeter bavegung.* Moscow: Shul un Bukh, 1928.

Litvakov, Moishe. *5 yor mlukhishe idisher kamer-teater 1919–1924*. Moscow: Shul un Bukh, 1924.

Lunacharskii, Anatoly V. *Pochemu nel'zia verit' v boga*. Moscow: Nauka, 1965.

Lurie, H. *Peisakh*. Kharkov: Put' Prosveshcheniia, 1924.

———. *Shabes*. Kharkov: Put' Prosveshcheniia, 1922.

———. *Toire*. Kharkov: Put' Prosveshcheniia, 1923.

———. *Yom Kipur*. Kharkov: Put' Prosvescheniia, 1923.

Merezhin, A. *Vegn Birobidzhan*. Kiev: Kultur-Ligè, 1929.

Mintz, L. "Bezrabotitsa sredi evreiskogo naseleniia," *Statisticheskoe obozrenie*, no. 8 (August 1928).

Nikol'skii, N. *Yidishe yomtoivim: zeier ufkum un antviklung*. Minsk: n.p., 1925.

1905 yor in Barditshev. Berdichev: n.p., 1925.

Novakovskii, Y. *Gots strapshes*. Kiev: Kultur-Ligè, 1930.

———. *Yidishe yontoivim un 'hailike' minhogim*. Kiev: Kultur-Ligè, 1930.

Osherovich, A. "Di baratung fun di yidpart-tuer bam TsKKP(B)V," *Shtern* (Minsk), VI, no. 1 (January 1930).

Rafes, M. G. *Dva goda revoliutsii na ukraine*. Moscow: Gosizdat, 1920.

———. "Jewish Bolsheviki in Russia," *Living Age* (Boston). November 13, 1920.

Reznik, Y., ed. *Programen fun der einheitlekher arbet shul*. Moscow: Tsentraler felker farlag fun FSSR, 1928.

Rives, Sh. *Ershte trit*. Minsk: M̄elukhe farlag in Veisrusland, 1926.

Rokhkind, V. "Ufdekn bizn sof di trotskistish-bundishe kontrobande," *Oktiabr* (Minsk), July 26, 1937.

Rossiiskaia komunisticheskaia partiia (bol'shevikov), *Spravochnik partiinogo rabotnika*. Moscow: Gosizdat, 1921.

Rubin, et al. *Gezelshaftkentenish*. Minsk: Veisruslendisher melukhe-farlag, 1928.

Shprakh, P. *Di tsionistn*. Kiev: Kultur-Ligè, 1928.

———. *Shovinizm.* Kiev: Kultur-Ligè, 1928.

Solts, B. and N. Veinholz, eds. *Yomim noiroim.* Minsk: Chervenaia zmena, 1926.

Stalin, Joseph. *Marxism and the National and Colonial Question.* New York: International Publishers, n.d.

Sudarskii, I. *Farvos kemfn mir kegn religie.* Kharkov: Tsentrfarlag, 1931.

———. *Vuhin gait di ekonomishe antviklung fun di yidishe arbetndike masn.* Kharkov: Melukhe farlag, 1929.

Tan-Bogoraz, B. D., ed. *Evreiskoe mestechko v revoliutsii.* Moscow-Leningrad: Gosizdat, 1926.

Vaganian, V. *O natsional'noi kulture.* Moscow-Leningrad: Gosizdat, 1927.

Veisrusishe Visnshaft Akademie—Yidsektor. *Tsum xv yortog fun der oktiaber revoliutsie: historisher zamlbukh.* Minsk: Melukhe farlag fun Veisrusland, 1932.

———. *Tsum xv yortog fun der oktiaber revoliutsie: sotsialekonomisher zamlbukh.* Minsk: Melukhe Farlag fun Veisrusland, 1932.

Veitzblit, I. I. *Di dinamik fun der yidisher bafelkerung in ukraine far di yorn 1897–1926.* Kharkov: Literatur un kunst, 1930.

Yaroslavskii, Emelian. *Tsiln un metodn fun antireligiezer propaganda.* Moscow-Kharkov-Minsk: Tsentrfarlag, 1930.

Zinger, L. *Evreiskoe naselenie v Sovetskom Soiuze.* Moscow-Leningrad: Gosudarstvennoe sotsial'no-ekonomicheskoe izdatel'stvo, 1932.

10. Memoirs

Abramovich, Raphael. "Di konferents in moskve ven der rusisher 'bund' hot zich geshpoltn," *Forverts* (Forward), February 1, 1942.

———. *In tsvai revolutsies: di geshikhte fun a dor.* 2 vols. New York: Arbeter Ring, 1944.

Agurskii, S., ed. *Di oktiabr revolutsie in Veisrusland.* Minsk: Histpart TsKKP(B)V, 1927.

———. *1905 in Veisrusland.* Minsk: n.p., 1925.

An-Man, P. (Rosental). "Di fareinigungs frage af der VII konferents fun bund," *Roiter pinkas,* no. 2, 1924.

Bogen, Boris D. *Born a Jew.* New York: Macmillan, 1930.

Charney, Daniel. *A yortzendlik aza.* New York: CYCO, 1943.

Chemeriskii, A. I. "Vospominaniia o 'evreiskoi nezavisimoi rabochei partii,'" *Krasnyi arkhiv,* I, Moscow: 1922.

Eliash, Yosef. *Zikhronot Tsioni MeRusiya* (Memoirs of a Russian Zionist). Tel Aviv: HaSifriya HaTsionit, 1955.

Gitlow, Benjamin. *The Whole of Their Lives.* New York: Charles Scribner's Sons, 1948.

Goldenveizer, A. A. "Iz kievskikh vospominanii," in G. V. Gessen, ed., *Arkhiv russkoi revoliutsii,* VI, Berlin: 1922.

Katz, Ben Zion. "Al Shisha Harugai Malkhut" (On Six Martyrs), *Hadoar.* New York: May 25, 1956.

———. *Zikhronot* (Memoirs). Tel Aviv: Twersky, 1963.

Kazhdan, Kh. Sh. *In di teg fun revolutsie.* Warsaw: Kh. Brzoza, 1928.

Liesin, A. *Geklibene verk: zikhronos un bilder.* New York: CYCO, 1954.

Lev, Yitzkhak. *In gerangl.* Tel Aviv: Y. L. Peretz farlag, 1958.

Maazeh, Jacob. *Zikhronot* (Memoirs). 4 vols. Tel Aviv: Jalkut, 1936.

Margolin, Arnold D. *From a Political Dairy: Russia, the Ukraine and America, 1905–1945.* New York: Columbia University Press, 1946.

Manevich, David. *In yene teg.* New York: Freiheit, 1926.

Medem, Vladimir. *Fun mein lebn.* 2 vols. New York: n.p., 1923.

Mill, John. *Pionern un boier.* 2 vols. New York: Veker, 1946.

Nir-Rafalkes, Nahum. *Ershte yorn.* Tel Aviv: Y. L. Peretz farlag, 1960.

Pestkovskii, S. "Vospominania o rabote v narkomnatse," *Proletarskaia revoliutsiia,* x, no. 6 (1930).

Rabinovich, Yitzkhak. *MiMoskva ad Yerushalayim* (From Moscow to Jerusalem). Jerusalem: Rubin Mass, 1957.

Shapiro, L. *Bakalakhat HaRusit: Pirkai Zikhronot* (In the Russian Stream: Some Memoirs). Jerusalem: Lustigman, 1952.

Trotsky, Leon. *My Life.* New York: Charles Scribner's Sons, 1930.

V bor'be za oktiabr' v Belorussii i na zapadnom fronte. Minsk: Gosizdat BSSR, 1957.

Weinrauch, Hershel. *Blut oif der zun.* New York: Mensh un yid, 1950.

11. Secondary Works

"A., Y." Unzer partai prese in rusland," *Unzer shtime* (Warsaw), 1918.

American Jewish Year Book, 5678, 5684, 5690, 5691. Philadelphia: Jewish Publication Society, 1917, 1923, 1929, 1930.

Aronson, Grigori. Articles in *Undzer shtime* (Paris), November 5, 1938, and January 14, 1939.

———. "Der blutiger sakh-hakol vos stalin hot gemakht fun dem 'bund' in rusland," *Forverts* (Forward), January 12, 1938.

———. *Di yidishe problem in sovet rusland.* New York: Veker, 1944.

———. "Farn bund un kegn bund," *Unzer gedank* (Berlin), September 1931.

———. *Rusish-idish inteligenz.* Buenos Aires: Yidbukh, 1962.

———. "Vi azoi stalin hot farnikhtet k'mat ale vikhtige idishe komunistn," *Forverts* (Forward), January 8, 1938.

———, Jacob Frumkin, Alexis Goldenweiser, Joseph Lewitan, *Russian Jewry.* New York: Thomas Yoseloff, 1969.

"Baal Dimyon." "Der idisher komunist, di kultur-lige un dos idishe bukh," *Di tsukunft,* xxxi, no. 1 (January 1923).

Barghoorn, Frederick C. *Soviet Russian Nationalism.* New York: Oxford University Press, 1956.

Baron, Salo W. *The Russian Jew under Tsars and Soviets.* New York: Macmillan, 1964.

Barzilai, Y. "Akhrito shel Aleksander Khashin" (Aleksander Khashin's Fate), *Molad* (Jerusalem), xxiii (July-August 1965), 201–02.

———. *Hatragedia Shel HaMahpekha HaSovietit* (The Tragedy of the Russian Revolution). Tel Aviv: Am Oved, 1968.

———. "Moshe Litvakov—Kavim Lidyokno al-pi Reshamim Ishiyim" (Moshe Litvakov—A Personality Sketch Based on Personal Notes), *Bekhinot* no. 1 (1970).

———. *Zohar bekhatsot* (Light at Midnight). Tel Aviv: Am Oved, 1963.

Bikel, Shlomo, ed. *Pinkes far der forshung fun der yidisher literatur un prese.* New York: n.p., 1965.

Blattberg, Wolf. "The Story of the Hebrew and Jewish Writers in the Soviet Union." New York: Institute of Jewish Affairs, World Jewish Congress, 1953 (mimeo).

Boersner, Demetrio. *The Bolsheviks and the National and Colonial Question.* Geneva: E. Droz, 1957.

Borys, Jurij. *The Russian Communist Party and the Sovietization of the Ukraine.* Stockholm: n.p., 1960.

Bugaev, E. *Voznikovenie bol'shevistkikh organizatsii i obrazovanie kompartii Belorussii.* Moscow: Gospolitizdat, 1959.

Bukhbinder, N. A. *Di geshikhte fun der yidisher arbeter bavegung in rusland.* Vilna: Tomor, 1931.

Burmistrova, T. Iu. *Bor'ba bol'shevistskoi partii za inter-*

natsional'noe splochenie trudiashchikhsia mass Rossii v 1917 godu. Leningrad: Izdatel'stvo Leningradskogo Universiteta, 1957.

———. *Leninskaia politika proletarskogo internatsionalizma v period obrazovanie RSDRP (1894–1903 gg.).* Leningrad: Izdatel'stvo Leningradskogo Universiteta, 1962.

———. *Natsional'naia politika partii bol'shevikov v pervoi russkoi revoliutsii.* Leningrad: Izdatel'stvo Leningradskogo Universiteta, 1962.

Buslova, K. P., ed. *Iz istorii bor'by za rasprostranenie marksizma v Belorussii (1893–1917 gg.).* Minsk: Akademiia nauk BSSR, 1958.

Carr, Edward H. *A History of Soviet Russia:* Vol. I: *The Bolshevik Revolution 1917–1923.* London: Macmillan, 1950.

———. *Socialism in One Country, 1924–1926.* London: Macmillan, 1961.

Chamberlin, William Henry. *The Russian Revolution 1917–1921.* 2 vols. New York: Macmillan, 1935.

Charney, Daniel. "Di merkvirdige geshikhte fun ershten idisher komisar (Dimanshtain)," *Der tog* (New York), January 18, 1926.

———. "Farvos redn di komunistn vegn a idisher republik in sovet rusland," *Der tog* (New York), January 18, 1926.

———. "Freint Khanin, ir zeint farfirt gevorn," *Bikher velt* (Warsaw), no. 4, April 1, 1929.

———. "Fun emes tsum emes," *Bikher velt,* no. 3, June 1, 1928.

Conquest, Robert. *Power and Policy in the USSR.* London: Macmillan, 1961.

Curtiss, John Shelton. *The Russian Church and the Soviet State.* Boston: Little, Brown and Company, 1953.

Dallin, David J. *Soviet Espionage.* New Haven: Yale University Press, 1955.

Daniels, Robert Vincent. *The Conscience of the Revolution.* Cambridge, Mass.: Harvard University Press, 1960.

Dawidowicz, Lucy S., ed. *The Golden Tradition: Jewish Life and Thought in Eastern Europe, 1772–1939.* New York: Holt, Rinehart and Winston, 1967.

Deutscher, Isaac. *The Non-Jewish Jew and Other Essays.* London: Oxford University Press, 1968.

———. *The Prophet Unarmed.* New York: Vintage Books, 1965.

Di y'surim fun libavitshn rebn in sovet rusland. Riga: n.p., 1928.

Dinur, Ben Zion. *Biymai Milkhama Umahpekha* (In Days of War and Revolution). Jerusalem: n.p., 1960.

Dubnov, Semën M. *Evrei v Rossii v tsarstvovanie Nikolaia II.* Petrograd: Kadima, 1922.

Dubnow, Simon. *History of the Jews in Russia and Poland.* 3 vols. Philadelphia: The Jewish Publication Society of America, 1916, 1918, 1920.

Eisenstein, Miriam. *Jewish Schools in Poland, 1919–1939.* New York: King's Crown Press, 1950.

Epstein, Melech. *The Jew and Communism, 1919–1941.* New York: Trade Union Sponsoring Committee, 1959.

Erlich, Alexander. *The Soviet Industrialization Debate.* Cambridge, Mass.: Harvard University Press, 1960.

Erlich, Henryk. "Esther Frumkin," *Der veker* (New York), December 27, 1930.

Eudin, Xenia J., and Harold H. Fisher. *Soviet Russia and the East, 1920–1927.* Stanford: Stanford University Press, 1957.

Fainsod, Merle. *Smolensk Under Soviet Rule.* New York: Vintage Books, 1963.

Falkovich, E. "Ester—der lebns veg fun der groiser revolutsionern," *Folksshtime* (Warsaw), May 22, 25, 26, 27, 29; June 1, 2, 1965.

Fink, Viktor. *Evrei v taige.* Moscow: Federatsiia, 1930.

Finkelshtain, M. "Der bund un di idishe arbeter bavegung in sovet rusland," *Di tsukunft,* xx, no. 2 (February 1920).

Frank, M. A. "Anshai S'arah" (People of the Storm), *Hadoar* (New York), May 1, 1964.

Frumkin, Ia. G., G. Ia. Aronson, and A. A. Gol'denveizer, eds. *Kniga o russkom evreistve.* New York: Union of Russian Jews, 1968.

Gergel, N. *Di lage fun di yidn in sovet rusland.* Warsaw: Kh. Brzoza, 1929.

———. "Yidn in der ruslendisher komunistisher partai un in komunistishn yugentfarband," *YIVO bleter,* I. Vilna, 1931.

Gershuni, A. A. *Yahadut Berusiya HaSovietit* (Judaism in Soviet Russia). Jerusalem: Mosad HaRav Kook, 1961.

Getzler, Israel. *Martov: A Political Biography of a Russian Social Democrat.* Cambridge: Cambridge University Press, 1967.

Grazkin, D. I. *Okopnaia pravda.* Moscow: Gosizdat, 1933.

Greenbaum, Alfred Abraham. "Jewish Scholarship in Soviet Russia, 1918–1941." Boston, 1959 (mimeo).

———. "Nationalism as a Problem in Soviet Jewish Scholarship," *Proceedings of the American Academy for Jewish Research,* xxx (New York, 1962).

———. "Soviet Jewry During the Lenin-Stalin Period," *Soviet Studies,* xvi, nos. 4 and 5 (April and July 1965).

Greenberg, Louis. *The Jews in Russia.* 2 vols. New Haven: Yale University Press, 1944, 1951.

Grinboim, Yitzkhak. "Un dos iz unzer goirel," *Letste naies* (Tel Aviv), November 15, 1963.

"Haroeh," "Di evsekn baneien zeier kamf mit der idisher religie," *Yidishes tageblat* (New York), September 27, 1926.

Heller, Abraham. *Di Lage der Juden in Russland von der Märzrevolution 1917 bis zur Gegenwart.* Breslau: M. and H. Marcus, 1935.

Hertz, J. S., ed. *Di geshikhte fun bund.* 2 vols. New York: Unser Tsait, 1960.

Hurvich, Sh. "Di idishe shul in sovet rusland," *Di tsukunft,* xxxvi, no. 5 (May 1928).

Hurwicz, Abraham A., ed. *Aspects of Contemporary Belorussia.* New Haven: Human Relations Area Files, 1954–1955.

———. *Aspects of Contemporary Ukraine.* New Haven: Human Relations Area Files, 1954–1955.

Iurenev, I. "Rabota R.S.D.R.P. v severo-zapadnom krae (1903–1913 gg.)," *Proletarskaia revolutsiia,* iv, no. 8–9 (31–32), August-September 1924.

Ivan, Wolf-Hersh. "A bezbozhnik a baal-teshuvah," *Dos yidishe vort—The Israelite Press* (Winnipeg), September 24, 1965.

Janowsky, Oscar. *The Jews and Minority Rights.* New York: Columbia University Press, 1933.

Joravsky, David. *Soviet Marxism and Natural Science 1917–1932.* London: Routledge and Kegan Paul, 1961.

Katkov, George. *Russia, 1917: The February Revolution.* New York: Harper and Row, 1967.

Katz, Moshe. "Di kultur lige in ukraine," *Di tsukunft,* xxix, no. 3 (March 1921).

Keep, J. L. H. *The Rise of Social Democracy in Russia.* Oxford: Clarendon Press, 1963.

Khanin, N. *Sovet rusland vi ikh hob ir gezen.* New York: Veker, 1929.

Khmurner, Y. "Di likvidatsie fun di likvidatorn," *Neie folksteitung* (Warsaw), March 20, 1930.

Kirzhnitz, A. "Bund un RS-DAP erev dem tsvaitn tsuzamenfor," *Visenshaftlekhe yorbikher,* Vol. I. Moscow, 1929.

———. "Der bund un di komunistishe partai in rusland," *Di tsukunft,* xxix, no. 8 (August 1921).

Kochan, Lionel, ed. *The Jews in Soviet Russia Since 1917.* London: Oxford University Press, 1970.

Kohn, Hans. *Nationalism in the Soviet Union.* New York: Columbia University Press, 1933.

Koralnik, Yisroel. "Di idishe komunistn in rusland," *Di tsukunft,* XXXI, no. 5 (May 1923).

Kossovski, V. "Farvos un vi azoi der bund hot zikh geshpoltn," *Di tsukunft,* XXIX, no. 1 (January 1921).

———. "Martov un die rusishe sotsial-demokratie," *Di tsukunft,* XXXII, no. 3 (March 1924).

Kostiuk, Hryhory. *Stalinist Rule in the Ukraine.* New York: Praeger, 1960.

Kretzer, Paul. *Die beruflichen und sozialen Verhältnisse der Juden in der Sowietunion.* Berlin: n.p., 1931.

Krushinsky, S. "Belorussian Communism and Nationalism: Personal Recollections." New York: Research Program on the USSR, Mimeographed Series, no. 34, 1953.

Lane, David. *The Roots of Russian Communism.* Assen, Netherlands: Van Gorcum, 1969.

Laqueur, Walter Z. *Communism and Nationalism in the Middle East.* 3rd ed. London: Routledge and Kegan Paul, 1961.

———. *The Soviet Union and the Middle East.* London: Routledge and Kegan Paul, 1959.

Lerner, Warren. *Karl Radek: The Last Internationalist.* Stanford: Stanford University Press, 1970.

Lestschinsky, Yaakov. *Der emes vegn di idn in rusland.* Berlin: Jalkut, 1925.

———. "Der shrek fun tsiferen," *Di tsukunft,* XXX, no. 9 (September 1922).

———. *Dos sovetishe idntum.* New York: Yidisher Kemfer, 1941.

Levitats, Isaac. *The Jewish Community in Russia, 1772–1844.* New York: Columbia University Press, 1943.

Liesin, A. "Tsederbaum-Martov," *Di tsukunft,* XXXI, no. 6 (June 1923).

Lifshits, Sh. *Vegn shtetl.* Kharkov-Kiev: n.p., 1932.

Linfield, H. S. "The Communal Organization of the Jews in Soviet Russia" (address delivered at the National Conference of Jewish Social Service, Toronto, Canada, June 25, 1924). New York: 1925.

Lipset, Zvi. "Batai HaSefer Hayehudiyim bivrit HaMoetsot Ushkiatam" (The Jewish Schools in the Soviet Union and Their Decline), *Bekhinot,* no. 1 (1970).

Low, Alfred D. *Lenin on the Question of Nationality.* New York: Bookman Associates, 1958.

Lvavi (Babitzky), Yaakov. *HaHityashvut HaYehudit Be-Birobijan* (Jewish settlement in Biro-Bidzhan). Jerusalem: Historical Society of Israel, 1965.

———. "OZET-GEZERD," *HeAvar,* No. 16 (1969).

Majstrenko, Iwan. *Borot'bism: A Chapter in the History of Ukrainian Communism.* New York: Research Program on the USSR, 1954.

Makarova, G. P. *Osushchestvlenie leninskoi natsional'noi politiki v pervye gody sovetskoi vlasti.* Moscow: Nauka, 1969.

Mansvetov, N. "Velikaia oktiabr'skaia sotsialisticheskaia revolutsiia i sozdanie narodnogo komissariata po delam natsional'nostei," *Voprosy istorii,* XXIV, no. 9 (August 1949).

Maor, Yitzkhak. *She'elat HaYehudim Batenua HeLiberalit veHaMehapkhanit Berusiya (1890–1914)* (The Jewish Question in the Liberal and Revolutionary Movement in Russia, 1890–1914). Jerusalem: Mosad Bialik, 1964.

Margolis, O. *Geshikhte fun yidn in Rusland.* Moscow-Kharkov-Minsk: Tsentraler felker farlag fun Ussr, 1930.

———. *Viazoi lebn yidn in sovetrusland.* Moscow: Emes, 1940.

———. *Yidishe folksmasn in kamf kegn zeiere unterdriker.* Moscow: Emes, 1940.

Markiianov, B. K. *Bor'ba kommunisticheskoi partii Belorussii za ukreplenie edinstva svoikh riadov v 1921–1925* gg. Minsk: Izdatel'stvo ministerstva vysshego, srednego, spetsial'nogo i professional'nogo obrazovaniia, BSSR, 1961.

Maslov, Sergius. "Opposition Movements in Russia," *Slavonic Review*, XII, no. 36 (April 1934).

Massell, Gregory J. "Law as an Instrument of Revolutionary Change in a Traditional Milieu," *Law and Society Review*, II, no. 2 (February 1968).

Mendelsohn, Ezra. *Class Struggle in the Pale*. Cambridge: Cambridge University Press, 1970.

Minsky, E. L. *The National Question in the Russian Duma*. London: Jewish Labor League, 1915.

Mishkinskii, Moshe. "Regionale faktorn bei der oisforemung fun der yidisher arbeter bavegung in tsarishn rusland." Paper for the YIVO Research Conference on Jewish Participation in Movements Devoted to the Cause of Social Progress, New York, September 10–13, 1964 (mimeo).

Monnerot, Jules. *Sociology and Psychology of Communism*. Boston: Beacon Press, 1953.

Nettl, J. P. *Rosa Luxemburg*. London: Oxford University Press, 1969.

Nikolaevskii, B. I. "Men'sheviki v dni oktiabr'skogo perevorota." New York: Inter-University Project on the History of the Menshevik Movement, Paper No. 8, 1962 (mimeo).

Nomberg, H. D. "Mein reize iber rusland," Vol. V, *Gezamlte verk*. Warsaw: Kultur-Ligè, 1928.

Olgin, Moishe. "Tsen yor," *Di tsukunft*, XV, no. 12 (December 1907).

ORT. "Evrei v SSSR: Materialy i isledovaniia." Vypusk IV. Moscow: 1929 (mimeo).

———. "Statisticheskie materialy po evreiskoi demografii i ekonomike." Moscow: 1929 (mimeo).

Park, Alexander G. *Bolshevism in Turkestan, 1917–1927.* New York: Columbia University Press, 1957.

Pat, Yaakov. "A shmues mit M. Litvakovn," *Neie folkstseitung* (Warsaw), February 7, 1936.

———. "Ainike zeitike bamerkungen vegn M. Litvakov," *Neie folkstseitung* (Warsaw), March 20, 1936.

Pechenik, Aaron. *Tsionism un idishkeit in sovet-rusland.* New York: 1943.

Pesikina, E. I. *Narodnyi komissariat po delam natsional'nostei i ego deiatel'nost' v 1917–1918 gg.* Moscow: Gosizdat, 1950.

Pines, Don. *Hekhalutz BeKur HaMahpekha* (The *Khalutz* Organization in the Furnace of Revolution). Tel Aviv: Davar, 1938.

Pinson, Koppel S. *Modern Germany: Its History and Civilization.* New York: Macmillan, 1954.

———, ed., Simon Dubnow. *Nationalism and History.* Philadelphia: Meridian Books and Jewish Publication Society, 1961.

Pipes, Richard. *The Formation of the Soviet Union: Communism and Nationalism, 1917–1923,* rev. ed. Cambridge, Mass.: Harvard University Press, 1964.

Poliakov, D. and L. Fursova. *Partiia i natsional'nye rezervy v oktiabr'skoi revoliutsii.* Moscow: Gospolitizdat, 1958.

Pomerantz, Alexander. *Di sovetishe harugai-malkhus.* Buenos Aires: YIVO (Argentina), 1962.

Popov, N. N. *Natsional'naia politika sovetskoi vlasti.* Moscow-Leningrad: Gosizdat, 1927.

Prakticheskoe rasreshenie natsional'nogo voprosa v Belorusskoi sotsialisticheskoi sovetskoi respublike: Chast' II-ia rabota sredi natsional'nykh men'shinstv. Minsk: 1928.

Radkey, Oliver Henry. *The Election to the Russian Constituent Assembly of 1917.* Cambridge, Mass.: Harvard University Press, 1950.

Rafes, M[oishe]. *Ocherki po istorii "Bunda."* Moscow: 1923.

Rafaeli (Tsentsifer), A. *BaMaavak Ligeulah* (In the Struggle for Redemption). Tel Aviv: Davar-Ayanot, 1956.

Reshetar, John S. *The Ukrainian Revolution 1917–1920.* Princeton: Princeton University Press, 1952.

Revutskii, A. "Der 'joint' un di idishe kolonizatsie in rusland," *Di tsukunft,* xxxiii, no. 6 (June 1925).

———. "Di vegn fun hilf far'n rusishn identum," *Di tsukunft,* xxxiii, no. 5 (May 1925).

———. "Idishe kolonizatsie in rusland in ihr emes'n geshtalt," *Di tsukunft,* xxxiii, no. 9 (September 1925).

Rosenberg, James N. *On the Steppes.* New York: Alfred A. Knopf, 1927.

Rubshtain, B. "Der khurbon fun dem idishn dorfsman in rusland," *Di tsukunft,* xxx, no. 5 (May 1922).

———. "Di idishe sektsie in moskve un di idishe 'teritorie' in krim," *Di tsukunft,* xxxii, no. 4 (April 1924).

———. "Di oisshtarbung fun di rusishe idn," *Di tsukunft,* xxx, no. 3 (March 1922).

———. "Idishe derfer oif kooperative yesodos in Ukraine," *Di tsukunft,* xxx, no. 9 (September 1922).

Schapiro, Leonard. *The Communist Party of the Soviet Union.* New York: Random House, 1959.

———. "The Role of the Jews in the Russian Revolutionary Movement," *Slavonic and East European Review,* xl (December 1961).

Schwarz, Solomon M. *Antisemitizm v sovetskom soiuze.* New York: Chekhov Publishing House, 1952.

———. *The Jews in the Soviet Union.* Syracuse: Syracuse University Press, 1951.

Shaheen, Samad. *The Communist (Bolshevik) Theory of National Self-Determination.* The Hague: W. Van Hoeve, 1956.

Sharapov, Iakub Sharapovich, *Natsional'nye sektsii RKP(b)*. Kazan: Izdatel'stvo Kazanskogo universiteta, 1967.

Shub, Boris. "Evrei v russkoi revolutsii," *Evreiskii mir*, Vol. II. New York: Union of Russian Jews, 1944.

Shulman, V. "Der bund in rusland fahr der tseit fun der revolutsie," *Unzer shtime*. Warsaw: August 1918.

Slutskii, B., Y. Liberberg, and H. Kozakevich. *Leksikon fun politishe un fremd verter*. Kiev: Kultur Lige, 1929.

Smoliar, Hersh. "Der ershter: tsum 80 geboirntog fun Shimon Dimanshtain," *Folksshtime* (Warsaw), February 24, 1965.

Sonin, A. "Vi azoi men hot gefeiert pesakh in sovet rusland," *Der tog*, April 21, 1926.

Shteinberg, I. N. "Di neie heroishe idishe yugent," *Di tsukunft*, xxxvi, no. 5 (May 1928).

Sullivant, Robert S. *Soviet Politics and the Ukraine, 1917–1957*. New York: Columbia University Press, 1962.

Tobias, Henry J. "The Bund and Lenin Until 1903," *The Russian Review*, xxix, no. 4 (October 1961).

Towster, Julian. *Political Power in the USSR, 1917–1947*. New York: Oxford University Press, 1948.

Trotski, Leon. *Stalin: an Appraisal of the Man and His Influence*. London: Hollis and Carter, 1947.

Tsentsifer (Refaeli), L. *Eser Sh'not Redifot* (Ten Years of Persecution). Tel Aviv: Akhdut, 1930.

———. *Paamai Geulah* (Footsteps of Liberty). Tel Aviv: Twersky, 1951.

Tsherikover, Elias. *Antisemitizm un pogromen in ukraine, 1917–1918*. Berlin: Yidisher Literarisher Farlag, 1923.

———. *Di ukrainer pogromen in yor 1919*. New York: YIVO, 1965.

———. *In der tkufe fun revolutsie: memoirn, materialn, dokumentn*, Vol. I. Berlin: Yidisher Literarisher Farlag, 1924.

———. *Yehudim BeItot Mahpekha* (Jews in the Time of Revolution). Tel Aviv: Am Oved, 1957.

"Tsivion" (B. Z. Hoffman). "Der bund un di sotsiale revolutsie in Rusland," *Di tsukunft*, XXIX, no. 2 (February 1921).

Vakar, Nicholas P. *Belorussia: The Making of a Nation.* Cambridge, Mass.: Harvard University Press, 1956.

Vest, B., ed. *Naftulai Dor* (Trials of a Generation). Tel Aviv: Hapoel Hatsair, 1945.

Viktor, Ab. *In Sovetishn geboi.* New York: Morgen-Freiheit, 1931.

Vishnitzer, M. "Di gezerd konferents in moskve," *Di tsukunft*, XXXV, no. 2 (February 1927).

Vit, L. E. *Birebidzhan.* Moscow: Gezerd, 1929.

Volin, S. "Men'sheviki na Ukraine (1917–1921)." New York: Inter-University Project on the History of the Menshevik Movement, Paper No. 11, 1962 (mimeo).

Vsia Moskva: adressnaia i spravochnaia kniga na 1927 god. Moscow: n.d. [1928].

Weinstein, Harold R. "Language and Education in the Soviet Ukraine," *The Slavonic Year Book* (vol. XX of the *Slavonic and East European Review*), 1941.

Wolfe, Bertram D. *Three Who Made a Revolution.* Boston: Beacon Press, 1948.

Yakhinson, Y. *Sotsial-ekonomisher shtaiger ba yidn in Rusland in XIX y"h.* Kharkov: Tsentraler farlag far di felker fun FSRR, 1929.

Yarblum, M. "60 Shana LaBaaya HaYehudit LeHalakha Ul'maase BeToldot HaBolshevizm" (Sixty Years of the Jewish Question in Theory and Practice in the History of Bolshevism) *Hapoel Hatsair*, November 26, 1963.

Yarmolinsky, Avrahm. *The Jews and Other Minor Nationalities under the Soviets.* New York: Vanguard Press, 1928.

Zhitnik, A. Y. *Di idn in sovet rusland.* Cleveland: n.p., 1925.

Zinger, Y. Y. *Nei rusland.* Vilna: B. Kletzkin, 1928.

Zipin, M. "Der idisher kongress in rusland," *Di tsukunft,* xxvii, no. 1 (January 1919).

———. "Di bolshevikes, di kadetn un di idn," *Di tsukunft,* xxvi, no. 9 (September 1918).

12. General Works

Ake, Claude. *A Theory of Political Integration.* Homewood, Ill.: Dorsey Press, 1967.

Apter, David E. *The Politics of Modernization.* Chicago: University of Chicago Press, 1965.

———. "System, Process and the Politics of Economic Development," in Jason L. Finkle and Richard W. Gable, eds., *Political Development and Social Change.* New York: John Wiley, 1966.

Barth, Fredrik. *Ethnic Groups and Boundaries.* London: George Allen and Unwin, 1969.

Black, C. E. *The Dynamics of Modernization.* New York: Harper and Row, 1966.

Connor, Walker. "Self-Determination: The New Phase," *World Politics,* xx, no. 1 (October 1967).

Deutsch, Karl W. "Social Mobilization and Political Development," *American Political Science Review,* lv, no. 3 (September 1961).

Eisenstadt, S. N. *Essays on Sociological Aspects of Political and Economic Development.* The Hague: Mouton, 1961.

———. *Modernization: Protest and Change.* Englewood Cliffs, N. J.: Prentice-Hall, 1966.

Finkle, Jason L., and Richard W. Gable, eds. *Political Development and Social Change.* New York: John Wiley and Sons, 1966.

Geertz, Clifford. *Old Societies and New States.* New York: The Free Press of Glencoe, 1963.

Inkeles, Alex. "Models and Issues in the Analysis of Soviet Society," *Survey*, no. 60 (July 1966).

Lewin, Kurt. *Resolving Social Conflicts*. New York: Harper and Row, 1948.

Linz, Juan Jr. "An Authoritarian Regime: Spain," in Erik Allard and Yrjö Littunen, eds., *Cleavages, Ideologies and Party Systems*. Transactions of the Westermarck Society, x. Helsinki: Academic Bookstore, 1961.

Lüthy, Herbert. "A Rehabilitation of Nationalism?" in K. A. Jelenski, ed., *History and Hope*. London: Routledge and Kegan Paul, 1962.

Nahirny, Vladimir C. "Some Observations on Ideological Groups," *American Journal of Sociology*, LXVII, no. 4 (January 1962).

Pye, Lucian W., and Sidney Verba, eds. *Political Culture and Political Development*. Princeton: Princeton University Press, 1965.

Rupin, Arthur. *The Jews of To-day*. New York: Henry Holt, 1913.

Rustow, Dankwart A. *A World of Nations*. Washington, D. C.: The Brookings Institution, 1967.

Shibutani, Tamotsu, and Kian M. Kwan. *Ethnic Stratification*. New York: The Macmillan Company, 1965.

Stonequist, Everett V. *The Marginal Man*. New York: Charles Scribner's Sons, 1937.

Theodorson, George A. "Acceptance of Industrialization and its Attendant Consequences for the Social Patterns of Non-Western Societies," *American Sociological Review*, 18, no. 5 (October 1953).

Index

Jewish Nationality and Soviet Politics: The Jewish Sections of the CPSU, 1917–1930, appears in a series of studies sponsored by the Research Institute on Communist Affairs of Columbia University, New York City. The Institute promotes studies on international communism and on various aspects of Marxist theory and practice. While the Institute does not assume responsibility for the views of the authors, it feels that these studies contribute to a better understanding of the role of communism in the world today.

Books Published for the Research Institute on Communist Affairs

Diversity in International Communism. Alexander Dallin, ed., in collaboration with the Russian Institute. Columbia University Press, 1963.

Political Succession in the USSR. Myron Rush. Published jointly with the RAND Corporation, Columbia University Press, 1965.

Marxism in Modern France. George Lichtheim. Columbia University Press, 1966.

Power in the Kremlin: Khrushchev to Kosygin. Michel Tatu. Published by Grasset, 1966, and by Viking Press, 1969.

Vietnam Triangle. Donald S. Zagoria. Pegasus Press, 1968.

The Soviet Bloc: Unity and Conflict. Zbigniew Brzezinski. Revised and enlarged edition. Harvard University Press, 1967.

Communism in Malaysia and Singapore. Justus van der Kroef. Nijhoff Publishers, 1968.

Radicalismo Cattolico Brasiliano. Ulisse Alessio Floridi. Instituto Editoriale Del Mediterraneo, 1968.

Marxism and Ethics. Eugene Kamenka. Macmillan, 1969.

Stalin and His Generals. Seweryn Bialer, ed. Pegasus Press, 1969.

Dilemmas of Change in Soviet Politics. Zbigniew Brzezinski, ed. Columbia University Press, 1969.

The USSR Arms the Third World: Case Studies in Soviet Foreign Policy. Uri Ra'anan. MIT Press, 1969.

Communists and Their Law. John N. Hazard. University of Chicago Press, 1969.

The Fulcrum of Asia. Bhabani Sen Gupta. Pegasus Press, 1970.

Le Conflit sino-soviétique et l'Europe de l'Est. Jacques Levesque. Les Presses de l'Université de Montreal, 1970.

Between Two Ages. Zbigniew Brzezinski. Viking Press, 1970.

Communism and Nationalism in India: M. N. Roy and Comintern Policy, 1920–1939. John Patrick Haithcox. Princeton University Press, 1971.

Les Régimes politiques de l'URSS et de l'Europe de l'Est. Michel Lesage. Presses Universitaires de France, 1971.

Bulgarian Communism, 1934–1944. Nissan Oren. Columbia University Press, 1971.